MATH Trailblazers®

A BALANCED MATHEMATICS PROGRAM INTEGRATING SCIENCE AND LANGUAGE ARTS

Teacher Implementation Guide

THIRD EDITION

KENDALL/HUNT PUBLISHING COMPANY
4050 Westmark Drive   Dubuque, Iowa   52002

A TIMS® Curriculum
University of Illinois at Chicago

Teacher Implementation Guide

Math Trailblazers®

A Balanced Mathematics Program Integrating Science and Language Arts

A TIMS® Curriculum from the University of Illinois at Chicago

---

Dedication

This book is dedicated to the children and teachers who let us see the magic in their classrooms and to our families who wholeheartedly supported us while we searched for ways to make it happen.

—*The TIMS Project*—

 UIC The University of Illinois at Chicago

The original edition was based on work supported by the National Science Foundation under grant No. MDR 9050226 and the University of Illinois at Chicago. Any opinions, findings, and conclusions or recommendations expressed in this publication are those of the authors and do not necessarily reflect the views of the granting agencies.

GRADE 5

Acknowledgments

Teaching Integrated Mathematics and Science (TIMS) Project Directors
Philip Wagreich, Principal Investigator
Joan L. Bieler
Howard Goldberg (emeritus)
Catherine Randall Kelso

Director
Third Edition   Joan L. Bieler

Curriculum Developers
Third Edition   Lindy M. Chambers-Boucher   Philip Wagreich
     Janet Simpson Beissinger

Contributors
Third Edition

Eileen Wynn Ball	Sandy Niemiera
Jenny Bay-Williams	Christina Nugent
Ava Chatterjee-Belisle	Janet M. Parsons
Elizabeth Colligan	Leona Peters
Marty Gartzman	Catherine Reed
Carol Inzerillo	

Editorial and Production Staff
Third Edition

Kathleen R. Anderson	Christina Clemons
Lindy M. Chambers-Boucher	Anne Roby

TIMS Professional Developers

Barbara Crum	Cheryl Kneubuhler
Catherine Ditto	Lisa Mackey
Pamela Guyton	Linda Miceli

TIMS Director of Media Services
Henrique Cirne-Lima

TIMS Research Staff

Stacy Brown	Catherine Ditto
Reality Canty	Kathleen Pitvorec
Alison Castro	Catherine Randall Kelso

TIMS Administrative Staff

Eve Ali Boles	Enrique Puente
Kathleen R. Anderson	Alice VanSlyke
Nida Khan	

Director

Second Edition   Catherine Randall Kelso

Curriculum Developers

Second Edition

Lindy M. Chambers-Boucher   Jennifer Mundt Leimberer
Elizabeth Colligan   Georganne E. Marsh
Marty Gartzman   Leona Peters
Carol Inzerillo   Philip Wagreich
Catherine Randall Kelso

Editorial and Production Staff

Second Edition

Kathleen R. Anderson   Georganne E. Marsh
Ai-Ai C. Cojuangco   Cosmina Menghes
Andrada Costoiu   Anne Roby
Erika Larsen

Principal Investigators

First Edition   Philip Wagreich   Howard Goldberg

Senior Curriculum Developers

First Edition

Janet Simpson Beissinger   Carol Inzerillo
Joan L. Bieler   Andy Isaacs
Astrida Cirulis   Catherine Randall Kelso
Marty Gartzman   Leona Peters
Howard Goldberg   Philip Wagreich

Curriculum Developers

First Edition

Janice C. Banasiak   Jenny Knight
Lynne Beauprez   Sandy Niemiera
Andy Carter   Janice Ozima
Lindy M. Chambers-Boucher   Polly Tangora
Kathryn Chval   Paul Trafton
Diane Czerwinski

Illustrator

First Edition   Kris Dresen

Editorial and Production Staff

First Edition

Glenda L. Genio-Terrado   Sarah Nelson
Mini Joseph   Birute Petrauskas
Lynette Morgenthaler   Anne Roby

Research Consultant

First Edition   Andy Isaacs

Mathematics Education Consultant

First Edition   Paul Trafton

National Advisory Committee

First Edition

Carl Berger   Mary Lindquist
Tom Berger   Eugene Maier
Hugh Burkhart   Lourdes Monteagudo
Donald Chambers   Elizabeth Phillips
Naomi Fisher   Thomas Post
Glenda Lappan

Preface

This third edition of *Math Trailblazers* is the product of about 20 years of concerted effort by the TIMS (Teaching Integrated Mathematics and Science) Project. The TIMS Project has its roots in the pioneering work of Howard Goldberg, Professor of Physics at the University of Illinois at Chicago (UIC) and a Carnegie Foundation Professor of the Year in 1995. Over the past two decades, the TIMS Project has worked with children, teachers, and administrators to improve the quality of mathematics and science curricula and instruction in the Chicago area and nationwide. In 1990, the TIMS Project was awarded a grant by the National Science Foundation to develop a new elementary mathematics curriculum to meet the needs of children who will be entering the world of work in the 21st century. After years of research and development, including pilot- and field-testing in hundreds of classrooms, the first edition of the curriculum was published as *Math Trailblazers* in 1997 and 1998.

The primary goal of *Math Trailblazers* has been to create an educational experience that results in children who are flexible mathematical thinkers, who see the connections between the mathematics they learn in school and the thinking they do in everyday life, and who enjoy mathematics. The curriculum is based on the premise that children can succeed in mathematics and that if more is expected of them, more will be achieved. The curriculum incorporates the best of traditional mathematics, while widening the horizons of students' mathematical thinking.

Since the initial publication of *Math Trailblazers*, the TIMS Project has continued its research and development work, studying how to implement the curriculum in the most effective ways. We have learned considerably more about the importance of teacher professional development and whole-school change. The dedication and insight of our teacher collaborators constantly encouraged us. Feedback from hundreds of teachers who tested early versions of *Math Trailblazers* and thousands of others who used the program over the past ten years significantly reshaped our view of the curriculum and inspires our continuing efforts to improve it.

The first edition of *Math Trailblazers* was grounded in mathematics education research literature as well as our own research and experience as curriculum and staff developers. It was also inspired by the 1989 publication of the National Council of Teachers of Mathematics *Curriculum and Evaluation Standards for School Mathematics*. In this edition we drew from advances in research over the decade as well as NCTM's updated vision for school mathematics, as embodied in the NCTM's *Principles and Standards for School Mathematics*.

New editions of *Math Trailblazers* have made the curriculum easier for teachers to use. The math facts program was realigned in the 2nd edition and in this edition assessment and review components of the curriculum are more clearly highlighted. This edition also features an improved format for the *Unit Resource Guide* as well as new content in the *Teacher Implementation Guide* aimed at teachers and administrators. This content was suggested and shaped by our experience as professional developers working with schools and districts across the country that implement *Math Trailblazers*. It includes **Building the *Math Trailblazers* Classroom,** strategies and tips gathered from classroom teachers; **Teaching the *Math Trailblazers* Student: Meeting Individual Needs,** integral structures and features of *Math Trailblazers* that make it accessible to all children, including sections on working with English Language Learners, Special Education students and gifted and talented students; **Language in the *Math Trailblazers* Classroom,** strategies to help students learn to effectively communicate in the math classroom; and an **Administrator Handbook,** strategies to successfully guide implementation of the curriculum.

This third edition of *Math Trailblazers* is one more step in the continuing evolution of the curriculum. The Project is now housed within UIC's Learning Sciences Research Institute, providing a permanent home for interdisciplinary collaboration between mathematicians, scientists, mathematics educators, learning scientists, and teachers as we continually work at providing the best possible mathematics curriculum. We hope that teaching *Math Trailblazers* will be an enjoyable and productive experience for you and your students.

Philip Wagreich
Professor, Department of Mathematics, Statistics, and Computer Science
Director Emeritus, TIMS Project
University of Illinois at Chicago

Joan L. Bieler and Catherine R. Kelso
Co-Directors, TIMS Project
University of Illinois at Chicago

GRADE
5

Teacher Implementation Guide
Table of Contents

Grade 5 Math Trailblazers
Table of Contents

This Table of Contents includes page numbers for the teacher material in the *Unit Resource Guide* plus corresponding page numbers in the student books (*Student Guide, Discovery Assignment Book,* and *Adventure Book*).

Introduction

Introduction

The Introduction outlines the *Teacher Implementation Guide's* various sections and explains how best to use them.

A teacher and a student explore equivalent fractions.

Introduction

What Is the *Teacher Implementation Guide?*

The *Teacher Implementation Guide* is the reference manual for *Math Trailblazers*®. It, combined with the *Grade 5 Facts Resource Guide* and the *Unit Resource Guide,* provides a comprehensive set of resources to assist in the implementating of the curriculum. The *Unit Resource Guide* is the teacher's working guide, providing information and instructions related to the planning and teaching of units and individual lessons—it is intended to be used on a day-to-day basis. The *Grade 5 Facts Resource Guide* is a compilation of the components of the fifth grade math facts program, including background material. The *Teacher Implementation Guide* supplements the *Unit Resource Guide* and the *Grade 5 Facts Resource Guide* by addressing larger issues related to the curriculum. Information in the *Teacher Implementation Guide* can be roughly categorized into three groups: general background about *Math Trailblazers;* specific information about the program; and deep background about important math and science concepts. The *Teacher Implementation Guide* is a valuable resource in long-range planning for math instruction, curriculum, related implementation issues, and staff development.

Brief descriptions of sections found in the *Teacher Implementation Guide* follow:

- **Foundations of *Math Trailblazers***
  The underlying philosophy of the program is described.

- **Components and Features Guide**
  Math Trailblazers is a multicomponent program. Grade 5 includes three books for students (the *Student Guide, Discovery Assignment Book,* and *Adventure Book*) and three volumes for teachers (the *Teacher Implementation Guide,* the *Grade 5 Facts Resource Guide,* and the *Unit Resource Guide*). A *Teacher Resource CD* is also available for teachers. The Components and Features Guide is a road map for understanding the purposes of the various components and where to find key information. Important features taken from actual student and teacher pages are illustrated.

- **Grade 5 Overview**
  The Overview is an extended table of contents for the Grade 5 curriculum. Pacing suggestions in unit outlines help you plan your instruction schedule. Unit summaries include a narrative description of each unit's content and a list of important math concepts covered. This provides a snapshot view of the curriculum for your grade.

- **Connections with the NCTM *Principles and Standards***
  Math Trailblazers was developed to reflect the goals and approaches outlined in the *Principles and Standards for School Mathematics* of the National Council of Teachers of Mathematics (NCTM). This section includes detailed information about how the program aligns with the *Principles and Standards.*

- **Scope and Sequence**
  The Scope and Sequence is organized to correspond with the NCTM *Principles and Standards,* providing additional detailed information about *Math Trailblazers'* alignment with the *Standards.* The scope and sequence

chart is divided into two sections—one for the unit lessons and one for the Daily Practice and Problems and the Home Practice.

- **Summary of Approaches to Math Facts and Whole-Number Operations**

  The *Math Trailblazers* program for presenting the math facts and whole-number operations is summarized in this section. Background information about our approach and expectations for the grades are outlined.

- **Daily Practice and Problems and Home Practice Guide**

  An essential component of *Math Trailblazers* is a carefully designed sequence of short problems in Grades 1–5, called the Daily Practice and Problems (DPP). In third through fifth grades, a component called Home Practice (HP) is introduced. This component provides additional practice with skills and concepts.

- **Assessment**

  Math Trailblazers includes a comprehensive program of student assessment. The philosophy and components of this program are described in the Assessment section. Assessment materials from the curriculum illustrate key ideas. Specific suggestions for implementing the assessment program are included.

- **TIMS Tutors: Background Information for Teachers**

  This section includes a series of documents called TIMS Tutors which provide extensive information on topics in pedagogy, mathematics, and science. The tutors serve as a source of deep background information. Some tutors, such as the tutor on math facts, supply specific information needed by teachers to plan particular portions of the *Math Trailblazers* program. Other tutors, such as the tutor on mass, focus on math and science content. Still others, such as the tutor on portfolios, address teaching strategies.

- **Building the *Math Trailblazers* Classroom**

  This section contains strategies and tips gathered from classroom teachers. Topics include the organization of materials and classrooms, as well as student groupings to best implement *Math Trailblazers*.

- **Teaching the *Math Trailblazers* Student: Meeting Individual Needs**

  From its earliest days, the authors developed the *Math Trailblazers* curriculum on a foundation of equity. This means that all children in all classrooms have the right to access rigorous mathematics. This section describes the integral structures and features of *Math Trailblazers* that make it accessible to all children. It also contains a section for working with English Language Learners and Special Education students, as well as suggestions for working with gifted and talented students.

- **Language in the *Math Trailblazers* Classroom**

  Language plays an important role in the *Math Trailblazers* Classroom. Language is used to convey mathematical problems. For example, vignettes of everyday situations are often used as contexts for establishing and exploring mathematical content. Both written and spoken language are essential to communicate mathematical ideas, strategies, and solutions. This section describes strategies to help students learn to effectively communicate in the math classroom, including tips on how to help students learn mathematical vocabulary in context.

- **Manipulatives List**
  A listing of the manipulatives required for program implementation is included in this section.
- **Literature List**
  Math Trailblazers uses commercially available trade books in many lessons. A listing of these trade books is included in this section.
- **Games List**
  Games are often used in *Math Trailblazers* to engage students in practicing basic arithmetic skills and other math concepts. Once introduced, these games can be used throughout the year for ongoing practice. A complete listing and description of the games for your grade are provided.
- **Software List**
  Math Trailblazers does not require the use of computers. We do, instead, suggest some software programs that can supplement the curriculum. A listing of these programs and some suggested uses for them are provided.
- **Suggestions for Working with Parents**
  When adopting a math program that is new and different, such as *Math Trailblazers*, it is important to keep parents informed and educated about the program. Some hints for working with parents regarding *Math Trailblazers* are outlined in this section. A brochure about the curriculum and a parent letter describing the math facts program are also provided. The documents are in both English and Spanish.
- **Glossary**
  Most *Math Trailblazers* lessons include mathematical terms relevant to the lesson. The glossary defines many of these terms and can also be used to locate key vocabulary in the lessons. Most definitions cite the locations of the term in the curriculum.
- **Index**
  The index is a list of major mathematical topics and their locations in the curriculum. The *Student Guide, Discovery Assignment Book, Adventure Book, Unit Resource Guides,* and *Teacher Implementation Guide* are all referenced in this index.

How to Use the *Teacher Implementation Guide*

Use of this guide will differ depending upon your purpose. Suggestions for using it for different purposes are described here.

If you are a teacher considering whether to use *Math Trailblazers:*
The *Teacher Implementation Guide* provides useful information for adoption committees or individual teachers who are considering *Math Trailblazers*. General information about the program that will be most helpful for this group includes the Foundations, alignment with the NCTM *Principles and Standards,* Scope and Sequence, and the Overview. The Components and Features Guide will help reviewers understand the purposes of the different student and teacher books. Other specific information, such as the Math Facts and Whole-Number Operations section and the Assessment section, may also be useful for potential users of the curriculum.

If you are a teacher who is about to use *Math Trailblazers* for the first time:

There is too much information in the *Teacher Implementation Guide* and the *Unit Resource Guide* for any teacher to digest all at once. To make effective use of the *Teacher Implementation Guide,* it is best to select portions to examine at different points in the curriculum implementation. Prior to using *Math Trailblazers,* glance at the Foundations section to get a sense of our overall philosophy. However, you will probably want to spend more time reviewing the sections that provide specific information

about using the curriculum. This information will help you get started and plan for the year.

Carefully review the Components and Features Guide to see the big picture of the program's components and features. This information will eventually become second nature as you gain experience with the curriculum, but it will be helpful at first to see what is included in the program. We suggest you review the Overview to get a feel for what is covered over the year and can plan ahead. It will be easier to make instructional decisions if you know what is planned for later lessons. The Assessment section and the Daily Practice and Problems Guide are essential and should be read prior to beginning the curriculum. Among the TIMS Tutors, we suggest that you first review *Math Facts.* It outlines our philosophy and plan for introducing the math facts. The

manipulatives and literature lists are useful tools if you are ordering manipulatives. The section on working with parents will also be useful to read prior to using the curriculum. Use the rest of the *Teacher Implementation Guide* as the need arises.

If you are a teacher who is already using *Math Trailblazers*:

During your first several years of using *Math Trailblazers,* you will likely refer to the *Teacher Implementation Guide* on an ongoing basis. You will find the TIMS Tutors particularly valuable in helping you better understand the content and approaches of key parts

of the curriculum. There are numerous pointers in the *Unit Resource Guide* to individual tutors. The Scope and Sequence supplements the Overview in providing detailed information about when specific concepts are covered. Review the Games List and Software List periodically to help you in lesson planning. Any background information not found in the *Unit Resource Guide* is probably in the *Teacher Implementation Guide.*

If you are a school administrator in a school using *Math Trailblazers:*

The school administrator is the leader of the *Math Trailblazers* implementation. As the instructional leader, the school administrator works with the staff to establish, communicate, and support the goals of the mathematics program as the implementation unfolds. The *Administrator Handbook* contains a description of the important components of a math implementation and explanations of strategies to successfully guide the implementation. It also contains blackline masters to use in presentations with staff and other audiences. Important sections from the *Teacher Implementation Guide* are also included.

If you are planning staff development sessions about *Math Trailblazers:*

Implementation of *Math Trailblazers* is most effective when accompanied by a comprehensive professional development program. An orientation to *Math Trailblazers* is made available to schools using *Math Trailblazers* through Kendall/Hunt Publishing. We recommend that schools continue their professional development throughout the lifetime of the implementation. The TIMS Project has developed presenters' guides for a variety of professional development sessions. These guides, called Teacher Enhancement Resource Modules (TERMs), contain a guide for presenters with explanatory text, discussion questions and answers, and blackline masters. Most TERMs include video that demonstrates the *Math Trailblazers* curriculum in action. Used together the 18 TERMs provide approximately 70 hours of staff development in both the content and pedagogy of *Math Trailblazers.* The TERMs are available through Kendall/Hunt Publishing.

For specific suggestions about planning local staff development related to *Math Trailblazers,* contact the Teaching Integrated Mathematics and Science (TIMS) Project at 800-454-TIMS or Kendall/Hunt Publishing Company at 800-542-6657. Information is also available on the *Math Trailblazers* Implementation Center website at *www.math.uic.edu/IMSE* and at *www.mathtrailblazers.com.*

Foundations of *Math Trailblazers*

The Foundations of *Math Trailblazers* describes the principles behind *Math Trailblazers* and discusses the curriculum's key features.

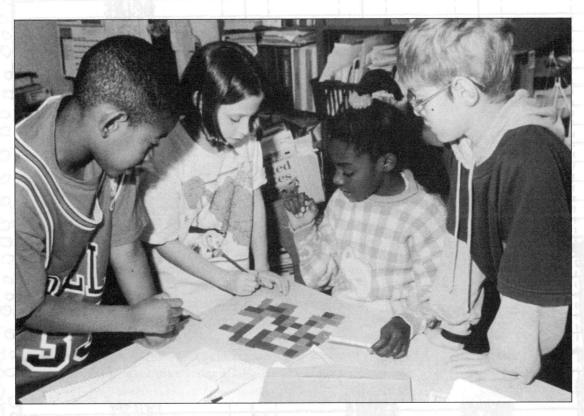

Students work together to solve problems.

Foundations of *Math Trailblazers*

Math Trailblazers is an elementary mathematics curriculum for schools that want their math programs to reflect the goals and ideas of the National Council of Teachers of Mathematics (NCTM) *Principles and Standards for School Mathematics.* With funding from the National Science Foundation (NSF) the TIMS (Teaching Integrated Mathematics and Science) Project at the University of Illinois at Chicago created a comprehensive program that embodies the *Principles and Standards.*

Math Trailblazers is based on the ideas that mathematics is best learned in real-world contexts that make sense to children; that all students deserve a richer and more challenging curriculum; and that a balanced and practical approach to learning mathematics is what students need and teachers want.

Features of *Math Trailblazers*
Alignment with Reform Recommendations

The *Principles and Standards,* which was released in 2000, is an update of three groundbreaking volumes published a decade earlier that collectively became known as the "NCTM *Standards.*" This publication was extended in 2006 with the release of the *Curriculum Focal Points for Prekindergarten through Grade 8 Mathematics: A Quest for Coherence,* which was "offered as a starting point in a dialogue on what is important at particular levels of instruction as an initial step toward a more coherent, focused curriculum in this country." (NCTM 2006, p. vii) However, in describing the relationship between the documents, the NCTM states that the *Principles and Standards* "remains the definitive reference on the development of mathematical content and processes across the grades." (NCTM 2006, p. 1)

The NCTM documents outline a vision for school mathematics that includes: a mathematically challenging curriculum that is coherent and covers a broad range of mathematical content; a strong focus on engaging students in mathematical problem solving; conceptually oriented instruction that stresses thinking, reasoning, and applying; appropriate uses of calculators and computers; and a strong commitment to promoting success in mathematics among all students—not merely those who traditionally have done well. Most states incorporated this vision for mathematics teaching and learning into their mathematics standards.

The first edition of *Math Trailblazers* took more than six years of work that included extensive pilot and field testing of the materials. After publication of the first edition, continued NSF support enabled the TIMS Project to develop implementation models and professional development materials that assisted teachers and schools as they adopted the program.

In developing the second edition of *Math Trailblazers,* we looked carefully at the NCTM *Principles and Standards* and reorganized portions of the *Math Trailblazers,* such as the math facts program, to keep *Math Trailblazers* closely aligned with the new NCTM recommendations. TIMS researchers also studied how the program impacted student achievement. The second edition of *Math Trailblazers* therefore represented more than twelve years of NSF-supported work related to the curriculum.

The third edition provides materials in an easier-to-use format, as well as new content for teachers and administrators. This content was suggested and shaped by other lessons learned from our years of professional development work with schools and districts across the country that implement *Math Trailblazers*.

The importance of a coherent, well-developed curriculum is clear in the *Principles and Standards,* which states:

A curriculum is more than a collection of activities: it must be coherent, focused on important mathematics, and well articulated across the grades. A school mathematics curriculum is a strong determinant of what students have an opportunity to learn and what they do learn. In a coherent curriculum, mathematical ideas are linked to and build on one another so that students' understanding and knowledge deepens and their ability to apply mathematics expands. An effective mathematics curriculum focuses on important mathematics—mathematics that will prepare students for continued study and for solving problems in a variety of school, home, and work settings. A well-articulated curriculum challenges students to learn increasingly more sophisticated mathematical ideas as they continue their studies. (NCTM, 2000, p. 14)

Math Trailblazers was developed with that goal in mind. It is a *Standards*-based curriculum in the truest sense—developed explicitly to reflect national standards for K–5 mathematics, and now revised to maintain close alignment with those standards as they have evolved.

More specific connections between *Math Trailblazers* and the NCTM *Principles and Standards* are discussed in Scope and Sequence & the NCTM *Principles and Standards* (Section 5).

High Expectations and Equity

The first principle in the *Principles and Standards* is the Equity Principle. It challenges a myth prevalent in the United States that only a few students are capable of rigorous mathematics. The Equity Principle states:

> *Excellence in mathematics education requires equity—high expectations and strong support for all students.* (NCTM, 2000, p. 12)

Accordingly, we introduce challenging content in every grade: computation, measurement, data collection, statistics, geometry, ratio, probability, graphing, algebraic concepts, estimation, mental arithmetic, and patterns and relationships.

Contexts for this demanding content begin with students' lives. Lessons are grounded in everyday situations, so abstractions build on experience. By presenting mathematics in rich contexts, the curriculum helps students make connections among real situations, words, pictures, data, graphs, and symbols. The curriculum also validates students' current understandings while new understandings develop. Students can solve problems in ways they understand while being encouraged to connect those ways to more abstract and powerful methods. Within the same lesson, some students may work directly with the manipulatives to solve the problems while other students may solve the same problems using graphs or symbols. The use of varied contexts and diverse representations of concepts allows children of varying abilities to access the mathematics.

Problem Solving

A fundamental principle of *Math Trailblazers* is that mathematics is best learned through actively solving real problems. Questions a student can answer immediately may be worthwhile exercises, but *problems,* by definition, are difficult, but not impossible.

The importance of problem solving is echoed in the NCTM *Principles and Standards,* which states:

> *Problem solving is the cornerstone of school mathematics. . . . The goal of school mathematics should be for all students to become increasingly able and willing to engage with and solve problems.*

> *Problem solving is also important because it can serve as a vehicle for learning new mathematical ideas and skills (Schroeder and Lester). A problem-centered approach to teaching mathematics uses interesting and well-selected problems to launch mathematical lessons and engage students. In this way, new ideas, techniques, and mathematical relationships emerge and become the focus of discussion. (NCTM, 2000, p. 182)*

As recommended by NCTM, problem solving in *Math Trailblazers* is not a distinct topic but permeates the entire program, providing a context for learning concepts and skills. Throughout the curriculum, students apply the mathematics they know and construct new mathematics as needed. Students' skills, procedures, and concepts emerge and develop as they solve complex problems.

Connections to Science and Language Arts

Real-world problems are naturally interdisciplinary, so any problem-solving curriculum should integrate topics that are traditionally separated. Accordingly, we have integrated mathematics with many disciplines, especially science and language arts.

Connections to Science

Math Trailblazers is a full mathematics program that incorporates many important scientific ideas. Traditionally, school science has focused on the results of science. Students learn about plate tectonics, the atomic theory of matter, the solar system, the environment, and so on. Knowing basic facts of science is seen as part of being educated, today more than ever. However, the facts of science, important and interesting as they are, do not alone constitute a comprehensive and balanced science curriculum.

Science has two aspects: results and method. The results of scientific inquiry have enriched human life the world over. More marvelous than the results of science, however, is the method that established those results. Without the method, the results would never have been achieved. *Math Trailblazers* aims to teach students the method of science through scientific investigation of everyday phenomena. During these investigations, students learn both mathematics and science.

The method scientists use is powerful, flexible, and quantitative. The TIMS Project has organized this method in a way that is simple enough for elementary school children to use. Students use the TIMS Laboratory Method in a rich variety of mathematical investigations. In these investigations, students develop and apply important mathematical skills and concepts in meaningful situations. Their understanding of fundamental scientific concepts is also enhanced through the use of quantitative tools.

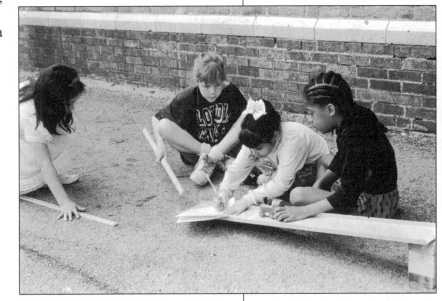

Investigations begin with discussions of experimental situations, variables, and procedures. Then students draw pictures that indicate the experimental procedures and identify key variables. Next students gather and organize data in data tables. Then they graph their data. By analyzing their data or studying their graphs, students are able to see patterns. These patterns show any relationships between the variables. Students can use the relationships to make predictions about future data. The last phase of the experiment is an in-depth analysis of the experimental results, structured as a series of exploratory questions. Some questions ask students to make predictions and then to verify them. Other questions probe students' understanding of underlying concepts and explore the role of controlled variables. As students advance through the curriculum, the questions progress from simple to complex, building eventually to problems that require proportional reasoning, multiple-step logic, and algebra.

The TIMS Laboratory Method initiates children into the authentic practice of science. Identifying variables, drawing pictures, measuring, organizing data in tables, graphing data, and looking for and using patterns are a major part of many scientists' work. This is a major goal of science: to discover and use relationships between variables—usually expressed in some mathematical form—in order to understand and make predictions about the world.

The science content in *Math Trailblazers* focuses on a small set of simple variables that are fundamental to both math and science: length, area, volume, mass, and time. Understanding these basic variables is an essential step to achieving scientific understanding of more complex concepts. Measurement is presented in meaningful, experimental situations.

Emphasizing the scientific method and fundamental science concepts helps students develop an understanding of how scientists and mathematicians think. These habits of mind will be important in all aspects of life in the 21st century. See the TIMS Tutor: *The TIMS Laboratory Method* for more discussion of these ideas.

Connections to Language Arts

Reading, writing, and talking belong in mathematics class, not only because real mathematicians and scientists read, write, and talk mathematics and science constantly, but also because these activities help students learn. The NCTM *Principles and Standards* emphasizes the importance of communication and discourse for students to achieve at higher levels.

In school mathematics, results should be accepted not merely because

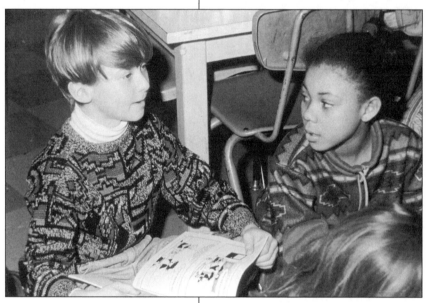

someone in authority says so, but rather because persuasive arguments can be made for them. A result and a reason are often easier to remember than the result alone. By discussing the mathematics they are doing, students increase their understanding. They also extend their abilities to discuss mathematics and so to participate in a community of mathematicians. Talking or writing about mathematics is part of every lesson. Journal and discussion prompts are standard features in the teacher's guide for each lesson.

Reading is also built into this curriculum. Many lessons, especially in the primary grades, use trade books to launch or extend mathematical investigations. The curriculum also includes many original stories, called *Adventure Books,* that show applications of concepts or sketch episodes from the history of mathematics and science. Literature is used to portray mathematics as a human endeavor, so that students come to think of mathematicians and scientists as people like themselves. Mathematics embedded in a narrative structure is also easier to understand, remember, and discuss. And, of course, everyone loves a good story. In addition, students regularly write about their mathematical investigations, even in the early grades.

Collaborative Work

Scientists, mathematicians, and most others who solve complex problems in business and industry have always worked in groups. The reasons for this are simple: Most interesting problems are too difficult for one person. Explaining one's work to another person can help clarify one's thinking. Another person's perspective can suggest a new approach to a problem. Ideas that have been tested through public scrutiny are more trustworthy than private notions.

All these are reasons for collaborating in schools as well. But there are other reasons, too. Students can learn both by receiving and by giving explanations. The communication that goes with group work provides practice in verbal and symbolic communication skills. In group discussion, a basic assumption is that mathematics and science ought to make sense—something, unfortunately, that many students stop believing after only a few years of school. Social skills, especially cooperation and tolerance, increase, and the classroom community becomes more oriented towards learning and academic achievement.

Assessment

There are three major purposes for assessment. First, assessment helps teachers learn about students' thinking and knowledge: information that can then be used to guide instruction. Secondly, it communicates the goals of instruction to students and parents. Finally, it informs students and parents about progress toward these goals and suggests directions for further efforts.

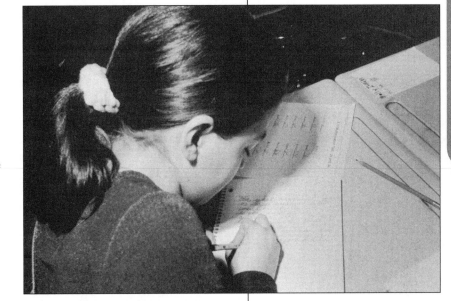

Assessment in *Math Trailblazers* reflects the breadth and balance of the curriculum. Numerous opportunities for both formal and informal assessment of student learning are integrated into the program. Many assessment activities are incorporated into the daily lessons; others are included in formal assessment units. Assessment activities include a mix of short, medium-length, and extended activities. Some are hands-on investigations, others are paper-and-pencil tasks. In all cases, assessment activities further students' learning.

For a detailed discussion of assessment in *Math Trailblazers,* refer to Assessment (Section 8) and the TIMS Tutor: *Portfolios.*

More Time Studying Mathematics

One cannot reasonably expect to cover all the concepts in a traditional program, add many new topics, and utilize an approach that emphasizes problem solving, communication, reasoning, and connections in the same amount of time used to teach a traditional math curriculum. In developing *Math Trailblazers,* we have attempted to achieve some efficiencies, such as building review into new concepts and using effective strategies to teach math facts and procedures. However, there is no magic in *Math Trailblazers.* Implementing a comprehensive, reform mathematics curriculum will require a significant amount of time. **We assume that in Grades 1–5 one hour**

every day will be devoted to teaching mathematics. In Kindergarten, the class make-up and the activity will determine the length of the class.

In some schools, finding an hour per day for math instruction may require a restructuring of the daily school schedule. Please note, however, that because *Math Trailblazers* includes extensive connections with science and language arts, *some* time spent with *Math Trailblazers* can be incorporated within science or language arts time. Thus, it may be possible to allot the one hour per day of mathematics instruction by simply scheduling math and science instruction back to back or including literature connections and journal writing in language arts.

Hard work on the part of students and more time engaged in mathematical problem solving are important ingredients to success in mathematics—no matter what program you are using. Because students using *Math Trailblazers* are actively involved in applying mathematics in meaningful contexts, our experience is that students will be highly motivated to spend extra time studying mathematics.

Staff Development and Broad School Support: Essential Ingredients

Developing the curriculum and working with schools over the last 20 years has taught us that implementing a *Standards*-based mathematics program will progress more smoothly if it is accompanied by a solid support system for teachers. Ideally, this includes a professional development program that includes workshops on content and pedagogy, leadership development, in-school support, and the means to address a variety of concerns as they arise.

Overall implementation of *Math Trailblazers* will be much easier in a school that organizes support for the new program. Necessary tools such as manipulatives, overhead projectors, and transparency masters need to be provided in adequate quantities. Institutional considerations, such as classroom schedules that allot necessary time for instruction and provide time for teachers to meet and plan together, need to be implemented. In-classroom support from resource teachers is extremely helpful. Storage and check-out systems for shared manipulatives need to be in place. Ways to engender parental support for the program, including possible ways to involve some parents in providing classroom assistance to interested teachers during math time, should be developed.

Administrators need to maintain a long-term perspective recognizing that program implementation will take some time—and they need to communicate this clearly to teachers. In short, schools need to examine their current situations and make necessary modifications to develop a school environment that supports the kind of teaching and learning that characterizes *Math Trailblazers*.

A Balanced Approach

A reform mathematics program should take a balanced and moderate approach. *Math Trailblazers* is balanced in many different ways with whole-class instruction, small-group activities, and individual work. New mathematical content is included, but traditional topics are not neglected.

Children construct their own knowledge in rich problem-solving situations, but they are not expected to reinvent 5000 years of mathematics. Concepts, procedures, and facts are important, but are introduced thoughtfully to engender the positive attitudes, beliefs, and self-image that are also important in the long run. Hands-on activities of varied length and depth, as well as paper-and-pencil tasks, all have their place. The program's rich variety of assessment activities reflects this broad balance.

Either-or rhetoric has too often short-circuited real progress in education: problem solving vs. back-to-basics, conceptual understanding vs. procedural skill, paper-and-pencil computation vs. calculators. *Math Trailblazers* is based on the view that these are false dichotomies. Students must solve problems, but of course they need basic skills to do so. Both concepts and procedures are important, and neglecting one will undermine the other. There is a place in the curriculum both for paper-and-pencil algorithms and for calculators, and for mental arithmetic and estimation. The careful balance in *Math Trailblazers* allows teachers and schools to move forward with a reform mathematics curriculum while maintaining the strengths of their current teaching practices.

Research Foundations of *Math Trailblazers*

The first edition of *Math Trailblazers* was completed in 1997. The roots of the curriculum, however, date back to the late 1970s and the work of Howard Goldberg, a particle physicist at the University of Illinois at Chicago (UIC). Building on the work of Robert Karplus and others, Goldberg developed a framework for adapting the scientific method for elementary school children and applied that framework within a series of elementary laboratory investigations (Goldberg & Boulanger, 1981). Goldberg was joined in 1985 by UIC mathematician Philip Wagreich and, together with others, formed the Teaching Integrated Mathematics and Science Project (TIMS).

Thus, the motivation behind TIMS came from two sources, one with roots in science and one with roots in mathematics. The scientific impetus stemmed from the desire to teach science to children in a manner that reflects the practice of scientists. Modern science is fundamentally quantitative; therefore, quantitative investigations should have an important role in children's science education. The mathematical impetus was to find a way to make mathematics meaningful to children. Engaging children in quantitative investigations of common phenomena harnesses their curiosity in a way that builds on their understanding of the natural world, which, in turn, helps promote study of rigorous mathematics (Isaacs, Wagreich, & Gartzman, 1997).

Initially, TIMS focused primarily on the development and implementation of a series of quantitative, hands-on activities, the *TIMS Laboratory Investigations* (Goldberg, 1997). The laboratory investigations continue the tradition of Dewey (1910) and others in focusing on the method of science and on exploring a relatively small set of fundamental scientific concepts in depth. Several studies provided clear evidence that the *TIMS Laboratory Investigations* are effective in promoting students' development of mathematics and science concepts (Goldberg & Wagreich, 1990; Goldberg, 1993).

Based largely on the success with the supplemental *TIMS Laboratory Investigations,* the National Science Foundation (NSF) supported the TIMS Project to develop a comprehensive, elementary mathematics curriculum that would align with the National Council of Teachers of Mathematics (NCTM) *Curriculum and Evaluation Standards for School Mathematics* (NCTM, 1989). The first edition of *Math Trailblazers* is the result of this work. As part of the revision process for the second edition, the authors made changes so that the new edition aligns with the current NCTM recommendations as outlined in the *Principles and Standards for School Mathematics* (NCTM, 2000).

The third edition provides materials in an easier-to-use format, as well as new content for teachers and administrators. This content embodies the lessons learned from our TIMS Project's 20 years of professional development work with schools and districts that implement *Math Trailblazers.*

In developing each edition of *Math Trailblazers,* the authors drew upon research findings from a wide variety of sources, as well as from the broad experiences of the authoring group. In this section we highlight a portion of the research that helped guide the curriculum's development and other current research that validates the approaches used.

A Problem-Solving Curriculum

A distinguishing element of any *Standards*-based mathematics curriculum is that problem solving is used as a context for students to learn new concepts and skills. Throughout *Math Trailblazers,* students apply the mathematics they know and construct new mathematics as needed. Students' skills, procedures, and concepts emerge and develop as they solve problems. Students also practice skills and procedures as they apply them in diverse and increasingly challenging contexts. Problem-solving contexts can emerge from real-life investigations or from more mathematical situations. The problems serve as the motivation for purposeful use of mathematics.

Using problem solving as a cornerstone of the mathematics curriculum has been promoted by educators dating back to Dewey and has received considerable support from current mathematics education researchers. (See Hiebert et al., 1996; Schoenfeld, 1985 and 1994; National Research Council, 2001; and NCTM 1989 and 2000 for a discussion of problem solving in the curriculum.)

A curriculum that emphasizes solving problems can use many different contexts. In developing *Math Trailblazers,* the authors first identified the key mathematical concepts and skills to be developed and then selected problem-solving contexts to support student learning in these areas. Our earlier work and that of others (e.g., Cognition and Technology Group at Vanderbilt, 1997) had confirmed the value of using quantitative laboratory investigations for this purpose. Drawing from this work, eight to ten laboratory investigations were adapted and integrated into *Math Trailblazers* in each grade, beginning with first grade. These investigations are supplemented by many other contexts for problem solving.

Challenging Mathematics in All Grades for All Students

An assumption in the development of *Math Trailblazers* was that students can learn more challenging mathematics than is covered in traditional mathematics curricula. This has been underscored in international comparison studies (Heibert, 1999; McKnight et al., 1987; Stigler & Perry, 1988; Schmidt, McKnight, & Raizen, 1996; Stigler & Hiebert, 1997; Stevenson & Stigler, 1992) and in analyses of U.S. mathematics instruction (Flanders, 1987; Lindquist, 1989). Maintaining high expectations and providing access to rigorous mathematics for all students has proven effective regardless of the socioeconomic status and ethnicity of the students (National Research Council, 2001; Newmann, Bryk, & Nagaoka, 2001; Smith, Lee, & Newmann, 2001). Therefore, mathematical expectations in *Math Trailblazers* are high and grow steadily. Review of concepts and skills is carefully built into new and increasingly challenging problems as the program builds upon itself both within and across grades.

Balancing Concept and Skill Development

The importance of developing a strong conceptual foundation is emphasized in research that guided the development of all content strands in *Math Trailblazers.* Many educators have long recognized the importance of balancing conceptual and skill development. New conceptual understandings are built upon existing skills and concepts; these new understandings in turn support the further development of skills and concepts.

A wide body of research affirms that instructional programs that emphasize conceptual development can facilitate significant mathematics learning without sacrificing skill proficiency (see Hiebert, 1999). Research affirms that well-designed and implemented instructional programs can facilitate both conceptual understanding and procedural skill.

This research had a profound effect on development of *Math Trailblazers.* For example, such research helped define the curriculum's program for developing number sense and estimation skills (Sowder, 1992) and for learning math facts and whole-number operations (Carpenter, Carey, & Kouba, 1990; Carpenter, et al., 1999; Fuson, 1987, 1992; Fuson & Briars, 1990; Fuson et al., 1997; Isaacs & Carroll, 1999; Lampert, 1986a, 1986b; Thornton, 1978, 1990a, 1990b). Work with fractions and decimals was informed by research that stressed the need to develop conceptual understandings of fractions and decimals prior to introducing procedures with the four arithmetic operations (see Behr & Post, 1992; Ball, 1993; Cramer, Post, & del Mas, 2002; Lesh, Post, & Behr, 1987; Mack, 1990; Hoffer & Hoffer, 1992). Similar research findings on student understanding of geometric concepts shaped the development of lessons in geometry (see Burger & Shaughnessy, 1986; Crowley, 1987; Fuys, Geddes, & Tishler, 1988).

In direct response to research such as that cited here, every content strand within *Math Trailblazers* interweaves the promotion of conceptual understanding with distributed practice of skills and procedures.

Field Testing and Research on the Curriculum in Classrooms

NSF funding allowed sequential development of the program to be coupled with extensive field testing in schools. As a result, curriculum development became an iterative process involving considerable interaction between the developers and field-test teachers. Comments and suggestions from teachers were incorporated into revisions that were often retested in classrooms one or more times before final revisions were made. Field-test teachers met regularly with the program's authors, and classrooms were often visited as part of the development process. Teachers using the early versions in their classrooms addressed content, language, format, practical considerations, and other issues related to each lesson.

In addition to assessing feedback from field-test teachers, independent researchers and TIMS Project staff conducted preliminary studies that helped affirm the efficacy of the content placement and approaches in the early versions of the materials (Burghardt, 1994; Perry, Whiteaker, & Waddoups, 1996; Whiteaker, Waddoups, & Perry, 1994). These preliminary studies provided an additional means for the authors to monitor the effectiveness of the developing program.

Early studies of student achievement in *Math Trailblazers* classrooms in both urban and suburban schools have shown that students using the curriculum performed as well, and often better, on mandated standardized tests than students in those schools prior to implementation of *Math Trailblazers*. (Carter, et al., 2003; Putnam, 2003) "[The results] indicate that the balanced problem-solving approach found in *Math Trailblazers* has been successful in improving student learning and achievement in mathematics." (Carter, et al., 2003)

In developing the second edition, we benefited from the suggestions and comments of teachers throughout the country who were using the published *Math Trailblazers* materials. Input from teachers, for example, resulted in the major changes to the second edition's teacher guides. Teachers' feedback also directed us to modify or eliminate some lessons.

In third edition development, changes were made to the format and content for teachers and administrators based on surveys, focus groups, and feedback from teachers and administrators. The format of the third edition materials is easier for teachers to use. New content for teachers and administrators assists with implementation issues in the classroom, school, and district. This content embodies 20 years of professional development work by the TIMS Project with schools and districts that implement *Math Trailblazers*.

Extensive field testing during the program's development, current research and evaluation in schools, and our ongoing conversations with *Math Trailblazers* teachers have helped us develop a challenging, yet grade-level-appropriate program that reflects the needs and realities of teachers and students.

References

The following references are cited in the above document. Additional references to research literature are included in many *Unit Resource Guides* following the Background and in many sections of the *Teacher Implementation Guide* including the Assessment section and the TIMS Tutors.

Ball, D. "Halves, Pieces, and Twoths: Constructing and Using Representational Contexts in Teaching Fractions." In T. P. Carpenter, E. Fennema, and T.A. Romberg (Eds.), *Rational Numbers: An Integration of Research,* pp. 157–195. Lawrence Erlbaum Associates, Hillsdale, NJ, 1993.

Behr, M.J., and T.R. Post. "Teaching Rational Number and Decimal Concepts." In *Teaching Mathematics in Grades K–8: Research Based Methods.* Allyn and Bacon, Boston, 1992.

Burger, W., and J.M. Shaughnessy. "Characterizing the Van Hiele Levels of Development in Geometry." *Journal for Research in Mathematics Education,* 17, pp. 31–48, National Council of Teachers of Mathematics, Reston, VA, 1986.

Burghardt, B. Results of Some Summative Evaluation Studies: 1993–1994 Evaluation Report. (An unpublished report to the National Science Foundation.) 1994.

Carpenter, T.P., D. Carey, and V. Kouba. "A Problem-Solving Approach to the Operations." J.N. Payne, ed., *Mathematics for the Young Child.* National Council of Teachers of Mathematics, Reston, VA, 1990.

Carpenter, T.P., E. Fennema, M.L. Franke, L. Levi, and S.E. Empson. *Children's Mathematics: Cognitively Guided Instruction.* Heinemann, Westport, CT, 1999.

Carter, M.A., J.S. Beissinger, A. Cirulis, M. Gartzman, C.R. Kelso, and P. Wagreich. "Student Learning and Achievement with *Math Trailblazers.*" S.L. Senk and D.R. Thompson, eds., *Standards-Based School Mathematics Curricula: What Does the Research Say about Student Outcomes?* Lawrence Erlbaum Associates, Inc., Hillsdale, NJ, 2003.

Cognition and Technology Group at Vanderbilt. *The Jasper Project: Lessons in Curriculum, Instruction, Assessment, and Professional Development.* Erlbaum, Mahwah, NJ, 1997.

Cramer, K., T. Post, and R. del Mas. "Initial Fraction Learning by Fourth- and Fifth-Grade Students: A Comparison of the Effects of Using Commercial Curricula with the Effects of Using the Rational Number Project Curriculum." *Journal for Research in Mathematics Education,* 33(2), pp. 111–144.

Crowley, M.L. "The Van Hiele Model of Development of Geometric Thought." *Learning and Teaching Geometry, K–12, 1987 Yearbook.* Edited by Mary Montgomery Lindquist. National Council of Teachers of Mathematics, Reston, VA, 1987.

Curriculum and Evaluation Standards for School Mathematics. National Council of Teachers of Mathematics, Reston, VA, 1989.

Dewey, J. "Science as Subject-Matter and as Method." *Science,* 31(787), pp. 121–127, 1910.

Flanders, J. "How Much of the Content in Mathematics Textbooks Is New?" *The Arithmetic Teacher,* 35(1), pp. 18–23, 1987.

Fuson, K.C. "Teaching Addition, Subtraction, and Place-Value Concepts." L. Wirszup and R. Streit (eds.), *Proceedings of the UCSMP International Conference on Mathematics Education: Developments in School Mathematics Education Around the World: Applications-Oriented Curricula and Technology-Supported Learning for All Students.* National Council of Teachers of Mathematics, Reston, VA, 1987.

Fuson, K.C. "Research on Whole Number Addition and Subtraction." *Handbook of Research on Mathematics Teaching and Learning,* pp. 243–275, D.A. Grouws, ed. Macmillan Publishing Company, New York, 1992.

Fuson, K.C., and D.J. Briars. "Using a Base-Ten Blocks Learning/Teaching Approach for First- and Second-Grade Place-Value and Multidigit Addition and Subtraction." *Journal for Research in Mathematics Education,* 21, pp. 180–206, 1990.

Fuson, K.C., D. Wearne, J. Hiebert, H. Murray, P. Human, A. Olivier, T. Carpenter, and E. Fennema. "Children's Conceptual Structures for Multidigit Numbers and Methods of Multidigit Addition and Subtraction." *Journal for Research in Mathematics Education,* 28, pp. 130–162, 1997.

Fuys, D., D. Geddes, and R. Tishler. "The Van Hiele Model of Thinking in Geometry among Adolescents." *Journal for Research in Mathematics Education, Monograph Number 3.* National Council of Teachers of Mathematics, Reston, VA, 1988.

Goldberg, H. *A Four Year Achievement Study: The TIMS Program.* University of Illinois at Chicago Institute for Mathematics and Science Education, Chicago, IL, 1993.

Goldberg, H. *The TIMS Laboratory Investigations.* Kendall/Hunt, Dubuque, IA, 1997.

Goldberg, H.S., and F.D. Boulanger. "Science for Elementary School Teachers: A Quantitative Approach." *American Journal of Physics,* 19(2), pp. 120–124, 1981.

Goldberg, H., and P. Wagreich. "A Model Integrated Mathematics Science Program for the Elementary School." *International Journal of Educational Research,* 14(2), pp. 193–214, 1990.

Goldberg, H., and P. Wagreich. "Teaching Integrated Math and Science: A Curriculum and Staff Development Project for the Elementary School." *Issues in Mathematics Education: Mathematicians and Education Reform.* N. Fisher, H. Keynes, and P. Wagreich, eds., American Mathematical Society, Providence, RI, 1990.

Hiebert, J. "Relationships between Research and the NCTM Standards." *Journal for Research in Mathematics Education,* 30(1), pp. 3–19, 1999.

Hiebert, J., T.P. Carpenter, E. Fennema, K.C. Fuson, P. Human, H. Murray, A. Olivier, D. Wearne. "Problem Solving as a Basis for Reform in Curriculum and Instruction: The Case of Mathematics." *Educational Researcher,* 25(4), pp. 12–21, 1996.

Hoffer, A.R., and S.A.K. Hoffer. "Ratios and Proportional Thinking." In *Teaching Mathematics in Grades K–8: Research Based Methods.* Allyn and Bacon, Boston, 1992.

Isaacs, A.C., and W.M. Carroll. "Strategies for Basic-Facts Instruction." *Teaching Children Mathematics,* 5(9), pp. 508–515, 1999.

Isaacs, A.C., P. Wagreich, and M. Gartzman. The Quest for Integration: School Mathematics and Science. *American Journal of Education,* 106(1), pp. 179–206, 1997.

Lampert, M. "Knowing, Doing, and Teaching Multiplication." *Cognition and Instruction,* 3 (4), pp. 305–342, 1986a.

Lampert, M. "Teaching Multiplication." *Journal of Mathematical Behavior,* 5, pp. 241–280, 1986b.

Lesh, R., T. Post, and M. Behr. "Representations and Translations Among Representations in Mathematics Learning and Problem Solving." C. Janvier, ed., *Problems of Representation in the Teaching and Learning of Mathematics.* Lawrence Erlbaum Associates, Hillsdale, NJ, 1987.

Lindquist, M.M., ed. *Results from the Fourth Mathematics Assessment of the National Assessment of Educational Progress.* National Council of Teachers of Mathematics. Reston, VA, 1989.

Mack, N.K. "Learning Fractions with Understanding: Building on Informal Knowledge." *Journal for Research in Mathematics Education,* 21(1), National Council of Teachers of Mathematics, Reston, VA, January 1990.

McKnight, C.C., F.J. Crosswhite, J.A. Dossey, E. Kifer, J.O. Swafford, K.T. Travers, and T.J. Cooney, *The Underachieving Curriculum: Assessing U.S. School Mathematics from an International Perspective.* Stipes Publishing Company, Champaign, IL, 1987.

National Research Council. *Adding It Up: Helping Children Learn Mathematics.* J. Kilpatrick, J. Swafford, and B. Findell, eds. National Academy Press, Washington, DC, 2001.

Newmann, F.M., A.S. Bryk, and J.K. Nagaoka. *Authentic Intellectual Work and Standardized Tests: Conflict or Coexistence?* Consortium on Chicago School Research, Chicago, 2001.

Perry, M., M. Whiteaker, and G.L. Waddoups. "Students' Participation in a Reform Mathematics Classroom: Learning to Become Mathematicians." In K. Fuson (Chair), *Effects of Reform Mathematics Curricula on Children's Mathematical Understanding.* Symposia conducted at the annual meeting of the American Educational Research Association, New York, 1996.

Principles and Standards for School Mathematics. National Council of Teachers of Mathematics, Reston, VA, 2000.

Putnam, R.T. "Commentary on Four Elementary Mathematics Curricula." S.L. Senk and D.R. Thompson, eds., *Standards-Based School Mathematics Curricula: What Does the Research Say about Student Outcomes?* Lawrence Erlbaum Associates, Inc., Hillsdale, NJ, 2003.

Schmidt, W.H., C.C. McKnight, and S.A. Raizen. *A Splintered Vision: An Investigation of U.S. Science and Mathematics Education.* Kluwer, Norwell, MA, 1996.

Schoenfeld, A.H. *Mathematical Problem Solving.* Academic Press, Orlando, FL, 1985.

Schoenfeld, A.H. "What Do We Know about Mathematics Curricula?" *Journal of Mathematical Behavior,* 13(1), pp. 55–80, 1994.

Schroeder, T.L., and F.K. Lester, Jr. "Developing Understanding in Mathematics via Problem Solving." In *New Directions for Elementary School Mathematics,* 1989 Yearbook. National Council of Teachers of Mathematics, Reston, VA, 1989.

Smith, J.B., V.E. Lee, and F.M. Newmann. *Instruction and Achievement in Chicago Elementary Schools.* Consortium on Chicago School Research, Chicago, 2001.

Sowder, J. "Estimation and Number Sense." *Handbook of Research on Mathematics Teaching and Learning,* pp. 243–275, D.A. Grouws, ed., Macmillan Publishing Company, New York, 1992.

Stevenson, H.W., and J.W. Stigler. *The Learning Gap.* Simon & Schuster, New York, 1992.

Stigler, J.W., and J. Hiebert. "Understanding and Improving Classroom Mathematics Instruction: An Overview of the TIMSS Study." *Phi Delta Kappan,* 79(1), pp. 14–21.

Stigler, J.W., and M. Perry. "Mathematics Learning in Japanese, Chinese, and American Classrooms." G.B. Saxe and M. Gearhart, eds., *New Directions for Child Development, No. 41: Children's Mathematics.* Jossey Bass, San Francisco, CA, 1988.

Thornton, C.A. "Emphasizing Thinking Strategies in Basic Fact Instruction." *Journal for Research in Mathematics Education,* 9 (3), pp. 214–227, 1978.

Thornton, C.A. "Solution Strategies: Subtraction Number Facts." *Educational Studies in Mathematics,* 21 (1), pp. 241–263, 1990a.

Thornton, C.A. "Strategies for the Basic Facts." *Mathematics for the Young Child,* pp. 133–151, J.N. Payne, ed. National Council of Teachers of Mathematics, Reston, VA, 1990b.

Whiteaker, M., G.L. Waddoups, and M. Perry. "Implementing a New Mathematics Curriculum: Constructing Models for Success." Paper presented at annual meeting of the American Educational Research Association, New Orleans, 1994.

Components and Features Guide

The Components and Features Guide presents reduced-size curriculum pages and descriptive boxes that cover each element of *Math Trailblazers*.

Students use Activity, Lab, and Game Pages, which are provided in the student books.

Components of *Math Trailblazers*

The following pages offer a walk-through of the *Teacher Implementation Guide, Unit Resource Guide, Facts Resource Guide, Teacher Resource CD, Student Guide, Discovery Assignment Book,* and *Adventure Book.*

Teacher Materials

TEACHER IMPLEMENTATION GUIDE (TIG)

- reference guide for teachers, containing program philosophy, overview, and in-depth reference documents, including a section on assessment
- black and white, nonconsumable
- glossary, including locations of key vocabulary terms in the curriculum
- curriculum index with page references to key vocabulary terms

TEACHER RESOURCE CD

Teacher resource containing:

- Daily Practice and Problems (DPP) items
- Observational Assessment Record
- Individual Assessment Record Sheet
- Letters Home (English and Spanish)
- Sections from the Facts Resource Guide
- Assessment, Transparency, and Blackline Masters
- Reproducibles
- Student and Teacher Rubrics

UNIT RESOURCE GUIDE (URG)

- comprehensive guide providing essential background information and materials for day-to-day planning, instruction, and assessment
- four-color, nonconsumable
- contains:
  Letters Home (English and Spanish)
  Unit Outlines
  Daily Practice and Problems
  Observational Assessment Record
  Lesson Guides
  Materials Lists
  Assessment Pages
  Transparency and Blackline Masters
  Answer Keys
  Glossary

FACTS RESOURCE GUIDE GRADES 2–5

- compilation of most math facts materials for each grade
- black and white, nonconsumable
- contains:
  DPP and Home Practice math facts items
  Facts Quizzes
  Games
  Lessons focusing on math facts
  Math Facts Philosophy
  Triangle Flash Cards

Student Materials

STUDENT GUIDE (SG)

- core materials for students
- four-color
- soft-cover, consumable: Grades 1, 2
- hard-cover, nonconsumable: Grades 3, 4, 5
- glossary and index: Grades 1, 2
- glossary-embedded index: Grades 3, 4, 5

DISCOVERY ASSIGNMENT BOOK (DAB) GRADES 3–5

- consumable student pages
- soft-cover, black and white
- double- and single-sided worksheets

ADVENTURE BOOK (AB)

- collections of illustrated stories focused on math and science concepts
- available in four-color Big Adventure Book and consumable black-and-white books in Grades 1, 2
- available in soft-cover, four-color, nonconsumable format in Grades 3, 4, 5

Administrator Materials

ADMINISTRATOR HANDBOOK

- Describes important components of a math implementation
- Strategies for administrators to successfully guide implementation
- Blackline Masters for presentations to staff, parents, or other audiences
- Important sections for administrators from *Teacher Implementation Guides*
- black and white, nonconsumable

Letter Home (Parent Letter)

The Letter Home is designed to be signed and sent by the teacher. It explains what students will study and how their families can help. Spanish versions of letters are also provided.

Carta al hogar
División y datos

Fecha: _____

Estimado miembro de familia:

En esta unidad, su hijo/a hallará las áreas de figuras y dividirá usando divisores de un dígito. Usando estas habilidades, su hijo/a hallará promedios de datos y practicará la estimación. Los estudiantes también participarán en una experiencia de laboratorio titulada Expandiendo.

El método de papel y lápiz que usa *Math Trailblazers®* para hacer la división larga es un poco diferente al modo tradicional que se enseña en los Estados Unidos. Este método, llamado método de división "que perdona", suele ser más fácil de aprender para los estudiantes. No tienen que borrar tanto, y aprenden más sobre división y estimación. Mientras trabajamos juntos en clase, éstas son algunas maneras en las que usted puede ayudar a su hijo/a en casa:

- Animando a su hijo/a a que le enseñe cómo está aprendiendo a dividir.
- Hablando acerca de medir áreas en su casa. Por ejemplo, pueden hablar sobre el número de pies cuadrados en diferentes habitaciones de la casa.
- Pidiéndole a su hijo/a que le cuente más acerca de la experiencia de laboratorio Expan
- Ayudando a su hijo a estudiar las tablas de multiplicación y división en casa. En esta u trabajamos con los números al cuadrado (2 × 2, 3 × 3, 4 × 4, etc.). Use las tarjetas tr para repasar las tablas.

Gracias por su apoyo.

Atentamente,

_____

iv   URG • Grade 5 • Unit 4

Letter Home
Division and Data

Date: _____

Dear Family Member:

In this unit, your child will find the areas of shapes and divide using one-digit divisors. Using these skills, he or she will average data and practice estimation. Students also participate in a lab experience, *Spreading Out*.

The paper-and-pencil method that *Math Trailblazers®* uses to do long division is somewhat different from the way long division is traditionally taught in the United States. This method, called the forgiving division method, is often easier for students to learn. They do not have to erase as much, and they learn more about division and estimation.

As we work together in class, these are some ways to help your child at home:

- Encourage your child to show you how he or she is learning division.
- Talk about measuring area in your home. For example, you might discuss the number of square feet in different rooms in your home.
- Ask your child to tell you more about the lab *Spreading Out*.
- Help your child study the multiplication and division facts at home. In this unit, we work with the square numbers (2 × 2, 3 × 3, 4 × 4, etc.). Use the *Triangle Flash Cards* to help review the facts.

Thank you for your support.

Sincerely,

_____

```
        92
  7 | 644
    - 140    20
      504
      350    50
      154
      140    20
       14
       14     2
        0     92
```

The forgiving division method is often easier for children to learn.

URG • Grade 5 • Unit 4   iii

Components & Features

Art — Most letters include an illustration relating to the unit's activities.

Outline

The Outline indicates the number of lessons, what they are about, supplies you will need for them, how much time they will take, and other materials you may want to introduce. The Outline also includes helpful planning information such as a summary of the unit, Pacing Suggestions, Assessment Indicators, related trade books and software as well as ideas for differentiation.

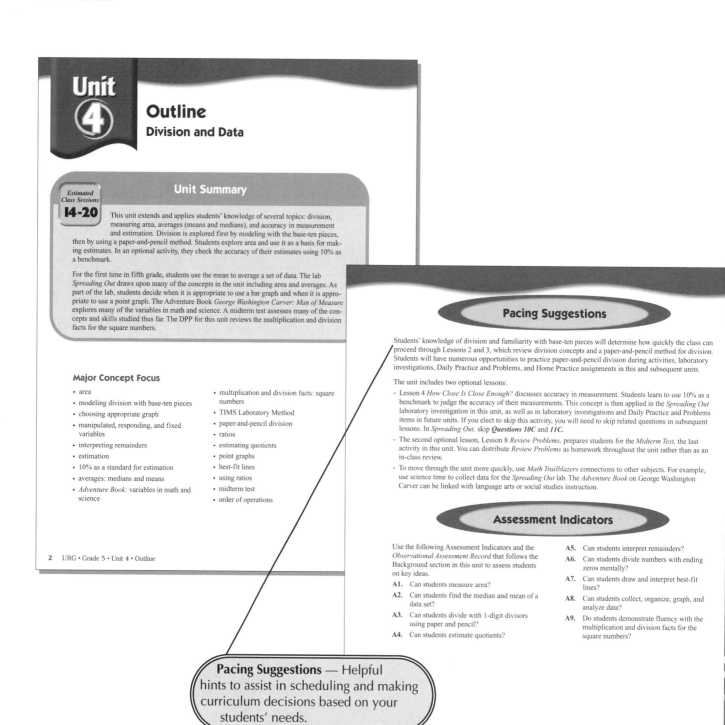

Unit 4

Outline
Division and Data

Estimated Class Sessions
14-20

Unit Summary

This unit extends and applies students' knowledge of several topics: division, measuring area, averages (means and medians), and accuracy in measurement and estimation. Division is explored first by modeling with the base-ten pieces, then by using a paper-and-pencil method. Students explore area and use it as a basis for making estimates. In an optional activity, they check the accuracy of their estimates using 10% as a benchmark.

For the first time in fifth grade, students use the mean to average a set of data. The lab *Spreading Out* draws upon many of the concepts in the unit including area and averages. As part of the lab, students decide when it is appropriate to use a bar graph and when it is appropriate to use a point graph. The Adventure Book *George Washington Carver: Man of Measure* explores many of the variables in math and science. A midterm test assesses many of the concepts and skills studied thus far. The DPP for this unit reviews the multiplication and division facts for the square numbers.

Major Concept Focus

- area
- modeling division with base-ten pieces
- choosing appropriate graph
- manipulated, responding, and fixed variables
- interpreting remainders
- estimation
- 10% as a standard for estimation
- averages: medians and means
- *Adventure Book:* variables in math and science

- multiplication and division facts: square numbers
- TIMS Laboratory Method
- paper-and-pencil division
- ratios
- estimating quotients
- point graphs
- best-fit lines
- using ratios
- midterm test
- order of operations

2   URG • Grade 5 • Unit 4 • Outline

Pacing Suggestions

Students' knowledge of division and familiarity with base-ten pieces will determine how quickly the class can proceed through Lessons 2 and 3, which review division concepts and a paper-and-pencil method for division. Students will have numerous opportunities to practice paper-and-pencil division during activities, laboratory investigations, Daily Practice and Problems, and Home Practice assignments in this and subsequent units.

The unit includes two optional lessons:

- Lesson 4 *How Close Is Close Enough?* discusses accuracy in measurement. Students learn to use 10% as a benchmark to judge the accuracy of their measurements. This concept is then applied in the *Spreading Out* laboratory investigation in this unit, as well as in laboratory investigations and Daily Practice and Problems items in future units. If you elect to skip this activity, you will need to skip related questions in subsequent lessons. In *Spreading Out*, skip **Questions 10C** and **11C**.
- The second optional lesson, Lesson 8 *Review Problems*, prepares students for the *Midterm Test*, the last activity in this unit. You can distribute *Review Problems* as homework throughout the unit rather than as an in-class review.
- To move through the unit more quickly, use *Math Trailblazers* connections to other subjects. For example, use science time to collect data for the *Spreading Out* lab. The *Adventure Book* on George Washington Carver can be linked with language arts or social studies instruction.

Assessment Indicators

Use the following Assessment Indicators and the *Observational Assessment Record* that follows the Background section in this unit to assess students on key ideas.

A1. Can students measure area?

A2. Can students find the median and mean of a data set?

A3. Can students divide with 1-digit divisors using paper and pencil?

A4. Can students estimate quotients?

A5. Can students interpret remainders?

A6. Can students divide numbers with ending zeros mentally?

A7. Can students draw and interpret best-fit lines?

A8. Can students collect, organize, graph, and analyze data?

A9. Do students demonstrate fluency with the multiplication and division facts for the square numbers?

URG • Grade 5 • Unit 4 • Outline   3

Pacing Suggestions — Helpful hints to assist in scheduling and making curriculum decisions based on your students' needs.

Supplies — Describes the type of manipulatives, lab equipment, and other materials essential for each lesson.

Lesson — Indicates the type of lesson (Activity, *Adventure Book,* Assessment, Game, or Lab) and outlines its contents.

Copies/Transparencies — Describes the pages and quantities needed for the lesson.

Component — Tells you where to find student and teacher print materials for each lesson.

Daily Practice and Problems Letters — These letters indicate the suggested DPP items for each lesson.

Math Facts — Highlights the math facts items in the DPP and lessons.

Assessment — Identified here to help you prepare and plan.

Sessions — The number of 60-minute class sessions needed to complete the lesson.

Homework — Alerts you to possible homework for planning.

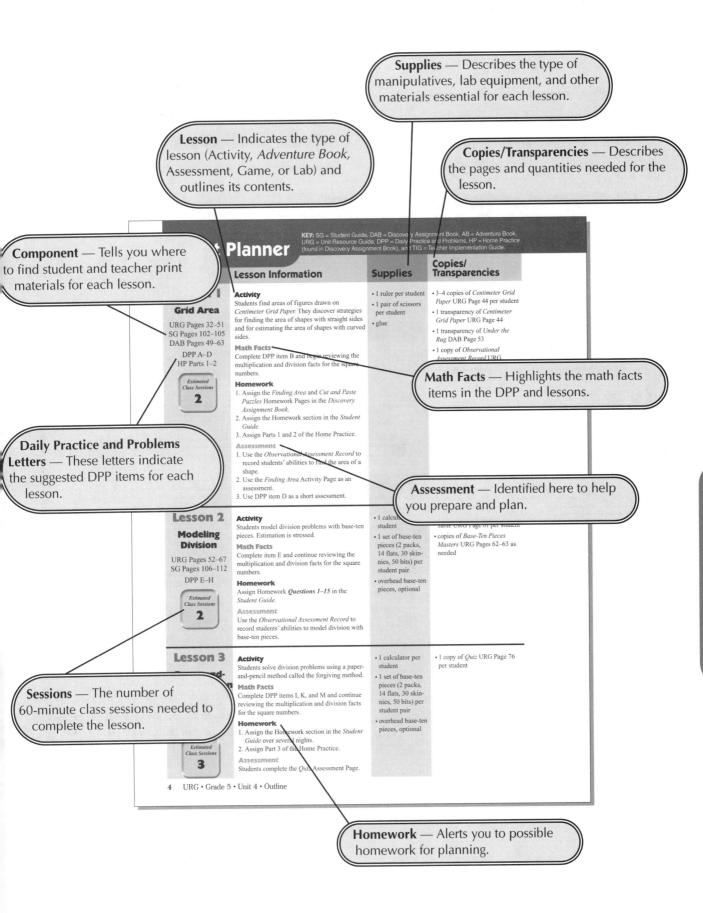

KEY: SG = Student Guide, DAB = Discovery Assignment Book, AB = Adventure Book, URG = Unit Resource Guide, DPP = Daily Practice and Problems, HP = Home Practice (found in Discovery Assignment Book), and TIG = Teacher Implementation Guide.

t Planner

	Lesson Information	Supplies	Copies/ Transparencies

Grid Area

URG Pages 32–51
SG Pages 102–105
DAB Pages 49–63
DPP A–D
HP Parts 1–2

Estimated Class Sessions **2**

Activity
Students find areas of figures drawn on *Centimeter Grid Paper.* They discover strategies for finding the area of shapes with straight sides and for estimating the area of shapes with curved sides.

Math Facts
Complete DPP item B and begin reviewing the multiplication and division facts for the square numbers.

Homework
1. Assign the *Finding Area* and *Cut and Paste Puzzles* Homework Pages in the *Discovery Assignment Book.*
2. Assign the Homework section in the *Student Guide.*
3. Assign Parts 1 and 2 of the Home Practice.

Assessment
1. Use the *Observational Assessment Record* to record students' abilities to find the area of a shape.
2. Use the *Finding Area* Activity Page as an assessment.
3. Use DPP item D as a short assessment.

Supplies:
- 1 ruler per student
- 1 pair of scissors per student
- glue

Copies/Transparencies:
- 3–4 copies of *Centimeter Grid Paper* URG Page 44 per student
- 1 transparency of *Centimeter Grid Paper* URG Page 44
- 1 transparency of *Under the Rug* DAB Page 53
- 1 copy of *Observational Assessment Record* URG

Lesson 2

Modeling Division

URG Pages 52–67
SG Pages 106–112
DPP E–H

Estimated Class Sessions **2**

Activity
Students model division problems with base-ten pieces. Estimation is stressed.

Math Facts
Complete item E and continue reviewing the multiplication and division facts for the square numbers.

Homework
Assign Homework *Questions 1–15* in the *Student Guide.*

Assessment
Use the *Observational Assessment Record* to record students' abilities to model division with base-ten pieces.

Supplies:
- 1 calcula... student
- 1 set of base-ten pieces (2 packs, 14 flats, 30 skinnies, 50 bits) per student pair
- overhead base-ten pieces, optional

Copies/Transparencies:
- ...*Table* URG Page 61 per student
- copies of *Base-Ten Pieces Masters* URG Pages 62–63 as needed

Lesson 3

URG Pages...

Estimated Class Sessions **3**

Activity
Students solve division problems using a paper-and-pencil method called the forgiving method.

Math Facts
Complete DPP items I, K, and M and continue reviewing the multiplication and division facts for the square numbers.

Homework
1. Assign the Homework section in the *Student Guide* over several nights.
2. Assign Part 3 of the Home Practice.

Assessment
Students complete the *Quiz* Assessment Page.

Supplies:
- 1 calculator per student
- 1 set of base-ten pieces (2 packs, 14 flats, 30 skinnies, 50 bits) per student pair
- overhead base-ten pieces, optional

Copies/Transparencies:
- 1 copy of *Quiz* URG Page 76 per student

4   URG • Grade 5 • Unit 4 • Outline

Components & Features

Preparing for Upcoming Lessons — Suggestions to help you plan ahead.

Connections — The material in *Math Trailblazers* lessons often can be related to books, magazine articles, and computer programs. When a Connection is recommended for use with a specific lesson, it is included in the Lesson Guide.

Preparing for Upcoming Lessons

Students use eyedroppers in Lesson 6. Provide an informal opportunity for students to practice using eyedroppers.

Connections

A current list of literature and software connections is available at *www.mathtrailblazers.com*. You can also find information on connections in the *Teacher Implementation Guide* Literature List and Software List sections.

Literature Connections
Suggested Titles

- Adair, Gene. *George Washington Carver: Botanist.* Chelsea House Publishers, New York, 1989. (Lesson 7)
- Carter, Andy, and Carol Saller. *George Washington Carver.* Carolrho... MN, 2001. (Lesson 7)
- Dodds, Dayle Ann. *The Great Divide: A Mathematical Marathon.* Ca... MA, 1999.
- Mitchel, Barbara. *A Pocketful of Goobers.* Carolrhoda Books, Inc., M...
- Moore, Eva. *The Story of George Washington Carver.* Scholastic, Ne...

Software Connections
- *The Factory Deluxe* promotes spatial reasoning and practices findi...
- *Graph Master* allows students to collect data and create their own gr...
- *Ice Cream Truck* develops problem solving, money skills, and arithm...
- *Math Mysteries: Advanced Whole Numbers* is a series of structured ... with whole numbers.
- *Mighty Math Calculating Crew* poses short answer questions about ...
- *Mighty Math Number Heroes* poses short answer questions about nu...
- *National Library of Virtual Manipulatives* website (http://matti.usu.e... manipulatives including geoboards, base-ten pieces, the abacus, and ...
- *Number Sense and Problem Solving: How the West Was One + Three ... order of operations.
- *TinkerPlots* allows students to record, compare, and analyze data in ...

Teaching All Math Trailblazers Students — Helps you plan lessons that challenge all your students.

Teaching All Math Trailblazers Students

Math Trailblazers lessons are designed for students with a wide range of abilities. The lessons are flexible and do not require significant adaptation for diverse learning styles or academic levels. However, when needed, lessons can be tailored to allow students to engage their abilities to the greatest extent possible while building knowledge and skills.

To assist you in meeting the needs of all students in your classroom, this section contains information about some of the features in the curriculum that allow all students access to mathematics. For additional information, see the Teaching the *Math Trailblazers* Student: Meeting Individual Needs section in the *Teacher Implementation Guide.*

Differentiation Opportunities in this Unit

Laboratory Experiments

Laboratory experiments enable students to solve problems using a variety of representations including pictures, tables, graphs, and symbols. Teachers can assign or adapt parts of the analysis according to the student's ability. The following lesson is a lab:

- Lesson 6 *Spreading Out*

Journal Prompts

Journal prompts provide opportunities for students to explain and reflect on mathematical problems. They can help both students who need practice explaining their ideas and students who benefit from answering higher order questions. Students with various learning styles can express themselves using pictures, words, and sentences. Teachers can alter journal prompts to suit students' ability levels. The following lessons contain a journal prompt:

- Lesson 1 *Grid Area*
- Lesson 4 *How Close Is Close Enough?*

DPP Challenges

DPP Challenges are items ... and Problems that usual ...

minutes to complete. These problems are more thought-provoking and can be used to stretch students' problem-solving skills. The following lessons have DPP Challenges in them:

- DPP Challenge L from Lesson 3 *Paper-and-Pencil Division*
- DPP Challenge P from Lesson 5 *Mean or Median?*
- DPP Challenges T and X from Lesson 6 *Spreading Out*
- DPP Challenge BB from Lesson 9 *Midterm Test*

Extensions

Use extensions to enrich lessons. Many extensions provide opportunities to further involve or challenge students of all abilities. Take a moment to review the extensions prior to beginning this unit. Some extensions may require additional preparation and planning. The following lessons contain extensions:

- Lesson 1 *Grid Area*
- Lesson 3 *Paper-and-Pencil Division*
- Lesson 5 *Mean or Median?*

Differentiation Opportunities in this Unit — This section identifies the games, laboratory experiments, journal prompts, and extensions you can use to meet the varying needs of your students.

8   URG • Grade 5 • Unit 4 • Outline

Background

The Background explains what students will learn in the unit and places the material in the larger context of the *Math Trailblazers* curriculum.

Unit 4

Background
Division and Data

This unit extends and applies students' knowledge of several topics: division, area, averages (means and medians), and accuracy in measurement and estimation.

Division

In Grade 4, students modeled division problems using base-ten pieces and began work with paper-and-pencil methods. In this unit, students use base-ten pieces to build a conceptual model of division as equal sharing. This type of division is referred to as **measurement division.** The number of groups and the total number of objects in the set are known. An example: Ms. Jones drove 144 miles in 6 trips of equal distance. How many miles did she drive each trip? Practice problems also include the other type of division situation known as equal grouping or **partitive division.** In this type of division, the number in each group and the total number are known. Division is used to find the number of groups. For example, a store sells tulip bulbs. The bulbs come in packages of 8. If they sold 216 bulbs, how many packages did they sell?

In this unit, an alternative division method is presented, rather than the one traditionally used in the United States. This method, which we call the **forgiving division method,** does not require that the greatest quotient be found at each step, eliminating the frequent erasing encountered with the standard algorithm. Research shows that students taught the forgiving division method are better at solving unfamiliar problems and better able to explain the meaning of the steps in the method than those taught the traditional method (van Engen and Gibb, 1956). The forgiving division method also gives students the opportunity to practice mental math.

As an example of the forgiving method, we divide 23 into 5256. (Note that even though the example here involves a two-digit divisor, in this unit the division problems involve one-digit divisors. In Unit 9 students will work with two-digit divisors.) There are 5256 marbles to be shared equally among 23 children. How many marbles will each child get? To begin, take a guess, say, 100. Then write:

Figure 1: *One possible first step in dividing 23 into 5256*

Students should be encouraged to multiply 23 × 100 mentally, as discussed in Unit 2. The 2300 is the number of marbles that have been taken care of, with 2956 marbles left to distribute. After subtracting, we see that 100 is a good choice for the next number as well.

```
   ____
23| 5256
  - 2300  | 100
   ------
    2956
    2300  | 100
   ------
     656
```

Figure 2: *A second possible step in dividing 23 into 5256*

Students should look at the size of the remainder. They should see that 100 is now too big. That is, we cannot give 100 more marbles to each child. A student might choose 10 here and then 10 again as shown below.

```
   ____
23| 5256
  - 2300  | 100
   ------
    2956
    2300  | 100
   ------
     656
     230  | 10
   ------
     426
     230  | 10
   ------
     196
```

Figure 3: *Two more steps in dividing 23 into 5256*

URG • Grade 5 • Unit 4 • Background   **9**

Observational Assessment Record

The *Observational Assessment Record* is a form used to record observations of students' progress.

Assessment Indicators — These are the Assessment Indicators listed in the Unit Outline. They highlight the skills and concepts you should look for as you observe students working on activities in the unit.

Additional lines are provided to help document students' progress with other content.

Observational Assessment Record

- (A1) Can students measure area?
- (A2) Can students find the median and mean of a data set?
- (A3) Can students divide with 1-digit divisors using paper and pencil?
- (A4) Can students estimate quotients?
- (A5) Can students interpret remainders?
- (A6) Can students divide numbers with ending zeros mentally?
- (A7) Can students draw and interpret best-fit lines?
- (A8) Can students collect, organize, graph, and analyze data?
- (A9) Do students demonstrate fluency with the multiplication and division facts for the square numbers?
- (A10) _____

Name	A1	A2	A3	A4	A5	A6	A7	A8	A9	A10	Comments
1.											
2.											
3.											
4.											
5.											
6.											
7.											
8.											
9.											
10.											
11.											
12.											
13.											

URG • Grade 5 • Unit 4 • Observational Assessment Record   13

Daily Practice and Problems

The Daily Practice and Problems (DPP) is a series of short exercises that provide continuing review of math concepts, skills, and facts. Each DPP set includes a Teacher's Guide, which provides specific information on the study and assessment of the math facts in the current unit.

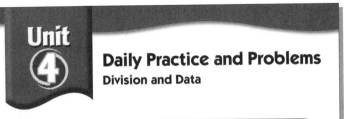

Unit 4

Daily Practice and Problems
Division and Data

A DPP Menu for Unit 4

Two Daily Practice and Problems (DPP) items are included for each class session listed in the Unit Outline. A scope and sequence chart for the DPP is in the *Teacher Implementation Guide*.

Icons in the Teacher Notes column designate the subject matter of each DPP item. The first item in each class session is always a Bit and the second is either a Task or Challenge. Each item falls into one or more of the categories listed below. A menu of the DPP items for Unit 4 follows.

N Number Sense	Computation	Time	Geometry
C, G, H, L, N–V, X, Y, BB	A, F, G, O, P, R–U, X, Z	J	D, W
Math Facts	Money	Measurement	Data
B, E, I, K, M, S, Z, AA	P	A, D, F, W	T, V, Y, BB

Refer to the *Daily Practice and Problems and Home Practice Guide* in the *Teacher Implementation Guide* for further information on the DPP. The guide includes information on how and when to use the DPP.

Review and Assessment of Math Facts

By the end of fourth grade, students in *Math Trailblazers* are expected to demonstrate fluency with the multiplication and division facts. The DPP for this unit continues the systematic, strategies-based approach to reviewing the multiplication and the division facts. This unit reviews the third group of facts, the square numbers (2×2, 3×3, 4×4, etc.). The *Triangle Flash Cards* for these facts follow the Home Practice for this unit in the *Discovery Assignment Book*. Blackline masters of all the cards, organized by group, are in the *Grade 5 Facts Resource Guide*.

The following describes how the facts for the square numbers will be practiced and assessed in the DPP for this unit.

1. DPP item B instructs students to quiz each other on the facts for the square numbers using the *Triangle Flash Cards*. Students sort the cards into three piles: those facts they know and can answer quickly, those they can figure out with a strategy, and those they need to learn. The DPP item also reminds students to update their *Facts I Know* charts, which they began in Lesson 2 of Unit 2.

2. DPP item E helps students practice the multiplication facts for the square numbers. DPP items I, K, and M use fact families to introduce the related division facts. Note that the fact families for the square numbers have only two number sentences (e.g., $4 \times 4 = 16$ and $16 \div 4 = 4$). (Item S also provides more practice with the division facts for the square numbers.)

URG • Grade 5 • Unit 4 • Daily Practice and Problems   15

DPP Menu — Sorts DPP items into categories for easy reference.

The Daily Practice and Problems may be used in class for practice and review, as assessment, or for homework. Notes for teachers provide the answers as well as suggestions for using the items.

Eight icons indicate the subject matter of each item:

N **Number Sense** (estimating, partitioning numbers, skip counting, etc.);

Computation (solving problems using paper-and-pencil methods, estimation, mental math, or calculators);

Time (telling time, solving problems involving elapsed time);

Geometry (work with shapes, coordinates, or other geometric topics);

Math Facts (practice with addition, subtraction, multiplication, or division facts);

$ **Money** (counting change, combining various coins, or estimating total cost);

Measurement (measuring length, area, mass, volume, or time); and

Data (collecting, organizing, graphing, or analyzing data).

Components & Features

There are two Daily Practice and Problems items for each nonoptional class session noted in a Unit Outline. The first of these is always a TIMS Bit and the second is either a TIMS Task or a TIMS Challenge.

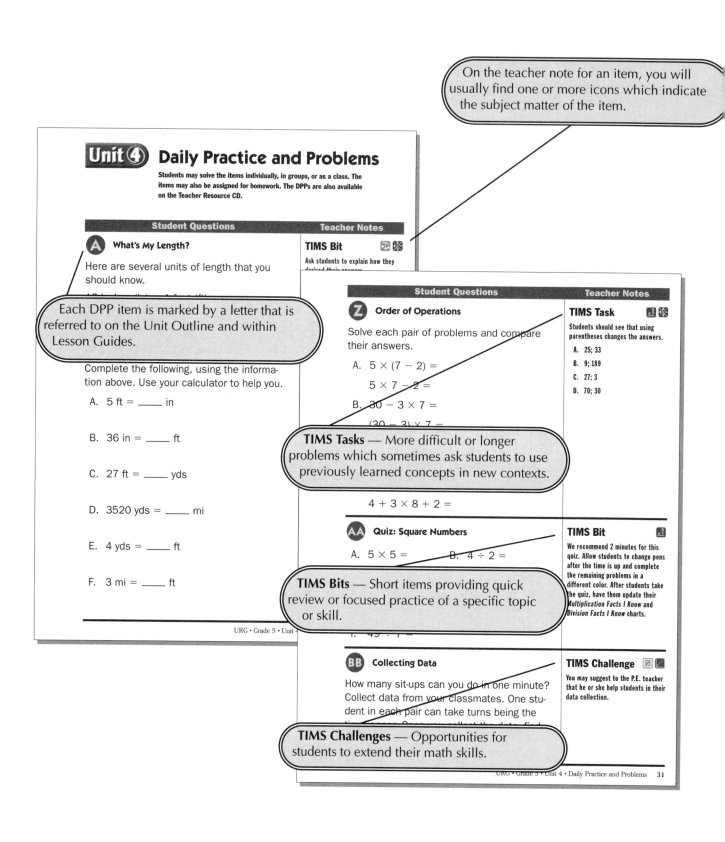

On the teacher note for an item, you will usually find one or more icons which indicate the subject matter of the item.

Unit 4 Daily Practice and Problems

Students may solve the items individually, in groups, or as a class. The items may also be assigned for homework. The DPPs are also available on the Teacher Resource CD.

Student Questions

A   What's My Length?

Here are several units of length that you should know.

Each DPP item is marked by a letter that is referred to on the Unit Outline and within Lesson Guides.

Complete the following, using the information above. Use your calculator to help you.

A. 5 ft = _____ in

B. 36 in = _____ ft

C. 27 ft = _____ yds

D. 3520 yds = _____ mi

E. 4 yds = _____ ft

F. 3 mi = _____ ft

Teacher Notes

TIMS Bit

Ask students to explain how they derived their answers.

URG • Grade 5 • Unit

Student Questions

Z   Order of Operations

Solve each pair of problems and compare their answers.

A. $5 \times (7 - 2) =$

    $5 \times 7 - 2 =$

B. $30 - 3 \times 7 =$

    $(30 - 3) \times 7 =$

TIMS Tasks — More difficult or longer problems which sometimes ask students to use previously learned concepts in new contexts.

$4 + 3 \times 8 + 2 =$

AA   Quiz: Square Numbers

A. $5 \times 5 =$ B. $4 \div 2 =$

TIMS Bits — Short items providing quick review or focused practice of a specific topic or skill.

BB   Collecting Data

How many sit-ups can you do in one minute? Collect data from your classmates. One student in each pair can take turns being the

TIMS Challenges — Opportunities for students to extend their math skills.

Teacher Notes

TIMS Task

Students should see that using parentheses changes the answers.

A. 25; 33

B. 9; 189

C. 27; 3

D. 70; 30

TIMS Bit

We recommend 2 minutes for this quiz. Allow students to change pens after the time is up and complete the remaining problems in a different color. After students take the quiz, have them update their *Multiplication Facts I Know* and *Division Facts I Know* charts.

TIMS Challenge

You may suggest to the P.E. teacher that he or she help students in their data collection.

URG • Grade 5 • Unit 4 • Daily Practice and Problems   31

Lesson Guide

The Lesson guide is a how-to manual explaining what you need for the lesson and what it involves.

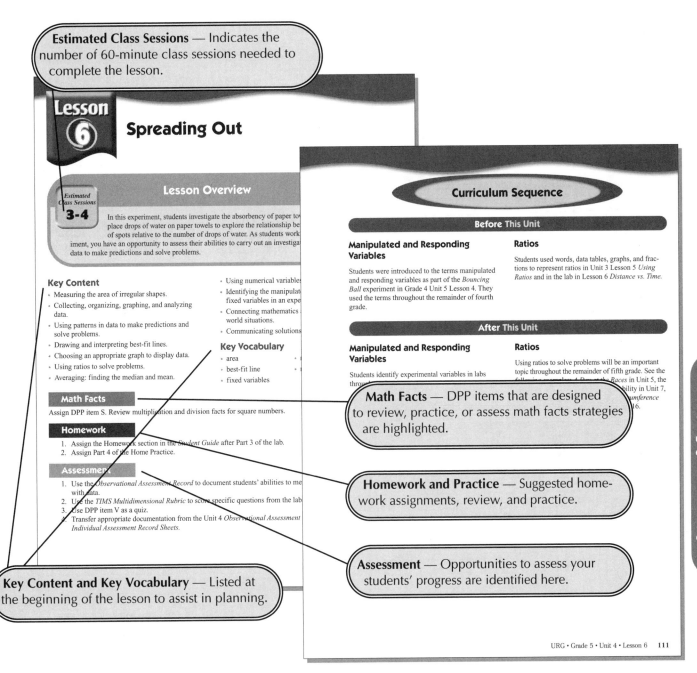

Estimated Class Sessions — Indicates the number of 60-minute class sessions needed to complete the lesson.

Lesson 6 — Spreading Out

Estimated Class Sessions 3-4

Lesson Overview

In this experiment, students investigate the absorbency of paper to place drops of water on paper towels to explore the relationship be of spots relative to the number of drops of water. As students work iment, you have an opportunity to assess their abilities to carry out an investiga data to make predictions and solve problems.

Key Content

- Measuring the area of irregular shapes.
- Collecting, organizing, graphing, and analyzing data.
- Using patterns in data to make predictions and solve problems.
- Drawing and interpreting best-fit lines.
- Choosing an appropriate graph to display data.
- Using ratios to solve problems.
- Averaging: finding the median and mean.

- Using numerical variables
- Identifying the manipulat fixed variables in an expe
- Connecting mathematics world situations.
- Communicating solutions

Key Vocabulary

- area
- best-fit line
- fixed variables

Math Facts

Assign DPP item S. Review multiplication and division facts for square numbers.

Homework

1. Assign the Homework section in the *Student Guide* after Part 3 of the lab.
2. Assign Part 4 of the Home Practice.

Assessment

1. Use the *Observational Assessment Record* to document students' abilities to me with data.
2. Use the *TIMS Multidimensional Rubric* to score specific questions from the lab.
3. Use DPP item V as a quiz.
4. Transfer appropriate documentation from the Unit 4 *Observational Assessment Individual Assessment Record Sheets*.

Curriculum Sequence

Before This Unit

Manipulated and Responding Variables

Students were introduced to the terms manipulated and responding variables as part of the *Bouncing Ball* experiment in Grade 4 Unit 5 Lesson 4. They used the terms throughout the remainder of fourth grade.

Ratios

Students used words, data tables, graphs, and fractions to represent ratios in Unit 3 Lesson 5 *Using Ratios* and in the lab in Lesson 6 *Distance vs. Time*.

After This Unit

Manipulated and Responding Variables

Students identify experimental variables in labs throu

Ratios

Using ratios to solve problems will be an important topic throughout the remainder of fifth grade. See the following examples: *Days at the Races* in Unit 5, the ... bility in Unit 7, ... *umference* ... 16.

Math Facts — DPP items that are designed to review, practice, or assess math facts strategies are highlighted.

Homework and Practice — Suggested homework assignments, review, and practice.

Assessment — Opportunities to assess your students' progress are identified here.

Key Content and Key Vocabulary — Listed at the beginning of the lesson to assist in planning.

Components & Features

Materials List

Supplies and Copies

Student	Teacher
Supplies for Each Student	**Supplies**
• calculator • ruler	
Supplies for Each Student Group	
• 1–2 pairs of scissors • eyedropper • 3–4 sheets of the same brand of paper towel • small container of water • 2 books or 1 geoboard (for drying the paper towels)	
Copies	**Copies/Transparencies**
• 1 copy of *Centimeter Grid Paper* per student or more as needed (*Unit Resource Guide* Page 44) • 1 copy of *Three-trial Data Table* per student or more as needed (*Unit Resource Guide* Page 129) • 2 copies of *Centimeter Graph Paper* per student (*Unit Resource Guide* Page 130)	• 1 transparency of *Centimeter Graph Paper*, optional (*Unit Resource Guide* Page 130) • 1 transparency of *Bar Graph or Point Graph?*, optional (*Unit Resource Guide* Page 127) • 1 transparency of *Spot Check*, optional (*Unit Resource Guide* Page 128)

All blackline masters including assessment, transparency, and DPP masters are also on the Teacher Resource CD.

Student Books

Spreading Out (*Student Guide* Pages 131–138)
Student Rubric: *Telling* (*Student Guide* Appendix C and Inside Back Cover), optional

Daily Practice and Problems and Home Practice

DPP items S–X (*Unit Resource Guide* Pages 27–29)
Home Practice Part 4 (*Discovery Assignment Book* Page 45)

Note: Classrooms whose pacing differs significantly from the suggested pacing of the units should use the Math Facts Calendar in Section 4 of the *Facts Resource Guide* to ensure students receive the complete math facts program.

Assessment Tools

Observational Assessment Record (*Unit Resource Guide* Pages 13–14)
Individual Assessment Record Sheet (*Teacher Implementation Guide*, Assessment section)

Materials List — Everything you and students need for the lesson, including curriculum pages and manipulatives.

Supplies — Indicates manipulatives and other supplies needed for the lesson.

Print Materials — Outlines all the copies and transparencies needed for the lesson and where to find them.

Student Books — Highlights which student books and pages are needed for the lesson.

Assessment Tools — Reminds you of opportunities to use the *Observational Assessment Record* and other Assessment tools.

DPP Items — To be completed as a warm-up or review.

Daily Practice and Problems

Suggestions for using the DPPs are on pages 122–124.

S. Bit: Multiplying and Dividing by Multiples of 10 (URG p. 27)

A. $800 \times 80 =$ B. $25,000 \div 50 =$
C. $4900 \div 7 =$ D. $10,000 \div 10 =$
E. $40 \times 400 =$ F. $8100 \div 90 =$

T. Challenge: Within 10%?
(URG p. 27)

Jerome, Lin, Nicholas, and Alexis each estimate the number of marshmallows in a jar. Jerome's estimate is 131. Lin's estimate is 120. Nicholas's estimate is 100. Alexis estimates there are 135 marshmallows in the jar. The jar actually contains 111 marshmallows. Which estimates are within 10% of 111? How do you know?

U. Bit: More Shortcut Division
(URG p. 27)

Use a paper-and-pencil method to solve the following problems. Estimate to make sure your answers are reasonable.

A. $3315 \div 6 =$
B. $927 \div 7 =$
C. $3476 \div 4 =$

V. Task: Ratios (URG p. 28)

Manny put 1, 2, and 4 drops of liquid on three pieces of the same brand of paper towel. He counted the area of each spot formed. His data are shown below.

N Number of Drops	A Area (sq cm)
1	7
2	15
4	28

1. Graph Manny's data on a piece of *Centimeter Graph Paper*. Graph the number of drops on the horizontal axis and the area on the vertical axis.
2. If Manny put 6 drops of liquid on the paper towel, predict the approximate area of the new spot.
3. Write three equal ratios, in the form of a fraction, for the ratio of the area to the number of drops. Use ratios from your graph.

W. Bit: Decorating the House
(URG p. 29)

Jackie wants to cut rectangles from material to make rugs for her miniature doll house. She measures the living room and family room floors. Her measurements are listed below. Find the area of the floor in each of these rooms.

Living room: 7 cm by 9 cm

Family room: 7 cm by 11 cm

X. Challenge: What's That Number? (URG p. 29)

Find a number between 200 and 300 that is divisible by 2, 3, and 5. What strategies did you use?

Before the Lab/Activity — Covers what you need to prepare ahead of time for the lesson.

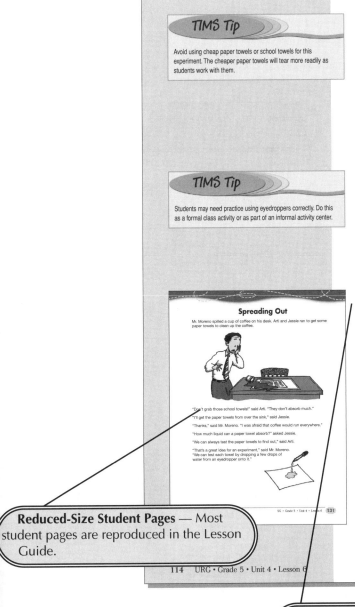

TIMS Tip

Avoid using cheap paper towels or school towels for this experiment. The cheaper paper towels will tear more readily as students work with them.

TIMS Tip

Students may need practice using eyedroppers correctly. Do this as a formal class activity or as part of an informal activity center.

Spreading Out

Mr. Moreno spilled a cup of coffee on his desk. Arti and Jessie ran to get some paper towels to clean up the coffee.

"Don't grab those school towels!" said Arti. "They don't absorb much."

"I'll get the paper towels from over the sink," said Jessie.

"Thanks," said Mr. Moreno. "I was afraid that coffee would run everywhere."

"How much liquid can a paper towel absorb?" asked Jessie.

"We can always test the paper towels to find out," said Arti.

"That's a great idea for an experiment," said Mr. Moreno. "We can test each towel by dropping a few drops of water from an eyedropper onto it."

SG • Grade 5 • Unit 4 • Lesson 6   131

114   URG • Grade 5 • Unit 4 • Lesson 6

Reduced-Size Student Pages — Most student pages are reproduced in the Lesson Guide.

Before the Lab

The extended list of concepts in the Key Content section at the beginning of the Lesson Guide shows that this lab provides a context for many math and science concepts. Students had some experience with most of these concepts in preceding grades and units. However, in this lab we ask students to apply the concepts in new ways. For example, although they used means and medians to average data in fourth grade, in this lab they must also consider which average (mean or median) best represents their data. As you read the Lesson Guide and prepare to teach the lab, consider your students' needs. For students new to the curriculum, you may decide to emphasize some concepts more than others, provide more guidance for some parts of the lab, or delete some questions. For example, students who did not complete optional Lesson 4 should not be assigned the problems using 10% as a standard for error in measurements. On the other hand, for students who have had experience with most of these concepts, this lab can challenge them to apply these important ideas in a real-world situation. Discussion prompts in the Lesson Guide and questions in the *Student Guide* are designed to help students make connections between the concepts.

Teaching the Lab

Part 1   Defining the Variables and Drawing the Picture

The first few *Spreading Out* Lab Pages in the *Student Guide* set the stage for this activity. Read these pages as a class or ask students to read the pages in small groups. The Identifying Variables section uses the terms "manipulated" and "responding variable" for the first time in fifth grade. (See the TIMS Tutor: *The TIMS Laboratory Method* for more information on variables in experiments.) Identify these two main variables in the lab. The number *(N)* of drops used is the **manipulated variable,** since Arti and Jessie chose the values for the number of drops before they began collecting data. The area *(A)* of the spots is the **responding variable** since they find the values for area by doing the experiment. Expand on this discussion of variables using the following prompts:

- *Think about the experiments we have done this year. For example, think about the lab* Distance vs. Time. *What are the two main variables in that lab?* (Distance and time)
- *Which variable had values we chose before we started collecting data?* (Distance. The three distances that were timed were measured out and written in the data table before data collection.)

Teaching the Lab/Activity — Describes what students will do in each activity.

Components & Features

After the discussion, students begin the experiment using *Questions 5–9* on the *Spreading Out* Lab Pages in the *Student Guide.* They draw a picture of the experimental setup and label the main variables *(Question 5A).* The picture allows you to see if students have a clear understanding of the method and variables and are ready to proceed.

Figure 20: *Sample student drawing*

As part of designing their experiments, students choose values for the number of drops. *(Question 5B)* Discuss the values that Jessie and Arti chose and decide as a class if these are the ones you will also use. Students should choose values that are manageable and show a pattern for the relationship of area to the number of drops. Note that *Questions 10–11* ask students to interpolate and extrapolate for 3 and 5 drops from their data. Students should not use these numbers of drops in their experiment.

Part 2 Collecting Data

Question 6 asks students to make decisions concerning the collecting and recording of the data. *Questions 6A–6B* ask them to decide how many trials they will make and how they will organize their data. You can provide further structure for students by giving them a copy of a blank *Three-trial Data Table.* Figure 21 shows sample data for the experiment.

Spreading Out

N Number of Drops	A Area (in sq cm)			
	Trial 1	Trial 2	Trial 3	Average
1	$5\frac{1}{2}$	4	$6\frac{1}{2}$	5
2	17	15	14	15
4	26	30	27	28

Figure 21: *Sample* Three-trial Data Table *using the mean (rounded to the nearest whole centimeter)*

Question 6C asks students how they can check for mistakes in dropping the water to make spots. Remind students that they should make their spots so each is clearly defined and they do not run together. Use the *Spot Check* Transparency Master to encourage students to check for obvious errors in making spots before they count square centimeters. The transparency shows three spots made by a fifth-grade student for one, two, and four drops of water. Ask:

- *Are the spots for each number of drops all about the same size? What should the experimenter do?* (No, one of the spots for one drop is much larger than the other spots for one drop. The experimenter should try to make another spot with one drop so all three drops are about the same size. Since one of the spots for two drops is much smaller than the other spots for two drops, the experimenter should again try to make spots of about the same size with two drops. The spots for four drops are about the same size, so the experimenter can measure the area of these spots by counting square centimeters.)

Students count square centimeters to measure the area of each spot *(Question 6D)* and record each area in their data tables. Then before they graph the data, they should check to see if their data are reasonable. No single measurement should be much bigger or smaller than the others. If students completed optional Lesson 4 *How Close Is Close Enough?*, they can use 10% as a standard for error among their measurements *(Question 6E).*

Observe students working and recording data. Are they carefully using the eyedroppers? Do the groups look over their measurements to see if they are reasonable? If they find data points that are not reasonable, encourage them to find reasons for the differences. Did the spots run together? Did they have trouble controlling the number of drops? Help them make informed decisions about how to handle the data.

Question 7 asks students to decide whether to use the mean or the median to average the data. The data in the table in Figure 21 shows the mean values rounded to the nearest whole centimeter. Since the mean and the median for this data are nearly the same, either average can be used to represent the data. If students use the mean, encourage them to use their calculators and to round to the nearest whole centimeter.

Content Note

Using 10% as a standard is not intended to involve lengthy arithmetic procedures nor to be used as a rigid rule. (See Lesson 4.) Instead, students should develop the number sense needed for rough mental calculations and estimates. For example, they should recognize that 10% of any measurement less than 10 sq cm is less than 1 sq cm. So, the areas made with 1 drop of water ($5\frac{1}{2}$ sq cm, 4 sq cm, and $6\frac{1}{2}$ sq cm) recorded in Figure 21 are not within 1 sq cm of one another, nor is 4 sq cm within 1 sq cm of the median value of $5\frac{1}{2}$ sq cm. These data do not strictly fall within our 10% limits. However, given the difficulty of controlling the variables, students can use this data.

If students did not complete Lesson 4, they do not need to use the 10% standard. However, they should check to see that their measurements are reasonable.

Samples of Student Work — Reproductions or transcriptions of work by actual students from the same grade level as your class allow you to compare your students' work to other students' work.

Graphs and Tables — Shows sample graphs and data tables.

Discussion Prompts — Italicized questions designed to use in class.

Content Notes — Specific content information relating to lesson activities.

In *Question 5* students should notice that one-half of the rectangle is shaded. The area of the rectangle is 27 sq cm. Since the triangle is one half of this area, divide by 2 and get $13\frac{1}{2}$ sq cm for the area of the triangle.

Students should see that a ruler is needed to find the area in *Question 7*. The area of the rectangle in sq cm is 7 cm × 5 cm or 35 sq cm. Students will also need rulers to draw the shapes in *Question 8*.

Journal Prompt

Explain two methods for finding the area of a rectangle. Show why the two methods both give the correct answer.

Math Facts

DPP item B introduces the multiplication and division facts for the square numbers.

Homework and Practice

- You can use the *Finding Area* Activity Page in the *Discovery Assignment* Book as homework after Part 1 of this lesson.
- You can also assign...

Journal Prompts — Suggested writing prompts that can be assigned to students in class or for homework.

Student Guide - page 138 (Answers on p. 132)

45 (Answers on p. 133)

Math Facts — DPP items designed to review, practice, or assess math facts are highlighted.

Homework and Practice — Suggested homework assignments, review, and practice.

calculator (644 sq cm ÷ 14 sq cm = 46 spots) we find that the paper towel would be covered by about 46 two-spot drops. So, the paper towel can absorb about 2 × 46 or about 90–100 drops. Student groups are likely to develop several alternative strategies for solving this problem.

Students must analyze the graph in Figure 24 to answer *Question 14.* Students should conclude that *Super Soak* paper towels are the most absorbent because each drop covers less area, so the towel can soak up more drops in a smaller area.

Figure 24: *Lines for different brands of paper towels*

Math Facts

DPP item S provides practice with multiplication and division with multiples of ten.

Homework and Practice

- The Homework section of the *Student Guide* and DPP item V provide practice plotting points and writing ratios. If you assign these before students solve *Question 13* in the Explore section, they will have practiced the skills needed in *Question 13.*
- DPP Bit U provides in-class practice with paper-and-pencil division. DPP Bit W provides practice finding area.
- Assign Part 4 of the Home Practice, which involves reading and interpreting graphs.

Answers for Part 4 of the Home Practice are in the Answer Key at the end of this lesson and at the end of this unit.

Components & Features

Extension

- Purchase two or more brands of paper towels. Give half the class one brand and the other half the second brand. Give each group 3–4 sheets of the same brand. Repeat the experiment. Compare differences in the data. Find the most absorbent and the least absorbent paper towel.
- Assign DPP Challenges T and X. Use item T only if students completed Lesson 4.

Software Connection

Use a graphing program, such as *Graph Master*, to graph and help analyze the data. If you use *Graph Master*, the manipulated variable in the experiment (number of drops in *Spreading Out*) is the independent variable and the responding variable (area of the spots in *Spreading Out*) is the dependent variable. Using a graphing utility allows students to easily modify components of the graph, such as the scales on the horizontal and vertical axes.

Extensions — Activities or suggestions for further exploration on the same topic.

Connections — How to connect the lesson to children's literature, computer programs, and other content areas such as science and social studies.

Assessment — How to evaluate your students' skills and their understanding of concepts.

Assessment

- Use the *Observational Assessment Record* in the *Unit Resource Guide* to record student success in measuring area, making an appropriate graph, and working with data.
- Use one or more dimensions of the *TIMS Multidimensional Rubric* to score student responses to **Question 13** in the Explore section of the *Student Guide*. Encourage students to use the Student Rubric: *Telling* to guide them as they describe their solution strategies. You can also encourage them to use the Student Rubrics: *Knowing* and *Solving*. Tell students your expectations before they work on the problem. If a student has trouble getting started, such as needing help finding the area of a paper towel, record this information and include it in your evaluation. After students solve the problem and write a draft, give them suggestions for improving their work. You may ask a student to correct some calculations, include all the steps in the process, display the data in an organized manner, or check the solution using another method. Score their revisions and add them to their collection folders for possible inclusion in their portfolios.

To grade the lab, teach...

At a Glance — Summarizes suggested steps for teaching the lesson and highlights math facts, practice, other DPP items, homework, and assessment.

Estimated Class Sessions 3-4

At a Glance

Math Facts and Daily Practice and Problems

Assign DPP items S–X. Review multiplication and division facts for square numbers.

Part 1. Defining the Variables and Drawing the Picture

1. Read the first few *Spreading Out* Lab Pages in the *Student Guide* to introduce the lab.
2. Use the Identifying the Variables section of the *Student Guide* to name the two main variables in the lab (the manipulated and responding variables) and the variables that must be held fixed.
3. Use the *Bar Graph or Point Graph?* Transparency Master and the discussion prompts in the Lesson Guide to help students choose the appropriate type of graph.
4. Discuss *Questions 1–4.*
5. Students draw pictures of their experiments. *(Question 5)*

Part 2. Collecting Data

1. Remind students of the procedures for collecting the data.
2. Students decide on the number of spots to use, the number of trials, how to check if their data are reasonable, and how to organize the data tables. *(Question 6)*
3. Students collect and record their data in their data tables.
4. Students decide whether to use the mean or the median. *(Question 7)*

Part 3. Graphing the Data

1. Students plot their data and add (0 drops, 0 sq cm) to their graphs. *(Question 8)*
2. Students use a ruler to draw the best-fit line. *(Question 9)*

Part 4. Exploring the Data

1. Students make predictions and check them. *(Questions 10–12)*
2. Use *Question 13* to assess students' abilities to solve an open-ended problem and communicate solution strategies.
3. Students discuss their responses to the questions.
4. Students add the labs and their solution to *Question 13* to their collection folders.

Homework

1. Assign the Homework section in the *Student Guide* after Part 3 of the lab.
2. Assign Part 4 of the Home Practice.

Assessment

1. Use the *Observational Assessment Record* to document students' abilities to measure area and work with data.
2. Use the *TIMS Multidimensional Rubric* to score specific questions from the lab.
3. Use DPP item V as a quiz.
4. Transfer appropriate documentation from the Unit 4 *Observational Assessment Record* to students' *Individual Assessment Record Sheets*.

Lesson Guide for the Adventure Book

The Lesson guide is a how-to manual explaining what you need and what is involved in each lesson.

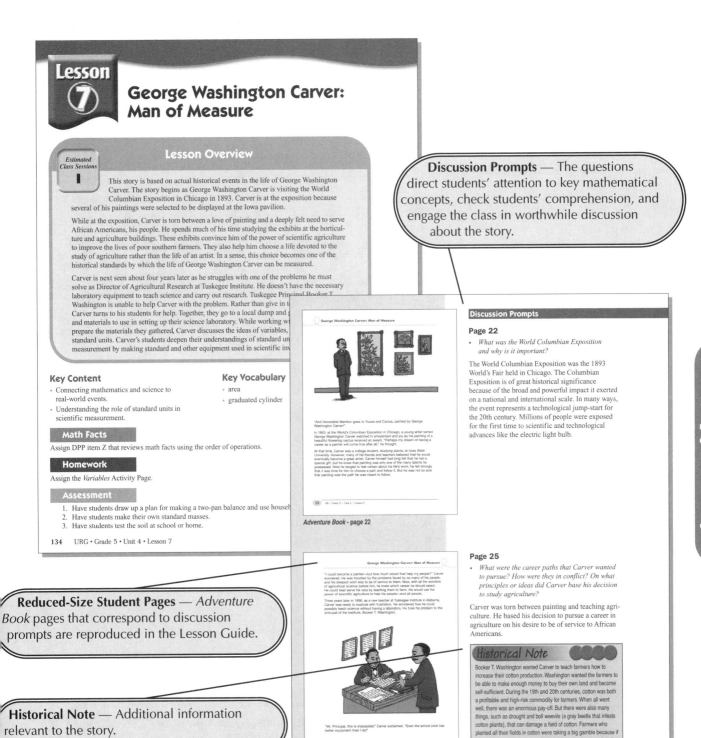

Discussion Prompts — The questions direct students' attention to key mathematical concepts, check students' comprehension, and engage the class in worthwhile discussion about the story.

Reduced-Size Student Pages — *Adventure Book* pages that correspond to discussion prompts are reproduced in the Lesson Guide.

Historical Note — Additional information relevant to the story.

Components & Features

Student Pages

Name _____ Date _____

Reproducibles — Frequently used pages to be photocopied. They can be printed from the *Teacher Resource CD.*

Name _____ Date _____

Number Changes

You need your abacus to complete this page.

1. Show the number 4,287,398,729 on your abacus. Then, record the number on the abacus picture below. Show only the beads that are pushed to the crossbar.

Now, make the changes described below. After each change, go back to the original number in Question 1 before you make the next change.

2. **A.** Show 500 less than 4,287,398,729.

   B. Write the new number. _____

3. **A.** Show 1 million more than 4,287,398,729.

   B. Write the new number. _____

Centimeter Graph Paper, Blackline Master

Copyright © Kendall/Hunt Publishing Company

Copyright © Kendall/Hunt Publishing Company

Blackline Masters, Transparency Masters, and Assessment Blackline Masters — Pages to be photo-copied as review, assessment, or transparency masters; located at the end of the Lesson Guide. They can be printed from the *Teacher Resource CD.*

120   URG • Grade 5 • Unit 2 • Lesson 4   Assessment B

Answer Key

An Answer Key at the end of each lesson provides answers to questions on *Student Guide, Unit Resource Guide,* and *Discovery Assignment Book* pages, including recommended Home Practice. The Home Practice Answer Key at the end of the unit includes the answers to all the Home Practice in the *Discovery Assignment Book* for that unit. Reduced pages showing the questions are provided beside the answers.

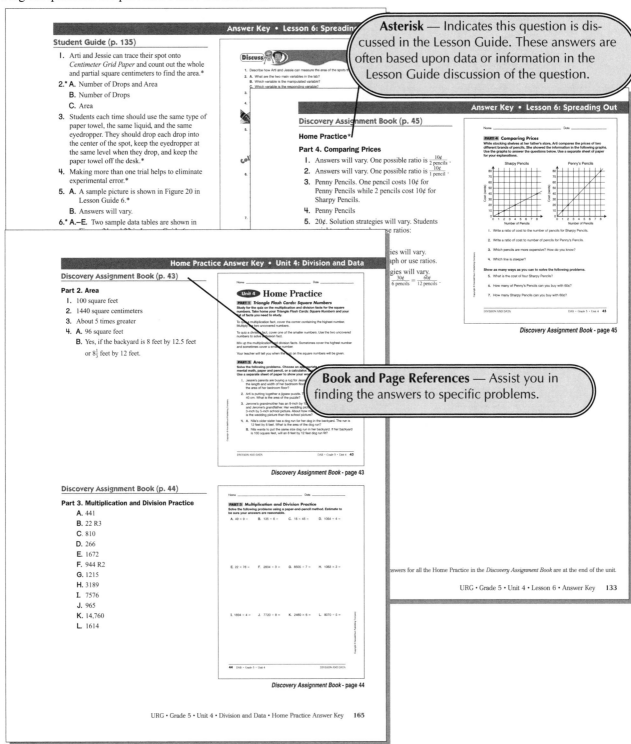

Asterisk — Indicates this question is discussed in the Lesson Guide. These answers are often based upon data or information in the Lesson Guide discussion of the question.

Book and Page References — Assist you in finding the answers to specific problems.

Components & Features

TEACHER IMPLEMENTATION GUIDE

The *Teacher Implementation Guide* is the reference manual for *Math Trailblazers.* Information in the *Teacher Implementation Guide* can be roughly categorized into three groups: general background about *Math Trailblazers,* specific information about the program, and deep background about important math and science concepts.

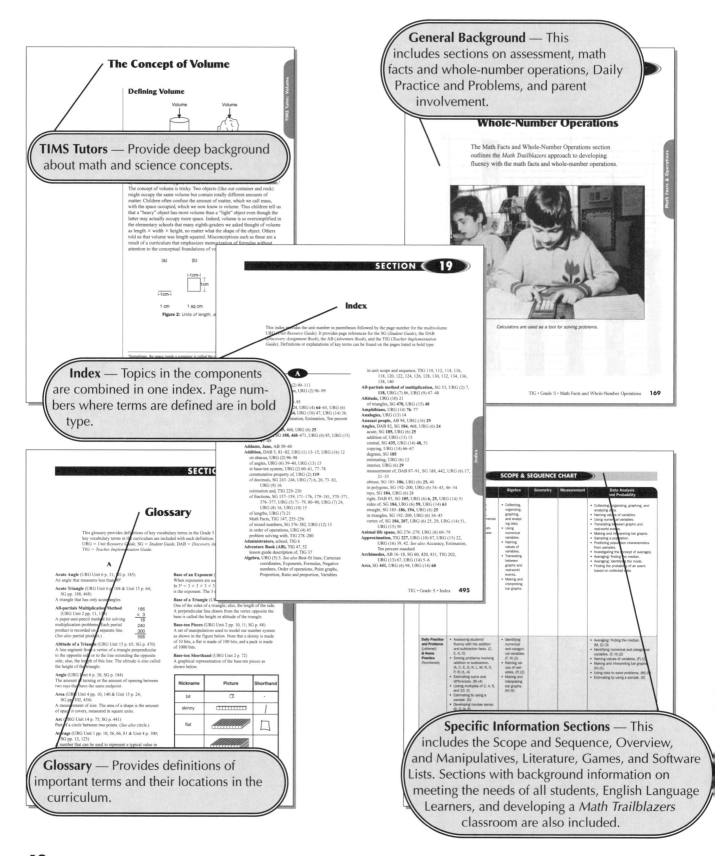

The Concept of Volume

Defining Volume

TIMS Tutors — Provide deep background about math and science concepts.

The concept of volume is tricky. Two objects (like our container and rock) might occupy the same volume but contain totally different amounts of matter. Children often confuse the amount of matter, which we call mass, with the space occupied, which we now know is volume. Thus children tell us that a "heavy" object has more volume than a "light" object even though the latter may actually occupy more space. Indeed, volume is so oversimplified in the elementary schools that many eighth-graders we asked thought of volume as length × width × height, no matter what the shape of the object. Others told us that volume was length squared. Misconceptions such as these are a result of a curriculum that emphasizes memorization of formulas without attention to the conceptual foundations of vo

Figure 2: *Units of length, a*

Index — Topics in the components are combined in one index. Page numbers where terms are defined are in bold type.

Glossary — Provides definitions of important terms and their locations in the curriculum.

General Background — This includes sections on assessment, math facts and whole-number operations, Daily Practice and Problems, and parent involvement.

Whole-Number Operations

The Math Facts and Whole-Number Operations section outlines the *Math Trailblazers* approach to developing fluency with the math facts and whole-number operations.

Calculators are used as a tool for solving problems.

TIG • Grade 5 • Math Facts and Whole-Number Operations **169**

Specific Information Sections — This includes the Scope and Sequence, Overview, and Manipulatives, Literature, Games, and Software Lists. Sections with background information on meeting the needs of all students, English Language Learners, and developing a *Math Trailblazers* classroom are also included.

FACTS RESOURCE GUIDE

The *Facts Resource Guide* provides a single location for all math facts materials for the grade and a schedule for classrooms that differ significantly from the suggested pacing of units. Almost all of the student materials in the *Facts Resource Guide* are also located in the *Student Guide, Discovery Assignment Book,* or *Unit Resource Guides.*

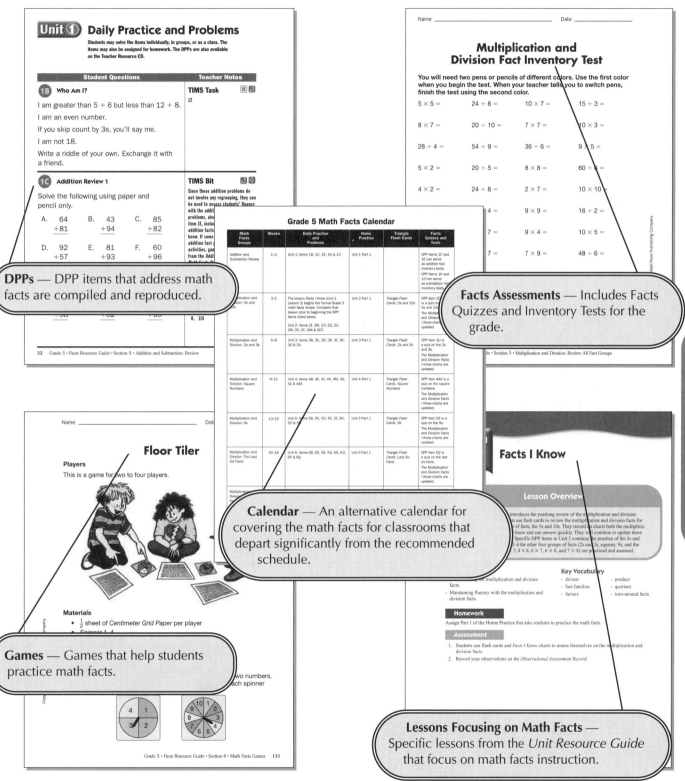

DPPs — DPP items that address math facts are compiled and reproduced.

Facts Assessments — Includes Facts Quizzes and Inventory Tests for the grade.

Calendar — An alternative calendar for covering the math facts for classrooms that depart significantly from the recommended schedule.

Games — Games that help students practice math facts.

Facts I Know

Lessons Focusing on Math Facts — Specific lessons from the *Unit Resource Guide* that focus on math facts instruction.

Components & Features

TEACHER RESOURCE CD

The *Teacher Resource CD* provides key items from other components of the curriculum. This CD includes: Letters Home (Spanish and English); Daily Practice and Problems (with and without teacher notes); *Observational Assessment Record* pages; *Individual Assessment Record Sheet;* all Blackline Masters and Transparency Masters; Teacher Rubrics and Student Rubrics; frequently used masters; and appropriate sections of the *Facts Resource Guide.*

Daily Practice and Problems — Allows you to search DPP items by topic and to print Student Questions without the Teacher Notes.

Observational Assessment Record and *Individual Assessment Record Sheet* — Interactive files can be copied to disk so you can enter and maintain data electronically.

Facts Resource Guide — Includes appropriate sections from the *Facts Resource Guide.*

Rubrics — All three student rubrics and the related teacher rubrics are included.

Blackline Masters — All Blackline Masters from the *Unit Resource Guide* are collated and included on the CD for convenient reproduction from your personal computer.

The *Student Guide* contains most nonconsumable student materials, including activities, labs, and games.

Unit Opener — A list of lesson numbers, names, and locations in the curriculum materials.

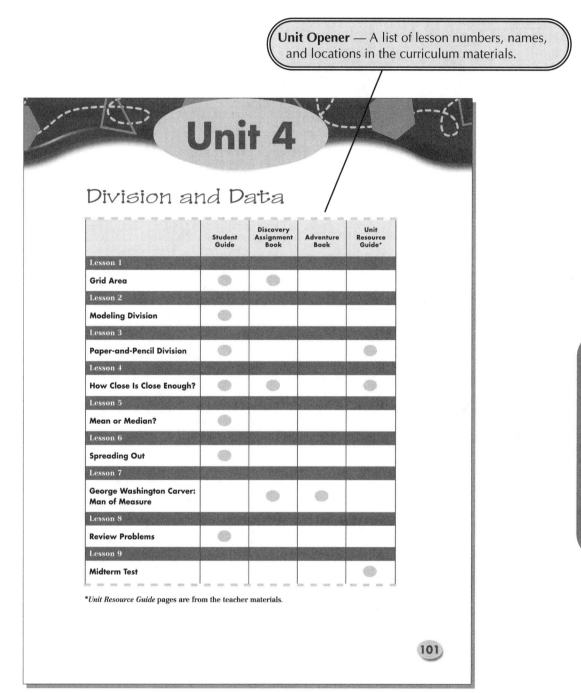

Unit 4

Division and Data

	Student Guide	Discovery Assignment Book	Adventure Book	Unit Resource Guide*
Lesson 1				
Grid Area	●	●		
Lesson 2				
Modeling Division	●			
Lesson 3				
Paper-and-Pencil Division	●			●
Lesson 4				
How Close Is Close Enough?	●	●		●
Lesson 5				
Mean or Median?	●			
Lesson 6				
Spreading Out	●			
Lesson 7				
George Washington Carver: Man of Measure		●	●	
Lesson 8				
Review Problems	●			
Lesson 9				
Midterm Test				●

Unit Resource Guide pages are from the teacher materials.

101

Components & Features

Spreading Out

Mr. Moreno spilled a cup of coffee on his desk. Arti and Jessie ran to get some paper towels to clean up the coffee.

"Don't grab those school towels!" said Arti. "They don't absorb much."

"I'll get the paper towels from over the sink," said Jessie.

"Thanks," said Mr. Moreno. "I was afraid that coffee would run everywhere."

"How much liquid can a paper towel absorb?" asked Jessie.

"We can always test the paper towels to find out," said Ar

"That's a great idea for an experiment," said Mr. Moreno. "We can test each towel by dropping a few drops of water from an eyedropper onto it."

"I think we should try three different numbers of drops so we have enough data to look for patterns," said Jessie. "We should start with numbers (of drops) that have a pattern. Then it will be easier to see how changing the number of drops changes the area of the spots. We should also do three trials as we did in *Distance vs. Time*. Then, if the areas of the spots for all three trials are close, we will know we didn't make any big mistakes."

Identifying Variables

"As you were talking, you identified the two main variables in your experiment," said Mr. Moreno. "The variables are number of drops (N) and area (A). The two main variables in an experiment have special names. The variable with values we know in the beginning of the experiment is called the **manipulated variable.** We often choose the values of the manipulated variable before collecting the data."

Arti and Jessie chose 1 drop, 2 drops, and 4 drops as the values for the number of drops, so that the spots they made would not be too big. They made three spots of water with 1 drop, three spots of water with 2 drops, and three spots with 4 drops of water on paper towels.

"The variable with values obtained by doing the experiment is called the **responding variable,**" said Mr. Moreno. "Your responding variable is the area of the spots. The area of each spot changes, depending upon the number of drops of water you use."

Mr. Moreno added, "There are other variables that can affect the size of the spots. For example, if we use a bigger eyedropper or a different liquid, the size of the spots might be different. These other variables should stay the same during the whole experiment. In this way, the only thing that affects the area of the spots is the number of drops. The other variables that stay the same are called **fixed variables.**"

When the spots had dried a little, Arti and Jessie traced around each spot with a pencil. They used scissors to cut out each spot. They then measured the area of each spot and recorded it in a data table.

Key Vocabulary — When appearing in student pages, key words in bold type are defined. The page number for each definition is noted in bold in the Curriculum Index and the *Student Guide* Index.

Homework

You will need a sheet of graph paper and a ruler to complete this homework.

1. Professor Peabody tested Whizzo brand paper towels. He noticed a very interesting pattern in his data. Then, his pet mouse, Milo, tracked ink across his data table. Look for a pattern in Professor Peabody's data.

N Number of Drops	A Area of Spot in sq cm
1	
2	
	8
8	16

A. Copy the data table on your paper and fill in the missing values.

B. Make a point graph of the data. Graph the number of drops on the horizontal axis and the area on the vertical axis. Use a ruler to fit a line to the points.

C. What would be the area of a spot made with no drops? Add this point to your graph.

2. A. Choose a point on the graph. Use it to write the ratio $\left(\frac{A}{N}\right)$ number of drops.

B. Using fractions, write two ratios equal to the ratio in Qu

3. A. What area would 6 drops make on a Whizzo brand pap

B. How many drops are needed to make a spot with an ar Show your work.

5. Design a lab to find out what happens to the of drops of water used to make the spot. Dra

A. Label the variables in your picture.

B. Choose values for the number of drops. (4 drops as Arti and Jessie did, or you may

Collect

6. Work with your partner(s) to collect data and following before you begin:

A. How many trials will you need to make? T make a spot for each number of drops?

B. How will you organize your data in a data

C. How can you check for mistakes in dropp spots?

D. What unit of measure will you use when fi

E. How will you check to be sure your data i

7. Look at the data you have collected. Will you to average the data?

Grade 5

Index/Glossary

This index provides page references for the *Student Guide*. Definitions or explanations of key terms can be found on the pages listed in bold.

Components & Features

DISCOVERY ASSIGNMENT BOOK

The *Discovery Assignment Book* contains consumable student materials for activities, labs, and homework.

Name and Date Lines — Since the *Discovery Assignment Book* is consumable, a name and date line has been provided.

The Home Practice is a series of problems that supplements homework assignments.

Each Home Practice is divided into several parts. Each part can be assigned separately.

Name _____ Date _____

Unit 4 Home Practice

PART 1 *Triangle Flash Cards: Square Numbers*

Study for the quiz on the multiplication and division facts for the square numbers. Take home your *Triangle Flash Cards: Square Numbers* and your list of facts you need to study.

To quiz a multiplication fact, cover the corner containing the highest number. Multiply the two uncovered numbers.

To quiz a division fact, cover one of the smaller numbers. Use the two uncovered numbers to solve a division fact.

Mix up the multiplication and division facts. Sometimes cover the highest number and sometimes cover a smaller number.

Your teacher will tell you when the quiz on the square numbers will be given.

PART 2 Area

Solve the following problems. Choose an appropriate method for each: mental math, paper and pencil, or a calculator. Explain your solutions. Use a separate sheet of paper to show your work.

1. Jessie's parents are buying a rug for Jessie's bedroom. Jessie measured the length and width of her bedroom floor. It is 10 feet by 10 feet. What is the area of her bedroom floor?

2. Arti is putting together a jigsaw puzzle. The finished puzzle is 36 cm by 40 cm. What is the area of the puzzle?

3. Jerome's grandmother has an 8-inch by 10-inch wedding picture of herself and Jerome's grandfather. Her wedding picture sits next to Jerome's 3-inch by 5-inch school picture. About how many times greater in area is the wedding picture than the school picture?

4. A. Nila's older sister has a dog run for her dog in the backyard. The run is 12 feet by 8 feet. What is the area of the dog run?

   B. Nila wants to put the same size dog run in her backyard. If her backyard is 100 square feet, will an 8 feet by 12 feet dog run fit?

Name _____ Date _____

Finding Area

Find the area of each shape. Then on a separate sheet found the area. You may wish to use number sentences

1. Area = _____

3. Area = _____

4. Area

5. Area = _____

6. Area = _____

Footer — The Home Practice footer provides you with information about the page location:

DAB:	*Discovery Assignment Book*
Grade __:	Grade Level
Unit __:	Unit Number and Name

Activity Page — Consumable activity pages are located in the *Discovery Assignment Book*.

ADVENTURE BOOK

Illustrated stories that present mathematics and science concepts.

George Washington Carver: Man of Measure

"And Honorable Mention goes to Yucca and Cactus, painted by George Washington Carver!"

In 1893, at the World's Columbian Exposition in Chicago, a young artist named George Washington Carver watched in amazement and joy as his painting of a beautiful flowering cactus received an award. "Perhaps my dream of having a career as a painter will come true after all," he thought.

At that time, Carver was a college student, studying plants, at Iowa State University. However, many of his friends and teachers believed that he would eventually become a great artist. Carver himself had long felt that he had a special gift, but he knew that painting was only one of the many talents he possessed. Now he longed to feel certain about his life's work; he felt strongly that it was time for him to choose a path and follow it. But he was not so sure that painting was the path he was meant to follow.

22   AB • Grade 5 • Unit 4 • Lesson 7

What I Want to Know	Where to Find It
What does this lesson cover?	*Unit Resource Guide*–Unit Outline *Unit Resource Guide*–Lesson Guide *Teacher Implementation Guide*–Overview
What are the "big ideas" in this lesson or the entire unit?	*Unit Resource Guide*–Lesson Guide–Key Content *Unit Resource Guide*–Unit Outline *Unit Resource Guide*–Unit Background *Teacher Implementation Guide*–Overview
What do I need to prepare for this lesson?	*Unit Resource Guide*–Unit Outline–Preparing for Upcoming Lessons *Unit Resource Guide*–Lesson Guide–Before the Activity *Unit Resource Guide*–Lesson Guide–Materials List
What manipulatives do I need for this lesson?	*Unit Resource Guide*–Unit Outline *Unit Resource Guide*–Lesson Guide–Materials List
What have students covered on this topic in previous grades or previous units?	*Unit Resource Guide*–Lesson Guide–Curriculum Sequence—Before This Unit *Teacher Implementation Guide*–Scope and Sequence *Teacher Implementation Guide*–Overview
What will students cover on this topic in later units?	*Unit Resource Guide*–Lesson Guide–Curriculum Sequence—After This Unit *Teacher Implementation Guide*–Scope and Sequence *Teacher Implementation Guide*–Overview
How do I teach this lesson?	*Unit Resource Guide*–Lesson Guide
Where is a quick summary of each lesson to help teach the lesson?	*Unit Resource Guide*–Lesson Guide–At a Glance
How long will it take to do this lesson (or the entire unit)?	*Unit Resource Guide*–Unit Outline–Estimated Class Sessions *Unit Resource Guide*–Lesson Guide *Teacher Implementation Guide*–Overview
How do I deal with potential trouble spots?	*Unit Resource Guide*–Lesson Guide–TIMS Tip *Unit Resource Guide*–Lesson Guide–Content Notes *Teacher Implementation Guide*–TIMS Tutors
How do I organize my class to do this lesson?	*Unit Resource Guide*–Lesson Guide
Where are the Blackline and Transparency Masters?	*Unit Resource Guide*–Letter Home *Unit Resource Guide*–Lesson Guide *Teacher Resource CD*
Where are Journal Prompts?	*Unit Resource Guide*–Lesson Guide
Where are the remediation activities?	*Unit Resource Guide*–Daily Practice and Problems *Unit Resource Guide*–Unit Outline–Optional Review Lessons *Facts Resource Guid*e–Addition and Subtraction Math Facts Review section
Where is the skill practice and review?	*Unit Resource Guide*–Daily Practice and Problems *Discovery Assignment Book*–Home Practice *Student Guide*–Homework section *Facts Resource Guide*–Daily Practice and Problems, Home Practice, Addition and Subtraction Math Facts Review section *Teacher Resource CD*

What I Want to Know	Where to Find It
Where are the enrichment activities?	*Unit Resource Guide*–Lesson Guide–Extensions *Unit Resource Guide*–Daily Practice and Problems–Challenges *Unit Resource Guide*–Optional Lessons

What information is available for parents?	*Teacher Implementation Guide*–Parents and *Math Trailblazers*–
	    Parent Brochure; Information for Parents: Math Facts Philosophy
	    (English and Spanish)
	Unit Resource Guide–Letter Home
	Unit Resource Guide–Unit 2–Information for Parents:
	    Math Facts Philosophy

What should I assign as homework?	*Unit Resource Guide*–Lesson Guide–Homework and Practice, At a Glance *Discovery Assignment Book*–Home Practice
How do I assess students' progress?	*Unit Resource Guide*–Unit Background–Assessment Indicators *Unit Resource Guide*–Daily Practice and Problems–Fact Quizzes *Unit Resource Guide*–Observational Assessment Record *Unit Resource Guide*–Assessment Units *Unit Resource Guide*–Assessment Lessons *Unit Resource Guide*–Lesson Guide–Assessment Pages *Unit Resource Guide*–Lesson Guide–Assessment *Unit Resource Guide*–Lesson Guide–Journal Prompts *Teacher Implementation Guide*–Assessment section *Teacher Implementation Guide*–Assessment section– *Individual Assessment Record Sheet*
Where do I find connections to literature, computer software, and other content areas such as social studies and science?	*Unit Resource Guide*–Unit Outline *Unit Resource Guide*–Lesson Guide–Connections *Teacher Implementation Guide*–Literature List *Teacher Implementation Guide*–Software List
How do I find background information about concepts underlying each activity?	*Unit Resource Guide*–Unit Background *Unit Resource Guide*–Lesson Guide–Content Notes *Teacher Implementation Guide*–TIMS Tutors
How does this activity or unit fit into the "big picture" for my grade?	*Teacher Implementation Guide*–Overview *Teacher Implementation Guide*–Scope and Sequence *Unit Resource Guide*–Unit Background *Unit Resource Guide*–Lesson Guide–Curriculum Sequence
What will my students do this year?	*Teacher Implementation Guide*–Overview *Teacher Implementation Guide*–Scope and Sequence
What manipulatives do I need for the entire year?	*Teacher Implementation Guide*–Manipulatives List
Where is the scope and sequence?	*Teacher Implementation Guide*–Scope and Sequence

Does this curriculum match my district's objectives?	*Teacher Implementation Guide*–Scope and Sequence & the
	    NCTM *Principles and Standards*
	Teacher Implementation Guide–Overview
	Teacher Implementation Guide–Assessment section–
	    Individual Assessment Record Sheet
	Unit Resource Guide–Unit Background–Assessment Indicators

Where is the *Student Guide* Index?	*Student Guide*—Index
Where is the index for the curriculum?	*Teacher Implementation Guide*—Index

Components & Features

Overview

The Overview presents brief descriptions and lists of featured concepts for each unit. It provides a quick reference to locate concepts and activities.

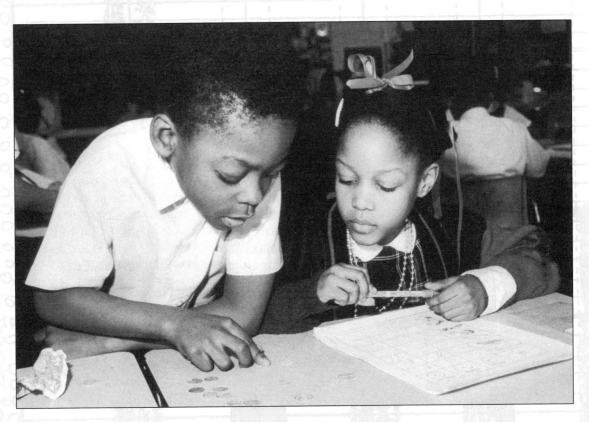

Students solve a problem using money.

Overview

The overview reflects the scope, sequence, and tone of the fifth-grade curriculum. The fundamental assumption of all the units is that math concepts and skills are best acquired through active involvement in problem solving. Thus, problem-solving activities are pervasive. Mathematics content—measurement, graphing, computation, logical reasoning, fractions, data analysis, geometry, and estimation—is included within problems in each unit. The TIMS Laboratory Method, used in laboratory experiments throughout the curriculum, incorporates experiences with some of the important tools for investigation and experimentation: drawing a picture, measuring, collecting and organizing data, constructing a graph, and posing and answering questions about the data.

Units also include:

- Suggestions for journal writing;
- Recommended homework assignments for most lessons;
- Parent letters that discuss the important ideas within the unit and provide suggestions for home activities that support lessons in school;
- Assessment, both through formal instruments and through the informal observations that a discourse-rich curriculum makes possible.

Many units include *Adventure Book* stories and recommendations for using related trade books and children's literature. A recommended software list accompanies most units. Some of the units in the first semester include activities that review materials from fourth grade so students new to the curriculum will have the necessary skills and concepts for fifth grade.

Home Practice. The Home Practice in the *Discovery Assignment Book* consists of short problems that can be assigned as homework or assessment throughout the unit. The Home Practice includes skill practice and problems that are related to the current unit or previous units. Problems can be solved in many ways with a variety of tools including calculators, data tables and charts, graphs, manipulatives, and paper-and-pencil strategies.

Daily Practice and Problems. The Daily Practice and Problems (DPP) is a vital component of the curriculum and can be found at the beginning of each unit in the *Unit Resource Guide* and on the *Teacher Resource CD*. These short exercises provide ongoing practice and review. Two DPP items are provided for each class session. TIMS Bits are short items that provide quick reviews of a topic or focused practice on a specific skill. TIMS Tasks and TIMS Challenges are problems that ask students to use previously learned concepts in a new context or to extend those concepts in a challenging new situation. The content includes:

- estimation
- computation
- number sense
- using data
- addition and subtraction facts review
- multiplication and division facts review

- counting and numeration
- money
- geometry
- problem solving

- time
- logic
- measurement
- using graphs

Summaries, pacing suggestions, and outlines of the fifth-grade units follow.

Unit 1: Populations and Samples · 9–12 Sessions

Unit Summary

This unit is designed to start the year off right by establishing a positive classroom atmosphere, introducing critical mathematics, and gathering baseline assessment data about students' mathematical abilities.

Students begin the unit with a lab called *Eyelets* that sets a cooperative atmosphere and reviews concepts used in earlier grades. Two activities from fourth grade review finding the median and collecting, organizing, and graphing data in bar graphs. Throughout the unit, students translate between graphs and real-world events. The *Searching the Forest* lab, which will help you gather baseline data on students' mathematical abilities, focuses on populations and samples.

The Adventure Book, *A Matter of Survival,* further explores these concepts. The DPP for this unit will allow you to assess students' fluency with the addition and subtraction facts.

Major Concept Focus

- numerical and categorical variables
- addition and subtraction fact review
- interpreting graphs
- finding the probability of an event
- *Adventure Book:* populations and samples
- choosing appropriate methods to solve problems
- TIMS Laboratory Method
- averages: medians and modes
- bar graphs
- populations and samples
- solving problems in more than one way

Pacing Suggestions

This unit is designed to be completed in nine to twelve days. However, several issues will impact how quickly a class will complete the unit:

- If students have had *Math Trailblazers* in previous grades, use the minimum number of class sessions for each lesson as a guide for lesson planning. If students have not had *Math Trailblazers,* use the maximum number of days as a guide.
- Lesson 2: *Review: Representing Data* is designed for students who did not have *Math Trailblazers* in fourth grade. The material is taken from Unit 1 of fourth grade and prepares students for data collection activities in fifth grade. Omit the lesson if students are already familiar with the content.
- The pacing schedule for the year assumes that mathematics instruction begins on the first day of school and that students receive 60 minutes of mathematics instruction each day. The first lesson is a data collection activity set in a context designed specifically to engage students on the first day of school.
- It is not necessary to stop and make sure students have mastered each skill before moving on to Unit 2, since later units will review and extend the skills and concepts developed in Unit 1. Students will also review skills in the Daily Practice and Problems (in each *Unit Resource Guide*) and Home Practice (in the *Discovery Assignment Book*).

The table below shows the location of resources that provide information on the development of concepts and skills throughout the year.

Resources for Pacing	Location
Curriculum Sequence	In Most Lesson Guides
Unit Scope and Sequence	*Teacher Implementation Guide*
Daily Practice and Problems and Home Practice Scope and Sequence	*Teacher Implementation Guide*
Individual Assessment Record Sheet	*Teacher Implementation Guide*

Preparing for Upcoming Lessons

Students will build an abacus in *The Chinese Abacus* in Unit 2 Lesson 4. Begin collecting 12 cm by 24 cm pieces of cardboard, string, and beads or ditali noodles (small noodles that can be found in most grocery stores) to make the abacuses.

Begin collecting pennies. Students will need about 20 pennies per group to complete *Stack Up* in Unit 2 Lesson 9.

Unit Planner

KEY: SG = Student Guide, DAB = Discovery Assignment Book, AB = Adventure Book, URG = Unit Resource Guide, DPP = Daily Practice and Problems, HP = Home Practice (found in Discovery Assignment Book), and TIG = Teacher Implementation Guide.

	Lesson Information	Supplies	Copies/Transparencies
Lesson 1 **Eyelets** URG Pages 28–49 SG Pages 2–9 DPP A–F HP Parts 1–2 *Estimated Class Sessions* **3**	**Lab** Students use the TIMS Laboratory Method to carry out a brief study of the number of eyelets in shoes in the classroom. **Math Facts** Use DPP Bits C and E to assess students' fluency with addition facts. Use the Addition and Subtraction Math Facts Review section of the *Facts Resource Guide* with students who need additional facts practice. **Homework** 1. Assign *Questions 1–4* in the Homework section in the *Student Guide*. 2. Assign Parts 1 and 2 of the Home Practice in the *Discovery Assignment Book*. **Assessment** Use the *Pockets at St. Crispin's* Assessment Page found at the end of the Lesson Guide.		• 1 copy of *Pockets at St. Crispin's* URG Page 41 per student • 2 copies of *Centimeter Grid Paper* URG Page 42 per student • 2 copies of *Two-column Data Table* URG Page 43 per student • 1 transparency of *Two-column Data Table* URG Page 43 or laminated data table wall chart or poster-size paper • 1 transparency of *Centimeter Grid Paper* URG Page 42 or laminated graph wall chart or poster-size paper
Lesson 2 **Review: Representing Data** URG Pages 50–75 *Estimated Class Sessions* **2-3**	OPTIONAL LESSON REVIEW FROM GRADE 4 **Optional Activity** This lesson is for students who did not use *Math Trailblazers* last year. The material is taken from Grade 4 Unit 1. It provides experiences with collecting, organizing, and graphing numerical data. **Math Facts** Use the Addition and Subtraction Math Facts Review section of the *Facts Resource Guide* as needed. **Homework** Assign the Homework sections of the *Collecting, Organizing, and Graphing* Activity Pages and the *Finding the Median* Activity Pages. **Assessment** Use the *Observational Assessment Record* and students' *Individual Assessment Record Sheets* to record students' abilities to make bar graphs.	• class-generated data table, Variables and Possible Values, from Lesson 1	• 1 copy of *Collecting, Organizing, and Graphing Data* URG Pages 63–65 per student • 1 copy of *Finding the Median* URG Pages 66–69 per student • 2 copies of *Centimeter Graph Paper* URG Page 70 per student • 1 transparency of *Bar Graph I: What's Wrong Here?* URG Page 61 • 1 transparency of *Bar Graph II: What's Wrong Here?* URG Page 62 • 1 transparency of *Three-column Data Table* URG Page 71 or laminated data table wall chart or poster-size paper • several transparencies of *Two-column Data Table* URG Page 43 or laminated data table wall chart or poster-size paper • 1 transparency of *Centimeter Graph Paper* URG Page 70 or laminated graph wall chart or poster-size paper • 1 copy of *Observational Assessment Record* URG Pages 13–14 to be used throughout this unit • 1 copy of *Individual Assessment Record Sheet* TIG Assessment section per student, to be used throughout the year

	Lesson Information	Supplies	Copies/Transparencies
Lesson 3 **Analyzing Data** URG Pages 76–89 SG Pages 10–16 DPP G–H HP Part 3 *Estimated Class Sessions* **1**	**Activity** Students analyze graphs and review averages (medians and modes). **Math Facts** Use the Addition and Subtraction Math Facts Review section of the *Facts Resource Guide* as needed. **Homework** 1. Assign the Homework section in the *Student Guide.* 2. Assign Part 3 of the Home Practice in the *Discovery Assignment Book.* **Assessment** Use *Question 1* in the Homework section as an assessment.		
Lesson 4 **A Matter of Survival** URG Pages 90–97 AB Pages 1–12 DPP I–J *Estimated Class Sessions* **1**	**Adventure Book** Betty and her parents sample animal populations in the Amazon rain forest. This story sets the stage for the lab in Lesson 5. **Math Facts** Use the Addition and Subtraction Math Facts Review section of the *Facts Resource Guide* as needed. **Homework** Assign item I from the Daily Practice and Problems.	• a map of South America, optional	
Lesson 5 **Searching the Forest** URG Pages 98–118 SG Pages 17–23 DPP K–P HP Parts 4–5 *Estimated Class Sessions* **3**	**Assessment Lab** Students model sampling an animal population in the forest by sampling a "population" of colored square-inch tiles in a bag. Students add this lab to their collection folders to collect baseline assessment data on their abilities to collect, organize, graph, and analyze data. **Math Facts** 1. Use Bits K and O to assess students' fluency with the subtraction facts. 2. Use the Addition and Subtraction Math Facts Review section of the *Facts Resource Guide* as needed. **Homework** 1. You can use Radio Favorites and Candy Grab in the Homework section of the *Student Guide* for homework during the lab. 2. Assign Parts 4 and 5 of the Home Practice. **Assessment** 1. Use *Jocelyn's Wildflowers* Assessment Page in the *Unit Resource Guide* as a quiz. 2. Evaluate students' labs based on the suggestions in the Assessment section of the Lesson Guide and in the Assessment section in the *Teacher Implementation Guide.*	• colored square-inch tiles, at least 50 in at least 2 colors per student group; more tiles in up to 5 colors is better • 1 brown lunch bag or opaque sack per student group • 1 letter-sized envelope per student group	• 1 copy of *Jocelyn's Wildflowers* URG Page 112 per student • 3 copies of *Centimeter Graph Paper* URG Page 70 per student • 1 copy of *Three-trial Data Table* URG Page 113 per student • 1 copy of *Three-column Data Table* URG Page 71 per student • 1 copy of *Two-column Data Table* URG Page 43 per student • 1 transparency of *Centimeter Graph Paper* URG Page 70, optional • 1 transparency or poster of Student Rubric: *Knowing* TIG, Assessment section, optional

(Continued)

	Lesson Information	Supplies	Copies/Transparencies
	3. Students save their labs in their collection folders.		
Lesson 6 **Practice Problems** URG Pages 119–124 SG Page 24 DPP Q–R HP Part 6 *Estimated Class Sessions* **1**	**Activity** Students solve a variety of multistep problems. **Math Facts** Use the Addition and Subtraction Math Facts Review section of the *Facts Resource Guide* as needed. **Homework** 1. Assign some or all of the problems for homework. 2. Assign Part 6 of the Home Practice.	• 1 calculator per student	

Unit 2: Big Numbers

Unit Summary

Students complete activities that involve reading and writing big numbers, using convenient numbers to estimate products, using paper and pencil to multiply, and reading scientific notation. This unit also provides opportunities to gather baseline data on students' mathematical abilities in these areas. Activities from fourth grade allow students to use base-ten pieces to review place value and addition and subtraction as needed. An Adventure Book, *Sand Reckoning,* tells the story of Archimedes and his estimate for the number of grains of sand needed to fill the universe. A short assessment problem, *Stack Up,* provides baseline data on students' abilities to solve multistep problems and communicate their solution strategies. The Student Rubrics: *Telling* and *Solving* are reintroduced and students begin collection folders to make portfolios. The yearlong review of the multiplication and division facts begins in this unit. Students use fact families to review the multiplication and division facts for the fives and tens.

Major Concept Focus

- addition and subtraction review
- multiplication with ending zeros
- paper-and-pencil multiplication
- measuring length in centimeters
- convenient numbers for computations
- Student Rubrics: *Telling* and *Solving*
- communicating solution strategies
- multiplication and division facts: 5s and 10s

- place value
- big numbers
- estimation
- exponents
- scientific notation
- using data to solve problems
- portfolios

Pacing Suggestions

This unit is designed to be completed in 15 to 21 days. Students' knowledge of place value, familiarity with base-ten pieces, and computational skills will determine how quickly the class completes the unit.

- In Lesson 2, students assess their fluency with the multiplication and division facts and begin a systematic review of the facts they need to study. They continue their review in the Daily Practice and Problems in this and succeeding units. In this unit they review the multiplication and division facts for the 5s and 10s. All students should continue learning new concepts and skills while reviewing the facts. For more information, see the TIMS Tutor: *Math Facts* in the *Teacher Implementation Guide.* (This review of the facts is also available in the *Grade 5 Facts Resource Guide.*)
- **Use Lesson 3 or Lesson 4, but not both.** Both lessons review place value. Lesson 3 *The Base-Ten Number System* reviews place value, addition, and subtraction with base-ten pieces using material from fourth grade. Use Lesson 3 if students did not use *Math Trailblazers* in previous grades. This will prepare them to use base-ten pieces in Grade 5 in lessons on multiplication and division. If students had *Math Trailblazers* in previous grades, use Lesson 4 *The Chinese Abacus* to review place value.
- For the remaining lessons, take advantage of the distributed practice and content spiral built into the curriculum. Move through the lessons using the minimum number of class sessions if students are familiar with *Math Trailblazers*. If they are not, use the maximum number of days as needed. Students will continue reviewing skills in the Daily Practice and Problems (in each *Unit Resource Guide*) and Home Practice (in the *Discovery Assignment Book*).

Preparing for Upcoming Lessons

If you plan to complete the optional Lesson 4 *The Chinese Abacus,* collect cardboard, string, and pony beads or ditali noodles to make the abacuses.

Students will need 20 pennies per group to complete Lesson 9 *Stack Up.*

Students will use *Triangle Flash Cards* to review the multiplication and division facts in Lesson 2 *Facts I Know.* You may want to laminate these cards or have students cut them out ahead of time to save class instruction time. The cards are in the *Discovery Assignment Book* following the Home Practice for this unit, and in the *Grade 5 Facts Resource Guide.*

Unit Planner

	Lesson Information	Supplies	Copies/Transparencies
Lesson 1 **Reading and Writing Big Numbers** URG Pages 32–48 SG Pages 26–34 DAB Pages 13–19 DPP A–D HP Part 2 *Estimated Class Sessions* **2-3**	**Activity** Students review reading and writing big numbers and use estimation skills to locate numbers on a number line. They play a game to practice reading large numbers. **Math Facts** Continue review of addition and subtraction facts as needed for individual students. **Homework** 1. Assign the Homework section in the *Student Guide.* 2. Assign the *Writing Big Numbers* Activity Page in the *Discovery Assignment Book.* 3. Assign the *Spin and Read Number Game.* 4. Assign Part 2 of the Home Practice. **Assessment** Use the Reading and Writing Big Numbers section of the *Student Guide* to assess writing numbers.	• 1 calculator per student • playing cards, optional • 1 clear plastic spinner or pencil and paper clip per student group	• 4 copies of *Digit Cards 0–9* URG Pages 43–44 per student group copied back to back • 1 transparency of *Population Lines* DAB Page 15, optional • 1 transparency of *Place Value Chart* DAB Page 19
Lesson 2 **Facts I Know** URG Pages 49–65 SG Pages 35–38 DAB Pages 21–24 DPP E–F HP Part 1 *Estimated Class Sessions* **1-2**	**Assessment Activity** This lesson launches the yearlong review of the multiplication and division facts that will continue in the DPP. **Homework** Assign Part 1 of the Home Practice that asks students to practice the math facts. **Assessment** 1. Students use flash cards and *Facts I Know* charts to assess themselves on the multiplication and division facts. 2. Record your observations on the *Observational Assessment Record.*	• 1 ruler per student • 1 pair of scissors per student and 1 pair for the teacher	• 1 copy of *Multiplication* and *Division Facts I Know* charts URG Pages 61–62 per student • 1 copy of *Information for Parents: Grade 5 Math Facts Philosophy* URG Pages 13–14 per student • 1 copy of *Centimeter Dot Paper* URG Page 63 per student • 1 transparency of *Triangle Flash Cards: 5s* DAB Page 21 • 1 transparency of *Triangle Flash Cards: 10s* DAB Page 23 • 1 transparency of *Centimeter Dot Paper* URG Page 63 • 1 copy of *Observational Assessment Record* URG Pages 15–16 to be used throughout this unit
Lesson 3 **The Base-Ten Number System** URG Pages 66–105 DPP G–J *Estimated Class Sessions* **2-3**	OPTIONAL LESSON DO EITHER LESSON 3 OR LESSON 4 **Optional Activity** This optional lesson reviews place value concepts using materials from fourth grade. This lesson is broken into three parts. In part 1, students represent numbers with base-ten pieces and review the Fewest Pieces Rule. In parts 2 and 3, students review the addition and subtraction algorithms by modeling these operations with the pieces. **Math Facts** Assign DPP item I.	• 1 set of base-ten pieces (2 packs, 14 flats, 30 skinnies, 50 bits) or 2 copies of bits and skinnies *Base-Ten Pieces Master* and 3 copies of flats and packs *Base-Ten Pieces Master* URG Pages 87–88 per student pair	• 1 copy of *The Base-Ten Number System* URG Pages 79–83 per student • 1 copy of *Addition with Base-Ten Pieces* URG Pages 89–91 per student • 1 copy of *Subtraction with Base-Ten Pieces* URG Pages 92–95 per student • 1 copy of *Recording Sheet* URG Page 86 per student

(Continued)

Overview

	Lesson Information	Supplies	Copies/ Transparencies
	Homework Assign the Homework sections in *The Base-Ten Number System, Addition with Base-Ten Pieces,* and *Subtraction with Base-Ten Pieces* Activity Pages.	• 40 connecting cubes per student group, optional • 1 pair of scissors per student group, optional • tape • overhead base-ten pieces, optional	• 1 copy of *Base-Ten Board Part 1* URG Page 84 per student group • 1 copy of *Base-Ten Board Part 2* URG Page 85 per student group • 1 transparency of *Recording Sheet* URG Page 86, optional • 1 transparency of *Base-Ten Board Part 1* URG Page 84, optional
Lesson 4 **The Chinese Abacus** URG Pages 106–130 SG Pages 39–45 DPP G–J *Estimated Class Sessions* **2-3**	OPTIONAL LESSON DO EITHER LESSON 3 OR LESSON 4 **Optional Activity** Students construct and use an abacus to represent numbers. They compare place value on the abacus to our base-ten number system. **Math Facts** Assign DPP item I. **Homework** 1. Assign *Question 1* in the Homework section of the *Student Guide.* Students need two copies of the *Abacus Pictures* Activity Page to complete the assignment. 2. Assign *Questions 2–13* in the Homework section of the *Student Guide.* Students may use their abacus to solve the problems. **Assessment** Use the *Number Changes* Assessment Pages to assess students' understanding of place value as modeled on the abacus.	• 1 piece of cardboard 14 cm by 24 cm per student • 11 pieces of string 16 cm long per student • 77 pony beads or ditali macaroni pieces per student • 1 strip of half-inch masking tape 24 cm long per student • 1 pair of scissors per student • 1 cm ruler per student • overhead abacus	• 1 copy of *Column Place Value Guides* URG Page 122 per student • several copies of *Abacus Pictures* URG Page 123 per student • 1 copy of *Number Changes* URG Pages 120–121 per student • 1 transparency of *Column Place Value Guides* URG Page 122 • 1 transparency of *Abacus Pictures* URG Page 123
Lesson 5 **Multiplication** URG Pages 131–156 SG Pages 46–55 DPP K–T HP Part 3 *Estimated Class Sessions* **5**	**Activity** Students multiply large numbers with ending zeros and look for patterns. They then review the all-partials method of multiplication as well as the traditional multiplication algorithm (the compact method). **Math Facts** Assign items M, O, and Q and review the multiplication and division facts for the 5s and 10s. **Homework** Assign the Homework section in the *Student Guide.* **Assessment** Use the *Making Money* Assessment Pages as a quiz.	• 1 set of base-ten pieces per student group • overhead base-ten pieces, optional	• 1 copy of *Making Money* URG Pages 147–149 per student • 1 table from *Multiplication Table* URG Page 146 per student • 1 copy of *Base-Ten Board Part 1 and 2* URG Pages 84–85 per student, optional • 1 copy of *Recording Sheet* URG Page 86 per student, optional • 1 transparency of *Base-Ten Board Part 1* URG Page 84, optional • 1 transparency of *Recording Sheet* URG Page 86, optional

	Lesson Information	Supplies	Copies/ Transparencies

Lesson 6

Estimating Products

URG Pages 157–166
SG Pages 56–59

DPP U–V
HP Part 4

Estimated Class Sessions
1-2

Activity
Students use convenient numbers to estimate products. Computational estimation is explored.

Math Facts
Assign item U and continue reviewing the multiplication and division facts for the 5s and 10s.

Homework
1. Assign *Questions 1–20* in the Homework section of the *Student Guide*.
2. Assign Part 4 of the Home Practice.

Assessment
1. Use some of the homework problems as assessments.
2. Use DPP item V to assess fluency with paper-and-pencil multiplication.

• 1 table from *Multiplication Table* URG Page 146 per student

Lesson 7

Sand Reckoning

URG Pages 167–171
AB Pages 13–20

DPP W–X

Estimated Class Sessions
1

Adventure Book
Using a story about the ancient mathematician Archimedes, students are prompted to think about large numbers.

Math Facts
Assign DPP items W and X for more practice with the multiplication and division facts for the 5s and 10s.

Lesson 8

Exponents and Large Numbers

URG Pages 172–181
SG Pages 60–63

DPP Y–Z

Estimated Class Sessions
1-2

Activity
Students review the use of exponents and then learn to read large numbers written in scientific notation. They read numbers on their calculator displays that are the result of calculations with large numbers.

Math Facts
Assign item Y.

Homework
1. Assign *Questions 1–20* in the Homework section of the *Student Guide*.
2. Assign DPP Task Z.

Assessment
Use the open-ended assessment problem in Lesson 9 *Stack Up*.

• 1 calculator per student

Overview

(Continued)

	Lesson Information	Supplies	Copies/Transparencies
Lesson 9 **Stack Up** URG Pages 182–198 DPP AA–BB *Estimated Class Sessions* **1-2**	**Assessment Activity** Students solve an open-response problem by estimating the number of pennies it will take to make a stack that reaches the moon. **Math Facts** Complete DPP item AA and continue reviewing the multiplication and division facts for the 5s and 10s.	• 1 calculator per student • 20 pennies per student group • 1 ruler per student	• 1 copy of *Stack Up* URG Pages 195–196 per student • 1 copy of *Centimeter Graph Paper* URG Page 197 per student, optional • 1 copy of *TIMS Multidimensional Rubric* TIG, Assessment section • 1 transparency or poster of Student Rubrics: *Solving* and *Telling* TIG, Assessment section, optional
Lesson 10 **Portfolios** URG Pages 199–206 SG Pages 64–65 DPP CC–DD *Estimated Class Sessions* **1**	**Assessment Activity** Students begin the process of putting together a portfolio. **Math Facts** Complete DPP item CC. **Assessment** 1. Begin student portfolios as a selection of best work. 2. Transfer appropriate documentation of the Unit 2 *Observational Assessment Record* to students' *Individual Assessment Record Sheets*.	• 1 folder per student • hanging rack or box for storing folders	• 1 copy of *Individual Assessment Record Sheet* TIG Assessment section per student, previously copied for use throughout the year

Unit 3: Fractions and Ratios .... 11–16 Sessions

Unit Summary

Students build a strong conceptual foundation for work with fractions, ratios, and proportions. They review fraction concepts with pattern blocks and use the concepts to develop skills and procedures such as finding equivalent fractions, ordering fractions, writing mixed numbers for improper fractions, and writing improper fractions for mixed numbers.

Students explore ratios using data tables, graphs, and symbols. In the lab *Distance vs. Time,* speed is defined as the ratio of distance moved to time taken. Students use this definition as they apply their knowledge of fractions and ratios. The Student Rubric: *Knowing* is reintroduced. The DPP for this unit reviews the multiplication and division facts for the twos and threes.

Major Concept Focus

- ratios
- mixed numbers
- Student Rubric: *Knowing*
- modeling fractions with pattern blocks
- writing number sentences using fractions
- measuring time with a stopwatch
- point graphs
- using data to solve problems
- multiplication and division facts: 2s and 3s
- improper fractions
- TIMS Laboratory Method
- comparing fractions
- ordering fractions
- equivalent fractions
- measuring length in yards
- best-fit lines
- speed

Pacing Suggestions

This unit begins work with fractions and ratios. The units that follow use the fraction concepts developed in this unit to build additional skills and concepts with fractions, ratios, decimals, and proportional reasoning. These skills and concepts are developed in a careful sequence as shown below.

Unit 4:   Application of ratios and proportional reasoning (Lesson 6)

Unit 5:   Equivalent fractions, mixed numbers, improper fractions, ordering fractions, addition and subtraction of fractions, application of ratios and proportional reasoning

Unit 7:   Decimals, percents, and probability

Unit 8:   Application and assessment of fractions, decimals, and percents (Lessons 5 and 6)

Unit 9:   Fractions and division, remainders as fractions

Unit 11: Fractions in lowest terms, common denominators, comparing fractions, addition and subtraction of fractions

Unit 12: Addition, subtraction, and multiplication of fractions, addition of mixed numbers, applications of fractions

Unit 13: Ratios and proportions

Unit 14: Application of ratios and proportional reasoning (Lesson 2)

Unit 16: Application and assessment of ratios and proportional reasoning (Lessons 2, 3, and 4)

- Teach the units in the order in which they were written. Students will revisit important concepts and skills as they experience them in new contexts as the units progress. Units that do not contain significant content on fractions and ratios will include practice and review in the Daily Practice and Problems and the Home Practice in the *Discovery Assignment Book.*

- Use the recommended session numbers for each lesson as a guide. It is not necessary to wait until students master each concept and skill as they will revisit them in later units and practice them in the Daily Practice and Problems and Home Practice throughout the year. Use the Assessment Indicators as a guide for the appropriate time to assess specific skills. The Assessment Indicators for all the units are listed on the *Individual Assessment Record Sheet* which is in the Assessment section of the *Teacher Implementation Guide.*

- Unit 3 Lesson 1 *Wholes and Parts* contains a review of pattern block fractions taken from fourth grade materials. This review is for students who have not had *Math Trailblazers* in previous years. These blackline masters are at the end of the Lesson Guide. If you use this review, students will need 2 days to complete the lesson.
- Unit 3 Lesson 7 *Speedy Problems* is an optional lesson. It is a series of word problems that are appropriate to assign for homework. The lesson is suitable for a substitute teacher since the preparation is minimal.

Preparing for Upcoming Lessons

In Lesson 6, students use stopwatches. You may want to place stopwatches in a learning center so students become familiar with their use before this activity.

Unit Planner

	Lesson Information	Supplies	Copies/Transparencies
Lesson 1 **Wholes and Parts** URG Pages 31–50 SG Pages 68–72 DAB Pages 35–38 DPP A–B HP Parts 1–2 *Estimated Class Sessions* **1-2**	**Activity** Students use pattern blocks to model fractions, to review the concept of a whole, and to write fractions. **Math Facts** Review the multiplication and division facts for the 2s and 3s. Complete DPP item B. **Homework** 1. Assign the *Homework: Wholes and Parts* Activity Pages found in the *Discovery Assignment Book.* 2. Assign Parts 1 and 2 of the Home Practice. **Assessment** Use the homework pages in the *Discovery Assignment Book* to assess students' abilities to represent a fraction given a whole.	• 1 set of pattern blocks (2–3 yellow hexagons, 6 red trapezoids, 10 blue rhombuses, 10 green triangles, 6 brown trapezoids, 12 purple triangles) per student pair • overhead pattern blocks, optional	• 1 copy of *Introducing Pattern Block Fractions* URG Pages 40–42 per student, optional • 1 transparency of *Pattern Block Record Sheet* DAB Page 35
Lesson 2 **Fraction Sentences** URG Pages 51–62 SG Pages 73–76 DPP C–D HP Part 4 *Estimated Class Sessions* **1-2**	**Activity** Using pattern blocks, students write number sentences for a whole divided into parts. They also write number sentences that equate mixed numbers with improper fractions. **Math Facts** Review the multiplication and division facts for the 2s and 3s. Complete DPP items C and D. **Homework** 1. Assign the Homework section in the *Student Guide.* 2. Assign Part 4 of the Home Practice.	• 1 set of pattern blocks (2–3 yellow hexagons, 6 red trapezoids, 10 blue rhombuses, 10 green triangles, 6 brown trapezoids, 12 purple triangles) per student pair • overhead pattern blocks, optional	• 1 copy of *Pattern Block Record Sheet* DAB Page 35 per student, optional
Lesson 3 **Equivalent Fractions** URG Pages 63–74 SG Pages 77–81 DAB Page 39 DPP E–H *Estimated Class Sessions* **2-3**	**Activity** Students investigate equivalent fractions using pattern blocks and number lines. They write equivalent fractions for a given number. **Math Facts** Review the multiplication and division facts for the 2s and 3s. Complete DPP item E. **Homework** Assign the homework in the *Student Guide.* **Assessment** 1. Choose questions in the Homework section as assessment. 2. Use the journal prompt as an assessment.	• 1 set of pattern blocks (2–3 yellow hexagons, 6 red trapezoids, 10 blue rhombuses, 10 green triangles, 6 brown trapezoids, 12 purple triangles) per student pair • 1 ruler per student • colored chalk, optional • overhead pattern blocks, optional	• 1 transparency of *Number Lines for Fractohoppers* DAB Page 39, optional

Overview

(Continued)

	Lesson Information	Supplies	Copies/Transparencies
Lesson 4 **Comparing Fractions** URG Pages 75–84 SG Pages 82–84 DPP I–J HP Parts 3 & 6 *Estimated Class Sessions* **1**	**Activity** Students compare fractions using 0, $\frac{1}{2}$, and 1 as benchmarks. They also compare fractions with like numerators or like denominators. **Math Facts** Review the multiplication and division facts for the 2s and 3s. Complete DPP item I. **Homework** 1. Assign Homework *Questions 1–6* in the *Student Guide.* 2. Assign Part 3 of the Home Practice. **Assessment** Use Part 6 of the Home Practice as an assessment.	• pattern blocks, optional	• 1 transparency of *Number Lines for Fractohoppers* chart SG Page 82
Lesson 5 **Using Ratios** URG Pages 85–109 SG Pages 85–93 DPP K–N HP Part 5 *Estimated Class Sessions* **2-3**	**Activity** Students use ratios to find the cost of items at a school fun fair. They express the ratios in words, tables, graphs, and symbols. **Math Facts** Review the multiplication and division facts for the 2s and 3s. Complete DPP item K. **Homework** 1. Assign the homework at the end of the lesson. Students will need enough graph paper to make three or four graphs. 2. Assign Part 5 of the Home Practice. **Assessment** 1. Use *Question 1* in the Homework section of the *Student Guide.* 2. Use the *Quiz Time* Assessment Pages.	• 1 ruler per student	• 1 copy of *Quiz Time* URG Pages 94–96 per student • 5 copies of *Centimeter Graph Paper* URG Page 100 per student • 1 copy of *Half-Centimeter Grid Paper* URG Page 101 per student, optional • 1 transparency of *Cost of Muffins Data Table* URG Page 97 • 1 transparency of *Cost of Muffins Graph* URG Page 98 • 1 transparency of *Using Ratios to Convert Feet to Yards* URG Page 99
Lesson 6 **Distance vs. Time** URG Pages 110–139 SG Pages 94–98 DPP O–V *Estimated Class Sessions* **4**	**Lab** Students use ratios to investigate the walking speed of a fifth grader. They review measurement, graphing, and data collection skills. **Math Facts** Review the multiplication and division facts for the 2s and 3s. Complete DPP item O. **Homework** 1. Assign the Homework section in the *Student Guide.* 2. Assign the problems in Lesson 7 *Speedy Problems.* **Assessment** 1. Use DPP item U to assess students' fluency with the multiplication and division facts for the 2s and 3s. 2. Use the *Observational Assessment Record* and the *Individual Assessment Record Sheet* as you observe students measuring length. 3. Assess students' graphing abilities by scoring their graphs.	• 3 stopwatches per student group • 1–2 metersticks per student group • chalk or tape • 1 calculator per student	• 1 copy of *Using Best-Fit Lines* URG Pages 126–131 per student, optional • 1 copy of *Centimeter Graph Paper* URG Page 100 per student • 1 copy of *Three-trial Data Table* URG Page 132 per student • 1 transparency of *Nila's Sit-Ups* URG Page 124, optional • 1 transparency of *What's Wrong with This Graph?* URG Page 125, optional • 1 transparency of *Centimeter Graph Paper* URG Page 100, optional • 1 transparency or wall chart of Student Rubric: *Knowing* TIG, Assessment section

Lesson Information	Supplies	Copies/Transparencies
4. Use the rubrics *Knowing* and *Telling* to assess students' work on **Questions 16–18** in the Explore section. 5. Use DPP item V to assess ratio concepts.		• 1 transparency or wall chart of Student Rubric: *Telling* TIG, Assessment section • 1 copy of *TIMS Multidimensional Rubric* TIG, Assessment section • 1 copy of *Observational Assessment Record* URG Pages 11–12 to be used throughout this unit • 1 copy of *Individual Assessment Record Sheet* TIG Assessment section per student, previously copied for use throughout the year

Lesson 7

Speedy Problems

URG Pages 140–143
SG Page 99

Estimated Class Sessions

1

OPTIONAL LESSON

Optional Activity
Students solve a variety of multistep word problems.

Homework
Assign some or all of the problems for homework.

Assessment
Assess students' work on **Question 6.**

• 1 calculator per student

Unit 4: Division and Data $\ldots\ldots\ldots\ldots\ldots\ldots\ldots\ldots\ldots$ 14–20 Sessions

Unit Summary
This unit extends and applies students' knowledge of several topics: division, measuring area, averages (means and medians), and accuracy in measurement and estimation. Division is explored first by modeling with the base-ten pieces, then by using a paper-and-pencil method. Students explore area and use it as a basis for making estimates. In an optional activity, they check the accuracy of their estimates using 10% as a benchmark. For the first time in fifth grade, students use the mean to average a set of data. The lab *Spreading Out* draws upon many of the concepts in the unit including area and averages. As part of the lab, students decide when it is appropriate to use a bar graph and when it is appropriate to use a point graph. The Adventure Book *George Washington Carver: Man of Measure* explores many of the variables involved in math and science. A midterm test assesses many of the concepts and skills studied thus far. The DPP for this unit reviews the multiplication and division facts for the square numbers.

Major Concept Focus
- area
- modeling division with base-ten pieces
- choosing appropriate graph
- manipulated, responding, and fixed variables
- interpreting remainders
- estimation
- 10% as a standard for estimation
- averages: medians and means
- *Adventure Book:* variables in math and science
- multiplication and division facts: square numbers
- TIMS Laboratory Method
- paper-and-pencil division
- ratios
- estimating quotients
- point graphs
- best-fit lines
- using ratios
- midterm test
- order of operations

Pacing Suggestions
Students' knowledge of division and familiarity with base-ten pieces will determine how quickly the class can proceed through Lessons 2 and 3, which review division concepts and a paper-and-pencil method for division. Students will have numerous opportunities to practice paper-and-pencil division during activities, laboratory investigations, Daily Practice and Problems, and Home Practice assignments in this and subsequent units.

The unit includes two optional lessons:

- Lesson 4 *How Close Is Close Enough?* discusses accuracy in measurement. Students learn to use 10% as a benchmark to judge the accuracy of their measurements. This concept is then applied in the *Spreading Out* laboratory investigation in this unit, as well as in laboratory investigations and Daily Practice and Problems items in future units. If you elect to skip this activity, you will need to skip related questions in subsequent lessons. In *Spreading Out,* skip **Questions 10C** and **11C.**

- The second optional lesson, Lesson 8 *Review Problems,* prepares students for the *Midterm Test*, the last activity in this unit. You can distribute *Review Problems* as homework throughout the unit rather than as an in-class review.
- To move through the unit more quickly, use *Math Trailblazers* connections to other subjects. For example, use science time to collect data for the *Spreading Out* lab. The *Adventure Book* on George Washington Carver can be linked with language arts or social studies instruction.

Preparing for Upcoming Lessons

Students use eyedroppers in Lesson 6. Provide an informal opportunity for students to practice using eyedroppers.

Overview

Unit Planner

KEY: SG = Student Guide, DAB = Discovery Assignment Book, AB = Adventure Book, URG = Unit Resource Guide, DPP = Daily Practice and Problems, HP = Home Practice (found in Discovery Assignment Book), and TIG = Teacher Implementation Guide.

	Lesson Information	Supplies	Copies/Transparencies
Lesson 1 **Grid Area** URG Pages 32–51 SG Pages 102–105 DAB Pages 49–63 DPP A–D HP Parts 1–2 *Estimated Class Sessions* **2**	**Activity** Students find areas of figures drawn on *Centimeter Grid Paper.* They discover strategies for finding the area of shapes with straight sides and for estimating the area of shapes with curved sides. **Math Facts** Complete DPP item B and begin reviewing the multiplication and division facts for the square numbers. **Homework** 1. Assign the *Finding Area* and *Cut and Paste Puzzles* Homework Pages in the *Discovery Assignment Book.* 2. Assign the Homework section in the *Student Guide.* 3. Assign Parts 1 and 2 of the Home Practice. **Assessment** 1. Use the *Observational Assessment Record* to record students' abilities to find the area of a shape. 2. Use the *Finding Area* Activity Page as an assessment. 3. Use DPP item D as a short assessment.	• 1 ruler per student • 1 pair of scissors per student • glue	• 3–4 copies of *Centimeter Grid Paper* URG Page 44 per student • 1 transparency of *Centimeter Grid Paper* URG Page 44 • 1 transparency of *Under the Rug* DAB Page 53 • 1 copy of *Observational Assessment Record* URG Pages 13–14 to be used throughout this unit
Lesson 2 **Modeling Division** URG Pages 52–67 SG Pages 106–112 DPP E–H *Estimated Class Sessions* **2**	**Activity** Students model division problems with base-ten pieces. Estimation is stressed. **Math Facts** Complete item E and continue reviewing the multiplication and division facts for the square numbers. **Homework** Assign Homework *Questions 1–15* in the *Student Guide.* **Assessment** Use the *Observational Assessment Record* to record students' abilities to model division with base-ten pieces.	• 1 calculator per student • 1 set of base-ten pieces (2 packs, 14 flats, 30 skinnies, 50 bits) per student pair • overhead base-ten pieces, optional	• 1 table from *Multiplication Table* URG Page 61 per student • copies of *Base-Ten Pieces Masters* URG Pages 62–63 as needed
Lesson 3 **Paper-and-Pencil Division** URG Pages 68–79 SG Pages 113–117 DPP I–N HP Part 3 *Estimated Class Sessions* **3**	**Activity** Students solve division problems using a paper-and-pencil method called the forgiving method. **Math Facts** Complete DPP items I, K, and M and continue reviewing the multiplication and division facts for the square numbers. **Homework** 1. Assign the Homework section in the *Student Guide* over several nights. 2. Assign Part 3 of the Home Practice. **Assessment** Students complete the *Quiz* Assessment Page.	• 1 calculator per student • 1 set of base-ten pieces (2 packs, 14 flats, 30 skinnies, 50 bits) per student pair • overhead base-ten pieces, optional	• 1 copy of *Quiz* URG Page 76 per student

	Lesson Information	Supplies	Copies/ Transparencies
Lesson 4 **How Close Is Close Enough?** URG Pages 80–96 SG Pages 118–122 DAB Page 65 *Estimated Class Sessions* **2-3**	OPTIONAL LESSON **Optional Activity** Students learn to find 10% of a number and use 10% as a standard for error analysis. **Homework** Assign the Homework section in the *Student Guide.*	• 1 calculator per student	• 1 copy of *Shapes 1–5* URG Page 91 per student • 1 copy of *Shapes 6 and 7* URG Page 92 per student • 1 copy of *Two-column Data Table* URG Page 93 per student group • 1 transparency of *Shapes 1–5* URG Page 91 • 1 transparency of *10% Chart* DAB Page 65 or large graph paper for a class data table • 1 transparency of *Centimeter Grid Paper* URG Page 44, optional • 1 transparency of *Two-column Data Table* URG Page 93, optional
Lesson 5 **Mean or Median?** URG Pages 97–109 SG Pages 123–130 DPP O–R *Estimated Class Sessions* **2**	**Activity** Students review methods for finding the mean value for a set of data. They compare mean and median. **Math Facts** Continue reviewing the multiplication and division facts for the square numbers. **Homework** Assign the Homework section in the *Student Guide.* **Assessment** Use DPP items Y and Z as quizzes.	• 1 calculator per student • 80 connecting cubes or square-inch tiles per student pair	
Lesson 6 **Spreading Out** URG Pages 110–133 SG Pages 131–138 DPP S–X HP Part 4 *Estimated Class Sessions* **3-4**	**Lab** Students look for the relationship between the number of drops on a paper towel and the area of the spot they create. They use the data to solve problems involving ratios. **Math Facts** Assign DPP item S. Review multiplication and division facts for square numbers. **Homework** 1. Assign the Homework section in the *Student Guide* after Part 3 of the lab. 2. Assign Part 4 of the Home Practice. **Assessment** 1. Use the *Observational Assessment Record* to document students' abilities to measure area and work with data. 2. Use the TIMS *Multidimensional Rubric* to score specific questions from the lab. 3. Use DPP item V as a quiz.	• 1 calculator per student • 1–2 pairs of scissors per student group • 1 eyedropper per student group • 3–4 sheets of the same brand of paper towel per student group • 1 ruler per student • 1 small container of water per student group • 2 books or 1 geoboard (for drying the paper towels) per student group	• 1 copy of *Centimeter Grid Paper* URG Page 44 per student or more as needed • 1 copy of *Three-trial Data Table* URG Page 129 per student or more as needed • 2 copies of *Centimeter Graph Paper* URG Page 130 per student • 1 transparency of *Centimeter Graph Paper* URG Page 130, optional • 1 transparency of *Bar Graph or Point Graph?* URG Page 127, optional • 1 transparency of *Spot Check* URG Page 128, optional

(Continued)

Overview

	Lesson Information	Supplies	Copies/Transparencies
	4. Transfer appropriate documentation from the Unit 4 *Observational Assessment Record* to students' *Individual Assessment Record Sheets*.		• 1 copy of *Individual Assessment Record Sheet* TIG Assessment section per student, previously copied for use throughout the year

Lesson 7

George Washington Carver: Man of Measure

URG Pages 134–143
DAB Page 67
AB Pages 21–34

DPP Y–Z

Estimated Class Sessions

1

Adventure Book
Students are introduced to George Washington Carver as he sets up his lab at Tuskegee Institute. He and his students improvise lab equipment to measure length, area, volume, time, and mass.

Math Facts
Assign DPP item Z that reviews math facts using the order of operations.

Homework
Assign the *Variables* Activity Page.

Assessment
1. Have students draw up a plan for making a two-pan balance and use household items to build it.
2. Have students make their own standard masses.
3. Have students test the soil at school or home.

Lesson 8

Review Problems

URG Pages 144–151
SG Pages 139–142
HP Part 5

Estimated Class Sessions

1

OPTIONAL LESSON

Optional Activity
Students solve problems that review concepts on the midterm test.

Math Facts
Continue reviewing the multiplication and division facts for the square numbers.

Homework
1. Assign all or part of this lesson as homework.
2. Assign Part 5 of the Home Practice.

• 1 calculator per student
• pattern blocks
• 1 ruler per student

• 2 copies of *Centimeter Graph Paper* URG Page 130 per student

Lesson 9

Midterm Test

URG Pages 152–164

DPP AA–BB

Estimated Class Sessions

1-2

Assessment Activity
Students take a short-item test that assesses skills and concepts studied in the first four units.

Math Facts
Assign DPP item AA.

• 1 calculator per student
• pattern blocks
• 1 ruler per student

• 2 copies of *Centimeter Graph Paper* URG Page 130 per student
• 1 copy of *Midterm Test* URG Pages 156–161 per student

Unit 5: Investigating Fractions . . . . 11–17 Sessions

Unit Summary

This unit connects two important strands in the curriculum: the study of fractions and the use of data to solve problems. Students review and expand their knowledge of fraction concepts to include models for finding common denominators.

Students use rectangles on dot paper, geoboards, and pattern blocks as their primary fraction models. They then use these models to develop procedures for comparing, adding, and subtracting fractions with unlike denominators. These concepts are further explored in the lab *A Day at the Races.* In this lab, students use the TIMS Laboratory Method and their knowledge of fractions to compare speeds by comparing ratios. The DPP for this unit reviews the multiplication and division facts for the nines.

Major Concept Focus

- representing fractions with models
- numerators and denominators
- unit whole
- fractional parts of wholes
- equivalent fractions
- common denominators
- communicating solution strategies
- multiplication and division facts: 9s
- comparing fractions
- adding fractions using models
- subtracting fractions using models
- estimating with fractions
- TIMS Laboratory Method
- measuring length
- speed and velocity
- point graphs
- best-fit lines
- using ratios
- Student Rubric: *Telling*

Pacing Suggestions

This unit extends concepts and skills developed in Unit 3 and the lab *Spreading Out* in Unit 4 Lesson 6. Students make connections among manipulatives, pictures, and symbols. This work allows them to choose among these tools to solve problems using fractions and ratios. Some students will be comfortable using symbols and others will depend on manipulatives and pictures. Most will move back and forth among the different representations. In later units, students will develop and practice paper-and-pencil procedures.

- Use the recommended session numbers for each lesson as a guide. It is not necessary to wait until students master each skill—especially paper-and-pencil procedures—as students will revisit them in later units. They will also practice them in the Daily Practice and Problems and Home Practice throughout the year. Use the Assessment Indicators as a guide for the appropriate time to assess specific skills. The Assessment Indicators for all units are listed on the *Individual Assessment Record Sheet* in the Assessment section of the *Teacher Implementation Guide.*

- Collect the data for Unit 5 Lesson 5 *A Day at the Races* during science time. This laboratory investigation explores speed and velocity.

- Unit 5 Lesson 8 *Shannon's Trip to School* is an optional lesson. This series of word problems is appropriate to assign for homework.

Unit Planner

	Lesson Information	Supplies	Copies/ Transparencies
Lesson 1 **Geoboard Fractions** URG Pages 26–43 SG Pages 144–151 DPP A–D HP Part 1 *Estimated Class Sessions* **2-3**	**Activity** Students build rectangles on geoboards and draw rectangles on dot paper. They use the rectangles to model fractions and mixed numbers. **Math Facts** Complete DPP items B–D and begin reviewing the multiplication and division facts for the 9s. **Homework** 1. Assign the Homework section in the *Student Guide*. 2. Assign Part 1 of the Home Practice. **Assessment** Use *Questions 5–6* from the Homework section to assess students' understanding of denominators and numerators.	• 1 geoboard per student pair • rubber bands • overhead geoboard	• 4–5 copies of *Centimeter Dot Paper* URG Page 36 per student • 1 transparency of *Centimeter Dot Paper* URG Page 36
Lesson 2 **Parts and Wholes** URG Pages 44–55 SG Pages 152–156 DPP E–F HP Part 2 *Estimated Class Sessions* **1-2**	**Activity** Students work in pairs to model fractions using both pattern blocks and rectangles on dot paper. **Math Facts** Assign DPP item E. Item E reviews math facts with multiples of ten. **Homework** 1. Assign the Homework section in the *Student Guide*. 2. Assign Part 2 of the Home Practice. **Assessment** 1. Use *Question 3* in the Homework section to assess students' abilities to model fractions using rectangles on dot paper. 2. Give a short quiz to assess students' abilities to represent fractions using rectangles on dot paper as you model various fractions using overhead pattern blocks. 3. Observe students as they are working in class. Record your observations on the *Observational Assessment Record* and students' *Individual Assessment Record Sheets*.	• 1 set of pattern blocks (2–3 yellow hexagons, 6 red trapezoids, 10 green triangles, 10 blue rhombuses, 6 brown trapezoids, 12 purple triangles) per student pair • overhead pattern blocks	• 3–4 copies of *Centimeter Dot Paper* URG Page 36 per student • 1 transparency of *Centimeter Dot Paper* URG Page 36 • 1 copy of *Observational Assessment Record* URG Pages 13–14 to be used throughout this unit • 1 copy of *Individual Assessment Record Sheet* TIG Assessment section, previously copied to be used throughout the year
Lesson 3 **Using Dot Paper Rectangles** URG Pages 56–66 SG Pages 157–159 DAB Pages 77–78 DPP G–H HP Part 4	**Game and Activity** Students write fraction sentences using dot paper rectangles in the game *Fraction Cover-All*. Students then model equivalent fractions using dot paper rectangles. **Math Facts** Continue reviewing the multiplication and division facts for the 9s using *Triangle Flash Cards*. **Homework** 1. Assign the Homework section in the *Student Guide*. 2. Assign the *Equivalent Fractions on Dot Paper* Activity Pages in the *Discovery Assignment Book*. 3. Assign Part 4 of the Home Practice.	• 1 set of 6 index cards with the following fractions: $\frac{1}{2}, \frac{1}{4}, \frac{1}{3}, \frac{1}{6}, \frac{1}{12}, \frac{1}{12}$	• 3–4 copies of *Centimeter Dot Paper* URG Page 36 per student • 1 transparency of *Centimeter Dot Paper* URG Page 36

(Continued)

Overview

	Lesson Information	Supplies	Copies/ Transparencies
Estimated Class Sessions **1-2**	**Assessment** Use *Question 1* in the Homework section.		
Lesson 4 **Using Common Denominators** URG Pages 67–75 SG Pages 160–163 DPP I–J HP Part 5 **Estimated Class Sessions** **1**	**Activity** Using rectangles on dot paper, students compare fractions with unlike denominators by rewriting the fractions with common denominators. **Math Facts** Complete DPP item I, which uses fact families to review the multiplication and division facts for the 9s. **Homework** 1. Assign *Questions 1–12* in the Homework section on the *Using Common Denominators* Activity Pages in the *Student Guide*. 2. Assign Part 5 of the Home Practice. **Assessment** Use two or three problems from the Homework section as assessment.		• 3–4 copies of *Centimeter Dot Paper* URG Page 36 per student • 1 transparency of *Centimeter Dot Paper* URG Page 36
Lesson 5 **A Day at the Races** URG Pages 76–96 SG Pages 164–170 DPP K–P HP Part 3 **Estimated Class Sessions** **3-4**	**Lab** In an experiment on speed, students compare ratios using both graphs and symbols. **Math Facts** Complete DPP items K and O, which review math facts. **Homework** 1. Assign the Homework section in the *Student Guide*. 2. Assign the word problems in Lesson 8 for homework. 3. Assign Part 3 of the Home Practice. **Assessment** 1. Assign points to one or more sections of the lab to determine a grade. 2. Use *Question 18* to assess students' abilities to draw a graph. Use *Questions 19–20* to assess the students' abilities to solve problems and communicate solutions. 3. Use the *Observational Assessment Record* and the Assessment Indicators to record students' skills in measuring length.	• 1–2 metersticks per student group • 1–2 stopwatches per student group • chalk or tape	• 2–3 copies of *Centimeter Graph Paper* or *Half-Centimeter Graph Paper* URG Pages 89–90 per student • 2 copies of *Three-trial Data Table* URG Page 91 per student • 3 copies of *Five-column Data Table* URG Page 92 per student group, optional • 1 transparency of *Centimeter Graph Paper* or *Half-Centimeter Graph Paper* URG Pages 89–90, optional • 1 copy of *TIMS Multidimensional Rubric* TIG Assessment section

	Lesson Information	Supplies	Copies/Transparencies
Lesson 6 **Adding Fractions with Rectangles** URG Pages 97–109 SG Pages 82, 171–176 DPP Q–T *Estimated Class Sessions* **2**	**Activity** Students estimate sums of fractions using 0, $\frac{1}{2}$, and 1 as benchmarks. Then, they use rectangles on dot paper to develop and use procedures for adding fractions. **Math Facts** Complete DPP item S, which is a quiz on the facts. **Homework** 1. You may assign *Questions 15–25* in the Explore section for homework. 2. Assign homework *Questions 1–10* in the *Student Guide*. **Assessment** 1. Use *Questions 5–6* in the Homework section to assess students' skills. 2. Use DPP Task T *Comparing Fractions* as a quiz.	• crayons or markers	• 3–4 copies of *Centimeter Dot Paper* URG Page 36 per student • 1 transparency of *Centimeter Dot Paper* URG Page 36
Lesson 7 **Adding and Subtracting Fractions** URG Pages 110–123 SG Pages 177–181 DPP U–V HP Part 6 *Estimated Class Sessions* **1-2**	**Activity** Students use rectangles on dot paper to subtract fractions. Then they develop paper-and-pencil procedures for adding and subtracting fractions. **Homework** 1. Assign homework *Questions 1–8* in the *Student Guide*. 2. Assign Part 6 of the Home Practice. **Assessment** Students complete the *Fraction Follow-Up* Assessment Pages.		• 1 copy of *Fraction Follow-Up* URG Pages 117–118 per student • 3–4 copies of *Centimeter Dot Paper* URG Page 36 per student • 1 transparency of *Centimeter Dot Paper* URG Page 36
Lesson 8 **Shannon's Trip to School** URG Pages 124–128 SG Page 182 HP Part 7 *Estimated Class Sessions* **1**	OPTIONAL LESSON **Optional Activity** Students complete a set of word problems using fractions. **Homework** 1. Assign some or all of the problems for homework. 2. Assign Part 7 of the Home Practice. **Assessment** Use any of the problems for assessment.	• 1 calculator per student	

Unit 6: Geometry .... 9–15 Sessions

Unit Summary
Students investigate patterns and concepts in geometry. They draw triangles and other plane figures and discover properties of the shapes. Students discover the relationship between the number of sides of a polygon and the sum of its angles. They describe and classify shapes. Tessellations are explored using quilt designs.

This unit contains a short assessment, *Making Shapes,* in which students draw shapes with specific properties and measurements. To complete the assessment, they use the *Telling* Rubric to guide their writing as they explain the strategies they used to draw the shapes.

The DPP for this unit reviews the last six multiplication facts (4 × 6, 4 × 7, 4 × 8, 6 × 7, 6 × 8, and 7 × 8) and the related division facts.

Major Concept Focus
- estimating angle measures
- acute, obtuse, right, and straight angles
- congruence
- naming polygons
- properties of triangles and polygons
- measuring angles with a protractor
- drawing angles and shapes
- communicating solution strategies

- multiplication and division facts: last six facts
- similarity
- tessellations
- sums of angles in polygons
- triangulation
- classifying shapes
- Student Rubric: *Telling*

Pacing Suggestions
This unit is designed to be completed in 9–15 days. Students' previous experience with the unit's geometric concepts, as well as the extent of students' explorations in each lesson, will determine how quickly the class completes the unit.

- The unit includes one optional lesson, Lesson 5 *Quilts and Tessellations,* which is an engaging investigation involving geometric patterns and reasoning. The lesson also provides many opportunities for connections to other subjects. Students can complete this lesson in conjunction with art or social studies classes, or individual students can work on it as an enrichment activity.

Preparing for Upcoming Lessons
Collect pennies and nickels for Unit 7 Lessons 7–8.

Unit Planner

	Lesson Information	Supplies	Copies/Transparencies
Lesson I **Angle Measures** URG Pages 27–41 SG Pages 184–191 DAB Pages 87–88 DPP A–D HP Part 1 *Estimated Class Sessions* **2**	**Activity** Students review benchmark angles (90°, 180°, 270°). They measure and draw angles with protractors. **Math Facts** Complete DPP items B and D for this lesson. Task B begins the review of the last six facts, while Challenge D uses operations to solve puzzles. **Homework** 1. Students complete homework *Questions 1–5* in the *Student Guide* after Part 1. 2. Students complete homework *Questions 6–8* in the *Student Guide* after Part 2. 3. Assign Part 1 of the Home Practice. Students use flash cards to review the last six facts. **Assessment** 1. Use *Question 8* in the Homework section in the *Student Guide* as an assessment. 2. Use the *Observational Assessment Record* to note students' abilities to measure angles.	• 1 protractor per student and 1 for the teacher • cardboard corners, optional	• 1 transparency of *Measuring Angles* DAB Pages 87–88, optional • 1 copy of *Observational Assessment Record* URG Pages 11–12 to be used throughout this unit
Lesson 2 **Angles in Triangles and Other Polygons** URG Pages 42–57 SG Pages 192–196 DAB Pages 89–90 DPP E–H HP Parts 2–3 *Estimated Class Sessions* **2**	**Activity** Students measure angles in polygons and discover that the sum of a triangle's interior angles is always 180 degrees. **Math Facts** Complete DPP items E and G. Item E provides practice with the last six facts. Item G introduces fact families. **Homework** 1. Assign *Questions 1–6* in the Homework section of the *Student Guide* after Part 1. 2. Assign *Questions 7–9* in the Homework section after Part 2. 3. Assign Parts 2 and 3 of the Home Practice. **Assessment** 1. Use DPP item M as an assessment. 2. Use the *Observational Assessment Record* to document students' abilities to identify, describe, and classify 2D shapes.	• 1 protractor per student and 1 for the teacher • 1 ruler per student and 1 for the teacher • 1 set of pattern blocks (6 green triangles and at least 1 each of the following: yellow hexagon, red trapezoid, blue rhombus, brown trapezoid, purple triangle, tan rhombus, and orange square) per student group • 1 pair of scissors per student • 2 blank unlined sheets of paper per student • cardboard corners or plastic right triangle, optional • pattern block templates, optional • overhead pattern blocks, optional • large blackboard protractor, optional	• 1 transparency of *Measuring Pattern Block Angles* DAB Pages 89–90, optional • 1 transparency of *Regular Polygons* URG Page 52

(Continued)

Overview

	Lesson Information	Supplies	Copies/Transparencies
Lesson 3 **Polygon Angles** URG Pages 58–69 SG Pages 197–200 DAB Page 91 DPP I–J HP Part 4 *Estimated Class Sessions* **1-2**	**Activity** Students investigate the sum of the interior angles of various polygons to find patterns. **Homework** 1. Students can complete the homework problems in the *Polygon Angles* Activity Pages in the *Student Guide* after completing the *Polygon Angles Data Table.* 2. Assign Part 4 of the Home Practice. **Assessment** Use the Journal Prompt as an assessment.	• 1 calculator per student • 1 protractor per student and 1 for the teacher • 1 ruler per student	• 1 transparency of *Polygon Angles Data Table* DAB Page 91, optional
Lesson 4 **Congruent Shapes** URG Pages 70–81 SG Pages 201–204 DPP K–L HP Part 6 *Estimated Class Sessions* **1**	**Activity** Students explore properties of triangles. They investigate the difference between congruence and similarity. **Math Facts** Complete DPP item K for this lesson. **Homework** 1. Assign the Homework section in the *Student Guide.* 2. Assign Part 6 of the Home Practice. **Assessment** 1. Use DPP Task L Drawing Shapes as a quiz. 2. Use the *Observational Assessment Record* to document students' abilities to identify congruent and similar shapes.	• 10 straws plus extras per student group and 10 for the teacher • 4 chenille sticks plus extras per student group and 4 cut into approximately 5-cm lengths for the teacher • 1 pair of scissors per student • 1 centimeter ruler per student • 1 protractor per student	• 1 transparency of *Congruent Shapes Examples* URG Page 78 • 1 transparency of *A Triangle* URG Page 79 • 1 transparency of *Congruent Shapes* SG Pages 201–202, optional
Lesson 5 **Quilts and Tessellations** URG Pages 82–96 SG Pages 205–209 *Estimated Class Sessions* **3**	OPTIONAL LESSON **Optional Activity** Students analyze the geometry of quilt patterns and investigate tessellations. **Homework** Students complete the homework questions on the *Quilts and Tessellations* Activity Pages in the *Student Guide.* **Assessment** Use homework *Questions 1–2* as an assessment.	• 1 set of pattern blocks (12 green triangles, 12 orange squares, 3 yellow hexagons, 6 red trapezoids, 6 blue rhombuses, 12 tan rhombuses) per student group • 1 protractor per student and 1 for the teacher • plain unlined paper, optional • overhead pattern blocks, optional	• 3 copies of *Triangle Grid Paper* URG Page 94 per student plus extras, optional • 1 transparency of *Jacob's Ladder Quilt* URG Page 89 • 1 transparency of *Detail View of Jacob's Ladder Quilt* URG Page 90 • 1 transparency of *Four Quilt Patterns* URG Pages 91–92 • 1 transparency of *Regular Hexagons* URG Page 93

	Lesson Information	Supplies	Copies/Transparencies
Lesson 6 **Classifying Shapes** URG Pages 97–112 SG Pages 210–217 DAB Page 93 DPP M–P HP Part 7 *Estimated Class Sessions* **2-3**	**Activity** Students compare classifications in science to classifying polygons. **Math Facts** Complete DPP items O–P for this lesson. **Homework** 1. Assign the Homework section in the *Student Guide* before Part 2. 2. Assign Part 7 of the Home Practice. **Assessment** You can use The Flatville Zoo section in the *Student Guide* as an assessment.	• large art paper • glue • 1 pair of scissors per student • dictionary	• 1 transparency of *Classifying Shapes* SG Pages 210 & 212, optional
Lesson 7 **Making Shapes** URG Pages 113–123 SG Pages 218–219 DPP Q–R HP Part 5 *Estimated Class Sessions* **1-2**	**Assessment Activity** Students draw two-dimensional shapes based on information on an "order" for a slab of stone. **Math Facts** Complete DPP item Q, which quizzes the last six facts. **Homework** 1. Use uncompleted orders on the *Making Shapes* Activity Pages as homework. 2. Assign Part 5 of the Home Practice. **Assessment** 1. Use the *Slab Orders* Assessment Page to assess students' understanding. Score **Question 4** on the *Telling* Rubric. 2. Transfer appropriate documentation from the Unit 6 *Observational Assessment Record* to students' *Individual Assessment Record Sheets*.	• 1 protractor per student and 1 for the teacher • 1 ruler per student • straws and chenille sticks, optional • overhead ruler	• 1 copy of *Slab Orders* URG Page 120 per student • 1 copy of *TIMS Multidimensional Rubric* TIG, Assessment section • 1 copy of *Individual Assessment Record Sheet* TIG Assessment section per student, previously copied for use throughout the year • 1 transparency or poster of Student Rubric: *Telling* TIG, Assessment section

Overview

Unit 7: Decimals and Probability .... 13–18 Sessions

Unit Summary

A major goal of this unit is to help students understand that often they can express a quantity as a fraction, decimal, and a percent. Students use two models to help them make connections between fractions and decimal symbols: centiwheels (circles divided into hundredths) and squares divided into tenths, hundredths, and thousandths.

Students work with these grids to reinforce place value concepts, compare decimals, round decimals, and model addition and subtraction of decimals. They use an area model to learn to place decimals in products of decimal multiplication problems. Students use their knowledge of decimals to explore probabilities.

They complete a lab, *Flipping Two Coins,* in which they explore the results of coin flipping experiments. The lab is related to a real-life story in the Adventure Book *Unlikely Heroes.* The DPP for this unit reviews all the multiplication and division facts.

Major Concept Focus

- reading and writing decimals
- decimal place value
- adding decimals
- multiplying decimals
- using fractions to write probabilities
- using decimals to write probabilities
- *Adventure Book:* probability
- bar graphs
- relationships between fractions, decimals, and percents

- multiplication and division facts
- rounding decimals
- comparing decimals
- subtracting decimals
- estimating with decimals
- probabilities of flipping coins
- law of large numbers
- TIMS Laboratory Method
- predictions from graphs

Pacing Suggestions

This unit extends the study of fractions to decimals and probability. If students had experiences with decimals and probability in earlier grades, use the smaller of the recommended number of sessions to guide your planning. If students have not previously worked with decimals, they will move more slowly through the lessons. However, it is not necessary to wait until all students have mastered all the skills, as they will use them in later units in new contexts and continue to practice them in the Daily Practice and Problems and Home Practice. In particular, Unit 8 *Applications: An Assessment Unit* reviews fractions, decimals, and percents.

- Omit Part 1 of Lesson 1 if your students have studied decimals before. This optional part of the lesson, *A Review: Tenths and Hundredths,* introduces decimals using base-ten pieces. The material is from third and fourth grades.
- Lesson 9 *Families with Two Children* is an optional lesson that can serve as an extension. The activity is a real-world application of probability.

Preparing for Upcoming Lessons

Pennies will be needed for Lesson 7. Pennies and nickels will be needed for Lesson 8.

Save the interlocking centiwheels and the small centiwheels made in Lesson 1 for use in Units 8, 9, and 14.

Bubble solution and wands will be needed for Unit 8.

Unit Planner

	Lesson Information	Supplies	Copies/Transparencies
Lesson 1 **Fractions, Decimals, and Percents** URG Pages 29–58 SG Pages 222–229 DAB Page 101 DPP A–D HP Parts 1–3 *Estimated Class Sessions* **2-3**	**Activity** Students explore the relationship between fractions, decimals, and percents. An optional part of the activity from Grades 3 and 4 is included for students with little experience with decimals. **Math Facts** DPP item C reviews math facts. **Homework** 1. Students complete homework *Questions 1–5* in the *Student Guide.* 2. Students complete the *Designing Quilts* Homework Page in the *Discovery Assignment Book.* They will use their quilt designs in Lesson 2. 3. Assign Parts 1 and 2 of the Home Practice in the *Discovery Assignment Book.* **Assessment** Use Part 3 of the Home Practice as a quiz.	• 1 pair of scissors per student • 1 hole punch per student, optional • 1 set of base-ten pieces (2 flats, 20 skinnies, 15 bits) per student pair, optional	• 1 copy of *Tenths and Hundredths* URG Pages 42–47 per student, optional • 1 copy of *Centiwheel Disks* URG Page 48 per student, 1 disk on colored paper and 1 disk on white paper • 1 small disk from *Small Centiwheels* URG Page 49 per student • 2 copies of *Three-trial Data Table* URG Page 50 per student • 1 copy of *Centiwheel Disks* URG Page 48, 1 enlarged disk on white paper and 1 enlarged disk on colored paper for demonstration, optional
Lesson 2 **Decimal Models** URG Pages 59–77 SG Pages 230–237 DAB Page 103 DPP E–F HP Part 4 *Estimated Class Sessions* **1-2**	**Activity** Students use an area model to review tenths, hundredths, and thousandths. They use a place value chart to help them read and write decimals. **Homework** 1. Assign the questions in the Homework section in the *Student Guide.* Students will need a *Decimal Grids* Activity Page to complete the homework. 2. Assign the game *Score One.* 3. Assign Part 4 of the Home Practice. **Assessment** Use some of the homework questions as an assessment.	• 1 pair of scissors per student, optional • 1 toothpick per student, optional	• 2 copies of *Decimal Grids* URG Page 70 per student • 1 transparency of *Decimal Place Value Chart* URG Page 69, optional • 1 transparency of *Decimal Grids* URG Page 70, optional
Lesson 3 **Comparing and Rounding Decimals** URG Pages 78–93 SG Pages 238–242 DAB Pages 105–111 DPP G–J HP Part 5 *Estimated Class Sessions* **2**	**Activity** Students compare and order decimals using an area model and benchmark numbers of 0, 0.1, 0.5, and 1. They also use the area model to round decimals to the nearest whole number, tenth, and hundredth. **Math Facts** DPP item G reviews the multiplication and division facts. **Homework** 1. Assign the Homework section in the *Student Guide.* Students will need a copy of the *Decimal Grids* Activity Page from the *Unit Resource Guide* to complete the assignment. 2. Assign the *Connect the Dots* Activity Page in the *Discovery Assignment Book* for homework. (optional) **Assessment** Use Part 5 of the Home Practice as a quiz.		• 1–3 copies of *Decimal Grids* URG Page 70 per student • 1 transparency of *Decimals: A Closer Look* DAB Pages 105–109, optional • 1 transparency of *Decimal Place Value Chart* URG Page 69 • 1 transparency of *Decimal Grids* URG Page 70

(Continued)

Overview

	Lesson Information	Supplies	Copies/ Transparencies
Lesson 4 **Adding and Subtracting Decimals** URG Pages 94–106 SG Pages 243–246 DAB Pages 113–118 DPP K–L *Estimated Class Sessions* **1-2**	**Activity** Students use their knowledge of place value to align numbers correctly and then solve addition and subtraction problems with decimals. **Math Facts** DPP item K reviews math facts. **Homework** Assign *Questions 1–10* in the Homework section on the *Adding and Subtracting Decimals* Activity Pages in the *Student Guide* for homework. **Assessment** 1. Use *Questions 7–8* in the Homework section on the *Adding and Subtracting Decimals* Activity Pages in the *Student Guide* as an assessment. 2. Use DPP Task L as an assessment.		• 1 transparency of *Adding Decimals with Grids* DAB Page 113 • 1 transparency of *Subtracting Decimals with Grids* DAB Page 117 • 1 transparency of *Decimal Place Value Chart* URG Page 69
Lesson 5 **Multiplying Decimals with Area** URG Pages 107–116 SG Pages 247–251 DPP M–N HP Part 6 *Estimated Class Sessions* **1-2**	**Activity** Students investigate multiplying decimals. They develop a sense for the placement of a decimal in a product through estimation and the use of an area model. **Homework** 1. Assign the Homework section in the *Multiplying Decimals with Area* Activity Pages in the *Student Guide*. 2. Assign Part 6 of the Home Practice.	• 1 ruler per student	• 1–3 copies of *Centimeter Grid Paper* URG Page 113 per student • 1 transparency of *Centimeter Grid Paper* URG Page 113
Lesson 6 **Paper-and-Pencil Decimal Multiplication** URG Pages 117–125 SG Pages 252–254 DPP O–P *Estimated Class Sessions* **1**	**Activity** Students learn a procedure for placing decimals in products. **Math Facts** DPP Bit O reviews the multiplication and division facts. **Homework** Assign the Homework section in the *Student Guide*. **Assessment** Use the *Decimal Quiz* as an assessment of students' skills.		• 1 copy of *Decimal Quiz* URG Page 123 per student

	Lesson Information	Supplies	Copies/Transparencies
Lesson 7 **Flipping One Coin** URG Pages 126–134 SG Pages 255–257 DPP Q–R HP Part 8 *Estimated Class Sessions* **1**	**Activity** Students flip a coin 40 times and count the number of times heads or tails show. The probability of flipping a head is discussed and compared to experimental results. **Homework** Assign Part 8 of the Home Practice in the *Discovery Assignment Book*.	• 1 penny per student group • 1 small paper cup per student group, optional • 1 small cloth for tossing coins to muffle the sound per student group, optional	• 1 copy of *Three-column Data Table* URG Page 132 per student, optional
Lesson 8 **Flipping Two Coins** URG Pages 135–153 SG Pages 258–264 DAB Pages 119–123 DPP S–X HP Part 7 *Estimated Class Sessions* **3**	**Lab** Students flip a penny and a nickel repeatedly and record the number of heads showing. Data is compared for 10, 100, and 1000 trials after pooling data with classmates. **Math Facts** DPP items S and W review the multiplication and division facts. **Homework** 1. *Questions 1–4* provide practice translating fractions, decimals, and percents. Assign these questions before students analyze their data. 2. Assign *Question 5* after students complete the lab. They play a game and use what they learned from the lab to decide if it is fair or unfair. 3. Assign Part 7 of the Home Practice. **Assessment** 1. Assign points to one or more sections of the lab and grade them as an assessment. 2. As students analyze their group data, record their abilities to make and interpret bar graphs on the *Observational Assessment Record*. 3. Transfer appropriate documentation to students' *Individual Assessment Record Sheets*	• 1 calculator per student group • 1 penny per student group • 1 nickel per student group • 1 small paper cup per student group, optional • 1 small cloth for tossing coins to muffle the sound per student group, optional	• 3 copies of *Centimeter Graph Paper* URG Page 147 per student • 1 transparency of *Coin Flipping Data Tables* DAB Page 121, optional • 1 copy of *Observational Assessment Record* URG Pages 13–14 to be used throughout this unit • 1 copy of *Individual Assessment Record Sheet* TIG Assessment section per student, previously copied for use throughout the year
Lesson 9 **Families with Two Children** URG Pages 154–158 SG Pages 265–267 *Estimated Class Sessions* **1**	OPTIONAL LESSON—EXTENSION **Optional Activity** Using ideas from the lab in Lesson 8, students investigate the probability that a family with two children will have 0, 1, or 2 boys. **Homework** Students collect data at home on two-children families.		

(Continued)

	Lesson Information	Supplies	Copies/Transparencies
Lesson 10 **Unlikely Heroes** URG Pages 159–165 AB Pages 35–46 DPP Y–Z *Estimated Class Sessions* **1**	**Adventure Book** Students read a story about John Kerrich, an Englishman who was imprisoned in Denmark during World War II. Kerrich completed experiments involving probabilities of coin tosses while in prison.	• pennies, optional	

Unit 8: Applications: An Assessment Unit

Unit Summary

This unit applies and expands concepts and skills learned in the first seven units. Assess students on these concepts and skills as they work on the activities and labs. They demonstrate their knowledge by solving problems that arise in several contexts that have strong connections to science and social studies.

Students review labs completed in the first half of the year in preparation for completing the assessment lab, *Comparing the Lives of Animals and Soap Bubbles.* As part of the lab, students apply their knowledge of percents and interpret graphs.

They also read the Adventure Book *Florence Kelley,* which describes the work of a social reformer in the late 1900s who—through data collection—was able to contribute to the passage of child labor laws in Illinois. This Adventure Book sets the stage for an assessment activity called *Florence Kelley's Report* in which students interpret Florence Kelley's data as she reported it to the governor.

This unit includes the *Midyear Test* and a portfolio review session. The DPP for this unit tests all the multiplication and division facts.

Major Concept Focus

- experiment review
- interpreting data tables and graphs
- portfolio review
- binning data
- *Adventure Book:* child labor
- communicating solution strategies
- midyear test
- representing quantities using fractions, decimals, and percents
- estimating products of decimals
- point and bar graphs
- TIMS Laboratory Method
- percents
- Student Rubric: *Telling*
- Student Rubric: *Knowing*
- multiplication and division facts

Pacing Suggestions

This unit will take 9 to 14 days to complete. It includes a variety of review and assessment activities that allow teachers to assess individual growth in mathematics as students continue learning while applying concepts and skills in new contexts.

- Lessons 2 and 7 are optional lessons. Lesson 2 *Three in a Row* is a challenging game that provides practice estimating with decimals. Lesson 7 *Review Problems* is a set of word problems that reviews skills and concepts from the first seven units. You can assign these problems for homework. Lesson 7 is also appropriate for use by a substitute teacher.
- Lesson 3 *Florence Kelley* is an Adventure Book story that provides a strong connection both to language arts and social studies. It sets the stage for the open-response assessment problem in Lesson 4 *Florence Kelley's Report.* Allow two days for Lesson 4 if you plan to let students revise their responses. Alternatively, you can use language arts time for students to read the story or write and revise their responses.
- Lesson 5 *Life Spans* and Lesson 6 *Comparing Lives of Animals and Soap Bubbles* provide connections to science. Students can collect data for the lab in Lesson 6 during science time.

Unit Planner

	Lesson Information	Supplies	Copies/Transparencies
Lesson 1 **Experiment Review** URG Pages 26–36 SG Page 270 DAB Pages 135–136 DPP A–B HP Part 1 *Estimated Class Sessions* **1**	**Activity** Students review experiments completed in the last seven units in preparation for the assessment lab in this unit. **Math Facts** Complete DPP Task B, which reviews multiplication and division facts. **Homework** Assign Part 1 of the Home Practice. **Assessment** Use the *Observational Assessment Record* to note students' abilities to organize, graph, and analyze data.	• student portfolios	• 1 transparency of *Distance vs. Time Graph* URG Page 34 • 1 transparency of *Experiment Review Chart* DAB Pages 135–136 or large sheet of paper for a class chart • 1 copy of *Observational Assessment Record* URG Pages 11–12 to be used throughout this unit
Lesson 2 **Three in a Row** URG Pages 37–41 DAB Pages 137–139 *Estimated Class Sessions* **1**	OPTIONAL LESSON—ENRICHMENT MATERIAL **Optional Game** Students play a game that involves estimating products of decimals. **Math Facts** Remind students to practice their facts at home using their *Triangle Flash Cards.* **Homework** Have students play the game at home.	• 8–10 game markers or tokens of one color per student • 1 calculator per student	• 1 transparency of *Three in a Row* game board DAB Page 139
Lesson 3 **Florence Kelley** URG Pages 42–52 SG Pages 271–272 AB Pages 47–60 DPP C–D HP Part 5 *Estimated Class Sessions* **1**	**Adventure Book** Students learn about the life of Florence Kelley, who helped reduce child labor in Chicago around 1900. They use data she collected to make predictions. **Math Facts** DPP item C practices multiplication and division facts using variables in number sentences. **Homework** 1. Assign DPP Task D, which provides practice with estimation and operations. 2. Assign Part 5 of the Home Practice, which reviews reading and interpreting data in a bar graph. **Assessment** Use Lesson 4 *Florence Kelley's Report* to assess students' abilities to analyze and display data as well as communicate mathematically.	• 1 calculator per student	• 1 transparency of *Increase in Work Done: Third Annual Report* URG Page 50

	Lesson Information	Supplies	Copies/Transparencies
Lesson 4 **Florence Kelley's Report** URG Pages 53–68 DPP E–F *Estimated Class Sessions* **1-2**	**Assessment Activity** Students use the Adventure Book in Lesson 3 to demonstrate their abilities to graph and analyze data. They describe their conclusions in writing. **Assessment** 1. Compare this lesson to work on *Stack Up* in Unit 2. 2. Assess students' abilities to work cooperatively. 3. Use DPP item F to assess students' abilities to communicate mathematically.	• 1 calculator per student	• 1 copy of *Florence Kelley's Report* URG Page 66 per student • 1–2 copies of *Centimeter Graph Paper* URG Page 67 per student • 1 copy of *TIMS Multidimensional Rubric* TIG, Assessment section • 1 transparency or poster of Student Rubric: *Knowing* TIG, Assessment section • 1 transparency or poster of Student Rubric: *Telling* TIG, Assessment section
Lesson 5 **Life Spans** URG Pages 69–82 SG Pages 273–275 DAB Page 141 DPP G–H HP Part 2 *Estimated Class Sessions* **1-2**	**Activity** Students compare human life span data from 1858 to life span data from 1997. They organize and graph the data, scaling the vertical axis using percents. **Homework** 1. For homework, students can complete the data table and graph for 1997 data. They find the median age at death for this data. *(Questions 9–12)* 2. Assign Part 2 of the Home Practice.	• 1 calculator per student	• 2 copies of *Centimeter Graph Paper* URG Page 67 per student • 1 transparency of *Graphing Life Spans* URG Page 80, optional • 1 transparency of *Life Spans Data Tables* DAB Page 141, optional
Lesson 6 **Comparing Lives of Animals and Soap Bubbles** URG Pages 83–96 SG Pages 276–279 DAB Page 143 DPP I–N HP Parts 3–4 *Estimated Class Sessions* **3**	**Assessment Lab** Students collect data about the life spans of soap bubbles. They compare this data to the life spans of animals. Students scale the vertical axis using percents. **Math Facts** DPP items I, K, and M review math facts. **Homework** 1. Assign some or all of the review problems in Lesson 7 for homework. 2. Assign Parts 3 and 4 of the Home Practice. **Assessment** 1. Grade the lab by assigning points to drawing the picture, collecting and recording the data, graphing, and solving problems. 2. Score student responses to *Questions 10–12* using the Telling dimension of the *TIMS Multidimensional Rubric*.	• 1 small jar of bubble solution per student group • 1 bubble wand per student group • 1 stopwatch or watch that measures seconds per student group • 1 calculator per student • paper towels	• 1 copy of *Centimeter Graph Paper* URG Page 67 per student • 1 transparency of *Soap Bubbles Data Table* DAB Page 143, optional • 1 transparency of *Centimeter Graph Paper* URG Page 67, optional • 1 copy of *TIMS Multidimensional Rubric* TIG, Assessment section

(Continued)

Overview

	Lesson Information	Supplies	Copies/ Transparencies
Lesson 7 **Review Problems** URG Pages 97–103 SG Pages 280–281 HP Part 6 *Estimated Class Sessions* **1**	OPTIONAL LESSON—REVIEW MATERIAL **Optional Activity** Students solve word problems using ratios, decimals, and percents. **Homework** 1. Assign some or all of the problems for review, homework, or use for assessment. 2. Assign Part 6 of the Home Practice.	• 1 centiwheel per student • 1 ruler per student • 1 calculator per student	• 1 copy of *Centimeter Graph Paper* URG Page 67 per student
Lesson 8 **Midyear Test** URG Pages 104–116 DPP O–P *Estimated Class Sessions* **1-2**	**Assessment Activity** Students take a short item test assessing skills and concepts learned in Units 1–8. **Math Facts** Remind students to study for the *Multiplication and Division Fact Inventory Test.*	• 1 ruler per student • 1 calculator per student • 1 protractor per student	• 1 copy of *Centimeter Dot Paper* URG Page 108 per student, optional • 1 copy of *Midyear Test* URG Pages 109–113 per student
Lesson 9 **Portfolio Review** URG Pages 117–123 SG Pages 282–283 DPP Q–R *Estimated Class Sessions* **1**	**Assessment Activity** Students update and review their portfolios. **Math Facts** DPP item Q assesses the multiplication and division facts using an inventory test. **Homework** You can assign DPP item R as homework. **Assessment** Transfer appropriate documentation from the Unit 8 *Observational Assessment Record* to students' *Individual Assessment Record Sheets.*	• collection folders • portfolio folders	• 1 copy of *Multiplication and Division Fact Inventory Test* URG Page 25 per student • 1 copy of *Individual Assessment Record Sheet* TIG Assessment section per student, previously copied for use throughout the year

Unit 9: Connections to Division · 10–12 Sessions

Unit Summary

This unit focuses on division and its applications. Students explore the relationship between fractions and division to find decimal equivalents for fractions. They extend paper-and-pencil division to two-digit divisors and interpret remainders.

An optional activity introduces a different multiplication method: lattice multiplication. The lattice method is connected to the compact and all-partials algorithms. Students use calculators to divide larger numbers and devise strategies to find whole number remainders with calculators.

To conclude the unit, students solve an open-response problem in which they estimate the number of blades of grass in a lawn. They use the Student Rubrics to help them communicate their solution strategies.

Major Concept Focus

- fractions and division
- decimal equivalents for fractions
- paper-and-pencil division
- interpreting remainders
- checking division with multiplication
- estimating quotients
- using multiplication and division to solve problems
- calculator strategies for dividing
- repeating decimals
- communicating solution strategies
- measuring area
- Student Rubric: *Knowing*
- Student Rubric: *Solving*
- Student Rubric: *Telling*

Pacing Suggestions

- Use the recommended number of sessions for each lesson as a guide. Students extend their division skills in this unit, but it is not necessary to wait until all students master each concept and skill. Distributed practice of small sets of division problems and sets of word problems are included in each succeeding unit in the Daily Practice and Problems and Home Practice.
- Lesson 3 *Multiplication Methods* is an optional lesson that challenges students to learn different methods for multiplication. You can use this lesson as an extension.

Unit Planner

KEY: SG = Student Guide, DAB = Discovery Assignment Book, AB = Adventure Book, URG = Unit Resource Guide, DPP = Daily Practice and Problems, HP = Home Practice (found in Discovery Assignment Book), and TIG = Teacher Implementation Guide.

	Lesson Information	Supplies	Copies/Transparencies
Lesson 1 **Fractions and Division** URG Pages 27–46 SG Pages 286–293 DAB Pages 151–152 DPP A–D HP Part 1 *Estimated Class Sessions* **2**	**Activity** Students explore the relationship between division sentences and fractions. Students use calculators to change fractions into their decimal equivalents or approximations and compare them. Repeating decimals are introduced. **Homework** 1. Assign the *Dividing Pizzas* Homework Pages in the *Discovery Assignment Book* after Part 1 of the lesson. 2. Assign the Homework section in the *Student Guide*. 3. Assign Part 1 of the Home Practice. **Assessment** 1. Use some of the questions on the homework pages as assessments. ***Question 3*** on the *Dividing Pizzas* Homework Pages and ***Questions 2–4*** in the *Student Guide* Homework section are good choices. 2. Use the *Observational Assessment Record* to note students' abilities to find decimal equivalents for fractions.	• 1 small centiwheel per student • 1 calculator per student	• 1 wheel from *Small Centiwheels* URG Page 38 per student, optional • 1 copy of *Centimeter Dot Paper* URG Page 39 per student, optional • 1 copy of *Observational Assessment Record* URG Pages 11–12 to be used throughout this unit
Lesson 2 **Division** URG Pages 47–63 SG Pages 294–298 DAB Pages 153–155 DPP E–J HP Part 2 *Estimated Class Sessions* **3**	**Activity** Students review a method for dividing. Estimation strategies are emphasized. Students use multiplication to check their work. **Math Facts** DPP item G provides practice with the division facts for the 5s and 10s. **Homework** 1. Assign the *More Estimation and Division* Activity Page in the *Discovery Assignment Book*. 2. Assign the Homework section in the *Student Guide*. 3. Assign Part 2 of the Home Practice. 4. Assign DPP Task J. **Assessment** 1. Use the Homework section of the *Student Guide* as an assessment. 2. Use the *Observational Assessment Record* to note students' abilities to estimate quotients and to divide using a paper-and-pencil method.	• base-ten pieces, optional	• 1 transparency of *Introducing Division* URG Page 58, optional

	Lesson Information	Supplies	Copies/ Transparencies

Lesson 3

Multiplication Methods

URG Pages 64–73
SG Pages 299–303
DAB Pages 157–158

Estimated Class Sessions
2

OPTIONAL LESSON—EXTENSION

Optional Activity
Students use paper-and-pencil methods for multiplying larger numbers. A new method, lattice multiplication, is introduced. Students compare multiplication methods.

Homework
1. Assign the *Lattice Multiplication Practice* Activity Pages.
2. Assign the Homework section in the *Student Guide*.

Lesson 4

Understanding Remainders

URG Pages 74–87
SG Pages 304–309

DPP K–N
HP Parts 3–4

Estimated Class Sessions
2

Activity
Students explore remainders in division problems. Students complete division problems in which the remainder is expressed as a fraction.

Math Facts
DPP items K and M review the multiplication and division facts for the 5s and 10s.

Homework
1. Assign *Questions 4–9* on the *Understanding Remainders* Activity Pages.
2. Assign homework *Questions 1–10* in the *Student Guide*.
3. Assign Parts 3 and 4 of the Home Practice.

Assessment
1. Students complete the *Tie Dye T-Shirts* Assessment Page.
2. Use DPP Task N as a quiz.
3. Use the *Observational Assessment Record* to note students' abilities to interpret remainders.

• 1 copy of *Tie Dye T-Shirts* URG Page 82 per student

Lesson 5

Calculator Strategies: Division

URG Pages 88–97
SG Pages 310–313

DPP O–P
HP Part 5

Estimated Class Sessions
1

Activity
Students use calculators to divide larger numbers. They divide money using a calculator so the quotient reflects both dollars and cents.

Homework
1. Assign homework *Questions 1–10* in the *Student Guide*.
2. Assign Part 5 of the Home Practice.

Assessment
1. Use homework *Questions 1* and *9* in the *Student Guide* as an assessment.
2. Use the *Observational Assessment Record* to note students' abilities to use a calculator to solve division problems.

• 1 calculator per student

Overview

(Continued)

	Lesson Information	Supplies	Copies/Transparencies

Lesson 6

Grass Act

URG Pages 98–114
SG Page 314
DPP Q–T

Estimated Class Sessions

2

Assessment Activity
Students solve an open-response problem and write their solution strategies. They estimate the number of blades of grass in a given area.

Math Facts
DPP items Q and S practice the facts for the 5s and 10s.

Homework
Assign the Journal Prompt for homework.

Assessment
1. Use DPP Challenge T as an assessment of concepts learned in this unit.
2. Transfer appropriate documentation from the Unit 9 *Observational Assessment Record* to students' *Individual Assessment Record Sheets*.

- 1 pair of scissors per student group
- 1 3" by 5" index card per student
- 1 ruler per student group
- 1 calculator per student
- a large grassy area or piece of sod, nylon netting, window screen, or large beach towel

- 1 copy of *Grass Act Questions* URG Page 113 per student
- 1 copy of *TIMS Multidimensional Rubric* TIG, Assessment section
- 1 transparency or poster of Student Rubrics: *Solving, Knowing,* and *Telling* TIG, Assessment section, optional
- 1 copy of *Individual Assessment Record Sheet* TIG Assessment section per student, previously copied for use throughout the year

Unit 10: Maps and Coordinates .... 8–14 Sessions

Unit Summary

This unit starts with a discussion of negative numbers within several real-world contexts, including measuring temperature and tracking money in a bank account. Then, positive and negative numbers are applied to the task of making coordinate maps. The activity *Mr. Origin* extends students' use of coordinates to four quadrants. An Adventure Book *Wherefore Art Thou, Romeo?* emphasizes the importance of the positive and negative signs in coordinate pairs. In optional activities, students develop their spatial visualization skills and their understanding of geometric concepts by investigating the results of flips and slides on shapes in the coordinate plane.

Major Concept Focus

- negative numbers
- four quadrants
- plotting points
- tessellations
- Cartesian coordinates
- coordinate pairs
- reading maps
- Student Rubric: *Knowing*
- slides and flips
- using the scale on a map
- *Adventure Book:* coordinates

Pacing Suggestions

- Students with previous experience with *Math Trailblazers* worked with coordinates in the first quadrant in third grade. They explored negative numbers in fourth grade. This unit extends their understanding of the coordinate system to four quadrants using negative numbers. If students have not previously worked with these concepts, they will move more slowly through the lessons. Use the maximum number of sessions as a guide for these students. If students have worked with these concepts in previous grades, use the minimum number.
- You can include Lesson 8 *Reading a Map* in a map-reading lesson during social studies time.

Lessons 6, 7, and 9 are optional lessons that provide enrichment and fuller understanding of the Cartesian coordinate system. Use Lessons 6 and 7 if state or local standards call for students to study transformations (flips and slides).

- Lesson 6 *These Boots Are Made for Sliding* shows students how to slide (translate) shapes along one coordinate and then both coordinates.
- Lesson 7 *These Boots Are Made for Flipping* shows students how to flip (reflect) shapes about the horizontal and vertical axes. This lesson includes Assessment Pages *Moving Shapes,* a written assessment for the activities in both Lessons 6 and 7. If you omit either lesson, do not use the assessment.
- Lesson 9 *Escher Drawings* allows students to explore the work of M.C. Escher and use tessellations to create art.

Unit Planner

KEY: SG = Student Guide, DAB = Discovery Assignment Book, AB = Adventure Book, URG = Unit Resource Guide, DPP = Daily Practice and Problems, HP = Home Practice (found in Discovery Assignment Book), and TIG = Teacher Implementation Guide.

	Lesson Information	Supplies	Copies/Transparencies
Lesson 1 **Negative Numbers** URG Pages 22–35 SG Pages 316–318 DPP A–B HP Parts 1–2 *Estimated Class Sessions* **1**	**Activity** Children expand the number line to include negative numbers. They explore negative numbers in real-world contexts. **Math Facts** DPP item A reviews the multiplication and division facts for the 2s and square numbers. **Homework** 1. Assign the Homework section in the *Student Guide.* 2. Assign Parts 1 and 2 of the Home Practice. **Assessment** Use *Questions 8–12* to assess students' progress in solving problems involving negative numbers. Record your observations on the *Observational Assessment Record* or students' *Individual Assessment Record Sheets.*	• indoor/outdoor thermometer, optional	• 2 copies of *Two-column Data Table* URG Page 33 per student, optional • 1 transparency of *Frank's Bank Statement* URG Page 31 • 1 transparency of *Reading a Thermometer* URG Page 32 • 1 copy of *Observational Assessment Record* URG Pages 11–12 to be used throughout this unit • 1 copy of *Individual Assessment Record Sheet* TIG Assessment section per student, previously copied for use throughout the year
Lesson 2 **Introducing Cartesian Coordinates** URG Pages 36–51 SG Pages 319–326 DPP C–F HP Part 3 *Estimated Class Sessions* **2-3**	**Activity** This activity introduces students to the use of Cartesian coordinates for locating objects in a plane. The game *Great Barrier Reef* is introduced. **Math Facts** DPP item E reviews division facts. **Homework** 1. Assign *Questions 11–18* in the Explore section. 2. Assign the game as homework. 3. Assign the Homework section in the *Student Guide.* **Assessment** 1. Use the Homework section in the *Student Guide* as an assessment. 2. Use Part 3 of the Home Practice as an assessment.		• 4 copies plus extras of *Four-Quadrant Grid Paper* URG Page 47 per student or 4 copies plus extras of *Centimeter Grid Paper* URG Page 48 per student with axes drawn • 1 transparency of *One Quadrant Plus* URG Page 45 • 1 transparency of *Quadrant Overlay* URG Page 46 • 1 transparency of *Four-Quadrant Grid Paper* URG Page 47
Lesson 3 **Wherefore Art Thou, Romeo?** URG Pages 52–59 AB Pages 61–76 DPP G–H *Estimated Class Sessions* **1**	**Adventure Book** This book follows the misfortunes of a student who does not understand coordinates and causes chaos in a school play as a result.	• flashlight, optional	

	Lesson Information	Supplies	Copies/Transparencies
Lesson 4 **Mr. Origin** URG Pages 60–75 SG Pages 327–329 DAB Page 165 DPP I–L HP Part 5 *Estimated Class Sessions* **2-3**	**Activity** Students map the location of objects in a room or playground on a four-quadrant coordinate map. They use the map to make predictions about the distance between the objects. **Math Facts** DPP items I and K review the multiplication and division facts for the 2s and the square numbers. **Homework** 1. Have students draw a coordinate map of a room in their home. 2. Students complete the *Label the Axes* Homework Page in the *Discovery Assignment Book*. 3. Assign Part 5 of the Home Practice. **Assessment** Use the *Coordinates: Getting to the Point* Assessment Page to assess students' abilities to graph points.	• 1 meterstick or trundle wheel per student group • 1 Mr. Origin per student group, optional and 1 for the teacher • 7 index cards to label objects • 1 centimeter ruler per student group	• 1 copy of *Coordinates: Getting to the Point* URG Page 71 per student • 2 copies of *Centimeter Grid Paper* URG Page 48 per student • 1 copy of *Three-column Data Table* URG Page 72 per student, optional
Lesson 5 **Plotting Shapes** URG Pages 76–85 SG Pages 330–331 DPP M–N HP Part 4 *Estimated Class Sessions* **1**	**Activity** Children plot ordered pairs in four quadrants, then connect the dots to make shapes. **Homework** 1. Students design their own shape in **Question 5,** which you can assign for homework. 2. Assign Part 4 of the Home Practice. **Assessment** Assess students' abilities to plot points as they complete **Questions 1–3.** Record your observations on the *Observational Assessment Record*.		• several copies of *Four-Quadrant Grid Paper* URG Page 47 per student • several copies of *Half-Centimeter Graph Paper* URG Page 83 per student • 1 transparency of *Four-Quadrant Grid Paper* URG Page 47 • 1 transparency of *Half-Centimeter Graph Paper* URG Page 83, optional
Lesson 6 **These Boots Are Made for Sliding** URG Pages 86–99 SG Pages 332–336 DAB Pages 167–171 *Estimated Class Sessions* **1**	OPTIONAL LESSON— ENRICHMENT MATERIAL **Optional Activity** Children explore slides on a coordinate grid. **Homework** Assign the homework problems in the *Student Guide*.		• several copies of *Four-Quadrant Grid Paper* URG Page 47 per student or several copies of *Centimeter Grid Paper* URG Page 48 per student with axes drawn • 1 copy of *Four-column Data Table* URG Page 94 per student • 1 transparency of *Four-Quadrant Grid Paper* URG Page 47 • 1 transparency of *Slides* DAB Pages 167–171, optional

Overview

(Continued)

	Lesson Information	Supplies	Copies/Transparencies
Lesson 7 **These Boots Are Made for Flipping** URG Pages 100–114 SG Pages 337–342 DAB Pages 173–174 *Estimated Class Sessions* **1-2**	OPTIONAL LESSON— ENRICHMENT MATERIAL **Optional Activity** Children explore flipping shapes across the horizontal and vertical axes. **Homework** Assign the Homework section in the *Student Guide.* **Assessment** Use the *Moving Shapes* Assessment Pages as a quiz.	• 1 pair of scissors per student pair	• 1 copy *of Moving Shapes* URG Pages 108–109 per student • several copies of *Four-Quadrant Grid Paper* URG Page 47 per student • 1 copy of *Centimeter Graph Paper* URG Page 110 per student • 1 transparency of *Flips* DAB Pages 173–174, optional • 1 transparency of *Four-Quadrant Grid Paper* URG Page 47
Lesson 8 **Reading a Map** URG Pages 115–126 SG Pages 343–344 DPP O–P HP Part 6 *Estimated Class Sessions* **1**	**Activity** Students practice map-reading skills from the perspective of one and then four quadrants. An assessment using the *Knowing* Student Rubric is included. **Math Facts** DPP item O reviews math facts. **Homework** 1. Assign the Homework section on the *Reading a Map* Activity Pages in the *Student Guide.* 2. Assign Part 6 of the Home Practice. **Assessment** Use the *Carol's Chicago Map* Assessment Pages as an assessment.		• 1 copy of *Carol's Chicago Map* URG Pages 121–122 per student • 1 transparency of *Chicago Grid* URG Page 123 • 1 transparency of *Chicago Map* URG Page 124 • 1 copy of *TIMS Multidimensional Rubric* TIG, Assessment section
Lesson 9 **Escher Drawings** URG Pages 127–133 SG Page 345 *Estimated Class Sessions* **1**	OPTIONAL LESSON— ENRICHMENT MATERIAL **Optional Activity** Children explore the work of M.C. Escher and make their own Escher-like artwork.	• several index cards per student • 1 piece of newsprint or other large paper preferably greater than 8″ × 10″ plus extras • 1 pair of scissors per student • tape	• 1 transparency of *Creating Escher-like Drawings* URG Page 132, optional

Unit 11: Number Patterns, Primes, and Fractions .... 11–14 Sessions

Unit Summary

Students investigate some of the underlying structures of arithmetic, often referred to as number theory. They play a game in which they must find all the factors of the numbers from one to forty. They identify prime and composite numbers using a 100 chart and a process developed by Eratosthenes, a famous Greek mathematician. They then examine and describe patterns in the chart. Students complete an assessment activity, *A Further Look at Patterns and Primes,* using the same process on a different chart. In a different activity, students investigate patterns in square numbers. In the latter part of the unit, students use common factors and common multiples to rename, compare, and reduce fractions.

Major Concept Focus

- factors
- multiples
- Sieve of Eratosthenes
- exponents
- prime factorization
- common denominators
- comparing fractions
- adding and subtracting fractions
- number patterns
- prime numbers
- composite numbers
- factor trees
- square numbers
- reducing fractions to lowest terms
- point graphs
- communicating mathematically
- Student Rubric: *Telling*

Pacing Suggestions

This unit is designed to be completed in 11 to 14 days. Students discover patterns and relationships among numbers as they investigate prime and composite numbers.

- Part 2 of Lesson 3 *Patterns with Square Numbers* is optional. Use these Challenge Questions as an extension.
- Lesson 8 *From Factors to Fractions* is an optional lesson in which students solve multistep problems. You can assign these problems for homework. They are also appropriate for use by a substitute teacher since preparation is minimal.

Unit Planner

KEY: SG = Student Guide, DAB = Discovery Assignment Book, AB = Adventure Book, URG = Unit Resource Guide, DPP = Daily Practice and Problems, HP = Home Practice (found in Discovery Assignment Book), and TIG = Teacher Implementation Guide.

	Lesson Information	Supplies	Copies/Transparencies
Lesson 1 **Factor 40** URG Pages 23–35 SG Pages 348–352 DAB Page 181 DPP A–D HP Part 1 *Estimated Class Sessions* **2**	**Game** Students play *Factor 40* to review factors. They review prime numbers and composite numbers. **Homework** 1. Assign the Homework section in the *Student Guide.* 2. Assign Part 1 of the Home Practice. **Assessment** 1. Use homework *Questions 6–8* as an assessment. 2. Use the *Observational Assessment Record* to note students' abilities to find all the factors of a number.	• 1 calculator per student	• 4 copies of *Three-column Data Table* URG Page 32 per student, optional • 1 transparency of *Factor 40 Game Board* DAB Page 181 • 1 copy of *Observational Assessment Record* URG Pages 11–12 to be used throughout this unit
Lesson 2 **Sifting for Primes** URG Pages 36–43 SG Pages 353–355 DAB Page 183 DPP E–F HP Part 2 *Estimated Class Sessions* **1**	**Activity** Students use the Sieve of Eratosthenes to find the prime numbers from 1 to 100. Students look for patterns and sift for prime numbers from 101–200. **Math Facts** DPP Bit E reviews the division facts for the 3s and 9s. **Homework** 1. Students sift for the prime numbers from 101 to 200 on the *200 Chart* Activity Page in the *Discovery Assignment Book.* 2. Assign Part 2 of the Home Practice. **Assessment** Use the *Observational Assessment Record* to note students' abilities to identify prime numbers.		• 1–4 transparencies of *200 Chart* DAB Page 183, optional
Lesson 3 **Patterns with Square Numbers** URG Pages 44–56 SG Pages 356–359 DPP G–J *Estimated Class Sessions* **2**	**Activity** Students develop a visual picture of square numbers. Students discover a relationship between square numbers and odd numbers. **Math Facts** DPP item I reviews the division facts for the 3s and 9s.	• 25 square-inch tiles per student	• 1 copy of *Three-column Data Table* URG Page 32 per student • 1 copy of *Centimeter Grid Paper* URG Page 53 per student • 1 copy of *Centimeter Graph Paper* URG Page 54 per student • 1 transparency of *Three-column Data Table* URG Page 32, optional • 1 transparency of *Centimeter Grid Paper* URG Page 53 • 1 transparency of *Centimeter Graph Paper* URG Page 54, optional

	Lesson Information	Supplies	Copies/ Transparencies
Lesson 4 **Finding Prime Factors** URG Pages 57–67 SG Pages 360–362 DAB Page 185 DPP K–L HP Part 3 *Estimated Class Sessions* **1-2**	**Activity** Students build factor trees of numbers using their calculators. Students write numbers as products of primes using exponents. **Homework** Assign *Questions 1–4* in the Homework section in the *Student Guide.* **Assessment** Use Part 3 of the Home Practice to assess students' fluency with factors, exponents, and prime numbers.	• 1 calculator per student	• 2–3 blank transparencies, optional
Lesson 5 **Comparing Fractions** URG Pages 68–77 SG Pages 363–367 DPP M–P HP Part 5 *Estimated Class Sessions* **2**	**Activity** Students compare fractions using common denominators. **Math Facts** DPP items M and P include a review of the division facts for the 3s and 9s. **Homework** 1. Assign the questions in the Homework section. 2. Assign Part 5 of the Home Practice. **Assessment** 1. Use DPP Task P as a quiz. 2. Use the *Observational Assessment Record* to note students' abilities to find common denominators and to compare fractions.		
Lesson 6 **Reducing Fractions** URG Pages 78–88 SG Pages 82 & 368–372 DPP Q–R HP Parts 4 & 6 *Estimated Class Sessions* **1-2**	**Activity** Students use common factors to reduce fractions to lowest terms. Students add and subtract fractions after finding common denominators, and they solve division problems whose quotients are mixed numbers. They then reduce answers to lowest terms. **Math Facts** DPP item Q reviews the division facts for the 3s and 9s. **Homework** 1. Assign the problems in the Homework section of the *Reducing Fractions* Activity Pages. 2. Assign Parts 4 and 6 of the Home Practice. **Assessment** Students complete the *Skills Check-Up* Assessment Page.		• 1 copy of *Skills Check-Up* URG Page 84 per student

(Continued)

Overview

	Lesson Information	Supplies	Copies/ Transparencies
Lesson 7 **A Further Look at Patterns and Primes** URG Pages 89–100 DPP S–V *Estimated Class Sessions* **2**	**Assessment Activity** Students use different colors to sift for prime numbers using a six-column 100 chart. Students write about the patterns they see in the completed chart. Included are patterns involving multiples, prime numbers, and factors. **Math Facts** DPP items S and U review math facts. **Homework** Assign some or all of the word problems in Lesson 8 as homework. **Assessment** 1. Have students put their work for this activity in their collection folders for possible inclusion in their portfolios. 2. Use the *Observational Assessment Record* to note students' abilities to identify and describe number patterns. Transfer your observations to students' *Individual Assessment Record Sheets.*	• 4 different-colored crayons per student	• 1 copy of *A Further Look at Patterns and Primes* URG Page 98 per student • 1 copy of *6-column 100 Chart* URG Page 99 per student • 1 copy of *TIMS Multidimensional Rubric* TIG, Assessment section • 1 copy of *Individual Assessment Record Sheet* TIG, Assessment section per student, previously copied for use throughout the year • 1 transparency or poster of Student Rubric: *Telling* TIG, Assessment section, optional
Lesson 8 **From Factors to Fractions** URG Pages 101–104 SG Page 373 *Estimated Class Sessions* **1**	OPTIONAL LESSON **Optional Activity** Students solve word problems using fractions and decimals. **Homework** Assign some or all of the problems for homework.	• 1 calculator per student	

Unit 12: Using Fractions

Unit Summary
Students continue their study of fractions by using pattern blocks and other models to represent fractions in different ways. This helps students generalize concepts and procedures that they can then apply in new situations. For example, they use pattern blocks to model addition of mixed numbers and multiplication of fractions to develop paper-and-pencil methods for these operations. They read an Adventure Book *Peanut Soup,* which uses the context of the work of George Washington Carver to explore the use of fractions in a real-life setting. The unit concludes with a *Midterm Test,* which assesses concepts and skills studied in this and previous units.

Major Concept Focus
- using patterns to build number sense
- multiplying fractions and whole numbers
- multiplying fractions
- estimating the product of fractions
- using fractions in everyday situations
- communicating mathematically
- renaming mixed numbers
- adding mixed numbers
- Student Rubric: *Solving*
- *Adventure Book:* fractions
- midterm test

Pacing Suggestions
This unit is designed to be completed in 7 to 9 days.

- Lesson 6 *Peanut Soup* is an *Adventure Book* story taken from a true incident in the life of George Washington Carver. Students can read this story during language arts or social studies time.
- Lesson 7 *Party Problems* is an optional lesson in which students solve multistep word problems. Assigning these problems for homework can prepare students for the midterm test in Lesson 8. They are also appropriate for a substitute teacher since preparation is minimal.

Preparing for Upcoming Lessons
Begin collecting lids and cans of different sizes for the lab *Circumference vs. Diameter* in Unit 14.

Overview

Unit Planner

KEY: SG = Student Guide, DAB = Discovery Assignment Book, AB = Adventure Book, URG = Unit Resource Guide, DPP = Daily Practice and Problems, HP = Home Practice (found in Discovery Assignment Book), and TIG = Teacher Implementation Guide.

	Lesson Information	Supplies	Copies/Transparencies
Lesson 1 **Hexagon Duets** URG Pages 20–29 SG Pages 376–379 DAB Page 193 DPP A–B *Estimated Class Sessions* **1-2**	**Activity** Addition of mixed numbers is introduced through the use of a game. Students find equivalent representations of mixed numbers. **Math Facts** DPP Bit A reviews the last six division facts. **Homework** Assign the Homework section in the *Student Guide.* **Assessment** 1. Use the Journal Prompt as an assessment. 2. Use *Question 1* of the Homework section to assess students' abilities to rename mixed numbers. 3. Use the *Observational Assessment Record* to note students' abilities to add mixed numbers.	• 1 set of pattern blocks (2–3 yellow hexagons, 6 red trapezoids, 10 blue rhombuses, 10 green triangles, 6 brown trapezoids, 12 purple triangles) per student pair • 1 spinner or paper clip and pencil per student group • overhead pattern blocks, optional	• 1 transparency of *Hexagon Duets Spinner* DAB Page 193, optional • 1 copy of *Observational Assessment Record* URG Pages 11–12 to be used throughout this unit
Lesson 2 **Adding Mixed Numbers** URG Pages 30–37 SG Pages 380–382 DPP C–D HP Parts 1–2 *Estimated Class Sessions* **1**	**Activity** Students model addition of mixed numbers using pattern blocks; then they develop paper-and-pencil methods. **Homework** 1. Assign the homework problems in the *Student Guide.* 2. Assign Parts 1–2 of the Home Practice. **Assessment** Use *Questions 3–4* of the Homework section as an assessment.	• 1 set of pattern blocks (2–3 yellow hexagons, 6 red trapezoids, 10 blue rhombuses, 10 green triangles, 6 brown trapezoids, 12 purple triangles) per student pair • overhead pattern blocks, optional	
Lesson 3 **Fractions of Groups** URG Pages 38–48 SG Pages 383–386 DPP E–F *Estimated Class Sessions* **1**	**Activity** Using diagrams, students develop procedures for multiplying a fraction times a whole number. **Math Facts** DPP Bit E reviews the last six division facts. **Homework** Assign the Homework section in the *Student Guide.* **Assessment** Use *Question 7* in the Homework section as an assessment.		

	Lesson Information	Supplies	Copies/ Transparencies
Lesson 4 **Multiplication of Fractions** URG Pages 49–60 SG Pages 387–389 DAB Pages 195–197 DPP G–H *Estimated Class Sessions* **1**	**Activity** Using pattern blocks, students multiply fractions times whole numbers and fractions times fractions. **Math Facts** DPP Bit G reviews the last six facts. **Homework** Assign the Homework section in the *Student Guide.* **Assessment** 1. Use DPP Task H as a quiz to assess students' abilities to add mixed numbers. 2. Check students' homework for their abilities to represent fractions using pattern blocks and number sentences.	• 1 set of pattern blocks (2–3 yellow hexagons, 6 red trapezoids, 10 blue rhombuses, 10 green triangles, 6 brown trapezoids, 12 purple triangles) per student pair • overhead pattern blocks, optional	• 1 transparency of *Pattern Block Record Sheet* DAB Pages 195–197, optional
Lesson 5 **Using Patterns to Multiply Fractions** URG Pages 61–70 SG Pages 390–391 DPP I–J HP Parts 3–4 *Estimated Class Sessions* **1**	**Activity** Students fold paper to model multiplication of fractions. The patterns they see help them develop procedures for multiplying fractions with paper and pencil. **Math Facts** DPP Bit I reviews math facts in number sentences with variables. **Homework** 1. Assign the Homework section in the *Student Guide.* 2. Assign Parts 3 and 4 of the Home Practice. 3. Use some or all of the *Party Problems* in Lesson 7 for homework. **Assessment** 1. Use *Questions 10–14* in the Homework section as an assessment. 2. Use the *Observational Assessment Record* to note students' abilities to multiply fractions. 3. Transfer your observations to students' *Individual Assessment Record Sheets.*	• several $8\frac{1}{2}$-by-11 inch sheets of scrap paper per student • crayons or colored pencils	• 1 copy of *Individual Assessment Record Sheet* TIG Assessment section per student, previously copied for use throughout the year
Lesson 6 **Peanut Soup** URG Pages 71–80 AB Pages 77–92 DPP K–L HP Parts 5–6 *Estimated Class Sessions* **1**	**Adventure Book** The story tells how George Washington Carver was able to convince businessmen of the economic value of peanuts by inviting them to a meal made from peanut products. As they prepare the meal, Carver's students use fractions to convert recipes to the needed size. **Math Facts** DPP Bit K reviews math facts in division sentences with quotients as mixed numbers. **Homework** Assign Parts 5 and 6 of the Home Practice.		

(Continued)

Overview

	Lesson Information	Supplies	Copies/ Transparencies
Lesson 7 **Party Problems** URG Pages 81–85 SG Pages 392–393 *Estimated Class Sessions* **1**	OPTIONAL LESSON **Optional Activity** Students solve word problems in the context of a birthday party. **Homework** Assign some or all of the problems for homework.	• 1 calculator per student	
Lesson 8 **Midterm Test** URG Pages 86–100 DPP M–N HP Part 7 *Estimated Class Sessions* **1**	**Assessment Activity** Students complete a test involving concepts covered in this and previous units. **Math Facts** DPP Bit M reviews the last six facts. **Homework** 1. Assign DPP Task N for homework. 2. Assign Part 7 of the Home Practice. **Assessment** Add this test to students' portfolios to compare to similar assessments.	• pattern blocks • 1 ruler per student • 1 calculator per student	• 1 copy of *Midterm Test* URG Pages 91–96 per student

Unit 13: Ratio and Proportion . . . . 10–15 Sessions

Unit Summary

This unit's goal is to use the concepts of ratio and proportion to develop formal concepts and procedures for solving problems that involve proportional reasoning. Students review the use of words, tables, graphs, and symbols to express ratios. They learn that a proportion is a statement that two ratios are equivalent and develop strategies for solving proportional reasoning problems. Students apply proportional reasoning to the study of density in the activity *Sink and Float* and the lab *Mass vs. Volume.*

Major Concept Focus

- ratios
- variables in proportion
- volume
- TIMS Laboratory Method
- using ratios and proportions to solve problems
- proportions
- mass
- density
- point graphs
- best-fit lines

Pacing Suggestions

This unit is designed to be completed in 10 to 15 days.

- Lesson 2 *Variables in Proportion* is an optional lesson that extends students' knowledge of algebraic concepts including using variables and proportional reasoning.
- Lesson 3 *Sink and Float* and Lesson 4 *Mass vs. Volume: Proportions and Density* make strong connections between mathematics and science. Students can collect the data for these investigations during science time.
- Lesson 5 *Problems of Scale* includes a series of word problems and a quiz. You can assign the problems for homework to prepare students for the quiz. They are also appropriate for use by a substitute teacher since preparation is minimal.

Preparing for Upcoming Lessons

In Unit 14 Lessons 1 and 2, students measure the circumference and diameter of cans and lids. Ask students to bring in cans and lids of various sizes. A good selection for students to measure includes empty spools of thread, film canisters, soup cans, masking tape rolls, coffee cans, and large lids.

Unit Planner

KEY: SG = Student Guide, DAB = Discovery Assignment Book, AB = Adventure Book, URG = Unit Resource Guide, DPP = Daily Practice and Problems, HP = Home Practice (found in Discovery Assignment Book), and TIG = Teacher Implementation Guide.

	Lesson Information	Supplies	Copies/ Transparencies
Lesson 1 **Ratios, Recipes, and Proportions** URG Pages 24–38 SG Pages 396–401 DPP A–D HP Parts 1–2 & 5 *Estimated Class Sessions* **2-3**	**Activity** Students explore ratios and proportions in recipes. **Math Facts** DPP Bit A reviews division facts for the square numbers. **Homework** 1. Assign the Homework section in the *Student Guide.* 2. Assign Parts 1–2 of the Home Practice. **Assessment** 1. Use *Questions 21–23* of the Peanut Cake section in the *Student Guide* to assess students' abilities to write ratios and use proportions. 2. Assign Part 5 of the Home Practice to assess students' fluency in solving problems involving ratio and proportion. 3. Use the *Observational Assessment Record* to note students' abilities to express ratios using words, tables, graphs, fractions, and colon notations.	• 1 calculator per student	• 1 copy of *Centimeter Graph Paper* URG Page 34 per student • 1 copy of *Observational Assessment Record* URG Pages 11–12 to be used throughout this unit • 1 transparency of *Centimeter Graph Paper* URG Page 34
Lesson 2 **Variables in Proportion** URG Pages 39–53 SG Pages 402–410 *Estimated Class Sessions* **2-3**	OPTIONAL LESSON **Optional Activity** Students review selected topics in the fifth-grade curriculum and explore them from the perspective of ratio and proportion. They extend their knowledge of algebraic concepts as they investigate properties of variables in proportion and explore the use of line graphs in solving proportions. **Homework** 1. Assign the Homework section in the *Student Guide.* 2. Assign problems from Lesson 5.	• 1 calculator per student • large graph paper, optional	• 2 copies of *Centimeter Graph Paper* URG Page 34 per student • 4 transparencies of *Centimeter Graph Paper* URG Page 34, optional
Lesson 3 **Sink and Float** URG Pages 54–73 SG Pages 411–414 DAB Page 205 DPP E–J HP Part 3 *Estimated Class Sessions* **3**	**Activity** Students measure the mass and volume of several objects. Then they find the ratio of the mass to the volume (density) of each object and use it to predict whether the object will sink or float in water. **Math Facts** Use DPP items E, H, and I to review division facts. **Homework** Assign Part 3 of the Home Practice. **Assessment** Use the *Observational Assessment Record* to note students' abilities to use ratios and proportions to solve problems.	• 1 two-pan balance per student group • 1 set of gram masses per student group • 1 250-cc graduated cylinder per student group • 1 100-cc graduated cylinder per student group • 1 small piece of clay for leveling the balance per student group • paper towels • water	• 1 copy of *Mass Review* URG Pages 64–65 per student, optional • 1 copy of *Volume Review* URG Pages 66–68 per student, optional

	Lesson Information	Supplies	Copies/ Transparencies
		• 1 eyedropper per student group • 1 cup or beaker for pouring water per student group • 1 large container (dishpan) of water per student group • several small objects that sink or float (rock, marble, cork, clay, 1-inch diameter steel or plastic sphere, wood, paraffin block) per student group • 1 ruler to measure paraffin per student group • 1 calculator per student group	
Lesson 4 **Mass vs. Volume: Proportions and Density** URG Pages 74–97 SG Pages 415–422 DPP K–R HP Part 4 *Estimated Class Sessions* **4-5**	**Lab** Students use ratios and graphs to explore whether the density of a material is constant or dependent upon the amount of the material. They use proportional reasoning to solve problems about mass, volume, and density. Then they explore patterns in graphs that help them predict whether objects will sink or float. **Math Facts** DPP items M and Q review division facts. **Homework** Assign homework *Questions 1–7* in the *Student Guide*. **Assessment** 1. Assign Home Practice Part 4. 2. Grade the lab by assigning points to each part. 3. Use the *Observational Assessment Record* to assess students' abilities to measure mass and volume. 4. Transfer appropriate documentation from the Unit 13 *Observational Assessment Record* to students' *Individual Assessment Record Sheets*.	• 5 $\frac{1}{2}$-inch-diameter steel spheres per student group • 1 1-inch-diameter steel sphere per student group • 1 1$\frac{1}{4}$-inch-diameter steel sphere per student group • enough clay to make 3 pieces about the same size as the steel spheres and a small piece for leveling the balance; (clay cannot be water soluble) per student group • 1 two-pan balance per student group • 1 set of gram masses per student group • 1 250-cc graduated cylinder per student group • 1 100-cc graduated cylinder per student group	• 2 copies of *Centimeter Graph Paper* URG Page 34 per student • 2 copies of *Three-column Data Table* URG Page 91 per student • 2 transparencies of *Centimeter Graph Paper* URG Page 34 • 1 copy of *Individual Assessment Record Sheet* TIG Assessment section per student, previously copied for use throughout the year

(Continued)

Overview

	Lesson Information	Supplies	Copies/Transparencies
		• paper towels • 1 eyedropper per student group • water • 1 cup or beaker for pouring water per student group • 1 calculator per student group • vegetable oil, corn syrup, clear soda, raisins, eggs, salt, and food coloring for the extension	
Lesson 5 **Problems of Scale** URG Pages 98–105 SG Page 423 DPP S–T *Estimated Class Sessions* **1**	**Activity** Students solve word problems and take a quiz on content from this unit. **Math Facts** DPP item S provides practice with the division facts. **Homework** Assign some or all of the questions for homework. **Assessment** Use the *Paint Quiz* as an assessment.	• 1 calculator per student • 1 ruler per student	• 1 copy of *Paint Quiz* URG Pages 102–103 per student

Unit 14: Using Circles

Unit Summary

Students apply many previously learned skills and concepts as they explore the geometry of circles. They investigate the relationship between the circumference and the diameter of a circle, first informally, then more formally as they complete a laboratory investigation, *Circumference vs. Diameter.*

In this lab they use data tables and graphs to find an accurate approximation for the ratio circumference to diameter (C/D), or pi (π). Then, they use this ratio to find a formula for the circumference of a circle. Students also learn to use a compass and a ruler to copy and construct circles and other shapes.

As they work through each activity, they use geometric terms as needed to name parts of the circle. Finally, they interpret and construct circle graphs.

Major Concept Focus

- circumference
- diameter
- chords, arcs, and radii
- circle graphs
- pi (π)
- point graphs
- relationship between circumference and diameter
- using ratios
- constructing circles and figures
- generating formulas
- measuring length
- TIMS Laboratory Method
- best-fit lines

Pacing Suggestions

This unit is designed to be completed in 12 to 14 days.

- Lesson 5 *Circle Graphs* makes connections between mathematics and science. Students can use science time for reading circle graphs on endangered species.
- Lesson 6 *Practice and Problems* includes a series of word problems about circles. The problems can serve as homework or assessment. They are also appropriate for use by a substitute teacher since preparation is minimal.

Preparing for Upcoming Lessons

In Lessons 1 and 2, students measure the circumference and diameter of cans and lids. Ask students to bring in cans and lids of various sizes. A good selection of circular objects for students to measure includes: empty spools of thread or film canisters for small objects, soup cans or masking tape rolls for medium objects, and coffee cans or large lids for large objects.

Overview

Unit Planner

KEY: SG = Student Guide, DAB = Discovery Assignment Book, AB = Adventure Book, URG = Unit Resource Guide, DPP = Daily Practice and Problems, HP = Home Practice (found in Discovery Assignment Book), and TIG = Teacher Implementation Guide.

	Lesson Information	Supplies	Copies/Transparencies
Lesson 1 **Exploring Circumference and Diameter** URG Pages 26–35 SG Pages 426–427 DAB Page 213 DPP A–B HP Part 1 *Estimated Class Sessions* **1**	**Activity** Students explore the circumference and diameter of circles. They estimate that the circumference is about three times the length of the diameter. **Homework** 1. Assign the *Gluing It Down* Homework Page in the *Discovery Assignment Book*. 2. Assign Part 1 of the Home Practice. **Assessment** Use the *Observational Assessment Record* to note students' abilities to identify the parts of a circle.	• glue • 2 five-foot-long lengths of string that do not stretch per student pair • scissors • 2–3 cans and lids of various sizes per student pair	• 1 copy of *Observational Assessment Record* URG Pages 11–12 to be used throughout this unit
Lesson 2 **Circumference vs. Diameter** URG Pages 36–56 SG Pages 428–434 DPP C–H HP Parts 2–3 *Estimated Class Sessions* **3-4**	**Lab** Students measure the circumference and diameter of circles. They plot their measurements in a graph and find that the circumference of any circle is π times the length of the diameter. **Math Facts** Assign DPP items E and G, which review division facts. **Homework** 1. Assign the Homework section in the *Circumference vs. Diameter* Activity Pages. 2. Assign Parts 2 and 3 of the Home Practice. **Assessment** 1. Use *TIMS Multidimensional Rubric* Solving to assess students' responses to **Question 20** in the Explore section. 2. Use some of the word problems in the *Student Guide* in Lesson 6 *Practice and Problems* as an assessment. 3. Students complete the *Going Around in Circles* Assessment Page in the *Unit Resource Guide.* 4. Note students' abilities to use words and symbols to express the relationship between the circumference and diameter of a circle on the *Observational Assessment Record*.	• cans and lids of various sizes • 1 centimeter ruler per student • string or adding machine tape that will not stretch • 1 calculator per student	• 1 copy of *Going Around in Circles* URG Page 49 per student • 1 copy of *Centimeter Graph Paper* URG Page 50 per student • 1 copy of *Three-trial Data Table* URG Page 51 per student • 1 copy of *TIMS Multidimensional Rubric* TIG Assessment section

	Lesson Information	**Supplies**	**Copies/ Transparencies**
Lesson 3 **Constructing Circles with Terry** URG Pages 57–71 SG Pages 435–439 DAB Page 215 DPP I–N HP Part 4 *Estimated Class Sessions* **3**	**Activity** Students learn about circles and use rulers and compasses to draw, measure, and label them. **Math Facts** DPP item K reviews the division facts. **Homework** 1. Assign the Homework section in the *Student Guide.* 2. Assign Part 4 of the Home Practice. **Assessment** 1. Use DPP Bit I *Quiz: Try Some Pi.* 2. Choose one of the homework questions to use as an assessment. 3. Use the *Observational Assessment Record* to note students' abilities to construct geometric figures using rulers, compasses, and protractors.	• 1 ruler per student • 1 compass per student • 1 protractor per student • several sheets of blank paper per student • cardboard corners, optional • crayons or markers, optional • piece of string about a meter long to tie around a piece of chalk to use as a compass on the board or a large compass, optional	• 1 transparency of *The Circle* URG Page 68 • 1 transparency of *Snowman* DAB Page 215
Lesson 4 **Complex Constructions** URG Pages 72–90 SG Pages 440–444 DPP O–T HP Part 5 *Estimated Class Sessions* **3**	**Activity** Students use a compass and a ruler to copy and construct shapes. **Math Facts** DPP Bits O and S use division facts to practice mental math. Task P uses math facts to review prime factorization. **Homework** 1. Students complete the Homework section in the *Student Guide. Question 8* can be left as a challenge. 2. Assign Part 5 of the Home Practice. **Assessment** Use the *Circles and Constructions* Assessment Pages.	• 1 ruler per student • 1 compass per student • 1 protractor per student • several sheets of blank paper per student • crayons, colored pencils, or markers, optional • cardboard corners, optional • large compass or chalk and string	• 1 copy of *Circles and Constructions* URG Pages 84–85 per student • 1 transparency of *Examples of Art* URG Page 86, optional

(Continued)

Overview

	Lesson Information	Supplies	Copies/Transparencies

Lesson 5
Circle Graphs

URG Pages 91–104
SG Pages 445–449
DAB Pages 217–219

DPP U–X
HP Part 6

Estimated Class Sessions
2

Activity
Students interpret data using circle graphs. They use fractions, decimals, and percents to represent data. They make circle graphs using small centi-wheels.

Math Facts
DPP Bit W reviews the division facts.

Homework
1. Assign homework *Questions 1–6* on the *Circle Graphs* Activity Pages in the *Student Guide* after students complete Part 1 of the lesson.
2. Assign the *Make a Circle Graph* Activity Pages in the *Discovery Assignment Book* after students complete Part 2.
3. Assign Part 6 of the Home Practice.

Assessment
1. Use the *Make a Circle Graph* Activity Pages as an assessment.
2. Use DPP item U as an assessment.
3. Use the *Observational Assessment Record* to note students' abilities to use fractions, decimals, and percents to represent the same quantity.
4. Transfer appropriate documentation from the Unit 14 *Observational Assessment Record* to students' *Individual Assessment Record Sheet*.

Supplies:
• 1 calculator per student
• 1 pair of scissors per student
• 1 ruler per student
• 1 small centi-wheel per student
• 1 compass per student

Copies/Transparencies:
• 1 copy of *Individual Assessment Record Sheet* TIG Assessment section per student, previously copied for use throughout the year

---

Lesson 6
Practice and Problems

URG Pages 105–108
SG Pages 450–451

Estimated Class Sessions
1

OPTIONAL LESSON

Optional Activity
Students solve a variety of problems using concepts learned in this and previous units.

Supplies:
• 1 calculator per student

Unit 15: Developing Formulas with Geometry . . . . 6–10 Sessions

Unit Summary

In this final unit on geometry, students build on previous knowledge to develop and use formulas for the area and perimeter of a rectangle and the area of a triangle. They first review strategies for finding the area of a rectangle, then develop the formula. The formula for the perimeter of a rectangle is developed through the observation that opposite sides of a rectangle are equal in length.

Major Concept Focus

- right triangles
- acute triangles
- squares
- perimeter
- area of rectangles
- perimeter of rectangles
- obtuse triangles
- rectangles
- geometry formulas
- area of triangles

Pacing Suggestions

This unit is designed to be completed in 6 to 10 days.

Lesson 6 *A Variety of Problems* is an optional lesson that is a series of word problems involving area and perimeter. The problems can serve as homework or assessment. They are also appropriate for use by a substitute teacher since preparation is minimal.

Unit Planner

KEY: SG = Student Guide, DAB = Discovery Assignment Book, AB = Adventure Book, URG = Unit Resource Guide, DPP = Daily Practice and Problems, HP = Home Practice (found in Discovery Assignment Book), and TIG = Teacher Implementation Guide.

	Lesson Information	Supplies	Copies/Transparencies
Lesson 1 **Finding Area–Rectangles** URG Pages 21–33 SG Pages 454–457 DAB Pages 227–228 DPP A–B HP Parts 1–2 *Estimated Class Sessions* **1-2**	**Activity** Students discuss strategies for finding the area of rectangles. They then develop a formula for finding the area of a rectangle. **Homework** Assign homework *Questions 1–3* in the *Student Guide* and the *Finding Area: Review* Activity Pages in the *Discovery Assignment Book.* **Assessment** 1. Use the *Finding Area: Review* Activity Pages to assess students' abilities to find the area of rectangles and other polygons. 2. Use the *Observational Assessment Record* to note students' abilities to find the area of polygons.	• 1 protractor or object with right corners to construct right angles per student • 1 calculator per student • 1 ruler per student	• 1–2 copies of *Centimeter Grid Paper* URG Page 29 per student • 1 transparency of *Finding Area: Review* DAB Pages 227–228, optional • 1 transparency of *Centimeter Grid Paper* URG Page 29 • 1 copy of *Observational Assessment Record* URG Pages 11–12 to be used throughout this unit
Lesson 2 **Rectangle Riddles** URG Pages 34–43 SG Pages 458–461 DPP C–D HP Part 3 *Estimated Class Sessions* **1**	**Activity** Students find the missing measures of rectangles. They use calculators and learn about the $\boxed{x^2}$ key. **Homework** Assign homework *Questions 1–9* in the *Student Guide.* **Assessment** Use DPP Bit C as a quiz to assess skills developed in Lessons 1 and 2.	• 1 protractor or object with right corners to construct right angles per student • 1 calculator per student • 1 ruler per student	
Lesson 3 **Finding Area–Right Triangles** URG Pages 44–60 SG Pages 462–467 DPP E–F HP Part 5 *Estimated Class Sessions* **1-2**	**Activity** Students use geoboards and dot paper to build right triangles. They use different strategies to find the area of the triangles. Students develop a formula for the area of right triangles. **Math Facts** DPP Bit E reviews division facts. Use DPP Task F to gain fluency with the order of operations while practicing the math facts. **Homework** Assign homework *Questions 1–12.* You can leave *Questions 11–12* as challenges. **Assessment** Use selected homework questions as an assessment.	• 1 geoboard per student pair • 4–5 rubber bands per student pair • colored pencils, crayons, or markers • 1 calculator per student • 1 ruler per student • overhead markers for the *Geoboard* transparency or overhead geoboard and rubber bands • 4-by-8 inch paper rectangle	• 8–10 copies of *Centimeter Dot Paper* URG Page 54 per student • 1 transparency of *Geoboard* URG Page 53 or overhead geoboard and rubber bands • 1 transparency of *Centimeter Dot Paper* URG Page 54, optional

	Lesson Information	Supplies	Copies/ Transparencies
Lesson 4 **More Triangles** URG Pages 61–79 SG Pages 468–478 DPP G–J *Estimated Class Sessions* **2**	**Activity** Students find the area of acute and obtuse triangles using a variety of strategies. They generalize a formula for finding the area of any triangle. **Math Facts** Use DPP Bit I to review the division facts. **Homework** 1. Assign homework *Questions 1–8* at the end of the Acute Triangles section. 2. Assign homework *Questions 9–12* at the end of the Obtuse Triangles section. **Assessment** Choose questions in the homework section to use as an assessment.	• 1 geoboard per student pair • 4–5 rubber bands per student pair • 1 ruler per student • colored pencils • 1 calculator per student • overhead markers for the *Geoboard* transparency or overhead geoboard and rubber bands	• 1 copy of *Four-column Data Table* URG Page 71 per student, optional • 4–5 copies of *Centimeter Dot Paper* URG Page 54 per student • 1 transparency of *Geoboard* URG Page 53 or overhead geoboard and rubber bands • 1 transparency of *Centimeter Dot Paper* URG Page 54, optional
Lesson 5 **Perimeter** URG Pages 80–95 SG Pages 479–483 DPP K–L HP Part 4 *Estimated Class Sessions* **1-2**	**Activity** Students find the perimeter of various shapes. They use perimeter to solve problems about rectangles. Students also take a short item quiz on concepts and skills from this unit. **Homework** 1. Assign the homework *Questions 1–6* in the *Student Guide.* 2. Assign Part 4 of the Home Practice that provides more practice with finding the area of rectangles and triangles. **Assessment** 1. Students complete the *Areas and Perimeters* Assessment Pages in the *Unit Resource Guide.* 2. Use the *Observational Assessment Record* to note students' abilities to find the perimeter of rectangles and other shapes. 3. Transfer appropriate documentation from the Unit 15 *Observational Assessment Record* to students' *Individual Assessment Record Sheets.*	• 1 calculator per student • 1 ruler per student • adding machine tape, optional	• 1 copy of *Areas and Perimeters* URG Pages 88–90 per student • several copies of *Centimeter Grid Paper* or *Centimeter Dot Paper* URG Pages 29 & 54 per student • 1 copy of *Individual Assessment Record Sheet* TIG Assessment section per student, previously copied for use throughout the year • 1 transparency of *Centimeter Grid Paper* or *Centimeter Dot Paper* URG Pages 29 & 54, optional
Lesson 6 **A Variety of Problems** URG Pages 96–101 SG Pages 484–485 HP Part 6 *Estimated Class Sessions* **1**	OPTIONAL LESSON **Optional Activity** Students complete word problems involving concepts from this unit. **Homework** Assign some or all of the questions for homework. **Assessment** Use Part 6 of the Home Practice.	• 1 calculator per student • 1 ruler per student	

Overview

Unit 16: Bringing It All Together:
An Assessment Unit · **10–12 Sessions**

Unit Summary

This unit reviews, extends, and assesses the concepts students studied throughout the year. Students revisit the labs they completed during the year in preparation for completing an assessment lab. This lab is based on the Adventure Book *Bats!* in which a family helps a scientist estimate the number of bats in a cave. In the lab *How Many Bats in a Cave?* students use beans in a container to model the sampling procedures used in the story.

Using a similar procedure and proportional reasoning, students estimate the number of beans in their containers. Students also use pattern blocks to solve an assessment problem, *Pattern Block Candy.* Finally, students take an *End-of-Year Test,* which assesses concepts from Units 13–15. The unit ends with a review of students' portfolios.

Major Concept Focus

- experiment review
- populations and samples
- point graphs
- communicating solution strategies
- using data to solve problems
- end-of-year test

- *Adventure Book:* estimating animal populations
- TIMS Laboratory Method
- ratios and proportions
- best-fit lines
- Student Rubric: *Solving*
- portfolio review

Pacing Suggestions

This unit will take 10 to 12 days to complete. It includes a variety of review and assessment activities that provide opportunities for teachers to assess individual growth in mathematics as students apply concepts and skills in new contexts.

- Lesson 2 *Bats!* is an *Adventure Book* story that provides a strong connection to language arts, social studies, and science. It sets the stage for the assessment lab in Lesson 4 *How Many Bats in a Cave?* It is appropriate to use language arts or science time for students to read and discuss the story.
- Lesson 3 *More Bats!* and Lesson 4 *How Many Bats in a Cave?* provide connections to science. Students can collect the data for the lab in Lesson 4 during science time.

Unit Planner

	Lesson Information	Supplies	Copies/Transparencies
Lesson 1 **Experiment Review** URG Pages 22–32 SG Page 488 DAB Pages 235–237 DPP A–D HP Part 1 *Estimated Class Sessions* **2**	**Activity** Students review the labs they worked on during the past year by recounting the important features of each lab. The class discusses the similarities and differences between the labs. **Homework** Assign Part 1 of the Home Practice.	• portfolios	• 1 transparency of *Comparing Lives of Animals and Soap Bubbles Lab* URG Page 30 • 1 transparency of *Experiment Review Chart* DAB Pages 235–237 or a large sheet of easel paper for a class chart
Lesson 2 **Bats!** URG Pages 33–42 AB Pages 93–106 DPP E–F HP Part 2 *Estimated Class Sessions* **1**	**Adventure Book** Students read a story about using a capture-recapture technique to estimate the size of a bat population in a cave. The story describes how scientists collected the data and used proportional reasoning to calculate an estimate. **Math Facts** DPP item E provides practice with division facts. **Homework** 1. Assign DPP Challenge F, which explores mass, volume, and density. 2. Assign Part 2 of the Home Practice, which reviews fractions, decimals, and percents.	• map of the United States, optional	
Lesson 3 **More Bats!** URG Pages 43–50 SG Pages 489–491 DPP G–H *Estimated Class Sessions* **1**	**Activity** Students expand on the story *Bats!* as they graph the data collected by a conservation club. This lesson reviews skills needed for Lesson 4. **Math Facts** Complete DPP item G, which reviews the division facts. **Assessment** Use the *Observational Assessment Record* to note students' abilities to express ratios using words, tables, graphs, and fractions.	• 1 calculator per student • 1 ruler per student	• 1 copy of *Centimeter Graph Paper* URG Page 49 per student • 1 copy of *Observational Assessment Record* URG Pages 9–10 to be used throughout this unit

(Continued)

Overview

	Lesson Information	Supplies	Copies/Transparencies
Lesson 4 **How Many Bats in a Cave?** URG Pages 51–66 SG Pages 492–497 DPP I–N HP Parts 3–4 *Estimated Class Sessions* **3**	**Assessment Lab** Using beans to represent bats in a cave, students simulate the capture-recapture technique described in the Adventure Book *Bats!* Using this technique and proportional reasoning, students find the approximate number of "bats" in their "cave." **Math Facts** Assign DPP item I, which reviews the division facts. **Homework** 1. Assign the homework in the *Student Guide*. Students will need a piece of *Centimeter Graph Paper*. 2. Assign Parts 3 and 4 of the Home Practice. **Assessment** Choose one or more sections of the lab to use as an assessment.	• brightly colored markers for tagging the beans per student group • 1 self-closing bag filled with 1 lb. of baby lima beans per student group • 3 sizes of scoops: small (about 2 tablespoons), medium (about 4 tablespoons), and large (about 6 tablespoons) per student group • 1 ruler per student • 1 calculator per student	• 1 copy of *Three-column Data Table* URG Page 63 per student, optional • 2 copies of *Centimeter Graph Paper* URG Page 49 per student • 1 transparency of *Centimeter Graph Paper* URG Page 49, optional • 1 copy of *TIMS Multidimensional Rubric* TIG Assessment section, optional
Lesson 5 **Pattern Block Candy** URG Pages 67–78 DPP O–P HP Part 5 *Estimated Class Sessions* **1-2**	**Assessment Activity** Students use pattern blocks to build patterns. Using the *Solving* Rubric, they use the patterns to solve problems and then write about their solutions. **Math Facts** Complete DPP item O, which reviews the division facts. **Homework** Assign Part 5 of the Home Practice. **Assessment** Use the *TIMS Multidimensional Rubric* to score students' work. Encourage students to compare their work on this activity to similar activities in their portfolios.	• 1 calculator per student • 1 set of pattern blocks (4 or 5 of each shape: red trapezoid, blue rhombus, green triangle, brown trapezoid, purple triangle) per student	• 1 copy of *Pattern Block Candy* URG Pages 76–77 per student • 1 transparency or poster of Student Rubric: *Solving* TIG Assessment section, optional • 1 copy of *TIMS Multidimensional Rubric* TIG Assessment section, optional
Lesson 6 **End-of-Year Test** URG Pages 79–91 DPP Q–R HP Part 6 *Estimated Class Sessions* **1-2**	**Assessment Activity** Students complete a short item test designed to assess skills and concepts learned during the final quarter of the year. **Assessment** 1. Students solve the problems on the *End-of-Year Test* using tools available to them in the classroom. 2. Assign Part 6 of the Home Practice.	• 1 ruler per student • 1 protractor per student • 1 compass per student • 1 calculator per student	• 1 copy of *End-of-Year Test* URG Pages 83–87 per student • 1 copy of *Centimeter Dot Paper* URG Page 88 per student

	Lesson Information	Supplies	Copies/ Transparencies
Lesson 7 **Portfolio Review** URG Pages 92–96 SG Pages 498–499 DPP S–T *Estimated Class Sessions* **1**	**Assessment Activity** Students review their portfolios, looking at their growth since the start of the school year. **Math Facts** Complete DPP item S, which involves finding a pattern in a data table and continuing it. **Assessment** Transfer appropriate documentation from the Unit 16 *Observational Assessment Record* to students' *Individual Assessment Record Sheets*.	• collection folders • portfolio folders	• 1 copy of *Individual Assessment Record Sheet* TIG Assessment section per student, previously copied for use throughout the year

Overview

Scope and Sequence
& the NCTM *Principles and Standards*

This section provides descriptions and tables that show how *Math Trailblazers* relates to the National Council of Teachers of Mathematics *Principles and Standards for School Mathematics*. A comprehensive scope and sequence for Grade 5 units and Daily Practice and Problems is included.

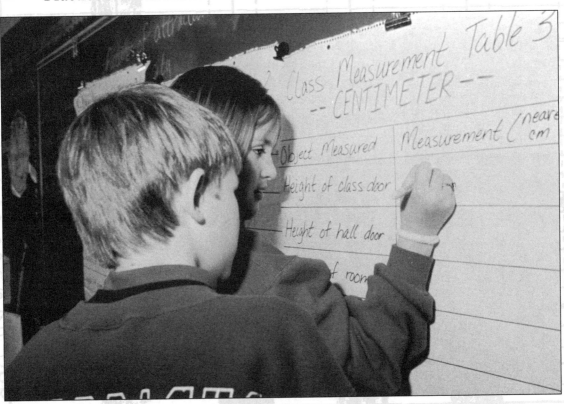

Students share their data by recording it on a class data table.

Math Trailblazers and the Principles and Standards

The National Council of Teachers of Mathematics (NCTM) *Principles and Standards for School Mathematics* and *Math Trailblazers* complement each other: The *Principles and Standards* is a vision of what school mathematics should be. *Math Trailblazers* is the curricular structure so teachers can turn that vision into reality. This section starts with an outline of how *Math Trailblazers* complements the five content and five process standards in the *Principles and Standards*. It concludes with a scope and sequence that specifies how the Grade 5 curriculum develops through the year. For information on the scope and sequence across the grades, see the *Math Trailblazers Scope and Sequence Chart* available from Kendall/Hunt Publishing Company.

Content Standards

Principles and Standards for School Mathematics outlines an articulated vision of how learning and teaching in each of five content areas should develop across the grades. These content areas are number and operations, algebra, geometry, measurement, and data analysis and probability. In *Math Trailblazers* the standards for all five content areas are addressed appropriately at every grade level, from Kindergarten through Grade 5. Five process standards prescribe a curriculum where problem solving, communication, reasoning, connections, and representation are integral, not ancillary, issues. By looking at the Scope and Sequence Chart in this section, one can see how mathematical ideas develop throughout the grade.

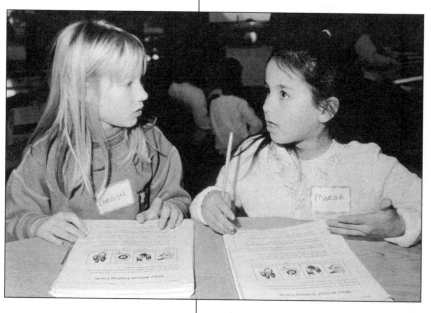

Many activities in *Math Trailblazers* address more than one of the content standards. Consider, for example, *Bouncing Ball,* a fourth-grade laboratory experiment in which students investigate the relationship between the drop height and the bounce height of a tennis ball. The investigation begins with a question: "What is the relationship between how far a tennis ball drops and how high it bounces?" Through class discussion, the variables are identified and named (D, the drop height and B, the bounce height) and experimental procedures are devised. A picture records this information. Next, the students drop the tennis balls repeatedly, measure drop height and bounce height each time, and record the data in a table. As students gather the data, they monitor the measurements for consistency and sense. Then when the data is complete, they examine the data table to see if they can discern a pattern. Next, students graph their data. As they work, they are asked how the data table and the graph relate to the physical system, what the relationship between drop height and bounce height is, and how that relationship is evident in the table and graph. Then students make and verify predictions. Finally, students generalize: "What would the graph look like for a Super ball?" "What would happen if the experiment were repeated on a carpeted floor?"

This single experiment involves measurement, data analysis, number sense, estimation, graphing, multiplication, patterns and functions (algebra), and mathematical reasoning. All these topics, moreover, relate to a single context that unites them. By weaving so many themes into one complex whole, that whole becomes more meaningful and the mathematics more powerful.

Lessons such as *Bouncing Ball* are embedded in a careful sequence of lessons and units that address all the standards. Other lessons develop single skills or concepts that students can then practice in the Daily Practice and Problems. These skills and concepts are extended and applied in more complex lessons and investigations. *Math Trailblazers* is therefore a comprehensive and balanced curriculum that includes geometry, statistics and probability, measurement, algebra, estimation, fractions, numeration, and computation—just what the *Principles and Standards* requires.

For more information on the *Math Trailblazers* approach to selected content areas, see the TIMS Tutors in Section 9 of this *Teacher Implementation Guide.*

Process Standards

The process standards highlight ways to acquire and use content knowledge. Each process standard is connected to the others. Moreover, the learning of mathematical processes is deeply embedded in the learning of content.

Problem Solving. A strong emphasis on problem solving is evident in the NCTM recommendations. Throughout *Math Trailblazers,* students are immersed in complex problem situations in which they both apply the mathematics they know and learn new mathematics. Students develop skills, procedures, and concepts as they work on the problems. For example, in the third-grade laboratory experiment, *The Better "Picker Upper,"* students explore the absorbency of various brands of paper towels by dropping water on each type of towel and comparing the areas of the spots. As students work through this complex problem, they learn about area (by tracing the spots on grid paper and counting square centimeters to find the areas), fractions (as they piece parts of square centimeters together to make whole square centimeters), averaging (as they aggregate the results of several trials), graphing (as they display and interpret their data in graphs), and computation (as they calculate the number of drops of water a whole paper towel absorbs). All this mathematics grows out of one problem: "Which is the more absorbent towel?"

Putting problems first is a different and difficult way to organize a mathematics curriculum. Having the focus on problems requires careful design, meticulous planning, and continual assessment to ensure the timely development of skills and concepts. Despite the difficulties, the benefits are clear: students not only master skills and concepts, they can apply them flexibly to solve problems.

Reasoning and Proof. This standard requires that reasoning permeate the curriculum. Students constantly explain their thinking and justify their solutions, first in small groups and then to the class as a whole. Sometimes they explain their thoughts orally and other times in writing or by using pictures and other tools. Students are always encouraged to find solutions in more than one way and to compare and contrast various solution methods. Thus, meaning and understanding are emphasized, and students find that mathematics makes sense.

"Mathematical reasoning develops in classrooms where students are encouraged to put forth their own ideas for examination. Teachers and students should be open to questions, reactions, and elaborations from others in the classroom. Students need to explain and justify their thinking and learn how to detect fallacies and critique others' thinking. They need to have ample opportunity to apply their reasoning skills and justify their thinking in mathematical discussion." (NCTM 2000, p. 188)

One example of an important area of mathematical reasoning that receives particular attention in *Math Trailblazers,* especially in Grades 3 through 5, is pre-proportional and proportional reasoning. This kind of reasoning is carefully developed over time through a sequence of real-life problems that students can solve with manipulatives, patterns, graphs, or symbols. Students choose the strategies and tools that make sense to them. Using these tools helps students create visual images of this important mathematical concept, which historically has largely been taught symbolically or procedurally and has been difficult for many students to grasp.

Communication. Students need frequent opportunities to communicate their mathematics. "Communication is an essential part of mathematics and mathematics education… Students gain insight into their thinking when they present their methods for solving problems, when they justify their reasoning to a classmate or teacher, or when they formulate a question about something that is puzzling to them." (NCTM 2000, p. 60) Communication is integral to *Math Trailblazers.* In many activities, students handle manipulatives, draw pictures, make graphs, and grapple with mathematical ideas. Many activities are collaborative exercises involving groups of students who work together to obtain, analyze, and generalize their results.

Just as people explain how they solve problems on the job, students who use the labs and activities talk about their mathematics. Students discuss, compare, contrast, and write about their problem-solving methods in both small-group and whole-class settings. This "publication" of students' mathematical thinking gives students access to a broader range of solution strategies and helps them become more reflective about mathematics.

Connections. This standard calls for connections within mathematics, between mathematics and other parts of the school curriculum, and between mathematics and their own interests. Integration of subject matter is a major focus of *Math Trailblazers.* Mathematics arises naturally in science, language, history, and daily life. *Math Trailblazers* does not artificially merge disparate ideas from distinct disciplines, but rather builds up the underlying unity between disciplines that we see in the real world. For example, the basic measurement variables that the curriculum covers extensively —length, area, volume, mass, and time—are fundamental not only to mathematics but also to science and daily life. The TIMS Laboratory Method effectively incorporates the method of science into the mathematics curriculum as a problem-solving tool.

The *Adventure Books* and Literature Connections integrate language arts and social studies with the mathematics curriculum. Some *Adventure Books* recount the history of science and mathematics; others show how the concepts and procedures students are learning apply to the work of real scientists or to everyday life. Students are continually required to communicate their mathematical thinking orally and in writing. *Math Trailblazers* is committed to the ideal of "writing across the curriculum."

Connections within mathematics are equally important. Like most real-world problems, activities in *Math Trailblazers* generally involve a combination of mathematical topics. A single laboratory experiment, for example, might involve arithmetic, data collection, estimation, geometry, probability, and algebraic concepts—each covered at an appropriate level for students.

Representation. "Representing ideas and connecting their representations to mathematics lies at the heart of understanding mathematics." (NCTM 2000, p. 136) *Math Trailblazers* is rich in the many opportunities it gives students to represent mathematical ideas. For example, whole numbers are represented as collections of objects (using manipulatives or drawings), as measurements, as points on a number line, or as items on a *100 Chart*. When children collect data they may organize it in a data table or represent it graphically. If there are patterns in the data, they can describe them numerically or graphically. Ultimately, they describe some relations symbolically.

Throughout *Math Trailblazers* students are encouraged to draw pictures and diagrams to illustrate their ideas and support their thinking. This communicates their reasoning, and as students create these representations, they clarify and build their thinking.

Developing a *Standards*-Based Classroom

The *Professional Standards for Teaching Mathematics* (NCTM, 1991) and the Teaching Principle in the *Principles and Standards* specify what classroom teachers, supervisors, teacher educators, and policy makers should do to improve mathematics instruction. Much of this discussion concerns four key areas: tasks, discourse, environment, and analysis. Teachers decide what tasks to set for students, foster discourse about mathematics, establish a classroom environment conducive to high achievement and positive attitudes, and engage in analysis of students' thinking and their own teaching. While accomplishing these things depends more on teachers' expertise than on curricula, materials that embody the *Principles and Standards* can make the work easier.

Tasks. *Math Trailblazers* provides a logical sequence of well-conceived tasks. Professional mathematicians and scientists helped develop the curriculum so lessons focus on significant concepts and skills. Teachers and mathematics educators also helped write the curriculum, so tasks are engaging, practical, and developmentally appropriate. Lessons develop both skills and concepts, so they make connections within mathematics and between mathematics and other subjects, portray mathematics as a human endeavor, and promote communication and problem solving.

Discourse. Many features of *Math Trailblazers* support discourse. Tasks in the curriculum have enough depth for significant discussion to be possible. An emphasis on multiple solutions to problems encourages students to talk about their own thinking. The *Student Guide* often displays and discusses multiple solutions to problems. Journal and discussion prompts in the teacher materials stimulate and focus classroom discussions. *Adventure Books* and children's literature help students understand that people really do talk about mathematics and science. The wide range of tools and technology in *Math Trailblazers*—manipulatives, calculators, pictures, tables, graphs, and symbols—enhance discourse by broadening the means of communication beyond what is traditional.

Environment. Creating a classroom environment conducive to the development of each student's mathematical power is necessary for the *Principles and Standards* to come alive. This involves arranging space, time, and materials in ways that maximize student learning. *Math Trailblazers'* diverse range of lessons—activities of varied length, activities for groups and individuals, hands-on and paper-and-pencil investigations, and activities that encourage multiple solution paths—all help teachers develop a classroom that builds mathematical understandings and skills for a wide range of students.

Analysis. The curriculum's activities and assessment program provide teachers with many opportunities to analyze students' learning. Teachers using the curriculum will know more about their students' mathematical abilities than they ever have before. The extensive background information in the unit guides and in the *Teacher Implementation Guide* provides accessible ways for teachers to gain additional insight into how students learn mathematics. This enhanced knowledge motivates the teaching of subsequent lessons. *Math Trailblazers* will help you become more attuned both to your students and to your teaching.

For additional discussion on these and related topics, see the following sections in the *Teacher Implementation Guide:*

- Building the *Math Trailblazers* Classroom
- Teaching the *Math Trailblazers* Student: Meeting Individual Needs
- Language in the *Math Trailblazers* Classroom
- Working with *Math Trailblazers* Parents and Families

Math Trailblazers:
A Standards-Based Curriculum

In summary, NCTM calls for curricula to be coherent within and across the grades, to be conceptually oriented, to involve students actively, to emphasize development of students' mathematical thinking and reasoning abilities, to emphasize applications, to include a broad range of content, and to make appropriate use of calculators and computers.

These are admirable goals and high expectations. No curriculum can finally and fully attain such goals and fulfill such expectations—not only will there always be improvements to be made, but in the end much depends upon individual teachers and students. Yet a curriculum that has been developed specifically to be aligned with the *Principles and Standards* will provide the foundation. The goals and characteristics described above are all hallmarks of *Math Trailblazers.*

The best test of alignment with the *Principles and Standards,* however, is to observe students using the curriculum. Are they actively involved? Do they grapple with significant concepts while learning and applying basic skills? Are they thinking and reasoning? Do they use a broad range of tools to solve realistic problems? We think you will find that *Math Trailblazers* more than meets this test.

References

An Agenda for Action: Recommendations for School Mathematics of the 1980s. National Council of Teachers of Mathematics, Reston, VA, 1980.

Assessment Standards for School Mathematics. National Council of Teachers of Mathematics, Reston, VA, 1995.

Curriculum and Evaluation Standards for School Mathematics. National Council of Teachers of Mathematics, Reston, VA, 1989.

Essential Mathematics for the 21st Century: The Position of the National Council of Supervisors of Mathematics. National Council of Supervisors of Mathematics, Minneapolis, MN, 1988.

National Research Council. "Conclusions and Recommendations." In *Adding It Up: Helping Children Learn Mathematics.* J. Kilpatrick, J. Swafford, and B. Findell (Eds.). National Academy Press, Washington, DC, 2001.

Principles and Standards for School Mathematics. National Council of Teachers of Mathematics, Reston, VA, 2000.

Professional Standards for Teaching Mathematics. National Council of Teachers of Mathematics, Reston, VA, 1991.

Scope and Sequence

Scope and Sequence for Units

Math Trailblazers was developed to meet the NCTM *Principles and Standards for School Mathematics.* The scope and sequence on white on the following pages indicates how each unit aligns with the *Principles and Standards.* By reading the chart horizontally, you will see the integration of the various standards within a given unit. By reading the chart vertically, you can track the development of a specific standard throughout the fifth-grade curriculum.

Scope and Sequence for the Daily Practice and Problems

Every unit includes a series of Daily Practice and Problems (DPP). The scope and sequence chart on gray on the following pages indicates how the DPP aligns with the *Principles and Standards.* By reading the chart vertically, you can track the development of a specific standard throughout the fifth-grade DPP. Each DPP item, which is denoted by a letter, has been correlated with one or more of the standards. The appropriate letters are indicated in parentheses following each entry. Thus the scope and sequence can also serve as a content map for the DPP.

For more information about the Daily Practice and Problems, see the Daily Practice and Problems Guide.

	Number and Operations	Algebra	Geometry	Measurement	Data Analysis and Probability
Unit 1: Populations and Samples **Lessons**	• Choosing appropriate methods and tools to calculate (calculators, pencil and paper, or mental math). • Choosing to find an estimate or an exact answer.	• Collecting, organizing, graphing, and analyzing data. • Using numerical variables. • Naming values of variables. • Translating between graphs and real-world events. • Making and interpreting bar graphs.			• Collecting, organizing, graphing, and analyzing data. • Naming values of variables. • Using numerical variables. • Translating between graphs and real-world events. • Making and interpreting bar graphs. • Sampling a population. • Predicting population characteristics from samples. • Investigating the concept of averages. • Averaging: finding the median. • Averaging: identifying the mode. • Finding the probability of an event based on collected data.
Daily Practice and Problems (Lettered) **& Home Practice** (Numbered)	• Assessing students' fluency with the addition and subtraction facts. (C, E, K, O) • Solving problems involving addition or subtraction. (A, C, E, G, K, L, M, N, O, P, R) (1, 4) • Estimating sums and differences. (R) (4) • Listing multiples of 2, 4, 5, and 10. (I) • Estimating by using a sample. (D) • Developing number sense. (B, D, N, P) • Developing mental math skills. (A, L, N, P, R) (1) • Solving multistep word problems. (B, G) (6) • Solving problems involving money. (J) (6) • Choosing appropriate methods and tools to calculate (calculators, pencil and paper, or mental math). (6) • Choosing to find an estimate or an exact answer. (6)	• Identifying numerical and categorical variables. (F, H) (2) • Naming values of variables. (F) (2) • Making and interpreting bar graphs. (H) (5)			• Averaging: finding the median. (M, Q) (3) • Identifying numerical and categorical variables. (F, H) (2) • Naming values of variables. (F) (2) • Making and interpreting bar graphs. (H) (5) • Using data to solve problems. (M) (5) • Estimating by using a sample. (D)

Problem Solving	Reasoning and Proof	Communication	Connections	Representation
• Promoting these beliefs: Problems can be solved by more than one method and different methods should yield solutions that agree. • Solving multistep word problems. • Choosing appropriate methods and tools (calculators, pencil and paper, or mental math) to calculate. • Choosing to find an estimate or an exact answer. • Using the *Knowing* Rubric to self-assess problem-solving skills.	• Predicting population characteristics from samples.	• Communicating solutions verbally and in writing.	• Connecting mathematics and science to real-world situations: surveying classmates and sampling populations. • Translating between graphs and real-world events.	• Collecting, organizing, graphing, and analyzing data. • Translating between graphs and real-world events. • Making and interpreting bar graphs. • Using numerical variables.
• Solving problems involving addition or subtraction. (A, G, L, M, N, P, R) (1, 4) • Solving multistep word problems. (B, G) (6) • Solving problems involving money. (J) (6) • Using data to solve problems. (M) (5) • Choosing appropriate methods and tools to calculate (calculators, pencil and paper, or mental math). (6) • Choosing to find an estimate or an exact answer. (6)	• Estimating by using samples. (D)			• Making and interpreting bar graphs. (H) (5)

Scope and Sequence

	Number and Operations	Algebra	Geometry	Measurement	Data Analysis and Probability
Unit 2: Big Numbers **Lessons**	• Self-assessing the multiplication and division facts. • Maintaining fluency with the multiplication and division facts with the 5s and 10s. • Representing large numbers using place value charts, abacuses, and base-ten pieces. • Reading and writing large numbers. • Comparing and ordering large numbers. • Using estimation to place large numbers on a number line. • Developing number sense for large numbers. • Rounding large numbers. • Understanding place value. • Translating between different representations of large numbers (concrete, pictorial, and symbolic). • Modeling multiplication with base-ten pieces. • Multiplying whole numbers using paper-and-pencil methods. • Using convenient numbers to estimate. • Estimating products. • Multiplying numbers with ending zeros. • Solving problems involving multiplication and division. • Using exponents. • Reading scientific notation.	• Using patterns in data to make predictions and solve problems. • Using turnaround facts (commutativity) to multiply. • Using exponents.		• Measuring length in centimeters.	• Using patterns in data to make predictions and solve problems. • Collecting and analyzing data.
Daily Practice and Problems (Lettered) **& Home Practice** (Numbered)	• Self-assessing the multiplication and division facts. (1) • Maintaining fluency with the multiplication and division facts with the 5s and 10s. (I, M, Q, U, W, X, Y, AA, CC) (1) • Using estimation to place numbers on a number line. (2) • Developing number sense. (G, H, J, N, P) (2) • Rounding large numbers. (K) • Estimating sums and differences. (A) (2) • Estimating products. (P, T, V, BB) (2, 3) • Estimating by using a sample. (J) • Comparing and ordering large numbers. (L, Z) • Reading and writing large numbers. (L) • Exploring patterns when multiplying with multiples of ten. (U, W, Y) • Multiplication place value games. (P) • Developing mental math skills. (U, W, X, Y, Z) • Understanding place value. (G, H, N, P, S) • Adding or subtracting with whole numbers using paper and pencil. (A) • Multiplying or dividing whole numbers using paper and pencil. (I, M, N, O, P, R, T, U, V) (3) • Solving problems involving addition and subtraction. (D, E, S, Z) • Solving problems involving multiplication and division. (B, I, M, N, P, R, U) (3, 4) • Solving multistep word problems. (3, 4) • Solving problems involving money. (B, E) (2) • Solving problems involving time. (C, D) • Choosing appropriate methods and tools to calculate (calculators, paper and pencil, or mental math). (O) (3, 4) • Reading scientific notation. (DD)	• Solving problems with unknowns. (Y)		• Measuring length in centimeters. (F) • Solving problems involving time. (C, D)	• Averaging: finding the median. (C, F) • Making predictions from samples. (J) • Estimating by using a sample. (J)

Problem Solving	Reasoning and Proof	Communication	Connections	Representation
• Solving open-response problems and communicating solution strategies. • Solving problems involving multiplication and division. • Collecting and using data to solve problems. • Using the *Solving* and *Telling* Rubrics to self-assess problem-solving skills.	• Translating between different representations of large numbers (concrete, pictorial, and symbolic).	• Communicating solutions verbally and in writing. • Using portfolios. • Using the *Solving* and *Telling* Rubrics to self-assess problem-solving skills.	• Translating between different representations of large numbers (concrete, pictorial, and symbolic). • Connecting mathematics and science to real-world situations. • Estimating the number of pennies in a stack to the moon: Archimedes' estimate of the number of grains of sand in the universe.	• Representing large numbers using place value charts, abacuses, and base-ten pieces. • Translating between different representations of large numbers (concrete, pictorial, and symbolic). • Modeling addition and subtraction of whole numbers with base-ten pieces. • Modeling multiplication of whole numbers with base-ten pieces. • Using exponents. • Reading scientific notation.
• Solving problems involving addition and subtraction. (D, E, S, Z) • Solving problems involving multiplication and division. (B, I, M, N, O, P, R, U) (3, 4) • Solving multistep word problems. (3, 4) • Solving problems involving money. (B, E) (3) • Solving problems involving time. (C, D) • Choosing appropriate methods and tools to calculate (calculators, pencil and paper, or mental math). (O) (3, 4)	• Making predictions from samples. (J)	• Communicating solution strategies. (BB) (4)		• Translating between different representations of numbers. (G, L, N) • Using estimation to place numbers on a number line. (2) • Solving problems with unknowns. (Y) • Reading scientific notation. (DD)

	Number and Operations	Algebra	Geometry	Measurement	Data Analysis and Probability
Unit 3: Fractions and Ratios **Lessons**	• Defining the numerator and the denominator. • Representing fractions using pattern blocks, number lines, and symbols. • Finding a fraction for a given quantity when a unit whole is given. • Writing improper fractions as mixed numbers and mixed numbers as improper fractions. • Finding equivalent fractions. • Comparing and ordering fractions using benchmarks of 0, $\frac{1}{2}$, and 1. • Writing number sentences using fractions. • Using words, pictures, tables, graphs, and fractions to express ratios. • Finding equal ratios. • Choosing appropriate methods and tools to calculate (calculator, pencil and paper, or mental math). • Choosing to find an estimate or an exact answer. • Solving problems involving fractions.	• Using numerical variables. • Using ratios to solve problems. • Using words, pictures, tables, graphs, and fractions to express ratios. • Drawing and interpreting best-fit lines. • Analyzing a situation with a constant rate of change. • Investigating how a change in one variable relates to a change in a second variable. • Using patterns in data to make predictions and solve problems.		• Measuring length in yards and feet. • Defining speed as a ratio. • Converting between feet and yards. • Dealing with precision and accuracy.	• Using data to solve problems. • Using words, pictures, tables, graphs, and fractions to express ratios. • Collecting, organizing, graphing, and analyzing data. • Drawing and interpreting best-fit lines. • Averaging: finding the median.
Daily Practice and Problems (Lettered) **& Home Practice** (Numbered)	• Self-assessing the multiplication and division facts. (B) (1) • Maintaining fluency with the multiplication and division facts with the 2s and 3s. (B, C, D, E, K, O, U) (1) • Developing number sense. (A, J, M, N, Q) (3) • Rounding large numbers. (2) • Estimating sums, differences, and products. (G, L) (4) • Comparing and ordering fractions. (M, N, Q) (3, 6) • Writing improper fractions as mixed numbers and mixed numbers as improper fractions. (I) (6) • Finding equivalent fractions. (6) • Skip counting by halves, thirds, and fourths. (J) • Multiplying by multiples of ten. (C) • Developing mental math skills. (C) • Understanding place value. (A) • Using words, pictures, tables, graphs, and fractions to express ratios. (5) • Finding a fraction for a given quantity when a unit whole is given. (H) • Adding, subtracting, multiplying, and dividing whole numbers using paper and pencil. (G, L) (4) • Solving problems involving addition, subtraction, multiplication, and division. (A, D, P, T) (4) • Solving problems involving time. (P, T) • Solving multistep word problems. (D)	• Using words, pictures, tables, graphs, and fractions to express ratios. (V) (5) • Drawing and interpreting best-fit lines. (V) (5) • Using patterns in data to make predictions and solve problems. (V) (5)		• Converting inches to feet and feet to yards. (R) • Choosing appropriate units of measure. (S)	• Using data to solve problems. (5) • Drawing and interpreting best-fit lines. (5) • Using words, pictures, tables, graphs, and fractions to express ratios. (V) (5) • Averaging: finding the median. (F) • Interpreting bar graphs. (F)

Problem Solving	Reasoning and Proof	Communication	Connections	Representation
• Using ratios to solve problems. • Solving multistep problems. • Solving problems involving fractions. • Using patterns in data to make predictions and solve problems. • Choosing appropriate methods and tools to calculate (calculator, pencil and paper, or mental math). • Using the *Knowing* and *Telling* Rubrics to self-assess problem-solving skills.	• Communicating solutions verbally and in writing.	• Using words, pictures, tables, graphs, and fractions to express ratios. • Communicating solutions verbally and in writing. • Using the *Knowing* and *Telling* Rubrics to self-assess problem-solving skills.	• Representing fractions using manipulatives and symbols. • Translating between graphs and real-world events. • Connecting mathematics and science to real-world situations: investigating walking speed.	• Representing fractions using manipulatives and symbols. • Using words, pictures, tables, graphs, and fractions to express ratios. • Collecting, organizing, graphing, and analyzing data. • Translating between graphs and real-world events. • Using numerical variables.
• Solving problems involving addition, subtraction, multiplication, and division. (A, D, L, P, T) (4) • Solving multistep word problems. (D) (4) • Using patterns in data to make predictions and solve problems. (V) (5)	• Explaining mathematical reasoning. (N) • Using patterns in tables and graphs to make predictions and solve problems. (V) (5)		• Using words, pictures, tables, graphs, and fractions to express ratios. (V) (5)	• Using words, pictures, tables, graphs, and fractions to express ratios. (V) (5) • Representing fractions using drawings. (H) • Representing numbers on number lines. (2)

Scope and Sequence

	Number and Operations	Algebra	Geometry	Measurement	Data Analysis and Probability
Unit 4: Division and Data **Lessons**	• Modeling division of whole numbers with base-ten pieces. • Dividing whole numbers using a paper-and-pencil method with 1-digit divisors. • Estimating quotients. • Interpreting remainders. • Comparing the mean and the median. • Using correct order of operations. • Using ratios to solve problems. • Using 10% as a standard for error analysis. • Averaging: finding the median and mean. • Choosing appropriate methods and tools to calculate (calculator, pencil and paper, or mental math). • Choosing to find an estimate or an exact answer. • Solving problems involving multiplication and division.	• Generalizing the area of a rectangle as length times width. • Using order of operations. • Using ratios to solve problems. • Using numerical variables. • Drawing and interpreting best-fit lines. • Analyzing a situation with a constant rate of change. • Translating between graphs and real-world events. • Using patterns in data to make predictions and solve problems.	• Measuring area. • Counting square centimeters to estimate the area of figures with curved sides. • Finding the area of polygons by counting square units. • Generalizing the area of a rectangle as length times width.	• Measuring area. • Counting square centimeters to estimate the area of a figure with curved sides. • Using 10% as a standard for error analysis. • Generalizing the area of a rectangle as length times width. • Understanding the role of standard units in scientific measurement. • Dealing with precision and accuracy.	• Averaging: finding the median and mean. • Comparing the mean and the median. • Collecting, organizing, graphing, and analyzing data. • Using numerical variables. • Identifying the manipulated, responding, and fixed variables in an experiment. • Translating between graphs and real-world events. • Drawing and interpreting best-fit lines. • Choosing an appropriate graph to display data. • Using patterns in data to make predictions and solve problems. • Using 10% as a standard for error analysis.
Daily Practice and Problems (Lettered) **& Home Practice** (Numbered)	• Self-assessing the multiplication and division facts. (B) (1) • Maintaining fluency with the multiplication and division facts with the square numbers. (E, I, K, M, Z, AA) (1) • Developing number sense. (H, L, R, X) • Estimating products and quotients. (G, L, O, R, U) (3) • Choosing appropriate methods and tools to calculate (calculators, pencil and paper, or mental math). (2, 5) • Comparing and ordering numbers written in scientific notation. (L) • Comparing and ordering fractions. (H) • Reading scientific notation. (L, Q) • Identifying the unit whole when a fractional part is given. (N) • Finding equivalent fractions. (C) • Using words, pictures, tables, graphs, and fractions to express ratios. (V) (4) • Divisibility by 2, 3, and 5. (X) • Multiplying and dividing by multiples of ten. (S) • Developing mental math skills. (S, X) • Multiplying and dividing whole numbers using paper and pencil. (G, O, P, U) (3) • Solving problems involving multiplication and division. (A, P) (2, 5) • Solving problems involving money. (P) (5) • Solving problems involving time. (J) • Using order of operations. (Z) • Using 10% as a standard for error analysis. (T)	• Generalizing the area of a rectangle as length times width. (W) (2) • Using words, pictures, tables, graphs, and fractions to express ratios. (4) (V) • Using ratios to solve problems. (4) • Using patterns in data to make predictions and solve problems. (V) • Drawing and interpreting best-fit lines. (V) (4) • Using order of operations. (Z)	• Measuring area. (D, F, W) (2) • Generalizing the area of a rectangle as length times width. (W)	• Measuring area. (D, F, W) (2) • Generalizing the area of a rectangle as length times width. (W) • Converting among English units of measure. (A)	• Using words, pictures, tables, graphs, and fractions to express ratios. (4) (V) • Using ratios to solve problems. (4) • Using patterns in data to make predictions and solve problems. (V) • Drawing and interpreting best-fit lines. (V) • Averaging: finding the median and mean. (Y, BB) (5)

Problem Solving	Reasoning and Proof	Communication	Connections	Representation
• Estimating quotients. • Interpreting remainders. • Comparing the mean and the median. • Using ratios to solve problems. • Using patterns in data to make predictions and solve problems. • Solving multistep word problems. • Solving problems involving multiplication and division. • Choosing appropriate methods and tools to calculate (calculator, pencil and paper, or mental math). • Choosing to find an estimate or an exact answer.	• Modeling division with base-ten pieces. • Collecting, organizing, graphing, and analyzing data. • Using patterns in data to make predictions and solve problems.	• Communicating solutions orally and in writing. • Choosing an appropriate graph to display data. • Using the *Telling* Rubric to self-assess communication skills.	• Connecting mathematics and science to real-world situations: George Washington Carver sets up his lab at Tuskegee Institute.	• Drawing and interpreting best-fit lines. • Modeling division of whole numbers with base-ten pieces. • Using numerical variables. • Collecting, organizing, graphing, and analyzing data. • Choosing an appropriate graph to display data. • Using patterns in data tables and graphs to make predictions.
• Choosing appropriate methods and tools to calculate (calculators, pencil and paper, or mental math). (2, 5) • Solving problems involving multiplication and division. (A, P) (2, 5) • Using ratios to solve problems. (4) • Solving multistep word problems. (P) (5) • Solving problems involving time. (J) • Solving problems involving money. (P) (5)	• Using patterns in data tables and graphs to make predictions. (V) (4) • Communicating solution strategies. (R, X) (2, 5)		• Using words, pictures, tables, graphs, and fractions to express ratios. (V) (4)	• Using words, pictures, tables, graphs, and fractions to express ratios. (V) (4) • Using patterns in data tables and graphs to make predictions. (V) (4) • Drawing and interpreting best-fit lines. (V) (4) • Reading and writing numbers in scientific notation, words, and symbols. (L, Q) • Representing fractions using drawings and symbols. (N) (4)

	Number and Operations	Algebra	Geometry	Measurement	Data Analysis and Probability
Unit 5: Investigating Fractions **Lessons**	• Defining the numerator and the denominator. • Representing fractions using pattern blocks, geoboards, pictures, and symbols. • Finding equivalent fractions. • Finding a fraction for a given quantity when a unit whole is given. • Identifying the unit whole when a fractional part is given. • Adding and subtracting fractions using manipulatives, pictures, or symbols. • Comparing and ordering fractions using pictures and symbols. • Estimating sums and differences of fractions. • Finding common denominators using pictures and symbols. • Writing number sentences using fractions. • Using symbols and graphs to express ratios. • Using ratios to solve problems. • Solving problems involving fractions. • Averaging: choosing the mean or median.	• Using ratios to solve problems. • Drawing and interpreting best-fit lines. • Using the steepness of a line to compare ratios. • Using numerical variables. • Translating between graphs and real-world events. • Analyzing a situation with a constant rate of change. • Investigating how a change in one variable relates to a change in a second variable.		• Measuring length in yards and feet. • Measuring time with a stopwatch. • Defining speed as a ratio. • Comparing speeds.	• Collecting, organizing, graphing, and analyzing data. • Drawing and interpreting best-fit lines. • Using the steepness of a line to compare ratios. • Averaging: choosing the median or mean. • Using numerical variables. • Translating between graphs and real-world events. • Using patterns in data to make predictions and solve problems.
Daily Practice and Problems (Lettered) **& Home Practice** (Numbered)	• Self-assessing the multiplication and division facts. (B) (1) • Maintaining fluency with the multiplication and division facts with the 9s. (B, C, D, E, I, K, O, S) (1) • Developing number sense. (Q, R, T) • Estimating sums, differences, products, or quotients. (M, N, Q, R) (5) • Comparing and ordering fractions or whole numbers. (N, T) (6) • Choosing appropriate methods and tools to calculate (calculators, pencil and paper, or mental math). (7) • Writing improper fractions as mixed numbers and mixed numbers as improper fractions. (4) • Finding equivalent fractions. (6) • Using order of operations. (C, D) (2) • Multiplying by multiples of ten. (E) • Developing mental math skills. (E, G) (5) • Using words, pictures, tables, graphs, and fractions to express ratios. (3) • Adding and subtracting fractions using manipulatives, number lines, pictures, or symbols. (R) (4, 6) • Identifying the unit whole when a fractional part is given. (L) • Adding, subtracting, multiplying, or dividing using paper and pencil. (M, N) (5) • Solving problems involving addition, subtraction, multiplication, or division. (D, M) (2) • Solving problems involving time. (A) • Solving problems involving money. (H) • Using ratios to solve problems. (P, V) (3) • Using 10% as a standard for error analysis. (J) • Solving multistep word problems. (F) (7)	• Using words, pictures, tables, graphs, and fractions to express ratios. (3) • Generalizing the area of a rectangle as length times width. (J) • Using ratios to solve problems. (P, V) • Using order of operations. (2)	• Estimating the area of a rectangle using pennies. (J) • Generalizing the area of a rectangle as length times width. (J)	• Estimating the area of a rectangle using pennies. (J) • Generalizing the area of a rectangle as length times width. (J) • Choosing appropriate units of measure. (U)	• Using words, pictures, tables, graphs, and fractions to express ratios. (3) • Averaging: finding the mean. (F)

Problem Solving	Reasoning and Proof	Communication	Connections	Representation
• Using ratios to solve problems. • Using patterns in data to make predictions and solve problems.	• Using patterns in data to make predictions and solve problems.	• Communicating solutions verbally and in writing. • Using the *Telling* Rubric to assess communication skills.	• Connecting mathematics and science to real-world situations: Investigating speeds. • Translating between graphs and real-world events.	• Representing fractions using pattern blocks, geoboards, pictures, and symbols. • Adding and subtracting fractions using manipulatives, pictures, or symbols. • Comparing and ordering fractions using pictures and symbols. • Finding common denominators using pictures and symbols. • Writing number sentences using fractions. • Using symbols and graphs to express ratios. • Drawing and interpreting best-fit lines. • Using numerical variables. • Collecting, organizing, graphing, and analyzing data. • Using patterns in data tables and graphs to make predictions.
• Solving problems involving addition, subtraction, multiplication, or division. (D, M) (2) • Using ratios to solve problems. (P, V) (3) • Choosing appropriate methods and tools to calculate (calculators, pencil and paper, or mental math). (7) • Solving multistep word problems. (F) (7) • Solving problems involving money. (H) • Solving problems involving time. (A)	• Using data to make predictions. (J) • Explaining mathematical reasoning. (F, T, V) (7)	• Explaining mathematical reasoning. (F, T, V) (7)	• Using words, pictures, tables, graphs, and fractions to express ratios. (3)	• Using words, pictures, tables, graphs, and fractions to express ratios. (3) • Adding and subtracting fractions using manipulatives, number lines, pictures, or symbols. (R) (4, 6) • Representing fractions using drawings. (L)

Scope and Sequence

	Number and Operations	Algebra	Geometry	Measurement	Data Analysis and Probability
Unit 6: **Geometry** **Lessons**		• Using numerical variables. • Expressing mathematical relationships using formulas. • Identifying, extending, and making generalizations about geometric and number patterns.	• Estimating angle measures using benchmarks. • Identifying acute, obtuse, and right angles. • Measuring angles with a protractor. • Drawing angles and shapes with determined measures. • Investigating properties of polygons. • Identifying and describing 2-dimensional shapes. • Investigating, describing, and reasoning about the results of subdividing polygons. • Identifying congruent and similar shapes. • Investigating tessellations. • Describing and classifying 2-dimensional shapes. • Constructing polygons with specific measures. • Making and testing conjectures about geometric properties. • Using geometric definitions.	• Estimating angle measures using benchmarks. • Measuring angles with a protractor. • Drawing angles of determined measures. • Identifying acute, obtuse, and right angles. • Constructing polygons with specific measurements (lengths of sides or angle measures).	
Daily Practice and Problems (Lettered) **& Home Practice** (Numbered)	• Self-assessing the multiplication and division facts. (B) (1) • Maintaining fluency with the multiplication and division facts with the last six facts. (B, E, G, O, P, Q) (1) • Developing number sense. (D, H, P, R) • Estimating sums, products, or quotients. (H, I, J) (2, 4) • Choosing appropriate methods and tools to calculate (calculators, pencil and paper, or mental math). (7) • Using order of operations. (D, P) • Adding, subtracting, multiplying, and dividing whole numbers and fractions using paper and pencil. (H, I, N) (2, 4, 6) • Comparing fractions using benchmarks. (H) • Developing mental math skills. (O) • Using ratios to solve problems. (A) (6) • Solving problems involving percents. (J) • Solving problems involving addition, subtraction, multiplication, or division. (D, I, K, N, O, P) (4, 7) • Solving multistep word problems. (N) (5, 7)	• Drawing and interpreting best-fit lines. (A) • Using patterns in data to make predictions and solve problems. (A) • Using order of operations. (D, P) • Using ratios to solve problems. (A) (6)	• Drawing angles and shapes with determined measures. (L) (3, 5) • Making and testing conjectures about geometric properties. (R) (3) • Constructing polygons with specific measures. (L) (5) • Estimating angle measures. (C) • Measuring area. (F) • Calculating angle measures. (M) • Recognizing similarity. (L) • Using geometric concepts and skills to solve problems. (L, M, R) (3, 5)	• Drawing angles and shapes with determined measures. (L) (3, 5) • Making and testing conjectures about geometric properties. (R) (3) • Constructing polygons with specific measurements (lengths of sides or angle measures). (L) (5) • Estimating angle measures. (C) • Measuring area. (F) • Calculating angle measures. (M) • Converting between units of measure. (6)	• Drawing and interpreting best-fit lines. (A) • Using patterns in data to make predictions and solve problems. (A)

Problem Solving	Reasoning and Proof	Communication	Connections	Representation
• Using geometric concepts and skills to solve problems. • Using the *Telling* Rubric to self-assess problem-solving skills.	• Developing deductive reasoning. • Making and testing conjectures about geometric properties. • Using geometric definitions. • Identifying, extending, and making generalizations about geometric and number patterns.	• Identifying and describing 2-dimensional shapes. • Using mathematical definitions. • Using the student Rubric: *Telling* as a guide for writing solutions.	• Connecting mathematics and art: investigating tessellations. • Connecting mathematics and science: classifying animals.	• Using numerical variables. • Drawing angles and shapes with determined measures.
• Solving problems involving addition, subtraction, multiplication, or division. (D, I, K, N, O, P) (4) • Choosing appropriate methods and tools to calculate (calculators, pencil and paper, or mental math). (7) • Solving multistep word problems. (N) (5, 7) • Solving problems involving percents. (J) • Using ratios to solve problems. (A) (6)	• Developing deductive reasoning. (R) (3, 5) • Explaining mathematical reasoning. (R) (3, 5) • Using geometric concepts and skills to solve problems. (L, M, R) (3, 5)	• Explaining mathematical reasoning. (R) (3, 5)		• Drawing angles and shapes with determined measures. (L) (3, 5) • Adding and subtracting fractions using manipulatives, pictures, or symbols. (6) • Translating between graphs and real-world events. (A)

	Number and Operations	Algebra	Geometry	Measurement	Data Analysis and Probability
Unit 7: Decimals and Probability **Lessons**	• Using fractions, decimals, and percents to represent the same quantity. • Representing decimals using place value charts, circles (centiwheels), and square grids. • Translating between different representations of decimals (concrete, pictorial, and symbolic). • Understanding place value. • Developing number sense for decimals. • Rounding decimals. • Reading and writing decimals to the thousandths. • Comparing and ordering decimals. • Estimating sums, differences, and products involving decimals. • Finding the probability of an event. • Expressing probabilities as fractions, decimals, and percents. • Adding and subtracting decimals using pictures. • Adding and subtracting decimals using paper-and-pencil methods. • Multiplying decimals using an area model. • Multiplying decimals using paper-and-pencil methods.	• Collecting, organizing, graphing, and analyzing data. • Translating between graphs and real-world events. • Making and interpreting bar graphs.		• Finding the area of rectangles. • Finding area by counting square centimeters.	• Making and interpreting bar graphs. • Collecting and organizing data from a random process. • Collecting, organizing, graphing, and analyzing data. • Understanding that random events are predictable "over the long run." • Analyzing fair and unfair games. • Exploring probabilities involved in flipping a coin. • Finding the probability of an event. • Expressing probabilities as fractions, decimals, and percents. • Using probability to predict outcomes. • Describing events as likely, unlikely, certain, impossible, more likely, and less likely.
Daily Practice and Problems (Lettered) **& Home Practice** (Numbered)	• Self-assessing the multiplication and division facts. (1) • Maintaining fluency with all the multiplication and division facts. (C, G, K, O, S, W) (1) • Developing number sense. (F, J, L, N, P, Q, U) • Estimating sums, differences, products, and quotients. (P, T, V, Z) (2, 6, 8) • Choosing appropriate methods and tools to calculate (calculators, pencil and paper, or mental math). (8) • Reading and writing large numbers. (5) • Adding, subtracting, multiplying, and dividing whole numbers and fractions using paper and pencil. (T, V, Y, Z) (2, 4, 6) • Representing decimals using place value charts, circles (centiwheels), or square grids. (L) (3) • Using fractions, decimals, and percents to represent the same quantity. (L) (3, 7) • Comparing and ordering fractions, decimals, or percents. (E, L, M, Q) (5) • Expressing probabilities as fractions, decimals, and percents. (7) • Skip counting. (I) • Understanding place value. (F, M, N, P, Q, U, V) (5) • Solving problems involving addition, subtraction, multiplication, and division. (H, R, T, V, Y, Z) (2, 4, 8) • Solving problems involving time. (H, J) • Solving problems with money. (J, X)	• Using patterns in data to make predictions and solve problems. (D) • Using ratios to solve problems. (E) • Solving problems with unknowns. (E)	• Calculating angle measures. (A) • Constructing polygons with specific measures. (B) • Using mathematical definitions. (B, R)	• Calculating angle measures. (A) • Constructing polygons with specific measures. (B) • Measuring length in centimeters. (R)	• Expressing probabilities as fractions, decimals, and percents. (7) • Using probability to predict. (7) • Using patterns in data to make predictions and solve problems. (D)

Problem Solving	Reasoning and Proof	Communication	Connections	Representation
• Using probability to predict outcomes. • Exploring probabilities involved in flipping a coin.	• Analyzing fair and unfair games. • Using probability to predict outcomes.		• Comparing probabilities with real-world events.	• Representing decimals using place value charts, circles (centiwheels), and square grids. • Translating between different representations of decimals (concrete, pictorial, and symbolic). • Using fractions, decimals, and percents to represent the same quantity. • Expressing probabilities as fractions and decimals. • Making and interpreting bar graphs.
• Solving problems involving addition, subtraction, multiplication, and division. (T, V, X, Y, Z) (2, 4) • Using probability to predict. (7) • Choosing appropriate methods and tools to calculate (calculators, pencil and paper, or mental math). (8) • Solving multistep word problems. (X) (8) • Solving problems with money. (I, J, X)	• Using mathematical definitions. (B, R) • Using mathematical reasoning. (J) • Explaining mathematical reasoning. (7)	• Explaining mathematical reasoning. (7)		• Representing decimals using place value charts, circles (centiwheels), or square grids. (L) (3) • Using fractions, decimals, and percents to represent the same quantity. (L) (3, 7) • Expressing probabilities as fractions, decimals, and percents. (7) • Translating between graphs and real-world events. (D) • Solving problems with unknowns. (E) • Reading and writing large numbers. (5)

SCOPE & SEQUENCE CHART

	Number and Operations	Algebra	Geometry	Measurement	Data Analysis and Probability
Unit 8: Applications: An Assessment Unit **Lessons**	• Using fractions, decimals, and percents to represent the same quantity. • Estimating products involving decimals. • Representing decimals using circles (centiwheels). • Solving multistep word problems. • Choosing appropriate methods and tools to calculate (calculator, pencil and paper, or mental math). • Choosing to find an estimate or an exact answer. • Finding equal ratios. • Using graphs and fractions to express ratios.	• Comparing and contrasting elements of different laboratory investigations: problems solved, types of graphs, and variables. • Drawing and interpreting best-fit lines. • Translating between graphs and real-world events. • Using numerical variables. • Analyzing a situation with constant rate of change. • Investigating how a change in one variable relates to a change in a second variable.		• Comparing and contrasting number of trials and measurement procedures of different laboratory investigations. • Measuring time with a stopwatch.	• Comparing and contrasting elements of different laboratory investigations: measurement procedures, number of trials, problems solved, types of graphs, and variables. • Collecting, organizing, graphing, and analyzing data. • Grouping data in bins to see patterns. • Making and interpreting bar graphs using binned data. • Drawing and interpreting best-fit lines. • Translating between graphs and real-world events. • Using data to make predictions and solve problems. • Averaging: finding the median.
Daily Practice and Problems (Lettered) **& Home Practice** (Numbered)	• Self-assessing the multiplication and division facts. (B) (1) • Maintaining fluency with the multiplication and division facts with all the facts. (C, I, K, M, Q) (1) • Developing number sense. (P) • Estimating sums, differences, products, or quotients. (D, O) (2) • Choosing appropriate methods and tools to calculate (calculators, pencil and paper, or mental math). (6) • Using fractions, decimals, and percents to represent the same quantity. (G) • Developing mental math skills. (K) • Understanding place value. (P) • Writing improper fractions as mixed numbers and mixed numbers as improper fractions. (3) • Finding equivalent fractions. (E) • Adding, subtracting, multiplying, or dividing whole numbers and fractions using paper and pencil. (D, L) (2, 3) • Solving problems involving addition, subtraction, multiplication, or division. (A) (2, 3, 4, 6) • Finding probabilities. (J)	• Drawing and interpreting best-fit lines. (R) • Using patterns in data to make predictions and solve problems. (R) • Solving problems with unknowns. (C, I, K)	• Measuring area. (A) (4) • Measuring angles with a protractor. (4) • Constructing polygons with specific measures. (H) • Using geometric concepts and skills to solve problems. (4)	• Measuring area. (A) (4) • Measuring angles with a protractor. (4) • Constructing polygons with specific measures. (H)	• Translating between graphs and real-world events. (R) (5) • Finding probabilities. (J) • Drawing and interpreting best-fit lines. (R) • Using patterns in data to make predictions and solve problems. (R)

Problem Solving	Reasoning and Proof	Communication	Connections	Representation
• Solving multistep word problems. • Choosing to find an estimate or an exact answer. • Using data to make predictions and solve problems. • Using the *Knowing* and *Telling* Rubrics to self-assess problem-solving skills. • Solving open-response problems and communicating solution strategies.	• Comparing and contrasting elements of different laboratory investigations: measurement procedures, number of trials, problems solved, types of graphs, and variables. • Making and interpreting bar graphs using binned data. • Drawing and interpreting best-fit lines. • Translating between graphs and real-world events. • Using data to make predictions and solve problems.	• Solving open-response problems and communicating solution strategies. • Using the *Knowing* and *Telling* Rubrics to self-assess problem-solving skills. • Using portfolios.	• Comparing and contrasting the following elements of different experiments: measurement procedures, number of trials, problems solved, types of graphs, and variables. • Using fractions, decimals, and percents to represent the same quantity. • Translating between graphs and real-world events. • Connecting mathematics and social studies to real-world situations: Collecting demographic data in the late 1800s to fight child labor. • Connecting mathematics and science to real-world situations: Investigating life spans of people and animals.	• Comparing and contrasting the types of graphs of different experiments. • Using fractions, decimals, and percents to represent the same quantity. • Representing decimals using circles (centiwheels). • Translating between graphs and real-world events. • Using patterns in tables and graphs to make generalizations about data. • Using numerical variables.
• Solving problems involving addition, subtraction, multiplication, or division. (D, L) (2, 3) • Choosing appropriate methods and tools to calculate (calculators, pencil and paper, or mental math). (6) • Solving multistep word problems. (N, P) (6) • Solving problems with unknowns. (C) (1) • Using geometric concepts and skills to solve problems. (4)	• Explaining mathematical reasoning. (O) (4, 5) • Using mathematical reasoning. (P)	• Solving open-response problems and communicating solution strategies. (F, N) (5) • Explaining mathematical reasoning. (O) (4, 5)	• Translating between graphs and real-world events. (R) (5) • Connecting mathematics to social studies. (R)	• Using fractions, decimals, and percents to represent the same quantity. (G) • Expressing probabilities as fractions. (J) • Translating between graphs and real-world events. (R) (5)

	Number and Operations	Algebra	Geometry	Measurement	Data Analysis and Probability
Unit 9: Connections to Division **Lessons**	• Interpreting fractions as division. • Dividing whole numbers using a paper-and-pencil method with 2-digit divisors. • Dividing whole numbers and money using calculators. • Estimating quotients. • Interpreting remainders. • Expressing a quotient as a mixed number. • Checking division using multiplication. • Finding decimal equivalents (or decimal approximations) for fractions. • Identifying repeating decimals. • Exploring different methods of paper-and-pencil multiplication. • Solving problems involving multiplication and division. • Developing number sense for large numbers.	• Interpreting fractions as division.	• Measuring area.	• Measuring area.	• Averaging. • Using data to solve problems. • Making predictions from samples.
Daily Practice and Problems (Lettered) **& Home Practice** (Numbered)	• Maintaining fluency with multiplication and division facts. (G, K, M, Q, S) • Developing number sense for decimals. (F, L, O, P) • Estimating sums, differences, products, and quotients. (A, E, J, L, N, O, P) (1, 3) • Comparing and ordering decimals. (F) • Choosing appropriate methods and tools to calculate (calculators, pencil and paper, or mental math). (A, J) (5) • Using fractions, decimals, or percents to represent the same quantity. (I) (2) • Expressing a quotient as a mixed number. (T) (4) • Finding equivalent fractions. (I) (2) • Interpreting remainders. (R, T) (4) • Multiplying and dividing with multiples of 10. (G, M, Q) • Developing mental math skills. (A, E, G, J, M, N, Q) (3) • Addition and subtraction of decimals place value game. (L, P) • Multiplying and dividing using paper and pencil. (A, H, J, N) (1, 3) • Solving problems involving multiplication and division. (C, H, T) (4) • Solving problems involving money. (C, H) • Solving problems involving time. (B) • Solving multistep word problems. (C, H) (5)	• Solving problems with unknowns. (K)			• Using data to solve problems. (C)

Scope and Sequence

Problem Solving	Reasoning and Proof	Communication	Connections	Representation
• Making predictions from samples. • Solving open-ended problems and communicating solution strategies. • Using the *Solving, Knowing,* and *Telling* Rubrics to self-assess problem-solving skills.	• Making predictions from samples. • Solving open-ended problems and communicating solution strategies. • Interpreting remainders.	• Solving open-ended problems and communicating solution strategies. • Using the *Solving, Knowing,* and *Telling* Rubrics to self-assess problem-solving skills.	• Connecting mathematics to real-world situations: Estimating the number of blades of grass in a lawn.	• Interpreting fractions as division. • Expressing a quotient as a mixed number. • Finding decimal equivalents (or decimal approximations) for fractions. • Identifying repeating decimals.
• Solving problems involving multiplication and division. (C, H, T) (4) • Choosing appropriate methods and tools to calculate (calculators, pencil and paper, or mental math). (A, J) (5) • Solving multistep word problems. (D, H) (5) • Solving problems involving money. (C, H) • Solving problems involving time. (B)	• Using patterns to solve problems. (D)	• Explaining mathematical reasoning. (E, O, T) (1, 5)		• Using fractions, decimals, or percents to represent the same quantity. (I) (2) • Expressing a quotient as a mixed number. (4) • Solving problems with unknowns. (K)

	Number and Operations	Algebra	Geometry	Measurement	Data Analysis and Probability
Unit 10: Maps and Coordinates **Lessons**	• Exploring negative numbers. • Representing negative numbers using a number line. • Solving problems using negative numbers. • Plotting points using ordered pairs in the four quadrants.	• Using coordinates to locate an object in a room, find a location on a map, or plot points on a graph. • Plotting points using ordered pairs in the four quadrants.	• Using coordinates to locate an object in a room, find a location on a map, or plot points on a graph. • Plotting points using ordered pairs in the four quadrants. • Graphing shapes in four quadrants. • Using slides to move shapes about the coordinate system. • Determining the image of a slide. • Using flips to move shapes about the coordinate system. • Determining the image of a flip. • Using a scale map to find distances. • Using tessellations to create art.	• Using a scale map to find distances. • Measuring length in centimeters and meters.	
Daily Practice and Problems (Lettered) **& Home Practice** (Numbered)	• Maintaining fluency with the multiplication and division facts. (A, E, I, K, O) • Developing number sense. (D, F) • Estimating sums, differences, products, or quotients. (C, D, J, L) (5) • Choosing appropriate methods and tools to calculate (calculators, pencil and paper, or mental math). (1, 6) • Exploring negative numbers. (2) • Representing negative numbers using a number line. (2) • Multiplying and dividing using multiples of 10. (I, K) (4) • Developing mental math skills. (I, K) (1, 4) • Dividing large numbers using calculators. (C) • Using the order of operations. (4) • Plotting points using ordered pairs in the four quadrants. (N) (3) • Adding, subtracting, multiplying, or dividing whole numbers and fractions using paper and pencil. (J, L) (1, 4, 5) • Solving problems involving addition, subtraction, multiplication, or division. (B, L) (6) • Solving problems involving money. (B, H) (6) • Solving problems using negative numbers. (G) (2) • Solving problems involving time. (B)	• Using coordinates to locate an object in a room, find a location on a map, or plot points on a graph. (3) • Plotting points using ordered pairs in the four quadrants. (3) • Plotting points using ordered pairs in the first quadrant. (N) • Solving problems with unknowns. (A) • Solving problems using negative numbers. (G)	• Plotting points using ordered pairs in the four quadrants. (N) (3) • Graphing shapes in four quadrants. (3) • Using geometric concepts and skills to solve problems. (N)		• Averaging: finding the median and mean. (H) • Finding probabilities involved in rolling a number cube. (M)

Problem Solving	Reasoning and Proof	Communication	Connections	Representation
• Using the *Knowing* Rubric to self-assess problem-solving skills.			• Connecting mathematics to real-world situations: Finding locations on a map of the Great Barrier Reef. • Connecting mathematics to real-world situations: Using coordinates to find locations on a stage in a school play. • Connecting mathematics and art: Investigating the art of M.C. Escher.	• Using coordinates to locate an object in a room, find a location on a map, or plot points on a graph. • Plotting points using ordered pairs in the four quadrants. • Representing negative numbers using a number line.
• Solving problems involving addition, subtraction, multiplication, or division. (B, L) (6) • Solving problems using negative numbers. (G) (2) • Choosing appropriate methods and tools to calculate (calculators, pencil and paper, or mental math). (1, 6) • Solving multistep word problems. (6) • Solving problems involving money. (B, H) (6) • Using tables to solve problems. (P) • Using geometric concepts and skills to solve logic problems. (N) • Solving problems involving time. (B)	• Using tables to solve logic problems. (P) • Explaining mathematical reasoning. (D, L) (5)			• Plotting points using ordered pairs in the four quadrants. (N) (3) • Representing negative numbers using a number line. (2) • Solving problems with unknowns. (A)

	Number and Operations	Algebra	Geometry	Measurement	Data Analysis and Probability
Unit 11: Number Patterns, Primes, and Fractions **Lessons**	• Finding all the factors of numbers. • Identifying prime, composite, and square numbers. • Finding the prime factorization of a number. • Using exponents. • Identifying and describing number patterns. • Using number patterns to solve problems. • Finding common denominators. • Comparing fractions. • Reducing fractions to lowest terms. • Adding and subtracting fractions using common denominators. • Expressing a quotient as a mixed number. • Solving multistep word problems. • Solving problems involving fractions. • Choosing appropriate methods and tools to calculate (calculators, paper and pencil, or mental math).	• Making and interpreting point graphs (curves). • Using variables in formulas. • Identifying and describing number patterns. • Using number patterns to solve problems. • Identifying, extending, and making generalizations about geometric and number patterns.			• Making and interpreting point graphs (curves). • Identifying and describing number patterns.
Daily Practice and Problems (Lettered) **& Home Practice** (Numbered)	• Maintaining fluency with the multiplication and division facts. (E, I, M, Q, S, U) • Developing number sense for decimals. (C, N) • Estimating sums, differences, products, or quotients. (A, K, N, R, T) (1, 5) • Choosing appropriate methods and tools to calculate (calculators, pencil and paper, or mental math). (6) • Comparing fractions. (O) • Identifying prime, composite, or square numbers. (G, J, P) • Divisibility rules. (L) • Finding the prime factorization of a number. (P) (3) • Finding all the factors of numbers. (G, P) (3) • Using exponents. (U) (3) • Reducing fractions to lowest terms. (H, R) (4) • Expressing a quotient as a mixed number. (5) • Using fractions and decimals to represent the same quantity. (H) • Adding and subtracting fractions. (R) (4) • Finding equivalent fractions. (O) • Writing fractions as mixed numbers. (R) • Plotting points using ordered pairs in the four quadrants. (D) • Solving problems involving addition, subtraction, multiplication, or division. (F) (2, 6) • Adding, subtracting, multiplying, or dividing whole numbers and decimals using paper and pencil. (A, K, N, T) (1, 5) • Developing mental math skills. (M, Q, U) • Solving problems involving money. (F) (2, 6) • Solving problems involving time. (B) • Dividing by multiples of 10. (M, Q)	• Using data to solve problems. (2) • Plotting points using ordered pairs in the four quadrants. (D) • Using unknowns to solve problems. (O, Q)	• Plotting points using ordered pairs in the four quadrants. (D)		• Using data to solve problems. (2) • Finding probabilities involving a number cube. (G)

Problem Solving	Reasoning and Proof	Communication	Connections	Representation
• Using number patterns to solve problems. • Using the *Telling* Rubric to self-assess problem-solving skills. • Solving multistep word problems. • Solving problems involving fractions. • Choosing appropriate methods and tools to calculate (calculators, pencil and paper, or mental math).	• Identifying, extending, and making generalizations about geometric and number patterns.	• Identifying and describing number patterns. • Communicating solutions verbally and in writing. • Using the *Telling* Rubric to self-assess communication skills.	• Translating between graphs and real-world events.	• Making and interpreting point graphs (curves). • Using variables in formulas. • Identifying and describing number patterns. • Using exponents. • Reducing fractions to lowest terms. • Expressing a quotient as a mixed number.
• Solving problems involving addition, subtraction, multiplication, or division. (F) (2, 6) • Choosing appropriate methods and tools to calculate (calculators, pencil and paper, or mental math). (6) • Solving problems involving money. (F) (2, 6) • Using tables to solve logic problems. (V) • Solving problems involving time. (B)	• Using tables to solve logic problems. (V) • Describing patterns in graphs. (D) • Explaining mathematical reasoning. (N, T) (1, 5)	• Describing patterns in graphs. (D)		• Using exponents. (3) • Plotting points using ordered pairs in the four quadrants. (D) • Using fractions and decimals to represent the same quantity. (H) • Using unknowns to solve problems. (O, Q) • Using exponents. (U) (3)

	Number and Operations	Algebra	Geometry	Measurement	Data Analysis and Probability
Unit 12: Using Fractions **Lessons**	• Using patterns to build number sense. • Reducing fractions to lowest terms. • Estimating sums of mixed numbers. • Adding fractions using pattern blocks and paper and pencil. • Adding mixed numbers using pattern blocks and paper and pencil. • Estimating products of fractions. • Multiplying a fraction and a whole number using diagrams, pattern blocks, and paper and pencil. • Multiplying fractions using pattern blocks, paper folding, and paper and pencil. • Choosing appropriate methods and tools to calculate (calculators, paper and pencil, or mental math). • Choosing to find an estimate or an exact answer. • Solving multistep word problems. • Solving problems involving fractions.	• Using patterns to build number sense.		• Creating a time schedule.	
Daily Practice and Problems (Lettered) **& Home Practice** (Numbered)	• Maintaining fluency with the multiplication and division facts. (A, E, G, I, K, M) • Estimating sums or products of fractions. (H, L) (3) • Estimating sums, differences, products, or quotients. (F) • Choosing appropriate methods and tools to calculate (calculators, pencil and paper, or mental math). (1, 2, 7) • Developing mental math skills. (E, I, K, M) (1, 2) • Reducing fractions to lowest terms. (H, K, L) (1, 2) • Expressing a quotient as a mixed number. (F, K) (1, 2) • Multiplying a fraction and a whole number. (J) (3) • Multiplying fractions. (L) (3) • Adding fractions and mixed numbers. (H) (5) • Adding, subtracting, multiplying, or dividing whole numbers and decimals using paper and pencil. (F, K) (1, 2, 5) • Multiplying and dividing using multiples of 10. (E, I, M) • Dividing large numbers using a calculator. (2) • Solving problems involving addition, subtraction, multiplication, or division. (B, D) (5) • Solving problems involving fractions, decimals, or percents. (4, 7) • Using ratios and proportions to solve problems. (B) (6)	• Plotting points using ordered pairs in the four quadrants. (6) • Using ratios and proportions to solve problems. (B) (6) • Using unknowns to solve problems. (G, I)	• Plotting points using ordered pairs in the four quadrants. (6) • Making and testing conjectures about geometric properties. (C) • Measuring area. (D)	• Making and testing conjectures about geometric properties. (C) • Measuring area. (D) • Using geometric concepts and skills to solve problems. (B) (6)	

SCOPE & SEQUENCE CHART

Problem Solving	Reasoning and Proof	Communication	Connections	Representation
• Promoting these beliefs: Problems can be solved by more than one method and different methods should yield solutions that agree. • Solving multistep word problems. • Solving problems involving fractions. • Choosing appropriate methods and tools to calculate (calculators, pencil and paper, or mental math). • Choosing to find an estimate or exact answer.	• Using patterns to build number sense.		• Connecting mathematics and social studies to real-world situations: Appreciating George Washington Carver's contributions as a scientist and teacher.	• Adding fractions using pattern blocks and paper and pencil. • Adding mixed numbers using pattern blocks and paper and pencil. • Multiplying a fraction and a whole number using diagrams, pattern blocks, and paper and pencil. • Multiplying fractions using pattern blocks, paper folding, and paper and pencil.
• Solving problems involving addition, subtraction, multiplication, or division. (B, D) (5) • Solving problems involving fractions, decimals, or percents. (4) • Choosing appropriate methods and tools to calculate (calculators, pencil and paper, or mental math). (1, 2, 7) • Solving multistep word problems. (N) (7) • Using geometric concepts and skills to solve problems. (B) (6) • Using ratios and proportions to solve problems. (B) (6)	• Using ratios and proportions to solve problems. (B) • Making and testing conjectures using geometric properties. (C) • Explaining mathematical reasoning. (F) (1, 3, 7) • Using mathematical reasoning. (N)	• Explaining mathematical reasoning. (F) (1, 3, 7)		• Expressing a quotient as a mixed number. (F, K) (1, 2) • Plotting points using ordered pairs in the four quadrants. (6) • Using unknowns to solve problems. (G, I)

Scope and Sequence

TIG • Grade 5 • Scope and Sequence & the NCTM Principles and Standards • Scope and Sequence **159**

	Number and Operations	Algebra	Geometry	Measurement	Data Analysis and Probability
Unit 13: **Ratio and** **Proportion** **Lessons**	• Using words, tables, graphs, fractions, and colon notation to express ratios. • Choosing appropriate methods and tools to calculate (calculators, paper and pencil, or mental math).	• Using words, tables, graphs, fractions, and colon notation to express ratios. • Translating between different representations of ratios (graphical and symbolic). • Using ratios and proportions to solve problems. • Drawing and interpreting best-fit lines. • Using numerical variables. • Using patterns in data tables and graphs to solve problems. • Translating between graphs and real-world events.		• Measuring mass. • Measuring volume by displacement. • Defining density as a ratio. • Dealing with precision and accuracy.	• Collecting, organizing, graphing, and analyzing data. • Drawing and interpreting best-fit lines. • Using patterns in data tables and graphs to solve problems.
Daily Practice and Problems (Lettered) **& Home Practice** (Numbered)	• Maintaining fluency with the multiplication and division facts. (A, E, H, I, M, Q, S) (1) • Estimating sums, differences, products, or quotients. (N) (3) • Choosing appropriate methods and tools to calculate (calculators, pencil and paper, or mental math). (N) (5) • Comparing and ordering fractions, decimals, and percents. (2) • Using exponents. (A) • Developing mental math skills. (A, C, E, I, M, Q) • Using words, tables, graphs, and fractions to express ratios. (4) • Using fractions, decimals, or percents to represent the same quantity. (F, H) • Finding equivalent fractions. (2) • Reducing fractions to lowest terms. (B) • Expressing a quotient as a mixed number. (H) (3) • Adding, subtracting, multiplying, or dividing whole numbers, fractions, or decimals using paper and pencil. (B, N) (3) • Dividing using multiples of 10. (E, I, M) • Using ratios and proportions to solve problems. (G, O, T) (4, 5) • Solving problems involving money. (R) • Solving problems involving addition, subtraction, multiplication, or division. (R) (5) • Solving problems involving time. (D) • Solving problems involving fractions, decimals, or percents. (R)	• Drawing and interpreting best-fit lines. (4) • Using ratios and proportions to solve problems. (G, O, T) (4, 5) • Using unknowns to solve problems. (I, M) (2)	• Measuring angles. (L) • Using geometric concepts and skills to solve problems. (L)	• Measuring length in cm. (G) • Measuring angles. (L)	• Using data to solve problems. (J) (4) • Organizing, graphing, and analyzing data. (4) • Drawing and interpreting best-fit lines. (4) • Finding probabilities. (P)

Problem Solving	Reasoning and Proof	Communication	Connections	Representation
• Using ratios and proportions to solve problems. • Choosing appropriate methods and tools to calculate (calculators, pencil and paper, or mental math). • Solving problems in more than one way. • Using patterns in data tables and graphs to make predictions and solve problems.	• Using ratios and proportions to solve problems. • Communicating solutions verbally and in writing.	• Using words, tables, graphs, fractions, and colon notation to express ratios. • Communicating solutions verbally and in writing.	• Using words, tables, graphs, fractions, and colon notation to express ratios. • Translating between different representations of ratios (graphical and symbolic). • Connecting mathematics and science to real-world situations: investigating density. • Connecting measurement, data analysis, and proportional reasoning. • Translating between graphs and real-world events.	• Using words, tables, graphs, fractions, and colon notation to express ratios. • Using numerical variables. • Translating between different representations of ratios (graphical and symbolic). • Translating between graphs and real-world events.
• Solving problems involving addition, subtraction, multiplication, or division. (R) (5) • Choosing appropriate methods and tools to calculate (calculators, pencil and paper, or mental math). (5) • Solving multistep word problems. (N) • Solving problems involving fractions, decimals, or percents. (R) • Using ratios and proportions to solve problems. (G, O, T) (4, 5) • Solving problems involving time. (D) • Using geometric concepts and skills to solve problems. (L) • Solving problems involving money. (R)	• Using ratios and proportions to solve problems. (G, O, T) (4, 5) • Using mathematical reasoning. (K) • Explaining mathematical reasoning. (N)	• Explaining mathematical reasoning. (N)	• Connecting mathematics and science. (4)	• Expressing a quotient as a mixed number. (H) (3) • Organizing, graphing, and analyzing data. (4) • Using exponents. (A) • Using fractions, decimals, and percents to represent the same quantity. (F, H) • Using unknowns to solve problems. (I, M) (2) • Using words, tables, graphs, and fractions to express ratios. (4)

	Number and Operations	Algebra	Geometry	Measurement	Data Analysis and Probability
Unit 14: Using Circles **Lessons**	• Defining π as the ratio of circumference to diameter. • Using words, tables, graphs, and fractions to express ratios. • Using fractions, decimals, and percents to represent the same quantity. • Choosing appropriate methods and tools to calculate (calculators, paper and pencil, or mental math).	• Defining π as the ratio of circumference to diameter. • Using variables in formulas. • Finding and expressing the relationship between the circumference and diameter of circles: $C = \pi \times D$. • Drawing and interpreting best-fit lines. • Translating between graphs and real-world events.	• Identifying the parts of a circle. • Finding and expressing the relationship between the circumference and diameter of circles: $C = \pi \times D$. • Finding the circumference of a circle. • Defining π as the ratio of circumference to diameter. • Drawing circles using rulers, protractors, and compasses. • Constructing simple figures with rulers, protractors, and compasses. • Making and interpreting circle graphs.	• Measuring length in centimeters. • Dealing with precision and accuracy. • Finding the circumference of a circle.	• Collecting, organizing, graphing, and analyzing data. • Drawing and interpreting best-fit lines. • Making and interpreting circle graphs. • Translating between graphs and real-world events.
Daily Practice and Problems (Lettered) **& Home Practice** (Numbered)	• Maintaining fluency with the multiplication and division facts. (E, G, K, O, S, W) • Developing number sense (D, H) • Estimating sums, differences, products, or quotients. (B, L) (1, 3) • Understanding place value. (C) (5) • Choosing appropriate methods and tools to calculate (calculators, pencil and paper, or mental math). (6) • Developing mental math skills. (B, C, G, O, Q, S) (2, 5) • Finding the prime factorization of a number. (P) • Using order of operations. (2) • Writing improper fractions as mixed numbers. (T) (5) • Reducing fractions to lowest terms. (B, T) • Adding, subtracting, multiplying, or dividing whole numbers and fractions using paper and pencil. (B, C, D, L, Q, R, S, T) (1, 2, 4, 5, 6) • Solving problems involving addition, subtraction, multiplication, or division. (D, I, L, R, S) (2, 4, 5) • Solving problems with unknowns. (J, K, N) (4) • Solving problems with functions. (J, N) (4) • Solving multistep word problems. (R) • Solving problems involving time. (A)	• Understanding the relationship between circumference and diameter. (I, M) (3) • Solving problems with functions. (J, N) (4) • Plotting points using ordered pairs in the four quadrants. (V) • Understanding translations in the four quadrants. (V) • Solving problems with unknowns. (J, K, N) (4)	• Understanding the relationship between circumference and diameter. (I, M) (3) • Identifying the properties of a circle. (U) • Drawing circles using rulers, protractors, and compasses. (U) • Plotting points using ordered pairs in the four quadrants. (V) • Understanding translations in the four quadrants. (V) • Using geometric concepts and skills to solve problems. (I, M)	• Understanding the relationship between circumference and diameter. (I, M) (3)	• Finding the mean of a data set. (F)

Problem Solving	Reasoning and Proof	Communication	Connections	Representation
• Solving problems involving circles. • Solving multistep word problems. • Choosing appropriate methods and tools to calculate (calculators, paper and pencil, or mental math).	• Finding and expressing the relationship between the circumference and diameter of circles: $C = \pi \times D$.	• Using words, tables, graphs, and fractions to express ratios. • Using fractions, decimals, and percents to represent the same quantity.	• Connecting mathematics and science: interpreting circle graphs about endangered species.	• Using words, tables, graphs, and fractions to express ratios. • Using fractions, decimals, and percents to represent the same quantity. • Using variables in formulas. • Finding and expressing the relationship between the circumference and diameter of circles: $C = \pi \times D$. • Drawing circles using rulers, protractors, and compasses.
• Solving problems involving addition, subtraction, multiplication, or division. (D, L, Q, S) (1, 2, 4, 5) • Solving problems with functions. (J, N) (4) • Choosing appropriate methods and tools to calculate (calculators, pencil and paper, or mental math). (6) • Solving multistep word problems. (R, X) (6) • Using geometric concepts and skills to solve problems. (I, M) • Solving problems with unknowns. (J, K, N) (4) • Using mathematical reasoning. (X)	• Explaining mathematical reasoning. (H, M, X) (1)	• Explaining mathematical reasoning. (H, M, X) (1)		• Comparing and ordering fractions, decimals, or percents using symbols. (D)

	Number and Operations	Algebra	Geometry	Measurement	Data Analysis and Probability
Unit 15: Developing Formulas with Geometry **Lessons**	• Using the correct order of operations. • Using exponents. • Using fractions and decimals to find area and perimeter.	• Developing formulas for finding the perimeters of rectangles and the areas of triangles. • Finding the area of rectangles and triangles using formulas. • Finding the perimeter of rectangles using formulas. • Using variables in formulas. • Solving multistep word problems.	• Identifying the legs and hypotenuse of a right triangle. • Identifying the base and height (altitude) of a triangle. • Finding the area of polygons by counting square units. • Developing formulas for finding the perimeter of rectangles and the area of triangles. • Finding the area of rectangles and triangles using formulas. • Finding the perimeter of rectangles using formulas. • Measuring the perimeter of polygons. • Using geometric concepts and skills to solve problems.	• Measuring length in centimeters. • Finding the area of polygons by counting square units. • Finding the area of rectangles and triangles using formulas. • Finding the perimeter of rectangles using formulas. • Measuring the perimeter of polygons.	
Daily Practice and Problems (Lettered) **& Home Practice** (Numbered)	• Maintaining fluency with the multiplication and division facts. (E, I) (1) • Developing number sense. (3) • Understanding place value. (3) • Estimating sums, differences, products, or quotients. (D) (5) • Choosing appropriate methods and tools to calculate (calculators, pencil and paper, or mental math). (6) • Adding, subtracting, multiplying, or dividing using a paper-and-pencil method. (D, F) (1, 3, 5) • Developing mental math skills. (A, P) (1, 2, 5) • Using order of operations. (F) (2) • Expressing a quotient as a mixed number. (5) • Using ratios and proportion to solve problems. (H) • Solving problems involving addition, subtraction, multiplication, or division. (C) (1, 3, 4, 5) • Solving problems with unknowns. (I) (2) • Solving problems about time. (B) • Solving problems using percents. (K)	• Solving problems with unknowns. (I) (2) • Using formulas to find the area of rectangles and triangles. (C, H, J) (4)	• Finding the area of rectangles and triangles using formulas. (C, H, J) (4, 6) • Making and interpreting circle graphs. (K) • Using geometric concepts, skills, and formulas to solve problems. (G, J) (4, 6)	• Finding the area of rectangles and triangles using formulas. (C, H, J) (4, 6)	• Making and interpreting circle graphs. (K)

Problem Solving	Reasoning and Proof	Communication	Connections	Representation
• Using geometric concepts and skills to solve problems. • Solving multistep word problems. • Choosing appropriate methods and tools to calculate (calculators, paper and pencil, or mental math). • Communicating solutions orally and in writing.	• Developing formulas for finding the perimeters of rectangles and the areas of triangles.	• Communicating solutions verbally and in writing.		• Developing formulas for finding the perimeters of rectangles and the areas of triangles. • Using variables in formulas. • Using exponents.
• Solving problems involving addition, subtraction, multiplication, or division. (C, D) (1, 3, 5) • Solving problems with unknowns. (I) (2) • Choosing appropriate methods and tools to calculate (calculators, pencil and paper, or mental math). (6) • Solving multistep word problems. (L) (6) • Using ratios to solve problems. (H) • Using geometric concepts, skills, and formulas to solve problems. (G, J) (4) • Using ratios and proportions to solve problems. (H) • Solving problems using percents. (K)	• Explaining mathematical reasoning. (A) (5) • Using mathematical reasoning. (L)	• Explaining mathematical reasoning. (A) (5)		• Translating between written and pictorial representations of data. (K)

	Number and Operations	Algebra	Geometry	Measurement	Data Analysis and Probability
Unit 16: Bringing It All Together: An Assessment Unit **Lessons**	• Using words, tables, graphs, and fractions to express ratios. • Using ratios and proportions to solve problems. • Identifying and describing number patterns. • Finding equal ratios.	• Comparing and contrasting elements of different laboratory investigations: problems solved, types of graphs, and variables. • Using words, tables, graphs, and fractions to express ratios. • Translating between different representations of ratios (graphical and symbolic). • Finding equal ratios. • Drawing and interpreting best-fit lines. • Translating between graphs and real-world events. • Using ratios and proportions to solve problems. • Using numerical variables. • Identifying and describing number patterns. • Using patterns to make predictions and solve problems.		• Comparing and contrasting elements of different laboratory investigations: problems solved, types of graphs, and variables.	• Collecting, organizing, graphing, and analyzing data. • Drawing and interpreting best-fit lines. • Sampling a population. • Making predictions from samples.
Daily Practice and Problems (Lettered) **& Home Practice** (Numbered)	• Maintaining fluency with the multiplication and division facts. (E, G, I, O) • Estimating sums, differences, products, or quotients. (B, J, M) (1, 5) • Choosing appropriate methods and tools to calculate (calculators, pencil and paper, or mental math). (B, J, M) (1, 6) • Developing mental math skills. (B, I, J, M) (1, 5, 6) • Finding all the factors of numbers. (D) • Adding, subtracting, multiplying, or dividing whole numbers and fractions using paper and pencil. (B, J, M, T) (1, 5) • Expressing a quotient as a mixed number. (5) • Dividing using multiples of 10. (I) • Solving problems involving addition, subtraction, multiplication, or division. (A, N, T) (2, 3, 4, 6) • Using ratios and proportions to solve problems. (F, L, Q) • Solving problems involving fractions, decimals, and percents. (A, C, T) (2, 3)	• Understanding the relationship between circumference and diameter. (4) • Using ratios and proportions to solve problems. (F, L, Q) • Using a formula to find the circumference of a circle. (4) • Using unknowns to solve problems. (G, O, P) • Using patterns in tables to solve problems. (S, P)	• Understanding the relationship between circumference and diameter. (4) • Generalizing the area of a rectangle as length times width. (R) • Solving problems using geometric concepts and skills. (H, K, R)	• Understanding the relationship between circumference and diameter. (4) • Exploring density. (F) • Finding the circumference of circles. (4) • Using formulas to find area and perimeter of rectangles. (H, K, R) (4)	• Interpreting circle graphs. (C)

Problem Solving	Reasoning and Proof	Communication	Connections	Representation
• Using ratios and proportions to solve problems. • Solving open-ended problems and communicating solution strategies. • Solving problems in more than one way. • Making predictions from samples. • Using the *Solving* and *Telling* Rubrics to self-assess problem-solving skills. • Using patterns to make predictions and solve problems.	• Using ratios and proportions to solve problems. • Solving open-ended problems and communicating solution strategies. • Making predictions from samples. • Using patterns to make predictions and solve problems.	• Comparing and contrasting elements of different laboratory investigations: problems solved, types of graphs, and variables. • Using words, tables, graphs, fractions, and colon notation to express ratios. • Identifying and describing number patterns. • Solving open-ended problems and communicating solution strategies. • Using the *Solving* and *Telling* Rubrics to self-assess problem-solving skills. • Using portfolios.	• Comparing and contrasting elements of different laboratory investigations: problems solved, types of graphs, and variables. • Connecting mathematics and science to real-world situations: estimating the number of animals in a population. • Using words, tables, graphs, and fractions to express ratios. • Translating between different representations of ratios (graphical and symbolic). • Translating between graphs and real-world events.	• Using words, tables, graphs, and fractions to express ratios. • Translating between graphs and real-world events. • Using numerical variables. • Translating between different representations of ratios (graphical and symbolic). • Translating between graphs and real-world events.
• Solving problems involving addition, subtraction, multiplication, or division of whole numbers and fractions. (A, N, T) (2, 3, 4, 6) • Choosing appropriate methods and tools to calculate (calculators, pencil and paper, or mental math). (B, J, M) (1, 5, 6) • Solving multistep word problems. (A, L, N, T) (6) • Using ratios and proportions to solve problems. (F, L, Q) • Solving problems with functions. (P, S) • Solving problems using geometric concepts and skills. (H, K, R) (4) • Using patterns in tables to solve problems. (P, S) • Solving problems involving fractions, decimals, and percents. (A, C, T) (2, 3)	• Using mathematical reasoning. (D, F) • Using ratios and proportions to solve problems. (F, L, Q)		• Connecting mathematics and science. (F)	• Interpreting circle graphs. (C) • Using unknowns to solve problems. (G, O, P) • Using a formula to find the circumference of a circle. (4)

Math Facts and Whole-Number Operations

The Math Facts and Whole-Number Operations section outlines the *Math Trailblazers* approach to developing fluency with the math facts and whole-number operations.

Calculators are used as a tool for solving problems.

Math Facts and Whole-Number Operations

Work with whole numbers pervades the elementary mathematics curriculum. A major goal of *Math Trailblazers* is to prepare students to compute accurately, flexibly, and appropriately in all situations. Standard topics in arithmetic—acquisition of basic math facts and fluency with whole-number operations—are covered extensively.

In this section, we briefly describe our approach to developing fluency with the math facts and whole-number operations. Table 1 outlines the development of these two topics in Grades K–5. We also summarize below the fundamental characteristics of our work with whole numbers. You can obtain more detailed information from the following sources:

- Two TIMS Tutors *Arithmetic* and *Math Facts;* and
- Background sections and lesson guides from individual *Math Trailblazers* units.

Introduction to the Math Facts in *Math Trailblazers*

In developing our program for the math facts, we sought a careful balance between strategies and drill. This approach is based on a large body of research and is advocated by the NCTM *Principles and Standards for School Mathematics*. The research indicates that the methods used in the *Math Trailblazers* math facts program lead to more effective learning and better retention of the math facts and also helps develop essential math skills.

The *Math Trailblazers* program for teaching the math facts is characterized by these elements:

- *Early emphasis on problem solving.* Students first approach the basic facts as problems to solve rather than as facts to memorize. Students invent their own strategies to solve these problems or learn appropriate strategies from others through class discussion. Students' natural strategies, especially for counting, are explicitly encouraged. In this way, students learn that math is more than memorizing facts and rules that "you either get or you don't."
- *De-emphasis of rote work.* Fluency with the math facts is an important component of any student's mathematical learning. Research shows, however, that overemphasizing memorization and frequent timed tests are counterproductive. We encourage the use of strategies to find facts, so students become confident they can find answers to fact problems that they do not immediately recall.
- *Gradual and systematic introduction of facts.* Students study the facts in small groups of problems that can be solved using similar strategies. Students first work on simple strategies for easy facts and then progress to more sophisticated strategies and harder facts. By the end of the process, they gain fluency with all the required facts.

- *Ongoing practice.* Work on the math facts is distributed throughout the curriculum, especially in the Daily Practice and Problems (Grades 1–5), Home Practice (Grades 3–5), and games. This practice for fluency, however, takes place only after students have a conceptual understanding of the operations and have achieved proficiency with strategies for solving basic fact problems. Delaying practice in this way means that less practice is required to achieve fluency.

- *Appropriate assessment.* Teachers assess students' knowledge of the facts through observations as they work on activities, labs, and games as well as through the appropriate use of written tests and quizzes. Beginning in first grade, periodic, short quizzes in the Daily Practice and Problems naturally follow the study of small groups of facts organized around specific strategies. As self-assessment in Grades 3–5, each student records his or her progress on *Facts I Know* charts and determines which facts he or she needs to study. Inventory tests of all facts for each operation are used sparingly in Grades 2–5 (no more than twice per year) to assess students' progress with fact fluency. The goal of the math facts assessment program is to determine whether students can find answers to fact problems quickly and accurately and retain this skill over time.

- *Multiyear approach.* In Grades 1 and 2, *Math Trailblazers* emphasizes strategies that lead to fluency with the addition and subtraction facts. In Grade 3, students gain fluency with the multiplication facts while reviewing the addition and subtraction facts. In Grade 4, students achieve fluency with the division facts and verify fluency with the multiplication facts. In Grade 5, the multiplication and division facts are systematically reviewed and assessed. This is outlined in Table 1.

- *Facts are not gatekeepers.* Students are not prevented from learning more complex mathematics because they do not perform well on fact tests. Use of strategies, calculators, and other math tools (e.g., manipulatives, hundreds charts, printed multiplication tables) allows students to continue to work on interesting problems and important mathematical concepts while still learning the facts.

Whole-Number Operations in *Math Trailblazers*

Math Trailblazers helps students develop efficient and accurate methods for computation with the four basic operations. The treatment of whole-number computation proceeds in several stages. The grade levels for the stages vary with the operation—full development of division, for example, comes long after addition—but the general pattern is similar for all the operations. Roughly speaking, the stages are:

- developing meaning for the operation,
- inventing procedures for solving problems, and
- becoming more efficient at carrying out procedures, all leading to
- developing mathematical power.

Developing mathematical power with an operation means that students understand *when* to apply the operation and *how* to use varied computational methods to solve problems, even complex or nonroutine problems.

With each operation, we seek a balance between conceptual understanding and procedural skill. Standard methods for solving problems are not introduced until students develop good conceptual and procedural understandings. Research has shown that introducing such procedures too early may short-circuit students' common sense, encouraging mechanical and uncritical behavior. As a result, formal instruction in some standard procedures is delayed slightly beyond the traditional time, but problems that would normally be solved by standard procedures are often introduced sooner than is customary. This forces students to use their prior knowledge to devise their own methods to solve the problems.

Students practice using the operations in activities, games, and laboratory investigations. More practice is provided in the Daily Practice and Problems in Grades 1–5 and in the Home Practice in Grades 3–5. Even after analyzing and practicing standard methods, students are still encouraged to solve problems in more than one way. Flexible thinking and mathematical power are our goals, not rote fluency with a handful of standard algorithms.

The *Math Trailblazers* approach to all mathematics topics promotes the coordinated development of both procedural skill and conceptual understanding. This is particularly apparent in our approach to computation.

The following table describes the development of math facts and whole-number operations in *Math Trailblazers*. The shaded portions of the table highlight development of the math facts program in each grade. Expectations for fluency with math facts are indicated in bold. The white portions of the table highlight development of the whole-number operations.

Grade	Addition	Subtraction	Multiplication	Division
K	Introduce concepts through problem solving and use of manipulatives.			
1	Develop strategies for addition facts.	Develop strategies for subtraction facts.	Develop concepts through problem solving and use of manipulatives.	
	Solve addition problems in context.	Solve subtraction problems in context.		
2	Continue use of addition facts in problems. Continue use of strategies for addition facts. **Assess for fluency with addition facts.**	Continue use of subtraction facts in problems. Continue use of strategies for subtraction facts. **Assess for fluency with subtraction facts.**	Continue concept development through problem solving and use of manipulatives.	
	Continue solving addition problems in context. Introduce procedures for multidigit addition using manipulatives and paper and pencil.	Continue solving subtraction problems in context. Introduce procedures for multidigit subtraction using manipulatives and paper and pencil.		
3	Diagnose and remediate with addition facts as needed.	Maintain fluency with subtraction facts through review and assessment.	Continue use of multiplication facts in problems. Develop strategies for multiplication facts. **Assess for fluency with multiplication facts.**	Continue use of division facts in problems. Develop strategies for division facts.
	Develop procedures for multidigit addition using manipulatives and paper and pencil. Practice and apply multidigit addition in varied contexts.	Develop procedures for multidigit subtraction using manipulatives and paper and pencil. Practice and apply multidigit subtraction in varied contexts.	Solve multiplication problems in context. Introduce paper-and-pencil multiplication (1-digit $\times$ 2-digits).	Continue concept development. Solve division problems in context.
4	Diagnose and remediate with addition facts as needed.	Diagnose and remediate with subtraction facts as needed.	Maintain fluency with multiplication facts through review and assessment.	Continue use of division facts in problems. Continue development of strategies for division facts. **Assess for fluency with division facts.**
	Practice and apply multidigit addition in varied contexts. Review paper-and-pencil procedures for multidigit addition.	Practice and apply multidigit subtraction in varied contexts. Review paper-and-pencil procedures for multidigit subtraction.	Develop procedures for multiplication using manipulatives and paper and pencil (1-digit and 2-digit multipliers). Practice and apply multiplication in varied contexts.	Solve division problems in context. Develop procedures for division using manipulatives and paper and pencil (1-digit divisors).
5	Diagnose and remediate with addition facts as needed.	Diagnose and remediate with subtraction facts as needed.	Maintain fluency with multiplication facts through review and assessment.	Maintain fluency with division facts through review and assessment.
	Practice and apply multidigit addition in varied contexts.	Practice and apply multidigit subtraction in varied contexts.	Review paper-and-pencil procedures. Practice and apply multiplication in varied contexts.	Develop paper-and-pencil procedures (1-digit and 2-digit divisors). Practice and apply division in varied contexts.

Table 1: *Math Facts and Whole-Number Operations Overview*

Daily Practice and Problems and Home Practice Guide

The Daily Practice and Problems (DPP) and Home Practice (HP) Guide explains the purpose and use of the DPP and HP within the curriculum.

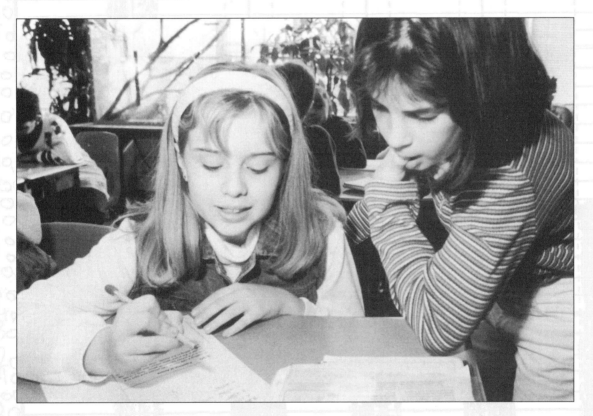

Students work cooperatively to solve a problem from the Daily Practice and Problems.

Daily Practice and Problems and Home Practice Guide

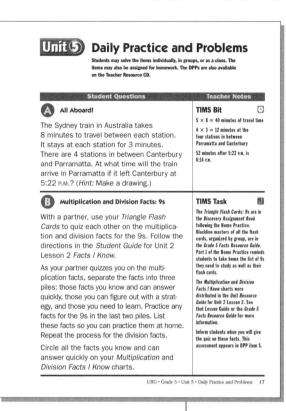

Figure 1: *DPP pages*

Daily Practice and Problems

The Daily Practice and Problems (DPP) is a set of short exercises that provides ongoing review, practice, and study of math concepts and skills. These exercises are in each *Unit Resource Guide* immediately preceding the lesson guides and on the *Teacher Resource CD*. The DPP should become a routine part of daily instruction since the problems serve several important functions in the curriculum:

- They provide distributed practice in computation and a structure for systematic study of the basic math facts.
- They develop concepts and skills such as number sense, telling time, and working with money throughout the year; and
- They review topics from earlier units, presenting concepts in new contexts and linking ideas from unit to unit.

There are three types of items: Bits, Tasks, and Challenges. Bits are short and should take no more than 5 or 10 minutes to complete. They often provide practice with a skill or the basic math facts. Tasks take 10 or 15 minutes to complete. Challenges usually take longer than 15 minutes to complete and the problems are more thought-provoking. Use them to stretch students' problem-solving skills.

Two DPP items are included for each class session listed on the Unit Outline. The first item is always a Bit and the second is either a Task or a Challenge. Each item is composed of Student Questions and Teacher Notes as shown in Figure 1.

The Teacher Notes give the answers and often discuss possible problem-solving strategies. Eight icons designate the subject matter of the problems. See Figure 2.

The Scope and Sequence chart in Section 5 of the *Teacher Implementation Guide* lists the topics covered in the DPP in each unit. This chart correlates the items in the DPP to the standards from the National Council of Teachers of Mathematics *Principles and Standards for School Mathematics*. Teachers can use this chart to track the development of a particular standard throughout third grade and locate items on particular topics to use for review, extra practice, or enrichment. For example, by looking at the Number and Operations column, teachers can follow the sequence of items providing computation and facts practice. By looking at the Measurement column in the same way, teachers can find all the items that deal with measuring length and area. For a specific description of the study and assessment of the math facts as organized in the DPP, see the TIMS Tutor: *Math Facts*.

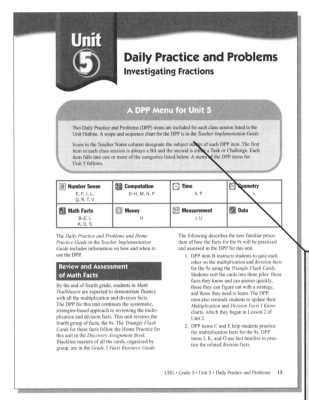

Grades 1–5 — Each set of DPP includes a Teacher's Guide which often provides specific information on the study and assessment of the math facts in the current unit.

Figure 2: *DPP icons and DPP menu on a DPP page*

Eight icons indicate the subject matter of each problem:

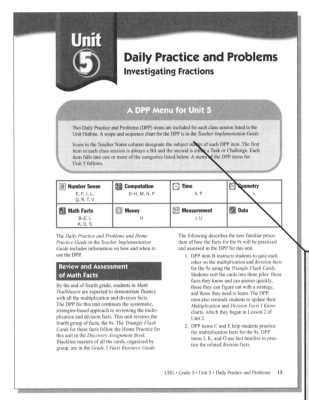 **Number Sense** (estimating, partitioning numbers, skip counting, etc.);

Math Facts (practice with addition, subtraction, multiplication, and division facts);

Computation (problems that may be solved using paper-and-pencil methods, estimation, mental math, or calculators);

$ Money (counting change, combining various coins, and estimating total cost);

Time (telling time, solving problems involving elapsed time);

Measurement (measuring length, area, mass, volume, and time);

Geometry (work with shapes, coordinates, and other geometric topics); and

Data (collecting, organizing, graphing, and analyzing data).

How to Use the Daily Practice and Problems

The Suggestions for Teaching the Lesson section and the At a Glance in most lessons provide suggestions on how and when to use each DPP item. These are only suggestions. The following provides further description on how to incorporate the DPP into your math instruction.

Assign a Bit each day to provide students with the review and fact practice they need. Bits are short, quick questions that need little instruction from the teacher. Students should be able to complete them independently. For many problems, it will be appropriate for students to work in pairs or groups. For other items such as facts quizzes, students should answer the questions individually. If students take more than 5 or 10 minutes to complete the problems, they are probably unfamiliar with a topic. For example, items intended to review second-grade topics may be new to students who are using *Math Trailblazers* for the first time in third grade. If students need more instruction on the material presented in the DPP, defer the problems and the instruction until a later date, possibly during an upcoming unit that covers similar subject matter.

Choose from the Tasks and Challenges as time permits according to the interests and needs of your students. Tasks can extend a topic or provide extra practice. Challenges can provide enrichment for those students who need less skill practice and are ready for more complex problems. Not all students will be able to complete all the Tasks and Challenges, but all should have the opportunity to try.

Teachers use the Daily Practice and Problems in many ways. Many problems can easily be written on the board or displayed using an overhead projector. Items can also be photocopied or printed (without the teacher portion) from the *Teacher Resource CD* and distributed to students daily, or several items can be stapled together in a packet and distributed weekly. For many items (such as facts practice or mental arithmetic), it is appropriate for students to just write answers on scrap paper. For others (such as skip counting), students can respond orally. One way to establish routines is to have students use their math journals for any written responses. This will also preserve a record of their work. Teacher notes sometimes recommend conducting a discussion of students' problem-solving strategies. These discussions are an important part of the problem-solving process, but they need not be extensive since topics are revisited many times.

When to Use the Daily Practice and Problems

At the Beginning of Math Class. Use Bits and other DPP items to begin class and focus students' attention on mathematics. Students immediately answer the questions and then the class can discuss the answers before they begin work on the current lesson. Alternatively, the teacher can assign the items at the beginning of a lesson and students can solve the problems as they have time during class. This is especially effective if students are collecting data for an experiment and have to take turns using equipment.

During Daily Routines. Bits can be used as part of morning (or afternoon) routines that also include taking the roll, calendar work, language arts practice, or geography questions. A "Problem of the Day" can also be part of the daily routine in which the teacher presents students with a Task or a Challenge that they can work on throughout the day or take home to complete for homework or as extra credit. For some Tasks and Challenges, it may be appropriate to ask students to describe their problem-solving process.

During Transition Times. You can use many items, especially practice with the math facts, during transition times throughout the day. Possible times include when students have completed an assignment, when money or permission slips are being collected, when an activity is delayed, or when an activity ends earlier than expected.

As Homework or Assessment. You can also assign problems for homework or use them for short assessments. See the TIMS Tutor: *Math Facts* for information on facts assessment in the DPP and the Assessment Overview in Part VI of the Assessment section for specific locations of Facts Quizzes and Fact Self-Assessment in the DPP.

Home Practice

The Home Practice (HP) is a series of problems that supplement the homework included in the lessons. The HP, like the DPP, distributes skill practice throughout the units and reviews concepts studied in previous units. For each unit, the *Discovery Assignment Book* begins with problems divided into different parts as shown in Figure 3.

How to Use the Home Practice

The At Glance in many lessons provides guidance for how and when to use the Home Practice. Here are further suggestions.

One way to assign the HP is to send all parts home with students at some point during the unit. Students are responsible for completing the pages and returning them on a given day. This schedule allows flexibility for the teacher, students, and students' families. If some evenings are filled with athletic practices, meetings, family commitments, or the completion of other homework, students can choose their own times to work on the HP.

The HP is designed to be used in addition to (not as a replacement for) the unit homework. Since some parts may include content directly related to the current unit, often it is not appropriate to assign these parts during the first week of the unit. Rather, use such HP items after students solve similar problems in class.

Another way to occasionally use the HP is for the teacher (or parents) to complete one or more parts of the assignment. The adult makes some intentional mistakes and shows how he or she solved the problems. Then, students grade the adult's work, justifying the number of points awarded to each problem.

From time to time, teachers may ask students to reflect on how they completed the HP either in a short paragraph attached to the homework or in math journals. Did they need help? Who helped them? Did the helper give them new strategies for solving problems? How did they organize their time?

Figure 3: *Home Practice pages*

Calculations: Paper-and-Pencil, Calculators, Mental Math, or Estimation?

The HP provides many opportunities for practice of computational skills. Practice of paper-and-pencil calculations is emphasized throughout the HP. However, besides developing skill with paper-and-pencil computations, students also need to be able to choose when it is appropriate to use paper-and-pencil procedures, calculators, mental math, or estimation.

The following problem serves as an example:

> *The Student Council is selling 1000 pencils to make money for a school project. They have already sold 450 pencils. How many more do they have to sell?*

Students may use paper-and-pencil procedures, but subtracting across zeros is difficult and not particularly efficient. They may estimate that the student council needs to sell about 500 more, but a more exact answer is probably needed in this situation. Using a calculator is possible, but probably not necessary. Using a mental math strategy of counting up is effective and efficient. (Count up 50 from 450 to 500, then count up 500 more to 1000 to arrive at the answer of 550 pencils.) Before sending home the HP, you may discuss the possible strategies for particular problems and whether or not it is appropriate to use a calculator or another method of calculating. For more information on helping students choose appropriate strategies for computation, see the TIMS Tutor: *Arithmetic* in Section 9 of the *Teacher Implementation Guide.*

Assessment

The Assessment section details the philosophy, goals, and components of assessment in the curriculum.

A teacher and her students assess their work on a problem.

Assessment

 PART I

Philosophy of the Assessment Program in *Math Trailblazers*

Assessment in *Math Trailblazers* is ongoing and reflects the program's content and goals. Throughout the program, assessment serves several purposes:

- It helps teachers learn about students' thinking and knowledge. This information is then used to guide instruction.
- It communicates the instruction goals to students, parents, and others.
- It informs students, parents, and others about progress toward these goals.

The assessment program is built around two main principles: assessment should reflect the breadth and balance of the curriculum; and assessment activities should be valuable educational experiences.

Alignment with Goals

The National Council of Teachers of Mathematics (NCTM) *Principles and Standards for School Mathematics* describes the understanding, concepts, and skills students need to acquire. These principles and standards call for a mathematically rich curriculum for all students. The curriculum must teach a broad range of content and develop mathematical processes including problem solving, reasoning, and communication.

Math Trailblazers is designed to meet recommendations in the *Principles and Standards.* As such, the program requires significant shifts in emphases relative to a traditional program—changes in content, learning, teaching, evaluation, and expectations. The implications with regard to student assessment are also significant. We can no longer focus narrowly on the assessment of only isolated skills and procedures, using single sources of information at the end of a learning cycle. Instead, assessment needs to shift toward collecting information over the course of the year from a variety of sources, covering a wide range of mathematical content, and incorporating the rich problem-solving situations that are characteristic of the curriculum. The NCTM *Principles and Standards for School Mathematics* describes this as follows:

> *Many assessment techniques can be used by mathematics teachers, including open-ended questions, constructed-response tasks, selected-response items, performance tasks, observations, conversations, journals, and portfolios.* (NCTM, 2000, p. 23)

Integral with Instruction

Assessment is an integral part of instruction. All assessment activities are valuable educational experiences that have their own merit. By making assessment both integral to instruction and reflective of the overall mathematical content of the curriculum, we communicate what we value in mathematics. Again, the NCTM *Principles and Standards* addresses this idea:

> *To ensure deep, high-quality learning for all students, assessment and instruction must be integrated so that assessment becomes a routine part of ongoing classroom activity rather than an interruption.* (NCTM, 2000, p. 23)

Our assessment program gives teachers frequent opportunities to assess student progress. It assesses concepts and skills in many different ways but especially within the context of solving problems. Assessments are designed to elicit more than just an answer. In solving problems, students show their thinking and give a picture of their understanding of mathematical concepts, strategies, tools, and procedures.

Integrating assessment with instruction has significant implications for the structure of the assessment program. There is no separate assessment book; assessment activities and other components of the assessment program are fully integrated into units. Furthermore, because much of the curriculum's content is revisited many times in varying contexts, students are assessed many times on many concepts. This flavors both instruction and assessment. Teachers can focus on student progress since they know there will be other opportunities to review and assess and thus do not expect mastery at every juncture. At the same time, students' mathematical progress is not put on hold until they pass any particular assessment.

Balanced Assessment

The assessment program reflects the curriculum's instruction in another important way: it is varied and balanced. The *Math Trailblazers* curriculum is balanced across several dimensions:

- **Math Content.** The program incorporates a broad range of mathematical content and procedures, and connections between different topics abound.
- **Communication.** Students are expected to communicate their mathematical work and represent mathematical ideas in many different ways, such as written and oral explanations, number sentences, tables, graphs, pictures, and models.

- **Student Groupings.** Students work individually, in pairs, and in small groups.
- **Length of Activities.** There are short activities (5–15 minutes), tasks that take a full class period, and longer investigations that take several days.
- **Amount of Teacher Direction.** Some activities involve considerable teacher direction; others are more student-directed.
- **Varied Contexts.** Mathematics is presented in a variety of contexts, such as laboratory experiments, real-life settings, word problems, and numerical problems.

Our assessment program is balanced in similar ways. A balanced assessment program gives each student an opportunity to demonstrate what he or she knows by allowing multiple approaches. It covers a wide range of content, allows access to tools when appropriate, varies the difficulty and pedagogy, and assesses within different kinds of contexts.

Using multiple sources of evidence improves the validity of judgments made about students' learning. With more than one source of information about students' progress, strengths in one source can compensate for weaknesses in others. It also helps teachers judge the consistency of students' mathematical work. (NCTM, 2000, p. 24)

Promoting Student Reflection

Assessment activities in *Math Trailblazers* do more than provide momentary snapshots of a student's progress. Students are often asked to revise work based on commonly understood criteria for excellence. In Grades K–2, these criteria are communicated largely by the teachers. Beginning in Grade 3, the Student Rubrics provide an additional source of information to students about what is expected of them. As students become more involved in the assessment process, they become more reflective and can make constructive, critical judgments about their work and the work of others.

Components in Grades 1–5

Watching students grow intellectually throughout the school year is one of the great satisfactions of teaching. The components of the assessment program provide teachers with the tools necessary to document students' progress over time as they acquire skills and concepts, develop their abilities to solve problems, and learn to communicate their thinking. While most components are included at all grade levels, the assessment program does vary from grade to grade based on the students' needs.

All materials provided to assess student learning are located in the units, either in the student materials or the *Unit Resource Guide.* Each unit contains assessment ideas and activities appropriate for the unit's content and goals. Many components are also available in electronic form on the *Teacher Resource CD.* This section describes the following components:

Observational Assessment
Assessment Indicators
Observational Assessment Record
Individual Assessment Record Sheet

Written Assessments
Assessment Pages
Math Journals
Assessment Section in
  the Lesson Guide
Assessment Lessons
  Assessment Labs
  Open-Response Problems
  Tests
Assessment Units
Portfolios
Facts Assessment

Observational Assessment

Teachers have always assessed student learning through informal classroom observations, thus integrating instruction and assessment. The NCTM *Principles and Standards* confirms the importance of these observations.

Observations and conversations in the classroom can provide insights into students' thinking, and teachers can monitor changes in students' thinking and reasoning over time with reflective journals and portfolios. (NCTM, 2000, p. 24)

Teachers use the information gathered from classroom observations to guide instruction. While watching, questioning, and listening to students, they make moment-to-moment instructional decisions that change the direction and emphasis of the lesson. Teacher evaluation of student responses during a lesson will also affect the content of succeeding lessons.

Teachers can also use classroom observations to evaluate student achievement and monitor student progress. Skills such as using a graduated cylinder to measure volume, habits such as estimating regularly to check results, and behaviors such as working effectively within a group are best assessed through observing students at work. Assessing students through observation is especially important in the primary grades, because students at this age can often communicate their thinking very well in a discussion, but not always in writing. Also, what we assess becomes what we value. If we only assess written work, we may neglect other important behaviors such as verbal communication. Finding a manageable way to organize and record these observations is critical to an effective assessment program.

Each unit includes two tools to help teachers organize and document informal assessments: Assessment Indicators and the *Observational Assessment Record*.

Assessment Indicators

The Background for each unit in Grades 1–5 lists several Assessment Indicators that orient teachers to important skills, behavior, and knowledge they should assess in the unit. See Figure 1.

Assessment Indicators

- Can students group and count objects by twos, fives, and tens?
- Can students divide a collection of objects into groups of a given size and count the leftovers?
- Can students collect, organize, graph, and analyze data?
- Can students identify the relationships among pennies, nickels, and dimes?

Figure 1: *Assessment Indicators from Grade 1 Unit 5*

Observational Assessment Record

An *Observational Assessment Record* similar to the one shown for Grade 1 Unit 5 in Figure 2 follows the Background in each unit. The Assessment Indicators for that unit are listed at the top of each sheet. Each indicator is identified with an icon. An additional line is provided for teachers to include their own ideas. Each sheet has 32 rows for student names with columns for recording observations and extra space for comments. It is not necessary to record an observation about each child in each column. The grid provides a snapshot of the class's understanding of the unit's main concepts, procedures, and skills.

Observational Assessment Record

(A1) Can students group and count objects by twos, fives, and tens?
(A2) Can students divide a collection of objects into groups of a given size and count the leftovers?
(A3) Can students collect and organize data in a table?
(A4) Can students identify the relationships among pennies, nickels, and dimes?
(A5)

Name	A1	A2	A3	A4	A5	Comments
1.						
2.						
3.						
4.						
5.						
6.						
7.						
8.						
9.						
10.						
11.						
12.						
13.						

URG • Grade 1 • Unit 5 • Observational Assessment Record   9

Figure 2: *Sample* Observational Assessment Record *from Grade 1 Unit 5*

In first and second grade, the icons are also placed in the At a Glance sections of the Lesson Guides. These indicate which skills and concepts described in the Assessment Indicators teachers might assess during that particular lesson. Figure 3 is a sample At a Glance section from Grade 1 Unit 5 Lesson 2. The use of the icon **A1** shows that during this lesson teachers can assess students on their abilities to count objects by twos, fives, and tens.

Individual Assessment Record Sheets

Information from the *Observational Assessment Record* can be transferred to *Individual Assessment Record Sheets*. The *Individual Assessment Record Sheet* is located at the end of Part VI of this section and provides an organizational tool for compiling a year-long, anecdotal record for each child. Assessment Indicators for the entire year are listed by unit along with a line for comments as shown in Figure 4.

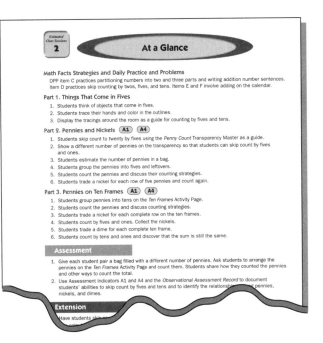

Figure 3: *Sample At a Glance from Grade 1 Unit 5 Lesson 2*

Figure 4: Observational Assessment Record *from Grade 5 Unit 1 and* Individual Assessment Record Sheet *from Grade 5*

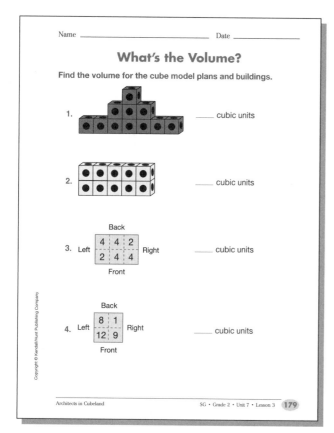

Figure 5: *Assessment Page from Grade 2 Unit 7*

Written Assessments

Assessment Pages

Many lessons in *Math Trailblazers* include short paper-and-pencil assessments that teachers can use to check skills or concepts developed in a unit. While teachers can use some assessment pages to assess students as they work in groups, they can often use these pages as quizzes to assess students individually. Checking student work gives both the teacher and the students feedback on their current abilities. The *What's the Volume?* Assessment Page from Grade 2 Unit 7 is shown in Figure 5. Students must combine their arithmetic skills with their measurement skills to complete the page correctly.

Math Journals

Students' entries in their math journals are a rich source of assessment information. Journal Prompts, a regular feature in the lesson guides, elicit information about students' understanding of specific concepts. Figure 6 shows an example of a Journal Prompt in Grade 5 Unit 1 Lesson 3.

A stream has an average depth of 1 meter. Can you wade across?

Figure 6: *A Journal Prompt from Grade 5 Unit 1 Lesson 3*

Figure 7: *A second-grade journal entry*

Regular journal writing provides teachers and parents with a means of documenting a student's growth in mathematical thinking, attitudes, and communication skills. (For information on math journals, see the TIMS Tutor: *Journals*.) Young children often begin by drawing pictures in their journals or combining pictures with a few words. The journal entry in Figure 7 is an early effort by Jayne, a second grader, at communicating her thoughts about a math lesson on doubling. Jayne used six circles and six squares to show two examples of doubling three. She also wrote a short paragraph about the class:

> *Today my class did some math. and we did some writ (write) some math too! I like it!*

Assessment Section

The Assessment section at the end of most lesson guides lists ideas for assessing the lesson's content. The following components are often recommended as assessment: Assessment Pages, Journal Prompts, classroom observations corresponding to the Assessment Indicators, and appropriate questions from the student pages and Homework sections. The teacher can also record the level of a student's response to these questions on the *Observational Assessment Record* or in a grade book. Figure 8 shows assessment for Grade 1 Unit 6 Lesson 2.

Assessment Lessons

Some units include specially designed assessment lessons. These lessons are generally one of three types: assessment labs, open-response problems, or written tests composed of short items. Each type provides different kinds of information to teachers so that they can develop and document a complete picture of their students' progress toward the curriculum's goals.

Assessment Labs

Two or three laboratory experiments in each grade are designated as assessment labs. Teachers can use them to assess students' abilities to work with a group on an investigation that takes several days. Teachers can also observe students to see if they are confident enough to tackle new ideas and to use previously learned mathematics in new contexts. Working on projects such as these—problems requiring integration and application of many concepts and skills over a period of time—more closely resembles the work of mathematicians and scientists (as well as working adults in many occupations) than any other kind of work students do in school. Suggestions for evaluating labs are included in Part III.

Open-Response Problems

In these lessons, students are given a task that requires them to demonstrate their problem-solving skills individually or while working in a group. Students are also assessed on their understanding of the mathematical content and their abilities to communicate their strategies. They must produce a product that allows teachers to examine their processes as well as their final answers. More than a few minutes are required to solve such a problem and students will often need a whole class period to find solutions and describe their strategies. To encourage students to give full explanations and improve their writing skills, teachers can comment on students' initial responses and ask them to make revisions. Part III includes rubrics for scoring student responses to these problems.

Math Facts Strategies

DPP item D provides practice with addition math facts.

Homework and Practice

- The *Two Car Roll-off* Homework Page shows a diagram of two cars that rolled down different ramps. Students count the links and compare the distances.
- DPP item C practices addition in a measurement context. For DPP item E, students estimate lengths of objects. Item F reviews even and odd numbers. Item G practices partitioning numbers. Students divide groups of cookies among 4 people and count leftovers. Item H asks students to solve problems using skip counting.

Assessment

- The *Brian's Class* Assessment Page asks students to examine the data for a fictional class. *Questions 1–4* are similar to questions found in the class discussion while *Question 5 is* a challenge.
- Use children's journal entries to assess whether students understand the connection between "fairness" and controlled variables.
- Use the *Observational Assessment Record* to record students' abilities to make and interpret bar graphs and also to solve problems using data involving length.

Extension

Provide additional measurement practice by leaving the ramp in an activity center for student use.

Figure 8: *Grade 1 Unit 6 Lesson 2—Math Facts Strategies, Homework and Practice, Assessment, and Extension*

Name _____ Date _____

Class Party

Suppose there are 25 students in your class and you have $10 for a class party. Use the prices in the table to plan a party.

Tell how you would spend the money, and explain why you would spend it that way. Use as much of the $10 as you can, but do not plan to spend more than $10. (There is no tax.) Be sure your plan works for a class of 25.

Write your plan on another piece of paper. Be sure to explain how you solved the problem and how you made your decisions.

Item	Cost
pitcher of lemonade (10 servings)	$2.50
paper cups (package of 24)	69¢
ice cream bars	30¢
oatmeal cookies (package of 16)	99¢
bag of popcorn (30 servings)	$1.09
napkins (package of 50)	49¢

Figure 9 shows Jayne's response to an open-response problem written at midyear of third grade. Jayne is the same student who wrote the journal entry shown in Figure 7. Compare her writing here with her paragraph from second grade and also with her work at the end of third grade on the Earning Money problem shown in Figure 19 in Part III. Comparing these three responses shows how she has developed her communication skills.

Tests

Tests that assess students' conceptual understanding and procedural skills are short items that teachers can easily grade. There is a test in the final unit of both first and second grade. In third grade, there is a midyear and an end-of-year test. In fourth and fifth grades, there is a midterm test in both the fall and spring semesters in addition to a midyear and end-of-year test.

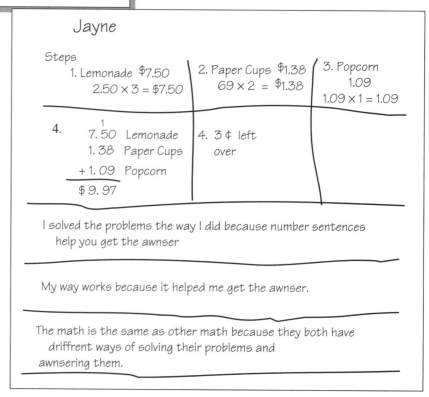

Figure 9: *Jayne's work for an open-response problem*

Assessment Units

In each grade, specific units are designated as assessment units. They include lessons that emphasize assessment at the same time that content is reviewed and new material is introduced. Teachers can assess students' abilities to apply previously studied concepts in new contexts and their willingness to approach new mathematics.

Assessment units at the beginning of each grade provide opportunities to observe students and collect baseline data on students' mathematical knowledge. Teachers can use this information to plan instruction that meets students' needs and to begin documenting students' mathematical growth over the course of the year. See the Assessment Overview in Part VI for specific information on the assessment units.

Portfolios

Portfolios are important tools for documenting students' growth throughout the year. They are collections of students' written work and teachers' anecdotal records. To provide a complete picture of a student's learning, a portfolio should include assessments that demonstrate the range of the child's abilities. Samples of student work on labs, open-response problems, assessment activity pages, and tests can be included along with samples of students' daily work. Work from the year's beginning to end will show students' growth over time. Certain lessons in the assessment units are especially appropriate for inclusion in portfolios. Refer to the TIMS Tutor: *Portfolios* for more information.

Facts Assessment

In *Math Trailblazers,* teachers assess students' knowledge of the facts by observing them as they work on activities, labs, and games and through the appropriate use of quizzes and tests. Periodic, short quizzes in the Daily Practice and Problems naturally follow the study of small groups of facts organized around specific strategies. As self-assessment in third, fourth, and fifth grades, each student can record his or her progress on *Facts I Know* charts and determine which facts he or she needs to study. The goal of the math facts assessment program is to determine the degree to which students can find answers to fact problems quickly and accurately and whether they can retain this skill over time. For more information on teaching and assessing the math facts, see the TIMS Tutor: *Math Facts.*

PART III | Implementing the Assessment Program

Evaluating and reporting on a broad range of student achievement throughout the school year is a complex task. It is only practical if the assessment process is built into day-to-day instruction. Components of the assessment program are designed so teachers can gather information about students as they are learning. This section outlines a plan for gradually introducing the various components of the assessment program during the first weeks of instruction and provides information on evaluating and scoring written work.

Getting Started

An assessment program that emphasizes the documentation of students' growth over time establishes a climate in which each child is valued for the knowledge and skills he or she brings to the classroom and in which each student is expected to make significant gains in mathematics. These are high expectations that also reflect reality. Students begin and end the school year with varying abilities, backgrounds, and accomplishments. Therefore, it is important to record what each student can do initially, as well as during the learning process, so that the teacher, student, and parents can fully appreciate progress throughout the year.

Begin Observational Assessments

Activities in the first two or three units of each grade provide many opportunities to observe students as they use mathematics. These observations provide a rich source of baseline information about students. For example, in Units 1–3 of first grade, students count objects in many contexts. By routinely observing four or five students during appropriate lessons, the teacher can note those students who can count and those who may need additional help. At the same time, all students are working on their counting skills as well as on related concepts such as comparing numbers and organizing data.

Unit 2 of third grade is also designated as an assessment unit. In this unit, students review strategies to maintain fluency with the subtraction facts. Students discuss strategies, play games, work with flash cards, assess themselves using *Facts I Know* charts, and use subtraction facts as part of a data collection activity. Observing students participating in these activities gives teachers information about students' knowledge of the facts and, more importantly, about students' abilities to use the facts to solve problems. Since students will continually use the facts in many activities as well as in the Daily Practice and Problems, the teacher need only record observations for a small number of students at a time. (For more information on assessment of the math facts, see the TIMS Tutor: *Math Facts.*)

Using the *Observational Assessment Record.* Before beginning assessment observations, teachers need a system for recording short, anecdotal records. Such a system should allow recording of a broad range of evidence of students' behavior, attitudes, and understanding of mathematics and should make recording and retrieving information easy and convenient. The *Observational Assessment Record* and the Assessment Indicators help organize data from observations. Teachers can develop their own shorthand to denote satisfactory progress toward a goal or proficiency with a skill or concept.

In Grades 1–5, information from the *Observational Assessment Record* can be transferred to *Individual Assessment Record Sheets* to create a year-long anecdotal record of growth for each child. The *Individual Assessment Record Sheet* is located at the end of Part VI of this section. Teachers can copy and place it in each student's portfolio. It is also available on the *Teacher Resource CD*. Teachers can use it to maintain records of each student's progress electronically.

As part of lesson planning, the teacher can choose one or two behaviors, concepts, or skills to check during class. The Assessment Indicators for each unit and the Assessment section in the lesson guides can facilitate this process. The teacher should choose no more than four or five students to observe in a day. Additional students can be observed in succeeding lessons or units to provide further information about individual students' progress and the improvement of the class as a whole.

Figure 10 is an example of an *Observational Assessment Record* for Grade 1 Unit 1 that shows one possible scheme for recording classroom observations. Note that the teacher chose to observe students' abilities to work together as well as counting skills.

Other suggestions from teachers for organizing anecdotal records follow:

Student Grid. A teacher can make a grid that allows note-taking about all students on one piece of paper as shown in Figure 11. The grids include as many cells as there are students in the class, labeling each cell with a student's name. Observations are written in the cells. Like the *Observational Assessment Record,* this provides a view of the entire class's progress.

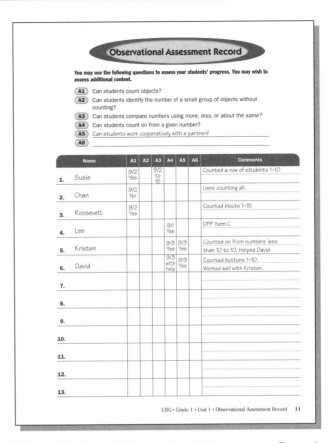

Figure 10: *Sample* Observational Assessment Record *for Grade 1 Unit 1*

Sally Adamji	Feliz Arnez	John Boyd	Barb Crown
Willie Darno	Sarah Frank	Lee Guzman	etc.

Figure 11: *Student grid*

Assessment

Flip Chart. A flip chart can be made by lining up index cards and taping them to a clipboard or a piece of heavy cardboard so they overlap by all but a strip of about $\frac{1}{2}$ inch as shown in Figure 12. Students' names are written on the uncovered area of each card, so the teacher can easily flip to a student's card and write a quick, dated note about the observation. As a card is filled, it can be removed to a card file or a student's portfolio and replaced with a new card.

Figure 12: *Flip chart*

Flip Cards. A variation of the flip chart can be made by fastening together a set of index cards—one card labeled for each student in the class. A binder ring is placed through a hole in a corner of each card.

Self-Adhesive Notes. Some teachers prefer to write their observations about individual students on self-adhesive notes, which are then attached to a sheet of paper in the student's portfolio. These notes have the advantage of being easily transferable, so they can be grouped and regrouped by student, subject, day, etc.

Begin Math Journals

At the beginning of the year, math journals provide a safe place for students to start communicating their insights. By writing regularly in their journals, they gain the experience necessary to write more and learn to express themselves clearly. Students can write in response to journal prompts or record answers to questions from the *Student Guide* or Daily Practice and Problems. See the TIMS Tutor: *Journals* for more information on using journals to assess students.

Begin Portfolios

The TIMS Tutor: *Portfolios* recommends establishing portfolios by starting small with modest goals. This implies using portfolios to document progress in one or two specific areas such as communicating mathematically or collecting and analyzing data. One way to begin is to assign each student a collection folder in which early examples of student work are saved. Later in the process, teachers can designate or students can select a smaller number of pieces that show growth in these areas.

It is important to choose examples of work from the beginning of the year so a student's first efforts can be compared to later work. The earliest entries in the portfolio will most likely show much less sophisticated results than those that are added toward the end of the year. For example, to compare students' use of the TIMS Laboratory Method at the beginning of the year to their abilities to conduct an experiment at the end of the year, include a data table and a graph from an early lab in each student's portfolio. Good choices of initial labs to collect in portfolios include the following: In Grade 1, save students' weather graphs from Unit 2; in Grade 2, use the Button Sizer Graph from Unit 3; and in Grade 3, choose student work from the lab *Kind of Bean* in Unit 1 or the graph and write-up from *Spinning Differences* in Unit 2. At the beginning of Grade 4, include *Arm Span vs. Height* from Unit 1 and *Perimeter vs. Length* from Unit 2. In Grade 5, begin portfolios with the labs *Searching the Forest* from Unit 1 and *Distance vs. Time* from Unit 3.

Scoring Open-Response Problems

In *Math Trailblazers,* most lessons involve multiple mathematical topics, skills, and processes. Assessing student progress requires tools that allow students to respond using multiple approaches and that let teachers evaluate student communication and problem-solving strategies as well as mathematical knowledge.

TIMS Multidimensional Rubric

To assist teachers in evaluating student performance and in communicating progress to students and parents, we have developed a rubric—a scoring guide—for evaluating student work on open-response problems. The *TIMS Multidimensional Rubric* addresses three dimensions of mathematical learning: (i) knowing, (ii) solving, and (iii) telling. Using these three dimensions broadens the assessment focus from the traditional emphasis on rote procedures to a more complete view of mathematics learning. The rubric outlines our criteria for excellence and provides an explicit indication of what we value in mathematics. Examples of using the rubric to score student work are included in lesson guides beginning in Grade 3. The ideas embodied in the rubric are generally applicable to younger children and can be modified for use in earlier grades. The rubric is displayed in Part V.

The three dimensions of mathematical understanding emphasized in the *TIMS Multidimensional Rubric* are described here briefly.

- *Solving.* This section focuses on students' understanding of a problem and their abilities to devise a plan for solving it, organize information, analyze results, and reflect on its mathematical implications.
- *Knowing.* This portion of the rubric examines students' comprehension of mathematical concepts and their abilities to apply procedures, rules, and facts to a given mathematical situation. This includes effective use of representations, such as written numbers, words, graphs, tables, or pictures, and the ability to make connections among different mathematical ideas.
- *Telling.* This part stresses students' abilities to explain their problem-solving strategies, justify their solutions, use symbols and terminology correctly, and discuss connections among mathematical topics.

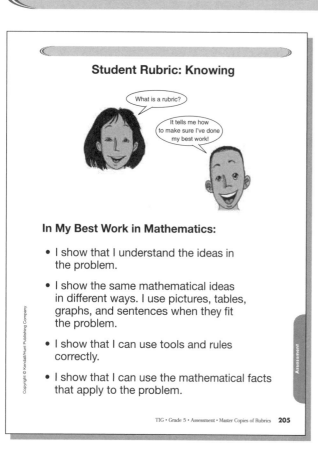

The *TIMS Multidimensional Rubric* specifies criteria for assigning scores on each dimension to one piece of student work. Level 4 is the highest and is intended to represent excellence in that particular dimension. A paper might earn, for example, a 3 in *Solving*, a 4 in *Knowing*, and a 3 in *Telling*. It is not necessary to assign a score for all three dimensions for every task. For many tasks, it may be more appropriate to give scores for only one or two dimensions.

Student Rubrics

Corresponding Student Rubrics for each dimension make the expectations of student performance clear. These rubrics provide students with goals as they solve problems, communicate their solutions, and revise their work. Students also use these rubrics as guides when assessing their own work. The student rubrics are introduced gradually in the *Student Guide* throughout the first semester of third, fourth, and fifth grades. They are included in lessons with open-response problems.

The Student Rubrics are shown in Figure 13.

The Student Rubrics are located in Appendices A, B, and C and on the inside backcover of the *Student Guides* for Grades 3–5. Blackline Masters of the Student Rubrics are included in Part V so teachers can make transparencies or use a copier to enlarge the rubrics to make classroom posters.

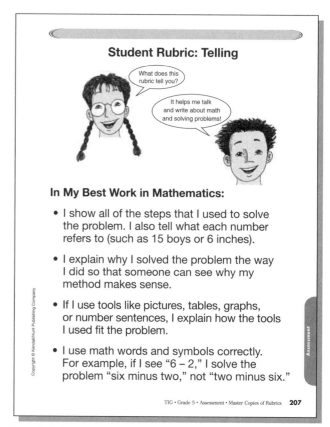

Figure 13: *Student Rubrics:* Knowing, Solving, *and* Telling

Using the Rubrics: An Early Example

Using the student rubrics to inform students of your expectations as well as using the *TIMS Multidimensional Rubric* to score student work is a process that evolves throughout the year. For example, Grade 3 Unit 2 includes the first assessment lesson with an open-response problem. This is the students' first exposure to the student rubrics. The problem is shown in Figure 14.

To begin the lesson the class reads and discusses the problem. It is similar to the problem in an earlier lesson (Unit 2 Lesson 2 *Spinning Sums*), so students should be familiar with the procedures. They also read and discuss the Student Rubric: *Knowing*. The teacher may ask students what tools, rules, and mathematical facts apply to the problem. She explains that she will grade their work based on the rubric.

After students understand the problem, they work in groups to plan a strategy for solving the problem and to carry out their plans. Then students write paragraphs describing their problem-solving processes and their results. The teacher directs students either to write the paragraph with their groups or to write the paragraph individually. When students have completed their paragraphs, the teacher reviews their work and makes suggestions for improvement.

It is a good idea to make transparencies of exemplary work from previous years or the lesson guide. The teacher discusses the exemplary work with the class, comparing the work to the rubric's standards. Finally, students revise their work based on the teacher's comments. A student response with teacher comments is shown in Figure 15.

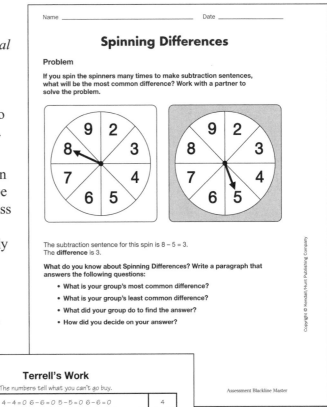

Figure 14: *Assessment lesson from Grade 3 Unit 2*

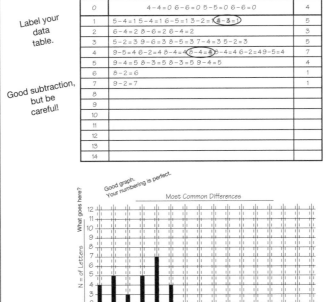

Figure 15: *A student response to a teacher's comments*

The teacher used the Knowing dimension of the *TIMS Multidimensional Rubric* to score students' work. The Lesson Guide provides questions specific to this problem to guide the teacher's scoring. The questions provided for this problem are given below:

- Were the data table and graph appropriately labeled?
- Was the graph scaled properly?
- Were the bars correctly drawn?
- Were the subtraction sentences correct?
- Were the most common differences identified?

Many of the criteria in the rubric overlap. In addition, the student's data table, graph, and written paragraphs tell us about more than one component of the problem. Consequently, the score for a dimension will result from the compilation of all the evidence, not necessarily from an arithmetic average of scores in each cell of the rubric. Figure 16 shows the Knowing dimension of the *TIMS Multidimensional Rubric* with the teacher's notations after she scored Terrell's paper.

How would you score Terrell's work? Terrell's teacher decided that he earned a 3. He worked with his group using tools to spin the spinners 30 times, record the results in a table, and display the data in a graph. The bars are drawn correctly on the graph and the axes are scaled correctly. However, the incorrect labels on both the data table ("The numbers that tell what you can't go buy") and graph ("Most Common Differences" and "$N =$ of Letters") indicate that he was not clear on his goal for collecting data and therefore did not completely understand the problem's concepts and applications. The incorrect labels also show major errors translating between tables, graphs, and real situations, although he did correctly identify the most common and least common differences. The correct number sentences are evidence that he knows the subtraction facts. (See the Lesson Guide for *Spinning Differences* in Grade 3 Unit 2 for other examples of student work scored using the rubric.)

Knowing	Level 4	Level 3	Level 2	Level 1
Understands the task's mathematical concepts, their properties and applications…	Completely	Nearly completely	Partially	Not at all
Translates between words, pictures, symbols, tables, graphs, and real situations…	Readily and without errors	With minor errors	With major errors	Not at all
Uses tools (measuring devices, graphs, tables, calculators, etc.) and procedures…	Correctly and efficiently	Correctly or with minor errors	Incorrectly	Not at all
Uses knowledge of the facts of mathematics (geometry definitions, math facts, etc.)…	Correctly	With minor errors	With major errors	Not at all

Figure 16: *Scoring an open-response problem using one dimension of the* TIMS Multidimensional Rubric

Using the Rubrics: A Second Example

During the school year, students become familiar with all three student rubrics and use them as they solve problems. Depending on the problem, they may use one or more of the rubrics. The results of these assessments are often saved in portfolios to show students and parents progress over time. The problem in Figure 17 is posed to students in the final assessment unit of third grade.

Before students begin solving the problem, the class reads and discusses the problem. Students should understand that play money will be available to help solve the problem and that they will be asked how they can use calculators to solve the problem. The teacher also reviews all three student rubrics and advises students that their work for this problem will be scored using all three dimensions.

Students use the tools available to them to find solutions and write about their strategies. The teacher may use samples of students' work to provide good examples for students to emulate. The teacher also comments on students' first drafts and students revise their work accordingly.

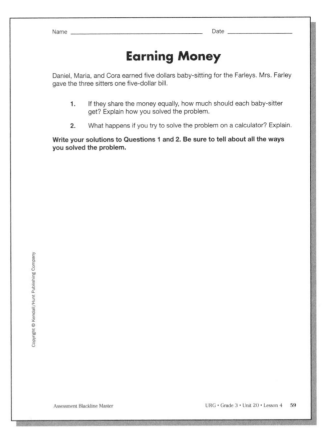

Earning Money

Daniel, Maria, and Cora earned five dollars baby-sitting for the Farleys. Mrs. Farley gave the three sitters one five-dollar bill.

1. If they share the money equally, how much should each baby-sitter get? Explain how you solved the problem.

2. What happens if you try to solve the problem on a calculator? Explain.

Write your solutions to Questions 1 and 2. Be sure to tell about all the ways you solved the problem.

Figure 17: *An open-response problem from Grade 3 Unit 20*

Samples of two students' work are shown in Figures 18 and 19. Scores for both students for all three dimensions of the *TIMS Multidimensional Rubric* are discussed below. The teacher was guided by additional questions in the Lesson Guide that are specific to this problem and that point out elements to consider while scoring.

The teacher gave Marco a 2 on Solving. Marco chose a legitimate problem-solving strategy—guess and check—but did not use it systematically or efficiently, nor did he organize his work. His work does show evidence that he persisted in the problem-solving process, but does not show that he

Marco's Work

Marco's response the first day:

$3.65
× 3 kids

three dollars and sixey five cenes times three kids, and five dollers minus one doller and foty five cenes egels fore dollers.

$5.00
− $1.45
$4.00   ← not good

Teacher comments:

I'm still not clear from your explanation what you tried. Maybe you should try to explain to me. Did you use the money or the calculator? Try to finish today.

Ms. Ho

Marco's response the second day:

I didn't use the money, But I used a calculator.

75¢ $4.50   165
75   3 ×   × 3
75           $1.50   4.95
225                         $1.70
                            × 3
3.13 $5.10
× 3
3.39   1.67
             × 3
3   5.01
$1.10   1.69
$1.10   × 3
+ $1.10   5.07
$3.30   1.66
             × 3
             4.98

Figure 18: *Marco's work*

identified all the elements of the problem since he does not indicate that he knows that there will be money left over. He makes no connections to previously studied mathematics or previously solved problems.

On the Knowing dimension, the teacher gave Marco a 3 since he correctly used his knowledge of mathematics and he used appropriate tools (a calculator) and procedures (repeated addition and multiplication) to solve the problem. He did not demonstrate that he completely understood the nature of the task or show that he can translate between symbols and real situations since he did not calculate the amount of money that would be left over.

Marco received a 1 on the Telling dimension. His explanation was very short and totally unclear, with no supporting arguments. Since he did not identify which trial was successful, we are not even sure of his final answer. He used symbols to show his trials, but made no attempt to organize them. Appropriate terminology is not present.

A second sample of student work on the Earning Money problem is shown below:

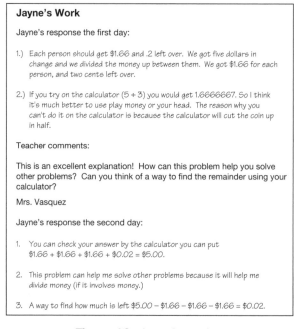

Jayne's Work

Jayne's response the first day:

1.) Each person should get $1.66 and .2 left over. We got five dollars in change and we divided the money up between them. We got $1.66 for each person, and two cents left over.

2.) If you try on the calculator (5 ÷ 3) you would get 1.6666667. So I think it's much better to use play money or your head. The reason why you can't do it on the calculator is because the calculator will cut the coin up in half.

Teacher comments:

This is an excellent explanation! How can this problem help you solve other problems? Can you think of a way to find the remainder using your calculator?

Mrs. Vasquez

Jayne's response the second day:

1. You can check your answer by the calculator you can put $1.66 + $1.66 + $1.66 + $0.02 = $5.00.

2. This problem can help me solve other problems because it will help me divide money (if it involves money.)

3. A way to find how much is left $5.00 − $1.66 − $1.66 − $1.66 = $0.02.

Figure 19: *Jayne's work*

Jayne's teacher gave her a score of 4 for Solving. She fully met the criteria in the rubric. She clearly identified the elements of the problem when she described the problem first as dividing the play money "up between them." She then found the amount left over and used a calculator to divide (5 ÷ 3) resulting in a repeating decimal. With prompting from the teacher, she looked for other strategies and found she could use repeated addition and subtraction to find the remainder. All her strategies are effective and they are presented in an organized fashion. Jayne's first conclusion that "you can't do it (find the remainder) on the calculator is because the calculator will cut the coin up in half" is insightful, although not quite correct mathematically. Using both repeated addition and subtraction on the calculator to find the remainder shows that she made meaningful connections between the operations and that she was willing to persist in the problem-solving process.

Jayne also received a 4 in Knowing since she clearly understood the problem's mathematical concepts. She readily translated the real situation into words when she described the process of dividing up the money and then translated words into symbols using correct addition, subtraction, and division sentences. The use of play money and a calculator is evidence that she can use tools correctly and efficiently and her calculations show that she can use the facts of mathematics correctly as well.

The teacher gave Jayne a score of 3 for the Telling dimension. Her explanations and responses were fairly complete and clear. However, we are not entirely sure how the group shared the money. Did they trade the dollars for quarters and then the quarters for dimes, etc., or were they able to make the process more efficient in some way? Her supporting arguments are sound, but they contain a few minor gaps. Did she use repeated subtraction or repeated addition first to find the remainder? Why did she choose these operations? She used many symbols and terms correctly. However, she reported that two cents were left over and wrote it first as ".2."

Like any new tool, using the rubric efficiently will require practice. As you begin to work with the rubric, we suggest that you work closely with other teachers. For example, you might score a half-dozen papers and ask one or more colleagues to score the same set; then compare and discuss the results, negotiating any differences. Repeating this process over the course of the year will help establish school-wide norms for applying the rubrics.

Using Assessment Observations, Math Journals, and Portfolios

The rubrics can be combined with other components of the assessment program to provide a more complete picture of students' skills at solving open-response problems. For example, to assess students' willingness to tackle new problems or work cooperatively in a group, teachers can observe students as they work on the problem or ask them to write in their journals about the process. For example, the Journal Prompt for the Earning Money problem concerns students' feelings about working in groups in math class. (See Figure 20.)

Journal Prompt

How did your group share the work on this problem? How do you feel about working with a group in math class?

Figure 20: *Journal prompt for Earning Money (Grade 3 Unit 20)*

Considerable growth in mathematical power is often evident when several write-ups of open-response problems from different times of the year are included in a student's portfolio. We can see growth in Jayne's problem-solving and communication skills when we look at her work on both the Class Party and Earning Money problems. (See Figure 9 in Part II and Figure 19.)

Evaluating Labs

Teachers have used the following ideas to evaluate student performance on labs:

Group Work
Students work in their groups to polish a lab write-up and turn in one completed lab or to prepare an oral report to be presented to the class. Their reports may include how the work was distributed among the group members. Students can also write a paragraph in their journals describing how each member functioned in the group and how to improve the process.

Using the Multidimensional Rubric
Choose one or two important questions to score using one or more dimensions of the *TIMS Multidimensional Rubric.* Often suitable questions are suggested in the Assessment section of the Suggestions for Teaching the Lesson in the Lesson Guide. These are usually open-response questions that ask students to make predictions or solve a problem using the data collected during the experiment.

Self-Assessment
Students can grade their own labs in class. This provides a forum for discussing the most important aspects of the lab.

Using a Point System
To grade a lab, teachers can assign a given number of points to each part of the lab and grade each part based on the criteria below. Teachers can also choose to grade only a portion of the lab such as the picture or the graph.

1. Drawing the Picture
   - Are the procedures and the materials clearly illustrated?
   - Are the variables labeled?
2. Collecting and Recording the Data
   - Are the data organized in a table?
   - Are the columns in the data table labeled correctly?
   - Are the data reasonable?
   - Are the correct units of measure included in the data table?
   - If applicable, did students average the data (find the median or mean) correctly?
3. Graphing the Data
   - Does the graph have a title?
   - Are the axes scaled correctly and labeled clearly? Labeling should be consistent with the picture and the data table and should include appropriate units of measure.
   - If it is a bar graph, are the bars drawn correctly?
   - If it is a point graph, are the points plotted correctly?
   - If the points suggest a straight line or a curve, did the student draw a best-fit line or fit a curve to the points?
   - Did the students show any interpolation or extrapolation on the graph?

4. Solving the Problems
   - Are the answers correct based on the data?
   - Did students use appropriate tools (calculators, rulers, graphs, etc.) correctly?
   - Are the answers, including the explanations, clear and complete?

References

Elementary Grades Assessment. *Balanced Assessment for the Mathematics Curriculum.* University of California. Dale Seymour Publications, White Plains, NY, 1999.

Lane, Suzanne. "The Conceptual Framework for the Development of a Mathematics Performance Assessment Instrument" in *Educational Measurement: Issues and Practice.* Vol. 12, Number 2. National Council on Measurement in Education, Washington, DC, 1993.

Mathematics Resource Guide for Fourth- and Eighth-Grade Teachers. Vermont Department of Education, Montpelier, VT, 1996.

Middle Grades Assessment. *Balanced Assessment for the Mathematics Curriculum.* University of California. Dale Seymour Publications, White Plains, NY, 2000.

Pellegrino, J.W., N. Chadowsky, and R. Glaser (Eds.) *Knowing What Students Know: The Science and Design of Educational Assessment.* National Research Council. National Academy Press, Washington, DC, 2001.

Performance Assessment in Mathematics: Approaches to Open-Ended Problems. Illinois State Board of Education, Springfield, IL, 1994.

Principles and Standards for School Mathematics. National Council of Teachers of Mathematics, Reston, VA, 2000.

Stenmark, J.K. (Ed.) *Mathematics Assessment: Myths, Models, Good Questions, and Practical Suggestions.* National Council of Teachers of Mathematics, Reston, VA, 1991.

Master Copies of Rubrics

This section contains the blackline masters of the *TIMS Multidimensional Rubric* and the three Student Rubrics: *Knowing, Solving,* and *Telling.* The Scoring Open-Response Problems section in Part III describes the rubrics and provides examples of their use in the curriculum. The *TIMS Multidimensional Rubric* is provided here so that teachers can use it to score student work. The copies of the three student rubrics in this section can be used to make transparencies for the overhead projector or enlarged to make posters for the classroom.

TIMS Multidimensional Rubric

Solving	Level 4	Level 3	Level 2	Level 1
Identifies the elements of the problem and their relationships to one another	All major elements identified	Most elements identified	Some, but shows little under-standing of relationships	Few or none
Uses problem-solving strategies which are . . .	Systematic, complete, efficient, and possibly elegant	Systematic and nearly complete, but not efficient	Incomplete or unsystematic	Not evident or inappropriate
Organizes relevant information . . .	Systematically and efficiently	Systematically, with minor errors	Unsystematically	Not at all
Relates the problem and solution to previously encountered mathe-matics and makes connections that are . . .	At length, elegant, and meaningful	Evident	Brief or logically unsound	Not evident
Persists in the problem solving process . . .	At length	Until a solution is reached	Briefly	Not at all
Looks back to examine the rea-sonableness of the solution and draws conclusions that are . . .	Insightful and comprehensive	Correct	Incorrect or logically unsound	Not present

Knowing	Level 4	Level 3	Level 2	Level 1
Understands the task's mathe-matical concepts, their properties and applications . . .	Completely	Nearly completely	Partially	Not at all
Translates between words, pictures, symbols, tables, graphs, and real situations . . .	Readily and without errors	With minor errors	With major errors	Not at all
Uses tools (measuring devices, graphs, tables, calculators, etc.) and procedures . . .	Correctly and efficiently	Correctly or with minor errors	Incorrectly	Not at all
Uses knowledge of the facts of mathematics (geometry definitions, math facts, etc.) . . .	Correctly	With minor errors	With major errors	Not at all

Telling	Level 4	Level 3	Level 2	Level 1
Includes response with an explanation and/or description which is . . .	Complete and clear	Fairly complete and clear	Perhaps ambiguous or unclear	Totally unclear or irrelevant
Presents supporting arguments which are . . .	Strong and sound	Logically sound, but may contain minor gaps	Incomplete or logically unsound	Not present
Uses pictures, symbols, tables, and graphs which are . . .	Correct and clearly relevant	Present with minor errors or somewhat irrelevant	Present with errors and/or irrelevant	Not present or completely inappropriate
Uses terminology . . .	Clearly and precisely	With minor errors	With major errors	Not at all

Student Rubric: Knowing

What is a rubric?

It tells me how to make sure I've done my best work!

In My Best Work in Mathematics:

- I show that I understand the ideas in the problem.

- I show the same mathematical ideas in different ways. I use pictures, tables, graphs, and sentences when they fit the problem.

- I show that I can use tools and rules correctly.

- I show that I can use the mathematical facts that apply to the problem.

Assessment

Student Rubric: Solving

In My Best Work in Mathematics:

- I read the problem carefully, make a good plan for solving it, and then carry out that plan.

- I use tools like graphs, pictures, tables, or number sentences to help me.

- I use ideas I know from somewhere else to help me solve a problem.

- I keep working on the problem until I find a good solution.

- I look back at my solution to see if my answer makes sense.

- I look back at my work to see what more I can learn from solving the problem.

Student Rubric: Telling

In My Best Work in Mathematics:

- I show all of the steps that I used to solve the problem. I also tell what each number refers to (such as 15 boys or 6 inches).

- I explain why I solved the problem the way I did so that someone can see why my method makes sense.

- If I use tools like pictures, tables, graphs, or number sentences, I explain how the tools I used fit the problem.

- I use math words and symbols correctly. For example, if I see "6 – 2," I solve the problem "six minus two," not "two minus six."

Assessment Overview for Fifth Grade

The assessment overview includes short descriptions of the components in the assessment program followed by a table that lists each assessment in fifth grade. The table names the assessments in each unit and gives the lesson name and number, the type of assessment, and the location of the assessment within the unit.

Component Summary

Assessment Indicators: A list of important topics covered in a given unit. The Assessment Indicators help the teacher focus on important skills and concepts.

Observational Assessment Record: A tool that helps teachers record student progress on the Assessment Indicators. Information about all students in the class can be recorded on the *Observational Assessment Record.* This provides a quick view of how both individual students and the class as a whole are progressing during the course of a unit. Student information can later be transferred to *Individual Assessment Record Sheets.*

Individual Assessment Record Sheet: A tool for tracking individual students' progress with the Assessment Indicators from all sixteen units.

Assessment Section in the Lesson Guide: Suggested ways to assess student progress during a lesson are included at the end of the lesson guides. This section might highlight particular parts of an activity as appropriate for observations, direct teachers to an assessment page or activity, or suggest a Daily Practice and Problems (DPP) item or homework questions for assessment.

Math Journals: As a part of the assessment for a lesson, students are sometimes asked to respond in their Math Journals to a specific question or prompt.

Assessment Pages: Short paper-and-pencil assessments that can be used to check skills or concepts developed in a unit. Some are designed for use in groups, while others are for individual work.

Assessment Lessons: Specially designed lessons to gauge student progress. There are three basic types of assessment lessons: assessment labs, open-response problems, and written tests composed of short items.

Assessment Labs: 2–3 laboratory investigations each year are designated as Assessment Labs. They are used to assess students' abilities to work in a group on an investigation that takes several days.

Assessment Units: Specific units in each grade that help teachers monitor student progress as part of the learning process. Units 1, 2, 8, and 16 are the Assessment Units in Grade 5.

Fact Self-Assessment: As part of the DPP, students regularly assess their knowledge of specific groups of math facts. Students categorize facts into three groups (facts I know quickly, facts I know using a strategy, facts I need to learn). They record this information on a special chart, which is updated regularly.

Fact Quizzes: Periodic quizzes of small groups of math facts are given as part of the DPP in the first eight units of fifth grade. Facts are grouped to encourage the use of strategies in learning facts. A test of the entire set of facts is given at midyear.

Portfolios: Collections of students' written work and teachers' anecdotal records. Portfolios are used to document students' growth over time.

Assessment Component	Component Description	Location
Unit 1—Populations and Samples		
Observational Assessment Record	**Assessment Record**	**URG**
Individual Assessment Record Sheet	**Assessment Record**	**TIG**
Lesson 1—Eyelets	**Lesson**	**URG**
DPP Item C—Addition Review 1	Addition Facts Assessment Item	URG
DPP Item E—Addition Review 2	Addition Facts Assessment Item	URG
Pockets at St. Crispin's	Assessment Page	URG
Lesson 5—Searching the Forest	**Assessment Lab**	**URG, SG**
DPP Item K—Subtraction Review 1	Subtraction Facts Assessment Item	URG
DPP Item O—Subtraction Review 2	Subtraction Facts Assessment Item	URG
Student Rubric: *Knowing*	Student Rubric	SG/TIG
Jocelyn's Wildflowers	Assessment Page	URG
Unit 2—Big Numbers		
Observational Assessment Record	**Assessment Record**	**URG**
Individual Assessment Record Sheet	**Assessment Record**	**TIG**
Lesson 2—Facts I Know	**Assessment Record**	**URG**
Multiplication Facts I Know	Assessment Page	URG
Division Facts I Know	Assessment Page	URG
Lesson 4—The Chinese Abacus	**Optional Lesson**	**URG**
Number Changes	Assessment Page	URG
Lesson 5—Multiplication	**Lesson**	**URG**
Making Money	Assessment Page	URG
Lesson 6—Estimating Products	**Lesson**	**URG**
DPP Item V—Multiplication Practice	Assessment Item	URG
Lesson 9—Stack Up	**Assessment Lesson**	**URG**
Stack Up	Open-Ended Problem	URG
Student Rubric: *Solving*	Student Rubric	SG/TIG
Student Rubric: *Telling*	Student Rubric	SG/TIG
TIMS Multidimensional Rubric	Scoring Guide	TIG
Lesson 10—Portfolios	**Assessment Lesson**	**URG, SG**
DPP Item CC—Quiz: 5s and 10s	Fact Quiz	URG

Assessment Component	Component Description	Location
Unit 3—Fractions and Ratios		
Observational Assessment Record **Individual Assessment Record Sheet**	**Assessment Record** **Assessment Record**	**URG** **TIG**
Lesson 1—Wholes and Parts DPP Item B—Multiplication and Division Facts: 2s and 3s	**Lesson** Fact Self-Assessment	**URG** URG
Lesson 4—Comparing Fractions Home Practice Part 6—A Fraction More	**Lesson** Assessment Page	**URG** DAB
Lesson 5—Using Ratios Quiz Time	**Lesson** Assessment Pages	**URG** URG
Lesson 6—Distance vs. Time DPP Item U—Quiz: 2s and 3s DPP Item V—Goldfish on Sale Student Rubric: *Knowing* Student Rubric: *Telling* TIMS Multidimensional Rubric	**Lesson** Fact Quiz Assessment Item Student Rubric Student Rubric Scoring Guide	**URG** URG URG SG/TIG SG/TIG TIG
Unit 4—Division and Data		
Observational Assessment Record **Individual Assessment Record Sheet**	**Assessment Record** **Assessment Record**	**URG** **TIG**
Lesson 1—Grid Area DPP Item B—Multiplication and Division Facts: Square Numbers DPP Item D—Area of Shapes Finding Area	**Lesson** Fact Self-Assessment Assessment Item Assessment Page	**URG** URG URG DAB
Lesson 2—Modeling Division DPP Item F—Counting Square Units	**Lesson** Area Assessment Item	**URG** URG
Lesson 3—Paper-and-Pencil Division Quiz	**Lesson** Assessment Page	**URG** URG
Lesson 5—Mean or Median? DPP Item Y—Medians and Means DPP Item Z—Order of Operations	**Lesson** Assessment Item Assessment Item	**URG** URG URG
Lesson 6—Spreading Out DPP Item V—Ratios	**Lab** Assessment Item	**URG** URG
Lesson 9—Midterm Test Item AA—Quiz: Square Numbers Midterm Test	**Assessment Lesson** Fact Quiz Written Test	**URG** URG URG

Assessment Component	Component Description	Location
Unit 5—Investigating Fractions		
Observational Assessment Record **Individual Assessment Record Sheet**	**Assessment Record** **Assessment Record**	**URG** **TIG**
Lesson 1—Geoboard Fractions DPP Item B—Multiplication and Division Facts: 9s	**Lesson** Fact Self-Assessment	**URG** URG
Lesson 5—A Day at the Races Student Rubric: *Telling* TIMS Multidimensional Rubric	**Lesson** Student Rubric Scoring Guide	**URG** SG/TIG TIG
Lesson 6—Adding Fractions with Rectangles DPP Item S—Quiz: 9s DPP Item T—Comparing Fractions	**Lesson** Fact Quiz Assessment Item	**URG** URG URG
Lesson 7—Adding and Subtracting Fractions Fraction Follow-Up	**Lesson** Assessment Pages	**URG** URG
Unit 6—Geometry		
Observational Assessment Record **Individual Assessment Record Sheet**	**Assessment Record** **Assessment Record**	**URG** **TIG**
Lesson 1—Angle Measures DPP Item B—Multiplication and Division Facts: The Last Six Facts	**Lesson** Fact Self-Assessment	**URG** URG
Lesson 2—Angles in Triangles and Other Polygons DPP Item M—What's Your Angle?	**Lesson** Assessment Item	**URG** URG
Lesson 3—Polygon Angles Journal Prompt	**Lesson** Math Journal	**URG** URG
Lesson 4—Congruent Shapes DPP Item L—Drawing Shapes	**Lesson** Assessment Item	**URG** URG
Lesson 7—Making Shapes DPP Item Q—Quiz: The Last Six Facts Student Rubric: *Telling* Slab Orders TIMS Multidimensional Rubric	**Assessment Lesson** Fact Quiz Student Rubric Assessment Page Scoring Guide	**URG, SG** URG SG/TIG URG TIG

Assessment

Assessment Component	Component Description	Location
Unit 7—Decimals and Probability		
Observational Assessment Record **Individual Assessment Record Sheet**	**Assessment Record** **Assessment Record**	**URG** **TIG**
Lesson 1—Fractions, Decimals, and Percents Home Practice Part 3—Fractions, Decimals, and Percents	**Lesson** Assessment Page	**URG** DAB
Lesson 3—Comparing and Rounding Decimals Home Practice Part 5—Reading, Writing, and Ordering Decimals	**Lesson** Assessment Page	**URG** DAB
Lesson 4—Adding and Subtracting Decimals DPP Item L—Using the Centiwheel	**Lesson** Assessment Item	**URG** URG
Lesson 6—Paper-and-Pencil Decimal Multiplication Decimal Quiz	**Lesson** Assessment Page	**URG** URG
Unit 8—Applications: An Assessment Unit		
Observational Assessment Record **Individual Assessment Record Sheet**	**Assessment Record** **Assessment Record**	**URG** **TIG**
Lesson 4—Florence Kelley's Report Florence Kelley's Report Student Rubric: *Knowing* Student Rubric: *Telling* TIMS Multidimensional Rubric	**Assessment Lesson** Open-Ended Problem Student Rubric Student Rubric Scoring Guide	**URG** URG SG/TIG SG/TIG TIG
Lesson 6—Comparing Lives of Animals and Soap Bubbles Student Rubric: *Telling* TIMS Multidimensional Rubric	**Assessment Lab** Student Rubric Scoring Guide	**URG, SG** SG/TIG TIG
Lesson 8—Midyear Test Midyear Test	**Assessment Lesson** Written Test	**URG** URG
Lesson 9—Portfolio Review DPP Item Q—Multiplication and Division Fact Inventory Test	**Assessment Lesson** Fact Test	**URG, SG** URG
Unit 9—Connections to Division		
Observational Assessment Record **Individual Assessment Record Sheet**	**Assessment Record** **Assessment Record**	**URG** **TIG**
Lesson 4—Understanding Remainders DPP Item N—Operations Tie Dye T-Shirts	**Lesson** Assessment Item Assessment Page	**URG** URG URG
Lesson 6—Grass Act DPP Item T—Remainders Grass Act Questions Student Rubric: *Knowing* Student Rubric: *Telling* Student Rubric: *Solving* TIMS Multidimensional Rubric	**Assessment Lesson** Assessment Item Open-Ended Problem Student Rubric Student Rubric Student Rubric Scoring Guide	**URG, SG** URG URG SG/TIG SG/TIG SG/TIG TIG

Assessment Component	Component Description	Location
Unit 10—Maps and Coordinates		
Observational Assessment Record **Individual Assessment Record Sheet**	**Assessment Record** **Assessment Record**	**URG** **TIG**
Lesson 2—Introducing Cartesian Coordinates Home Practice Part 3—Working with Coordinates	**Lesson** Assessment Page	**URG** DAB
Lesson 4—Mr. Origin Coordinates: Getting to the Point	**Lesson** Assessment Page	**URG** URG
Lesson 7—These Boots Are Made for Flipping Moving Shapes	**Optional Lesson** Assessment Pages	**URG** URG
Lesson 8—Reading a Map Carol's Chicago Map Student Rubric: *Knowing* TIMS Multidimensional Rubric	**Lesson** Assessment Pages Student Rubric Scoring Guide	**URG** URG SG/TIG TIG
Unit 11—Number Patterns, Primes, and Fractions		
Observational Assessment Record **Individual Assessment Record Sheet**	**Assessment Record** **Assessment Record**	**URG** **TIG**
Lesson 4—Finding Prime Factors Home Practice Part 3—Using Exponents	**Lesson** Assessment Page	**URG** DAB
Lesson 5—Comparing Fractions DPP Item P—Finding Factors	**Lesson** Assessment Item	**URG** URG
Lesson 6—Reducing Fractions Skills Check-Up	**Lesson** Assessment Page	**URG** URG
Lesson 7—A Further Look at Patterns and Primes A Further Look at Patterns and Primes 6-column 100 Chart Student Rubric: *Telling* TIMS Multidimensional Rubric	**Lesson** Open-Ended Problem Assessment Page Student Rubric Scoring Guide	**URG** URG URG SG/TIG TIG
Unit 12—Using Fractions		
Observational Assessment Record **Individual Assessment Record Sheet**	**Assessment Record** **Assessment Record**	**URG** **TIG**
Lesson 4—Multiplication of Fractions DPP Item H—Adding Mixed Numbers	**Lesson** Assessment Item	**URG** URG
Lesson 8—Midterm Test Midterm Test	**Assessment Lesson** Written Test	**URG** URG

Assessment

Assessment Component	Component Description	Location
Unit 13—Ratio and Proportion		
Observational Assessment Record **Individual Assessment Record Sheet**	**Assessment Record** **Assessment Record**	**URG** **TIG**
Lesson 1—Ratios, Recipes, and Proportions Home Practice Part 5—In Proportion	**Lesson** Assessment Page	**URG** DAB
Lesson 3—Sink and Float Mass Review Volume Review	**Lesson** Assessment Pages Assessment Pages	**URG** URG URG
Lesson 4—Mass vs. Volume: Proportions and Density Home Practice Part 4—Measuring the Density of Rocks	**Lesson** Assessment Page	**URG** DAB
Lesson 5—Problems of Scale Paint Quiz	**Lesson** Assessment Pages	**URG** URG
Unit 14—Using Circles		
Observational Assessment Record **Individual Assessment Record Sheet**	**Assessment Record** **Assessment Record**	**URG** **TIG**
Lesson 2—Circumference vs. Diameter Going Around in Circles	**Lesson** Assessment Page	**URG** URG
Lesson 3—Constructing Circles with Terry DPP Item I—Try Some Pi	**Lesson** Assessment Item	**URG** URG
Lesson 4—Complex Constructions Circles and Constructions	**Lesson** Assessment Pages	**URG** URG
Lesson 5—Circle Graphs DPP Item U—Constructions	**Lesson** Assessment Item	**URG** URG
Unit 15—Developing Formulas with Geometry		
Observational Assessment Record **Individual Assessment Record Sheet**	**Assessment Record** **Assessment Record**	**URG** **TIG**
Lesson 2—Rectangle Riddles DPP Item C—Area—Rectangles Quiz	**Lesson** Assessment Item	**URG** URG
Lesson 5—Perimeter Areas and Perimeters	**Lesson** Assessment Pages	**URG** URG
Lesson 6—A Variety of Problems Home Practice Part 6—Building a Park	**Lesson** Assessment Page	**URG** DAB

Assessment Component	Component Description	Location
Unit 16—Bringing It All Together: An Assessment Unit		
Observational Assessment Record **Individual Assessment Record Sheet**	**Assessment Record** **Assessment Record**	**URG** **TIG**
Lesson 4—How Many Bats in a Cave? Student Rubric: *Telling* TIMS Multidimensional Rubric	**Assessment Lab** Student Rubric Scoring Guide	**URG, SG** SG/TIG TIG
Lesson 5—Pattern Block Candy Pattern Block Questions Student Rubric: *Solving* TIMS Multidimensional Rubric	**Assessment Lesson** Open-Ended Problem Student Rubric Scoring Guide	**URG** URG SG/TIG TIG
Lesson 6—End-of-Year Test End-of-Year Test	**Assessment Lesson** Written Test	**URG** URG
Lesson 7—Portfolio Review	**Assessment Lesson**	**URG, SG**

Individual Assessment Record Sheet

Name _____

Unit 1: Populations and Samples   ✔   Date and Comments:

A1. Can students collect, organize, graph,
and analyze data? _____ _____

A2. Can students make and interpret bar graphs? _____ _____

A3. Can students find the median of a data set? _____ _____

A4. Do students work well in small groups? _____ _____

A5. Do students solve problems in more than one way? _____ _____

A6. Do students demonstrate fluency with the addition and
subtraction facts? _____ _____

A7. _____ _____ _____

Unit 2: Big Numbers   ✔   Date and Comments:

A1. Can students compare and order large numbers? _____ _____

A2. Can students read and write large numbers? _____ _____

A3. Can students multiply using paper and pencil? _____ _____

A4. Can students multiply numbers with ending
zeros mentally? _____ _____

A5. Can students estimate products? _____ _____

A6. Can students solve open-response problems and
communicate solution strategies? _____ _____

A7. Do students demonstrate fluency with the
multiplication and division facts for the 5s and 10s? _____ _____

A8. _____ _____ _____

Unit 3: Fractions and Ratios   ✔   Date and Comments:

A1. Can students represent fractions using pattern blocks
and number lines? _____ _____

A2. Can students find equivalent fractions? _____ _____

A3. Can students name fractions greater than one as mixed
numbers or improper fractions? _____ _____

A4. Can students compare and order fractions? _____ _____

A5. Can students collect, organize, graph, and analyze data? _____ _____

A6. Can students draw and interpret best-fit lines? _____ _____

A7. Can students use ratios to solve problems? _____ _____

A8. Can students measure length in yards? _____ _____

A9. Do students demonstrate fluency with the multiplication
and division facts for the 2s and 3s? _____ _____

A10. _____ _____ _____

Name _____

Unit 4: Division and Data   ✔   **Date and Comments:**

A1.   Can students measure area?   _____   _____

A2.   Can students find the median and mean of a data set?   _____   _____

A3.   Can students divide with 1-digit divisors using paper and pencil?   _____   _____

A4.   Can students estimate quotients?   _____   _____

A5.   Can students interpret remainders?   _____   _____

A6.   Can students divide numbers with ending zeros mentally?   _____   _____

A7.   Can students draw and interpret best-fit lines?   _____   _____

A8.   Can students collect, organize, graph, and analyze data?   _____   _____

A9.   Do students demonstrate fluency with multiplication and division facts for the square numbers?   _____   _____

A10. _____   _____   _____

Unit 5: Investigating Fractions   ✔   **Date and Comments:**

A1.   Can students represent fractions using pattern blocks and rectangles on dot paper?   _____   _____

A2.   Can students find equivalent fractions?   _____   _____

A3.   Can students compare and order fractions?   _____   _____

A4.   Can students collect, organize, graph, and analyze data?   _____   _____

A5.   Can students draw and interpret best-fit lines?   _____   _____

A6.   Can students use ratios to solve problems?   _____   _____

A7.   Can students measure length in yards and feet?   _____   _____

A8.   Can students add and subtract fractions using manipulatives, pictures, or symbols?   _____   _____

A9.   Do students demonstrate fluency with the multiplication and division facts for the 9s?   _____   _____

A10. _____   _____   _____

Unit 6: Geometry   ✔   **Date and Comments:**

A1.   Can students measure angles?   _____   _____

A2.   Can students draw shapes and angles with given measures?   _____   _____

A3.   Can students identify and describe 2-dimensional shapes?   _____   _____

A4.   Can students classify 2-dimensional shapes?   _____   _____

A5.   Can students identify congruent and similar shapes?   _____   _____

A6.   Can students make and test conjectures about geometric properties?   _____   _____

A7.   Can students use geometric concepts and skills to solve problems?   _____   _____

A8.   Can students use numerical variables?   _____   _____

A9.   Do students demonstrate fluency with the last six multiplication and division facts $(4 \times 6, 4 \times 7, 4 \times 8, 6 \times 7, 6 \times 8, 7 \times 8)$?   _____   _____

A10. _____   _____   _____

Assessment

Unit 7: Decimals and Probability   ✔   **Date and Comments:**

A1.   Can students represent decimals using centiwheels and decimal grids?   _____   _____

A2.   Can students use fractions, decimals, and percents to represent the same quantity?   _____   _____

A3.   Can students read and write decimals to thousandths?   _____   _____

A4.   Can students compare and order decimals?   _____   _____

A5.   Can students add and subtract decimals?   _____   _____

A6.   Can students multiply decimals?   _____   _____

A7.   Can students collect, organize, graph, and analyze data?   _____   _____

A8.   Can students make and interpret bar graphs?   _____   _____

A9.   Can students use fractions and percents to give the probability of an event?   _____   _____

A10. _____   _____   _____

Unit 8: Applications: An Assessment Unit   ✔   **Date and Comments:**

A1.   Can students collect, organize, graph, and analyze data?   _____   _____

A2.   Can students make and interpret bar graphs and point graphs?   _____   _____

A3.   Can students translate between graphs and real-world events?   _____   _____

A4.   Can students use numerical variables?   _____   _____

A5.   Can students choose appropriate methods and tools to calculate (calculators, pencil and paper, or mental math)?   _____   _____

A6.   Can students solve open-response problems and communicate solution strategies?   _____   _____

A7.   Can students use fractions, decimals, and percents to represent the same quantity?   _____   _____

A8.   Do students choose appropriately whether to find an estimate or an exact answer?   _____   _____

A9.   Do students demonstrate fluency with the multiplication and division facts?   _____   _____

A10. _____   _____   _____

Unit 9: Connections to Division   ✔   **Date and Comments:**

A1.   Can students divide with 2-digit divisors using paper and pencil?   _____   _____

A2.   Can students estimate quotients?   _____   _____

A3.   Can students interpret remainders?   _____   _____

A4.   Can students write quotients as mixed numbers?   _____   _____

A5.   Can students use a calculator to solve division problems?   _____   _____

A6.   Can students check division using multiplication?   _____   _____

A7.   Can students solve open-response problems and communicate solution strategies?   _____   _____

A8.   Can students find decimal equivalents for fractions?

A9. _____   _____   _____

Name _____

Unit 10: Maps and Coordinates   ✔   **Date and Comments:**

A1. Can students represent negative numbers using a
number line?   _____   _____

A2. Can students solve problems using negative numbers? _____   _____

A3. Can students plot points using ordered pairs in the
four quadrants?   _____   _____

A4. Can students locate objects or find locations on maps
using coordinates?   _____   _____

A5. Can students use a scale map to find distances?   _____   _____

A6. _____   _____   _____

Unit 11: Number Patterns, Primes, and Fractions   ✔   **Date and Comments:**

A1. Can students find all the factors of a number?   _____   _____

A2. Can students identify prime, composite, and
square numbers?   _____   _____

A3. Can students find the prime factorization of a number? _____   _____

A4. Can students reduce fractions to lowest terms?   _____   _____

A5. Can students find common denominators?   _____   _____

A6. Can students compare fractions?   _____   _____

A7. Can students add and subtract fractions using
common denominators?   _____   _____

A8. Can students use variables in formulas?   _____   _____

A9. Can students identify and describe number patterns? _____   _____

A10. _____   _____   _____

Unit 12: Using Fractions   ✔   **Date and Comments:**

A1. Can students add and subtract fractions using
pattern blocks and paper and pencil?   _____   _____

A2. Can students reduce fractions to lowest terms?   _____   _____

A3. Can students rename mixed numbers?   _____   _____

A4. Can students estimate sums of mixed numbers?   _____   _____

A5. Can students add mixed numbers using pattern blocks
and paper and pencil?   _____   _____

A6. Can students estimate products of fractions?   _____   _____

A7. Can students multiply a fraction and a whole number? _____   _____

A8. Can students multiply fractions using pattern blocks,
paper folding, and paper and pencil?   _____   _____

A9. Do students solve problems in more than one way? _____   _____

A10. _____   _____   _____

Assessment

Name _____

Unit 13: Ratio and Proportion   ✔   **Date and Comments:**

A1.   Can students use words, tables, graphs, fractions, and colon notation to express ratios?   _____   _____

A2.   Can students use ratios and proportions to solve problems?   _____   _____

A3.   Can students measure mass?   _____   _____

A4.   Can students measure volume by displacement?   _____   _____

A5.   Can students collect, organize, graph, and analyze data?   _____   _____

A6.   Can students draw and interpret best-fit lines?   _____   _____

A7.   Do students solve problems in more than one way?   _____   _____

A8.   Can students choose appropriate methods and tools to calculate (calculators, pencil and paper, or mental math)?   _____   _____

A9.   _____   _____   _____

Unit 14: Using Circles   ✔   **Date and Comments:**

A1.   Can students identify the parts of a circle?   _____   _____

A2.   Can students express the relationship between the circumference and diameter of a circle using words and symbols?   _____   _____

A3.   Can students use variables in formulas?   _____   _____

A4.   Can students measure length in centimeters?   _____   _____

A5.   Can students collect, organize, graph, and analyze data?   _____   _____

A6.   Can students draw and interpret best-fit lines?   _____   _____

A7.   Can students use words, tables, graphs, and fractions to express ratios?   _____   _____

A8.   Can students use fractions, decimals, and percents to represent the same quantity?   _____   _____

A9.   Can students construct geometric figures using rulers, compasses, and protractors?   _____   _____

A10.   Can students make and interpret circle graphs?   _____   _____

Unit 15: Developing Formulas with Geometry   ✔   **Date and Comments:**

A1.   Can students identify the legs and hypotenuse of a right triangle?   _____   _____

A2.   Can students identify the base and height (altitude) of a triangle?   _____   _____

A3.   Can students find the area of rectangles and triangles?   _____   _____

A4.   Can students measure the perimeter of rectangles and other shapes?   _____   _____

A5.   Can students use variables in formulas for area and perimeter?   _____   _____

A6.   Can students measure length in centimeters?   _____   _____

A7.   Can students use geometric concepts and skills to solve problems?   _____   _____

A8.   Can students use the correct order of operations?   _____   _____

A9.   _____   _____   _____

Name _____

Unit 16: Bringing It All Together: An Assessment Unit   ✔   **Date and Comments:**

A1.   Can students collect, organize, graph, and analyze data?   _____   _____

A2.   Can students draw and interpret best-fit lines?   _____   _____

A3.   Can students translate between graphs and real-world events?   _____   _____

A4.   Can students use words, tables, graphs, and fractions to express ratios?   _____   _____

A5.   Can students use ratios and proportions to solve problems?   _____   _____

A6.   Can students use numerical variables?   _____   _____

A7.   Can students identify and describe number patterns?   _____   _____

A8.   Can students solve open-response problems and communicate solution strategies?   _____   _____

A9.   Do students solve problems in more than one way?   _____   _____

A10.   _____   _____   _____

Additional Comments:

TIMS Tutors

The TIMS Tutors section provides an in-depth exploration of the mathematical concepts and ideas behind *Math Trailblazers*.

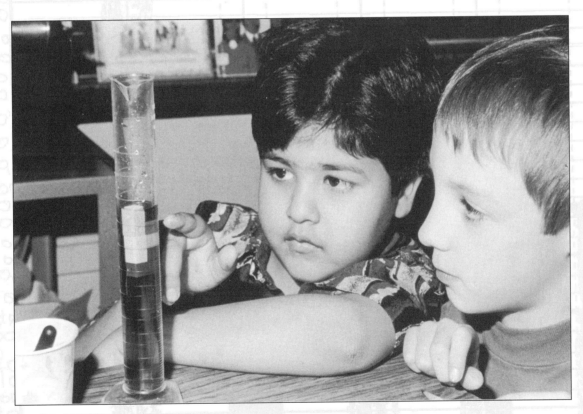

Students use a graduated cylinder to find the volume of small objects.

Introduction

TIMS Tutors

Arithmetic

Introduction

The last half-century has seen many changes in elementary school mathematics. For many people, "mathematics" is synonymous with "arithmetic." But today, while reasonable people can still debate the proper content of an elementary mathematics curriculum, nearly all agree that a curriculum focused largely on rote arithmetic will not meet the needs of students in the twenty-first century.

Much more than just arithmetic is now expected—geometry, probability, statistics, measurement, graphing, even algebra. Technology is dramatically changing the world, making it hard to imagine what our children will need to know in 20 or 40 more years, but also ensuring that many skills critical 50 years ago are less essential. Despite recent advances in psychology, educational research, and curriculum design, we are far from resolving all the uncertainties of the elementary school mathematics curriculum. A few things, however, do seem clear:

<table>
<tr><td>

Outline

This tutor is organized as follows:

</td></tr>
</table>

- The school mathematics curriculum can and must be more rigorous.
- Arithmetic is only one piece, albeit an important one, of a broad mathematics curriculum.
- We need to do better at helping children connect marks on paper to the real world. Too many children and adults fail to use common sense when dealing with mathematical symbolism. Discussing mathematics and integrating subject matter may help students make these connections.
- As we correct for the overemphasis on skills in the traditional mathematics curriculum, we should avoid over-correcting. Problem solving requires both procedural skill and conceptual understanding. As William Brownell (1956) noted during a previous period of reform, "In objecting to the emphasis on drill prevalent not so long ago, we may have failed to point out that practice for proficiency in skills has its place too." In *Math Trailblazers,* we consistently seek a balance between conceptual understanding and procedural skill.

The National Council of Teachers of Mathematics' (NCTM) *Principles and Standards for School Mathematics* advocates learning mathematics with understanding. "In recent decades, psychological and educational research on the learning of complex subjects such as mathematics has solidly established the important role of conceptual understanding in the knowledge and activity of persons who are proficient. Being proficient in a complex domain such as mathematics entails the ability to use knowledge flexibly, applying what is learned in one setting appropriately in another. One of the most robust findings of research is that conceptual understanding is an important component of proficiency, along with factual knowledge and procedural facility" (Bransford, Brown, and Cocking, 1999). The alliance of factual knowledge, procedural proficiency, and conceptual understanding makes all three components usable in powerful ways. Students who memorize facts or procedures without understanding often are not sure when or how to use what they know, and such learning is often quite fragile (Bransford, Brown, and Cocking, 1999; NCTM, 2000).

Several arguments support the NCTM position. One is that the computational proficiency of American students comes at too high a cost. The hundreds of hours devoted to arithmetic computation in elementary school leave too little time for other important topics. The traditional rote approach to computation undermines higher-level thinking: children learn that mathematics is blindly following rules, not thinking.

Another argument for shifting away from the traditional arithmetic curriculum is that technology has altered the role of paper-and-pencil calculation. As noted in the NCTM *Principles and Standards,* ". . . most of the arithmetic and algebraic procedures long viewed as the heart of the school mathematics curriculum can now be performed with handheld calculators. Thus more attention can now be given to understanding the number concepts and the modeling procedures used in solving problems." (NCTM, 2000) More practical topics—probability and statistics, geometry, measurement, mental computation and estimation—deserve more attention.

A final and most important argument in favor of the changes NCTM recommends is that new approaches to arithmetic instruction are more effective in helping students learn both appropriate calculation skills and how to apply those skills in solving problems. These new approaches build on students' own knowledge and intuitive methods and engage their common sense. This more meaningful approach helps students to be efficient and flexible in their computation and can reduce, though not eliminate, the amount of practice required. Thus a greater emphasis on conceptual understanding can lead to better procedural skills and problem-solving abilities (Brown & Burton, 1978; Skemp, 1978; Hiebert, 1984; Van Lehn, 1986; Carpenter, 1986; Baroody and Ginsburg, 1986; Good, Mulryan, and McCaslin, 1992; Hiebert, 1999; National Research Council, 2001).

A final and most important argument in favor of the changes NCTM recommends is that new approaches to arithmetic instruction are more effective in helping students learn both appropriate calculation skills and how to apply those skills in solving problems.

Numeration and Place Value

Numeration in kindergarten emphasizes developing oral counting skills, making one-to-one correspondence between objects and numbers, developing the concept of cardinality, discovering patterns in our number system, and writing numbers. Students in Grade 1 continue to develop these skills and concepts. They take part in activities that help them become familiar with the structure of the number system.

In kindergarten and Grade 1, students practice their counting skills. They learn to count past 100 by ones, twos, fives, and tens. They count forward and backward from any given number. They group objects for counting.

Students use counting to solve addition and subtraction problems. They learn to write numbers up to and beyond 100. Beginning in kindergarten, a ten frame is frequently used as a visual organizer. See Figure 1. The *100 Chart* is introduced and used for a variety of purposes, including solving problems and studying patterns. Students partition, or break apart, numbers in several ways ($25 = 20 + 5$, $25 = 10 + 10 + 5$, and so on). These activities help children develop number sense that allows them to use numbers flexibly.

Figure 1: *Sample ten frame*

While formal study of place value is not a focus in kindergarten or Grade 1, the multiple grouping and counting experiences described above provide children with a foundation for building an intuitive sense for the meaning of place value.

Work with counting continues in Grade 2, especially skip counting and counting backwards. Place value is explored in the context of counting and grouping by tens. Children continue to count and group everyday objects such as buttons or beans. They use connecting cubes to represent these objects and often group the cubes by tens. Later, base-ten pieces represent these same objects, thus linking the base-ten representations with quantities of actual objects.

Students explore numbers well into the hundreds. Counting is still used for problem solving, but more elaborate procedures may be employed. For example, a student may solve $885 - 255$ by counting up, first by hundreds (355, 455, 555, 655, 755, 855) and then by tens (865, 875, 885), yielding 630 as the answer.

More elaborate partitions of numbers are investigated in Grade 2. Particularly important are partitions in which every part is a single digit times 1, 10, 100, or 1000: $359 = 300 + 50 + 9$ and so on. Attention is also given to partitioning numbers in more than one way:

$$359 = 300 + 50 + 9$$
$$= 200 + 150 + 9$$
$$= 100 + 250 + 9$$

This work with multiple partitioning is closely related to multidigit addition and subtraction. One way to think about addition and subtraction—indeed, one way to think about much of elementary mathematics—is as procedures for renaming numbers in more convenient forms. For example, $563 + 13$ is a number we usually rename as 576. Another number, $875 \div 25$, is renamable as 35 when it suits our purposes.

In Grade 3, more formal study of place value takes place. Students work in varied contexts involving numbers through the thousands. For example, students draw an outline of a coat and determine how many square centimeters of material are required to make the coat. Using contexts such as this encourages students to associate quantities of actual objects with representations of the quantities using base-ten pieces and with the numerals that represent them. Most of this work is closely connected with addition and subtraction of multidigit numbers. Indeed, a good reason for studying computational algorithms is that they provide a context for learning about place value.

In Grade 4, large numbers up to the millions are studied and used in various contexts. Continued efforts are made to connect the numbers with actual quantities. For example, the class creates its own base-ten pieces for large numbers—pieces we call super skinnies (10,000), super flats (100,000), and megabits (1,000,000). See Figure 2.

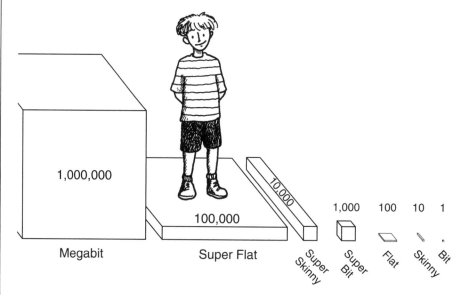

Figure 2: *Base-ten pieces for small and large numbers*

After reviewing and establishing the basics of the base-ten place value system for whole numbers, the system is extended to include decimals beginning in third grade. In Grade 4, the ten-for-one trading rules and other aspects of our number system are extended to the right of the decimal point for the first time.

In Grade 5, we extend the number system to even larger numbers. The story of Archimedes' attempt to calculate the number of grains of sand that would fill the observed universe introduces students to numbers far beyond what we encounter in everyday life. With the use of scientific calculators in Grade 5, scientific notation for large numbers is needed and introduced.

Basic Number Facts

In developing the math facts program, we sought a careful balance between strategies and drill. This approach is based on a large body of research and advocated by the NCTM *Principles and Standards for School Mathematics*. The research indicates that the methods used in the *Math Trailblazers* math facts program lead to more effective learning and better retention of the math facts and also helps develop essential math skills.

The *Math Trailblazers* program for teaching the math facts is characterized by these elements:

- *Early emphasis on problem solving.* Students first approach the basic facts as problems to solve rather than facts to memorize. Students invent their own strategies to solve these problems or learn appropriate strategies from others through class discussion. Students' natural strategies, especially counting strategies, are explicitly encouraged. In this way, students learn that math is more than memorizing facts and rules that "you either get or you don't."

- *De-emphasis of rote work.* Fluency with the math facts is an important component of any student's mathematical learning. Research has shown that an overemphasis on memorization and the frequent administration of timed tests are counterproductive. (National Research Council, 2001) We encourage the use of strategies to find facts, so students become confident they can find answers to fact problems they do not immediately recall.

- *Gradual and systematic introduction of facts.* Students study the facts in small groups that can be solved using similar strategies. Students first work on simple strategies for easy facts and then progress to more sophisticated strategies and harder facts. By the end of the process, they gain fluency with all the required facts.

- *Ongoing practice.* Work on the math facts is distributed throughout the curriculum, especially in the Daily Practice and Problems, Home Practice, and games. This practice for fluency, however, takes place only after students conceptually understand the operations and are proficient with strategies for solving basic fact problems. Delaying practice in this way means students need less practice to achieve fluency.

- *Appropriate assessment.* Teachers assess students' knowledge of the facts through observations as they work on activities, labs, and games as well as through the appropriate use of written tests and quizzes. Beginning in first grade, periodic, short quizzes in the Daily Practice and Problems naturally follow the study of small groups of facts organized around specific strategies. As self-assessment in Grades 2–5, students record their progress on *Facts I Know* charts and determine which facts they need to study. Inventory tests of all facts for each operation are used sparingly in Grades 2–5 (no more than twice per year) to assess students' progress with fact fluency. The goal of the math facts assessment program is to determine the degree to which students can find answers to fact problems quickly and accurately and whether they can retain this skill over time.

- *Multiyear approach.* In Grades 1 and 2, *Math Trailblazers* emphasizes strategies that lead to fluency with the addition and subtraction facts. In Grade 3, students gain fluency with the multiplication facts while reviewing the addition and subtraction facts. In Grade 4, students achieve fluency with the division facts and verify fluency with the multiplication facts. In Grade 5, the multiplication and division facts are systematically reviewed and assessed. This is outlined in Table 1.
- *Facts are not gatekeepers.* Students are not prevented from learning more complex mathematics because they do not perform well on fact tests. Use of strategies, calculators, and other math tools (e.g., manipulatives, hundreds charts, printed multiplication tables) allows students to continue to work on interesting problems and important mathematical concepts while they are still learning the facts.

The *Math Trailblazers* approach to the math facts is discussed more fully in the TIMS Tutor: *Math Facts*.

Concepts of Whole-Number Operations
Concepts and Skills

Throughout the past 150 years, there were numerous attempts to teach mathematics meaningfully rather than by rote. Unfortunately, as Lauren Resnick points out in *Syntax and Semantics in Learning to Subtract,* ". . . the conceptual teaching methods of the past were inadequate to the extent that they taught concepts instead of procedures and left it entirely to students to discover how computational procedures could be derived from the basic structure of the number and numeration system." (1987, p. 136)

Many educators have long recognized, however, that there is no real conflict between skills and concepts. (Whitehead, 1929; Dewey, 1938; Brownell, 1956; May, 1995; National Research Council, 2001) New conceptual understandings are built on existing skills and concepts; these new understandings in turn support the further development of skills and concepts. Thomas Carpenter describes the relationship in this way: ". . . It is an iterative process. Procedures are taught that can be supported by existing conceptual knowledge, and the conceptual knowledge base is extended to provide a basis for developing more advanced concepts. At every point during instruction, procedures are taught that can be connected to existing conceptual knowledge." (1986, p. 130) This integration of concepts and skills underlies our work with arithmetic in *Math Trailblazers.*

Subtraction in Grades K to 5

To illustrate how concepts and skills are balanced in *Math Trailblazers,* we outline in this section how one operation—subtraction—is developed with whole numbers in Grades K–4. Though the details may differ for the other operations, the same general approach described here with subtraction applies to all four arithmetic operations.

In kindergarten and Grade 1 of *Math Trailblazers,* students solve a variety of problems involving subtraction of numbers up to and even beyond 100. These problems are based on hands-on classroom activities and realistic situations from children's experiences. Different subtraction problem types are represented, including take-away, comparison, part-whole, and missing addend problems. (See the TIMS Tutor: *Word Problems* for a discussion of these and other problem types.)

Students in even the earliest grades are thus faced with problems for which they have no ready solution methods, problems that in the traditional view are beyond their ability. They do, however, have much prior knowledge that is relevant. They have their common sense—their conceptual knowledge of the problem situations. They know, for example, that if Grace begins with 50 marbles and loses 17, then she must end with fewer than 50 marbles. Young students also have considerable procedural knowledge, including various kinds of counting skills: ordinary counting, counting on, counting back, and skip counting by twos, fives, and tens. Students have tools to solve the problems. These include connecting cubes, links, *100 Charts,* ten frames, other manipulatives, paper and pencil, calculators, and number lines. Researchers note that initial work with any operation should involve classroom activities that use real-world or imaginary contexts, manipulatives, or drawings that highlight the attributes of the numbers and operations. (Carpenter et al., 1998; Fuson and Briars, 1990, Hiebert et al., 1997) This research further emphasizes the importance of long-term use of the manipulatives and of linking the manipulatives with written notation.

On one side, then, are hard problems involving many types of subtraction. On the other side are the kindergartners and first-graders, with their common sense, their counting skills, and tools. Traditionally, word problems and other applications involving subtraction (and other operations) were introduced only after students had extensive practice with a subtraction algorithm. Research on students' learning of addition and subtraction (Carpenter et al., 1998) strongly suggests that it is more effective to have students solve and pose word problems and other context-based problems (such as problems in the laboratory investigations in *Math Trailblazers*) before they learn formal, paper-and-pencil procedures for subtraction. As students apply their resources to solve the problems, they build their conceptual and procedural understanding of subtraction. They devise methods to solve the problems, make records of their work, and discuss their methods with their teacher and classmates. Their new knowledge about subtraction is closely linked to their prior knowledge, especially their out-of-school knowledge and their counting skills. (Baroody and Ginsburg, 1986)

You comment on students' methods and may show students how to use conventional symbols to describe their work, but you make no attempt to standardize students' methods. Any method that yields a correct result is acceptable—as long as it makes sense. The goal is to encourage students to apply their prior knowledge to problems they encounter and to let students know that their intuitive methods are valid.

As students apply their resources to solve the problems, they build their conceptual and procedural understanding of subtraction. They devise methods to solve the problems, make records of their work, and discuss their methods with their teacher and classmates.

First grade focuses on various strategies students can use to solve single-digit subtraction problems. For example, they can solve a problem like 9 − 3 by counting back 3 from 9: 8, 7, 6. This work aims not at achieving fluency with the subtraction facts, but rather at building conceptual understanding of subtraction and procedural skill with various strategies. (See the TIMS Tutor: *Math Facts.*)

At the beginning of Grade 2, the problem-solving approach to subtraction continues. Problems with numbers up to 1000 are introduced, but again no standard solution method is taught at this point. Students devise their own ways to solve the problems, drawing on their prior knowledge of the problem situations and the number system, and share their thinking with the class.

The strategies approach to the subtraction facts continues in Grade 2. As students' fluency with the addition facts and simple subtraction facts increases, more sophisticated strategies become feasible. For example, a child may solve 14 − 6 by reasoning that "to take away 6 from 14, I first can take away 4, which leaves 10. Then I take away 2 more, which equals 8." These new strategies, sometimes called derived fact strategies or reasoning from known facts, illustrate how new knowledge builds on prior skills.

Giving children only multidigit problems that do not involve borrowing encourages the development of a rote and faulty algorithm that may not carry over into problems that require borrowing.

Later in Grade 2, systematic work begins on paper-and-pencil methods for subtracting two-digit numbers. Students solve two-digit subtraction problems using their own methods and record their solutions on paper. The class examines and discusses the various procedures that students devise. At this time, if no student introduces a standard subtraction algorithm, then the teacher does so, explaining that it is a subtraction method that many people use. The standard method is examined and discussed, just as the invented methods were. Students who do not have an effective method of their own are urged to adopt the standard method.

Problems that require borrowing are included from the beginning. Though this differs markedly from traditional approaches, we view it as important in developing a sound conception of subtraction algorithms. Giving children only multidigit problems that do not involve borrowing encourages the development of a rote and faulty algorithm that may not carry over into problems that require borrowing.

By the beginning of Grade 3, students have a strong conceptual understanding of subtraction and significant experience devising procedures to solve subtraction problems with numbers up to 1000. They also have some experience with standard and invented paper-and-pencil algorithms for solving two-digit subtraction problems. In Grade 3, this prior knowledge is extended in a systematic examination of paper-and-pencil methods for multidigit subtraction.

This work begins with a series of multidigit subtraction problems that students solve in various ways. Many of these problems are set in a whimsical context, the TIMS Candy Company, a business that uses base-ten pieces to keep track of its production and sales. Other problems are based on student-collected data, such as a reading survey.

As in Grade 2, the class discusses and compares the several methods students use to solve these problems. Again, any method that yields correct results is acceptable, but now a greater emphasis is given to methods that are efficient and compact. This work leads to a close examination of one particular subtraction algorithm. See Figure 3. Students solve several problems with base-ten pieces and with this standard algorithm, making connections between actions with the manipulatives and steps in the algorithm. After a thorough analysis of the algorithm, including a comparison of the standard algorithm and other methods, students are given opportunities to practice the algorithm or other methods of their choice.

$$
\begin{array}{r}
\overset{3\ \ \ 16}{7\ \cancel{4}\ \cancel{0}} \\
-\ 4\ 3\ 9 \\
\hline
3\ 0\ 7
\end{array}
$$

Figure 3: *A standard subtraction algorithm*

Practice in paper-and-pencil methods for multidigit subtraction is distributed throughout Grades 3 and 4. Students encounter sets of problems that encourage them to look at each problem and choose an efficient method to solve it. For many of these problems, a standard algorithm will be the most efficient choice. For others, students can use mental math or counting strategies. For example, students should identify the problem $4001 - 3998$ as a problem they can easily solve by counting up three from 3998 to 4001.

By the beginning of Grade 4, basic work with whole number subtraction is complete. Students have a firm conceptual understanding of subtraction and a diverse repertoire of methods they can use to solve subtraction problems. Work in Grade 4 is designed to maintain and extend these skills and understandings. Fluency with the subtraction facts is verified and remediation is provided for students who need it. In the laboratory experiments and other work, students solve a wide variety of subtraction problems using methods of their own choosing. The Daily Practice and Problems and Home Practice include distributed practice in paper-and-pencil subtraction so that those skills do not deteriorate.

In Grade 5 students continue to use subtraction in activities and labs. As in earlier grades, they are encouraged to decide when it is appropriate to use paper and pencil, calculators, or estimation. A review of subtraction modeled with base-ten pieces is included for students who have not used *Math Trailblazers* in previous grades. Distributed practice is provided in the Daily Practice and Problems and the Home Practice. Fluency with the subtraction facts is assessed in the first unit, and remediation is provided in the Addition and Subtraction Math Facts Review section in the *Facts Resource Guide.*

Whole-Number Computation in *Math Trailblazers*

Many other topics in *Math Trailblazers*—addition, multiplication, division, fractions, and decimals—are treated in ways similar to that sketched for subtraction above. In all these areas, we seek a balance between conceptual understanding and procedural skill. For all operations, standard methods for solving problems are not introduced until students have developed good conceptual and procedural understandings—the too-early introduction of such procedures may short-circuit students' common sense, encouraging mechanical and uncritical behavior. (Brownell & Chazall, 1935; Resnick & Omanson, 1987; Rathmell & Huinker, 1989; Perry, 1991; Hiebert, 1999)

> *We seek a balance between conceptual understanding and procedural skill. For all operations, standard methods for solving problems are not introduced until students have developed good conceptual and procedural understandings—the too-early introduction of such procedures may short-circuit students' common sense, encouraging mechanical and uncritical behavior.*

Grade	Addition	Subtraction	Multiplication	Division
K	• concepts of the operation	• concepts of the operation	• concepts of the operation	• concepts of the operation
1	• concepts of the operation • informal methods	• concepts of the operation • informal methods	• concepts of the operation	• concepts of the operation
2	• concepts of the operation • invented algorithms • standard methods for small numbers	• concepts of the operation • invented algorithms • standard methods for small numbers	• concepts of the operation • informal methods	• concepts of the operation • informal methods
3	• invented algorithms • standard methods for larger numbers	• invented algorithms • standard methods for larger numbers	• concepts of the operation • invented algorithms • standard methods for small numbers	• concepts of the operation
4	• review, practice, apply, and extend	• review, practice, apply, and extend	• invented algorithms • standard methods for larger numbers	• invented algorithms • standard methods for larger numbers
5	• review, practice, apply, and extend	• review, practice, apply, and extend	• review, practice, apply, and extend	• standard methods for larger numbers

Table 1: *Whole-number operations scope and sequence*

Even after analyzing and practicing standard methods students are still encouraged to solve problems in more than one way. Flexible thinking and mathematical power are our goals, not rote fluency with a handful of standard algorithms.

Even after analyzing and practicing standard methods students are still encouraged to solve problems in more than one way.

Varieties of Computation

There is much more to computation than the standard paper-and-pencil algorithms for adding, subtracting, multiplying, and dividing. These algorithms are good for obtaining exact answers with simple technology, but, depending on the resources available and the result desired, there are many other kinds of computation. For example, if you are in a supermarket check-out line with several items and you find only $10 in your wallet, then a quick judgment whether you have sufficient funds is desirable. In this case, a rough mental estimate of the total cost of your purchases is what you want. If you are planning an addition to your house, however, different computational demands must be met. The situation is more complex than the supermarket checkout, and the penalty for making a mistake is more severe, so greater care must be taken. You will want more resources—paper and pencil, a calculator, time to work, perhaps a computer spreadsheet—and you will probably want rather precise estimates for the cost of various alternative designs for the addition.

A well-rounded mathematics program should prepare students to compute accurately, flexibly, and appropriately in all situations. Figure 4 shows a classification of computational situations using two criteria, the result desired and the resources available. Although you may want to move some of the questions to other cells or insert your own examples, these six categories of computation indicate the scope required of a complete mathematics curriculum (Coburn, 1989).

Resources Available

		Paper & Pencil	Machine	Mental
Result Desired	Exact	How many students are in the three third grades at my school?	How much will my monthly payment be on my car loan?	How much baking soda do I need if I am tripling a recipe that calls for 2 teaspoons?
	Approximate	What is my share of the national debt?	House remodeling: Which design(s) can I afford?	Supermarket checkout: Do I have enough money for these items?

Figure 4: *Six varieties of computation*

The TIMS Philosophy: Meaning, Invention, Efficiency, Power

The treatment of computation in *Math Trailblazers* proceeds in several stages. The grade levels for the stages vary with the operation—ideas of division, for example, develop long after addition—but the general pattern is similar for all the operations. Roughly speaking, the stages are

- developing meaning for the operation,
- inventing procedures for solving problems, and
- becoming more efficient at carrying out procedures, all leading to
- developing mathematical power.

Developing mathematical power with an operation means that students understand *when* to apply the operation and *how* to use varied computational methods to solve problems, even complex or nonroutine problems.

The goal of the first stage is to help students understand the meaning of the operation. Most of the work involves solving problems, writing or telling "stories" that involve operations, and sharing solution strategies. These methods typically involve a great deal of mental arithmetic and creative thinking. The use of manipulatives, pictures, and counting is encouraged at this stage. Discussing these informal methods helps develop students' understanding of the operation.

In the next stage, the focus shifts from developing the concept of the operation to devising and analyzing procedures to carry out the operation. At this stage, students "invent" methods for carrying out the operation, explaining, discussing, and comparing their procedures. Multiple solution strategies—mental, paper and pencil, manipulative, calculator—are encouraged, and parallels between various methods are explored. There is evidence that this "invented algorithms" approach enhances students' number and operation sense and problem-solving abilities (Madell, 1985; Sawada, 1985; Kamii, Lewis & Jones, 1991; Burns, 1992; Kamii, Lewis & Livingston, 1993; Porter & Carroll, 1995; Carroll & Porter, 1997). Inventing their own methods helps make mathematics meaningful for children by connecting school mathematics to their own ways of thinking. The expectation that mathematics should make sense is reinforced.

In the third stage, a standard algorithm for the operation is introduced. This algorithm is not presented as the one, true, and official way to solve problems, but rather as yet another procedure to examine. The algorithms used in *Math Trailblazers* are not all identical to the traditional ones taught in school. The addition and subtraction algorithms are only a little different, but the procedures for multiplication and division are considerably different. (See Figures 5 and 6.)

$$
\begin{array}{r}
5\ 8 \\
\times\ 3\ 6 \\
\hline
4\ 8 \\
3\ 0\ 0 \\
2\ 4\ 0 \\
1\ 5\ 0\ 0 \\
\hline
2\ 0\ 8\ 8
\end{array}
$$

Figure 5: *All-partials multiplication*

```
                1  9 R 31
        3 2 ) 6  3  9
             -3  2  0     10
              3  1  9
             -1  6  0      5
              1  5  9
             -   9  6      3
                 6  3
             -   3  2      1
                 3  1    19
```

Figure 6: *A division algorithm*

We chose these alternative algorithms for multiplication and division for several reasons. First, they are easier to learn than the traditional methods. Second, they are more transparent, revealing what is actually happening. Third, they provide practice in multiplying by numbers ending in zero, an important skill for estimation. Finally, even though they are less efficient than the traditional algorithms, they are good enough for most purposes—any problem that is awkward to solve by these methods should probably be done by machine anyway.

Students who have no reliable method of their own are urged to adopt the standard algorithm. However, even after introducing and analyzing a standard algorithm for an operation, alternative methods are still accepted, even encouraged, for students who are comfortable with them. In particular, the standard algorithm is very inefficient with some problems. For example, students using *Math Trailblazers* should be able to compute 40×30 mentally to get 1200. Using the standard algorithm here would be inefficient. Or consider $16,000 - 5$. Using a standard algorithm to solve this problem is tedious and often results in errors.

In the last stage, students achieve mathematical power through the mastery of procedures that solve entire classes of problems: efficient and reliable computational algorithms. This procedural fluency, moreover, is based on solid conceptual understandings so that it can be applied flexibly to solve problems. These procedures become part of the students' base of prior knowledge—on which they can build more advanced conceptual and procedural understandings.

Fractions and Decimals

The approach to fractions and decimals in *Math Trailblazers* parallels that for whole numbers. At first, the focus is on developing concepts and meanings for fractions and decimals. Next comes a period in which students invent procedures for solving problems, connecting school mathematics to their own informal methods and common sense. Finally, formal procedures are investigated, not as substitutes for common sense, but as more efficient methods for achieving desired results.

Fraction Meanings

One of the problems with fractions is that they are so useful. Consider some of the meanings for $\frac{1}{2}$:

- half of a cookie (a part-whole fraction)
- $1 \div 2$ (division)
- one cup water to two cups flour (a ratio, sometimes written 1:2)
- $\frac{1}{2}$ mile (a measurement)
- the point midway between 0 and 1 (the name of a point on a number line)
- the square root of $\frac{1}{4}$ (a pure number)
- the chance a fair coin will land heads up (a probability)

Because the same notation can mean so many different things, children and even adults sometimes become confused and may manipulate fraction symbols haphazardly, often with unfortunate results. A better approach develops sound meanings for the symbols before focusing on how to manipulate them (Mack, 1990).

Part-Whole Fractions

Early fraction work focuses on part-whole fractions. Many fractions in daily life are part-whole fractions, so even young children are familiar with terms like one-half and three-fourths in part-whole contexts. Also, many key ideas about fractions are well illustrated in part-whole situations.

There are two concepts that are fundamental in understanding part-whole fractions: knowing what the whole is and understanding what a part is in relation to the whole. For example, to understand the statement, "Last night I ate three-fourths of a carton of ice cream," requires knowing what the whole is. Just how big a carton of ice cream was it? One must also understand that the parts into which the whole is divided must be equal—they should have the same area or mass or number, etc. A way to make this clear to children is to talk about "fair shares."

The whole in a part-whole fraction can be either a single thing (e.g., a pizza) or a collection (e.g., a class of students). When the whole is a collection, then counting is generally used to make fair shares; when the unit is a single thing, the fairness of the shares depends on some measurable quantity. Half of one pizza is different from half of three pizzas. Often, area is the variable that must be equally allocated among the parts; such a situation may be called an area model for fractions.

Symbols and Referents

A key idea in the *Math Trailblazers* approach to fractions is that fractions should be represented in several ways and that students should be able to make connections between those representations. The fraction two-thirds, for example, can be expressed in words, symbols, pictures, or real objects (Figure 7).

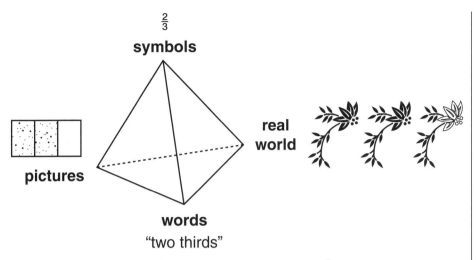

Figure 7: *Representations of* $\frac{2}{3}$

The ability to move freely between these several representations is an essential component of the mathematical understanding of fractions (Lesh, Post & Behr, 1987). Especially important are connections between fraction symbols and the real-world situations to which those fractions refer. Given symbols for a fraction, can students draw an illustrative picture or tell a story? Can students explain the relationship between a group of five girls and two boys and the fraction $\frac{5}{7}$?

Math Trailblazers makes extensive use of manipulatives in teaching fractions in all grades. Pictures, pattern blocks, geoboards, paper folding, and number lines are among many tools used to promote students' conceptual understanding of fractions. When paper-and-pencil procedures for adding, subtracting, multiplying, and dividing fractions are introduced in Grades 4 and 5, they are always linked closely with other representations of fractions, such as manipulatives or pictures.

Decimals

Decimals are treated in two ways in *Math Trailblazers:* first, as another way to write certain common fractions—those with denominators that are powers of ten—and second, as an extension of the whole number place value system. Similar to the coverage of other topics in *Math Trailblazers,* considerable attention is placed upon developing a solid conceptual foundation about decimals before formal, paper-and-pencil operations are introduced. Students with strong conceptual understandings of decimals learn procedures more easily and can apply those procedures to problem situations more effectively

> *The ability to move freely between these several representations is an essential component of the mathematical understanding of fractions. Especially important are connections between fraction symbols and the real-world situations to which these fractions refer.*

(Ball, 1993; Behr & Post, 1992; Hiebert, Wearne & Taber, 1991; Lesh, Post & Behr, 1987). Connections between fractions (common fractions) and decimals (decimal fractions) are stressed throughout.

As with work with whole numbers and fractions, work with decimal fractions includes extensive work with manipulatives. Often these models are used to make strong connections between fractions, decimals, and percents. Figures 8 and 9 show two examples of tools used in Grade 5 lessons on decimals. These representations create visual images of the decimal fractions and link those images with students' previous work with fractions and percent.

Figure 8: *Interlocking centiwheel disks model $\frac{1}{4}$, 0.25, and 25%.*

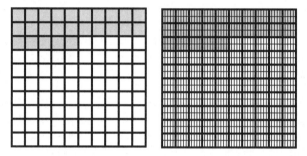

Figure 9: $\frac{25}{100} = 0.25$ *and* $\frac{250}{1000} = 0.250$

A Developmental Approach

Kindergarten fraction work emphasizes the idea that the fractional parts of a whole must be the same size. Work with symbols is not emphasized.

Fraction work in Grades 1–3 of *Math Trailblazers* focuses primarily on establishing links between symbols and referents for part-whole fractions. Children learn to make connections between marks on paper and the real world. Concepts of the unit—identifying the unit, knowing how the size of the unit affects the value of the fraction, appreciating the importance of fair shares—are also explored (Figure 10). Decimals are treated primarily as an alternative notation for certain fractions, and some attention is given to the interpretation of decimals that appear on calculators. Real-world situations, especially fair sharing, and area models predominate.

If is $\frac{1}{3}$,

then what is one whole?

Figure 10: *A concept-of-unit exercise*

In Grade 3, students continue to develop concepts of the unit, but they begin to use more varied models. Children explore the relative size of fractions, especially with respect to the benchmark numbers 0, $\frac{1}{2}$, and 1. They also study equivalent fractions in Grade 3. Fractions are represented with a variety of manipulatives—paper folding, pattern blocks, geoboards. Collections of objects are divided to represent fractions.

Decimals are investigated more extensively in Grade 3, again being treated as a kind of fraction. Decimals in metric length measurement and on number lines are investigated. Base-ten pieces are used to create concrete and visual representations of decimal fractions. Translating between common fractions and decimals is again stressed.

In Grade 4, work on operations with fractions and decimals begins, but standard procedures are not taught. As discussed above, modeling concepts and procedures with manipulatives is intended to establish a basis for more algorithmic work in Grade 5. In fourth grade, students solve problems involving addition and subtraction, largely with the aid of manipulatives and other fraction models.

Operations with fractions and decimals include more than simply the four arithmetic operations. Putting fractions and decimals in order by size, renaming the same number in several equivalent forms, and estimating sums, differences, and so on, are all operations that can be carried out with fractions and decimals. Again, manipulatives, such as pattern blocks and base-ten pieces, are used to develop conceptual understanding and provide a concrete representation of the symbols.

In Grade 5, paper-and-pencil procedures for addition, subtraction, and multiplication of fractions and decimals are explored, including use of common denominators and reducing. Repeating decimals are introduced. Students also use calculators to rename fractions as decimals for comparing and ordering common fractions.

Many contexts are used to reinforce students' understanding of fraction and decimal concepts. For example, in a Grade 5 laboratory investigation, *Comparing Lives of Animals and Soap Bubbles,* students collect data about the "life spans" of soap bubbles. As they analyze the data, they convert the data first to a fractional quantity, then to the equivalent decimal fraction. Making these connections between mathematical concepts and real-world situations helps students make sense of the mathematics they are learning.

Conclusion

Our goal in developing *Math Trailblazers* is to create a balanced program that promotes the coordinated development of both procedural skill and conceptual understanding. Students will connect school mathematics with intuitive knowledge and informal procedures. They will use a variety of techniques and manipulatives for modeling the mathematical ideas. In doing so, students will not only develop skills and concepts, but will be able to use those skills and concepts to solve problems.

References

Ball, D. "Halves, Pieces, and Twoths: Constructing and Using Representational Contexts in Teaching Fractions." In T.P. Carpenter, E. Fennema, and T.A. Romberg (Eds.), *Rational Numbers: An Integration of Research.* pp. 157–195. Lawrence Erlbaum Associates, Hillsdale, NJ, 1993.

Baroody, A.J., and H.P. Ginsburg. "The Relationship between Initial Meaning and Mechanical Knowledge of Arithmetic." In J. Hiebert (ed.), *Conceptual and Procedural Knowledge: The Case of Mathematics.* Lawrence Erlbaum Associates, Hillsdale, NJ, 1986.

Behr, M.J., and T.R. Post. "Teaching Rational Number and Decimal Concepts." In *Teaching Mathematics in Grades K–8: Research Based Methods.* Allyn and Bacon, Boston, MA, 1992.

Bransford, J.D., A.L. Brown, and R.R. Cocking, eds. *How People Learn: Brain, Mind, Experience, and School.* National Academy Press, Washington, DC, 1999.

Brown, J.S., and R.R. Burton. "Diagnostic Models for Procedural Bugs in Basic Mathematical Skills." *Cognitive Science, 2,* pp. 155–192, 1978.

Brownell, W.A., and C.B. Chazal. "The Effects of Premature Drill in Third-Grade Arithmetic." *Journal of Educational Research, 29* (1), 1935.

Brownell, W.A. "Meaning and Skill—Maintaining the Balance." *Arithmetic Teacher, 34* (8), pp. 18–25 (Original work published in 1956), 1987.

Carpenter, T.P. "Conceptual Knowledge as a Foundation for Procedural Knowledge." In J. Hiebert (ed.), *Conceptual and Procedural Knowledge: The Case of Mathematics.* Lawrence Erlbaum Associates, Hillsdale, NJ, 1986.

Carpenter, T.P., E. Fennema, and M.L. Franke. *Cognitively Guided Instruction: Building the Primary Mathematics Curriculum on Children's Informal Mathematical Knowledge.* A paper presented at the annual meeting of the American Educational Research Association, San Francisco, CA, April 1992.

Carpenter, T.P., M.L. Franke, V.R. Jacobs, E. Fennema, and S.B. Empson. "A Longitudinal Study of Invention and Understanding in Children's Multidigit Addition and Subtraction." *Journal for Research in Mathematics Education, 29,* pp. 3–20, 1998.

Carroll, W., and D. Porter. "Invented Algorithms: Helping Students to Develop and Use Meaningful Mathematical Procedures." *Teaching Children Mathematics,* pp. 370–374, March 1997.

Coburn, T.G. "The Role of Computation in the Changing Mathematics Curriculum." In P.R. Trafton (ed.), *New Directions for Elementary School Mathematics.* National Council of Teachers of Mathematics, Reston, VA, 1989.

Dewey, J. *Experience and Education.* Macmillan, New York, 1938.

Finn, C.E., Jr. "What If Those Math Standards Are Wrong?" *Education Week,* 20 January 1993.

Fuson, K.C., and D.J. Briars. "Using a Base-Ten Blocks Learning/Teaching Approach for First- and Second-Grade Place-Value and Multidigit Addition and Subtraction." *Journal for Research in Mathematics Education,* 21, pp. 180–206, 1990.

Good, T.L., C. Mulryan, and M. McCaslin. "Grouping for Instruction in Mathematics: A Call for Programmatic Research on Small-Group Processes." In D.A. Grouws (ed.), *Handbook of Research on Mathematics Teaching and Learning: A Project of the National Council of Teachers of Mathematics* (Chapter 9). Macmillan, New York, 1992.

Greenes, C., M. Cavanagh, L. Dacey, C. Findell, and M. Small. *Navigating through Algebra in Pre-kindergarten–Grade 2.* National Council of Teachers of Mathematics, Reston, VA, 2001.

Hiebert, J. "Children's Mathematical Learning: The Struggle to Link Form and Understanding." *Elementary School Journal,* 84 (5), pp. 497–513, 1984.

Hiebert, J. "A Theory of Developing Competence with Written Mathematical Symbols." *Educational Studies in Mathematics,* 19, pp. 333–355, 1988.

Hiebert, J. "Relationships between Research and the NCTM Standards." *Journal for Research in Mathematics Education,* 30 (1), pp. 3–19, 1999.

Hiebert, J. and D. Wearne. "Procedures over Concepts: The Acquisition of Decimal Number Knowledge." In J. Hiebert (Ed.), *Conceptual and Procedural Knowledge: The Case of Mathematics.* Lawrence Erlbaum Associates, Hillsdale, NJ, 1986.

Hiebert, J., D. Wearne, and S. Taber. "Fourth Graders' Gradual Construction of Decimal Fractions during Instruction Using Different Physical Representations." *Elementary School Journal,* 91 (4), pp. 321–341, 1991.

Hiebert, J., T. Carpenter, E. Fennema, K.C. Fuson, D. Wearne, H. Murray, A. Oliver, and H. Piet. *Making Sense: Teaching and Learning Mathematics with Understanding.* Heinemann, Portsmouth, NH, 1997.

Kamii, C., B.A. Lewis, and S. Jones. "Reform in Primary Mathematics Education: A Constructivist View." *Educational Horizons,* 70 (1), pp. 19–26, 1991.

Kamii, C., B.A. Lewis, and S.J. Livingston, "Primary Arithmetic: Children Inventing Their Own Procedures." *Arithmetic Teacher,* 41 (4), pp. 200–203, 1993.

Lesh, R., T. Post, and M. Behr. "Representations and Translations among Representations in Mathematics Learning and Problem Solving." C. Janvier, ed., *Problems of Representation in the Teaching and Learning of Mathematics.* Lawrence Erlbaum Associates, Hillsdale, NJ, 1987.

McKnight, C.C., F.J. Crosswhite, J.A. Dossey, E. Kifer, J.O. Swafford, K.J. Travers, and T.J. Cooney. *The Underachieving Curriculum: Assessing U.S. School Mathematics from an International Perspective.* Stipes, Champaign, IL, 1987.

Mack, N.K. "Learning Fractions with Understanding: Building on Informal Knowledge." *Journal for Research in Mathematics Education,* 21 (1), pp. 16–32, 1990.

Madell, R. "Children's Natural Processes." *Arithmetic Teacher,* 32 (7), pp. 20–22, 1985.

Mathews, J. "Psst, Kid, Wanna Buy a Used Math Book? They're Old-Fashioned and a Bit Tedious, but John Saxon's Books are Hot Stuff in the Education Underground." *Newsweek,* 121, pp. 62–63, 1993.

May, L. "Reflections on Teaching Mathematics Today." *Illinois Mathematics Teacher,* 46 (3), pp. 5–8, 1995.

National Council of Teachers of Mathematics. *Curriculum Focal Points for Pre-kindergarten through Grade 8 Mathematics: A Quest for Coherence.* Reston, VA, 2006.

National Research Council. *Adding It Up: Helping Children Learn Mathematics.* National Academy Press, Washington, DC, 2001.

National Research Council. "The Strands of Mathematical Proficiency." *Adding It Up: Helping Children Learn Mathematics.* pp. 115–156, J. Kilpatrick, J. Swafford, and B. Findell, eds. National Academy Press, Washington, DC, 2001.

Perry, M. "Learning and Transfer: Instructional Conditions and Conceptual Change." *Cognitive Development,* 6, pp. 449–468, 1991.

Porter, D., and W. Carroll. "Invented Algorithms: Some Examples from Primary Classrooms." *Illinois Mathematics Teacher,* pp. 6–12, April 1995.

Press, M. "Drill and Practice Add Up." *San Jose Mercury News,* 27 February 1995.

Principles and Standards for School Mathematics. National Council of Teachers of Mathematics, Reston, VA, 2000.

Rathmell, E.C., and D.M. Huinker. "Using 'Part-Whole' Language to Help Children Represent and Solve Word Problems." In P.R. Trafton (ed.), *New Directions for Elementary School Mathematics,* pp. 99–110. National Council of Teachers of Mathematics, Reston, VA, 1989.

Resnick, L.B. "Syntax and Semantics in Learning to Subtract." In R. Glaser (ed.), *Advances in Instructional Psychology* (Vol. 3). Lawrence Erlbaum Associates, Hillsdale, NJ, 1987.

Resnick, L.B., and S.F. Omanson. "Learning to Understand Arithmetic." In *Advances in Instructional Psychology* (Vol. 3). Lawrence Erlbaum Associates, Hillsdale, NJ, 1987.

Resnick, L.B., S. Lesgold, and V. Bill. *From Protoquantities to Number Sense.* A paper prepared for the Psychology of Mathematics Education Conference, Oaxtapec, Mexico, 1990.

Sawada, D. "Mathematical Symbols: Insight through Invention." *Arithmetic Teacher,* 32 (6), pp. 20–22, 1985.

Shuard, H. "CAN: Calculator Use in the Primary Grades in England and Wales." In J. T. Fey (ed.), *Calculators in Mathematics Education,* Reston, VA, 1992.

Skemp, R.R. "Relational Understanding and Instrumental Understanding." *Arithmetic Teacher,* 26 (3), pp. 9–15, 1978.

Swart, W.L. "Some Findings on Conceptual Development of Computational Skills." *Arithmetic Teacher* 32 (5), pp. 36–38, 1985.

Usiskin, Z. "Paper-and-Pencil Skills in a Calculator/Computer Age." *UCSMP Newsletter,* 16, pp. 7–14, 1994.

Van Lehn, K. "Arithmetic Procedures Are Induced from Examples." In J. Hiebert (ed.), *Conceptual and Procedural Knowledge: The Case of Mathematics.* Lawrence Erlbaum Associates, Hillsdale, NJ, 1986.

Whitehead, A.N. "The Rhythmic Claims of Freedom and Discipline." In *The Aims of Education and Other Essays.* Macmillan, New York, 1929.

Averages

Introduction

"Average" is one of those words that mean different things to different people. Baseball players talk about their batting averages. A teacher might confide to a colleague that "Jim is just an average student." At the university, students always want to know what the class average is on an exam. Sometimes you hear the statement that the temperature will be about average for this time of year. When someone asks you how you feel, you may reply, "Just average." In everyday usage, "average" is a word that can be anything from a synonym for "typical," "normal," or "usual," to a number derived according to some formula or rule. This TIMS Tutor lays out some of the different numerical meanings of "average" and explains some of the importance of averages in mathematics and science.

The Mean—A Wage Dispute

In his wonderful little book, *How to Lie with Statistics,* Darrell Huff gives the example of a factory owner and his workers who are arguing over wages. There are 25 workers including the owner. The owner pays himself $45,000. The others make $15,000, $10,000, $10,000, $5700, $5000, $5000, $5000, $3700, $3700, $3700, $3700, $3000, $2000, $2000, $2000, $2000, $2000, $2000, $2000, $2000, $2000, $2000, and $2000. The owner says the average wage is $5700 but the workers claim the average wage is only $3000. Even though prices have gone way up since Huff wrote his book 50 years ago, the discrepancy is clear: there is a big disagreement over what people are being paid, let alone what they should be paid.

So, what's going on here? Who's right, the owner or the workers? Both! The factory owner's average is the (arithmetic) mean; the workers' average is the median. There are other averages too, such as the **mode** (the number or value that occurs most often in a data set). However, in *Math Trailblazers,* we primarily use the mean and/or the median when finding average values. These two averages will be the focus of our discussion in this tutor.

Usually when people use the term "average," they are referring to the **mean.** This is the familiar add-up-all-the-numbers-and-divide average you learned in school. The mean has many useful properties that make it beloved by schoolteachers, statisticians, and scientists alike. Consider finding the average height of all the children in a class. Data for 23 children from a third-grade class is shown in Figure 1.

The mean height of these 23 children is

$$\langle H \rangle = \frac{\text{sum of heights}}{\text{number of children}}$$

$$= \frac{(133 + 136 + \ldots + 129 + 134) \text{ cm}}{23}$$

$$= \frac{3064 \text{ cm}}{23}$$

$$= 133.2 \text{ cm}$$

Name	H Height (in cm)
Karina	133
Federico	136
Ramon	135
Kiela	127
Aesha	126
Bravlia	128
Zuzia	133
Anthony	139
Iorta	146
Cordeli	135
Mary	137
Gennice	124

Name	H Height (in cm)
Curtis	139
Brian C	125
David	135
Anna	141
Brian M	131
Adriana	137
Boberto	134
Lucas	131
Gennifer	129
Amber	129
Nathan	134

Figure 1: *Data from a third-grade class*

Although no child may have this mean height, it gives everyone a point for making comparisons. For scientists, the mean is often the first number they calculate when looking at a data sample.

There is another way to interpret the mean height of this class. This may seem strange, but consider the following situation. Suppose you walk into another class and find 23 students all exactly the same height. The mean is clearly that height. If the mean height of this new class and the mean in our class are the same, then the sum of the heights of the children is the same. That is, imagine making two stacks of the children, one for our class and one for the new class. Stack the children one on top of another. Then the two stacks would be the same height. So, if two class means are the same and the number of children in each class is the same, then the sums of the heights in the classes are the same, even if the individual heights that make the sums are vastly different.

Statisticians like the mean because it is often the "best" estimate of an unknown quantity like a length, an area, or a mass. For example, suppose you are trying to measure the mass of a large steel sphere. You have an unbiased balance, and you know you need to take repeated readings to get an accurate measurement. So, suppose you make eleven measurements and find the sphere's mass to be 129 gm, 133 gm, 132 gm, 130 gm, 128 gm, 129 gm, 130 gm, 131 gm, 130 gm, 129 gm, and 131 gm. Then

$$\frac{(129 + 133 + \ldots + 130 + 129 + 131) \text{ gm}}{11}$$

$$= \frac{1432 \text{ gm}}{11}$$

$$= 130 \text{ gm}$$

This is the best estimate of the "true" mass of the sphere, given these measurements. (Notice that the quotient above is actually equal to 130.18181818 . . . gm. However, since our original measurements are to the nearest gram, it makes sense to give the average only to the nearest gram.)

Similar situations arise all the time in everyday life. Our factory owner is using the mean. He computes the average wage by adding up everyone's salary (including his big fat one) and dividing by the total number of workers:

$$\frac{\$142,500}{25} = \$5,700$$

As one final example, suppose Marty scores 85, 84, 86, 87, 84, 87, 85, 85, 83, and 85 on 10 rounds of golf and Ellen scores 83, 83, 95, 97, 81, 83, 82, 84, 96, and 84. Then Marty's mean score is

$$= \frac{85 + 84 + 86 + 87 + 84 + 87 + 85 + 85 + 83 + 85}{10}$$

$$= 85.1$$

and Ellen's mean score is

$$= \frac{83 + 83 + 95 + 97 + 81 + 83 + 82 + 84 + 96 + 84}{10}$$

$$= 86.8$$

So, it would appear that Marty is a better golfer than Ellen. (In golf, a lower score is a better score.)

But anyone who plays golf and bets will notice that if Marty and Ellen played 10 rounds against each other and scored as above, then Marty would win three times and Ellen would win seven times. And the factory workers still feel underpaid, despite that nice mean salary. So to get some perspective on what is happening here, let's look at another average, the median.

The Median

The **median** is the number in the middle. That is, roughly speaking, the median splits a set of numbers into two halves: one half is less than the median; the other half is more than the median.

The **median** is the number in the middle. That is, roughly speaking, the median splits a set of numbers into two halves: one half is less than the median; the other half is more than the median. So to find the median, rank the numbers from smallest to largest and take the one in the middle.

Suppose you want to find the median selling price of homes in your town. At the town office you find that 15 homes sold in the last six months. The selling prices, in rank order, were $134,000, $156,000, $164,000, $170,000, $184,000, $194,000, $224,000, $236,000, $250,000, $264,000, $266,000, $278,000, $334,000, $350,000, and $372,000. The median price was $236,000: seven houses sold for less than $236,000 and seven houses sold for more than $236,000.

When there is an even number of values, then the median can be a little harder to find. Say only 14 of the homes above have sold. Suppose that the highest-priced house, the one costing $372,000, went unsold. What is the new median? Counting up seven from the $134,000 house, we end up at the $224,000. Counting down seven from the $350,000 house, we end up at $236,000. The seventh house from the bottom is not the seventh house from the top! What to do? Easy. Go halfway between the two numbers closest to the middle. Halfway between $224,000 and $236,000. That comes out to be $230,000. So the median price of the 14 homes that sold would be $230,000.

Going back to our factory workers' example, there were 25 employees including the owner. The thirteenth salary (from the top or from the bottom) is $3000: there are 12 employees who make less than $3000, and 12 who make more than $3000. So, the median salary is $3000.

One common situation where the median may be preferred is when there are extreme values. In such cases, the mean can give a distorted picture of the "average" because the extreme values tend to "pull" the mean away from the typical values.

Sometimes the median is a better average to use than the mean. One common situation where the median may be preferred is when there are extreme values. In such cases, the mean can give a distorted picture of the "average" because the extreme values tend to "pull" the mean away from the typical values. Statisticians say the median is more "robust" than the mean; that is, the median is less affected by extreme values than the mean. This is why the factory workers prefer the median: it gives a truer picture of what a typical worker earns than the mean, which is pulled up by the owner's big salary.

The median offers some insight into our golfing example, too. Marty's (ranked) golf scores were 83, 84, 84, 85, 85, 85, 85, 86, 87, and 87. The two numbers in the middle are 85 and 85, so Marty's median score is 85. Ellen's scores were 81, 82, 83, 83, 83, 84, 84, 95, 96, and 97. The two numbers in the middle are 83 and 84, so Ellen's median score is 83.5. Thus, using medians, Ellen is a slightly better golfer, on average. Every few rounds she has a high score, but her typical score is better than Marty's typical score, so she usually wins.

Obviously, the median has several advantages with respect to the mean: it is less affected by extreme values; it requires little computation; it can be a better indicator of what is typical. You will want to be flexible, sometimes using the mean, sometimes using the median.

The Mode

The **mode** of a data set is the number that appears most often. For example, in Ellen's golf scores, the number that appears most often is 83. In our first example from *How to Lie with Statistics,* we considered the factory owner and his 25 workers who are arguing over wages. The owner pays himself $45,000. The others make $15,000, $10,000, $10,000, $5700, $5000, $5000, $5000, $3700, $3700, $3700, $3700, $3000, $2000, $2000, $2000, $2000, $2000, $2000, $2000, $2000, $2000, $2000, $2000, and $2000. To present their best argument, the workers could have argued that the modal salary was $2,000, since 12 workers had that salary.

Making Sense of Measures of Central Tendency

The median, mean, and mode are all "measures of central tendency." They each tell us something about the way the information in the data set clusters. Of course, when we replace a whole data set with one number, we lose a lot of information. Depending on the nature of the data set, the mean, median, or mode may or may not provide us with useful information. These measures of central tendency are most useful when the data clusters around some value.

Averaging in the *Math Trailblazers* Classroom

So how are averages used in *Math Trailblazers?* Suppose your second-grade students collected the data shown in Figure 2 for the TIMS Laboratory Investigation, *Rolling Along in Centimeters.* There are three experimental values for each car, and students need some measure of the middle that fairly represents their data for each car. In this case, the median is a perfectly respectable average.

T Type of Car	*D* Distance (in cm/unit)			
	Trial 1	Trial 2	Trial 3	Median
Red	83	93	86	
Blue	44	44	43	
Orange	39	53	46	
Black	194	199	189	

Figure 2: *Data from* Rolling Along in Centimeters

One way to get a median from data like this is illustrated in Figure 3. The students cross out the largest and smallest numbers in each row and use the one that is left as their average value. Finding the median value of the three trials does not require young children to do any arithmetic and conceptually illustrates quite nicely the idea of an average representing a middle value.

T	**D**			
Type of Car	**Distance (in** $\frac{cm}{unit}$ **)**			
	Trial 1	**Trial 2**	**Trial 3**	**Median**
Red	~~88~~	~~88~~	(86)	86
Blue	~~44~~	(44)	~~45~~	44
Orange	~~39~~	~~55~~	(46)	46
Black	(194)	~~189~~	~~189~~	194

Figure 3: *Finding the median*

42
45
47

You can illustrate finding the median more concretely by using links (or string, adding machine tape, etc.) to create "lengths" that match the actual distance the cars roll each time. At the end of three rolls, students will have three lengths of links each representing the distance a car rolled in a trial.

This is illustrated in Figure 4. The median value can then be found by comparing the lengths and discarding the shortest and longest; the remaining length represents the median. A similar process is used in the first-grade experiment *Rolling Along with Links.*

In fourth grade, students begin finding the mean as well as the median. Again the concepts are introduced concretely. For example, students find the median value for several towers of cubes by lining them up from shortest to tallest and

Figure 4: *Finding the median in* Rolling Along with Links selecting the tower in the middle. This is illustrated in Figures 5a and 5b. Figure 6 illustrates an even number of trials. To find the median here, students have to find the halfway point between the two middle towers.

Figures 5a and 5b: *Finding the median with cubes*

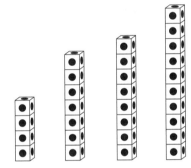

Figure 6: *The median number of cubes is $7\frac{1}{2}$.*

You can also use cubes to introduce the mean. For example, suppose students begin with the same five towers illustrated in Figure 5a. They first estimate the mean by figuring out a way to "even out the towers," as illustrated in Figure 7. The mean, to the nearest whole cube, is ten cubes. In this manner, the concept of the mean as a representative measure is stressed rather than focusing purely on the arithmetic procedure. Students then learn to calculate the mean using numerical values.

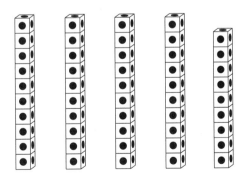

Figure 7: *Estimating the mean by "evening out" towers of cubes*

Students will often use calculators to calculate the mean of a data set. For example, the mean distance for the red car in Figure 2, when found by calculator, is:

$$\frac{(83 + 93 + 86) \text{ cm}}{3} = 87.333333 \text{ cm}$$

This is an example of too much of a good thing. In this case, the calculator gives many more digits than are meaningful. Students have to determine an appropriate level of significance. Keep in mind that our goal is to get a reasonable number to use as an average. Here, the original measurements were made to the nearest cm, so it makes sense to also report the mean value also to the nearest cm.

Why Average?

Finding the average is critical in a *Math Trailblazers* experiment. It is an important step from raw data to understanding. Errors are inevitable when making measurements, and averaging is one way to detect and control them. If a group of students makes the same measurement three times and gets 67 cm, 64 cm, and 84 cm, they should notice that the 84 cm is way off. They can detect their error and redo that measurement.

When we take a measurement, many factors prevent us from getting an exact answer. First is the precision of our measuring tools. A meterstick can measure only to the nearest tenth of a centimeter. When we measure the area of an irregular figure by counting square centimeters, we have to estimate the area of the fraction pieces of square centimeters, and so on. In addition, when we perform an experiment, we might get somewhat different measurements each time. If we drop a ball from a height of 100 centimeters and try to measure how high it bounces, we will get different answers each time. This is due to the difficulty in controlling variables (can we be sure we dropped the ball exactly the same way each time?) and the difficulty in measuring how high a moving object bounces. Nevertheless, if students are careful and practice measuring, they should get answers that are reasonably close. Even when all the measurements are close, the average minimizes error. If the measurements are 67 cm, 64 cm, and 67 cm, then the mean, 66 cm, is a more accurate prediction of future measurements than any of the actual measurements.

Another function of averaging is to aggregate raw data. Unlike computers, people cannot handle too many numbers at once. If I tell you the height of every child in a school, then you will be overwhelmed by numbers. If I tell you the median height of children in the school, you know less but probably understand more. The situation in a typical *Math Trailblazers* experiment is similar. From 12 actual measurements in *Rolling Along in Centimeters,* we cut down to four medians that are then used to display the data in a graph.

References

Huff, Darrell. *How to Lie with Statistics.* W.W. Norton & Co., New York, 1954.

Johnson, Robert. *Elementary Statistics,* 3rd ed., Wadsworth, Inc., Belmont, CA, 1980.

Estimation, Accuracy, and Error

For many people, one of the most attractive aspects of mathematics is that it is exact. The story problems that we worked on in our youth were reassuring (or terrifying) in the certainty of their answers. If one potato weighs 2 pounds, then 100 potatoes weigh 200 pounds. The only problem is that the real world is not so exact. One potato does not weigh exactly 2 pounds and 100 potatoes probably do not weigh 200 pounds. In this tutor, we discuss ways we deal mathematically with situations where exactness is not called for (when we estimate) or impossible (when we measure within a certain degree of accuracy).

Virtually all mathematics educators agree that estimation should be an important part of any elementary curriculum. Unlike content areas such as number and operation and geometry, there is very little traditional curriculum on estimation as well as some disagreement about exactly what is meant by estimation. Some mathematicians and educators make a distinction between estimation and approximation, but there is no generally agreed definition of these terms. This tutor provides a general overview of the concept of estimation and discusses some of the more common strategies and applications. For a more exhaustive treatment of estimation, we recommend the NCTM yearbook (1986).

What Is Estimation?

According to *Webster's Eleventh New Collegiate Dictionary,* **to estimate** means to judge tentatively or approximately the value, worth, or significance of something. Alternatively, it means to calculate approximately. **An estimate** is a general calculation of size, value, and so on, especially an *approximate* computation of the probable cost of a piece of work. This leads one to ask for the definition of **approximate.** The dictionary states that approximate means located close together, or nearly correct or exact. Moreover, **an approximation** is an *estimate,* guess, or mathematical result that is close in value but not the same as a desired quantity.

Although these definitions appear to be circular (an estimate is an approximation and an approximation is an estimate), the dictionary does give us a general idea of what these words mean. As with most words, these words have several meanings and their exact meaning is determined by the particular context in which they are used. In particular, these words are used in a variety of ways in mathematics. You should first note that unlike most mathematical concepts, estimate and approximate do not have precise definitions. What does it mean for two numbers to be "near in position, close together?" Is 5 close to 10? Is 1250 close to 1300? Is 1000 close to 3000? It's hard to say. In spite of our inability to precisely define closeness, we shall see that the varied uses of estimation are an important ingredient in mathematical problem solving.

Pedagogical Aspects of Estimation

In her survey article, "Estimation and Number Sense," Judith Threadgill-Sowder (1992) points out that

> *Good estimators are flexible in their thinking, and they use a variety of strategies. They demonstrate a deep understanding of number and operations, and they continually draw upon that understanding. Poor estimators seem to be bound, with only slight variations, to one strategy—that of applying algorithms more suitable for finding an exact answer. Poor estimators have only a vague notion of the nature and purpose of estimation; they believe it to be inferior to exact calculation (Morgan, 1988) and equate it with guessing.*

It follows from this view that teaching estimation is a complex task. Rather than being a simple skill that follows a few basic rules, estimation requires a variety of strategies. Rather than being a separate subject, estimation is a habit of mind that is carried out in many mathematical activities. Thus, there are few lessons in the *Math Trailblazers* curriculum devoted solely to estimation, while many lessons offer opportunities for estimation. While estimation is not a simple skill, a number of simple skills, such as rounding and mental multiplication, are extremely useful when doing estimation.

Students often have difficulty with estimation because they are uncomfortable about having more than one correct answer. They want to know "the right answer" and dislike being told "that's a good estimate." So it is your task to keep reminding students of the purpose of estimation and that different strategies can result in different correct answers. The laboratory experiments in *Math Trailblazers* help students develop an appreciation of the approximate nature of measurement and the fact that some problems can have more than one solution.

To help organize our thoughts about estimation, we will break the uses of estimation in the elementary mathematics curriculum into four major categories:

1. Estimating the result of a calculation (in particular, addition, subtraction, multiplication, and division) to see if the answer is reasonable.
2. Measurement error, experimental error, and predictions.
3. Estimating the magnitude of a measurement; for example, the height of a building, the area of a wall, the volume of a jar, or the weight of a person.
4. Estimating how many; for example, the number of peanuts in a jar, the number of students in a school, the number of people at a concert.

Good estimators are flexible in their thinking, and they use a variety of strategies. They demonstrate a deep understanding of number and operations, and they continually draw upon that understanding.

It is your task to keep reminding students of the purpose of estimation and that different strategies can result in different correct answers.

Estimating the Results of a Calculation

Two primary reasons for estimating calculation results are:

1. To check that the exact answer is (possibly) correct. The estimation can be done either before or after the calculation. Getting an answer that is far from your estimate indicates that the calculation is incorrect. On the other hand, an estimate close to the calculation does not guarantee that it is correct.
2. As a substitute for the exact answer. In many situations an exact answer is not needed and may not even make sense.

We will discuss a few of the more common strategies used to estimate the results of a calculation. Undoubtedly, you and your students will find other good strategies.

Addition and Subtraction

For estimation purposes, the most important digits in a number are the ones to the left, i.e., the leading digits. When estimating a sum or difference, one strategy you can usually carry out mentally is to look at the first one or two *place-value columns.* For example, here are some statistics on the New England states from a 1987 almanac:

	Population (1984)	Area (sq mi)
Maine	1,164,000	33,215
New Hampshire	998,000	9304
Vermont	535,000	9609
Massachusetts	5,822,000	8257
Rhode Island	968,000	1214
Connecticut	3,174,000	5009

When estimating a sum or difference, one strategy you can usually carry out mentally is to look at the first one or two place-value columns.

If we wanted to estimate the total population of New Hampshire and Vermont in 1984 using "front end estimation," we could look at the first column on the left. In this case, it is the hundred thousands column. Adding the 9 and the 5 we get 14, which tells us that the sum is approximately 14 hundred thousands; in other words, one million, four hundred thousand. In fact, the first two digits of the sum must be either 14 or 15 (depending on whether or not there is any carrying when we do the addition algorithm). Your estimate can be 1,400,000 or you can look at the next digits to see if there is likely to be any carrying. In this case, the digits in the ten thousands column are 9 and 3, so there will be carrying. Thus, 1,500,000 is an even better estimate. Of course, the whole point of estimation is to get a quick, approximate answer. If you start looking at too many digits, you might as well find the exact answer.

A second quick method for this estimate is to think that the population of New Hampshire was approximately 1 million and that of Vermont was about $\frac{1}{2}$ million, so the total is about 1.5 million. Since the "exact" answer is 1,533,000, an estimate of 1.5 million is only off by about 2 percent. A more rule-bound approach that says, "round off the nearest million" would give us 1 million plus 1 million which is 2 million. This is not a very close estimate (it's about 30 percent off). In fact, there is no simple rule that gives a good estimate in all situations. A rule that often gives good results is "round each number to one significant digit and then add." (A whole number has one significant digit if all digits after the first one equal zero.) That's what we did in this case, rounding 1,164,000 to 1,000,000 and 535,000 to 500,000.

You can apply the same strategies to estimate the results of subtraction calculations. For example, if we wanted to know how much larger the population of New Hampshire was than the population of Vermont, we could round each population to one significant digit, and subtract 500,000 from 1 million to get 500,000. Rounding to the nearest million definitely doesn't work in this problem, since both populations round to 1 million, and we would get the nonsensical estimate that there were no more people in New Hampshire than there were in Vermont! It should be noted that looking at the difference between two numbers is not always the best way of comparing them. If we wanted to compare the populations of New Hampshire and Vermont, it might be better to look at the ratio of their populations and say that New Hampshire had twice the population of Vermont.

The fact that the population figures are rounded off to the nearest thousand in the table is an acknowledgment that census figures themselves are estimates. In this case, there are two reasons that the data is not exact. Population data for the United States is based on census data. Since the U.S. population is so large and not everyone cooperates with the census takers, it is impossible to count everyone in the country. The population is also a moving target. Every day, tens of thousands of people are born or die. Finally, the figures for 1984 population are obtained by starting with the 1980 figures and extrapolating based on assumptions about the rate of population growth. Since many factors affecting population growth change, it is highly unlikely that predictions for population would be very accurate.

Rounding is also one effective strategy for mentally estimating the sum of a series of numbers. For example, to find the total population of New England from the individual state populations above, you might round the numbers in the population column to the nearest half million, namely 1, 1, $\frac{1}{2}$, 6, 1, and 3 million. Adding these mentally gives $12\frac{1}{2}$ million, which is pretty close to the actual total of 14,238,888 people. Try to estimate the total area of New England, mentally. The exact answer is 62,810 square miles.

Note that these are not the only strategies for estimating the sum or difference of several numbers. For example, if you want to purchase items that cost $3.79, $4.19, $2.23, and $6.49, you might add the dollars mentally (3 + 4 + 2 + 6 = 15) and then round the cents to the nearest quarter, i.e., 79 cents is about 75 cents, etc. This way, you see you need about $1.75 more (or 7 quarters). So, the total is pretty close to $16.75.

Multiplication: Rounding and Mental Math

The most basic technique for estimating the result of a multiplication problem is to replace (if necessary) the original numbers in the problem with other numbers that permit us to do the calculation mentally, or rapidly with paper and pencil. For example, if you want to know the number of minutes in a day, you would multiply 24 hours by 60 minutes per hour. Finding 24 × 60 is too hard for most people to do mentally, but 25 × 60 can be done by many fourth- and fifth-graders. Now, 25 × 60 is the same as 25 × 6 × 10, and 25 × 6 is 150. (Think of 6 quarters as a dollar-fifty. Most of us are pretty good at calculating

The most basic technique for estimating the result of a multiplication problem is to replace (if necessary) the original numbers in the problem with other numbers that permit us to do the calculation mentally . . .

with multiples of 5, 10, and 25, since we have had a lot of practice doing mental arithmetic with money.) Finally, if 6 × 25 is 150, then 6 × 25 × 10 is 1500. This is a pretty good estimate for 24 × 60. Note that we repeatedly used the commutative property of multiplication—i.e., the order in which we multiply several numbers does not affect the result. An alternative estimate for 24 × 60 can be obtained by rounding off 24 to 20 and multiplying 20 by 60 to get approximately 1200 minutes in a day. This estimate is not as close, but it may suffice for many purposes.

A basic skill fundamental to being able to estimate in multiplication and division situations is the ability to multiply and divide by ten and powers of ten (100, 1000, etc.). Thus, as early as third grade in *Math Trailblazers,* we observe the pattern that multiplying a whole number by 10 amounts to adding the digit 0 to the right of the number, i.e., 10 × 57 = 570, 10 × 365 = 3650, and so on. Similarly, multiplying by 100 amounts to adding two 0 digits to the right, and so on. When we start to work with decimals, we observe that multiplying a decimal by 10 amounts to moving the decimal point to the right one place. For example, 10 × 45.76 = 457.6. This is really the same pattern we see with whole numbers, since 10 × 57.0 = 570, etc.

Another fundamental process in the examples above was finding convenient numbers that were close to the numbers we started with. Here, convenient means numbers with which we can calculate mentally. For example, we rounded 24 to 25, since multiples of 25 are easy to figure out. Often, the convenient numbers are what we call round numbers. For example, when we used our second strategy to estimate 24 × 60, we rounded 24 to the nearest 10, which gave us 20. All this means is that 20 is the multiple of 10 that is nearest to 24 (since 24 is between 20 and 30 but is closer to 20).

Rounding

Traditionally, students were taught a lot of rules about rounding, but they often are not able to apply them successfully since they did not understand the purpose of rounding, nor did they have a good understanding of place value. When we are doing mental estimation, we frequently want to round a number in the hundreds to the nearest hundred, a number in the thousands to the nearest thousand, and so on. For example, 457 rounded to the nearest hundred is 500, while 447 rounded to the nearest hundred is 400. That's because both numbers are between 400 and 500, and 457 is closer to 500 and 447 is closer to 400. Now 450 is exactly halfway between 400 and 500, so it is not obvious how to round 450 to the nearest hundred. Strictly speaking, it does not make sense to talk about **the** nearest hundred in this situation, since 450 is 50 away from 400 and 50 away from 500. In the context of estimation, this means that you can use either 400 or 500 as an estimate for 450. For example, if we wanted to estimate 450 × 321, we could say 400 × 300 = 120,000 is an estimate for the answer. This estimate is certainly smaller than the actual answer, since 400 is less than 450 and 300 is less than 321. On the other hand, 500 × 300 = 150,000, which is probably bigger than the actual answer. So the answer is probably between 120,000 and 150,000 (it's actually 144,450).

It used to be taught that numbers halfway between should always be rounded up, but there is really no reason for doing so. In general, the choice is determined by the context in which the rounding takes place and the reason you are rounding. For example, if you want to make sure you have enough money to purchase the items in your grocery cart, it is probably best to make a conservative estimate and round items that cost $12.50 up to $13.

Division

It may be surprising to realize that the operation we need to estimate most frequently in daily life is division. This is because many decisions we have to make are based on proportional reasoning. How many miles per gallon is your car getting? Which brand of cereal is the least expensive? (One costs $2.65 for 14 oz and the other costs $3.55 for 24 oz.) A calculator can answer all these easily, but we often do not have a calculator handy. More significantly, students often perform the wrong calculations on the calculator. Letting students first solve their problem using convenient numbers allows them to focus on the essential parts of the problem, without being distracted by a lot of digits and a lot of mechanical manipulations. Once they have found a reasonable solution strategy, they can return to solve the original messy problem.

The easiest problems are ones that we can turn into a problem that requires dividing by a power of 10. Dividing by 10 is the inverse of multiplying by 10. Thus we can divide by 10 mentally by moving the decimal point one place to the left. For example, $\frac{279}{10} = 27.9$, $\frac{456.2}{10} = 45.62$, and so on. Similarly, we can divide by 100 by moving the decimal point two places to the left. When dividing a whole number by 10, we get a fairly good estimate for the result by just dropping the ones digit. For example, $\frac{279}{10}$ is approximately 27. Note that the estimate we get this way is always smaller than the exact answer.

One method for estimating the results of a division problem is to replace each number by a suitable nearby convenient number and then carry out the first step in the division algorithm. The rounding is chosen to make the division easy. For example, suppose we wanted to estimate the population density of Maine in 1984. The data in Table 1 tells us that the density is 1,164,000 people ÷ 33,215 square miles. We can round off the divisor to 30,000 square miles and round off the dividend to 1,000,000 people. To estimate 1,000,000 ÷ 30,000, we can ask what times 30,000 gives 1,000,000. Multiplying 30,000 by 10 gives 300,000 and multiplying this by 3.3 gets us near 1,000,000. So, our estimate is about 33. Another method is to replace the divisor and dividend with nearby convenient numbers. For example, 33,215 is near 30,000 and 1,164,000 is close to 1,200,000. We chose this pair of numbers because 12 is divisible by 3. So, our estimate now amounts to 1,200,000 people ÷ 30,000 square miles. Again, we see we need to multiply 30,000 by 40 to get 1,200,000. So 40 people per square mile is a reasonable estimate for the population density of Maine. Putting the numbers back into the context of the problem is important for checking any result.

A powerful technique for estimating the result of a division problem is to consider the division as a ratio. For example, suppose you traveled 637 miles and used 22 gallons of gas. To find miles per gallon, divide 22 into 637. Write the ratio 637 miles/22 gallons. Rounding 637 to 600 and 22 to 20 we get

$$\frac{637 \text{ mi}}{22 \text{ gal}} \approx \frac{600 \text{ mi}}{20 \text{ gal}}$$

Note that we used the symbol $\approx$ instead of the equal sign. This symbol means "approximately equal." Now, we can simplify the ratio $\frac{600}{20}$ by dividing both numerator and denominator by 10. So

$$\frac{600 \text{ mi}}{20 \text{ gal}} = \frac{60 \text{ mi}}{2 \text{ gal}}$$

and dividing numerator and denominator by 2 gives us

$$\frac{60 \text{ mi}}{2 \text{ gal}} = \frac{30 \text{ mi}}{1 \text{ gal}}$$

Putting this all together, we get 637 mi/22 gal $\approx$ 30 mi/1 gal; in other words, our estimate is 30 miles per gallon.

A note on canceling. Many people learned to simplify ratios by "canceling" the same thing in the numerator and the denominator. You might be tempted to say that when we wrote 600 mi/20 gal $\approx$ 60 mi/2 gal, we "canceled a 0" in the numerator and the denominator. Unfortunately, this can lead to some bad habits. For example, can you cancel the fives in $\frac{875}{25}$ to get $\frac{87}{2}$, or cancel the fives in $(X + 5)/(Y + 5)$ to get X/Y? You better not, since this amounts to subtracting the 5 from the numerator and denominator and results in a fraction that is not equal to the one we started with.

$$\frac{875}{25} \neq \frac{87}{2}$$

$$\frac{X + 5}{Y + 5} \neq \frac{X}{Y}$$

So canceling does not always result in an equal ratio. For this reason, we always say exactly what we are doing, dividing numerator and denominator by the same number, rather than using the word "cancel."

Here are some examples of estimation in a division context:

Example 1: Estimate the quotient $\frac{80,000}{30}$. This is approximately $\frac{8000}{3}$, which is between $\frac{7500}{3}$ and $\frac{9000}{3}$, i.e., between 2500 and 3000. Note that if we estimated $\frac{80,000}{30}$ by replacing 30 with 40 (since 40 goes into 80,000 evenly) we get $\frac{80,000}{40} = \frac{8000}{4} = 2000$, which is not as good as our previous estimate. This might be a little surprising, since we only made a change of 10 in replacing 30 by 40. But what is important here is not the size of the change (10), but the relative size of the change (10 out of 30 is 33%).

Here are some additional examples of estimation in a division context. See if you can follow the reasoning in these estimates. Can you make an estimate in a different way?

$$\frac{6206}{8271} \approx \frac{6000}{8000} = \frac{6}{8} = \frac{3}{4} = 0.75$$

$$\frac{78,221}{987} \approx \frac{80,000}{1000} = 80$$

$$\frac{77,921}{289} \approx \frac{75,000}{250} = \frac{7500}{25} = 300$$

$$\frac{828}{38,765} \approx \frac{800}{40,000} = \frac{8}{400} = \frac{2}{100} = .02$$

Measurement Error, Experimental Error, and Predictions

The theme of this tutor is the way to deal with "inexactness" in real-world mathematics. One class of situations that involve inexactness is measurement error or experimental error.

Measurement error is the unavoidable error that occurs due to the limitations inherent to any measurement instrument. Any measurement in the real world is an approximation. It is not really possible to guarantee that an object is exactly 1 meter long since any measuring instrument has a limit to its accuracy. For example, our centimeter ruler can only measure to the nearest tenth of a centimeter and the two-pan balance usually used in *Math Trailblazers* can only measure mass to the nearest gram.

Experimental error is the variation in measurement that results from the inability to control extraneous variables in an experiment.

These two types of error are closely related. Let's consider three examples of measurement in real-world contexts to get some idea of the meaning of measurement and experimental error:

Example 1: A volunteer is selected from the class and every student measures the circumference of her head to the nearest tenth of a centimeter. Most students get between 47 and 49 centimeters. One student gets 37.4 centimeters.

Example 2: Students drop a ball from a height of 80 centimeters three times to see how high it bounces. They get 41 centimeters, 45 centimeters, and 44 centimeters.

Example 3: Students measure the volume of a marble using a graduated cylinder. Most students get either 7 or 8 cubic centimeters. Two students get 67 cubic centimeters.

Example 4: A student finds that the mass of one blue pattern block is 11 grams. She predicts that 2 blue pattern blocks will have a mass of 22 grams and 4 blue pattern blocks will have a mass of 44 grams. When she checks her results, she finds that 2 pattern blocks do have a mass of 22 grams, but 4 pattern blocks have a mass of 42 grams.

Measurement error is the unavoidable error that occurs due to the limitations inherent to any measurement instrument. . . .
Experimental error is the variation in measurement that results from the inability to control extraneous variables in an experiment.

Errors vs. Mistakes

In Examples 1, 2, and 3, there were repeated measurements of the same thing that produced seemingly different answers. The fact that most students obtained slightly different answers in Example 1 is due to slight variations in how they performed the measurement—where they placed the tape measure, how tight they held it, etc. All these measurements are "close" to each other (see below for a discussion of "what's close?").

However, the student whose measurement was 37.4 centimeters probably made a *mistake* such as reading the tape measure incorrectly or placing the tape measure in the wrong position. In mathematics, we try to distinguish between the words "error" and "mistake." Of course, "mistake" is one of the common meanings of "error." *Webster's New World Dictionary of the American Language* gives as its first definition of the word "error," "the state of believing what is untrue, incorrect, or wrong."

In the current context, however, "error" has a different meaning. This is the fifth definition given for "error" in that dictionary, namely "the difference between a computed or estimated result and the actual value as in mathematics." The dictionary goes on to explain that "error implies deviation from truth, accuracy, correctness, right, [while] mistake suggests an error resulting from carelessness, inattention, misunderstanding, etc."

Most of the measurements in Example 1 involved some measurement error, but those measurements were correct. However, the student who measured 37.4 centimeters must have made a mistake. In this case, the teacher would help the student find the reason for the mistake and then repeat the measurement correctly.

In Example 2, it is not surprising that repeating the activity, that is, dropping the ball from 80 centimeters, results in a different measurement. It's pretty hard to measure how high the ball bounces, since the ball does not stop at the height of its bounce and wait for you to measure its distance from the floor. Also, there can be slight variations because different parts of the ball or different spots on the floor are "bouncier." This is a typical example of the experimental error that results from the inability to control all the fixed variables in an experiment. (See the TIMS Tutor: *The TIMS Laboratory Method,* Fixed Variables in Controlled Experiments.)

In Example 3, students used a graduated cylinder to measure the volume by displacement. Two students forgot to subtract the volume of the water in the cylinder, so they obtained measurements that were very different from the others. This is a clear example of a mistake. The actual volume of the marble was between 7 and 8 cubic centimeters.

Reducing Experimental Error

In Examples 1 through 3, we saw that repeating a measurement does not always give the same answer. To get more reliable and accurate results, scientists often repeat a measurement several times and then take the average of all the measurements. The "average" that we use in this situation can be

> In mathematics, we try to distinguish between the words "error" and "mistake."

> To get more reliable and accurate results, scientists often repeat a measurement several times and then take the average of all the measurements.

either the mean or the median. (See the TIMS Tutor: *Averages.*) In Example 2, we can take the median of the three measurements and say that dropping the ball from 80 centimeters results in a bounce height of 44 centimeters. We could also use the mean, in which case the bounce height would be nearly the same—approximately 43 centimeters.

In many experiments, we have another way of minimizing experimental error. If the data points plotted on a graph appear close to a straight line, we find a best-fit line that is close to all the data points. (See the TIMS Tutor: *The TIMS Laboratory Method.*) Using the best-fit line is a way of averaging out the experimental error. In *Math Trailblazers,* we draw a best-fit line "by eye," using a transparent ruler. In addition to averaging out the error, these lines help scientists and mathematicians make predictions based upon the patterns in the data. Scientists, mathematicians, and statisticians use a variety of sophisticated methods to find best-fit lines for data, but the "eyeball" method is pretty good for making approximate predictions.

> *Scientists, mathematicians, and statisticians use a variety of sophisticated methods to find best-fit lines for data, but the "eyeball" method is pretty good for making approximate predictions.*

One example of an activity that uses both averaging and best-fit lines to minimize experimental error is the *Math Trailblazers* fourth-grade lab, *The Bouncing Ball.* In this lab, students drop a ball from heights of 40, 80, and 120 cm and record their data in a data table. See Figure 1. Note that the ball was dropped three times from each height. When the data is graphed, we can see that the data points lie close to a straight line. In Figure 2, we see an estimated best-fit line drawn by a student. For further information, see the TIMS Tutor: *The TIMS Laboratory Method,* Point Graphs: Fitting Lines and Curves.

Tennis Ball

D Drop Height in cm	B Bounce Height in cm			
	Trial 1	Trial 2	Trial 3	Average
40	27	22	21	22
80	50	40	43	43
120	72	62	68	68

Figure 1: The Bouncing Ball *data table*

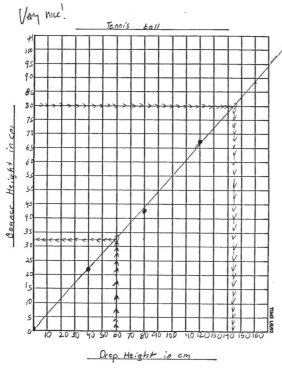

Very nice!

Figure 2: The Bouncing Ball *graph*

What's Close?

Recall that the notions of approximation and estimation involve the notion of finding a number that is close to a desired number. But how do we decide what is close? The most fundamental idea about closeness is that it is a **relative** idea. For example, suppose two merchants are selling the same item and the prices differ by $1. Are the prices close? If the merchants were selling cars that cost around $30,000, you would not make your decision based on a $1 difference in price. On the other hand, if you could buy a cup of coffee in one restaurant for $1 and it cost $2 at another restaurant, you might go out of your way for the $1 coffee (provided the quality was not vastly different). Why are these two choices for coffee significantly different? Because one brand costs twice as much as the other! This leads us to the fundamental idea for discussing closeness: when comparing closeness of numbers or measurements, we should look at the **ratio** of the two numbers, rather than the difference. The only problem with this approach is that the concept of ratio is difficult to understand fully. Developing this concept requires time and exposure to many experiences. We deal with this problem in two ways. First, instead of using ratios, we use a related concept—percent. Second, instead of calculating specific percentages (another difficult concept), we make comparisons to certain benchmark percentages, such as 10%. Using 10% as a benchmark for closeness, we see that $1 is not close to $2 since $2 is more than 10% bigger than $1 (in fact, it's 100% bigger). On the other hand, if we compare $30,000 and $30,001 we see that the difference, $1, is a lot less than 10% of $30,000.

*The most fundamental idea about closeness is that it is a **relative** idea.*

In Example 1, the one in which many students measured the head circumference of one person, most measurements fell between 47 and 49 centimeters. A rough estimate for 10% of these numbers is 4 cm. Now the difference between 47 cm and 49 cm is 2 cm, so there is clearly less than 10% variation between the largest and smallest measurement. We can safely say these measurements are "close." On the other hand, the student who got 37.5 cm was almost 10 cm less than 47 cm. This is nowhere close to being within 10% of the other measurements, so we should suspect a mistake in that measurement. In Example 2, students took three measurements of the bounce height of a ball—41 cm, 45 cm, and 44 cm. Again, the variation is less than 10%. Finally, in Example 3, when students measured the volume of a marble, most obtained a value between 7 cc and 8 cc, while a few measured 67 cc. Now, 10% of 7 or 8 cc is less than 1 cc, so the students who measured 67 cc are nowhere close to the others. It should be pointed out that in situations such as Example 3, we do not decide who had the correct measurements by taking a majority vote. While the majority is usually right, it is not always right. The different results are a warning flag telling us to seek out the reasons for the discrepancies. Someone is making a mistake, but we can only find out who by looking more closely. Once we find the mistake, then we discard the incorrect information.

The 10 Percent Solution

It's natural to ask why we use 10% as a standard of closeness. We have a variety of reasons:

1. It's easy to find 10% of a number, or at least to estimate it. Just divide by 10. For whole numbers bigger than 10, the simplest estimate for 10% is obtained by dropping the last digit. Thus 10% of 187 is about 18 (it's between 18 and 19) and 10% of 5623 is about 562.
2. In many of the *Math Trailblazers* hands-on experiments, 10% is about the accuracy we can expect from students using the equipment they have, while 10% accuracy is still good enough for seeing the patterns in the data on graphs.
3. Psychologically, 10% is near the limit of our visual estimating ability. For example, if a person sees two drawings in sequence, one an enlargement of the other, in most cases that person will have difficulty distinguishing pictures that are less than 10% different in size, but will be able to distinguish figures that are much more than 10% different in size. Of course, this 10% borderline is not exact, and the point at which different people will be able to make distinctions is different.

Estimating the Magnitude of a Measurement

The basic measurement variables in the *Math Trailblazers* curriculum are length, area, volume, mass, and time. While much of the discussion that follows will apply to any type of measurement, it is a good idea to keep these few variables in mind. The examples given in this section will use these five variables.

There are two important types of knowledge used in many measurement estimation exercises. First, you need to know the measurements of some objects to use as a reference point. Second, you must know how to estimate unknown measurements by comparison with things you know. Very often this will involve some kind of proportional reasoning. The first type of knowledge is gained from experience. Therefore, students should have a wide variety of hands-on experiences as well as knowledge gained from external sources. For example, students should know the height of an average adult in English and metric systems ($5\frac{1}{2}$–6 feet, 160–185 cm), the length of their feet, and the width of their hands. We would hope that students have a general idea of the width of the continental United States from east to west (3000 miles) and from north to south (1000 miles). These facts can be used to make other estimates. For example, what is the area of the United States? The continental United States looks as though it would fit in a rectangle that is 3000 miles long and 1000 miles wide. This gives us an estimate of 3 million square miles. The actual area is close to 3.6 million square miles. To estimate the height of a three-story building (Figure 3), we could first estimate the height of one floor. Looking at an adult standing in the room, we might estimate that the distance from floor to ceiling is twice the height of the person. If the person is about 6 feet tall, then we get an estimate of 12 feet from floor to ceiling. If there are three floors, then the total height of the building is approximately $3 \times 12 = 36$ feet high.

Figure 3: *Estimating the height of a three-story building*

Accuracy and Precision

The accuracy required in a measurement depends on how we are going to use the measurement. By its very nature, any measurement we make in the real world is an estimation. What does it mean to say that a sheet of paper is 21.6 cm wide? How does one find this out? One way is to put the 0 cm mark on the ruler even with the left-hand edge of the paper and see that the right-hand edge of the paper is even with the 22.6 cm mark. If the paper is really 22.61 cm wide, we could not tell this with our ruler, which is only divided into tenths of a centimeter. So the measurements we make are really estimates that are accurate to the nearest tenth of a centimeter. Measuring the width of a piece of paper to an accuracy of more than a tenth of a centimeter would probably not make sense, since the sides cannot be perfectly even and measuring the width in different places would give different answers (like 22.613 cm and 22.615 cm). In any case, a measurement of 22.6 cm is probably more than sufficient for our purpose.

> *By its very nature, any measurement we make in the real world is an estimation.*

Dealing with Decimal Digits

One important fact to note is that in the course of solving a problem we can end up with a number that has many digits, most of which do not make sense in the real world (although they make mathematical sense). For example, suppose we wanted to share 16 ounces of orange juice among three students. When I divide 16 by 3 on my calculator, I get 5.3333333333. It makes no sense at all to say that we should give each student 5.3333333333 ounces of juice, since, with the tools we have, we cannot measure more accurately than to the nearest tenth of an ounce. In fact, when we say that we want to share 16 ounces of orange juice, we do not mean that we have exactly 16 ounces of juice. Unless we were using unusually sensitive measuring instruments, it would only make sense to say that we would give each student 5.3 ounces or $5\frac{1}{3}$ ounces of juice. Although 5.3 and $5\frac{1}{3}$ are not equal, they are approximately equal in this context.

Estimating "How Many"

In this type of estimation, we estimate the number of objects in some collection. It could be the number of trees in the United States, the number of students in a school district next year, or the number of beans in a jar. This class of problems has a lot in common with the estimation problems we have already discussed. Many problems that require estimating "how many" are similar to estimating a measurement in that they involve knowing how many objects there are in some known set and then comparing the unknown with the known. Here are some examples:

Example 1: Students are asked to estimate the number of peanuts in a jar. If students have no previous experience with peanuts or jars, this is not really an estimate, but rather a guess. Answers will vary widely because students do not have any idea of what the answer might be and no strategies to use to get a sensible answer. A more reasonable exercise is to give them a small jar and have them count how many peanuts can fit in the jar. If they are now given a larger jar, they should be able to make a sensible estimate by comparing the large jar to the small one. How many small jars would they think fit in the large jar? If the small jar holds 10 peanuts and it appears that 12 small jars fit in the large one, what is a reasonable estimate for the number of peanuts that fit in the large jar?

Example 2: How many students are in your school? The reference set here can be the number of students in a class. Students should know how many students are in their class. They should also be able to estimate the number of classes in the school. This gives an estimate for the number of students in the school (using multiplication).

Example 3: How many total hours of television were watched by all the children in the school? We can find the *exact* answer by asking every student how much they watched and then adding the number of hours. The answer can be *estimated* using a very important technique called sampling. Take a survey of some of the children in the school (say one class or two students in each class) and then scale up.

Example 4: We have a picture of the crowd at a basketball game. How can we determine the number of people at the game? It would be tedious to count the number of people in the picture. We could draw a square on the picture and count the number of people in that square. Then multiply that result by the number of such squares needed to cover the crowd. Figure 4 from the *Math Trailblazers* fourth-grade curriculum shows a picture used to pose a similar problem.

Figure 4: *Picture of a basketball game crowd*

Example 5: Will more people vote for Fred or Amy in the next election? This is another example of a kind of problem that frequently occurs in the real world. The common technique for estimating the answer is to take a sample of the voters and use the sample to predict the results for the whole population. For example, if 40% of the sample says they will vote for Fred and 60% says they will vote for Amy, we might predict that Amy will win. We might even predict that Fred will get 40% of the vote and Amy 60%. We know from real life that predictions like this are not always accurate. Some things that affect the accuracy of such estimates are the size of the sample (compared to the whole population) and the randomness of the sample (how well the sample represents the whole population).

Example 6: How many households are there in the United States? We can only make this estimate if we know enough facts about the population of the United States. We know that the population of the United States is about 250 million people and that the average family has 2.3 children. If we think that some households have only one person, while others have several generations living together, we might say that the average household size is about 4 or 5 people. Using a household size of 5 for our estimate (since 5 goes evenly into 25) we get a figure of 50 million households.

> *The best way to become a good estimator is to estimate.*

Conclusion

We hope that this tutor gives you an overview of the way estimation is treated in the *Math Trailblazers* curriculum. Naturally, it could not deal with all the types of estimation situations and all kinds of estimation strategies. The best way to become a good estimator is to estimate. The best way for children to learn to be good estimators is to be given meaningful situations that require estimation and to be given the opportunity to discuss their strategies with others. As with all mathematics instruction, the teacher plays a valuable role by moderating discourse and by adding new strategies when appropriate.

References

Schoen, Harold L., and Marilyn J. Zweng (eds.). *Estimation and Mental Computation—1986 Yearbook.* National Council of Teachers of Mathematics, Reston, VA, 1986.

Sowder, J., "Estimation and Number Sense," in *Handbook of Research on Mathematics Teaching and Learning.* Douglas A. Grouws (ed.). Macmillan Publishing Co., New York, 1992.

Threadgill-Sowder, J. "Computational Estimation Procedures of School Children." *Journal of Educational Research,* 77 (6), 1984.

Webster's Eleventh New Collegiate Dictionary. Merriam-Webster, Inc., Springfield, MA.

Functions

Introduction

Function is one of those words with a mathematical meaning that is not the same as its everyday meaning. In everyday life, a function can be an important celebration, a role someone or something has, or the purpose for something. In mathematics and science, a function is a special and very important kind of relationship between variables. Discovering functional relationships between variables is what science is all about.

> *In mathematics and science, a function is a special and very important kind of relationship between variables. Discovering functional relationships between variables is what science is all about.*

Three Blind Men and an Elephant. There is a story about three blind men who encounter an elephant. The first comes up against one of the elephant's legs and says, "An elephant is like a tree." The second touches the side of the elephant and says, "No, no. An elephant is like a wall." The third blind man finds the elephant's trunk and claims, "You're both wrong. An elephant is like a big snake."

Each blind man has some notion of what an elephant is. The story doesn't tell whether they eventually resolve their differences and come to a proper understanding of elephants; we can only hope so. Our approach to functions will be similar: We will begin with three different views of functions. This, we hope, will lead to a fuller and more proper understanding of functions.

Tables

Many functions are displayed as tables. For example, consider this data table from the experiment *Mass vs. Number,* shown in Figure 1.

N Number of <u>Erasers</u>	M Mass (in gm)
1	39 gm
2	79 gm
4	158 gm

Figure 1: Mass vs. Number *data table*

This table displays a functional relationship between the variables N and M. For each value of N we have a value of M; we say that the mass is a function of the number of erasers. That is, if we know what N is, then we can find M. This is the essence of a function: knowing one variable's value enables us to find the corresponding value of the other variable. In this example, the data has a distinctive pattern: within experimental error, doubling one variable causes the other to double. N and M are said to be (directly) proportional.

Many functions we encounter in everyday life come to us as tables. You can think of stock tables, for example, as functions: one variable is the company, the other is the closing price. If you know the company, you can look up the price. Almanacs are filled with tables of information, most of which you can think of as functions: one variable is the name of the country, the other is the population, and so on. The sports pages are filled with tabular functions of team standings and individual statistics.

Many functions come to us first as tables, and some, like batting averages or almanac information, are normally given only as tables. Tables of numbers, however, can be very difficult to understand. Patterns in the data can go undetected—patterns that might help us better understand the function. One of the best ways to get a handle on patterns is to make a visual image of the data in the form of a graph.

Graphs

If a picture is worth a thousand words, a graph is worth a billion numbers. The graph of the *Mass vs. Number* data, seen in Figure 2, is a good example.

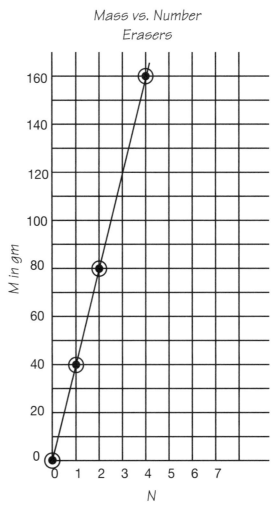

Figure 2: *Graph of* Mass vs. Number *data*

The key thing about this graph is that the data points lie on a straight line through (0,0). This confirms that N and M are proportional: we can fit a straight line through (0,0) if and only if the variables are proportional. Many other types of functions besides direct proportion are characterized by their graphs.

Often, experimental error obscures the nature of the relationship between the variables until the data is plotted. Like taking multiple measurements and averaging, graphing the data and fitting a curve can help control error. With error minimized, the true nature of the relationship between the variables may become clearer. Stock analysts graph their data to spot trends in order to make predictions (and money); such trends are unlikely to be noticed in the stock tables. Scientists graph their data almost as soon as they get it because the graph is so much more likely to be revealing than the raw data.

The graph is a crucial step on the road from the concrete apparatus to formal understanding. Sometimes, this formal understanding can be distilled in a few symbols, as in a formula.

> *The graph is a crucial step on the road from the concrete apparatus to formal understanding.*

Formulas

A more abstract way to consider a function is as a formula. In our *Mass vs. Number* example, we can exploit the fact that when variables are proportional, their ratio is constant. The value of this constant ratio is the slope of the best-fit line. So,

$$\frac{M}{N} = \frac{39.5 \text{ gm}}{1 \text{ eraser}} .$$

This can be rewritten to give a formula for M as a function of N:

$$M = \frac{39.5 \text{ gm}}{1 \text{ eraser}} \times N$$

Such formulas are very useful when they can be found. When we do manage to obtain a formula, it allows us to solve problems quickly and accurately. We can also use formulas to ascend to higher levels of abstraction. This movement to ever greater abstraction and generality is the driving force behind much of science and mathematics.

G Number of Generations	A Number of Ancestors
1	2
2	4
3	8
4	16

Figure 3: *Ancestors data table*

Often students are not able to understand formulas, but they are, nevertheless, able to continue a pattern in a data table or devise a rule that works. For example, the pattern in the table shown in Figure 3 is easy to extend. Five generations back, you have 32 ancestors: each further generation doubles the number of ancestors (ignoring the inevitable overlap). Extending patterns like this is a first step towards formulas. Later, the students may be able to give a rule for a data table. For example, consider the table in Figure 4, the number of fence posts needed for a given length of fence.

L Length of Fence in _feet_	N Number of Fence Posts
10	2
20	3
30	4
40	5

Figure 4: _Fence posts data table_

The rule may be stated: the number of fence posts is just one more than $\frac{1}{10}$ the number of feet in the fence.

$$N = \frac{L}{10} + 1$$

It is not much harder for us to express this sentence as a formula, but this type of expression may be confusing to a third-grader. Often, a rule stated in ordinary language is more accessible.

Formulas are the most powerful way to look at functions but are often not appropriate for elementary school students. The great temptation is to move to formulas as quickly as possible. This sometimes leads to quick gains, but over the long run it is often problematic. Pushing formulas at children is like building a house of cards: students need to build a conceptual foundation by handling apparatus, gathering data, and graphing and analyzing it. Only after students develop an understanding of the relationship of the variables is it proper to distill that understanding into a formula. Extending patterns and figuring out rules are excellent alternatives for younger students moving towards higher levels of abstraction.

What Is a Function?

A **function** is a special kind of relationship between variables that can often be expressed as a data table, graph, or formula. One variable is the manipulated (or independent) variable; the other is the responding (or dependent) variable.

But not every relationship is a function. The main requirement for a relationship to be a function is that for each value of the manipulated variable, there is only one value of the responding variable. For example, suppose the manipulated variable is the edge length of a cube and the responding variable is the surface area. Then, for each given edge length there is exactly one surface area: if the edge is 3 cm, then the surface area is 54 sq cm, and so on. Or consider the manipulated variable to be the company and the responding variable to be the closing price: each stock has exactly one closing price each day. Notice that many stocks may have the same closing price; that's okay. The requirement says only that each value of the manipulated variable must have exactly one value of the responding variable. Values of the responding variable may repeat, and often do. One way to visualize this requirement is to think about functions as mappings. Figure 5 shows a map of a squaring function.

> . . . not every relationship is a function. The main requirement for a relationship to be a function is that for each value of the manipulated variable, there is only one value of the responding variable.

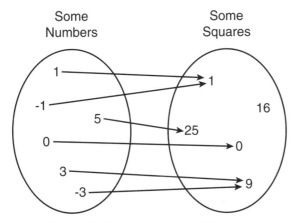

Figure 5: *Map of a squaring function*

Every number has exactly one square; this corresponds to the single arrow leaving each number on the left above. Notice that more than one arrow can end at a single number; the requirement is only that exactly one arrow leave each of the starting numbers. The mapping in Figure 6 is not a function because two arrows leave each number.

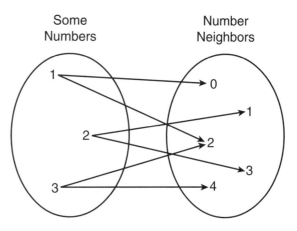

Some Numbers   Number Neighbors

1
0
2
1
3
2
3
4

Figure 6: *Map of a relationship that is not a function*

But you may object, saying that when we do experiments we often have several different values of the responding variable for each value of the manipulated variable. Isn't there a functional relationship between variables like the drop height and the bounce height in *The Bouncing Ball?* In a word, yes. But with real data, things get more complicated. Experimental error creeps in; there are other uncontrolled variables; there is uncertainty inherent in all our measurements.

One useful way to think about the situation is to suppose there is some "true" value of the responding variable that we cannot measure exactly. So, instead we measure the responding variable several times and then take the average as our best estimate of the true value.[1] Then we have a function: for each value of the manipulated variable there is exactly one *true* value of the responding variable. The only trouble is, in most real-world situations, we usually don't know what that true value is.

Mathematicians have precise and abstract definitions of function. We could go on and on describing more precisely the requirements a relationship must have to be a function. We could spell out the meanings of technical terms having to do with functions—terms like *domain, range, one-to-one, many-to-one,* and so on. For most purposes, however, thinking about functions in the terms outlined above is enough.

Functions in the Classroom

The concept of a function is a powerful one for organizing and extending mathematical ideas. From time to time, we have activities that deal with functions, for example, *Function Machines* in second grade. The best approach to functions, however, is just doing the *Math Trailblazers* lessons. As your students do TIMS Laboratory Investigations and other activities, they will move naturally from the apparatus to the data table, graph, and questions. Much of the data analysis is designed to help children see how changes in one of these correspond to changes in the others. Thus, in each experiment the students will deal with specific functions in several guises and will gain facility in moving between different representations of functions. This is the best possible preparation for the explicit study of functions later in high school and beyond.

[1]See the TIMS Tutor: *Averages.*

Journals

Writing about mathematics and science helps students consolidate ideas, see connections between school and life, and think more abstractly.

We at TIMS embrace the idea of writing across the curriculum. We see helping students to write better as part of every teacher's job.

By writing in mathematics and science class, students improve their communication skills and develop their subject-matter understanding. Writing about mathematics and science helps students consolidate ideas, see connections between school and life, and think more abstractly.

Another reason to have students write about mathematics and science lessons is so you can gain insight into how those lessons are being received and what the students are learning. Collecting and saving students' writing is also an excellent way to document long-term student progress.

We incorporate writing into *Math Trailblazers* in several ways. We often ask for students to write a short or extended answer to a question and we may also ask students to explain how they obtained their solutions. Students may be asked to write about problems they solved in cooperative groups.

Journals are another effective way to use writing in mathematics and science. Typically, a journal is a small, bound book in which students write regularly. The writing can be in response to various prompts, or it can be rather undirected. Because each student responds at his or her own level and rate, journal writing is accessible to all students.

The teacher reads students' journals regularly, possibly responding in writing to what students wrote. Usually journal writing is not corrected for grammar, spelling, and punctuation—the focus is on the content of the writing, not the form.

The physical form of the journal is not important. A cloth-covered bound book, a spiral notebook, or even several sheets of paper stapled together all work just fine.

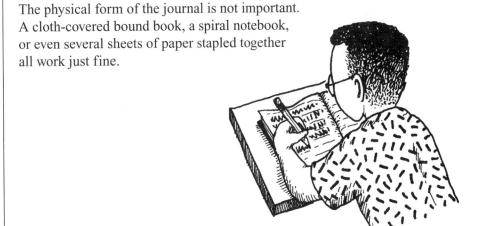

Journal Prompts

We urge you to have your students write regularly, every day or at least every week. Start with short periods and gradually extend the amount of time. When a student fills up one journal, give him or her another. Students will also enjoy reading their writing aloud and discussing it.

Your students' journal writing should take a variety of forms. Here are some suggestions for assignments ranging from highly structured to rather open-ended.

Sentence Completion

Give part of a sentence and ask students to complete it (Azzolino, 1990). For example, you might ask students to complete sentences like these:

"A shape is symmetric when . . ."
"Today we learned . . ."
"Before you use an equal-arm balance it's important to . . ."

A variation of this activity is to give one or more complete sentences and then to ask students to continue.

Explanations of Procedures

Ask students to explain how to measure the area of a leaf, how to use an equal-arm balance, how to add two three-digit numbers, or how to make a graph of some data. This may require an explanation of an entire procedure or only of certain steps.

Answers to Specific Questions

Sometimes you may pose a specific question about a lesson. For example, ask students to describe the shape of the graph for a certain experiment and to explain why the graph has that shape. Many *Math Trailblazers* lessons include questions that require some writing; these questions can be answered in the journals.

A question to ask sometimes is, "How did working in your group turn out?" You may get valuable information that can help you improve the dynamics of your small groups.

Descriptions of Solutions

There are usually many ways to solve a mathematics problem; it is often worth exploring multiple solutions. To correct the common misconception that there is usually only one way to solve a problem, students need to learn that the process of problem solving is often as important as the answer. In *Math Trailblazers,* they see connections by comparing different solutions. They learn that mathematics makes sense because their own ideas are validated. They are exposed to advanced ideas through other students' solutions, but without undue stress if they fail to understand those advanced ideas.

One way to encourage multiple solutions is to ask students to write about how they solved a problem. Ask them to describe all the ways they solved a problem or to describe a single way in depth. Ask them to write about failed solutions or what they did when they got stuck. Such assignments will encourage students to see such efforts not as failures but as periodic by-products of the problem-solving process.

Definitions

Ask students to define a key concept like area or volume. You may be surprised at some of their answers.

Advice to Adventure Book Characters

Often the characters in the *Adventure Books* and other activities encounter problems that yield to the techniques the students have been learning in the labs and activities. You might stop part way through an *Adventure Book* story and ask your students to write some advice, perhaps in the form of a letter, to the hero. When you finish the book, compare what the hero actually did to the students' advice.

Reactions

Ask students what they liked or didn't like about a certain lab, activity, or adventure book. Or, ask what they learned or what confused them.

Word Banks

Supply a list of words or phrases and ask students to use those words in a piece of writing (Azzolino, 1990). For example, you might supply the following words, "ten, hundred, thousand, less than, seven, more than, nine."

Problems

Students enjoy writing their own problems. Ask them to write another problem like a given problem; to write an addition, subtraction, or sharing problem; to write a number riddle; or to make up any problem that classmates would find interesting to solve.

Free Writing

Other times, simply tell students to write whatever they want about a certain lesson.

Some Tips for Getting Started

- Start with brief periods of writing and gradually extend the amount of time.
- Encourage pictures, data tables, graphs, number sentences, and other mathematical and scientific forms of communication.
- Vary the prompt. Sometimes be very specific; other times make the assignment more open-ended.
- Do not worry about grammar, spelling, and punctuation. Focus on content.

One way to encourage multiple solutions is to ask students to write about how they solved a problem. Ask them to describe all the ways they solved a problem or to describe a single way in depth. Ask them to write about failed solutions or what they did when they got stuck.

Conclusion

The name of our project—TIMS (Teaching Integrated Mathematics and Science)—expresses our conviction that the teaching of mathematics and science should be integrated. But we also believe strongly that integration should not stop there; language arts and social studies can and should be integrated with mathematics and science. Journals are one way to use writing in mathematics and science. Reading and writing are too important to be confined to language arts lessons.

References

Azzolino, A. "Writing as a Tool for Teaching Mathematics: The Silent Revolution." In *Teaching and Learning Mathematics in the 1990s: 1990 Yearbook.* T.J. Cooney and C.R. Hirsch, Eds. National Council of Teachers of Mathematics, Reston, VA, 1990.

Burns, Marilyn, and Robyn Sibley. "Incorporating Writing into Math Class." *So You Have to Teach Math? Sound Advice for K–6 Teachers.* Math Solutions Publications, Sausalito, CA, 2000.

Countryman, Joan. *Writing to Learn Mathematics.* Heinemann, Portsmouth, NH, 1992.

Math Facts

Students need to learn the math facts. Estimation, mental arithmetic, checking the reasonableness of results, and paper-and-pencil calculations require the ability to give quick, accurate responses when using basic facts. The question is not if students should learn the math facts, but how. Which teaching methods are most efficient and effective? To answer this question, we as authors of *Math Trailblazers* drew upon educational research and our own classroom experiences to develop a comprehensive plan for teaching the math facts.

Philosophy

The goal of the *Math Trailblazers* math facts strand is for students to learn the basic facts efficiently, gain fluency with their use, and retain that fluency over time. A large body of research supports an approach that is built on a foundation of work with strategies and concepts. This not only leads to more effective learning and better retention, but also to development of mental math skills. Therefore, the teaching and assessment of the basic facts in *Math Trailblazers* is characterized by the following elements:

- *Early emphasis on problem solving.* Students first approach the basic facts as problems to solve rather than as facts to memorize. Students invent their own strategies to solve these problems or learn appropriate strategies from others through class discussion. Students' natural strategies, especially counting strategies, are explicitly encouraged. In this way, students learn that math is more than memorizing facts and rules that "you either get or you don't."

- *De-emphasis of rote work.* Fluency with the math facts is an important component of any student's mathematical learning. Research shows that overemphasizing memorization and frequent administration of timed tests are counterproductive. Both can produce undesirable results (Isaacs and Carroll, 1999; Van de Walle, 2001; National Research Council, 2001). We encourage the use of strategies to find facts, so students become confident they can find answers to fact problems they do not immediately recall.

- *Gradual and systematic introduction of facts.* Students study the facts in small groups they solve using similar strategies. Students first work on simple strategies for easy facts and then progress to more sophisticated strategies and harder facts. By the end of the process, they gain fluency with all required facts.

- *Ongoing practice.* Work on the math facts is distributed throughout the curriculum, especially in the Daily Practice and Problems (DPP), Home Practice, and games. This practice for fluency, however, takes place only after students have a conceptual understanding of the operations and have achieved proficiency with strategies for solving basic fact problems. Delaying practice in this way means that less practice is required to achieve fluency.

- *Appropriate assessment.* Teachers assess students' knowledge of the facts through observations as they work on activities, labs, and games as well as through the appropriate use of written tests and quizzes. Beginning in first grade, periodic, short quizzes in the DPP naturally follow the study of small groups of facts organized around specific strategies. As self-assessment in Grades 3–5, students record their progress on *Facts I Know* charts and determine which facts they need to study. Inventory tests of all facts for each operation are used sparingly in Grades 2–5 (no more than twice per year) to assess students' progress with fact fluency. The goal of the math facts assessment program is to determine the degree to which students can find answers to fact problems quickly and accurately and whether they can retain this skill over time.

- *Multiyear approach.* In Grades 1 and 2, *Math Trailblazers* emphasizes strategies that lead to fluency with the addition and subtraction facts. In Grade 3, students gain fluency with the multiplication facts while reviewing the addition and subtraction facts. In Grade 4, students achieve fluency with the division facts and verify fluency with the multiplication facts. In Grade 5, the multiplication and division facts are systematically reviewed and assessed.

- *Facts are not gatekeepers.* Students are not prevented from learning more complex mathematics because they do not perform well on fact tests. Use of strategies, calculators, and other math tools (e.g., manipulatives, hundred charts, printed multiplication tables) allows students to continue to work on interesting problems while still learning the facts.

Expectations by Grade Level

The following goals for the math facts are consistent with the recommendations in the National Council of Teachers of Mathematics *Principles and Standards for School Mathematics:*

- In kindergarten, students use manipulatives and invent their own strategies to solve addition and subtraction problems.

- By the end of first grade, all students can solve all basic addition and subtraction problems using some strategy. Fluency is not emphasized; strategies are. Some work with beginning concepts of multiplication takes place.

- In second grade, learning efficient strategies for addition and especially subtraction continues to be emphasized. Work with multiplication concepts continues. By the end of the year, students are expected to demonstrate fluency with all the addition and subtraction facts.

- In third grade, students review the subtraction facts. They develop efficient strategies for learning the multiplication facts and demonstrate fluency with the multiplication facts.

- In fourth grade, students review the multiplication facts and develop strategies for the division facts. By the end of year, we expect fluency with all the division facts.

- In fifth grade, students review the multiplication and division facts and are expected to maintain fluency with all the facts.

This is summarized in the following chart:

Grade	Addition	Subtraction	Multiplication	Division
K	• invented strategies	• invented strategies		
1	• strategies	• strategies		
2	• strategies • practice leading to fluency	• strategies • practice leading to fluency		
3	• review and practice	• review and practice	• strategies • practice leading to fluency	
4	• assessment and remediation as required	• assessment and remediation as required	• review and practice	• strategies • practice leading to fluency
5	• assessment and remediation as required	• assessment and remediation as required	• review and practice	• review and practice

Table 1: *Math Facts Scope and Sequence*

Strategies for Learning the Facts

Students are encouraged to learn the math facts by first employing a variety of strategies. Concepts and skills are learned more easily and are retained longer if they are meaningful. By first concentrating on concepts and strategies, we increase retention and reduce the amount of time necessary for rote memorization. Researchers note that over time, students develop techniques that are increasingly sophisticated and efficient. Experience with the strategies provides a basis for understanding the operation involved and for gaining fluency with the facts. In this section, we describe possible strategies for learning the addition, subtraction, multiplication, and division facts. The strategies for each operation are listed roughly in order of increasing sophistication.

Strategies for Addition Facts

Common strategies include counting all, counting on, doubles, making or using 10, and reasoning from known facts.

Counting All

This is a particularly straightforward strategy. For example, to solve $7 + 8$, the student gets 7 of something and 8 of something and counts how many there are altogether. The "something" could be beans or chips or marks on paper. In any case, the student counts all the objects to find the sum. This is perhaps not a very efficient method, but it is effective, especially for small numbers, and is usually well understood by the student.

Counting On

This is a natural strategy, particularly for adding 1, 2, or 3. Counters such as beans or chips may or may not be used. As an example, consider $8 + 3$. The student gets 8 beans, and then 3 more, but instead of counting the first 8 again, she simply counts the 3 added beans: "9, 10, 11."

Even if counters are not used, finger gestures can help keep track of how many more have been counted on. For example, to solve $8 + 3$, the student counts "9, 10, 11," holding up a finger each time a number word is said; when three fingers are up, the last word said is the answer.

Doubles

Facts such as $4 + 4 = 8$ are easier to remember than facts with two different addends. Some visual imagery can help, too: two hands for $5 + 5$, a carton of eggs for $6 + 6$, a calendar for $7 + 7$, and so on.

Making a 10

Facts with a sum of 10, such as $7 + 3$ and $6 + 4$, are also easier to remember than other facts. Ten frames can create visual images of making a 10. For example, 8 is shown in a ten frame like the one in Figure 1:

Figure 1: *A ten frame*

This visual imagery helps students remember, for example, that $8 + 2 = 10$.

Using a 10

Students who are comfortable partitioning and combining small numbers can use that knowledge to find the sums of larger numbers. In particular, there are many strategies that involve using the number 10. For example, to find $9 + 7$, we can decompose 7 into $1 + 6$ and then $9 + 7 = 9 + 1 + 6 = 10 + 6 = 16$. Similarly, $8 + 7 = 8 + 2 + 5 = 10 + 5 = 15$.

Reasoning from Known Facts

If you know what $7 + 7$ is, then $7 + 8$ is not much harder: it's just 1 more. So, the "near doubles" can be derived from knowing the doubles.

Strategies for Subtraction Facts

Common strategies for subtraction include using counters, counting up, counting back, using 10, and reasoning from related addition and subtraction facts.

Using Counters

This method models the problem with counters like beans or chips. For example, to solve $8 - 3$, the student gets 8 beans, removes 3 beans, and counts the remaining beans to find the difference. As with using the addition strategy "counting all," this relatively straightforward strategy may not be efficient but it has the great advantage that students usually understand it well.

Counting Up

The student starts at the lower number and counts on to the higher number, perhaps using fingers to keep track of how many numbers are counted. For example, to solve $8 - 5$, the student wants to know how to get from 5 to 8 and counts up 3 numbers: 6, 7, 8. So, $8 - 5 = 3$.

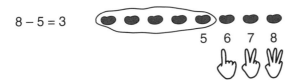

$8 - 5 = 3$

5 6 7 8

Figure 2: *Counting up*

Counting Back

Counting back works best for subtracting 1, 2, or 3. For larger numbers, it is probably best to count up. For example, to solve $9 - 2$, the student counts back 2 numbers: 8, 7. So, $9 - 2 = 7$.

$9 - 2 = 7$ 9 8 7

Figure 3: *Counting back*

Using a 10

Students follow the pattern they find when subtracting 10, e.g., $17 - 10 = 7$ and $13 - 10 = 3$, to learn close facts, e.g., $17 - 9 = 8$ and $13 - 9 = 4$. Since $17 - 9$ will be 1 more than $17 - 10$, they can reason that the answer will be 8, or $7 + 1$.

Making a 10

Knowing the addition facts that have a sum of 10, e.g., $6 + 4 = 10$, can be helpful in finding differences from 10, e.g., $10 - 6 = 4$ and $10 - 4 = 6$. Students can use ten frames to visualize these problems as in Figure 4. These facts can then also be used to find close facts, such as $11 - 4 = 7$.

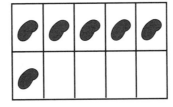

$10 - 4 = 6$

Figure 4: *Using a ten frame*

Using Doubles

Students can use the addition doubles, e.g., $8 + 8 = 16$ and $6 + 6 = 12$, to learn the subtraction "half-doubles" as well: $16 - 8 = 8$ and $12 - 6 = 6$. They can then use these facts to figure out close facts, such as $13 - 6 = 7$ and $15 - 8 = 7$.

Reasoning from Related Addition and Subtraction Facts

Knowing that $8 + 7 = 15$ would seem to be of some help in solving $15 - 7$. Unfortunately, however, knowing related addition facts may not be so helpful to younger or less mathematically mature students. Nevertheless, reasoning from known facts is a powerful strategy for those who can apply it and should be encouraged.

Strategies for Multiplication Facts

Common strategies for multiplication include skip counting, counting up or down from a known fact, doubling, breaking a product into the sum of known products, and using patterns.

Skip Counting

Students begin skip counting and solving problems informally that involve multiplicative situations in first grade. By the time they begin formal work with the multiplication facts in third grade, they should be fairly proficient with skip counting. This strategy is particularly useful for facts such as the 2s, 3s, 5s, and 10s, for which skip counting is easy.

Counting Up or Down from a Known Fact

This strategy involves skip counting forwards once or twice from a known fact. For example, if children know that 5×5 is 25, then they can use this to solve 6×5 (5 more) or 4×5 (5 less). Some children use this for harder facts. For 7×6, they can use the fact that $5 \times 6 = 30$ as a starting point and then count on by sixes to 42.

Doubling

Some children use doubling relationships to help them with multiplication facts involving 4, 6, and 8. For example, 4×7 is twice as much as 2×7. Since $2 \times 7 = 14$, it follows that 4×7 is 28. Since 3×8 is 24, it follows that 6×8 is 48.

Breaking a Product into the Sum of Known Products

A fact like 7×8 can be broken into the sum $5 \times 8 + 2 \times 8$ since $7 = 5 + 2$. See Figure 5. The previous two strategies are special cases of this more general strategy.

$$7 \times 8 =$$
$$5 \times 8 + 2 \times 8 =$$
$$40 + 16 = 56$$

Figure 5: *Breaking up 7 × 8*

Patterns

A. Perhaps the best-known examples of patterns are the nines patterns:

   1. When the nines products are listed in a column, as shown below, it is easy to see that the digits in the tens place count up by one (0, 1, 2, 3, . . .) and that the digits in the ones place count down by one (9, 8, 7, . . .).

      9
     18
     27
     36
     45
     54
     63
     72
     81

   2. The sums of the two digits in each of the nines products above are all equal to nine. For example, the sum of the digits in 36 is $3 + 6 = 9$; the sum of the digits in 72 is $7 + 2 = 9$. Adding the digits of a number to see whether they add up to nine can be a strategy in remembering a nines fact. For example, a student might think, "Let me see, does 9×6 equal 54 or 56? It must be 54 since $5 + 4$ is 9, but $5 + 6$ is not 9."

   3. The digit in the tens place in a nines fact is one less than the number being multiplied. For example, $4 \times 9 = 36$, and 3 is one less than 4. This can be combined with the previous pattern to derive nines facts. For example, 3×9 is in the twenties. Since $2 + 7$ is 9, 3×9 must be 27.

   4. Nines can easily be computed using the counting down strategy. Nine times a digit is the same as 10 times the digit, minus the digit. For example, 9×6 is $10 \times 6 - 6 = 54$.

B. Other patterns.

   Other patterns that are useful in remembering other special facts:

   1. 0 times a number equals 0.

   2. 1 times a number equals the number.

   3. 2 times a number is double the number.

   4. 5 times a number ends in 0 or 5; even numbers times 5 end in 0 and odd numbers times five end in 5.

   5. 10 times a number is the same number with a 0 on the end.

Sequencing the Study of Multiplication Facts

In kindergarten, children solve word problems involving multiplication situations. Beginning in first grade, the curriculum develops a conceptual foundation for multiplication through a variety of multiplication models, including repeated addition, the array model, and the number-line model. Fluency with the multiplication facts is expected by the end of third grade. Strategies are often introduced in specific, third-grade lessons. Practice is continued in subsequent lessons and especially in the Daily Practice and Problems and Home Practice. We do not introduce the multiplication facts in the order in which they are traditionally taught (first learning the 2s, then the

3s, then the 4s, etc.). Rather, we emphasize thinking strategies for the facts, introducing fact-groups in the following order:

2s, 3s, 5s, and 10s. The 2s, 3s, 5s, and 10s are easily solved using skip counting.

Square numbers such as $3 \times 3 = 9$, $4 \times 4 = 16$, and $5 \times 5 = 25$. These are introduced by arranging tiles into square arrays.

Nines. Students explore patterns for nines.

Last six facts. After students have learned the facts listed above and their turn-around facts ($9 \times 6 = 6 \times 9$), there are only six more facts to learn: 4×6, 4×7, 4×8, 6×7, 6×8, and 7×8.

Strategies for the Division Facts

The main strategy for learning the division facts is to think of the related multiplication fact. Therefore, students review the multiplication facts and develop fluency with the division facts by working with fact families. (Fact families are groups of related facts. An example of a fact family is $3 \times 4 = 12$, $4 \times 3 = 12$, $12 \div 3 = 4$, and $12 \div 4 = 3$.)

Using the Right Strategy

Different strategies appeal to different students. Students should not feel overburdened with the need to determine which is the "correct" strategy for a given fact. We do not intend to give them a new layer of things to learn. For example, when asked to explain a strategy for a fact, a student may say, "I've used it so much that now I just remember it." "Just remembering" is obviously an efficient strategy. The purpose of suggesting and discussing various strategies is to give students other, perhaps helpful, ways of learning the facts and to give them the confidence to think problems through when necessary. Students should have the opportunity to choose the strategies that work best for them or to invent their own.

Math Facts Lessons

The *Math Trailblazers* math facts program pervades most of the curriculum's components. Work with math facts are in different kinds of lessons. These are described in this section.

Figure 6: *Discussing fact strategies*

Everyday Work

As students work on problems in the labs and activities, encourage them to use and discuss various strategies for solving math facts problems. A number of important goals can best be reached through such discussions.

One goal is to legitimize all valid strategies, even those that may be less efficient. When students see their intuitive methods recognized and validated, they tend to perceive mathematical knowledge as continuous with everyday knowledge and common sense. We thus hope to avoid the unfortunate tendency of many students to separate their knowledge of mathematics from their knowledge of the real world.

By discussing strategies as they arise in context, students and teachers can explore how the strategies work and can verify that they are being used properly. Students should come to realize that a fact strategy that gives wrong answers is not very useful.

A second goal of our approach is to encourage students to communicate mathematical ideas. There are several reasons to stress communication: Students can learn from one another; communicating a method requires higher orders of thinking than simply applying that method; and skill at communicating is important in itself. We are social creatures. Mathematics and science are social endeavors in which communication is crucial.

A third goal of encouraging discussions of various methods is to give the teacher opportunities to learn about how students think. Knowing more about students' thinking helps the teacher ask better questions and plan more effective lessons.

Strategy Lessons

We feel that occasionally it is appropriate for lessons to focus on certain strategies that are developmentally appropriate for most students. Our plan is to begin with simple strategies that should be accessible to all students and to progress gradually to more complex forms of reasoning. For example, in the fall of first grade, we have several lessons that stress counting on to solve certain addition problems. Later, we explicitly introduce making a 10 and other, more sophisticated, strategies.

In general, you should expect your students to come up with effective strategies on their own. Our strategy lessons are intended to explore how and why various strategies work and also to codify and organize the strategies the students invent. They are not meant to dictate the only appropriate strategy for a given problem or to discourage students from using strategies they understand and like. They should be seen as opportunities to discuss strategies that may be appropriate for many students and to encourage their wider use.

Practice

Our ultimate goal is to produce students who can think mathematically, who can solve problems and deal easily with quantified information, and who enjoy mathematics and are not afraid of it. It is easier to do all of the above if one has fluency with the basic math facts. Practice strengthens students' abilities to use strategies and moves students towards fluency with the facts. Practice that follows instruction that stresses the use of strategies has been shown to improve

As students work on problems in the labs and activities, they should be encouraged to use and to discuss various strategies for solving math facts problems.

Our ultimate goal is to produce students who can think mathematically, who can solve problems and deal easily with quantified information, and who enjoy mathematics and are not afraid of it. It is easier to do all of the above if one has fluency with the basic math facts.

students' fluency with the math facts. We recommend, and have incorporated into the curriculum, the following practice to gain this fluency.

Practice in Context

The primary practice of math facts will arise naturally for the students as they participate in the labs and other activities in the curriculum. These labs and activities offer many opportunities to practice addition, subtraction, multiplication, and division in a meaningful way. The lessons involve the student visually with drawings and patterns, auditorily through discussion, and tactilely through the use of many tools such as manipulatives and calculators.

Pages of problems on the basic facts are not only unnecessary, they can be counterproductive. Students may come to regard mathematics as mostly memorization and may perceive it as meaningless and unconnected to their everyday lives.

Structured Practice

Student-friendly, structured practice is built into the curriculum, especially in the DPP, Home Practice, and games. One small group of related math facts is presented to the students at a time. The practice of groups of facts is carefully distributed throughout the year. A small set of facts grouped in a meaningful way leads students to develop strategies such as adding doubles, counting back, or using a 10 for dealing with a particular situation. Furthermore, a small set of facts is a manageable amount to learn and remember.

Beginning in the second half of first grade and continuing through fifth grade, a small group of facts to be studied in a unit is introduced in the DPP. Through DPP items, students practice the facts and take a short assessment. Beginning in second grade, students use flash cards for additional practice with specific groups of facts. Facts are also practiced in many word problems in the DPP, Home Practice, and individual lessons. These problems allow students to focus on other interesting mathematical ideas as they also gain more fact practice.

Games

A variety of games are included in the curriculum, both in the lessons and in the DPP items of many units. A summary of the games used in a particular grade can be found in the Games section. Once students learn the rules of the games, they should play them periodically in class and at home for homework. Games provide an opportunity to encourage family involvement in the math program. When a game is assigned for homework, a note can be sent home with a place for the family members to sign, affirming that they played the game with their student.

Figure 7: *Playing a game*

Use of Calculators

The relationship between knowing the math facts and the use of calculators is an interesting one. Using a multiplication table or a calculator when necessary to find a fact helps promote familiarity and reinforces the math facts. Students soon figure out that it is quicker and more efficient to know the basic facts than to have to use these tools. The use of calculators also requires excellent estimation skills so that one can easily check for errors in calculator computations. Rather than eliminating the need for fluency with the facts, successful calculator use for solving complex problems depends on fact knowledge.

When to Practice

Practicing small groups of facts often for short periods of time is more effective than practicing many facts less often for long periods of time. For example, practicing 8 to 10 subtraction facts for 5 minutes several times a week is better than practicing all the subtraction facts for half an hour once a week. Good times for practicing the facts for 5 or 10 minutes during the school day include the beginning of the day, the beginning of math class, when students have completed an assignment, when an impending activity is delayed, or when an activity ends earlier than expected. Practicing small groups of facts at home involves parents in the process and frees class time for more interesting mathematics.

> *Practicing small groups of facts often for short periods of time is more effective than practicing many facts less often for long periods of time.*

Assessment

Throughout the curriculum, teachers assess students' knowledge of the facts through observations as they work on activities, labs, and games. In Grades 3–5, students can use their *Facts I Know* charts to record their own progress in learning the facts. This type of self-assessment is very important in helping each student to become responsible for his or her own learning. Students are able to personalize their study of facts and not waste valuable time studying facts they already know.

In the second half of first grade, a sequence of facts assessments is provided in the Daily Practice and Problems. A more comprehensive facts assessment program begins in second grade. This program assesses students' progress in learning the facts, as outlined in the Expectations by Grade Level section of this tutor. As students develop strategies for a given group of facts, short quizzes accompany the practice. Students know which facts will be tested, focus practice in class and at home on those facts, then take the quiz. As they take the quiz, they use one color pencil to write answers before a given time limit, then use another color to complete the problems they need more time to answer. Students then use their *Facts I Know* charts to make a record of those facts they answered quickly, those facts they answered correctly but with less efficient strategies, and those facts they did not know at all. Using this information, students can concentrate their efforts on gaining fluency with those facts they answered correctly, but not quickly. They also know to develop strategies for those facts they could not answer at all. In this way, the number of facts studied at any one time becomes more manageable, practice becomes more meaningful, and the process less intimidating.

Tests of all the facts for any operation have a very limited role. They are used no more than two times a year to show growth over time and should not be given daily or weekly. Since we rarely, if ever, need to recall 100 facts at one time in everyday life, overemphasizing tests of all the facts reinforces the notion that math is nothing more than rote memorization and has no connection to the real world. Quizzes of small numbers of facts are as effective and not as threatening. They give students, parents, and teachers the information needed to continue learning and practicing efficiently. With an assessment approach based on strategies and the use of small groups of facts, students can see mathematics as connected to their own thinking and gain confidence in their mathematical abilities.

Conclusion

Research provides clear indications for curriculum developers and teachers about the design of effective math facts instruction. These recommendations formed the foundation of the *Math Trailblazers* math facts program. Developing strategies for learning the facts (rather than relying on rote memorization), distributing practice of small groups of facts, applying math facts in interesting problems, and using an appropriate assessment program— all are consistent with recommendations from current research. It is an instructional approach that encourages students to make sense of the mathematics they are learning. The resulting program will add efficiency and effectiveness to your students' learning of the math facts.

References

Ashlock, R.B., and C.A. Washbon. "Games: Practice Activities for the Basic Facts." In M.N. Suydam and R.E. Reys (eds.), *Developing Computational Skills: 1978 Yearbook*. National Council of Teachers of Mathematics, Reston, VA, 1978.

Beattie, L.D. "Children's Strategies for Solving Subtraction-Fact Combinations." *Arithmetic Teacher,* 27 (1), pp. 14–15, 1979.

Brownell, W.A., and C.B. Chazal. "The Effects of Premature Drill in Third-Grade Arithmetic." *Journal of Educational Research,* 29 (1), 1935.

Carpenter, T.P., and J.M. Moser. "The Acquisition of Addition and Subtraction Concepts in Grades One through Three." *Journal for Research in Mathematics Education,* 15 (3), pp. 179–202, 1984.

Cook, C.J., and J.A. Dossey. "Basic Fact Thinking Strategies for Multiplication—Revisited." *Journal for Research in Mathematics Education,* 13 (3), pp. 163–171, 1982.

Davis, E.J. "Suggestions for Teaching the Basic Facts of Arithmetic." In M.N. Suydam and R.E. Reys (eds.), *Developing Computational Skills: 1978 Yearbook*. National Council of Teachers of Mathematics, Reston, VA, 1978.

Fuson, K.C. "Teaching Addition, Subtraction, and Place-Value Concepts." In L. Wirszup and R. Streit (eds.), *Proceedings of the UCSMP International Conference on Mathematics Education: Developments in School Mathematics Education Around the World: Applications-Oriented Curricula and Technology-Supported Learning for All Students*. National Council of Teachers of Mathematics, Reston, VA, 1987.

Fuson, K.C., and G.B. Willis. "Subtracting by Counting Up: More Evidence." *Journal for Research in Mathematics Education,* 19 (5), pp. 402–420, 1988.

Fuson, K.C., J.W. Stigler, and K. Bartsch. "Grade Placement of Addition and Subtraction Topics in Japan, Mainland China, the Soviet Union, Taiwan, and the United States." *Journal for Research in Mathematics Education,* 19 (5), pp. 449–456, 1988.

Greer, B. "Multiplication and Division as Models of Situations." In D.A. Grouws (ed.), *Handbook of Research on Mathematics Teaching and Learning: A Project of the National Council of Teachers of Mathematics* (Chapter 13). Macmillan, New York, 1992.

Hiebert, James. "Relationships between Research and the NCTM Standards." *Journal for Research in Mathematics Education,* 30 January, pp. 3–19, 1999.

Isaacs, A.C., and W.M. Carroll. "Strategies for Basic Facts Instruction." *Teaching Children Mathematics,* 5 May, pp. 508–515, 1999.

Kouba, V.L., C.A. Brown, T.P. Carpenter, M.M. Lindquist, E.A. Silver, and J.O. Swafford. "Results of the Fourth NAEP Assessment of Mathematics: Number, Operations, and Word Problems." *Arithmetic Teacher,* 35 (8), pp. 14–19, 1988.

Myers, A.C., and C.A. Thornton. "The Learning-Disabled Child—Learning the Basic Facts." *Arithmetic Teacher,* 25 (3), pp. 46–50, 1977.

National Research Council. *Adding It Up: Helping Children Learn Mathematics.* National Academy Press, Washington, DC, 2001.

Principles and Standards for School Mathematics. National Council of Teachers of Mathematics, Reston, VA, 2000.

Rathmell, E.C. "Using Thinking Strategies to Teach the Basic Facts." In M.N. Suydam and R.E. Reys (eds.), *Developing Computational Skills: 1978 Yearbook.* National Council of Teachers of Mathematics, Reston, VA, 1978.

Rathmell, E.C., and P.R. Trafton. "Whole Number Computation." In J.N. Payne (ed.), *Mathematics for the Young Child.* National Council of Teachers of Mathematics, Reston, VA, 1990.

Swart, W.L. "Some Findings on Conceptual Development of Computational Skills." *Arithmetic Teacher,* 32 (5), pp. 36–38, 1985.

Thornton, C.A. "Doubles Up—Easy!" *Arithmetic Teacher,* 29 (8), p. 20, 1982.

Thornton, C.A. "Emphasizing Thinking Strategies in Basic Fact Instruction." *Journal for Research in Mathematics Education,* 9 (3), pp. 214–227, 1978.

Thornton, C.A. "Solution Strategies: Subtraction Number Facts." *Educational Studies in Mathematics,* 21 (1), pp. 241–263, 1990.

Thornton, C.A. "Strategies for the Basic Facts." In J.N. Payne (ed.), *Mathematics for the Young Child.* National Council of Teachers of Mathematics, Reston, VA, 1990.

Thornton, C.A., and P.J. Smith. "Action Research: Strategies for Learning Subtraction Facts." *Arithmetic Teacher,* 35 (8), pp. 8–12, 1988.

Van de Walle, J. *Elementary and Middle School Mathematics: Teaching Developmentally.* Addison Wesley, New York, 2001.

Portfolios

A portfolio is a purposeful collection of a student's work that provides evidence of the student's skills, understandings, or attitudes. If the portfolio includes work collected over time, then it may also reflect the student's growth.

This tutor outlines reasons portfolios may be useful and provides some guidance for getting started and going further. A bibliography includes suggestions for additional reading.

Why Portfolios?

Portfolios can help teachers:

- better assess student learning;
- foster student autonomy;
- communicate the goals of instruction to students and parents; and
- improve their own teaching.

Student Assessment

Since a portfolio contains direct samples of student work, it may, for certain purposes, be superior to indirect indicators like grades. For example, an actual graph shows a student's skill at graphing better than a grade; and the juxtaposition of two graphs, one from September and the other from January, documents learning over time much more accurately than two grades could ever do.

Portfolios can assess many outcomes that are hard to assess by more conventional methods—communication, reasoning, problem solving, confidence, perseverance, flexibility, and so on. They also can help you learn more about how students think and track the development of that thinking.

Student Autonomy

Portfolios can encourage students to assess their own learning. Students become more self-directed and motivated by examining and reflecting on their own work and the work of their peers.

Portfolios can assess many outcomes that are hard to assess by more conventional methods . . . They also can help you learn about how students think and track the development of that thinking.

Communication

Concrete examples of student work reveal much that is not easily conveyed in grades or comments. Parents and others can see progress and achievement for themselves.

The examples of student work in a portfolio also convey the content and goals of the curriculum in a specific way that complements the generalities of curriculum philosophies and scope and sequence charts. Portfolios focus on the work students actually do, not on ideology or wishful thinking. You can enhance communication between students and their parents, teachers, and peers by having particular examples to discuss.

Portfolios can help establish public norms for mathematics achievement. Focusing assessment on tests and grades communicates a narrow concept of what is valuable in mathematics. When assessment is more broadly based, it promotes a broader vision of mathematics.

Improvement of Instruction

Student portfolios are useful both for making instructional decisions and for evaluating and improving instruction.

Certainly, better understanding of how students think and feel can help you make better decisions about directions for future instruction. But portfolios can also help teachers improve their teaching more generally. Portfolios can facilitate discussions with professional colleagues about different approaches to the same topic; they can reflect the range of instructional opportunities offered; and they can indicate the use of manipulatives, group work, and technology in an implemented curriculum.

Student portfolios might be included in a Teaching Portfolio that a teacher can use for self-evaluation. You can refine your own teaching by collecting and examining several years of student portfolios. Some benefits that portfolios promise for students—collegiality, establishment of public norms, improvement of higher-level skills—may thus become available to teachers.

Getting Started

The beginnings of all things are small.

—CICERO

There is no single right way to do portfolios. The suggestions offered below have worked for others and may work for you, but you should expect to learn by trial and error and to rely on your own judgment. If you have used portfolios for writing or some other subject, then your experience will be invaluable. If you possibly can, work with a colleague as you implement portfolios for the first time.

Starting small, with modest goals, is a good idea. For example, you may organize your portfolio program around one well-defined area that is hard to assess by more traditional methods. For instance, choose one of the following areas as a theme for the portfolios:

- measurement,
- graphing,

There is no single right way to do portfolios.

- drawing pictures and diagrams, or
- communicating solution methods.

Besides starting small, start early so you have a baseline of student attitudes and achievement. Before and after comparisons are useful, but impossible without early samples. All materials in a portfolio must be dated.

A box with a file folder for each child's work is a simple way to start. If the box is easily accessible, then the portfolios are more likely to fit into classroom routines. Anticipate the need for more room as items are added to the portfolios.

What goes in the portfolios is a key decision. Figure 1 shows some kinds of materials you might include in a portfolio, although clearly no real portfolio will have such a wild collection. Figure 2 is a table of contents for a possible third-grade portfolio.

You might aim for balance in the selection of materials: group vs. individual assignments; short problems vs. longer projects; real life vs. purely mathematical problems; on-demand vs. no-deadline tasks; attitude vs. skill vs. concept-oriented work; and so on. The number of pieces should not be so few that there is not enough evidence about important outcomes, nor so many that there is no judgment about what is important or worthwhile. About eight to ten pieces might be enough for a semester.

You must also decide how to pick what to put in the portfolios. We suggest that students select items subject to constraints imposed by the teacher. Constraints might range from requiring particular items, to selecting items that meet certain criteria, to allowing complete freedom of choice by students. The amount of latitude you allow will depend on your class and goals. Younger children, for example, usually need more direction. Putting fewer constraints on what goes in the portfolios may foster student autonomy, but may result in portfolios with few overlapping items so comparisons between students are difficult, or may even yield useless collections of random scraps.

> *The number of pieces should not be so few that there is not enough evidence about important outcomes, nor so many that there is no judgment about what is important or worthwhile. About eight to ten pieces might be enough for a semester.*

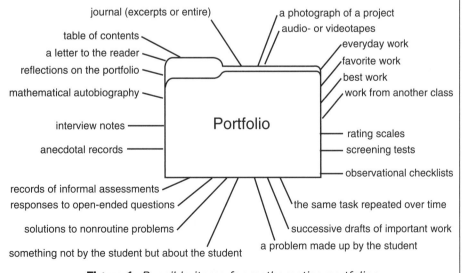

Figure 1: *Possible items for mathematics portfolios*

One way to organize the selection process is to have two folders for each child—a collection folder and the portfolio proper. Then, from time to time (once every several weeks or so), students can harvest the collection folder and add a few select items to the portfolio. At the same time, they can weed the portfolio so the total number of items does not become too large. Students can do this selection in small groups or pairs subject to teacher constraints as described above. Keep remaining items in the collection folder or send them home.

Eight to ten well-chosen and chronologically arranged pieces of work are most useful. You will have specific examples that communicate at parent conference time what your curriculum is and how your students are progressing; you will have a sampling of the products of your instruction so you can critically examine your teaching; and your students will see a cross section of their own work so they can attain greater self-awareness and autonomy. You have accomplished much even if your portfolios are no more than this.

Going Further

There are, however, other things you might want to try as you gain experience with portfolios, especially if you are working with older students. Periodic reviews of the portfolios, writing about the portfolios, and assessing the portfolios are worth considering.

Jarrett's Portfolio • Table of Contents		
Item	**Description**	**Date**
Letter to Reader	My letter tells what my portfolio shows about my math work this semester.	9/22
Journal	A few times a week we write about math in our journals. Mine has 35 pages so far!	
Spinning Differences	I used a spinner to make subtraction problems and then graphed how many times I got each difference.	9/27
The Better "Picker Upper"	I used water to make spots on different kinds of paper towels. Then I counted square cm to find the areas of the spots.	10/25
Joe the Goldfish	Joe needed a raincoat and I figured out how much cloth he would need to make it.	11/1
Palindromes	A palindrome is a number that is the same frontwards and backwards. I used addition to make numbers into palindromes.	11/10
Lemonade Stand	This was the first line graph I ever made.	11/15
Mass vs. Number	I measured the mass of different numbers of marbles. Then I made a line graph and used it to make some predictions.	12/5
Stencilrama	This was my favorite. We made stencils out of index cards and then used the stencils to make designs. We had to figure out how many times we would have to move the stencil to make a border around the bulletin board.	1/15

Figure 2: *Sample third-grade portfolio with an emphasis on graphing*

Portfolio Review

Most teachers will be hard-pressed to find time to meet with individual students to review portfolios. Whole-class discussion and peer consultations, however, can accomplish many of the same goals.

For example, ask students to look through their collection folders for their best graphs to add to their portfolios. First, through whole-class discussion, help students identify characteristics of a good graph. Then in small groups or pairs, students can examine their collections to pick out the best graphs. This opportunity for students to examine one another's work can help establish public norms for excellence.

Portfolio Writing

Asking students to write about the contents of their portfolios encourages reflection and self-assessment. This writing can take a variety of forms.

The most basic writing is a table of contents with the name of each piece, a brief description, and the date it was completed. Students can also include who chose the piece and why, who worked on the piece, and what was learned or liked or hard about the piece.

You might ask students to write a letter to the reader of the portfolio. The letter can identify favorite pieces and explain why they are favorites, or best work, or work that shows the most progress. The letter might show you what the portfolio reveals about the student as a learner of mathematics.

Assessing the Portfolios

You do not have to assess the portfolios. Most likely you already graded the work included in them, and the collection is itself a direct indicator of achievement and attitude. This indicator may be sufficient for your purposes.

Assessing the portfolios, however, can have advantages, especially if you are working with older students. For one, it shows that you care about the portfolios and so communicates to students that they should take them seriously. It can also model processes you want students to apply in peer- and self-assessment of the portfolios.

If you do intend to grade the portfolios, you should make your expectations known to the students in advance. The establishment of such public criteria for excellence, like the TIMS Student Rubrics, will help students know what they should aim for so their work can be better focused. You might concentrate on how well the portfolios are organized—table of contents, correct chronological order, completeness, etc.—or on the quality of the reflective writing about the portfolio. You may encourage a balanced selection of items, documentation of improvement over time, clarity of communication, accuracy of self-assessment, neatness, or something else. As long as your students know the criteria and you have the time to do it, such grading can be useful.

Conclusion

Portfolios will not solve all the problems of mathematics education. And there are some costs for using them. Using portfolios as part of an assessment program will certainly take extra time and can be difficult, especially at first. Getting students to reflect on their own learning is particularly hard. But despite such pitfalls, portfolios offer great promise for improving your teaching and your students' learning. The basic idea is simple: collect, select, reflect.

References

Crowley, Mary L. "Student Mathematics Portfolio: More Than a Display Case." *Mathematics Teacher,* 86 (7), pp. 544–547, 1993.

Kuhs, Therese. "Portfolio Assessment: Making It Work for the First Time." *Mathematics Teacher,* 87 (5), pp. 332–335, 1994.

Lambdin, Diana V., and Vicki L. Walker. "Planning for Classroom Portfolio Assessment." *Arithmetic Teacher,* 41 (6), pp. 318–324, 1994.

Mumme, Judith. *Portfolio Assessment in Mathematics.* (A publication of the California Mathematics Project.) University of California, Santa Barbara, CA, 1990.

Stenmark, Jean Kerr, ed. *Mathematics Assessment: Myths, Models, Good Questions, and Practical Suggestions.* National Council of Teachers of Mathematics, Reston, VA, 1991.

Word Problems

> In fact, word problems should not just be integrated into the mathematics curriculum; they should form the basis of the curriculum.
>
> —CARPENTER, FENNEMA, AND PETERSON, 1987

Although word problems are not the basis of the *Math Trailblazers* curriculum, we do agree that students should confront a wide variety of challenging word problems and exercises. Word problems can highlight applications of the mathematics students are learning. They can introduce, motivate, and develop new mathematics in meaningful contexts.

This tutor provides teachers with a summary of research and background information about word problems. It outlines the theoretical and practical frameworks that underlie the extensive use of word problems in *Math Trailblazers*.

Problem Representations

Problems are presented to us in different ways. Sometimes a problem arises from a real situation; other times we give problems in words, pictures, or symbols. These different ways are sometimes called modes of representation.

Real Situations

Consider this problem: "Jessica and Meri Joy baked 36 cookies. Then, Meri Joy dropped 12 cookies on the floor. How many were left?" Now this problem has a basis in reality: Jessica and Meri Joy are the daughters of two members of the *Math Trailblazers* development team; they really did bake cookies; some cookies really were dropped and spoiled. Note that Meri Joy and Jessica could answer the question simply by counting the cookies that were not dropped.

Such real-life situations are the most concrete level of problem representation. People rarely go wrong when they solve such problems. (Resnick, 1987)

Concrete Model

If, however, some time has passed and the cookies are no longer at hand, we can still ask and answer the question. One way is to get some beans and to pretend they are cookies. To solve the problem, we can count out 36 beans, separate 12, and count how many remain.

This use of beans to represent cookies is one step up the ladder of abstraction: a concrete model represents a real situation. Good evidence exists that even kindergarten students can handle complex problems that are represented by concrete models. (Carpenter, Ansell, Franke, Fennema, and Weisbeck, 1993)

Figure 1: *Twelve of 36 cookies dropped*

Pictures

Another way to approach the problem is via pictures. Each cookie can be represented by a circle. We can solve the problem by drawing 36 circles, crossing out 12, and counting those left.

This sort of pictorial representation is often useful in mathematics and science. Even when the picture does not lead immediately to a solution, it often helps us understand the problem situation and starts us on the road to a solution.

Verbal Representations

Most school problems are stated in words. This is often necessary (How else could we present our cookie problem in this essay?) and builds on a well-developed set of skills your students have—their language skills.

Language is the first and most powerful symbol system we learn. The recent emphasis on discourse and communication in learning is based at least in part on a recognition of the importance of language in human thought.

Symbols

We can also represent Jessica and Meri Joy's cookies in symbols:

$$36 - 12 = \Box$$

Such symbolic representations are abstract and powerful. Much of the explosive growth of mathematics in the last 400 years is due to the invention of more efficient symbol systems.

Unfortunately, for too many students, mathematical symbolism is a code they never crack. Such students do not see the marks on paper as meaningful or related to the real world in any way. Instead, they see the marks as part of an arcane game.

When writing number sentences, it is important to use units. Of course, constantly writing the units can be tedious. One compromise is to omit the units in the middle of a sequence of symbolic representations, but be sure to include them at the beginning and again at the end.

> *Even when the picture does not lead immediately to a solution, it often helps us understand the problem situation and starts us on the road to a solution.*

We want students to learn to write, read, and understand mathematical symbolism, especially number sentences. Here, word problems can be particularly useful. The situations in many word problems are straightforward enough that the corresponding number sentences are simple.

Usually, several number sentences are appropriate for each problem. Consider, for example, the following problem: "Janice had 9 stickers. Then her mother gave her some more. Now Janice has 16 stickers. How many stickers did Janice's mother give her?"

An adult might see this as a subtraction problem and write

$$16 - 9 = 7 \tag{a}$$
or
$$16 - 9 = \square \tag{b}$$

These number sentences are in the normal or "canonical" form. That is, the known quantities are on the left-hand side of the equals sign and the unknown or the answer is on the right-hand side.

Many students, however, write something like

$$9 + \square = 16 \tag{c}$$
or
$$9 + 7 = 16 \tag{d}$$

These "non-canonical" forms reflect the students' way of thinking about the problem: Janice had 9 stickers, then she got some more, and now she has 16 stickers. Often a student who writes (c) or (d) will solve the problem by counting on from 9 to 16 rather than by subtracting 9 from 16. We consider these non-canonical number sentences to be as correct as the canonical forms. They can also be more understandable for the students.

Translations between Representations

So we have a hierarchy of levels of representation: real objects, physical models, pictures, words, symbols.

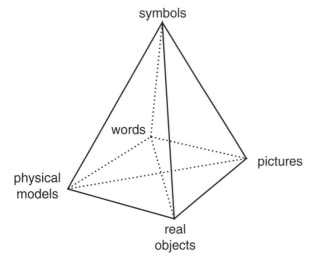

Figure 2: *Modes of representation*

But perhaps "hierarchy of levels" is not quite the right phrase; it may be better to consider that there are a number of different modes of representation, each of which has certain strengths and weaknesses. Recent cognitive theory indicates that the ability to translate from one representation to another is a crucial part of conceptual understanding and problem-solving skill. Connecting symbols with real referents, for example, permits one to understand symbolic manipulations and results in terms of real situations. Earlier, we saw how translating a problem from a real or verbal presentation to a concrete model could yield a solution by an elementary method.

Unfortunately, too much instruction in mathematics focuses exclusively on symbols. While symbolic representations are compact and powerful, they cannot stand alone. Our goal is to have students create mental "two-way streets" between symbols, words, concrete models, pictures, and real situations. Word problems are an excellent vehicle for reaching this goal.

Solving Problems

One view of problem solving is that the most critical step is developing the right representation: when we see the problem in the correct light, then the solution is obvious. Of course, the right representation for me might not be right for you. Accordingly, just as multiple representations should be part of the mathematics curriculum, so should multiple solutions. Estimation and attention to the reasonableness of results must also be part of instruction in problem solving.

Multiple Solutions

Many students think the main thing in mathematics is to get the right answer. Incorrect or partial answers are seen as failures, and re-solving a problem in a different way is considered futile.

On the contrary, students can learn much by solving problems in several ways. When different methods yield the same answer, students gain confidence both in the answer and in the various methods. This can be particularly useful for students learning more abstract and powerful methods: if a more powerful method gives the same answer as a more familiar method, then students are more likely to understand and trust the powerful method.

Students can also see connections within mathematics by comparing the points of view that generate different solutions to a problem. Making such connections is a key goal of the National Council of Teachers of Mathematics *Principles and Standards for School Mathematics* (NCTM, 2000). If students share their solution methods, then not only do they learn new methods from one another, but they also learn to communicate mathematically, another *Principles and Standards* goal.

Even incorrect or partial answers can be useful. Wrong answers are almost always the result of a student's honest attempt to get the problem right. Examining and discussing wrong answers and the procedures that generated them can make students' thinking explicit so that misconceptions can be identified and cleared up.

Sometimes a partial answer is the best we can reasonably hope for. In fact, many practical problems are impossible or prohibitively expensive to solve exactly. In some real situations, a partial answer may be all that is required.

A partial solution may be based on an idea that can be modified or extended to yield a complete solution. If a problem is hard, then making progress towards an answer is perfectly respectable, and certainly far better than giving up.

One way to get the most out of partial solutions is to encourage students to talk and write about the problem even if they cannot solve it. This will also help students stay with difficult problems longer.

Estimation

A common reason for estimating is that an exact answer is not necessary. If we have $5 and want to buy milk, bread, and eggs, a quick estimate will tell us if we have enough money. Sometimes an estimate must serve because an exact answer is impossible or impractical to obtain. The exact number of piano tuners who live in Chicago, for example, can only be estimated.

Another reason to estimate an answer is to verify the accuracy of a result obtained in some other way. This is especially important in our age of computing machines—if we do not have some idea what the answer should be, then we may be at a loss to know whether the answer the machine gives us is reasonable.

A less commonly recognized reason to make an estimate is as a step on the way to an exact answer. As one of our favorite teachers used to say, "Never solve a problem until you know the answer." We think he meant that finding an approximate answer can help in the search for the exact answer. By estimating an answer, we come to understand the problem better.

Learning to estimate builds number sense and encourages students to rely on their common sense rather than on rote procedures. Making a good estimate requires a flexible combination of common sense, experience, rules of thumb, and specific knowledge. Estimation is a high-level skill that takes a long time to develop. Estimation is, accordingly, built into *Math Trailblazers* from the beginning.

Reasonableness of Results

How often have you seen a student's paper with patently absurd answers? Such answers indicate that the student is not working at a meaningful level. Rather some procedures—half-understood, half-remembered—were carried out and something was produced, but the relationship of that product to the problem at hand is far from clear. No connection exists in the student's mind between the real situation and the symbolic manipulations.

Looking back when an answer is obtained, mapping the result of symbolic or other manipulations back onto the original problem statement, is a crucial part of the problem-solving process. George Polya, in his famous book *How to Solve It* (1957), included looking back as one of four basic steps in solving a problem. (Polya's other steps are to understand the problem; to make a plan to solve the problem; and to carry out the plan.)

When students look back at a solution, they should assess whether it is reasonable and correct. They can also look for ways to improve the solution, simplify it, or generalize it. By comparing their solution to other solutions, they can obtain further evidence of correctness and they have an opportunity to make connections between different approaches.

Addition and Subtraction Problem Types

Children typically use many varied methods to solve word problems. This, in part, relates to the fact that there is an underlying variety of problem types. Educational researchers in the last 20 years or so have explored the different problem types extensively. Several different examples are discussed here. Additional discussion about the methods children use to solve problems are in the TIMS Tutor: *Math Facts*.

Students should experience solving many different types of word problems. It is important to note, however, that in discussing the different problem types, we are not suggesting a new level of material for children to learn, i.e., we do not expect nor want children to have to learn about the different types of problems as a study in and of itself. Rather, we discuss the diversity in problem types so teachers recognize that this variety exists and subsequently are better prepared to present their students with a rich and varied collection of word problems.

Thomas Carpenter and his colleagues (Carpenter, Fennema, and Peterson, 1987; Carpenter, Carey, and Kouba, 1990; Carpenter, et al., 1999) have devised a classification scheme for problems that most adults would solve by simple addition or subtraction. They identify four general types of situations that give rise to 11 different kinds of addition or subtraction problems. (Other researchers have devised similar schemes. See, for example, Riley, Greeno, and Heller, 1983, and Rathmell and Huinker, 1989.)

Join Situations

Carpenter begins with "join" situations. Here, something is joined to a beginning quantity so a new quantity results. We think of these situations like this:

$$\text{start} + \text{change} = \text{result}$$

If the result is unknown, then we have an addition situation. Otherwise, we have a subtraction situation. Children often have more difficulty with problems in which the start is unknown than those in which the change is unknown.

Join/Result Unknown
Erick had 8 action figures. Then his father gave him 3 new ones. How many does he have now?

Join/Change Unknown
Janice had 9 stickers. Then her mother gave her some more. Now Janice has 16 stickers. How many stickers did Janice's mother give her?

Join/Start Unknown
Maria had some pennies. Then she found 3 more. Now she has 12 pennies. How many pennies did Maria have at first?

Separate Situations

Adults most often think of these situations as take-away problems:

$$\text{start} - \text{change} = \text{result}$$

If the result or change is unknown, then we have a subtraction (or take-away) situation. Otherwise, we have an addition situation.

Separate/Result Unknown
Thomas had 8 cookies. Then he ate 6. How many cookies does he have left?

Separate/Change Unknown
Leah had 12 dolls. She gave some of her dolls away. Then she had 7 dolls left. How many dolls did Leah give away?

Separate/Start Unknown
Michael had some marbles. He lost 5 of his marbles. Then he had 7 marbles. How many marbles did Michael have at first?

Part-Whole Situations

Carpenter's third category is part-whole. Here, a single whole is broken into two parts:

$$\text{part} + \text{part} = \text{whole}$$

This is similar to the join situation. The difference is that part-whole situations are static, the two parts coexisting from the beginning, whereas in join situations, two things are put together to form a new whole.

If the whole is unknown in a part-whole situation, then we have an addition situation. Otherwise, we have a subtraction situation.

Part-Whole/Whole Unknown
Ian has some action figures. He has 8 good guys and 3 bad guys. How many action figures does Ian have altogether?

Part-Whole/Part Unknown
There are 14 children who live in Clayton's building. Five of the children are boys. How many girls live in Clayton's building?

Compare Situations

Carpenter's last category is "compare." Here, two independent quantities are being compared:

$$q_1 - q_2 = \text{difference}$$

If the difference or q_2 is unknown, then we subtract. If q_1 is unknown, we add.

Compare/Difference Unknown
Samantha has \$14. Kristin has \$5. How much more money does Samantha have?

Compare/Q_2 Unknown
Jason has 13 crayons. Angela has 6 fewer than Jason. How many crayons does Angela have?

Compare/Q_1 Unknown

Lamar has some markers. Robin has 15 markers. Robin has 7 fewer markers than Lamar. How many markers does Lamar have?

Compare problems seem to be the hardest for children to solve. The other three types—join, separate, and part-whole—all involve a whole with parts in situations that are either static or dynamic. In compare problems, on the other hand, there is no whole. Rather, there are two independent quantities and a difference between them.

Need for Diversity in Problem Types

Traditionally, just two of these 11 kinds of problems have dominated American elementary mathematics textbooks, a dominance that contrasts sharply with customary practice abroad (Stigler, Fuson, Ham, & Kim, 1986; Fuson, Stigler, & Bartsch, 1988). These favored problem types, moreover, are the easiest to solve. Most of the subtraction problems are take-away situations (separate/result unknown). Most of the addition problems are join/result unknown. By presenting such a limited variety of problems, these texts give students a wrong impression about what addition and subtraction are. Carpenter's four situations—join, separate, part-whole, and compare—and the various types of problems reflect a much wider conception of addition and subtraction. In *Math Trailblazers,* we present this full range of addition and subtraction problems beginning in the earliest grades.

Diversity in Strategies

The description of the various problem types identified addition and subtraction situations. However, students may approach the problems in different ways. For example, while adults may immediately subtract when they encounter a take-away situation (8 cookies − 6 cookies = 2 cookies) some children may choose to use an addition strategy and count up. (Thomas ate 6 cookies and he has 2 left. Two more than 6 is 8 cookies.) Both are valid strategies.

Types of Multiplication and Division Problems

Researchers who have studied multiplication and division have identified different types of multiplication and division problems. While students do not need to be able to identify these different types of problems by name, it is important that they encounter and solve them. The different types of multiplication and division problems are outlined below.

Problems Involving a Number of Equivalent Sets

These sets can be groups of objects, arrays, or jumps on the number line. An example: Ask a class of 20 students to stand in a group. Instruct them to break into teams of four.

Using this situation, three different questions emerge. One question is interpreted as a multiplication problem, the other two as division problems.

Traditionally, just two of these 11 kinds of problems have dominated American elementary mathematics textbooks, a dominance that contrasts sharply with customary practice abroad. . . . These favored problem types, moreover, are the easiest to solve.

The Unknown Is the Total Number in All the Groups

If there are 5 teams with 4 members on each team, how many players are there in all? There are two known factors and a missing product. Using established knowledge, students often interpret this correctly as a repeated addition problem (4 + 4 + 4 + 4 + 4 = 20). Through classroom experiences with many such problems, they can connect the repeated addition sentence to a multiplication sentence (5 × 4 = 20).

The Unknown Is the Number of Groups

Twenty members of a class are divided into teams of four members each. How many teams are there? The problem gives the total number in all the groups and the measure or size of each group. This aspect of division is called *measurement division.*

The Unknown Is the Number in Each Group

Twenty members of a class are divided equally into five teams. How many students are on each team? The problem gives the total number of students and the number of partitions or groups. This aspect of division is known as *partitive division.*

Jumps on a number line and arrays provide additional experience with the multiplication and division of equivalent sets. Successive jumps of equal size on a number line provide a model for multiplication as repeated addition and division as repeated subtraction. In *Math Trailblazers,* we model this situation using mythical creatures called "mathhoppers." For example, a +2 mathhopper starts at 0 and hops 4 times. On what number will it land? (8)

An array is a group of objects arranged in rows and columns. For example, a candy box that contains 5 rows with 6 pieces in each row is a 5 × 6 array. One virtue of the array model is that it makes it very clear that 5 × 6 = 6 × 5. You can rotate the box 90 degrees to form a 6 × 5 array. Another advantage is that it creates a visual image for both multiplication and division problems.

Problems Involving Scale Factors

This type of problem is often found in TIMS Laboratory Investigations. For example, after students have rolled different cars down a ramp, they might be asked if one car rolled three times as far as another. Similarly, when finding the mass of objects, they may be asked if the mass of one object is one-half the mass of another object.

A Cartesian Product

This problem involves two sets of objects (such as shirts and pants) that must be joined into pairs (shirt-and-pant sets). The answer for this type of problem then becomes the number of unique pairs that students can form from these two sets. While this type of problem is difficult for young children, they are able to solve it using manipulatives and diagrams.

Experiences with many types of problems should provide a strong conceptual foundation not only for multiplication and division, but for fractions, ratios, and proportional reasoning as well.

Problem Contexts

Most word problems in *Math Trailblazers* are embedded in a larger context; this is often an advantage since situational problems are more meaningful to students than abstract problems. Sometimes, however, providing a context is constraining or distracting. Also, problems may come to us without context; often, we have to provide extra information to make sense of a problem. Accordingly, in an attempt to provide a balance between problems embedded in situations and problems that are self-contained, we often provide free-standing word problems.

Teaching Word Problems

A variety of approaches to teaching word problems can be useful and stimulating. Here are several:

Whole Class, Then Small Groups

First, present a sample problem to your whole class. Discuss the problem and ask students to estimate the answer. Also ask students to explain how they made their estimates. Neither the estimates nor the explanations are likely to be very good, but this is only the beginning.

Next, ask students to solve the problem in groups of two or three students. Tell them you want (1) an answer for the problem, (2) an explanation of how they obtained the answer, and (3) a number sentence for the problem.

Require students who need help to seek it first from other students in their groups. Clearly, this is beneficial for the students who need the help, but those who give the help also benefit since they must make explicit what they may understand only implicitly. You will also be freed up since your students will be helping one another instead of depending so much on you.

As students work, move among the groups, listening to the various strategies. Use your judgment about what questions to ask and how much help to give, but try to restrain yourself. It is often better if students struggle on their own and find a solution themselves.

When the groups have answers, reconvene the whole class and ask students to explain their solutions and number sentences for the problem. Be sure they assess the reasonableness and correctness of their results. During these discussions, emphasize that every student is responsible for understanding his or her group's solution. One way to accomplish this is to call on random students to explain each group's work.

Encourage students to solve problems in more than one way by accepting only novel solutions during class discussions. This will motivate students to search for multiple solutions so they can contribute to the class discussion.

Small Groups, Then Whole Class

As your students gain experience, you can abbreviate or eliminate the whole-class introduction to the problem. Again, a whole-class discussion of solutions is appropriate.

Individual Work, Then Small Groups

Another approach is for students to work individually first and then to come together in pairs or small groups to compare solutions. Then, the small-group solutions can be shared with other groups during a class discussion.

Other Suggestions

Find some word problems appropriate for homework or for individual seatwork. Other problems may be so hard that no student is able to solve them; use such problems for whole-class investigations. You may use certain problems to introduce new mathematics like multiplication and division. Use an interesting problem as an "opener" when students arrive or when math class begins.

TIMS Tips

- If students cannot solve a problem, ask them to describe the problem and to restate it in their own words or ask them to draw a picture. This may lead to a better understanding of the problem and then to a solution.
- Do only a few problems at a time. Distributed practice will be more effective than bunched practice.
- Vary the format: individual, small group, whole class, homework.
- Be sure to discuss multiple solution strategies. Compare and contrast strategies, and point out advantages of each, but accept all correct strategies.
- Discuss several number sentences for each problem. Ask students to explain how a given number sentence fits the problem situation.
- Ask students to explain why their answers are reasonable.
- Provide manipulatives and calculators to each group. Just having them available in the room may not be enough—these resources should be immediately at hand.

Conclusion

As your students work word problems and share solutions, they will be applying mathematics they already know and learning new mathematics. Word problems deserve a prominent place in your mathematics lessons.

References

Carpenter, T.P., E. Fennema, M.L. Franke, L. Levi, and S.E. Empson. *Children's Mathematics: Cognitively Guided Instruction.* Heinemann, Westport, CT, 1999.

Carpenter, T.P., E. Fennema, and P. Peterson. "Cognitively Guided Instruction: The Application of Cognitive and Instructional Science to Mathematics Curriculum Development." In *Developments in School Mathematics Education Around the World,* I. Wirszup and R. Streit, eds. National Council of Teachers of Mathematics, Reston, VA, 1987.

Carpenter, T.P., D. Carey, and V. Kouba. "A Problem-Solving Approach to the Operations." In *Mathematics for the Young Child,* J.N. Payne, ed. National Council of Teachers of Mathematics, Reston, VA, 1990.

Carpenter, T.P., E. Ansell, M.L. Franke, E. Fennema, and L. Weisbeck. "Models of Problem Solving: A Study of Fourth Grade Children's Problem-Solving Processes." *Journal for Research in Mathematics Education,* 24 (5), pp. 428–441, 1993.

Fuson, K.C., J.W. Stigler, and K. Bartsch. "Grade Placement of Addition and Subtraction Topics in Japan, Mainland China, the Soviet Union, Taiwan, and the United States." *Journal for Research in Mathematics Education,* 19 (5), pp. 449–456, 1988.

National Council of Teachers of Mathematics. *Principles and Standards for School Mathematics.* National Council of Teachers of Mathematics, Reston, VA, 2000.

Polya, G. *How to Solve It.* Princeton University Press, Princeton, NJ, 1957.

Rathmell, E.C., and D.M. Huinker. "Using Part-Whole Language to Help Children Represent and Solve Word Problems." In *New Directions for Elementary School Mathematics,* P.R. Trafton, ed. National Council of Teachers of Mathematics, Reston, VA, 1989.

Resnick, L.B. "Presidential Address: Learning In School and Out." *Educational Researcher,* 16 (9), pp. 13–20, 1987.

Riley, M.S., J.G. Greeno, and J.I. Heller. "Development of Children's Problem-Solving Ability in Arithmetic." In *The Development of Mathematical Thinking,* H.P. Ginsburg, ed. Academic Press, New York, 1983.

Stigler, J.W., K.C. Fuson, M. Ham, and M.S. Kim. "An Analysis of Addition and Subtraction Word Problems in American and Soviet Elementary Mathematics Textbooks." *Cognition and Instruction,* 3 (3), pp. 153–171, 1986.

The TIMS Laboratory Method

Math Trailblazers is a comprehensive mathematics program that incorporates many important scientific ideas. Scientific concepts often provide contexts for developing and practicing math concepts and skills. The tools and processes of science are integral to mathematical problem solving throughout the curriculum.

This tutor expands upon the *Math Trailblazers* connection with science. It outlines the Teaching Integrated Math and Science (TIMS) Project's view of science and describes the TIMS Laboratory Method, a version of the scientific method. This method forms a framework throughout the curriculum for students to explore science in much the way scientists work.

 ## The TIMS View of Science

Traditionally, school science has focused on the results of science. Students learn about parts of the body, types of rocks, the solar system, evolution, and so on. Knowing basic facts of science is seen as part of being educated, today more than ever. However, the facts of science, important and interesting as they are, do not alone comprise a comprehensive and balanced science curriculum.

The great educator and philosopher John Dewey expressed this idea some 100 years ago. In 1910, he wrote:

At times, it seems as if the educational availability of science were breaking down because of its sheer mass. There is at once so much of science and so many sciences that educators oscillate, helpless, between arbitrary selection and teaching a little of everything.

Visit schools where they have taken nature study conscientiously. This school moves with zealous bustle from leaves to flowers, from flowers to minerals, from minerals to stars, from stars to the raw materials of industry, thence back to leaves and stones.

Thus,. . . science teaching has suffered because science has been so frequently presented just as so much ready-made knowledge, so much subject-matter of fact and law, rather than as the effective method of inquiry into any subject-matter.

Surely if there is any knowledge which is of most worth it is knowledge of the ways by which anything is entitled to be called knowledge instead of being mere opinion or guess-work or dogma.

Such knowledge ... is not information, but a mode of intelligent practise, an habitual disposition of mind.

In 1996, the National Research Council (NRC) published the *National Science Education Standards* for K–12 science education. Among the many recommendations of the NRC document is a direction for decreased emphasis on teaching scientific facts and information, and increased emphasis on teaching for understanding of scientific concepts and developing abilities of inquiry. The NRC *Standards* state:

Emphasizing active science learning means shifting away from teachers presenting information and covering science topics. The perceived need to include all the topics, vocabulary, and information in textbooks is in direct conflict with the central goal of having students learn scientific knowledge with understanding.

These points of view underlie the TIMS approach to science. If we were to describe the TIMS approach in the most concise way possible, we would choose two words, *variable* and *experiment.* The essence of modern science, as it is practiced by scientists, is to understand the relationships among variables. Out of the great sea of variables we have selected those that we feel are fundamental to the understanding of all areas of science, namely: length, area, volume, mass, and time. These variables might be considered the fundamental vocabulary of science. They are integral to the everyday work of biologists, chemists, physicists, astronomers, and earth scientists. The more a child explores these variables, the greater will be his or her command of scientific language and the more complete will be his or her ability to take up the adventure of science.

We have therefore made these variables the focus of experiments and activities in Grades K through 5 of *Math Trailblazers.* Explorations in kindergarten are conceptual in nature. As the curriculum progresses through the grades, students revisit the variables many times in increasingly more sophisticated ways. In Grade 5, students are able to move on to compound variables such as density and velocity, which involve two of the basic variables. For example, density involves both mass and volume while velocity involves both length and time. To understand these compound variables, it is important that students are first familiar with the more basic variables. Through repeated investigation of the variables in different contexts, fundamental science concepts and skills become generalized.

> *If we were to describe the TIMS approach in the most concise way possible, we would choose two words, variable and experiment.*

PART II   Variables in Scientific Experiments

A **variable** is a quantity that may assume any one of a set of values. The variable is the heart and soul of science because the variable is to scientific investigation what the word is to language—its foundation and the basis of its structure. All experiments center around at least two variables, and the ability to measure these variables satisfactorily will determine the success or failure of the experiment.

Variables and Values

Variables fall into two broad categories: categorical and numerical. Would you say that a person's hair color is a categorical or a numerical variable? Would you say that a person's height is a categorical or numerical variable? A **numerical variable** is one that may assume a numerical set of values. In contrast, a **categorical variable** is one that does not assume numerical values.

Color, then, which can take on values such as red, blue, or yellow, is a categorical variable. Other categorical variables are shape, kind of object, and type of material the object is made of. In each case, you have the broad classification, the variable, and then the values the variable can assume.

The simplest kind of numerical variable is the number of objects in a set. For example, if we were studying the number of students who came to class each day, the variable would be "Number of Students," and the possible values of the variable would be 0 students, 1 student, 2 students, etc. A second category of numerical variable involves measurement. The basic measurement variables stressed in *Math Trailblazers* are length, area, volume, mass, and time. The values for these variables are what we measure during the course of an experiment. For example, if we are investigating the variable length, the values might be the number of meters, centimeters, millimeters, or other appropriate unit of length. When the variable is area, the values might be the number of square centimeters. Or if volume is the variable, the value might be the number of cubic centimeters, and so on. The variable is the broad classification; the **values** for the variable describe what we are counting or measuring for that variable.

One point in studying variables that will take repeated practice for your students to master is the regular use of units of measure. In science, we never deal with numbers without understanding what their units are. For example, say that we tell you that Mary dropped a ball from a height of 30. A question your students will learn to ask is, "Thirty what?" Was it 30 centimeters, 30 feet, or 30 miles? The name after the number 30 is what we call the unit of measure, and every variable has a set of them. $5 + 4 = 9$ can be meaningless unless we know 5 of what. 5 apples + 4 apples = 9 apples, but 5 apples + 4 pears does not equal either 9 apples or 9 pears. The sum is equal to 9 pieces of fruit. Invariably, children will give you the numerical value of the variable and leave off its unit. Learning to use units is merely a matter of discipline; that is, using them correctly so often that you feel uncomfortable when you either forget them or use them incorrectly. Developing this discipline in your students will help them later in their schooling as they examine more complicated scientific concepts.

Manipulated and Responding Variables in Controlled Experiments

In an experiment, a scientist tries to find a relationship between two variables. Where possible, the experimenter chooses ahead of time the values of one of the variables. This variable is called the **manipulated variable.** The values of the second variable are determined by the results of the experiment—something that the experimenter does not know ahead of time. We shall call the variable whose values result from the experiment, the **responding variable.**

For example, consider the following situation from a fourth-grade experiment, *The Bouncing Ball.* In this experiment, children study how high a ball bounces. They drop a ball from various heights and measure how high it bounces. As the experimenters, they decide what drop heights they want to use in the experiment, say 40 cm, 80 cm, and 120 cm. The drop height is the manipulated variable. But the height to which the ball bounces can only be determined after you drop the ball. It is not known ahead of time. So, the bounce height is the responding variable.

Or, say you fill a plastic jar with different-colored blocks and choose red, yellow, and blue as the colors of your blocks. You then ask a child to reach in and pull out as many pieces as he or she can in one grab, sort the blocks by color, and count them. Color is the manipulated variable in this experiment. The number of each color that he or she pulls out is the responding variable. You choose the values of the colors that go in but you have no choice over the number of each color that comes out.

Beginning in the first grade of *Math Trailblazers,* the experimental variables are identified in all laboratory experiments. This is an essential part of conducting any scientific experiment. It is not until fourth grade, however, that we introduce the formal terms "manipulated" and "responding."

Note that in *Math Trailblazers,* we have elected to use the terms "manipulated" and "responding" to describe experimental variables. We have found manipulated and responding to be less abstract for children (and adults) and easier to understand than the more commonly used terms for variables, "independent" and "dependent."

Fixed Variables in Controlled Experiments

Experiments often have more than two variables. In an ideal experiment, more easily realized in the laboratory than in the real world, a scientist focuses on only two variables—the ones we have called manipulated and responding—and strives to hold all others constant. If too many variables change simultaneously in an experiment, obtaining meaningful results can be difficult or impossible.

Consider a laboratory experiment done in second grade, *Rolling Along in Centimeters.* Students roll different kinds of cars down a ramp and use metersticks to measure the distance each car rolls. Here, the "type of car" is the manipulated variable and the distance each car rolls is the responding variable. The height of the ramp, the starting line, the floor onto which the cars roll, and the method for releasing the car are all held constant each time a car is rolled down the ramp. We refer to these as the **fixed variables** (or controlled variables) in the experiment. Children intuitively understand this as "keeping things fair" while the data are collected during the course of the experiment.

In many situations, some variables in an experiment are hidden; that is, they are not immediately obvious, although changing them will greatly alter the results of your experiment. Consider an experiment in which you collect data on the kinds of pets owned by each child in the classroom. The kind of pet is the manipulated variable and the number of each kind of pet is the

In an ideal experiment, more easily realized in the laboratory than in the real world, a scientist focuses on only two variables—the ones we have called manipulated and responding—and strives to hold all others constant. If too many variables change simultaneously in an experiment, obtaining meaningful results can be difficult or impossible.

responding variable. If you think about it, you can see that your results depend on where the pet owners live—in a high rise or a single-family house, in the city or a farm community, and even in which country. Thus the variable, "location," can drastically change the results.

One of the reasons cancer research is so difficult is because there are so many variables which are either difficult or impossible to control (such as environmental factors, personality traits, multitudinous viruses) that it is hard to pinpoint the variables that might be the cause of cancer. It is the complexity of biological and sociological systems that makes doing repeatable experiments in these areas very difficult.

Nonetheless, children can learn how to deal with simple physical systems where three or four variables are present. They should learn how to recognize the different variables involved and understand the importance of controlling all but two—the manipulated and the responding variable.

The TIMS Laboratory Method

Throughout *Math Trailblazers,* children carry out quantitative investigations in which they explore the relationships between variables. Each investigation is carried out with the same general format, which we call the TIMS Laboratory Method. One may call this our version of the scientific method. There are four phases: beginning the investigation and drawing the picture, collecting and organizing the data, graphing the data, and analyzing the experimental results. We discuss these four phases below, illustrating our discussion with references to *The Bouncing Ball* experiment described above and to *Marshmallows and Containers,* a second-grade experiment in which children study the number of marshmallows that fit into different-sized jars.

Phase 1: Beginning the Investigation and Drawing the Picture

Most investigations begin with a question. The question does not have to be momentous, but it must be meaningful to children. If the question connects in some authentic way with their experience, children will need no flashy inducements to want to find the answer. This is illustrated in the following classroom anecdote involving *Marshmallows and Containers.*

> *As class begins, students sit together in groups of three. Each group has three different containers: a margarine tub, a 100 cc graduated cylinder, and a small paper cup. The teacher shows the class a bag of miniature marshmallows and asks, "Which container will hold the most marshmallows? Why do you think so?"*
>
> *The teacher encourages the groups to discuss their predictions and explanations and to record their ideas in their journals. When the groups report to the class, many groups think that the graduated cylinder will hold the most because it is the tallest. One boy explains that he thinks the cylinder holds the most because even if he could stretch the plastic in the bowl so it was tall like the cylinder, it still would not be as tall and would not hold as much. Other groups choose the tub because it is fatter than the other containers.*

The teacher then asks, "How could you find out which container holds the most marshmallows?" This question leads naturally to an experiment: The students will fill each of the containers with marshmallows, count them, and record the numbers in a data table.

Once a suitable question has been posed—and posing such questions is far from trivial—then you must identify variables related to the question. *Marshmallows and Containers* examines the kind of container and the number of marshmallows. The size of the marshmallows and the method for packing the marshmallows into the jars is held fixed. In *The Bouncing Ball,* students measure the drop heights and bounce heights of a ball, while holding fixed the type of ball, the floor on which the ball is dropped, and the method for dropping the ball.

Through class discussion, the original question has been refined into a precise query about the relationship between two variables. These variables become defined well enough so children know how to gather information about them. Drawing a picture is an excellent way to summarize and communicate this beginning phase, and also to plan what is to come.

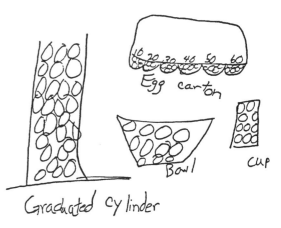

Figure 1: *Picture for* Marshmallows and Containers

Scientists often make sketches in experimental situations. In the TIMS Laboratory Method, drawing pictures helps children understand and organize what they are to do. A sketch gives the child time to think, to see relationships between variables, to place diverse relationships in a compact form, and to "explain" the experiment or problem to someone at a glance. Pictures also help teachers assess whether students are ready to proceed. Figure 1 shows one student's picture for

Figure 2: *Picture for* The Bouncing Ball

Marshmallows and Containers. The picture indicates the student's understanding of the experimental variables and the procedure. Note that the student is using an egg carton to make groups of 10 when counting marshmallows. Figure 2 shows a picture from *Bouncing Ball,* indicating the manipulated and responding variables (the drop height and the bounce height) and the procedure for the experiment. The students who drew these pictures are ready to go on to the next step, gathering data.

Scientists often make sketches in experimental situations. In the TIMS Laboratory Method, drawing pictures helps children understand and organize what they are to do. A sketch gives the child time to think, to see relationships between variables, to place diverse relationships in a compact form, and to "explain" the experiment or problem to someone at a glance.

Phase 2: Collecting and Organizing the Data

In Phase 2 of the TIMS Laboratory Method, children gather the data and organize it in a table. To illustrate, we return to our classroom anecdote involving *Marshmallows and Containers:*

On the next day, the children use their pictures to review the experiment before beginning the data collection. Each group receives a two-column data table, fills in the column headings, and writes the names (or draws pictures) of the containers in the first column. The teacher emphasizes the need for accuracy in counting, and the children discuss various methods for grouping and counting the marshmallows. As students begin to collect the data, the teacher circulates among the groups, coaching and assessing.

After the children complete their data tables (Figure 3), the teacher leads a discussion in which the groups compare their results. This discussion centers on whether the groups' results are reasonable or not. Most groups report about 130 marshmallows in the graduated cylinder. Students agree that numbers close to 130, but not exactly 130, are acceptable. Based on this discussion, a group that had recorded only 110 marshmallows for the cylinder decides to refill the cylinder and count again.

Container	N Number of Marshmallows
Graduated cylinder	133
cup	121
bowl	181

Figure 3: *Data table from* Marshmallows and Containers

Tennis Ball

D Drop Height in cm	B Bounce Height in cm			
	Trial 1	Trial 2	Trial 3	Average
40	27	22	21	22
80	50	40	43	43
120	72	62	68	68

Figure 4: *Data table from* The Bouncing Ball

Figure 3 shows a student's data table for *Marshmallows and Containers.* Figure 4 is a student's data table from *The Bouncing Ball.* The name of a variable, including units if appropriate, heads each column.

When creating data tables, scientists and mathematicians generally place the manipulated variable in the left column and the responding variable in the right column. Since the experimenter chooses values for the manipulated variable before the experiment begins, the first column of the data table can be filled out prior to the experiment. Values of the responding variable can only be filled in as the experiment is conducted.

When creating data tables, scientists and mathematicians generally place the manipulated variable in the left column and the responding variable in the right column. Since the experimenter chooses values for the manipulated variable before the experiment begins, the first column of the data table can be filled out prior to the experiment. Values of the responding variable can only be filled in as the experiment is conducted.

Data tables are tools for organizing data. In a real laboratory experiment, scientists have to record the data clearly and correctly the first time, during the experiment. It has to be recorded in such a way that not only you can read it, but also your colleagues and even a stranger. A story is told about the Nobel Prize-winner James Watson, who helped discover DNA. His teacher at Indiana University was asked if he suspected that Watson might go on to great things when he graduated. Yes, he answered. Watson would go far. Why? The teacher replied that although Watson did not take great care of his personal appearance, and his desk was a mess, he kept a neat notebook. That is a lesson that even young children can understand.

The data table is also useful in controlling error and identifying patterns. Children can detect blunders when a measurement deviates too much from established patterns (as in the *Marshmallows and Containers* anecdote above), and they can control inevitable measurement error by averaging several trials.

Note that in *The Bouncing Ball* lab, the students performed three trials for each measurement. In other words, to answer the question of how high does the ball bounce when dropped from 40 centimeters, they dropped the ball three times from 40 centimeters and recorded the bounce height, in this case (Figure 4), 27, 22, and 21 centimeters. The students then take the average (they used the median for the average) bounce height for their value of the bounce height. This is done to minimize the effect of measurement and experimental error on the experiment. (See the TIMS Tutors: *Averages* and *Estimation, Accuracy, and Error.*)

Phase 3: Graphing the Data

Graphing is the heart of scientific analysis. Graphs are powerful communication tools that create a picture of the data and "tell its story." They allow you to compare, predict, and infer. If there is a pattern in the relationship between the variables, you are more likely to see it clearly in a graph. Being able to read a graph and produce a graph from data should be a major goal of school science. Graphing cuts across many disciplines: biology, chemistry, sociology, and economics. Students using *Math Trailblazers* work extensively with graphs from kindergarten on.

Bar Graphs vs. Point Graphs

In *Math Trailblazers,* data are mostly graphed as either a bar graph or a point graph; these two types of graphs will thus be the focus of our discussion in this section. Since a graph is a visual representation of the relationship between variables, the type of graph used depends upon the types of variables studied in the experiment.

When both variables are numerical, a point graph is often (though not always) appropriate. In *The Bouncing Ball,* for example, both variables—the drop height and the bounce height—are numerical. Since the values for these variables are numbers and are not discrete—that is, there are values between the data points that make sense, such as 52.5 cm—it is possible to use points and lines on the graph instead of bars to represent the data. Drawing a line or a curve makes sense only when the variables are numerical and there is a pattern in the data. Figure 5 shows a student's graph from *The Bouncing Ball.*

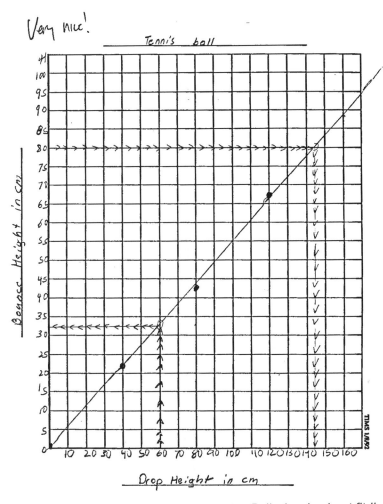

Figure 5: *Point graph from* The Bouncing Ball *showing best-fit lines, interpolation, and extrapolation*

Point graphs are introduced in *Math Trailblazers* in third grade and are used to represent a variety of different mathematical situations as well as to display data from laboratory experiments.

A bar graph is usually best when one of the variables is categorical (qualitative). In *Marshmallows and Containers,* for example, the type of container is a categorical variable and the number of marshmallows is numerical. Figure 6 shows the graph for *Marshmallows and Containers.* There are no values that make sense between the types of containers. Thus it does not make sense to connect them on the graph with a line. A bar graph, therefore, is appropriate for these kinds of situations.

A bar graph is usually best when one of the variables is categorical (qualitative).

Although point graphs are most often used when both experimental variables are numerical, that is not always the case. For example, in the experiment *First Names* from third grade, students collect data about the number of letters in the first names of classmates. The two primary variables in this experiment are the number of letters (the manipulated variable) and the number of names (the responding variable). A graph for the experiment is shown in Figure 7. While both variables in this experiment are numerical, they are also discrete—that is, it is not meaningful to speak of $6\frac{1}{2}$ letters in a name or $3\frac{1}{4}$ people who have that number of letters in their names. Thus, we can see why a point graph, in which values between the data points are represented, would not be appropriate in this case. Instead, the data is best represented on a bar graph.

Figure 6: *Bar graph from* Marshmallows and Containers

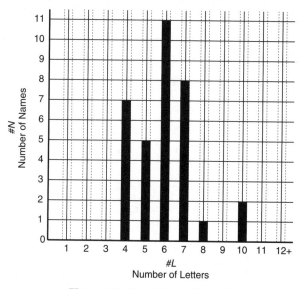

Figure 7: *Graph from* First Names

Labeling the Axes

With most types of data, it is conventional in science to place the manipulated variable along the horizontal axis and the responding variable along the vertical axis. The horizontal axis is labeled with a word or letter describing the manipulated variable and the vertical axis with a word or letter describing the responding variable. In Figure 7, for example, the horizontal axis—the manipulated variable—is labeled "#*L*, Number of Letters" and the vertical axis—the responding variable—is labeled "#*N*, Number of Names."

Once the axes are in place, the children can label the axes with the values for each variable. In the case of the *Marshmallows and Containers* in Figure 6, the student wrote in labels to represent the different kinds of containers.

> *With most types of data, it is conventional in science to place the manipulated variable along the horizontal axis and the responding variable along the vertical axis.*

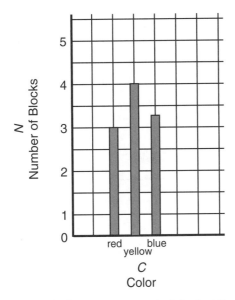

Figure 8: *Common errors in labeling the axes*

A common error in labeling axes is illustrated in Figure 8. This graph shows irregular spacing on both axes. The vertical axis in Figure 8 is incorrect with one space between 0 and 1 and two spaces between the other numbers. Technically, the categorical variables displayed on the horizontal axis do not have to be equally spaced, but it is a good idea to get your students into the habit of spacing their bars across the axis in regularly spaced intervals. This is because when dealing with numerical data, the values *must* be equally spaced.

Scaling the axes for numerical data requires an analysis of the range of the data and comparing it with the number of available intervals on your particular graph paper. Scaling by ones, two, fives, tens, or other numbers might be appropriate depending on the data for a particular experiment. What is essential, however, is that the intervals are all equal along a given axis. Students will learn that it is best to determine the appropriate interval ahead of time. Otherwise they will end up plotting their initial data points and later discovering that other points will not fit on the graph.

In most cases, the scale on the horizontal axis is independent of the scale on the vertical axis. Students should number the axes in ways that make sense for the data. For example, the horizontal axis in *The Bouncing Ball* graph

(Figure 5) is scaled by tens but the vertical axis is scaled by fives. One exception to this is when making scale maps. Here, using different scales for the different axes would create a distorted image and make it difficult to find distances on the map.

As scientists do, students using the TIMS Laboratory Investigations often use their graphs to make predictions about physical phenomena. When making point graphs, therefore, we often encourage students to scale their axes to allow room for extrapolation. (See the section below entitled *Predictions from Point Graphs: Interpolation and Extrapolation* for information about extrapolation.)

Bar Graphs in *Math Trailblazers*

As early as kindergarten, students using *Math Trailblazers* work on graphing concepts, including making and interpreting simple graphs. A quick way to make bar graphs of classroom data is to place self-adhesive notes on a labeled graph. An example of this with *First Names* is illustrated in Figure 9. In this graph, each student placed a self-adhesive note with the data for his or her name on the graph. The data are clearly represented. The one-to-one correspondence between data points and the number of students in the class is particularly apparent in this type of graph, which we use primarily in kindergarten, first, and second grades.

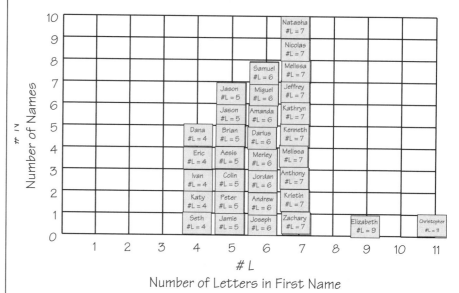

Figure 9: First Names *graph using self-adhesive notes*

In first grade, we introduce a graphing protocol that is different in *Math Trailblazers* than in some other programs. When making bar graphs, we encourage students to create their bars along the vertical lines in the graph rather than in the spaces between the lines. (See Figures 6, 7, and 9.) This does not affect the data or the reading of the graph. Rather it prepares students for making point graphs, where data points are plotted at the intersection of lines extending from the horizontal and vertical axes.

To assist students with this, we have created a special graph paper for making bar graphs. A version of this graph paper is shown in Figure 10. The dark vertical grid lines across the page are where the data for the manipulated variable is plotted. These lines are surrounded on both sides by a pair of dashed guide lines. Students make bars by coloring in the space on either side of the dark vertical lines. The result is a straight bar that is centered along a vertical line. The values for the manipulated variable are indicated on the horizontal axis directly below each bar.

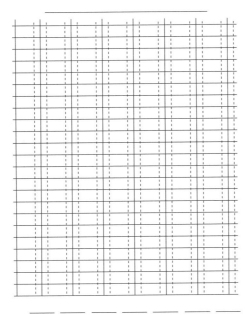

Figure 10: *TIMS bar graph paper*

The benefit of making bar graphs in this manner is most apparent in third grade as students make the transition to creating point graphs. To simplify students' initial attempt at creating a point graph, they first graph a data set as a bar graph and then convert the bar graph to a point graph. This is shown in Figure 11.

Figure 11: *Transition from bar graphs to point graphs in third grade*

Point Graphs: Fitting Lines and Curves

With point graphs, the data are plotted at the junction of the values of each variable. Once the data are plotted, we look for patterns. If the data points form a line or close to a line, we try to fit a line through the points. If the data form a curve, we try to fit a smooth curve through the points.

Figure 11 shows a graph in which the data points lie exactly on a straight line. Fitting a line to these data points is simply a matter of laying down a ruler and connecting the points.

For most experiments, we cannot expect the data to be so precise. In these experiments, the data may lie close to, but not exactly on a straight line. The "zigzags" in the data are due to experimental error. (See the TIMS Tutor: *Estimation, Accuracy, and Error.*) To average the error, one fits a line that comes as close to the data points as possible even though the line may not pass through any of these points. To assure a good fit, you would like as many points above the curve as below. You do not want to force the line through two points while missing the third by a mile. It is better to miss them all but come close to all than be too far from any one point.

As shown on *The Bouncing Ball* graph in Figure 5, you can fit a line to the data points, not by using some complicated statistical procedure, but simply "by eye." The student uses a clear ruler or a thread and moves it around until it fits the data points as closely as possible. This best-fit line is useful for minimizing error and making predictions.

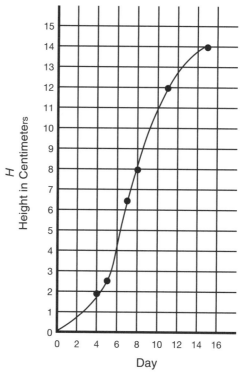

Figure 12: *Graph from* Plant Growth

Of course, not all experimental relationships result in data that yields straight lines on graphs. In *Math Trailblazers,* we also explore data that exhibits other kinds of patterns. Figure 12 shows the graph from a fourth-grade experiment, *Plant Growth,* where the data shows a pattern, but not a straight line.

When you can fit a smooth curve through the data points, you have uncovered one of nature's secrets—that the variables are related, that there is a predictable pattern to the data. We are then not restricted only to our specific data points, but can now use the pattern to predict what the value of the responding variable will be for any value of the manipulated variable.

Predictions from Point Graphs: Interpolation and Extrapolation

A major goal of mathematics and science is to find patterns in data and to use the patterns to make predictions. Interpolating and extrapolating on a point graph are two ways to do this.

Using the graph to find data points that lie between those in your data table is called **interpolation.** *Inter* means between or among. The simplest situation is when the pattern of data points produces a straight line. In the graph in Figure 5, the student interpolated to predict that a ball dropped from 60 cm would bounce about 32 cm. Note that in Figure 5 the student showed how she made her interpolation by starting at 60 cm on the horizontal axis, drawing a line (with arrows) up to the best-fit line, and then drawing a horizontal line to find the corresponding value of the bounce height—about 32 cm.

Extrapolation is an attempt to predict information beyond the last data point. *Extra* means outside or beyond. To extrapolate, we must extend the line into a region where there is no data. You can do this easily by laying a ruler on the straight line, extending the line, and reading off your prediction. In Figure 5, the student extrapolated to predict that a ball that bounced 80 cm was dropped from a height of about 144 cm. Here, the student began with values on the vertical axis (the bounce height) and predicted a value on the horizontal axis (the drop height). It is possible to interpolate and extrapolate in either of two directions: from values on the horizontal axis to values on the vertical axis or vice versa.

Having used these techniques to make predictions, it is important to have the children check their predictions experimentally and see how close their new data comes to the curve. This is one of the joys of science—to see that nature is often regular and predictable and that you can make predictions that come true! Checking predictions, though time-consuming, is worthwhile because it reinforces connections between mathematical abstractions and the real world.

Phase 4: Analyzing the Data

After making the graph, students explored the relationship between the variables in four ways: with the physical materials, in the picture, in the data table, and in the graph. The last phase of the TIMS Laboratory Method is the analysis of the entire situation, where students explore the relationship quantitatively and represent it symbolically (i.e., with numbers).

> A major goal of mathematics and science is to find patterns in data and to use the patterns to make predictions. Interpolating and extrapolating on a point graph are two ways to do this.

One way to structure this analysis is to ask a series of questions. The questions usually begin on the literal level: *Did the tallest container hold the most marshmallows? How high did the tennis ball bounce when dropped from 60 cm?* More demanding questions require prediction: *How many marshmallows would two bowls hold? If a ball bounced to 45 cm, what height was it dropped from?* Asking what would happen if one of the fixed variables is changed can build a broader understanding of the situation: *What would happen if we used large instead of miniature marshmallows? What would happen if we used a Super ball instead of a tennis ball?* This quantitative analysis of the data is one place in *Math Trailblazers* where students regularly practice and reinforce arithmetic and other math skills.

The end of the investigation may be a completely satisfying answer to the original question, but, more often than not, the end is another question that can lead to further investigations. *Marshmallows and Containers,* for example, might lead to an investigation of the liquid capacities of other short and tall containers. After an initial experiment with tennis balls in *The Bouncing Ball,* children carry out an investigation using another type of ball and compare the results from the two experiments.

Picture, Table, Graph, and Questions: Putting It Together

Each of the four phases previously described may require one or more class periods. In addition, you may spend time becoming familiar with the equipment at the beginning and on further experiments at the end. Thus, a lab is an extended activity that may last a week or even longer. This is much longer than a typical mathematics or science lesson, but there are significant benefits.

First, the four phases simplify the scientific method enough for children to use, but not so much that it fails to resemble what scientists do. Identifying variables, drawing pictures, measuring, organizing data in tables, graphing data, and looking for patterns are part of many scientists' work. Students are thus inducted via this method into the authentic practice of science.

The method fosters children's sense-making. Children handle numbers they have generated themselves by counting or measuring, numbers that are thus meaningful to them. As they deal with experimental error, they develop number sense and estimation skills. As they look for patterns in their tables and graphs, they make sense of the numbers before them. Arithmetic in context is more understandable.

The approach is multimodal, which has benefits for both individual students and heterogeneous groups of students. The multiple representations of relationships between the variables permit problems to be solved in more than one way, allowing different students to approach the same content in ways they understand. The container that holds the most marshmallows, for example, can be found from the graph, from the data table, or from the marshmallows themselves. A prediction about a bounce height might be obtained by extrapolating on the graph or by extending patterns in the data table, and can then be verified using the apparatus. Students can compare these various approaches, thus helping them make connections within mathematics as well as between the informal mathematics of their everyday experience and more formal mathematics.

Identifying variables, drawing pictures, measuring, organizing data in tables, graphing data, and looking for patterns are part of many scientists' work. Students are thus inducted via this method into the authentic practice of science.

Mathematics in Context

Two principles underlie the TIMS Laboratory Method. First, an investigation should begin within the children's own experiences. Children use objects from their everyday lives to investigate a familiar situation. Children's everyday knowledge, like a scientist's theory, provides a framework for interpreting the results of the investigation. Without that framework, the investigation would remain hollow and meaningless.

The second principle is that an investigation should also transcend children's everyday experiences. The exploration must go somewhere; it must lead the children both to a better understanding of the immediate situation and to improved skills, understandings, habits, and attitudes. The concepts can then be extended and transferred to new contexts.

Balancing these principles requires teacher judgment. The key is to enable students to follow their own ideas, but with the intention that those ideas will lead somewhere. How much scaffolding to provide, how much to guide students in directions that are fruitful rather than sterile, must be decided by the teacher in context. The goal is that students should advance not only in skill and understanding, but also in autonomy and perseverance. Just how much structure to provide along the way is perhaps a teacher's most important and difficult job.

The TIMS Laboratory Method helps children connect their everyday experiences with formal mathematics. As they investigate everyday situations quantitatively, children handle variables, explore relationships between variables, master a few powerful techniques for representing these relationships, and use these multiple representations to generate a wide variety of problem solutions. By beginning and ending in familiar situations, the abstractions of mathematics are linked to children's everyday knowledge. As students master this method, they become increasingly autonomous and flexible in its application. Then we can truly say they understand the fundamentals of *doing* science.

References

Archambault, Reginald D. (ed.), *John Dewey on Education: Selected Writings.* Modern Library, 1964.

Bruner, Jerome S. "The Course of Cognitive Growth." *American Psychologist* 19 (1), pp. 1–15, 1964.

Dewey, John. "Science as Subject-Matter and as Method." *Science* 31 (787), pp. 121–7, January 28, 1910.

Goldberg, Howard, and F. David Boulanger. "Science for Elementary School Teachers: A Quantitative Approach." *American Journal of Physics* 49 (2), pp. 120–124, 1981.

Goldberg, Howard, and Philip Wagreich. "Focus on Integrating Science and Math." *Science and Children* 2 (5), pp. 22–24, 1989.

Goldberg, Howard, and Philip Wagreich. "A Model Integrated Mathematics and Science Program for the Elementary School." *International Journal of Educational Research* 14 (2), pp. 193–214, 1990.

Hiebert, James. "A Theory of Developing Competence with Written Mathematical Symbols." *Educational Studies in Mathematics* 19, pp. 333–355, 1988.

Isaacs, Andrew C., and Catherine Randall Kelso. "Pictures, Tables, Graphs, and Questions: Statistical Processes." *Teaching Children Mathematics* 2 (6), pp. 340–345, 1996.

Isaacs, Andrew C., Philip Wagreich, and Martin Gartzman. "The Quest for Integration: School Mathematics and Science." *American Journal of Education* 106 (1), pp. 179–206, 1997.

Lesh, Richard, Thomas Post, and Merlyn Behr. "Representations and Translations among Representation in Mathematics Learning and Problem Solving." In C. Janvier (ed.), *Problems of Representation in the Teaching and Learning of Mathematics.* Lawrence Erlbaum Associates, Hillsdale, NJ, 1987.

National Research Council. *National Science Education Standards.* National Academy Press, Washington, DC, 1996.

Silver, Edward. "Using Conceptual and Procedural Knowledge: A Focus on Relationships." In J. Hiebert (ed.), *Conceptual and Procedural Knowledge: The Case of Mathematics.* Lawrence Erlbaum Associates, Hillsdale, NJ, 1986.

The Concept of Length

Units

In dealing with scientific problems, we must often know such things as the location of an object, the distance between objects, how tall or wide an object is, or how fast it is moving. Central to all these ideas is the concept of length. In this tutor, we shall examine the various disguises in which length can appear.

First, however, we must note the messy problem of units. The kinds of units chosen for length were for a long time quite arbitrary. The cubit, used by several ancient civilizations, was the length of a forearm between the tip of the middle finger and the elbow. The fathom was the width of a Viking sailor's embrace. (Fathom that!)

The foot was a convenient length defined as the length of a person's foot. Of course, everyone has a different-sized foot, so if we want to use, say, the king's foot as a standard, we will have to mark it permanently; we cannot very well lug the king around! Since the king is the ruler of the land, it was both rational and proper to call this marker a ruler as well. To show students the chaos caused by not having a standard length, have them measure the length of their desks in cubits or the width of the room in feet with each child using his or her own body measurements. You will have as many different values as measurers.

> *The foot was a convenient length defined as the length of a person's foot. Of course, everyone has a different-sized foot, so if we want to use, say, the king's foot as a standard, we will have to mark it permanently; we cannot very well lug the king around! Since the king is the ruler of the land, it was both rational and proper to call this marker a ruler as well.*

Nonstandard Units

At first, we have the children measure length using nonstandard units, often links. A link is shown in Figure 1 along with a chain of links. The measurement of the object shown is $4\frac{1}{2}$ links. The reasons we go to links are: (1) to make counting the unit length easy and (2) to keep the numbers manageable. Rather than dealing with hundreds of cm, we can count 50 links. And to count a link is easy since they are so large.

By alternating link colors (2 reds, 2 whites, 2 reds, etc.), one can make the counting even easier by skip counting by 2s. If you want to have the children skip count by 5s, then have a chain with 5 blues, 5 yellows, 5 blues, etc.

With links, it is also easy to round off to $\frac{1}{2}$ link as shown in Figure 1. If the edge we are measuring is near the middle, then the length is $4\frac{1}{2}$ links. If shorter, then the length is 4 links; if longer, the length is 5 links.

$4\frac{1}{2}$ links

Figure 1: *Links*

The Metric System

Of course, links are not a commonly used standard of measure. In the United States, it is feet. Unfortunately, many objects are smaller than a foot. This means one must subdivide the standard unit. For some miserable reason, the smaller unit, the inch, is $\frac{1}{12}$ of a foot. Who likes to divide by 12? So, the French scientific community at the time of the French Revolution (c. 1790) chose as the standard unit of length a distance that they called a meter. It was chosen so that 10^7 (10 million) metersticks laid end to end would just fit between the North Pole and the equator, as shown in Figure 2. A platinum-iridium rod was constructed with two marks a meter apart and stored in a vault near Paris. Every meterstick, albeit indirectly, comes from this standard. Having defined the meter, the French were smart enough to define all subsequent subdivisions of the meter as integral powers of ten. The foot is divided into $\frac{1}{12}$s and $\frac{1}{48}$s, and other equally horrible numbers; for the meter, the divisions are $\frac{1}{10}$s, $\frac{1}{100}$s, and $\frac{1}{1000}$s. We shall now explore this point further.

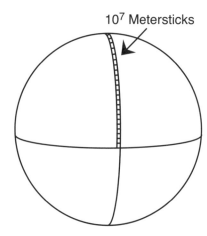

10^7 Metersticks

Figure 2: *Metersticks from the North Pole to the equator*

For measuring ordinary objects in the classroom, the meter is divided into three other units; the millimeter, the centimeter, and the decimeter (although the latter is rarely used). Without being specific as to the size of each unit, we can order them using the greater than (>) or less than (<) sign. Starting with the smallest, we have:

$$1 \text{ millimeter} < 1 \text{ centimeter} < 1 \text{ decimeter} < 1 \text{ meter}.$$

Reversing the order and starting with the largest, we have:

$$1 \text{ meter} > 1 \text{ decimeter} > 1 \text{ centimeter} > 1 \text{ millimeter}.$$

It is important that students know at least this much before going on to more exact relations.

The key to the subdivision of the meter is the prefix *milli*. Milli is related to the word mile. Mile was the distance it took a Roman soldier to step off 1000 paces, a pace being two steps. Since an average pace is approximately 5 feet (try it and see), a mile would be approximately 5000 feet. The crucial point is the number 1000 as related to the word mile. Milli is the prefix for "$\frac{1}{1000}$ of." Thus, a millimeter is one-thousandth of a meter. There are 1000 millimeters in a meter just as there are 1000 paces in a mile. In each case, we have a subunit that is one-thousandth of the main unit. The word mile is to remind us that there are 1000 paces in a mile. The word millimeter is to remind us that there are 1000 millimeters in a meter. One should try to picture this in one's mind. Millimeters are tiny; it takes a lot of them to make up any macroscopic length. (By macroscopic, we are referring to something one can see unaided versus microscopic where one would need a magnifying glass or microscope to see it.) On the other hand, because a meter is large, a millimeter is usually a fraction of most lengths one would measure in the lab. Thus, it is reasonable that a third-grader knows how to measure the length of his thumb as 3 cm or 30 mm, but not as 0.03 m.

How are mm, cm, dm, and m related? Let's start with the smallest and see how many mm are in a cm, a dm, and a meter.

1 centimeter contains 10 mm;
1 decimeter contains 100 mm;
1 meter contains 1000 mm.

Based on these relationships, we should be able to figure out how many centimeters are in a decimeter or in a meter. Here, however, the French have made it easy for us; the prefix for each word gives the answer away. *Centi* stands for 100th and *deci* stands for one-tenth. Thus one centimeter is one-hundredth of a meter; there are 100 cm in a meter. A decimeter is one-tenth of a meter; there are 10 dm in a meter. What this boils down to then is the following:

1 decimeter contains 10 cm;
1 meter contains 100 cm;
1 meter contains 10 dm.

Everything depends upon the size of the meter. Once that is fixed (by our rod in Paris), the sizes of all other metric units are determined.

Measuring Length

The simplest way to get started in the metric system is to count, using a meterstick, the number of mm or cm (and if they do not equal fractions, dm or meters) in a given length. Say we measure the width of the sheet of paper in cm. Then depending upon the accuracy of the meterstick (a cheap one could be off a bit) and the judgment of the student, one can see that there are between 21 and 22 cm across the page. If you stick to cm, then for students who are not yet comfortable with fractions or decimals, this is all you can say. As they begin to learn decimals, the children can determine the width as 21.6 cm. However, you can get still better accuracy even without decimals by going to mm instead of cm. Here, all one has to be able to do is count beyond 100. Thus, the width is 216 mm. In fact, one of the neat things about the metric system is that you can always choose a set of units to obtain almost any accuracy you want without going to fractions or decimals. On the other hand, you can purposely choose units that will give decimal or fractional answers. As we just saw, in cm units, the width of the page is a decimal, 21.6 cm. We could have asked for the width in meters. Since the width is less than a meter, we are dealing with fractions. In this case, the width is 0.216 meters or roughly $\frac{1}{5}$ of a meter. Clearly, there is great potential in the metric system for teaching math and linking this to scientific measurement.

With regard to addition, when adding numbers they must always have the same units. For example:

(a) 5 cm + 6 m = ? This is a "no-no"; the units are mixed.

(b) 5 cm + 600 cm = 605 cm. This is okay—we are adding the same units.

(c) 8 mm + 50 cm = ? We should convert the cm to mm and get:

8 mm + 500 mm = 508 mm.

Thus, if we ask a student to measure the length of his arm by separately measuring his hand (say in mm), his lower arm (say in cm), his upper arm (say in decimeters), and then adding them, he will first have to convert to a set of consistent units that he or she can handle. If you do not choose to have the students work with fractions, the students can change the units to millimeters as shown above. If you want to give the students a chance to work on decimal fractions, they can change the units to centimeters.

$$.8 + 50 \text{ cm} = 50.8 \text{ cm}$$

This brings us to another point—how to use a ruler. At first it seems quite apparent: just place the end of the ruler at the end of the object and read the length directly (Figure 3). However, a better test of whether students really understand how to use a ruler as well as a test of their ability to subtract is to place the object in the center of the ruler. Clearly, the length of the object should not depend upon its position vis-a-vis the ruler, but we have found that many young people (and even a few at our university) have trouble understanding how to find the length in the latter case.

Figure 3: *How to use a ruler*

Since we do not always have a ruler handy, a few "natural" rulers might be fun to discuss and use. For example, say the length of a person's upper thumb from knuckle to tip is generally about 3 cm while his spread-out fingers span about 20 cm, as shown in Figure 4. Either can now be used to measure the length of an object. Of course, as shown in Figure 3, there is the foot, a convenient measure for stepping off distances. This person's foot, without his shoes, is 23 cm or about 9 inches. Anyway, you should have the children measure a few objects using natural rulers and have them compare their results with that of a meterstick.

Figure 4: *Natural rulers*

The Concept of Area

Defining Area

The area of a shape or object can be defined in everyday words as the "amount of stuff" needed to cover the shape. Common uses of the concept of area are finding the amount of tile needed to cover a floor, the amount of wallpaper needed to cover a wall, and the amount of paint needed to cover a ceiling. You can often directly compare areas of different objects without measurement. For example, if one piece of carpet completely covers another, we know the top piece has more area.

Just as with length, to measure area we need a unit of measure. Many different units have been used throughout history. The acre is still used as a measure of land area, along with square miles. The square inch, square foot, and square yard are area units in the English system. For example, square yards is the unit of area measure for carpeting in the United States. Most of the world and all scientists use the metric system. For the classroom, the most frequent metric unit of area is the square centimeter. It is defined as the amount of flat surface within a square that is 1 cm on a side. This is illustrated in Figure 1.

Figure 1: *Units of length and area*

A note on terminology: Scientists often use the term "centimeters squared" in place of "square centimeters." This may be due to the fact that one way of writing the symbol for square centimeters is cm^2. We prefer to use sq cm for square centimeters. On occasion, the use of cm^2 can confuse students. Since 7 squared is 49, they may reason that 7 centimeters squared is 49 square centimeters. Unfortunately, the symbols $7 \, cm^2$ and $(7 \, cm)^2$ sound the same when spoken, if you say cm^2 as "centimeters squared." For that reason, we stick to "square centimeters" and sq cm.

Measuring Area by Counting Square Centimeters–Part I

One way to find an area is to count the number of sq cm needed to cover a surface. To count the number of sq cm, you can construct unit squares within the desired area. For example, the rectangle in Figure 2 is 3 cm wide and 4 cm high. You can find its area by completing the following steps.

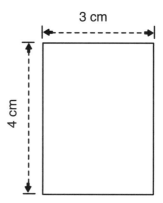

Figure 2: *A rectangle*

1. Draw a grid of lines so that each square in the grid is 1 cm on a side. (Figure 3.)

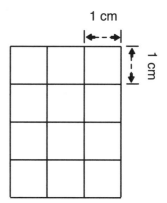

Figure 3: *A rectangle tiled with centimeter squares*

2. Count the number of sq cm enclosed in the rectangle. (Figure 4.)

1	2	3
4	5	6
7	8	9
10	11	12

Figure 4: *Counting square centimeters*

There are 12 sq cm in a rectangle that is 3 cm wide and 4 cm high. So the area of the rectangle is 12 sq cm.

Why Not Use Length × Width?

You may be wondering why we did not use the formula *length × width* to find the area of the rectangle. After all, $4 \times 3 = 12$. The formula works. Indeed, the reason the formula works is precisely because the rectangle can be represented by an ordered array of squares, 3 squares in each row and 4 rows of 3 squares each.

In any ordered array, you can count the total number of elements by multiplying the number of rows by the number of columns. Figure 5 shows 24 apples arrayed in 6 rows. Instead of counting each apple, we take advantage of the array and multiply 4×6 to obtain 24 apples. Using the length times width formula does give the area of a rectangle, but we delay teaching the formula for two reasons. First, we want students to build a mental image of the concept of area. Premature use of the formula for area of rectangles leads to rote use of the formula without understanding. In particular, many students are led to believe that the definition of area is length times width and that this formula works for any shape. While there are formulas for the areas of rectangles, circles, and other geometric shapes, there is no formula for the area of a leaf!

Premature use of the formula for area of rectangles leads to rote use of the formula without understanding. In particular, many students are led to believe that the definition of area is length times width and that this formula works for any shape.

Figure 5: *An array of apples*

Furthermore, using the formula can be harder than counting square centimeters when the sides of the rectangle are not whole numbers.

For example, what is the area of the rectangle, $3\frac{1}{2}$ cm wide and $2\frac{1}{2}$ cm high, shown in Figure 6? We asked a group of sixth-graders to find the area of this rectangle. Even though the students knew the length × width formula, 80 percent could not find the area. They were not able to multiply fractions. It is likely that these students would have been able to find the area by counting sq cm, as we shall see in the next section.

Figure 6: *Another rectangle*

Counting Square Centimeters–Part II

In Figure 7, we set up the square cm grid. To keep track of the sq cm, we first number the whole square centimeters. There are six whole sq cm in the rectangle. Next, we turn to the fractions of sq cm. Students can manipulate sq cm pieces of paper to complete the task. The two half sq cm on the right make up the seventh sq cm and so both are numbered 7. The two half sq cm along the bottom make up the eighth sq cm and are numbered 8. One half sq cm and one fourth square cm make up the remaining areas. The area is $8\frac{3}{4}$ sq cm.

Figure 7: *Whole and part centimeter squares*

Most students can count squares to find area—no multiplication is necessary. But what if there is no "order" to the figure? The shape in Figure 8 has no unique length or width; the formula *length × width* does not apply. The only way to find the area is to count the number of sq cm contained within the boundary of the figure.

Figure 8: *A blob*

First, construct a sq cm grid to fit over the shape of Figure 8. It's often easier if the horizontal and vertical boundary of the grid each touch the figure at one point. The grid should extend beyond the figure. The completed grid would look similar to the grid in Figure 9.

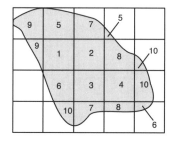

Figure 9: *Finding area by counting centimeter squares*

Next, count and number the whole sq cm. There are four. Now estimate which fractions of grid squares add together to form one square centimeter. For example, square centimeter number 5 is a big piece upper left and a little piece farther to the right. Number 6 is two pieces, a big piece on the left and a smaller piece in the lower right corner. Square centimeter number 7 is two pieces, each around a half square cm. Square centimeter 8 is made up of a $\frac{3}{4}$ and $\frac{1}{4}$ square cm piece. So is square centimeter 9. Three pieces make up square centimeter 10, two half square cm pieces and a smaller piece to the right.

Now all the shape is covered and counted in square centimeters. The shape has an area of about 10 square cm. While the method does not give an exact area, the result is usually close. And the primary benefit of this method is that students will have the opportunity to "see" area, aiding their understanding of this important mathematical concept.

Surface Area

Often, students who understand area quite well seem to have difficulty with the notion of surface area. One problem may be that they were led to believe that area and surface area are two different things. This is not surprising, since we use two different words. However, area and surface area are identical; a measure of the number of sq cm (or square units) needed to cover an object. Customarily, the term "surface area" is usually used for three-dimensional shapes and "area" for two-dimensional shapes.

To measure the surface area of a three-dimensional object, we count the number of square centimeters needed to cover it, just as with flat shapes. In some cases, this is easy as in the case of a rectangular box (since it is made up of flat pieces). Another easy example can be made by taking a sheet of flat paper and rolling it to make a cylinder (Figure 10). As long as the edges do not overlap, the surface area of the outside of the cylinder will be the same as the flat piece of paper. Another way to find the area of a cylinder is to cover it with one square centimeter "stamps." As with flat shapes, you may need some fractional pieces. With more complex shapes, like a sphere, it is hard to get an exact measurement of the surface area, but we can approximate the surface area by covering the object with square centimeters or smaller squares.

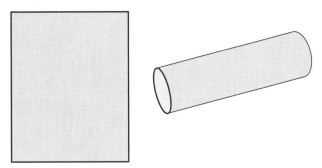

Figure 10: *Paper flat and rolled*

The Concept of Volume

Defining Volume

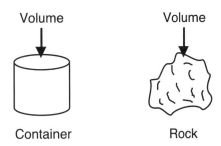

Figure 1: *Two meanings of volume*

Figure 1 shows a container and a rock. The space that the container surrounds (and is occupied by air) and the space that the rock takes up (and is occupied by elements such as oxygen, silicon, and aluminum) are both called **volume.**[1] The concept of volume is tricky. Two objects (like our container and rock) might occupy the same volume but contain totally different amounts of matter. Children often confuse the amount of matter, which we call mass, with the space occupied, which we now know is volume. Thus children tell us that a "heavy" object has more volume than a "light" object even though the latter may actually occupy more space. Indeed, volume is so oversimplified in the elementary schools that many eighth-graders we asked thought of volume as length × width × height, no matter what the shape of the object. Others told us that volume was length squared. Misconceptions such as these are a result of a curriculum that emphasizes memorization of formulas without attention to the conceptual foundations of volume.

Figure 2: *Units of length, area, and volume*

---

[1]Sometimes, the space inside a container is called the capacity of the container. For simplicity, we prefer to use one term, volume, to denote both "space inside" and "space occupied."

Units

As with length and area, if we wish to measure volume, we need to decide on a unit of measure. In the metric system, the metric unit of length is the centimeter (Figure 2a), and the unit of area is the square centimeter (the extent of the plane surface that is bounded by a square 1 cm on a side) (Figure 2b), so it is not unreasonable that we take as our unit of volume the space occupied within a cube that is 1 cm on a side (Figure 2c). The volume occupied by such a cube is defined as 1 cubic centimeter whether that volume is occupied by a solid object (Figure 3a) or by empty space (Figure 3b).

Figure 3: *Full and empty cubic centimeter*

Unlike area, it is very hard to divide an object up and count cubic cm. We can't trace the volume the way we trace areas on square cm paper. In theory we could slice it up into 1 cubic cm pieces, but this process will destroy the object. Therefore, learning to understand and measure volume can be more difficult than understanding and measuring area.

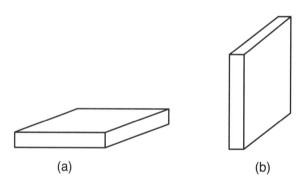

Figure 4: *Flat vs. tall shapes*

In everyday life, we are accustomed to a variety of other units of volume measure. Gallons, quarts, pints, and fluid ounces are one set of units, usually used to measure the capacity of a container. Cubic feet and cubic inches are also frequently used. For example, in the United States, air conditioners are often rated on the volume of space they can cool, measured in cubic feet. The remainder of this tutor uses metric units of measure, but many of the same underlying ideas apply to any system of measure.

Problem of Dimensionality

Another great difficulty in understanding volume is that the concept deals with three dimensions. As Piaget pointed out, it is much easier, and therefore usual, for a child to focus on one dimension. They will decide that a tall object has lots of volume because they only focus on the height and fail to take into account the other two dimensions to make a proper estimate. In Figure 4, the two objects have the same volume, but because (a) is flat and (b) is upright, young children will tell you that (b) has the greater volume.

Volume is an extremely important scientific variable. The way it is related to area and to mass and the manner in which it may change with time are all intrinsic to every area of scientific investigation. It is well worth our time to do a good job on volume.

Measuring Volume–Early Activities

Kindergarten students explore volume by filling containers with rice, water, pasta, sand, or beans. Another way to deal with volume in the primary grades is to have the children make figures out of a set of cubes. In first and second grade, we usually use connecting cubes that are about $\frac{3}{4}$-inch on a side. At the end of second grade, we start using standard centimeter linking cubes. For example, you can give each child 10 cubes and ask him or her to make a figure whose volume is 10 cubic units. You will get a variety of shapes, all of which have the same volume. This will begin to impress upon the children the idea that many different shapes can have the same volume.

Another centimeter cube activity to build the children's understanding at this level involves building shapes with different volumes. Give each child a few (3–10) centimeter cubes. Have each child make a shape with his or her centimeter cubes. Then have the children sort themselves into groups according to the volume of their shapes.

You can bring in some simple solid shapes, like a piece of chalk, a match box, a pile of washers, etc., and have the children make figures out of cubic units that approximate the volume (size and shape) of these objects. In this way, they can estimate the volume of the original object by keeping track of the number of cubic cm they used. An example is given in Figure 5 of a marking pen and cubic cms linked together to make a shape of approximately the same volume.

Figure 5: *A marker and a cm cube model*

> Another great difficulty in understanding volume is that the concept deals with three dimensions. As Piaget pointed out, it is much easier, and therefore usual, for a child to focus on one dimension. They will decide that a tall object has lots of volume because they only focus on the height and fail to take into account the other two dimensions to make a proper estimate.

The next step would be for you to make several cube models and have children count the number of unit cubes in each. Pictures of three typical models, each a bit more complex than the previous, are given in Figures 6a, b, and c. There are two potential problems here. The children may confuse surface area and volume and count the faces of the cubes calling each face a cubic cm. A subtle problem, exemplified by Figure 6c, is when there are one or more "hidden" cubic centimeters buried inside the figure.

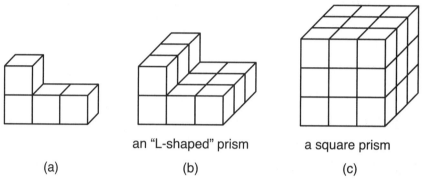

an "L-shaped" prism   a square prism

(a)   (b)   (c)

Figure 6: *Shapes made from centimeter cubes*

We want the children to learn to be systematic, look for patterns, and use simple addition and multiplication to count the cubic cm.

A very basic problem is learning to count the cubic centimeters properly. It is relatively easy to pick up 12 cubic centimeters, make a figure, and say the volume is 12 cc. It is quite another to hold a centimeter cube figure like that in Figure 6b, turn it over, and keep track of all the centimeters. We want the children to learn to be systematic, look for patterns, and use simple addition and multiplication to count the cubes. For example, Figure 6a is easy since it is only 4 cc. Figure 6b is made up of three layers, each of which is exactly like Figure 6a. Your students can then use addition to see that the volume is 4 cc + 4 cc + 4 cc, or use multiplication, 3 × 4 cc. Likewise in Figure 6c, it would be difficult to find and keep track of each cubic cm. A systematic approach allows the children to solve the problem easily. There are 9 cc in the top layer, and there are three layers; therefore the volume is

$$9 \text{ cc} + 9 \text{ cc} + 9 \text{ cc} = 27 \text{ cc}.$$

Note that Figures 6b and 6c are labeled as prisms. This means they are made of a number of identical layers. Figure 6b has three "L-shaped" layers and 6c has three "square-shaped" layers. It is important to know that these are prisms. Otherwise, there might be some hidden cubes behind the object that we cannot see, or there might be missing cubes "inside" the object.

A more difficult skill is finding the volume of an object directly from a perspective drawing, without actually building the object. You can develop this kind of spatial visualization skill by first having students build cube models from pictures. Students as early as first grade can build simple models from pictures. As the models get more complex, this task can become quite difficult. One important subtlety is that pictures such as 6b and 6c do not give enough information to reconstruct the model. For example, there might be some unexpected cubes hidden behind the model in Figure 6c (see Figure 7).

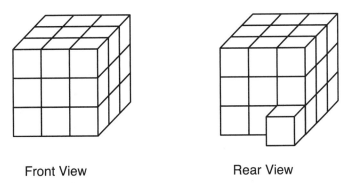

Front View   Rear View

Figure 7: *Front and rear views of Figure 6c*

For example, in Figure 7 we see what appears to be a 3 × 3 × 3 cm cube from the front, but when we view the model from the rear, we see there is an "extra" cube stuck on.

Finally, and hardest of all, you can ask the children to try to draw a figure with a given number of cubic centimeters. It is very hard for anyone to draw a cube, and a figure with several cubic centimeters is harder still. Nevertheless, it is worth a try since doing so will help them improve their spatial perception and will force them to think in three dimensions.

Let's review the four steps we just described:

1. Make figures out of a given number of centimeter cubes.
2. Count cubic centimeters in a cube model.
3. Count cubic centimeters in the drawing of a cube model—usually prisms.
4. Draw a figure with a given number of cubic centimeters.

This discussion covers volumes of objects made from cubes. The most important tool, however, for determining volume will be the graduated cylinder which we will discuss in the section after next. But first we want to talk about how to calculate the volume of prisms.

Calculating Volume—An Upper Grade Exercise

The volume of a rectangular prism made of cubic centimeters can be found using multiplication. The number of cubic centimeters in the top layer is just the product of 3 × 6 since there are 3 rows of 6 cubic cm (see Figure 8). Thus, in each layer there are 18 cc. Because there are 5 layers, the total number of cubic centimeters is 5 × 18 cc = 90 cc. As often written in math books, this type of counting is expressed as

$$V = l \times w \times h.$$

You should interpret this as the number of cubic cm in the top layer (given by the value of $l \times w$) times the number of layers (given by the value of h).

Figure 8: *A rectangular prism*

If the top layer is not rectangular but the figure is a right solid (sides perpendicular to top and bottom), then we can still find the volume by the above technique. The formula *length* × *width* × *height* will no longer work since the layers are not rectangular. However, since each horizontal slice has the same shape (see Figure 9), all we have to do is find the number of cubic cm in the top layer and multiply this by the number of layers. To find the number of cubic centimeters in the top layer, we have to find the number of square centimeters in the top surface, since each square centimeter of the surface is attached to a cubic centimeter in the top layer. Thus, if in Figure 9 by counting square cm we find that there are 22 sq cm on the top surface, then there must be 22 cubic cm in the top layer and in each subsequent layer. The total volume, then, is:

$$\frac{22 \text{ cubic cm}}{1 \text{ layer}} \times 5 \text{ layers} = 110 \text{ cubic cm}$$

for the object shown in Figure 9. As a general formula we have:

$$V = A \times h,$$

where the area A of the top tells us the number of cc in the top layer, and the value of h tells us the number of layers. Children should not just memorize each formula; they should understand what is behind the formulas.

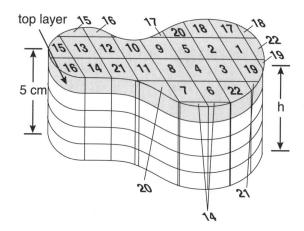

Figure 9: *A right solid*

When using a formula like $l \times w \times h$, the old bugaboo of units reappears. Since l, w, and h are all measured in centimeters, it is tempting to say that the

units of volume are centimeters cubed written as $(cm)^3$. And indeed this is what is often done in scientific texts. Yes, it's technically correct to write $(cm)^3$ or cm^3, but again it can be misleading for children just as "centimeter squared" can be misleading for area. If we say a volume is 7 centimeters cubed, is that $(7\ cm)^3 = 343\ cc$? We can avoid this confusion by writing what we mean; that the volume is 7 cubic centimeters or 7 cc.

Figure 10: *Graduated cylinders*

Clearly, the ability to calculate volume is rather limited to certain special shapes. An irregularly shaped container or object will require a different approach.

A Volume Measurer: The Graduated Cylinder

We have seen that a ruler which is calibrated in cm can be used to measure length. There is no comparably simple device for measuring area, but there is one for measuring volume. It is the graduated cylinder calibrated in cubic centimeters. Two graduated cylinders are shown in Figure 10. They can be made of glass or Pyrex, both of which are breakable, or plastic, which is not. The cylinder most suitable for classroom use would be calibrated in 1 cc, 5 cc, or 10 cc divisions and have a capacity of 100 to 150 cc. When filled with a liquid (usually water) or a fluid substance like sand or salt, one can read the volume of the material off the side of the graduated cylinder. One cannot use this device to directly measure the volume of a number of marbles since the marbles piled in the cylinder will leave an unknown volume of air spaces between them. This is illustrated in Figure 11b. As we shall see in the next section, we can find the volume of solid objects like marbles by the method of displacement. The rest of this section will discuss using the graduated cylinder for finding the volume of liquid, particularly water.

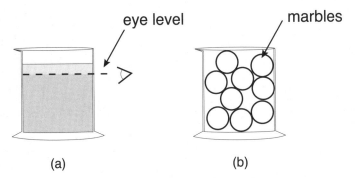

Figure 11: *Liquid and marbles in graduated cylinder*

To read the volume of water in a graduated cylinder, your eyes must be level with the liquid, as shown in Figure 11a. Since water is pulled up at the sides of the cylinder into a curved surface called a meniscus, one must measure the water level at the center of the cylinder. This is done by using the lower of the two lines that one sees (Figure 12) when looking at the water from the side. The top line is due to the pulled up water and should be ignored. (This phenomenon tends to be more pronounced when using glass rather than plastic graduated cylinders.)

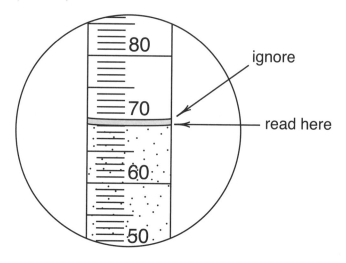

Figure 12: *The meniscus*

One must be careful about what one puts into a graduated cylinder. A tall, narrow one will generally have 1 cc divisions and thus can be used for accurate measurements. The trouble is, that because it is narrow, you can use only small objects. Many a time a student has misjudged the size of an object and found it stuck in the narrow cylinder never to come out again.

Chalk off one cylinder. A good general size that we like is one about 4 cm in diameter with a 150 cc capacity and made of plastic. The divisions are usually 5 or 10 cc. We shall discuss in the next section how to use a "big" graduated cylinder to measure the volume of small objects.

Many graduated cylinders that you purchase will have several different scales along the sides. This is due to the diversity of units for liquid measurements. Many cylinders will have a scale for fluid ounces and another for milliliters. The metric unit of volume is the milliliter, which is defined to be 1 cubic cm:

$$1 \text{ ml} = 1 \text{ cc.}$$

The liter is often encountered in daily life (for example, soda bottles are often 1 or 2 liters). It is exactly 1000 ml.

One of the first exercises the children can do with a graduated cylinder is simply to fill the cylinder to a specified level—10 cc, for example. An eyedropper is handy for getting the volume exactly right, since by pouring one usually overshoots or undershoots the mark. Whatever the divisions of the cylinder are, choose some volumes that fall right on a major division and some that fall between divisions, where the children will have to interpolate. An example is shown in Figure 13 for a cylinder with 10 cc divisions.

Figure 13: *A graduated cylinder exercise*

Once the second- or third-graders are good at reading the scale, they can use the graduated cylinder to find the capacity or volume of a set of three jars (Figure 14). You should build up a collection of jars of all shapes and volumes, from small baby food jars, through peanut butter containers, to large coffee jars. Exotic shapes are nice. To find the volume of a jar, one can either fill the jar to the brim and then keep pouring the water into the graduated cylinder, or one can keep filling the graduated cylinder and pour the water into the jar until it is filled. Either way, the children have to keep track of the number of times the graduated cylinder is filled and the total volume of water accumulated this way. This activity appears as a lesson called *Fill 'er Up* in third grade.

Figure 14: *A capacity exercise*

Volume Measurement by Displacement

How would you measure the volume of a small rock? This problem is dealt with in lessons on volume beginning in Grade 2. The technique is illustrated in Figure 15. First, you fill the graduated cylinder with a convenient amount of water, for example, 40 cc rather than 43 cc. Then you place the rock in the graduated cylinder without losing any water (there must be enough water in the cylinder initially to cover the object). You then read the new volume V. Since the volume of water V_{water} stays constant, the volume V is due to the water plus the rock. The rock displaces, or pushes aside, its volume in water and the water level rises. Thus, we have:

$$V_{rock} = V - V_{water}.$$

For example, in Figure 15 the volume of the rock is 22 cc. Note that subtraction is easier if you start with a multiple of ten for the volume of water. The technique works for any solid object no matter what its shape. To start with, then, ask children to find the volume of a wide variety of objects, some spheres, cubes, rocks, coins, washers, etc.

V_w $V = V_{rock} + V_{water}$

Figure 15: *Volume by displacement*

But what if the object is too big to fit into the graduated cylinder? If a bigger graduated cylinder isn't handy, then use your graduated cylinder to calibrate a large jar, and then away you go. One word of warning: When you place a large object in a graduated cylinder or jar, a considerable amount of water may splash out, even though you are very careful. You can get around this by placing the object in the graduated cylinder first and then pouring in a known amount of water V_w, and then read $V = V_{rock} + V_{water}$ off the scale. An alternative method is to find a large container and fill it with water to the brim. When the object is carefully placed in the container, it overflows, and the volume of the overflow liquid is equal to the volume of the object. If you catch all the overflow liquid in a second container, you can then use a graduated cylinder to find the volume of that liquid.

Finding the volume of small objects is also a problem, since the object may be so small you can't see the water level rise. Of course, you can always use a smaller graduated cylinder, one with 1 cc divisions instead of 5 or 10 cc divisions. The trouble is that sometimes even 1 cc per division is too large. The only way out is to measure the volume of several of the small objects at once (Figure 16b). (The volume of the several objects are identical.) For example, suppose you have 10 identical objects. To find the volume of one object, subtract the volume of the water and divide by 10. In this fashion, children can find the volume of small washers, paper clips, pins, and so on. Using 10 objects is a good idea since it is easy to divide by 10.

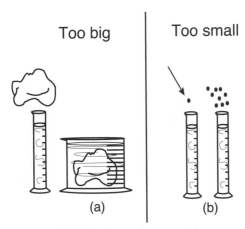

Too big   **Too small**

(a)   (b)

Figure 16: *Finding volumes of large or small objects*

Obtaining Accurate Results

A few words about accuracy are appropriate here. Most of the time you have to interpolate between divisions in order to read the volume. This usually leads to a reading error of about 20% of the value between the scale marks. Thus, if your graduated cylinder has 10 cc divisions, you might expect an error (i.e., children will get readings that differ) by up to 2 cc. This is illustrated in Figure 17a. If the object has raised the water level several divisions, then this 20% per division uncertainty is not a serious problem. For example, our rock changed the water level from 40 cc to 62 cc. If a reading error is up to 2 cc, then three children who read the same graduated cylinder might read 62 cc, but possibly 61 cc or 63 cc (if they are careful; maybe even more if they are not). But the volume of the rock is 62 cc − 40 cc = 22 cc for one child, but 23 cc for another, and 21 cc for the third. Thus we have a spread in reading of about 2 parts in 22 or 10%. A bigger rock, with a volume of, say, 46 cc would still have the same reading error of 2 cc, but its volume error would only be 2 parts in 46 or about 5%.

$V = 62 - 40 \text{ cc} = 22 \text{ cc}$
or
$V = 63 - 40 \text{ cc} = 23 \text{ cc}$
or
$V = 61 - 40 \text{ cc} = 21 \text{ cc}$

$V = 105 \text{ cc or } 106 \text{ cc or } 107 \text{ cc}$

$V = \dfrac{105 - 40 \text{ cc}}{3} = \dfrac{65}{3} = 21.67 \text{ cc}$

$V = \dfrac{106 - 40 \text{ cc}}{3} = \dfrac{66}{3} = 22.0 \text{ cc}$

$V = \dfrac{107 - 40 \text{ cc}}{3} = \dfrac{67}{3} = 22.33 \text{ cc}$

(a)   (b)

Figure 17: *Measurement error*

A good rule of thumb is that your reading will not be accurate unless the object raises the water level by more than one division. There are two ways to achieve this. One, use a narrow graduated cylinder, or two, use several identical objects if they are available. In the case of the latter, you find the volume of one object by dividing by the number of identical objects, as we did above for very small objects. For example, three objects would still produce a reading error of 2 cc but a volume error of only 2 cc/3 = 0.67 cc. This is illustrated in Figure 17b where three marbles give a volume spread of only 0.67 cc in 22 cc or 3%, compared to 10% for one marble. Of course, this would not work for finding the volume of a rock, since it would be difficult to find three identical rocks.

If the object floats, you have to push it under in order to measure its volume. In this situation, what is important is how you push it under. If you use your finger, then what you measure is the volume of the object plus the volume of your submerged finger. Since the volume of your finger may be comparable to the volume of the object, this is clearly not a good idea. What you need is a pusher whose volume is much less than the volume of the object. A straightened paper clip or a pin will do (Figure 18).

Figure 18: *Finding the volume of something that floats*

Two Misconceptions

Early on, the children should come to grips with two important ideas concerning volume:

1. The volume of an object is independent of the material it is made of.
2. The volume of an object does not change when its shape changes.[2]

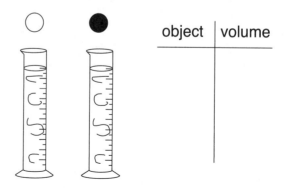

Figure 19: *Volume vs. material*

---

[2]Usually. See later discussion.

As to the first point, you can study spheres of the same volume but made of a wide variety of materials (steel, lucite, glass, even wood). The children should discover that their volumes are the same. As illustrated in Figure 19, students can fill two identical cylinders to the same level with water, carefully place both objects in, and see that the volume displaced is the same. Initially, many children will say that the heavier object has more volume and that the water will go up higher in its graduated cylinder. They are confusing mass and volume. If you take a clay cube and mash it into a thin disk, many children will say that the disk has less volume than the cube. Here they confuse one dimension, thinness, with volume: they mistakenly assume all thin objects have a small volume. Again, using the graduated cylinder the child can see that the volumes are the same. Figure 20. They can make all kinds of shapes out of a single piece of clay and determine that they all have the same volume. Indeed, the only way they can change its volume is to tear off a piece.

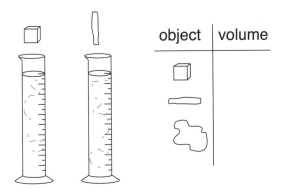

Figure 20: *Volume vs. shape*

The Concept of Mass

Defining Mass

Mass is one of the most difficult variables to understand. It is also one of the most important. Length, area, and volume have straightforward definitions. The volume of an object, for example, is defined as a measure of the space it occupies. Does mass have a similar straightforward definition? In a sense it does and in a sense it does not. Basically, **mass** is a measure of the quantity of matter in an object. That is its simple definition. Unfortunately, that begs the question. One can ask, what is matter, and we are back to where we started. So we have to look more closely at mass. And that is where things get difficult. Mass is defined through what it *does,* and this sets it apart from length, area, and volume. Moreover, mass does two things which means, in a sense, it has two definitions.

One of the things that mass does is absolutely crucial for the existence of our universe. Mass is the cause of the force of gravity. Without mass, there would be no gravity, and without gravity, matter would not have clumped into galaxies and stars and us. Since mass causes gravity, we can define mass through the pull of gravity—the greater the pull, the greater the mass an object has.

The other thing that mass does has to do with the motion of an object. All other variables being equal, the mass of an object determines how much the velocity of an object will *change* when subject to a given force. In layman's terms, the larger the mass of an object, the harder you have to push to change its speed. Since we are not ready to study motion, we will not discuss the details of this aspect of mass. Nevertheless, we might note that it was Einstein's contemplation of both properties of mass (gravity and motion) that led him to his general theory of relativity.

> Basically, **mass** is a measure of the quantity of matter in an object.

One way, then, to determine which of two objects has more mass is to determine which one is pulled on more strongly by the Earth's gravitational force. One possible way to do this is to drop two objects, as shown in Figure 1, and see which reaches the ground first. You might suppose, since the more mass an object has, the bigger the force of gravity, that the more massive object would fall faster and reach the ground first. If you do this exercise, however (as Galileo did), you will find that

Figure 1: *Dropping two objects*

both objects reach the ground at the same time! What went wrong? Well, we are breaking one of our cardinal rules, which is keeping variables fixed. When the objects fall, we not only have gravity pulling on them, but their velocity is changing as well. Therefore, both definitions of mass are involved and the overall effect is no longer obvious. It appears that in some way the effects cancel!

So we need a way of measuring the pull of gravity (i.e., using definition 1) without having the object move (i.e., eliminating definition 2). As we shall see in the next section, we can do this with a two-pan balance.

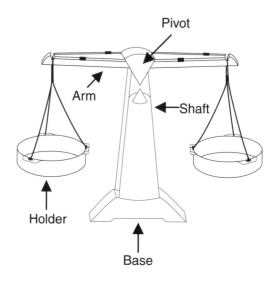

Figure 2: *A balance*

Equal Arm Balance

The equal arm, or two-pan, balance is the key to our operational definition of mass for children. If two objects balance, they have the same mass. If the arm tilts to one side, the object in the lower of the two pans has more mass than the object in the other pan.

Basically, the balance is a stick that is pivoted at its center and has two holders that are mounted on at points which are equidistant from the pivot (hence the name equal arm balance). Figure 2 pictures a balance that we often use in *Math Trailblazers*. It is quite sturdy and accurate enough for use in the elementary classroom. The tall shaft and long arms of the balance make it very useful in a variety of balancing experiments. If you would like to make your own, you can use a block of wood (Figure 3a) or a book to hold the pivot rod (Figure 3b). A ruler can act as the arm and the bottom of paper cups as pans. These latter pieces can be attached to the arm with string and paper clips.

The equal arm, or two-pan, balance is the key to our operational definition of mass for children. If two objects balance, they have the same mass. If the arm tilts to one side, the object in the lower of the two pans has more mass than the object in the other pan.

(a)

(b)

Figure 3: *Making a balance*

Once you have put your two-pan balance together, it must be zeroed. That is, the arm must be level before any masses are added. We suggest that you zero each balance and then have the children check to see that it is level before and during each experiment.

A	B	**More Mass**
Cube	Ball	Cube
Scissors	Ball	Scissors

Figure 4: *Comparing masses*

We are now ready to find out which of two objects, A or B, has greater mass. One is placed in each pan. Since the object with more mass will experience the bigger gravitational pull, the balance will tilt either one way or the other. If A has more mass it will tilt to the left, as shown in Figure 4, while if B has more mass it will tilt to the right. If the masses in the pans are equal, the pull of gravity on both is the same and the balance will remain level. One word of caution, though: If the masses are the same and the arm is tilted when the masses are placed on the balance, then the ruler will often remain tilted. Thus, to be sure, bring the arm back to level and see if it remains there.

One of the first exercises you can do with children in kindergarten through second grade is to have them compare, two at a time, the masses of a wide variety of objects. Then they should order the objects from the most massive to the least massive (see *Putting Masses in Order* in Grade 2 Unit 10). You can use a washer, connecting cube, small scissors, steel ball, and so on. Notice that the two-pan balance does away with the motion definition of mass since the balance is at rest when the measurement is made. Thus, the balance allows us to relate the object's mass directly to the pull of gravity.

Measuring Mass: The Mass Standard

The above is fine for comparing masses, but how do we measure *the* mass of an object? In other words, how do we assign a number to the mass of our object? Just as when we measure length, area, and volume, we need to decide on a unit. Say that we take as our standard masses a set of identical washers (paper clips would do as well). Let's call the mass of each washer 1 *ugh.* Then, if our object is balanced by 4 washers, its mass is 4 ughs, as shown in Figure 5. If the mass of the object is between 4 and 5 ughs, then the balance will not level out but tilt one way for 4 washers and the other way for 5. In this way, the child can assign unique masses to a wide range of objects. Clearly, the smaller the washer, the more accurately one can determine the mass of an object.

*The Paris Academy of Sciences submitted a report to the French National Assembly in which 1 cc of water was defined to have a mass of 1 gm, the **gram** being the name chosen for the unit of mass.*

But washers are not a very satisfactory standard. The washers in your class may not have the same mass as those used in another school in your district, much less in another city or another country. What we need is a universal standard that is accepted by the entire scientific community. This problem was recognized by scientists a long time ago and was resolved when the Paris Academy of Sciences submitted a report to the French National Assembly in which 1 cc of

Object	Number of Washers	Mass in ughs
Ball	4	4
Cube	2	2

Figure 5: *Measuring masses*

water was defined to have a mass of 1 gm, the **gram** being the name chosen for the unit of mass. Then, using this definition, a platinum cylinder was made and declared to be the standard for 1000 grams. In 1875, an international treaty was signed by most "civilized" nations which established an International Bureau of Weights and Measures in Sevres, France, near Paris. The international prototype kilogram, made of platinum iridium alloy, is kept there. If you want your own kilogram, you have to go to Paris with an equal arm balance and some material and hack away at the material until it balances the platinum iridium standard. The National Bureau of Standards in Washington, DC, has an accurately constructed copy as do other governments throughout the world.

For small measurements, one needs a mass that is smaller than a kilogram, just as one needs a length that is smaller than a meter. The gram, like the centimeter, is perfect for this. Most objects you will deal with in the elementary school science program will have masses between 1 and 100 grams. Masses are commercially available, usually in 1-, 5-, 10-, 20-, 50-, 100-, 200-, 500-, and 1000-gram pieces. It might be a good idea to have one good set of very accurate standard masses for your school (locked in a closet marked "Paris," of course), but they are expensive. For general classroom use, there are less expensive sets of plastic masses available. However, since the plastic masses may not be as accurate, you may wish to compare them to a good set of standard masses or find their mass using a triple beam balance or other accurate scales.

The cheapest standard mass is a nickel. It has a mass very close to 5 grams! But alas, a dime does not have a mass of 10 grams. There are two ways to get around having to buy sets of expensive standard masses. To determine the mass of a small object, measure the mass of several of the objects and then divide the total mass by the number of objects. For example, if it turns out that 10 small objects balance a 5-gram piece, then each object will have a mass of 0.5 grams. (5 grams ÷ 10 objects = 0.5 grams per object.)

Figure 6: *Using washers as standard masses*

If you go to a hardware store and make a pest of yourself—bring your two-pan balance—you can usually find washers that have "nice" masses, like 1, 2, 5, 8 grams, etc. Figure 6 shows such a collection that can be used as standard masses. Once you have the washers, give each child several of each and a lot of objects whose mass you want them to determine. A good data table is a big help since you want to keep track of the number of different washers it takes to balance the object.

Then, as shown in Figure 7, a little multiplication and addition is necessary to obtain the final mass in grams. In the example above, the total mass is:

$$m_{total} = 3 \times 1 \text{ gm} + 1 \times 2 \text{ gm} + 2 \times 5 \text{ gm} + 2 \times 8 \text{ gm} = 31 \text{ gm}.$$

Finding masses in grams is a great way to practice multiplication, addition, and mental math.

Object	Number of Standard Masses				Mass in gm
	1 gm	2 gm	5 gm	8 gm	
Plastic Cylinder	3	1	2	2	31

Figure 7: *Finding mass using washers*

A second way to get around using expensive standards is again to use washers but place them in packages of sets of 1, 5, 10, 20 grams, etc. The package can be composed of several washers wrapped in masking tape with enough tape or small washers to make an even 5 gm, 10 gm, and so on. Either way, the cost of a washer is small enough that children can have a set of masses for a few dollars.

Mass vs. Weight

In everyday language, we talk about the weight of an object rather than its mass. Are these two words for the same thing? Technically, weight and mass are distinct concepts. In scientific terms, the **mass** of an object is the amount of matter in the object. Mass is measured in kilograms and grams in the metric system and in pounds and ounces in the English system. The **weight** of an object is the measure of the pull of gravity on that object. Sir Isaac Newton first explained the importance of gravity for the motions of the planets and for the fall of an object more than 300 years ago.

Because of the awareness of space travel, most children know that the pull of gravity is different on different planets and that there is essentially no gravity in outer space. Many museums and planetariums have exhibits that show your weight on the moon and various planets. For example, since the moon's gravity is weaker than the Earth's, the pull on an individual object would be less. Thus, a human being would weigh less on the moon than on Earth.

How is the mass of an object affected by gravity? The mass of an object remains constant regardless of space travel since gravity does not influence mass. Since we use a two-pan balance to measure mass, both sides of the balance are equally affected by gravity. If an 11-gram pencil balances one 1-gram and two 5-gram standard masses on Earth, it will balance those same masses on the moon.

However, since most of us are likely to spend our lives on Earth, the distinction between mass and weight may be lost on many students.

We suggest two pedagogical alternatives with regard to the distinction between mass and weight:

1. Ignore it. This point is fairly subtle and eludes many adults.
2. Provide a simple explanation, but don't worry about it too much.

Building the *Math Trailblazers* Classroom

This section focuses on establishing a flexible and challenging learning environment for all students. Strategies include addressing classroom culture, effectively grouping students, managing manipulatives, and pacing instruction.

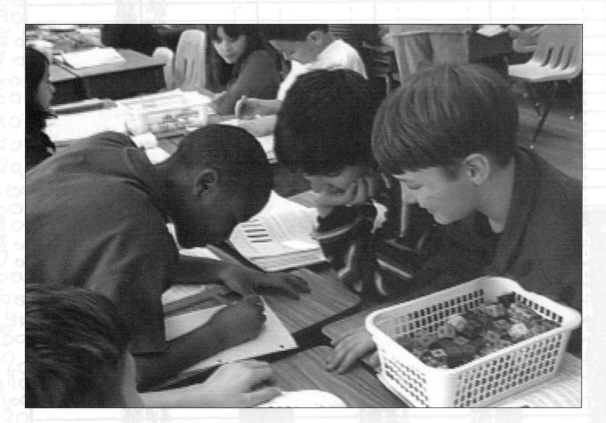

Students work effectively in groups assisted by easy access to math manipulatives.

Building the *Math Trailblazers* Classroom

> *Using strategies like those described here enables students to develop confidence and expertise in problem solving.*

Two factors essential to student learning are the curriculum and a classroom environment that supports and challenges students (NCTM, 2000; Reys & Bay-Williams, 2003). Data on classroom implementation of the *Math Trailblazers* curriculum came from pilot test results, classroom observations, videos of lessons, and teacher feedback. From these sources, effective classroom management and teaching strategies emerged. These strategies enable students to develop confidence and expertise in problem solving. This section summarizes the following teaching and classroom management strategies: addressing classroom culture, student grouping, organization and management of manipulatives, and curriculum pacing.

Classroom Culture

Creating a classroom culture that promotes thinking and learning requires an explicit focus on high student expectations and cooperation. The following strategies result in high performance among students (Kersaint, 2007) and should become part of *Math Trailblazers* classrooms:

- *Allow time for students to reason mathematically.* While many teachers may think they have high expectations, their well-intentioned actions can lower the difficulty level of students' work (Smith, Stein, Henningson, & Silver, 2000). For example, a teacher may model a detailed solution path for a challenging problem. However, when students mimic the teacher's solution path, they lose the opportunity to think about the problem and attempt their own strategies. This reduces the challenge of the problem. Instead, develop a challenging classroom culture that encourages mathematical reasoning by allowing students to discuss their strategies and ideas with classmates prior to starting the problem.

- *Provide opportunities for students to freely discuss mathematical understandings.* One noticeable characteristic of an effective *Math Trailblazers* classroom is the nature of the discussion that takes place consistently. When discourse is part of the classroom culture of learning, students are confident in sharing their ideas and questioning other students' contributions. Good classroom discourse is vital to the implementation of *Math Trailblazers*. "Academically Productive Talk" (Chapin & O'Connor, 2007) is the vehicle through which students make sense of new concepts. The Language in the *Math Trailblazers* Classroom section explores the connection between classroom discourse and learning.

- *Have students explain how they solve problems.* Teachers can encourage students to persevere in the problem-solving process by having them try different approaches or seek help from their classmates. Support students' thinking and classroom discourse by asking them to reflect on earlier completed tasks. References to previously completed tasks helps students make connections in their learning and in their problem-solving processes. Once students have drawn parallels in their learning, have them communicate their understandings in writing or share their ideas in class discussions.

- *Let students be responsible for their own learning.* One indicator of a classroom culture that supports and challenges students is that students realize they alone are responsible for solving problems. The teacher only provides the tools that assist students in solving problems. Students further understand that the teacher is not the owner of answers. Students should solve problems and offer explanations, not the teacher. The following two anecdotes are examples of students taking responsibility for their learning:

Jeremy, a fifth grader, whispered to a math coach who came regularly to his classroom, "I think you've known the answers all year! But you want us to figure them out!"

Hannah, a second grader, raised her hand to answer a question the teacher had posed. She paused and before responding, asked, "Will I have to explain my answer?" When the teacher assured her she would have to explain, she said, "Then let me think about it a little longer."

Use of the above strategies results in students who value mathematics, increase their persistence in solving a problem, become confident in their ability to do mathematics, become mathematical problem solvers, and believe that mathematics makes sense.

Establishing Classroom Norms

Establishing a classroom culture that promotes high expectations and inquiry means establishing classroom norms for participation. When you enter a classroom that "works" it seems effortless. The students and teacher respect each other's ideas. There is a true sense of collaboration and exploration. To create such an environment requires intentional and ongoing effort on the part of the teacher. The following recommendations represent ideas from numerous effective *Math Trailblazers* teachers.

> *To create an environment of true collaboration and exploration requires intentional and ongoing effort on the part of the teacher.*

- *Set clear expectations and remind students of them daily.* Some teachers use a "Rights and Responsibilities" approach to classroom rules. These rights and responsibilities can be framed in a positive way and encourage student ownership. Some examples include:

1. I have the right to be heard when speaking.
2. I will speak clearly.
3. I will not interrupt others.
4. I will listen carefully when others speak.
5. I have the right to learn.
6. I will ask questions when I do not understand.
7. I will not distract others from learning.

Chapin and O'Connor (2007) use the concept of "obligations" when considering students' participation in classroom discourse. Regardless of the rules you select, or whether you negotiate those rules with students or set them yourself, it is essential that you teach and model those expectations for students. In the beginning of the year, dedicate time each day to teaching and practicing students' rights and responsibilities. Take easy tasks and use them to teach desired behaviors. Be explicit and let students know which outcomes are being practiced. Some teachers discuss the expectations and post them in the front of the room. The investment in the beginning of the year and daily reminders are powerful in creating a risk-taking learning environment. For video examples of how some teachers prepare for and begin the year with *Math Trailblazers* go to www.Trailblazers.com.

- *Teach children to be mathematicians.* Provide opportunities for students to work in groups, struggle to find a solution path, argue their mathematics solution, and settle differences. These opportunities mirror the work of mathematicians.

- *Create a flexible and dynamic classroom environment.* Allow opportunities for further exploration or extensions of a topic. Often as students explore new problems, they make connections to other mathematical teaching opportunities.

 Grouping Students for Effective Instruction

Working with a partner or in small groups enhances students' opportunities to communicate about mathematics in a nonthreatening environment. Students learn from and help each other. However, selecting and managing effective groups requires important considerations. They include:

- Do I group heterogeneously?
- What size groups should I use?
- Do I just choose names randomly?
- Do I plan groups that mix students by ability, temperament, or both?
- Do I give students in a group "jobs" to ensure that everybody works?
- What individual accountability measures can I use?
- Will each student prepare a product, or will the group produce one shared product?

There are many ways to group students to ensure success. Some important considerations in grouping and facilitating group work follow.

Grouping needs to be flexible. Flexibility in grouping means that the number of people in the group changes based on the task. Also, sometimes pairing students with like abilities makes more sense then pairing a struggling learner with a very strong student. It may be effective to establish cooperative groups of three to four students that remain constant for a period of time, such as one month or one unit. Some days students may work in their cooperative group and other days they may be in a new partnership, based on your decision of what size group will best support student thinking and engagement.

Flexibility in grouping means that the number of people in the group changes based on the task.

The following are appropriate ways to group students for instruction:

- Small groups of two, three, or four students seem to be the most successful. In primary classrooms, pairs are the most effective groupings with the occasional exception of bringing two strong pairs together to form a group of four. Sometimes groups of three work best depending on the task. For example, in third grade, the *The Better Picker Upper* lab compares the absorbency of three types of paper towels. In this case it is best to assign each member of the group the responsibility of examining one type of paper towel. When it comes to grouping in your classroom, the important idea is to keep groupings flexible and to stress the importance of cooperation and respect no matter the group size.

- Teach pair-sharing where students turn quickly to a partner and discuss new concepts, strategies, or new vocabulary with a classmate. This breaks up teacher talk time and allows students to scaffold ideas for one another.
- Pick names randomly from a hat or jar when you want to increase the flexibility of students' working relationships.
- Have children choose partners.
- Place children in groups that match how they best work—the quiet ones all in one group and the boisterous all together.
- Assign groups by ability, heterogeneous or homogeneous when targeting specific skills with specific students.
- Keep the whole class together in one group.

While whole-class instruction and working individually are not often considered grouping strategies, both are appropriate and essential in learning mathematics. Whole-class instruction is especially useful when explaining the day's problem, introducing a new manipulative, correcting a common mistake, or summarizing the lesson. Whole-group instruction is most effective when it is brief, focused, and the information applies to all students. Clarity is enhanced when teachers provide a few minutes for pairs to discuss new ideas.

Working alone is powerful and effective as well. Giving students time to reflect and record their strategies before joining the group increases participation and helps students assess their own needs. When students do begin group time, they are able to focus on the lesson's goals and contribute thoughtfully to the discussion. In concluding the lessons, individual reflection in the form of journal writing can be a powerful assessment tool. Teachers can keep close tabs on student thinking as they develop from each day's lesson and also help catch any misinformation before big gaps in learning take place (DeBellis & Rosenstein, 2007).

Giving students time to reflect and record their strategies before joining the group increases participation and helps students assess their own needs.

Room Arrangement Matters. Seating students at tables or with desks pulled together does not necessarily guarantee that students will work well together, but sitting in rows and columns makes cooperation much more difficult. Have students sit around a group of desks that may be pulled together as a work surface to facilitate discussion and focus.

Build in Individual Accountability. Individual accountability is also important when students work in groups. To balance individual responsibility with cooperation, some teachers adopt a procedure that numbers students in each group 1, 2, 3, 4. The teacher prompts the class by saying, "3s may start the conversation at each table" or "odds talk to each other" or "1s and 3s talk and 2s and 4s listen." The important things to remember are that all students are held accountable and that the questions for groups are rich enough to push understanding.

Group members also need to be accountable to each other. They need to use one another as a resource before consulting the teacher. Be disciplined and not answer questions from group members unless they have carefully consulted each member. It is especially when working together on laboratory investigations that it is the group's responsibility to make sure all members have appropriate and accurate data tables and graphs. Students need to learn to rely on and trust one another for group work to be successful.

Here is a summary of how a *Math Trailblazers* classroom might use different student groupings:

- Students work independently giving each child a chance to think through a question and come up with a way to problem solve.

- Students turn to a partner to rehearse their answers or to make their answers more complete.

- Students work in groups to complete a task. They share ideas, responsibilities, and materials. These tasks would be difficult to complete independently. There are many ways to choose groups so that all students benefit from working with others.

- Students work as a whole class evaluating peer problem-solving strategies or receiving direction from the teacher.

Managing Math Manipulatives

Most *Math Trailblazers* lessons suggest or require the use of manipulatives. Manipulatives facilitate student learning, but effective manipulative use requires attention to their management. The following suggest ways to manage manipulatives within the classroom:

Manipulatives need to be prepared and organized ahead of time.

- When appropriate, the "Preparing for Upcoming Units" section of the Unit Planner identifies a manipulative to be used in the next unit. Gather manipulatives in advance and place them in a center for exploration.

- At the appropriate grade, have laminated copies of full-size or desk-size ten frames, *100* or *200 Charts,* and multiplication tables available for students.

- Store commonly used materials such as laminated flash cards and base-ten boards in accessible locations such as pocket charts. Make copies of these for students and allow them to take home their originals for practice.

- Allow students to explore manipulatives during indoor recess or center time. This casual experience helps them to be more focused when the lesson begins.

- Try all the manipulatives yourself before using them with students. Some grade levels use common planning time to try the lab activities together.

- Prepare and store copies of frequently-used items such as data tables and graphs. These can be copied in bulk before the school year saving both time and money.

Store manipulatives with easy access for students in mind.

- Have the most frequently used manipulatives, such as connecting cubes, links, coins, and base-ten pieces, available all year at student desks, on counters, or stored in nearby tubs for quick availability.

- If sharing a manipulative kit between teachers, develop a system to catalog manipulatives for easier accessibility.

- Store manipulatives in clear plastic bags, boxes, or cartons. Organize them so there are enough pieces in each bag or box for partners or whole tables. Have students who needs practice counting arrange links and connecting cubes in sets of ten by color.

- When working in groups with manipulatives, assign one person in each group the responsibility of collecting and returning items to their original location.

- Create a personal Daily Practice and Problem (DPP) manipulative kit for students to use when solving their DPPs each day. These kits include manipulatives frequently used to solve DPP problems. They may include things like links, coins, and connecting cubes at the primary grades, and base-ten pieces and pattern blocks at the middle grades.

- Label manipulative kits with quantities of materials to help prevent their loss. A label such as "This kit should contain 4 rulers, 4 calculators, and 4 sets of base-ten pieces" will help students (and teachers) track all materials before they are stored.

- Easy accessibility and visibility are key to efficient use of storage devices. Organizers, such as those with clear plastic shoe pockets designed to be hung on a door are a good resource for storing calculators or other manipulatives. By adding students' names to the outside of each pocket, you can tell quickly who has or has not returned their manipulatives.

Use manipulatives in instruction to promote understanding.

- Introduce each manipulative and discuss its use. For example, when students first use graduated cylinders, say, "What do you see when you look at a graduated cylinder?" Or for a balance ask, "What do you notice about this balance?" The conversations that groups have first and then share with the whole class are rich and exciting. Students often see interesting things that teachers may not.

Use manipulatives in instruction to promote understanding.

- Include calculators as an option for students. As with most tools, the more they use them, the more commonplace they become. Be open about discussing when calculators are an appropriate choice.

- Post a list of the day's manipulatives to be used for each lesson. Make older students responsible for retrieving and returning their own supplies according to that list.

- Designate a "hands off" area on the desk or table for manipulatives to be kept while listening to a student or teacher.

Above all, remember that the more experience students have with manipulatives, the more equipped they will be for solving problems.

Ideas on the Pacing of *Math Trailblazers* Lessons

Teach math 60 minutes per day, every day. The National Council of Teachers of Mathematics established a standard of 60 minutes per day of mathematics instruction for children beginning in grade 1. *Math Trailblazers* is designed to be used for 60 minutes per day, every day. Sequence activities that follow the day's schedule and the children's ability to focus. For example, you can begin the day with a Daily Practice and Problem item, do a math activity that keeps the children working in groups at tables, and do an activity that has the children walking around to gather data later in the day. Not all 60 minutes of instruction need to be offered continuously.

The National Council of Teachers of Mathematics established a standard of 60 minutes per day of mathematics instruction for children beginning in grade 1.

Building the MTB Classroom

The early units in each grade contain many opportunities for teachers to get to know the children and to assess their math abilities from the first day. Encourage your colleagues to join you in reaching the goal of a full hour of math, every day.

Use the Pacing Suggestions in the *Unit Resource Guide*. Suggestions for pacing are given within each *Unit Resource Guide* at the beginning of the lessons and Unit Outlines. They are also in the Overview section of the *Teacher Implementation Guide*. Often the suggestions will recommend omitting or adding certain lessons if this is your first year with *Math Trailblazers*. For example, pacing suggestions for fifth grade will sometimes direct you to add a lesson from fourth grade or skip sections of the unit if your students are new to *Math Trailblazers*.

Use the multidisciplinary structure of *Math Trailblazers* to your advantage. Teach the lessons involving *Adventure Books* during literature blocks or read aloud times. Pull the science-heavy lessons or units into your science time. The lessons involving "Mr. Origin" can be completed during Social Studies lessons to address map skills. There are many creative ways to incorporate more mathematics into each day.

If this is your first year teaching *Math Trailblazers*, work towards teaching as much of the material as possible. This is especially true for teachers at grades 3–5. Teachers in the primary grades often complete all the lessons as outlined in the *Unit Resource Guide* with little trouble. To do this, teachers must start on the first day of school and dedicate an hour to math instruction each day through the last day of school. Completing all the lessons in the primary grades greatly impacts students at grades 3–5.

Teachers in the upper grades should strive to complete more and more of the curriculum each year. However, there is more content in grades 4–5 than can be taught in one school year. *Math Trailblazers* is aimed at a national audience. Because content expectations vary from state to state, some content included in Grade 5 may be taught in grade 5 in your district. Thus, you and your colleagues need to carefully choose what content to teach at what time.

Upper-grade teachers in their first year with *Math Trailblazers* should teach the lessons as described and try not to stay too long on any one concept. Although this may be the first time your students see concepts presented in this way, they will have several opportunities to explore the ideas. Each lesson is not designed to be taught for mastery. The concepts will spiral back throughout the year in the Daily Practice and Problems and later units. Each time a concept is presented, the approach is slightly different. If students struggled the first time, they will have more opportunities as the year progresses to acquire the concept or skill.

Respecting differences in classrooms. Some schools or districts establish a pacing chart for each grade so classrooms stay together and all students will receive the same mathematics instruction. Asking teachers to move through a curriculum at exactly the same rate is very difficult to implement. Sometimes individual teachers find that students need more time with one concept and less time with another. We find that schools and districts with the best implementations recommend the lessons and units that need to be completed within a quarter and allow teachers some flexibility in the weekly pacing of the materials.

Rearranging lesson order. If changes must be made to the order of the lessons, make decisions as a grade level in a school or district. These decisions should be made with the advice of a math specialist or coordinator who understands the development of the mathematics content within and across grades. It is very important to the integrity of the curriculum that individual teachers not make pacing decisions on their own. Sometimes the timing of state tests determines when a particular unit should be covered. In these cases, teachers benefit from cross-grade level discussions.

Whole-group decisions can consider timing of the math facts program and Daily Practice and Problems. Teachers can use the *Facts Resource Guide* at grades 2–5 to keep on track with the math facts while making adjustments to other content. When making decisions as a school, teachers from one grade to the next can adjust for gaps in learning when items are missed or altered. It is very helpful to have at least one person with access to the entire curriculum to help guide these types of discussions for your school or district. If you do not have a qualified person in your district contact Kendall/Hunt for additional resources.

This section is just the beginning of what the *Math Trailblazers* classroom can be. The conversation continues with other sections of the *Teacher Implementation Guide.* Sections on classroom discourse, working with parents, and meeting the needs of individual students add to the information presented here. Also the online communities at Mathtrailblazers.com and the listserv give you direct access to teachers in the field. To join the *Math Trailblazers* Listserv, send a note to TIMS@uic.edu.

References

Chapin, Suzanne H., and Catherine O'Connor. "Academically Productive Talk: Supporting Students' Learning in Mathematics." *The Learning of Mathematics*. Portia C. Elliot, W. Gary Martin, and Marilyn E. Strutchens, eds., pp. 113–128. National Council of Teachers of Mathematics, Reston, VA, 2007.

Curriculum and Evaluation Standards for School Mathematics, National Council of Teachers of Mathematics, Reston, VA, 1989.

DeBellis, Valerie A., and Joseph G. Rosenstein. "Creating an Equitable Learning Environment for Teachers of Grades K–8 Mathematics." *The Learning of Mathematics*. Portia C. Elliot, W. Gary Martin, and Marilyn E. Strutchens, eds., pp. 271–288. National Council of Teachers of Mathematics, Reston, VA, 2007.

Kersaint, Gladis. "The Learning Environment: Its Influence on What is Learned." *The Learning of Mathematics*. Portia C. Elliot, W. Gary Martin, and Marilyn E. Strutchens, eds., pp. 83–96. National Council of Teachers of Mathematics, Reston, VA, 2007.

Principles and Standards for School Mathematics, National Council of Teachers of Mathematics, Reston, VA, 2000.

Reys, B.J., and J.M. Bay-Williams. "The Role of Curriculum Materials In Implementing the Curriculum and Learning Principles." *Mathematics Teaching in the Middle School.* 9(2), pp. 120–124, 2003.

Stein, M.K., M.S. Smith, M.A. Henningson, & E.A. Silver. *Implementing Standards-based Mathematics Instruction: A Casebook for Professional Development.* Teacher's College Press, New York, 2000.

Teaching the *Math Trailblazers* Student: Meeting Individual Needs

This section concentrates on meeting the needs of individual students, specifically focusing on the needs of English Language Learners, special education students, and talented or gifted students as they access the rigorous mathematics in *Math Trailblazers*.

Student and teacher working together to access the rigorous mathematics in Math Trailblazers.

Teaching the MTB Student

Teaching the *Math Trailblazers* Student: Meeting Individual Needs

Today's world is increasingly more diverse, and educators frequently need to attend to this diversity. New issues, ideologies, and calls for accountability surface almost daily, highlighting the need for teachers to address all forms of diversity within their classrooms. It may be surprising to some, but every classroom is diverse in some ways. Students vary in their prior knowledge, interests, and learning styles, among other things. Many classrooms have students from different cultures or ethnic groups. Within a student group, some may have special learning needs while others are gifted or talented in mathematics. All have the right to access the rigorous mathematics in *Math Trailblazers*.

The importance of making rigorous mathematics available to all students is articulated in the Equity Principle in the *Principles and Standards for School Mathematics* (NCTM, 2000). The Equity Principle states:

> Excellence in mathematics education requires equity—high expectations and strong support for all students. . . . All students, regardless of their personal characteristics, backgrounds, or physical challenges must have opportunities to study and support to learn mathematics. Equity does not mean that every student should receive identical instruction. . . . All students need access each year to a coherent, challenging mathematical curriculum taught by competent and well-supported mathematics teachers. (p. 12)

> *All students, regardless of their personal characteristics, backgrounds, or physical challenges must have opportunities to study and support to learn mathematics.*

From its inception, the *Math Trailblazers* writers intended to design a curriculum that would support all learners. According to Robert Marzano (2003), the school-level factor that has the most impact on student achievement for all students is a "guaranteed and viable curriculum." Marzano defines a guaranteed and viable curriculum as one in which students are provided with both the opportunity to learn and the time in which to learn. This means that the sequence and organization of the curriculum must support students as they learn.

Math Trailblazers materials (lessons, labs, games, and assessments) include a variety of strategies that address the needs of students of differing learning styles, cultural and linguistic differences, and mathematical abilities. To assist teachers in creating a flexible learning environment, these strategies as well as some of the opportunities for meeting the needs of a wide variety of learners are identified in the Unit Outline in grades 1–5.

While the design of *Math Trailblazers* makes great strides in supporting a wide range of learners, it is still important to consider the unique needs of learners and adapt lessons appropriately. English Language Learners, for example, benefit from the use of the language that is part of the *Math Trailblazers* design, but these learners will be more successful when teachers implement additional language support. Gifted learners certainly benefit from the challenging open-ended tasks that are found throughout the curriculum, but can learn more when these tasks include extensions or adaptations. Special education students are supported with the language, models, and strategies used throughout the curriculum, but additional scaffolding and reading and writing support can enhance their experience.

This section was created for teachers to understand how the curriculum design supports specific groups of learners *and* to provide ideas for additional strategies that can further support each learner. The populations addressed in this section are:

Part 1. English Language Learners

Part 2. Special Education Students

Part 3. Talented and Gifted Students

These sections are not a review of all research in the field nor are they intended to be exhaustive lists of appropriate strategies. Instead they are an overview of some math-specific issues that are likely to be true in many classrooms. They also include some tried and true strategies that *Math Trailblazers* teachers have found to support their efforts to provide a challenging and supportive learning environment for their students.

Resources

Marzano, Robert. *What Works in Schools: Translating Research into Action.* Association for Supervision and Curriculum Development, Alexandria, VA, 2003.

Principles and Standards for School Mathematics. National Council of Teachers of Mathematics, Reston, VA, 2000.

Using *Math Trailblazers* with English Language Learners

A. Introduction

Mathematics classrooms no longer operate within a universal environment of "just numbers." Students are now expected to reason, explore, justify, and record their strategies for solving complex problems. This shift in practice, while excellent in rigor, presents a different challenge for students who are learning English. Their needs are unique and, therefore, warrant special attention.

Whether your district has adopted a small group instruction model or a mainstream classroom model for English Language Learners (ELLs), they deserve access to the rich mathematics presented throughout *Math Trailblazers.* If you teach in a district that has adopted or is considering adopting *Math Trailblazers,* be prepared to instruct all students with this curriculum. You can be confident that students with special needs, whether linguistic or academic, will benefit immensely from the hands-on, concept-based instruction provided in *Math Trailblazers.*

Whether your district has adopted a small group instruction model or a mainstream classroom model for English Language Learners (ELLs), they deserve access to the rich mathematics presented throughout Math Trailblazers.

With the move away from isolated computation as the primary focus of mathematics instruction, it is important to ask, "How can I help English Language Learners succeed in a language-rich math class?" Rather than seeing the amount of listening, reading, writing, and speaking in *Math Trailblazers* as an obstacle, consider it as an opportunity for ELLs to learn and use their new language in a meaningful way. In fact, the only way they will learn English and mathematics is if they have the opportunity to use language in their math class.

The section in the *Teacher Implementation Guide,* titled Language in the *Math Trailblazers* Classroom, provides many ideas for supporting language use in general. In this section, the focus is on the unique needs of ELLs. While certainly not exhaustive, the ideas presented in this section offer a starting point for further thought, discussion, and collaboration. The section begins with a brief overview of research and theory related to language learning. It identifies and discusses tools already in the structure of *Math Trailblazers* and shares additional strategies that will increase access to the content.

B. Second Language Learning: Theory in Review

Early theories of second language learning were rooted in behaviorist theories of education. Behaviorists believed that language was learned through exposure to controlled grammar and language structure with minimal thought to social or cultural impact. (Ricard-Amato and Snow, 2005) In a time when much of education was decontextualized and rote, language instruction was no different.

From research in the field of second language learning starting in the late 1970s, we now know that second languages are not "learned" through rules and structures. Rather, they are acquired through context-embedded interactions much as children learn their first language. The work of Stephen Krashen, James Cummins, and others greatly shape our current views of how children acquire a language (*Schooling and Language Minority Students: A Theoretical Framework* Pp. 3–79, 1991).

Krashen (ibid, 1991) proposes that children acquire a second language naturally as they are exposed to comprehensible input through a low affective filter. In other words, as students interact in a safe, concrete environment they are able to understand and take risks in language. Through high motivation and purposeful use of the new language over time, students move towards proficiency in that language.

Cummins (ibid, 1991) adds further insight into second language learning by documenting the amount of time it takes most students to become proficient in the target language as described above. According to his research, it takes approximately two years for a student to master face-to-face, context-embedded communicative fluency. This level of competency is necessary to succeed in day-to-day social conversations such as those on the playground for example.

Ease at simple exchanges by ELLs, however, is often mistaken for advanced fluency in the new language. Therefore, Cummins (1984) identified an important distinction between the ease of social language and the unique demands required to succeed in the classroom's academic environment. To become proficient in the cognitively demanding language of the classroom, students need five to seven years to reach the level of their native English-speaking peers. That means even though students seem proficient in everyday conversations, they have years of academic language to master. The distinction between the two language proficiencies is crucial in ensuring the success of English Language Learners in our schools. The distinction allows teachers and researchers to identify and address the unique demands of academic language instruction.

Donaldson (1978) predated Cummins in her identification of "embedded and disembedded thought and language." By expanding on Donaldson's ideas, Cummins developed a framework for defining language use in the classroom. Cummins (1984) cites her framework when explaining why students acquire conversational language more rapidly due to the embedded contextual clues and high motivation of face-to-face communication. In addition, the framework reiterates the difficulty experienced by students in completing the cognitive demands of abstract tasks within the classroom. Cummins articulates the major aim of schooling as developing students' abilities to manipulate and interpret abstract texts. Therefore, the more we can do as educators to relate the abstract, academic world to the concrete, familiar world of students, the more accessible that knowledge becomes.

C. Tools in *Math Trailblazers* to Support English Language Learners

By using *Math Trailblazers* you are already well on your way to providing ELLs access to rigorous mathematics. This curriculum has numerous effective tools for making the abstract come to life. As you plan your lessons using the *Unit Resource Guide* consider the following features:

- Abundance of visuals
- Extensive use of manipulatives
- Graphic organizers
- Labs
- Problem solving from everyday life
- Connections to literature
- Group and partner work
- Opportunities to write and read in English

Math Trailblazers uses many of these features daily. Simply implementing all aspects of the curriculum will increase the support of your English Language Learners.

By using Math Trailblazers *you are already well on your way to providing English Language Learners access to rigorous mathematics.*

D. Language-rich Approach to Instruction

We now know that English Language Learners develop skills in listening, speaking, reading, and writing at the same time, although we once believed they progressed in a linear fashion (Richard-Amato and Snow, 2005). Therefore, every lesson should provide meaningful opportunities for English Language Learners to experience and use language. *Math Trailblazers* provides excellent opportunities for students to use and learn language in a safe environment. Language is two-way communication: receptive (listening and reading) and productive (speaking and writing). This section takes each of these four domains and explains what is built into *Math Trailblazers* along with a discussion of the related needs and strategies of English Language Learners.

Listening. *Math Trailblazers* provides problem solving in motivating scenarios. In these tasks, students listen to others in their groups as they work on solutions. For example, students sell lemonade and plan class parties in third grade. They track the weather and investigate healthy eating habits in first grade. They take trips to famous places to study mathematical concepts. They consider the height of the Sears Tower and the circumference of the large Ferris wheel at Navy Pier in Chicago. They even predict the number of pennies in a stack from Earth to the moon!

Students listen to original or adapted literature in the *Adventure Book* and trade books recommended in the curriculum. The *Unit Resource Guides* and the *Teacher Implementation Guides* list literature selections that are either suggested or essential to completing each unit. Research is overwhelming as to the benefits of daily read alouds for all students, especially English Language Learners (Krashen, 1993; Trelease, 2001). If you are unable to read each selection to the students, add math-related titles to your listening center, or for high motivation, your podcasting center.

For English Language Learners it is essential that you monitor their abilities to listen and comprehend what they hear, whether it is listening to you or their peers. Use strategies like "numbered heads together" where each group member is assigned a number for the teacher to use in monitoring participation or drawing names from a cup to ensure that all students share. Be careful, of course, to allow generous wait time for ELLs to form their thoughts, and even allow them to share in alternative ways like drawings or motions. Allow students to be the teacher as they share their strategies for solving problems. By limiting the sharing of duplicate strategies, you also encourage students to listen carefully and evaluate each other's ideas.

There are teacher actions that can improve the listening and comprehension skills of English Language Learners. These include:

- As you speak to your English Language Learners, use clear language with lots of expression and movement.
- Be your own dictionary, always explaining difficult words as you use them.

> *Every math lesson should provide meaningful opportunities for English Language Learners to experience and use language.*

- Use Art Costa's 10/2 principle. Do not speak for more than 10 minutes without giving students at least 2 minutes to process and make connections with the new information (Brechtel, 1998).

- Familiarize students with the process of turning quickly to their neighbor and interacting with what they are hearing.

- Allow students time to draw a picture or do a quick write.

However you manage it, just give students time to connect the new learning to a familiar idea.

Reading. Math class is a great opportunity for students to apply all their reading skills in a different context. English Language Learners benefit from paired reading especially when paired with strong English readers. (Diaz-Rico and Weed, 2002) They also benefit when expository texts, such as the *Student Guide,* are reworded into summary statements. (Echevarria and Graves, 2003) These strategies encourage groups of students to rewrite each paragraph or section using one sentence. Summarizing helps English Language Learners focus on the important information and not get lost in the details.

Again, use all the reading resources in the curriculum:

- Use the literature in the Literature Connections and the *Adventure Book* in addition to the *Student Guide.*

- Transfer key sentences from the *Student Guide* to sentence strips for English syntax examination.

- Omit key words for vocabulary development or "cloze" activities where students use the context of the sentence to find the missing key term or terms.

- Consider using math-related words in your spelling or vocabulary program.

- Do NOT focus on teaching key words like "in all" or "how many left" as indicators of certain operations. These terms can mislead and distract students from thinking about the whole problem. Instead teach students to read the problem carefully by focusing on its action or by considering the picture it creates.

Speaking. Use cooperative groups to put English Language Learners into situations where they can use their language and hear other native speakers. The Lesson Guides suggest ways for students to work in groups. Keep the groups flexible while varying their size and purpose. Students may work in groups to complete labs or in pairs to share strategies for problem solving. Because students need constant guidance and encouragement when working with others, spend the time needed to create a classroom environment of constructive student-to-student relationships. Give children the language needed to help each other or clarify ideas. Be sensitive to cultural and dominance issues that hinder equity among students. Do not be discouraged if it takes longer than you expect for students to work well together. Suggestions include:

- Provide sentence frames and sentence starters for discussion.

- Teach new vocabulary. (For more information and teaching ideas refer to the end of this section.)

- In primary classes use a key term as the "word of the day." Each time you transition within the lesson use the new term as a signal to move or begin work. You may even want to associate a physical movement or sound with the term to further involve the children with the new concept. (Brechtel, 1998)

- Encourage students to share their thinking by refusing to be the only expert in the room.

- Foster a safe environment where students are not ridiculed for making mistakes in English (or in math). For more information on establishing classroom norms, see the Building the *Math Trailblazers* Classroom section.

- Try numbering the participants in each group to encourage each student to speak. Use numbers or other identifiers as triggers to begin conversations. For example, "Twos, begin the conversation on prime numbers." Or "Fours, be ready to report back to the class at the end of your discussion." Using numbers or other identifiers in this way provides gentle accountability for all students.

- Keep in mind that the less time you talk, the more time students will have to talk.

- Set time for students to 1) work alone, 2) work in small groups before coming together in a whole-group discussion. This gives students a chance to think about the problem and test their ideas with a few others, before sharing with the whole class.

Writing. Take advantage of the many opportunities for children to write that exist in *Math Trailblazers*. English Language Learners need to see good writing modeled for them everyday, especially in math class. Even native speaking English students struggle to express their thinking and strategies for problem solving. All students need the language of thought. They need words for what is happening in their head. Therefore, encourage the use of terms such as counting on, skip counting, and regrouping. Use this vocabulary in class, not as words to be tested, but rather as language that gives meaning to the solution paths that students present. In the beginning you do the drawing and the writing; students give the ideas. Little by little as students become more confident, encourage them to draw, and later write, about their solutions. Save student work and show problem-solving examples to your students. You can score those just as you would score formal writing pieces in other subjects.

In addition, consider the following suggestions for improving writing for English Language Learners:

- Use the journal prompts. Make the journal prompts interactive by responding to the students in writing whenever possible.

- Model mathematical language by using shared writing strategies in which you and your students write together (McCarrier, Pinnell, and Fountas, 2000).

- Use the writing required in *Math Trailblazers* to support good writing in general. For example, reinforce transition words in strategy explanations as you would in expository writing.

- Use sentence frames or sentence starters to help English Language Learners model correct structure.

- Develop a respectful safe environment for students to share their strategies, so that English Language Learners will have more opportunities to develop that inner sense of what "sounds right" in English.

E. Issues Frequently Raised in Discussions with Teachers of English Language Learners

Planning Lessons When Some or All of the Students are ELLs

Use the *Unit Resource Guide* in planning your lessons. This component remains the center of each daily activity. The *Unit Resource Guide* outlines the content goals for each lesson. For the English Language Learners in your room, it is extremely important that the grade-level content goals are as close to the goals of their peers as possible. Not only do they need access to the same rich mathematics, for English Language Learners each new lesson is another opportunity for language growth as well. Therefore every lesson now needs to accomplish two goals: learning rigorous mathematics content and improving English skills (Echevarria, Vogt, and Short, 2000).

The following lesson from Grade 2 Unit 3 is an example of one way you might adapt a *Math Trailblazers* lesson to accommodate English Language Learners. This level of detail is NOT necessary for each lesson, but might be useful in getting started. Once you become more familiar with these strategies, the lesson planning will become second nature. You will be more confident making the adaptations right from the *Unit Resource Guide.*

English Language Learners need access to the same rich mathematics as their classmates, and each new lesson is another opportunity for language growth as well.

Teacher:	Grade 2 Unit 3 Lesson 3	Date:

Envision Outcomes:

Content Goals:
- Sorting objects by size.
- Collecting and recording data in a table.
- Making and interpreting bar graphs.

Posted goal for students:

"Students will sort buttons into groups by size, record the numbers in each group in a data table, and study them in a graph"

Language Goals:
- "There are ___ (small, medium, large) buttons in our handful."
- _____ buttons are the most common in our handful.
- _____ buttons are the least common in our handful.
- See Journal Prompt.
- Student pairs discuss how to sort their piles of buttons.
- Students review their graph at the end of class focusing on trends in the data.

Vocabulary:

sort	size*
button	small
medium	large
data table	graph
label	handful
most/least	common
tally	

*Word of the day

Enlist Help:

Consult the TIMS Tutor: *The TIMS Laboratory Method*. Ask adult helpers, if available, to monitor partner discussions.

Equip the Learners:
- Ask partners to identify a small, medium, and large object in the room and share with their table. Report a few examples to the class.
- Break down the word "handful." Ask students to predict its meaning from its construction.
- Bring in a soup can to show an example of a label. Discuss the function of a label.
- Review the pictures from *The Button Box* by M. Reid read in Unit 3 Lesson 1.

Engage Motivation:
- Give student pairs a handful of buttons and ask them to sort them into three groups: small, medium, and large. Show the transparency and model with a small group of buttons.
- Remind students of the sentence starters listed in the "Language Goals" they can use for discussion.
- Walk around and observe students as they work together. Praise appropriate use of mathematical language and cooperative behavior.

Execute the Lesson:
- Using the data table as a visual, remind students how to fill out the bottom of page 57 in their *Student Guide*. Ask pairs how they can record "Number of Buttons."
- If no groups suggest it, remind them how to draw tallies to keep track of the buttons.
- On a transparency or chart paper, review the parts of a graph. Pay close attention to the "labels" on each axis. Remind them of the soup can.
- Ask students to graph their data.
- Refer to the sentence frames to help students discuss their graphs with the class. Encourage student pairs to share.

Evaluate the Progress:
- Use the addition and subtraction problems suggested on page 34 of the *Unit Resource Guide* to continue problem solving in pairs.
- Have groups compare and contrast their graphs using sentence starters like, "Our group had ___ more/less buttons than…" or "Our graph looks like a _____, while their graph looks like a _____."
- Place graphs in portfolios to use as a baseline for future activities.
- Interact with the students' entries in their math journals.
- Record observations as groups work together. (See the Assessment section.)

Teacher: **Grade __ Unit __ Lesson __**   **Date:**

Envision Outcomes:

Content Goals:	Language Goals:	Vocabulary:

Enlist Help:

Equip the Learners:

Engage Motivation:

Execute the Lesson:

Evaluate the Progress:

Effective Lesson Planning for English Language Learners using the *Unit Resource Guide:*

ENVISION OUTCOMES:

Content Goals: These should be clear and posted for students at the beginning of the lesson. They may be in the form of a question that students will answer or a task they can complete. The Key Content section of the Lesson Guide is a good place to start formulating your goals. Regardless of their form, review them before the lesson begins and as you progress to help the students (and you) keep focus.

Language Goals: Here is the major adjustment needed for English Language Learners. As you review the lesson in the *Unit Resource Guide,* consider what language needs will arise for your students. Identify the English structure or vocabulary you must address as you proceed through the lesson. Be direct and explicit as you teach the language lessons. See below for more ideas on teaching new vocabulary.

ENLIST HELP:

Connect with other teachers in your building if you need help making your goals accessible to English Language Learners. If you have staff trained specifically in providing instruction to English Language Learners, ask them to team teach with you on occasion. If they work with some of your students in a small group either outside or inside the classroom, have them build background knowledge for your upcoming lessons. Be careful, however, to keep them from giving direct instruction before students have a chance to develop the concepts for themselves. Consult the *Teacher Implementation Guide* for any content-related questions involving the curriculum. You can also use the Background and Content Notes in the *Unit Resource Guides* to review the mathematics for yourself.

EQUIP THE LEARNERS:

Take a few minutes at the beginning of the lesson to awaken the background knowledge of your students. This is a great time to use picture or literature books recommended in the *Unit Resource Guide.* Also, as you review the *Unit Resource Guide* record any new vocabulary words that might pose a challenge to English Language Learners. This includes at least the Key Vocabulary section, but most likely additional terms as well. Remember to highlight new definitions of familiar terms or homophones relating to math. Take time to introduce new vocabulary before you begin the lesson as long as it does not take away from student exploration and discovery. (See the vocabulary section for more ideas.)

ENGAGE MOTIVATION:

Motivate students by providing manipulatives or engaging them in a real-life problem-solving scenario. Again the *Unit Resource Guide* is your best source for ideas regarding appropriate manipulatives for each lesson. Remind students of previous work they have done related to this topic. The *Student Guide* includes many opportunities for problem solving that relate to students.

EXECUTE THE LESSON:

Teach the lesson once the students are engaged. Use lots of visuals and graphic organizers to increase comprehension. For every ten minutes of instruction, give two minutes of process time. Remember to keep focused on the goals, language, and content that were introduced at the beginning of the lesson. Help the students remember the important, not just the interesting.

EVALUATE THE PROGRESS:

Finish the lesson by checking for understanding. Review the goals and check students' progress. Use response journals or pictures. Ask students to monitor their own learning as to how well they met the lesson's goals. Consult the lesson's Assessment section in the *Unit Resource Guide* for suggestions on assessment activities.

Strategies to Help English Language Learners Remember all the New Academic Language

The amount of new academic vocabulary can be overwhelming. As teachers we want to make every effort to familiarize the students with new vocabulary within the context of the lesson (Coggins, et al. 2007). This is not a directive for isolated vocabulary instruction.

- Help students to see new words all over the classroom.

- Include them in spelling lists and on word walls.

- Use a "word of the day" to signal transition times between activities.

- Create personal dictionaries that students update daily with pictures and descriptions of new terms.

- Remember that many terms specific to mathematics have multiple meanings from common words. For example, mean, average, foot, product, and difference are a few of the words that have new meanings related to math content. Other words are homophones like sum, whole, plane, or weight that have common definitions when spelled differently. It is important to acknowledge these nuances in meaning when it comes to content-specific vocabulary.

Help English Language Learners explore new words on a deeper level:

- Look for patterns between words and how words relate to each other.

- Uncover root words and prefixes to predict meanings.

- Map words according to their relationship to other words.

- Compare and contrast words.

- Consider non-examples as a way to define unfamiliar terms.

- Take words out of their original sentences or paragraphs to help students focus on context clues. This familiar technique is referred to as a "cloze" exercise, and it has been effective for years at helping students uncover meanings of new words from their surroundings.

Ultimately, students will leave your classroom and have to take responsibility for their own learning:

- Move students toward independence by teaching them to use available tools.
- Teach them to use the glossary or index section at the back of their *Student Guides.*
- Remind them that when they look up an unknown term in a standard dictionary, the definition relating to math may not be the first one mentioned.
- Help students assess their knowledge when they come across familiar or unfamiliar words. Teach them to ask themselves questions like, "Where have I heard that term before?" or "How is this familiar word being used in a new way?" Then, they can evaluate where they need to go for more information.

Strategies to Increase Use of Nonverbal Communication in the Classroom

Math Trailblazers includes many opportunities for students to discover knowledge and content through experience. Capitalize and extend those daily opportunities. For example, in the first-grade activity called *Sharing Cookies,* bring in a box of cookie-shaped cereal for the students to use instead of cubes. Use cardboard pizzas in third grade for the *Pizza Problems.* Have kids make a paper T-shirt to decorate for *T-shirt Factory Problems,* also in third grade. Collect actual coins for money problems. Whenever possible, use real or close to real objects in presenting lessons.

If the objects are too hard to gather, bring in pictures, videos, or online images to show new concepts. Save old magazines and laminate pictures to use for vocabulary development. Make your own Shape Book using digital photography during the first-grade *Shape Walk* activity. Enlist the help of older classes to make resources for the younger grades. Video and internet services like UnitedStreaming.com can also be useful for collecting visuals. Save your work in an organized file from year to year to make the task more manageable.

Help build background knowledge by setting up an exploratory center of the coming unit. Use the Preparing for Upcoming Lessons section of the *Unit Resource Guide* to give you ideas of what is coming. Have your English Language Learners explore some of the new vocabulary with a native speaking peer. Just try not to give direct instruction robbing the learner of the joy of future discovery.

In this growing field of education stay connected to current research through national organizations such as the National Council of Teachers of Mathematics, TODOS: Mathematics for All, and National Association of Bilingual Education.

> Math Trailblazers *includes many opportunities for students to discover knowledge and content through experience.*

References

Blachowicz, Camille, and Peter J. Fisher. *Teaching Vocabulary in All Classrooms.* Pearson Education, Upper Saddle River, NJ, 2002.

Brechtel, Marcia. *Bringing the Whole Together: An Integrated Whole Language Approach for the Multilingual Classroom.* Dominie Press, Carlsbad, CA, 1998.

Coggins, Debra, et al. *English Language Learners in the Mathematics Classroom.* Corwin Press, Thousand Oaks, CA, 2007.

Cummins, James. "Language Proficiency, Bilingualism, and Academic Achievement." *Academic Success for English Language Learners: Strategies for K–12 Mainstream Teachers.* Patricia A. Richard-Amato, and Marguerite Ann Snow, eds., pp. 76–86. Pearson Education, White Plains, NY, 2005.

Donaldson, Margaret. *Children's Minds.* Collins, Glasgow, 1978.

Diaz-Rico, L., and K. Weed. *The Crosscultural, Language, and Academic Development Handbook.* Allyn & Bacon, Needham Heights, MA, 2002.

Echevarria, Jana, and Anne Graves. *Sheltered Content Instruction: Teaching English-Language Learners with Diverse Abilities.* Allyn & Bacon, Boston, MA, 2003.

Echevarria, Jana, MaryEllen Vogt, and Deborah J. Short. *Making Content Comprehensible for English Language Learners: The SIOP Model.* Allyn and Bacon, Boston, MA, 2000.

Herrell, Adrienne, and Michael Jordan. *Fifty Strategies for English Language Learners.* Pearson Education, Upper Saddle River, NJ, 2004.

Hill, Jane D., and Kathleen M. Flynn. *Classroom Instruction That Works with English Language Learners.* Association for Supervision and Curriculum Development, Alexandria, VA, 2006.

Krashen, Stephen. "Bilingual Education and Second Language Acquisition Theory." *Schooling and Language Minority Students: A Theoretical Framework.* Charles F. Leyba, ed., pp. 51–79. Evaluation, Dissemination and Assessment Center, Los Angeles, CA, 1991.

Krashen, Stephen. *The Power of Reading.* Libraries Unlimited, Englewood, CO, 1993.

Leyba, Charles F, ed. *Schooling and Language Minority Students: A Theoretical Framework.* Evaluation, Dissemination and Assessment Center, Los Angeles, CA, 1991.

McCarrier, Andrea, Gay Su Pinnell, and Irene C. Fountas. *Interactive Writing: How Language and Literacy Come Together, K–2.* Heinemann, Portsmouth, NH, 2000.

Ortiz-Franco, Luis., et al., eds. *Changing the Faces of Mathematics: Perspectives on Latinos.* National Council of Teachers of Mathematics, Reston, VA, 1999.

Richard-Amato, Patricia A., and Marguerite Ann Snow, eds. *Academic Success For English Language Learners: Strategies for K–12 Mainstream Teachers.* Pearson Education, White Plains, NY, 2005.

Trelease, Jim. *The Read Aloud Handbook.* Penguin Books, New York, NY, 2001.

PART II | # Using *Math Trailblazers* with Special Education Students

A. Introduction

Finding appropriate strategies for working effectively with students who receive special education services is a challenge in any classroom. Depending on a student's disability, he or she may struggle with some or many aspects of mathematics instruction. This section highlights strategies designed to help all students, including those who experience difficulties with mathematical concepts, access the mathematics concepts and skills as presented in the *Math Trailblazers* curriculum.

In particular, this section focuses on issues related to using *Math Trailblazers* with students who have mathematics learning disabilities. You may find the information useful for other students who do not have a diagnosed disability but are experiencing learning difficulties in mathematics.

The 2004 reauthorization of the *Individuals with Disabilities Education Act* (IDEA) and associated regulations on implementing the law outline the parameters that schools must follow in providing specially designed instruction for students with disabilities. This includes the provision that students with disabilities must receive education in the least restrictive environment possible, where they have access to the general education curriculum and role models of typically developing classmates. This often means that students with disabilities have opportunities to learn challenging curricula alongside their peers without disabilities.

As part of the *No Child Left Behind Act* (NCLB) of 2001, school districts are held accountable for ensuring that all students, including those with special needs, make adequate yearly progress in reading and mathematics. The combination of IDEA and NCLB regulations has created new challenges for teachers and schools. With special-needs students being assessed on the full mathematics curriculum and schools being held accountable for the progress in mathematics of most students with disabilities, schools and districts are exploring new ways to ensure that all students including those with disabilities have access to the district's general mathematics curriculum.

Math Trailblazers was developed with a strong commitment to providing high-quality mathematics instruction for all students, including those with special needs. As such, the authors of *Math Trailblazers* incorporated approaches and tools into the curriculum to address the diverse learning needs of a wide range of students and to assist teachers with the task of differentiating their instruction. The authors of *Math Trailblazers* have designed this section to provide greater detail about strategies to support teachers to effectively plan their *Math Trailblazers* lessons for use by students in need of additional support in mathematics.

> *This section highlights strategies designed to help all students, including those who experience difficulties with mathematical concepts, access the mathematics concepts and skills as presented in the* Math Trailblazers *curriculum.*

The following section (Part B) highlights how the approaches used in *Math Trailblazers* align with the best practice research on differentiating mathematics instruction for students with disabilities. Part C includes additional resources developed by the Addressing Accessibility in Mathematics Project at Education Development Center (EDC) that can help teachers develop appropriate accommodations for students who have special learning needs in mathematics. References are included at the end of Part II.

B. *Math Trailblazers* Instruction and Special Education Research

The study of mathematics learning disabilities is relatively new when compared with research into reading disabilities (Geary, 2005; Gersten et al., 2004). Much of the work with mathematics learning disabilities has focused on simple arithmetic competencies, with little research on more complex arithmetic and other mathematical domains (Geary, 2004). While more research is needed, there is a research base of modifications and accommodations that can support (or inhibit) a student with learning disabilities. Some of the most promising strategies are shared here.

There is no single method or approach you can adopt for all students with disabilities or even all those with a specific disability. By definition, appropriate services for students with disabilities must be individualized. An essential element of working effectively with a student struggling with mathematics is identifying the source(s) of the student's difficulties. Accurately diagnosing mathematics learning disabilities is tricky (Ginsburg, 1997; Geary, 2005; Gersten et al., 2005). Different cognitive competencies are required for counting, recalling basic facts quickly; developing effective arithmetic procedures with whole numbers, fractions, and decimals; and learning mathematics that requires visual or spatial understandings, such as geometry or data representation. Students may have disabilities in one domain but function well in another.

It is also true that a student with significant language-based disabilities may appear to have a mathematical-based disability. It is therefore important that the full range of available assessment data be utilized to determine appropriate accommodations for each child.

However, there are general research-based teaching practices that seem to enhance learning for children with some mathematics learning disabilities. This section discusses those practices in relation to *Math Trailblazers*.

Strategies used within *Math Trailblazers* for all students are consistent with approaches researchers recommend for students who either are struggling with mathematics or those receiving special education services. As a result, accommodations for many special needs students will not likely require the development of drastically different approaches or lessons. Rather, teachers will need to examine lessons in relation to the learning preferences and needs of individual students, and highlight the specific approaches and strategies from within *Math Trailblazers* that make good instructional sense for the individual child. Good instruction for children with special needs ultimately depends upon reflective, knowledgeable, and flexible teachers who plan lessons carefully (Kilpatrick et. al., 2001).

Good instruction for children with special needs ultimately depends upon reflective, knowledgeable, and flexible teachers who plan lessons carefully.

Math Facts and Computation

Many students who are diagnosed with mathematics learning disabilities also have memory-related difficulties. Memory deficits can impact students' abilities to quickly recall math facts or routinely follow multiple steps in arithmetic procedures, but memory demands differ with the task. For example, the memory demands required for retrieval of math facts differ from those required for the recall of steps in a multistep procedure or to learn geometric shapes and properties.

Students with memory difficulties must use effective strategies to work around rote memorization of facts, procedures, or definitions. Following are examples that show how the design of the curriculum supports students with special needs.

Math Trailblazers interweaves conceptual understanding with development of procedural competency.

1. Instruction on the math facts focuses on patterns and connections among and between facts. *Math Trailblazers* approach for teaching and learning math facts is an example of how a strategies-based approach can assist some students who are not able to memorize the math facts. For those children, explicitly teaching strategies for figuring out the answers to math facts can be helpful. Such instruction connects the learning of one fact with knowledge of another. Research has consistently affirmed that carefully constructed, explicit instruction on problem-solving strategies provides students with learning disabilities more opportunities to figure out the correct answer and can dramatically improve their computation skills (Bottge, 2001; Gersten and Chard, 2001). See the TIMS Tutor: *Math Facts* for more information on this strategies-based approach.

2. *Math Trailblazers* interweaves conceptual understanding with development of procedural competency. This aligns with best-practice recommendations for instructing students with learning disabilities (Bottge et al., 2001; Thorton & Jones, 1996; Rittle-Johnson et al., 2001; Ginsburg, 1997). The *Math Trailblazers* approach to teaching arithmetic operations draws attention to tools within the curriculum that can assist special-needs learners to develop the needed conceptual understanding of the operations in order to gain fluency with the procedures.

3. Students use a variety of strategies for doing computation. The introduction of more than one valid procedure for each arithmetic operation offers students alternative options that might align better with their learning strengths. The regular use of calculators may be of great assistance and is a common accommodation for students who can effectively set up problems but have difficulty developing facility with paper-and-pencil procedures.

4. Extensive and ongoing use of multiple representations of arithmetic operations, such as manipulatives (e.g., connecting cubes and base-ten pieces), pictures (e.g., tallies, base-ten shorthand), and other visual representations (e.g., mathhoppers, rulers and number lines, part-part-whole mats) support students with special needs by providing different "entry points" for understanding the operations.

Use of multiple representations or alternative procedures are not panaceas in and of themselves. Most learners, but especially those with learning disabilities, will require instruction that explicitly helps them connect the various models and visual representations with the symbolic (numerical) representations of the concept (Fuson, 1992; Ginsberg, 1997). Students with learning disabilities often have difficulty making choices when multiple options are presented, and they often need more practice than other students. Introducing too many representations or alternative procedures may make it difficult for some students to make effective use of the information (Gersten & Chard, 2001). A lesson adaptation may include more explicit guidance identifying which procedures and representations are best suited to individual students at different times.

5. Daily Practice and Problems (DPPs) provide additional opportunities to practice. Once an appropriate method is identified as best suited for an individual student, additional practice is important. Most times, the practice opportunities are within the DPP or simple extensions of problem-solving contexts in daily lessons. Occasionally, the teacher may need to seek other resources for the extra practice.

Facts about Practice

- Arithmetic worksheets with many practice problems may not be helpful to many students with learning disabilities.
- Shorter, carefully constructed problem sets may be more effective in helping students with special needs develop fluency with facts and procedures (Diezman et al., 2003).
- In their meta-analysis of research on learning disabilities, Swanson and Deshler (2003) stated, "Although intensive practice of newly learned information in the early stages of learning is necessary, the cognitive intervention literature suggests that distributed practice is better for retention. Several studies have also suggested that the long-term retention of all kinds of information and skills is greatly enhanced by distributed practice" (p. 129).

Problem Solving

A fundamental assumption in *Math Trailblazers* is that students learn mathematics more effectively if they are using mathematics in meaningful contexts to solve problems. Engagement in mathematical problem solving is particularly important for students with special needs. Rich problems add context that may help such students make sense of the mathematics, build upon their previous knowledge, and judge the reasonableness of results. The problems also provide a source for the extra practice that students may require. As such, researchers caution against holding off problem solving because some basic skills are not yet in place (Bottge et al., 2001; Ginsburg, 1997; Gersten & Chard, 2001). The games and puzzles included in every grade of *Math Trailblazers* provide another source of motivation and practice that can be used effectively with special needs students.

Engagement in mathematical problem solving is particularly important for students with special needs.

Problem-solving situations in *Math Trailblazers* require students to transfer their mathematical knowledge to new situations. While these situations may be challenging for some students with learning disabilities, researchers emphasize that these students not be excluded from this important part of the mathematics curriculum. The kinds of mathematics problems they will encounter in *Math Trailblazers* can be successfully solved by the great majority. Some recommendations for supporting students are offered here:

1. Explicitly teach strategies for solving different kinds of problems (Fuchs and Fuchs, 2002; Fuchs and Fuchs, 2003; Baker et al., 2002; Swanson and Deschler, 2003). Such instruction often offers a series of steps that help students navigate through a problem, find the relevant information, and connect the problem with previous learning.

2. Consistently use tools such as advance organizers, picture-based models, or other explicit learning strategies that help students successfully work through complicated problems (Swanson and Deschler, 2003).

3. Help students make connections between varied aspects of instruction. Students with learning disabilities may need extra assistance making the connection between problem-solving experiences, concrete representations, and formal procedures (Gersten and Baker, 1998; Gersten and Chard, 1999; Ginsburg, 1997). They also will likely require additional, specific assistance with decision making, information use, vocabulary, sequencing, and patterning (Bley and Thorton, 1995).

4. Explicitly connect current or upcoming lessons with previous learning in the form of advance organizers. This may also be helpful, particularly with older students (Swanson and Deshler, 2003; Gersten and Baker, 1998).

Communication about Mathematics

Regular communication of mathematical ideas using different representations is a hallmark of instruction with *Math Trailblazers*. Classrooms that

> *Classrooms that encourage students to discuss their solution strategies and justify their answers enable students with learning disabilities to communicate their mathematical understandings in ways that align with their strengths—using actions, symbols, words, or manipulatives.*

encourage students to discuss their solution strategies and justify their answers enable students with learning disabilities to communicate their mathematical understandings in ways that align with their strengths—using actions, symbols, words, or manipulatives. Students with learning disabilities are more likely to understand and retain concepts when they:

- rephrase problems in their own words;
- describe solution approaches and results; and
- summarize what others have reported. (Diezman et al., 2003).

Multiple modes of classroom communication also provide teachers with richer data to assess student progress and offer regular feedback to students. Evidence suggests that students with learning disabilities tend to overestimate their academic performance and therefore depend even more than

Communication Strategies

Deizmann et al. (2003) suggest the following communication strategies, among others, to assist students with learning difficulties:

- Allow students to communicate their thinking and solution strategies in ways that align with their preferred learning styles and strengths, using actions, symbols, words, or manipulatives.
- Use a buddy system or other means to highlight the links between what is said, manipulated, and written during a task.
- Ask students to rephrase a task or problem in their own words because virtually all these students need to hear themselves so they can understand and retain ideas; ask them to repeat the solution strategies shared by other students in the class.
- Break tasks into smaller parts and require students to report in as each part is finished.
- Ask students to write on a slate or the board as opposed to paper.

other students on consistent feedback from teachers about their progress (Heath and Glenn, 2005; Bottge, 1999).

The balance in *Math Trailblazers* of whole class instruction, small group interactions, and individual work is well-suited to promoting the communication and learning needs of students with learning disabilities. Many special needs educators recommend varying group sizes to provide students with a range of opportunities for participation. Smaller groups also allow students with learning difficulties to experiment with ideas prior to sharing with a larger group.

Homework

Homework in *Math Trailblazers* presents special challenges because it often is atypical of parents' own experiences with mathematics homework. Parents may feel ill-equipped to assist with math homework and will likely need additional, explicit discussions about expectations for mathematics learning, homework policies, and ways to assist their children. Students with learning disabilities will benefit from strong, at-home homework support structures (parents, siblings, other relatives or adults, peers). The following suggestions may be helpful as teachers plan their homework assignments for students with learning disabilities. (ERIC/OSEP, 2001).

- Be sure the homework is meaningful and focuses on the essential mathematics that students must learn.

- The assignment should be clear and doable.

- Communicate clearly, taking extra time to explain assignments and use various means to remind students about the homework and due dates.

- Adjust the length of the assignment; assign the homework in small units.

- Adapt the assignment to address the individual needs and strengths of students; allow alternative methods for students to turn in their work, e.g., audio taping rather than writing assignments.

- Provide learning tools, such as calculators or manipulatives; don't assume those tools will be available at home.

- Identify a peer tutor or assign the student to a study group.

- Use various methods to communicate with parents about homework assignments; try to develop at-home homework support structures (e.g., parents, siblings, peers, other adults).

C. Lesson Planning Tools

The preceding section underscored two major points:

- The instructional approaches used regularly in *Math Trailblazers* align with the prevailing research on teaching students with learning disabilities.

- The curriculum already has many embedded tools and structures that can help students with mathematics learning disabilities succeed in mathematics.

Homework that prepares students for an upcoming lesson may be particularly useful for those with learning disabilities. Such homework may review previously taught concepts and skills needed in the upcoming lesson or preview some individual pieces of the upcoming lesson giving students some extra time prior to class to think about and process parts of problems they will see in class.

Careful lesson planning is the cornerstone of effective work with students who have mathematics learning disabilities. The Addressing Accessibility in Mathematics Project, based at the Education Development Center, has developed a lesson planning process and a set of tools that can assist teachers using *Math Trailblazers.* The project's goals are to make mathematics curricula and instruction more accessible to students with disabilities and to promote collaboration between mathematics teachers and special needs educators.

The Project's lesson planning process provides a framework for thinking proactively about the kinds of barriers that students may encounter in a lesson. Like many suggested planning routines for working with special needs students, the concept behind the Addressing Accessibility in Mathematics Project lesson planning process is that once barriers are identified, they can be addressed by providing the scaffolding and support that students need to reach the mathematics goals.

As part of the lesson planning, the Project suggests that teachers begin by considering instructional practices, such as pairing students or using large visuals, before deciding to alter the curriculum materials. They caution that some strategies can go too far and lose the integrity of the mathematics content and pedagogy or set expectations too low for students (Brodesky et al., 2004).

The steps in the Addressing Accessibility in Mathematics Project lesson planning process are summarized in the following table. Keep the guiding questions in mind as you plan. Making lessons accessible is a combination of proactive planning and on-the-spot decision-making. The expectation is not to make an individual lesson plan for each student; the goal is for teachers to create one lesson plan with accessibility strategies built in, recognizing that additional accommodations will be needed for some individuals. By examining the lesson through an accessibility lens, teachers can anticipate potential barriers for their students, plan strategies, and "keep them in their back pockets" to use as needed.

> *Careful lesson planning is the cornerstone of effective work with students who have mathematics learning disabilities.*

Addressing Accessibility in Mathematics Project Lesson Planning Process[1]	
Step	**Guiding Questions**
1. Focus on the mathematics of the lesson.	• What are the mathematics goals? What are the tasks? • What is most important for *all* students to learn?
2. Focus on the students.	• What are the student's strengths and weaknesses?
3. Identify potential barriers.	• What is the match or mismatch between the lesson's mathematics content and tasks and the student's strengths and weaknesses?
4. Consider accessibility strategies.	• What strategies might meet the student's needs and enable them to reach the mathematics goals?
5. Plan and implement the lesson.	• How do I integrate the accessibility strategies into my lesson plan? • How do I collect evidence to see if the strategies were effective?
6. Plan follow-up actions.	• Did the student achieve the mathematics goal for the lesson? Did the accessibility strategies help? How do you know? • How do the results of this lesson impact planning for future lessons?

[1] Adapted from Brodesky et al., 2004.

Tools for Planning Lessons

To assist *Math Trailblazers* teachers, we include several tools here that were developed by the Addressing Accessibility in Mathematics Project. These documents are reprinted here with permission from the Education Development Center for use by *Math Trailblazers* teachers. Teachers and school and district-based staff developers may make up to 10 copies. ***For all other uses, please contact Fred Gross (fgross@edc.org) for permission.*** These and other documents can also be accessed in electronic format from the Addressing Accessibility in Mathematics web site (http://edc.org/accessmath/).

• *Instructional Strategies to Increase Accessibility*
This one-page document lists strategies to consider for planning and teaching accessible lessons. It is a good introduction to a more detailed resource developed by the Addressing Accessibility in Mathematics Project: the *Accessibility Strategies Toolkit for Mathematics,* which is available from the project web site (http://edc.org/accessmath/resources/strategies.asp).

The goal of the *Accessibility Strategies Toolkit for Mathematics* is to provide an organized list of strategies for making mathematics more accessible to students with disabilities. Students' strengths and needs in six areas—conceptual processing, language, visual-spatial processing, organization, memory, and attention—are examined. For each of these six areas, the authors identified common types of tasks in *Standards*-based mathematics curricula, student needs and challenges, and corresponding teaching strategies for promoting accessibility.

- *Accessibility Planners*

  The Accessibility Planners are templates that provide guiding questions for identifying mathematical goals, potential barriers, and strategies to enable students to reach the goals. The planners are typically used in professional development workshops and with groups where teachers work together to analyze lessons and brainstorm accessibility strategies. They can, however, be used by individual teachers. Two different Planners are included here. Additional Planners are available from the Addressing Accessibility in Mathematics web site (http://edc.org/accessmath/resources/planners.asp).

  - *Individual Focal Student Planner*

    This planner is designed for recording observations on the strengths and weaknesses of an individual student. There is a space for listing accessibility strategies that are helpful for the student.

  - *Lesson Planner*

    This template can be used to plan accessibility strategies for individual lessons.

Instructional Strategies to Increase Accessibility

Helping Students Understand Tasks

- Reword directions or questions
- Have students paraphrase directions and questions
- Provide visual *and* auditory directions
- Preview vocabulary
- Have students highlight key information
- Change context to make it more familiar or appealing to students
- Show examples of the finished product

Helping Students Access Math in Varied Ways

- Build on students' prior math knowledge
- Make connections across math topics
- Move from concrete to representational to abstract
- Use multiple representations
- Provide additional examples
- Offer manipulatives
- Use technology strategies
- Use visuals like charts or projected images
- Offer alternative ways for students to show what they know
- Provide kinesthetic learning opportunities

Building Student Independence

- Offer timers to help students with pacing
- Teach highlighting and color-coding
- Use "think alouds" and other metacognitive strategies
- Teach *and* model strategies for:
  - Organization
  - Self-questioning and self-monitoring
  - Problem-solving
  - Memory (such as mnemonics)
- Clarify expectations (use rubrics)

Providing Tools and Handouts

- Provide study guides with key information to reduce copying and note-taking
- Offer calculators and multiplication charts
- Provide resource sheets
- Provide templates for tables, graphs, writing, and other tasks
- Use graphic organizers
- Provide practice problems
- Provide a word bank with key vocabulary words and visuals

Promoting Understanding through Discourse

- Have students work in pairs or small groups
- Use cooperative learning
- Keep class discussions short and focused
- Provide timely and constructive feedback
- Check in frequently with students
- Use questions, prompts, and hints

Helping Students Manage Tasks and Organization

- Reformat handouts to provide more workspace
- Reduce amount of copying
- Provide a checklist
- Provide time management cues
- Set up a notebook organizational system
- Provide project organizers to help the students keep track of tasks
- Offer tools such as highlighters and post-its to help students focus

Adjusting Tasks to Student Needs

- Adjust level of difficulty
- Use friendlier numbers
- Break complex tasks into smaller parts
- Adjust amount of time for tasks
- Adjust amount of work
- Create multiple versions of a problem, in order to offer alternatives to a range of learners
- Adjust pacing to optimize attention

Creating a Supportive Environment

- Post and reinforce classroom expectations
- Post homework assignments in a consistent location
- Seat students strategically, based on needs like vision or hearing. Seat distractible students away from windows or doors.
- Use nonverbal signals to cue attention or behavior
- Use consistent and familiar routines
- Provide easy access to manipulatives, templates, and other tools in the classroom

Teaching the MTB Student

Observations and Strategies for Focal Student: _____

	Student's Strengths	Student's Difficulties
Conceptual		
Language		
Visual-Spatial		
Organization		
Memory		
Attention		
Other		

Helpful Strategies for this Student

Lesson Planner for _____

Math Goals: *What are the priorities?*		
Lesson Demands *What's involved for students?* *Consider tasks and content.*	**Potential Barriers** **& Student Difficulties** *What difficulties do you anticipate?*	**Accessibility Strategies** *What strategies would you* *use to meet students' needs?*

References

Baker, S., R. Gersten, and D. Lee. "A Synthesis of Empirical Research on Teaching Mathematics to Low-achieving Students." *The Elementary School Journal,* 103(1), pp. 51–74, 2002.

Bley, N.S., and C.A. Thornton. *Teaching Mathematics to Students with Learning Disabilities.* Pro-Ed, Austin, TX, 1995.

Bottge, B.A. Reconceptualizing Mathematics Problem Solving for Low-achieving Students. *Remedial and Special Education,* 22(2), pp. 102–112, 2001.

Bottge, B.A., M. Heinrichs, S.Y. Chan, and R.C. Serlin. "Anchoring Adolescents' Understanding of Math Concepts in Rich Problem-solving Environments." *Remedial and Special Education,* 22(5), pp. 299–326, 2001.

Brodesky, A.R., C. Parker, M. Murray, and L. Katzman. *Accessibility Strategies Toolkit for Mathematics.* Education Development Center, Newton, MA, 2002.

Brodesky, A.R., F.E. Gross, A.E. McTigue, and C.C. Tierney. "Planning Strategies for Students with Special Needs: A Professional Development Activity." *Teaching Children Mathematics,* 11(3), pp. 146–154, 2004.

Diezmann, C.M., C.A. Thornton, and J.J. Watters. "Addressing the Needs of Exceptional Students Through Problem Solving." F.K. Lester & R.I. Charles, eds. *Teaching Mathematics Through Problem Solving: Prekindergarten–Grade Six,* pp. 169–182. National Council of Teachers of Mathematics, Reston, VA, 2003.

ERIC/OSEP Special Project. "Homework Practices That Support Students with Disabilities." *Research Connections in Special Education No. 8.* (EC 308348), Spring 2001.

Fuchs, L.S., and D. Fuchs. "Enhancing the Mathematical Problem Solving of Students with Mathematics Disabilities." H.L. Swanson, K.R. Harris, and S.E. Graham, eds. *Handbook on Learning Disabilities,* pp. 306–322. Guilford, New York, 2003.

Fuchs, L.S, and D. Fuchs. "Mathematical Problem-solving Profiles of Students with Mathematics Disabilities with and without Comorbid Reading Disabilities." *Journal of Learning Disabilities,* 35(6), pp. 563–573, 2002.

Fuson, K.C. "Research on Learning and Teaching Addition and Subtraction of Whole Numbers." G. Lenihardt, R. Putnam, and R. Hattrup, eds. *Analysis of Arithmetic for Mathematics Teaching.* Lawrence Erlbaum Associates, Hillsdale, NJ, 1992.

Geary, D.C. "Mathematics and Learning Disabilities." *Journal of Learning Disabilities,* 37(1), pp. 4–15, 2004.

Geary, D.C. "Role of Cognitive Theory in the Study of Learning Disability in Mathematics." *Journal of Learning Disabilities,* 38(4), pp. 305–307, 2005.

Geary, D.C., M.K. Hoard, J. Byrd-Craven, and M.C. DeSoto. "Strategy Choices in Simple and Complex Addition: Contributions of Working Memory and Counting Knowledge for Children with Mathematical Disability." *Journal of Experimental Child Psychology,* 88, pp. 121–151, 2004.

Gersten, R., and D. Chard. "Number Sense: Rethinking Arithmetic Instruction for Students with Mathematical Disabilities." *The Journal of Special Education,* 33(1), pp. 18–28, 1999.

Gersten, R., N.C. Jordan, and J.R. Flojo. "Early Identification and Interventions for Students with Mathematics Difficulties." *Journal of Learning Disabilities,* 38(4), pp. 293–304, 2005.

Gersten, R., and S. Baker. "Real World Use of Scientific Concepts Integrating Situated Cognition with Explicit Instruction." *Exceptional Children,* 65(1), pp. 23–25, 1998.

Ginsburg, H.P. "Mathematics Learning Disabilities: A View from Developmental Psychology." *Journal of Learning Disabilities,* 30, pp. 20–33, 1997.

Heath, N., and T. Glen. "Positive Illusory Bias and the Self-protective Hypothesis in Children with Learning Disabilities." *Journal of Clinical Child and Adolescent Psychology.* 34 (2), pp. 272–281, 2005.

Kilpatrick, J., J. Swafford, and B. Findell, eds. *Adding It Up: Helping Children Learn Mathematics.* National Academy Press, Washington, DC, 2001.

Lovin, L., M. Kyger, and D. Allsopp. "Differentiation for Special Needs Learners." *Teaching Children Mathematics,* pp. 158–167, 2004.

Marolda, M.R., and P.S. Davidson, eds. "Assessing Mathematical Abilities and Learning Approaches" C.A. Thornton and N.S. Bley, eds. *Windows of Opportunity: Mathematics for Students with Special Needs,* pp. 41–60. National Council of Teachers of Mathematics, Reston, VA, 1994.

McGilly, K., ed. *Classroom Lessons.* Bradford, Cambridge, MA, 1994.

Rittle-Johnson, B., R.S. Siegler, and M.W. Alibali. "Developing Conceptual Understanding and Procedural Skill in Mathematics: An Iterative Process." *Journal of Educational Psychology,* 93(2), pp. 346–362, 2001.

Smith, D.D., ed. *Introduction to Special Education: Teaching in an Age of Opportunity* (5th ed.). Pearson Education, Inc., Boston, MA, 2004.

Swanson, H.L., and D. Deshler. "Instructing Adolescents with Learning Disabilities: Converting a Meta-analysis to Practice." *Journal of Learning Disabilities,* 36(2), pp. 124–35, 2003.

Thornton, C.A., and N.S. Bley, eds. *Windows of Opportunity: Mathematics for Students with Special Needs.* National Council of Teachers of Mathematics, Reston, VA, 1994.

Thornton, C.A., and G.A. Jones. "Adapting Instruction for Students with Special Learning Needs, K–8." *Journal of Education,* 178(2), pp. 59–69, 1996.

Womack, D. *Special Needs in Ordinary Schools: Developing Mathematical and Scientific Thinking in Young Children.* Cassell Educational Limited, London, 1988.

PART III

Meeting the Needs of the Mathematically Gifted or Talented Student in the *Math Trailblazers* Classroom

A. Introduction

Talented or gifted students are quite different from other students in the classroom. For example, they remember things easily, needing very little review. They like to be engaged in problem solving, can work with abstract concepts beyond the scope of their peers, and approach problems in novel ways (Wilkens, Wilkens, & Oliver, 2006). A teacher's challenge with talented or gifted students is unique; rather than finding ways to make the content comprehensible to students, the teacher must move beyond the curriculum to provide additional challenge. Given this fact and that high stakes assessments focus on bringing low achieving students up to proficient levels, attention has shifted away from the talented or gifted student. Fortunately, the design of *Math Trailblazers* is well aligned with the needs of talented or gifted students, and the curriculum provides many opportunities for extending and differentiating instruction.

According to Zaccaro (2006), mathematically gifted children need to be given material that truly and appropriately challenges them. Assouline and Lupkowski-Shoplik (2005) list key elements of a curriculum that supports mathematically talented or gifted students. These elements include a broad scope of content studied in depth and at a high level with problem solving at the core of the instruction. Students solve problems, communicate solution strategies, represent problem situations in a variety of ways, and reflect on the efficiency of their problem-solving methods. Students should discover mathematical content that connects to real life as well as to other subjects.

The *Math Trailblazers* curriculum was developed with a commitment to both equity and excellence for all students, including the talented or gifted student. The following are some *Math Trailblazers* features that align with the needs of talented or gifted students:

- Students construct new knowledge as well as practice mathematical concepts through rigorous and authentic problem-solving situations.
- Students are frequently asked to communicate their solution strategies orally and in writing.
- Students solve problems using multiple problem-solving processes and provide multiple representations for their solutions.
- Students are encouraged to reflect and evaluate the efficiency of both their problem-solving strategies and the strategies of others.

B. Talented or Gifted Students in Mathematics

The following topics explore issues related to teaching talented or gifted children. Information includes insights from research, work with teachers, and how the structure of *Math Trailblazers* addresses these issues.

Identifying Talented or Gifted Students

One prevailing myth about mathematically talented students is that only students identified for a gifted program can be mathematically talented. There are a range of ways to identify students as gifted, some based on IQ scores (above 130) or on standardized test scores (above 95%). These types of criteria, however, can eliminate a student who has a special talent in one area and average or above average abilities in other areas. As a result a mathematically talented student may not meet the criteria for his or her school's gifted program (Assouline and Lupkowski-Shoplik, 2005).

The National Association for Gifted Children (NAGC) calls for a more comprehensive definition of a gifted student. They describe a gifted person as:

. . . someone who shows, or has the potential for showing, an exceptional level of performance in one or more areas of expression.

Some of these abilities are very general and can affect a broad spectrum of the person's life, such as leadership skills or the ability to think creatively. Some are very specific talents and are only evident in particular circumstances, such as a special aptitude in mathematics, science, or music. The term giftedness provides a general reference to this spectrum of abilities without being specific or dependent on a single measure or index. It is generally recognized that approximately five percent of the student population, or three million children, in the United States are considered gifted.

A person's giftedness should not be confused with the means by which giftedness is observed or assessed. Parent, teacher, or student recommendations, a high mark on an examination, or a high IQ score are not giftedness; they may be a signal that giftedness exists. Some of these indices of giftedness are more sensitive than others to differences in the person's environment.

(http://www.nagc.org/index.aspx?id=574)

In this discussion, we consider the talented or gifted student as those formally identified as gifted in the area of mathematics through assessment procedures and those students not formally identified as talented, but whom a teacher determines, through assessments, observations, and classroom assessments to be talented in mathematics.

Content Note

Although students are referred to as being either talented or gifted, programs developed for such students use the title Talented and Gifted.

While every student is different, talented or gifted students in mathematics commonly exhibit particular traits in a mathematics classroom. They begin to grasp mathematical concepts at an early age. Many of these students enter school having established their own theories of number sense, computational strategies, problem solving, and patterns. Teachers describe these children as being able to see connections among topics and ideas without formal instruction. They are often able to discern answers with unusual speed and accuracy. Also, due to their intuitive understanding, they may skip steps and be unable to explain how they arrived at their answer (Rotigel & Fello, 2005). According to Sheffield (1999), students who demonstrate giftedness in mathematics may demonstrate uneven understanding of mathematical concepts. These students are frequently less interested in the computational "how to," preferring to engage in problem solving that is both challenging and interesting (Zaccaro, 2006).

Though these students are usually able to understand difficult mathematical concepts more readily than their same age peers, these same students may also appear to be disinterested or unmotivated in a one-size-fits-all classroom. Diezmann and Watters (2005) identify boredom as a major concern for gifted students, which results from a lack of challenging academic tasks and from a perception that the learning experience has limited value to them. This lack of challenge may be furthered when teachers try to address the needs of these students by: simply increasing the amount of work the students are to complete without addressing the complexity of the task; assigning these students to help others who are still working; or asking them to work on something else quietly while they wait for others to finish (Tomlinson, 1999; Diezmann and Watters, 2005). Both the *Principles and Standards* (NCTM, 2000) and Zaccaro (2006) caution educators that the practice of simply pushing students through the curriculum at a faster pace is not the answer.

The NCTM *Principles and Standards* states:

> One traditional way for students to learn additional mathematics in which they have a particular interest is differential pacing—allowing some students to move rapidly through the mathematical content expected of all so that they can go on to additional areas. However, some alternatives to differential pacing may prove advantageous. For example, curricula can be offered in which students can explore mathematics more deeply rather than more rapidly. This model allows them to develop deep insights into important concepts that prepare them well for later experiences instead of experiencing a more cursory treatment of a broader range of topics. (p. 369)

Zaccaro (2006) explains that expecting more work from students increases the likelihood that gifted students will develop a lack of interest. More work does not nurture the student's passion for mathematics. He compares this to "teaching all scales and no music." (p. 3)

This model (differential pacing) allows them [students] to develop deep insights into important concepts that prepare them well for later experiences instead of experiencing a more cursory treatment of a broader range of topics.

Teaching Talented or Gifted Students: Classroom Learning Community

Providing the best classroom support for talented or gifted students begins with a classroom learning community that focuses on deep understanding of important mathematics for all learners. Hiebert et al. (1997) explain that effective learning means providing rich environments for developing deep understanding of mathematics through collaboration, communication, and the creation of cognitive conflict. Having these foundations in place allows the teacher to facilitate the most effective work with talented or gifted students.

The literature suggests that there are some common foundations present in a healthy classroom learning community. They include:

- Ideas and methods expressed by all students deserve and are given respect.
- Students are encouraged to work out their own methods and communicate them with understanding to others.
- Teachers help students make their own sense of ideas and methods.
- Teachers provide high expectations and the necessary scaffolding to move each child to his or her next learning benchmark.
- Mistakes are seen as sites for learning. Challenge and frustration are a part of learning and life and should be viewed as part of the learning process.
- The authority for determining whether something is correct and sensible lies with the logic of the subject rather than with the status of the teacher. The teacher strives for student independence. (Hiebert, et al., 1997; Tomlinson, 1999; Zaccaro, 2006; Kilpatrick, Swafford, & Findell, 2001)

For additional information on establishing and maintaining effective classrooms, see the Building the *Math Trailblazers* Classroom section.

> Providing the best classroom support for talented or gifted students begins with a classroom learning community that focuses on deep understanding of important mathematics for all learners.

Teaching Talented or Gifted Students: Homogeneous and Heterogeneous Grouping

Appropriate grouping of students in math class is often a concern of both new and experienced teachers. In an attempt to meet the needs of all learners, educators have often separated students by achievement, grouping them with students who have similar achievement levels. Many educators believed that these homogeneous classrooms would allow students to learn at their own pace and would allow teachers to meet the needs of the students more consistently. According to the National Research Council, however, data from international comparisons (especially Asia) support the assumption that all students can achieve important mathematical learning goals within heterogeneously grouped classrooms. Tomlinson (1999) further argues that students learn best in a heterogeneous classroom only when teachers create "effective communities of learning in which all learners are specifically and systematically addressed." (p. 22) She further states that classroom learning communities grounded in best-practice and that are responsive to the diverse needs of the learners benefit all students through differentiation of instruction.

Math Trailblazers is designed for heterogeneous grouping and contains the strategies described above to support and challenge talented or gifted students. The tasks within lessons are challenging and involve problem solving and reasoning—curriculum qualities appropriate for the talented or gifted child. In addition, tasks are solved using a range of strategies, which allows those more advanced to implement more sophisticated strategies. *Math Trailblazers* lessons provide the support for discussion about math concepts. These supports help students learn to be effective communicators and to work collaboratively. Many of the lessons involve working in pairs or small groups. This sets the stage for providing the differentiation and individualization that may not occur in classrooms that are more teacher directed or designed exclusively for whole class instruction.

Tasks That Support the Learning of Mathematically Talented or Gifted Students

According to Doyle (1983, 1988) students learn from the kind of work they do. The tasks students are asked to complete determine the nature of that work. When designing mathematical tasks for talented or gifted students, Diezmann and Watters (2005) identify four defining characteristics, each of them at the heart of the *Math Trailblazers* curriculum.

Defining Characteristics of Curriculum that Challenges and Supports Talented or Gifted Students (Diezmann and Watters 2005)

1. The tasks are authentic. Students are able to emulate the practices of mathematicians at an appropriate level.

2. The tasks develop mathematical abstract reasoning. These allow the student who is gifted mathematically to explore patterns and relationships, produce holistic and lateral solutions, and work abstractly.

3. The tasks develop meta-cognitive skills. Hiebert et al. (1997) describes this as knowing how to use information as a result of understanding how it is connected or related to new knowledge or skills. Additionally, meta-cognition is being able to decide when to use a strategy by judging whether or not it is efficient.

4. The tasks increase motivation and passion for mathematics. Tasks that are challenging and meaningful allow mathematically talented students to construct meaning and develop autonomy as a learner.

One of the unique strengths of the *Math Trailblazers* curriculum is its integration with science and language arts. This interdisciplinary approach to problem solving allows students to emulate the real-world work of mathematicians and scientists. Throughout the curriculum, students are involved in scientific investigations of everyday phenomena that develop and apply mathematical skills and concepts to generate meaningful situations.

The laboratory experiments in *Math Trailblazers* are examples of authentic tasks, crucial to the success of talented or gifted students. In each experiment, students identify variables, draw pictures of their methodology, collect and organize data in tables and graphs, and look for and use patterns to analyze their data. For example, in second grade, students compare the distance different vehicles can roll. Students are introduced to the concept of "multiple trials" in an investigation and to the use of the median as a way to average their data.

Students in fifth grade first explore the geometry of circles informally and then formally. Students use collected data to find an accurate approximation for the ratio of the circumference to diameter of a circle. Discussion ensues to cement the connection between this investigation and the constant pi (π). Students then use the constant to find a formula for the circumference of a circle. In each activity, the context of authentic tasks helps the talented or gifted students make connections between previous learning and new information. Students are able to apply what they have learned in a new or different context. According to the *Principles and Standards* (NCTM, 2000), students develop deeper and more lasting understanding when they can identify the rich connection among mathematical topics in contexts they can relate to other subjects, their own interests, and their experience. For a more in-depth discussion about *Math Trailblazers* integration with science and language arts, refer to the Foundations of *Math Trailblazers* section.

Communication is also an integral part of the *Math Trailblazers* curriculum. Students increase their understanding of mathematics by discussing the mathematics they are doing. Students are expected to share their strategies for problem solving during classroom discourse and through written explanations. Journal and discussion prompts are standard features in the lesson guide for many lessons. You can use these prompts to focus classroom discussions. Asking talented or gifted students to communicate the results of their thinking to others provides them an opportunity to clarify and deepen their understanding. Students become better able to justify their solution paths to others, especially when there are divergent solution paths. For a more in-depth discussion about communication in the *Math Trailblazers* classroom refer to the Language in the *Math Trailblazers* Classroom section.

The *Math Trailblazers* curriculum also emphasizes problems that have multiple solution paths. These problems give students opportunities to talk about their own thinking in both small group and whole-class discussions. As students share their problem-solving strategies with their classmates and teacher, and as they listen to the strategies of others, they become more reflective about mathematics. The consistent inclusion of opportunities for reflection helps the talented or gifted student think about his or her own learning and leads to more efficient strategies for problem solving.

Problems with multiple solutions give students opportunities to talk about their own thinking in both small group and whole-class discussions.

A Sample Task from *Math Trailblazers*

This sample task from *Math Trailblazers* includes the components discussed above, especially the importance of communication between student and teacher. Sharing such a task with parents, teachers of talented or gifted students, or administrators can illustrate the opportunities and challenge in this curriculum that make it appropriate for the talented or gifted student.

To develop an understanding of the base-ten number system, the students in first grade are asked to fill in numbers on an empty 50's chart, consisting of

5 rows of 10 squares per row, as shown in Figure 1. The students begin by choosing a number from a deck of digit cards. They then use a variety of strategies to determine where to record the selected number. Students continue this way until all the cards are used.

Figure 1: *A partially completed 50's chart*

Lessons are designed to encourage students to develop efficient strategies for problem solving as they build deep conceptual understandings of the mathematics.

This activity provides a launching point for developing important concepts in mathematics. The classroom described at left demonstrates that, when students are given the opportunity to construct meaning through open-ended problem solving and when they are provided the opportunity to reflect on and share their thinking with others, they are able to discover patterns and relationships, and deepen their understanding of mathematics.

C. Planning for Instruction

The *Math Trailblazers* curriculum was developed to provide high quality, rigorous mathematics for all students. Lessons are designed to encourage students to develop efficient strategies for problem solving as they build deep conceptual understandings of the mathematics. The teacher's role is integral to this process as he or she designs complex instruction with the needs of each learner in mind. Complex instruction is defined by Cohen (1994) as, "a rich strategy developed to deal with the sorts of academic ranges that frequently exist in classrooms that are academically, culturally, and linguistically heterogeneous." (p. 68)

Cohen's definition creates the underlying foundation for differentiated classrooms. In education, differentiation is defined as a teacher's responsive reaction to the needs of the learners in the classroom. In other words, differentiation is responding to individual or small group needs as opposed to teaching as if the class were a singular unit in which all students are alike.

50's Chart: From the Classroom

First graders were observed completing the task described above. They used a variety of problem-solving strategies to determine where to place the number represented on the selected card. Some students made a representation of that number using trains (or groups) of connecting cubes. The cubes were made into groups of tens and leftovers. The students placed the cubes directly onto the 50's chart to help them identify the correct box in which to record the number. Other students counted the squares, placing the number in the correct box. Still other students used the strategy of counting by tens and then by ones to identify where to place the number.

As the students continued to work, one child began to see a pattern emerging on the chart and was able to use this pattern to place the numbers. For example, he recognized that the number 47 would go in the same column as 17 only down 3 rows because 4 is 3 more than 1. This student may have been beginning to develop an abstract understanding of the value of 10 and using this to understand the relationship between the various numbers on his chart. He then asked the teacher, "Does this always work?" He was trying to make sense of the situation, make connections to what he knew, and devise a rule that explained how this system worked. The teacher continued to stretch this child's understanding by encouraging him to try to think about numbers greater than 50 asking, "Where would the number 93 fit on your chart?" He pointed to 43 and said, "Under this number, just more tens."

The goal of differentiation is maximum student growth and individual success (Tomlinson & Allen, 2000).

In the differentiated classroom, effective instruction begins with teacher planning. Tomlinson (1999) identifies the following three critical elements of the curriculum that must be linked for effective instruction:

- Content—The content is what we want students to know, understand, or do as a result of instruction. The content is the "input" for instruction.
- Process—The process includes the activities or tasks that allow a student to make sense of the content.
- Product—The product is the "output." The product represents the way in which a student demonstrates what he or she understands and can do as a result of learning.

The lessons in the *Math Trailblazers* curriculum are designed and organized to clearly focus on the content, the process, and the products so students develop understandings of the key concepts, guiding principles, essential skills, and necessary facts of mathematics. For the talented or gifted student, the teacher must consider if the content, processes, and products are appropriately challenging, and when necessary, to adapt the lesson.

There are many effective instructional strategies for working with talented or gifted students in a heterogeneous setting. Centers, stations, and using tiered lessons provide the greatest flexibility since the teacher can use these instructional strategies to differentiate instruction for all students in the classroom.

Instructional Strategies for Differentiation in the *Math Trailblazers* Classroom

In any lesson plan, a teacher needs to consider three important questions: What should be differentiated? For what purpose? And, how will this be accomplished? (Tomlinson, 1999)

When considering what to differentiate, a teacher needs to remember the three critical elements of the curriculum: content, process, and product. Additionally the teacher needs to consider the learning profile of each student, student interest, and student readiness. Another aspect that can be differentiated is the physical learning environment. Differentiating the physical learning environment might include the classroom configuration, use of specific grouping strategies, use of manipulatives both real and virtual, and student choice of product.

Key Principles of a Differentiated Classroom

- The teacher is clear about the key concepts of the unit.
- The teacher is clear about which skills are fundamental to supporting conceptual learning.
- The teacher understands, appreciates, and builds upon student differences.
- Assessment and instruction are inseparable.
- The teacher adjusts content, process, and product in response to student readiness, interests, and learning profile.
- All students participate in respectful work.
- Students and teachers are collaborators in learning.
- Goals of a differentiated classroom are maximum growth and individual success.
- Flexibility is the hallmark of a differentiated classroom. (Tomlinson, 1999)

There are many effective instructional strategies for working with talented or gifted students in a heterogeneous setting. Centers, stations, and using tiered lessons provide the greatest flexibility since the teacher can use these instructional strategies to differentiate instruction for all students in the classroom.

Centers. There are two types of centers that a teacher may use in a classroom to provide differentiation of instruction. The first, a learning center, is an area of the classroom that contains activities designed to teach, reinforce, or extend a skill or concept. Teachers can design classroom centers to focus on current instruction, review past instruction, or preview and explore an upcoming concept or skill set. The second type is the interest center. This center is designed to increase a student's motivation by providing opportunity to explore topics of interest to the student. In general a center provides students with materials and activities that address a wide range of instructional levels and learning styles. Center activities can vary from structured to open-ended, and promote individual learning toward a defined goal.

In the *Math Trailblazers* classroom, teachers can use centers effectively with talented or gifted students. A teacher may set up learning or interest centers with activities or materials that focus on practice or extension of a core concept or skill. Configuring a center for talented or gifted students is more than just giving them more work. The skillful use of centers permits the teacher to challenge talented or gifted students with content appropriate to their levels of understanding.

Stations. While similar to a center, stations provide a structure in which teachers can assign students to specific areas of the room to complete different tasks. The tasks can be varied according to the ability level of students assigned to that station. Stations invite flexibility in the classroom in that not all students need to go to every station. Stations may also be used sequentially to build desired skills or conceptual understandings.

Teachers in a *Math Trailblazers* classroom may develop stations in which all students are working on the same content but where each station represents a different entry point into the content. For example, at one station, students may work with manipulatives to construct concrete models for problem solving while at another station students might be asked to solve problems using more abstract representations for their solutions. The essential consideration in doing such lesson design is that each station is still focused on the goals of the lesson and of the unit. It is inappropriate to have stations that are limited to more trivial expectations—this interpretation of differentiated lessons has resulted in the propagation of inequities in the classroom.

In grades 3–5, the task and challenge items in the Daily Practice and Problems can be a rich resource for both centers and stations. The items identified as a task are designed to take about 15 minutes to complete, and often expand a concept or provide extra practice on a skill. Challenge items are designed to be more thought provoking and to stretch a student's problem-solving skills.

Tiered Lessons. Using tiered lessons is a differentiation strategy that allows teachers to develop multiple pathways for students to take as they address the same concept or skill. Although much of the content in *Math Trailblazers* is intentionally structured as tiered lessons, understanding how a tiered lesson is structured helps teachers more efficiently and effectively reach the talented or gifted student. Teachers can identify the challenge of each of the defined tiers in a lesson to determine which best meets the learning needs of the students in the classroom (Kingore, 2006; Pierce & Adams, 2005; Kettler & Curliss, 2005; Tomlinson, 1999).

Factors that Influence the Complexity of Tiered Learning Experiences

Degree of Assistance and Support

- Teacher directs instruction
- Teacher as facilitator
- Small group support
- Individual autonomy

Degree of Structure

- Clearly defined parameters
- Open ended

Complexity of Activity or Task

- Process and product are concrete
- Process and product involve abstract thinking

Complexity of Process

- Pacing
- Number and complexity of steps
- Simple to high levels of thinking
- Sophisticated research skills are required

Complexity of Product

- Simple, correct answers
- Varied and complex responses
- Integration of advanced skills and concepts is required

Adapted from Kingore (2006)

While there are several different models for developing a tiered lesson, some general characteristics span them all. The following list, which describes the tiered structure found in *Math Trailblazers* is adapted from Tomlinson (1999); Kingore (2006); and Pierce & Adams (2005).

1. Identify the key concepts, skills, or generalizations that are the focus of the lesson. Ask yourself the following: What do I want students to know and be able to do as a result of this lesson?

2. Think about the students in your classroom. Keep in mind that tiered lessons assume that all children are able to learn the same essential concepts, skills, or generalizations in different ways. The groups of students working at each tier should be flexible depending on the

content, process, and products assigned at each tier. As you define your groups consider the range of readiness in your classroom, as well as the interests, talents, and learning styles of each student.

3. Determine the complexity of the activity along a continuum from least complex to greatest complexity. In other words, will the task challenge your most talented or gifted students, your students working at grade level, or your less advanced students. Once you determine where this activity falls on the continuum you can determine if the task meets the needs of all in your classroom. One example of a lesson's tiered structure is that in the laboratory experiments, the questions are successively more difficult.

4. If you find that this activity does not meet the level of your most talented or gifted student, identify who needs another version of the learning experience.

5. Only when necessary, create a different version of the task to address the learners in your classroom. You will find that different *Math Trailblazers* lessons have different quantities of tiers depending on the concepts and skills.

6. Use appropriate assessment for the lesson. Assessments will vary depending on the tier.

Math Trailblazers was designed with many of its lessons structured according to the characteristics of tiered lessons. Lessons begin by clearly identifying the key content that is the focus for all students. Throughout the lesson students are presented with tasks and questions that allow for multiple solution paths that vary in complexity. The following is an example of a tiered lesson from *Math Trailblazers*.

In the fourth-grade lesson *Perimeter vs. Length,* students explore the relationship between the area and perimeter of a rectangle as the area is increased in a specified way. Students first create the rectangles with square inch tiles. They then record the rectangle on grid paper. This lesson is tiered because students are asked increasingly more complex questions about the area and perimeter of the rectangle. Students are provided multiple entry points to the problems presented. Some students will use the square-inch tiles to build concrete models to represent each figure and count the number of tiles to determine either the area or the perimeter. Other students will create representations of the figures using grid paper and rely on the figures they draw to solve the problem. Still others will begin to use mathematical formulas to find the area or perimeter of the figures as they build them.

Because this lesson is already "tiered," it allows children to access the mathematics in ways that make sense to them and to push their understanding as far as possible. The talented or gifted students engaged in this lesson are likely to apply mathematical formulas to find the area or perimeter of geometric figures. These learners are more likely to see that they can decompose more complex figures into simpler geometric shapes. For example they may decompose a trapezoid into a rectangle and two triangles. These students may also see the relationship between shapes, for example two triangles might make a square. These learners benefit from lessons such as this one that contain challenges that are an integral part of the curriculum.

D. Resources for Teachers

Meeting the needs of all learners in the classroom can be challenging but also very exciting. The *Math Trailblazers* curriculum provides many resources for teachers in the *Teacher Implementation Guide* (TIG). This resource includes information for teachers that explores mathematical concepts and ideas addressed in the curriculum.

To learn more about working with students identified as talented or gifted in the classroom the following websites may be helpful:

National Association for Gifted Children (NAGC) The NAGC has been in existence for more than 50 years. This organization is dedicated to serving professionals who work on behalf of gifted children. NAGC publishes a journal for professionals entitled, Gifted Child Quarterly.
http://www.nagc.org

The Association for the Gifted (TAG) TAG is a special interest group of the Council for Exceptional Children (CEC).
http://www.cec.sped.org

American Association for Gifted Children (AAGC) The AAGC is the oldest organization dedicated to advocacy for gifted children.
http://www.aagc.org

Hoagies Gifted Education Page An extensive listing of conferences, resources, articles, and support for teachers.
http://www.hoagiesgifted.com

References

Assouline, S., and A. Lupkowski-Shoplik. *Developing Mathematical Talent: A Guide for Challenging and Educating Gifted and Advanced Learners in Math.* Prufrock Press, Waco, TX, 2005.

Diezmann, C., and J. Watters. "Catering for Mathematically Gifted Elementary Students." *Math Education for Gifted Students.* S. Jensen and J. Kendrick, eds., pp. 33–46. Prufrock Press, Waco, TX, 2005.

Hiebert, J., T. Carpenter, E. Fennema, K. Fuson, D. Wearne, H. Murray, A. Olivier, and P. Human. *Making Sense Teaching and Learning Mathematics with Understanding.* Heinemann, Portsmouth, NH, 1997.

Kettler, T., and M. Curliss. "Mathematical Acceleration in a Mixed-Ability Classroom." *Math Education for Gifted Students.* S. Jensen and J. Kendrick eds., pp. 83–92. Prufrock Press, Waco, TX, 2005.

Kilpatrick, J, J. Swafford, and B. Findell, eds. *Adding it Up: Helping Children Learn Mathematics.* National Research Council (NRC), Washington, DC, 2001.

Kingore, B. "Tiered Instruction: Beginning the Process." *Teaching for High Potential.* NAGC, winter 2006.

Pierce, R., and C. Adams. "Tiered Lessons." *Math Education for Gifted Students.* S. Jensen and J. Kendrick, eds., pp. 49–60. Prufrock Press, Waco, TX, 2005.

Principles and Standards for School Mathematics. National Council of Teachers of Mathematics, Reston, VA, 2000.

Reed, C. "Mathematically Gifted in the Heterogeneously Grouped Mathematics Classroom." *Math Education for Gifted Students.* S. Jensen and J. Kendrick, eds., pp. 17–31. Prufrock Press, Waco, TX, 2005.

Rotigel, J., and S. Fello. "Mathematically Gifted Students How Can We Meet Their Needs?" *Math Education for Gifted Students.* S. Jensen & J. Kendrick, eds., pp. 3–16. Prufrock Press, Waco, TX, 2005.

Sheffield, L.J., ed. *Developing Mathematically Promising Students.* National Council of Teachers of Mathematics, Reston, VA, 1999.

Shore, B.M., and M.A.B. Delcourt. "Effective Curricular and Program Practices in Gifted Education and the Interface with General Education." *Journal for the Education of the Gifted* 20(2), pp. 138–154, 1996.

Tomlinson, C. *The Differentiated Classroom Responding to the Needs of all Learners.* Association for Supervision and Curriculum Development, Alexandra, VA, 1999.

Wilkins, M.M., J.L. Wilkins, and T. Oliver. "Differentiating the Curriculum for Elementary Gifted Mathematics Students." *Teaching Children Mathematics,* 13(1), pp. 6–13, 2006.

Zaccaro, E. "The Seven Components of Successful Programs for Mathematically Gifted Children." *Teaching for High Potential,* NAGC, winter 2006.

Language in the *Math Trailblazers* Classroom

This section focuses on the use of language while students read, write, speak, and listen in the *Math Trailblazers* classroom. Students' language abilities increase while using a curriculum rich in opportunities to communicate mathematically.

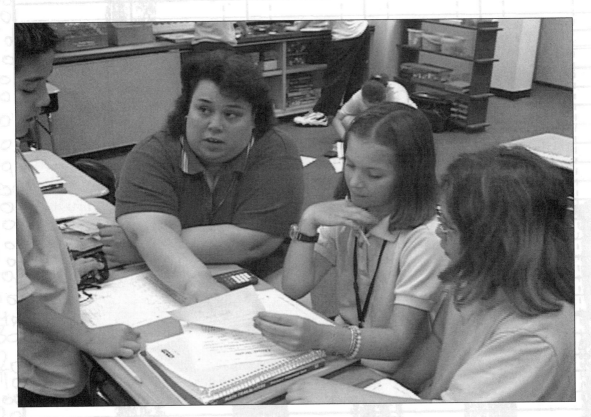

A teacher helps students solidify their understanding of mathematical concepts by listening to their explanations, helping them read the problems, and write their solutions.

Language in the Classroom

Language in the Math Trailblazers Classroom

The use of language—listening, reading, speaking, and writing—is emphasized throughout the *Math Trailblazers* curriculum. This enables students to consider and communicate ideas and solidify their understanding of mathematical concepts. In the past, many mathematics textbooks and lessons limited students' use of language. Parents, administrators, and other teachers may not understand the need for so much reading and writing in a mathematics class. Moreover, getting students to read, write, speak, and listen, while crucial to the learning process, is sometimes a challenge.

This section offers support for developing language use in your classroom. Part I provides a brief rationale of why language is important and how it is used in *Math Trailblazers*. This information is useful in working with colleagues and parents who may not understand the need for reading and writing in mathematics class. Part II provides additional background and support for incorporating language into your daily lessons. Specifically, support is provided on three overlapping areas of language use: reading, writing, and discourse strategies.

Listening, reading, speaking, and writing enable students to consider and communicate ideas and solidify their understanding of mathematical concepts.

Incorporating Language into Mathematics Lessons

Using language to learn mathematics is grounded in learning theory and research. While there are many reasons to incorporate reading, writing, listening, and speaking into mathematics instruction, we discuss issues that may arise when discussing language with parents, administrators, and other teachers.

Reasons to Focus on Language in Mathematics Lessons

Language can help students understand mathematics. The value of studying mathematics is to learn both processes and skills necessary for solving real-life problems. In *Math Trailblazers,* students investigate and solve mathematical problems in real-world contexts. They design accurate and efficient strategies. Discussing possible approaches during the problem-solving process and presenting various solution strategies broadens and deepens students' understanding. It also solidifies their ideas as they learn to use mathematics language.

The context of many mathematics lessons are language-dependent. *Math Trailblazers* uses real-life contexts to develop mathematical concepts in a concrete, visual manner. The contexts actually help students understand math concepts and promote student interest in the math lessons. The contexts provide meaning and concrete examples for thinking about abstract concepts.

Incorporating problem-solving contexts into the lessons, however, requires increased use of language in the text and in implementing of the lesson (through speaking, listening, and writing). For example, second-grade students use the context of a car moving through a neighborhood to develop initial concepts of geometry known as slides, flips, and turns. Without this context, which requires students to both read and listen as they solve the problems, the lesson would not be accessible to all learners. In later grades, these language-dependent contexts provide an opportunity for students to make sense of symbolic representations; e.g., 9×4 becomes 9 groups of 4 boxes, and so on. While tempting to remove the contexts to reduce the language demands, such adaptations interfere with a student's ability to make sense of what they are doing. The contexts also connect ideas within mathematics and between mathematics and their world.

Using language in mathematics results in improved literacy. Some teachers, parents, or principals may believe that the increased use of language interferes with the learning of mathematics. This is most often suggested for English-language learners and students with language-related learning disabilities. While such students may need additional support in interpreting the language in the problem, having a familiar context to ground thinking is more often a support to students, not a hurdle. In addition, English-language learners will only learn the language of mathematics if there is significant use of productive (speaking and writing) and receptive (listening and reading) forms of language. Language use in a mathematics classroom has the benefit of not just improving students' abilities to communicate mathematically, but to communicate in general. Everyday language is improved while using it within the context of math class.

Proficiency in mathematics language is essential for success in mathematics. There are three types of language involved in mathematical discourse. The first is conversational language used for giving instruction, explaining a process, and so on. The second is discrete language used for understanding symbols such as $+$, $-$, $\times$, $\div$, and the words and meaning attached to symbols. The third is mathematical language, which includes terms such as *range, product,* and *sample.* These have definitions specific to mathematics that are different from everyday usage. All three types of mathematical language are important to effectively communicate. Since mathematical language is not often a part of students' experiences outside the mathematics classroom, it is particularly important to make them a regular part of their mathematics learning.

Where Students Encounter Language in the *Math Trailblazers* Curriculum

In *Math Trailblazers,* students engage in all facets of language use including:

- reading introductory vignettes at the start of many lessons,
- explaining the process they used to solve a problem,
- listening to and comparing solution strategies,
- working collaboratively with classmates,
- writing responses to open-ended problems,
- reporting observations either orally or in writing, and
- reading and discussing the trade books and *Adventure Books.*

PART II

Assisting Students with Reading, Writing, and Discourse

Reading

> *Only if students comprehend the text can they begin to understand the problem and engage in doing mathematics.*

Reading Comprehension: Background

George Polya (1973) outlined a 4-step problem-solving process. "Understand the problem" is the first step, followed by devising a plan, carrying out the plan, and looking back. Understanding first involves comprehending the text and then understanding what the mathematics is within the text. If students do not comprehend the text, they can't begin to understand the problem, therefore they cannot engage in doing mathematics. This is true even for reading symbolic expressions as simple as $8 \div 2 = 4$. At the beginning of the problem-solving process, it is important to realize the complexity of reading in mathematics. Mathematics text is different from other text; it is very dense, containing more ideas per sentence than any other type of text (Kenney, 2005). In addition, it can contain words as well as numeric and nonnumeric symbols. Students may have to comprehend illustrations that relate to the text, including tables, graphs, charts, pictures, and coordinate axes. Finally, the syntax of mathematics story problems is different from everyday language. Making these distinctions explicit supports reading comprehension for all students and is absolutely essential for those struggling with language or learning English.

Reading Comprehension: Strategies

The following strategies can increase students' reading comprehension:

1. Help students understand the goal of the lesson. Understanding the lesson's goal helps them with reading comprehension.
2. Find out whether the context is familiar to students. Bring meaning to that context. For example, students may not know the meaning of sampling a population. Ask, "Can you share how you have heard the word 'sampling' used?" Students may report on sampling food, samples of wallpaper or paint, or other experiences. If not, share a personal experience such as when you participated in a survey.
3. Model the process of interpretation through "think aloud." This includes articulating what dilemmas or questions arise as you read and what words and phrases help you figure out what to do.
4. Ask students what difficulties they have understanding the problem. As students try to find words to describe what they don't understand, they often solve the problem themselves. Sometimes, other students offer helpful input.
5. Restate the problem in an interactive manner. Ask students to use the pair-share strategy: one partner tells what the problem is about (e.g., finding volunteers to work at the science fair) and the other partner tells the question they will need to answer (e.g., how many people will be needed).

6. Help students with phrases and their meanings. For example, consider the question: "Which group has twice as many small lids as large lids?" Ask students to think about what that phrase "twice as many . . . as" means and then describe how they know. Add these phrases to a journal or math word wall. Note that this helps students see how the meaning of words are influenced by other words around them. This is very different from a key-word approach, which can result in limited comprehension (see the section on using key words later in this document).

7. Allow students time to read aloud and time to listen to others read aloud. Follow with "What is this question asking you to do?" and "How did you know?" Asking "how" makes explicit the connection between words and mathematical concepts and procedures.

To support students as they read (or listen to) children's books connected to *Math Trailblazers* lessons, we recommend the following strategies:

- Preview or review vocabulary that may be problematic.
- Ask students to predict or summarize story contents.
- Ask questions related to the story, but beyond the discussion prompts.

Grades 1–5 in *Math Trailblazers* each has a series of *Adventure Books,* short stories written like graphic novels (comic book style) or illustrated, connected text. The stories are used to illustrate a math or science concept with children as the problem solvers.

You can share these stories in a variety of ways:

1. Read the story as students follow along.
2. Read the story, then have students read it with a partner.
3. Students read the story with a partner.
4. Assign the story for homework the night before for students to pre-read with family members.
5. Students read the story in a reader's theater format.
6. Record the story and place it in a listening center with accompanying questions for students to answer.

Reading Levels

In any classroom there is a range of reading abilities. While the curriculum is written to be accessible to all students, struggling readers or nonreaders may need additional support. One way is to read the text first as a whole class. Another is to group the nonreaders with the teacher at the start to be sure they understand the text. Heterogeneous grouping can support nonreaders or reluctant readers, especially if you insist that when you visit the group every student can explain the task. The following story demonstrates how one second-grade teacher organized her classroom with reluctant and nonreaders to provide access to all students.

A Classroom Example of Accommodating Different Reading Levels

(This second-grade lesson deals with making a map on the *x*- and *y*-axis with Mr. Origin (a referent object) at the origin of the coordinate plane.)

The room is full of second graders with varying degrees of reading abilities. I had planned the Mr. Origin lab for one class period, but didn't think we would get to the questions about the map. But these kids were wonderful and finished making their maps and measuring with ease. So, since they were in groups, I said to each group as they finished, "Go ahead and start answering the questions about your map."

There were groans, but each group began to read the questions and respond to them. One group put their heads together and answered all the questions. A second group got started but one child asked to be excused for a moment (a nonreader). A third group immediately split into two pairs and began answering questions (but didn't finish). When group 4 was stuck, I asked one boy to read the questions to the group. There was a nonreader in that group and he wouldn't listen to the questions being read. So, I asked him to read. He read the words but obviously couldn't read for meaning (yet). The first boy read it one more time and then the group answered the questions. Before they were finished they had read the question a total of 6 times and then answered the question.

Afterwards, I reflected on the lesson, in particular how the students were able to answer the questions. I thought that pairs might be better than larger groups for tasks involving reading.

I also thought about which child needed to be paired with which child during a reading part of a math lesson. One idea I had was to pull my nonreaders together and read to them before having them work in pairs on the questions.

When I looked at the papers, I found that only two children had not answered all or most of the questions successfully, both nonreaders. I made a mental note that I need to ask each nonreader to respond to me orally to check for understanding.

Working together, the students had helped each other understand the questions and respond to them successfully.

Caution: Key-Word Approach Can Limit Comprehension

Some reading strategies can inhibit learning. In mathematics, the most common is searching the story problem for key words that indicate a specific operation. Research shows that while teachers help identify what are sometimes called "key words" to support student thinking, students use these words to abandon reasoning about the problem (Kenney, Hancewicz, Heuer, Metsisto, Tuttle, 2005; Sowder, 1988). The reasons why a "key-word approach" can be detrimental to comprehension include:

1. Key words often have multiple meanings.
2. The list of key words continues to grow over the years making it difficult to remember.
3. The key words might indicate an operation, but the question may be asking for more than the response to a computation.
4. Key-word search doesn't help students understand the meaning of the problem.
5. For problems involving multiple steps, it doesn't work and students are then ill-prepared to read for understanding. Instead, students need opportunities to find meaning in the reading.
6. Phrases can shift the meaning of words in the phrase. For example "how," "many," and "how many" signify different things in mathematics.
7. Addition of (or removal of) a single letter changes meaning (e.g. "percent of" versus "percent off," "ten" versus "tens").

Appropriate Attention to Key Words

It is important to develop vocabulary that is specific to mathematics. Although, this point may seem to contradict the previous section, there is an important distinction. In the "keyword" approach, students memorize that a word (e.g., difference) means to "subtract" regardless of the content of the sentence; in a precision-of-vocabulary approach, students become familiar with the common phrases (e.g., more than) and relationships among words (e.g., if-then) and how they interact with the rest of the sentence. As a teacher, one way to support student-reading skills is to make explicit some of these vocabulary considerations specific to mathematics. Some common examples of the subtleties in mathematics language follow:

1. Here are two problems using the term *more than,* one requiring subtraction (or counting down) and one requiring addition (or counting up):
   - Jenny has 9 apples. She has 3 *more than* Linda. How many apples does Linda have?
   - Jenny has 9 apples. Linda has 3 *more than* Jenny. How many does Linda now have?
2. Here are two problems in which "by" indicates two different operations:
   - Linda had four cats in her stuffed animal collection. After her birthday, the number of cats *increased by* three. How many cats does Linda have?
   - Linda had four cats in her stuffed animal collection. After her birthday, the number of cats was *multiplied by* three. How many cats does Linda now have?

3. In this example, the operation is the same, but a different response is required for each:
   * The third grade went on a field trip. There are 50 students in the third grade. Twenty students fit on each bus. How many buses were needed?
   * The third grade went on a field trip. There are 50 students in the third grade. Twenty students fit on each bus. How many buses were full?
4. In these statements the key word *of* is used in different ways:
   * What is the area *of* a triangle? (indicating find the space inside)
   * What is one-half *of* 24? (indicating $\frac{1}{2} \times 24$ or $24 \div 2$)
     Find the perimeter *of* the rectangle. (indicating where the perimeter is).

Writing

Writing: Background

The value of having students write in math is quite simply that writing improves learning. Pugalee (2005) explains:

As students write, they manipulate, integrate, and restructure knowledge through using and reflecting on what they know and believe. This process facilitates the development of meaningful understanding: the more a student works with ideas and concepts, the more likely those ideas and concepts will be understood and remembered. (p. xii)

Writing can allow more flexibility in how much time a student has to describe a solution and provides the opportunity for reflection and correction. If students struggle with the words to explain, they can supplement or replace with illustrations. While writing has clear benefits, it is also very challenging. Students are learning to write as they are learning mathematics, so the thought processes are demanding, the precision required in communicating mathematically increases the difficulty of this task, and even students willing to share orally, may be reluctant to share their ideas in writing. Because writing does improve learning, but is difficult, it is essential that students have ample opportunity and support for writing.

Math Trailblazers offers many opportunities for students to write. Just as in a writing lesson, students benefit when they submit a written explanation, receive input from the teacher, and then revise the explanation based on feedback. In the early grades, writing might include a simple process of asking students to tell in words or sentences how many objects they found altogether. Teachers can help primary students learn to write by having them dictate their thinking to an adult or by drawing pictures. Teachers at all grade levels, including kindergarten, should expect students to submit written work, even if the thoughts are incomplete or inaccurate. Students become better writers by writing. As noted earlier, as students improve their writing in mathematics, they improve their writing skills in general. Math class is just one of many situations in which students need to learn effective written communication.

Writing: Strategies

Because writing may be the most difficult literacy skill, it is important to explicitly teach students to write (or illustrate) their work. Here are some ways teachers support student writing:

1. Use and display the *Math Trailblazers* Student Rubrics in grades 3–5. If students have the rubrics in front of them as they work, they will produce better products. If you use a sample, have students collectively respond to whether the sample meets the expectations in the *Telling* or other rubrics. Students will learn how to be more clear and thorough in their writing. For more information on rubrics, see the Assessment section.

TIMS Tip

Post enlargements of the rubrics in the classroom where they are easy to point to and read.

2. Prior to writing, ask students to verbally summarize the important concepts of the lesson. You can even list key points on the board so students can synthesize the information into complete sentences in their own way. Sharing key points can serve as a good review and an opportunity for speaking and reading that further solidifies the concept for students.

3. For students having trouble beginning, sentence starters are a good tool. Another related tool is a graphic organizer with sections where students are prompted to write the question, process, and solution. Some teachers use Polya's (1973) 4-step problem-solving process as a guide, asking students to (1) state the problem, (2) tell what approach they used, (3) explain what solution they got, and (4) tell how their solution answers the original problem.

4. Incorporate creative writing prompts that engage your students. For example, use a genre introduced in language arts, like poetry, fables, or persuasive narratives.

5. Ask students to draw pictures, diagrams or, for older students, concept maps of what they later explain in words. Using pictures can support writing and help you to see what they are trying to explain.

6. Have students keep a math journal of the written summaries of lessons or problems. In this way students can see their improvement in explaining mathematics and have a resource for looking up information they might have forgotten. See the TIMS Tutor: *Journals* for a range of prompts and tips on keeping a math journal.

7. Make a transparency of a well-written response to share with students. To preserve anonymity, use a sample from another class or save samples from year to year.

8. Ask students to fold a paper in half, solve the problem on the first half, and then open the paper and write the steps on the second half.

Regardless of the strategies you use, it is important to remember that the goal is to capture students' ideas and thinking. Creativity and novel solutions are important, and writing opportunities should not impose ways for students to begin or solve a problem.

Language in the Classroom

> *Because* Math Trailblazers *engages students in problem solving and inquiry, there are opportunities for students to approach a problem differently and share different solution strategies.*

Discourse: Background

Those who start teaching with a *Standards*-based curriculum like *Math Trailblazers* often see a change in their classroom discourse. Because *Math Trailblazers* engages students in problem solving and inquiry, there are opportunities for students to approach a problem differently and share different solution strategies. Students learn from hearing others' approaches, and such conversations allow teachers to help students focus on key mathematical ideas. This is different from asking questions to get students to a particular teacher-determined endpoint, a model of questioning often referred to as funneling, where the teacher uses questions to funnel students to a particular formula, approach, or term (Herbel-Eisenmann and Breyfogle, 2005).

Post-exploration discussions are essential to the learning process. As Chapin, O'Conner, and Anderson (2003) write, "When a teacher succeeds in setting up a classroom in which students feel obligated to listen to one another, to make their own contributions clear and comprehensible, and to provide evidence for their claims; that teacher has set in place a powerful context for student learning." (p. 9)

Discourse is not only a concluding activity in a lesson, however, but is important as student work is in progress. This can help stimulate new ideas across working groups. Whitin & Whitin (2000) call this "rough draft thinking" and argue that it allows classmates and the teacher to get a glimpse into other students' thought processes and to revise one's own thinking (p. 220).

Having classroom discourse means establishing norms for how students interact with each other. Hiebert, et al. (1996) describe four critical features of establishing a social culture for learning mathematics, shared in brief here:

Ideas are the currency of the classroom. Ideas, expressed by any participant, have the potential to contribute to everyone's learning and consequently warrant respect and response.

Students have autonomy with respect to the methods used to solve problems. Students must respect the need for everyone to understand their own methods and must recognize that there are often a variety of methods that will do the job.

The classroom culture exhibits an appreciation for mistakes as learning sites. Mistakes afford opportunities to examine errors in reasoning and thereby raise everyone's level of analysis. Do not cover up mistakes; use them constructively.

The authority for reasonability and correctness lies in the logic and structure of the subject, rather than in the social status of participants. The persuasiveness of an explanation or the correctness of a solution depends on the mathematical sense it makes, not on the popularity of the presenter. (pp. 9–10)

Discourse: Strategies

Facilitating discourse improves with practice. As students become more accustomed to explaining their thinking, listening to others, and asking their own questions, knowing what questions you should ask and when to ask them is an important skill. Discourse that "focuses" rather than "funnels" is less predictable and requires skills on your part. Some strategies to support effective discourse include the following:

1. Allot time for students to share and compare strategies and solutions at the end of the lesson, even if it is not the end of the period. It takes time for students to articulate their ideas. If you are running out of time, build it into the next day. Reflecting about the lesson helps children develop an understanding of math concepts and helps you to understand what it is they learned.

2. Shift classroom procedures from general ones like "listen to one another" to specific ones, such as "We need to listen and understand what the speaker is saying. We all have an obligation to ask questions when we don't understand."

3. Focus on the important mathematical concepts in the lesson. If these objectives are written on the board it helps both you and students keep the dialogue focused.

4. Ask good questions. Interesting questions that have answers not already known support good classroom discussions. Use questions that prompt students to listen to each other. For example, "Can you repeat in your own words what you just heard?" "How is this strategy similar to or different from your strategy?" and "What can you add to what was just said?" "Do you agree or disagree with it? Why or why not?" In all cases, the response is neither punitive nor evaluative. If the student who is asked these questions cannot answer, he or she can always ask, "I didn't understand, could you please repeat what was said?" These questions communicate to students that you expect them to listen and learn from each other. Good questions for facilitating discourse are offered in *Professional Standards for Teaching Mathematics* (NCTM, 1991) or can be accessed through Public Broadcasting Service Teacherline.

5. Engage all students in discussion. Participation is not optional. If students are sharing with the whole group, stop at times and ask them to share their thoughts with a partner. Ask students to write an idea on paper or in their journals so they are ready to share.

6. Focus on student understanding. Kenney, et al. (2005) characterize three types of discourse. First, the traditional, in which the teacher and several students talk. Second is a "probing" discussion, where the teacher is still generating the questions, but the questions are more open-ended. Third, is "discourse-rich," where students are working together toward mathematical understanding. An important distinction in the third type is the student-to-student and student-to-class interactions.

7. Decide when to guide students and when to wait, when to ask a student for further elaboration and when to elicit input from others. Quiet pauses should not be uncomfortable dead time, but "think time" for all students to think about what was just said, process it, and then respond.

In addition to these strategies, Easley (1990) offers guidelines for establishing an environment that fosters discourse (see below).

Ten Suggestions for Practice in Communication

From *Dialogue and Conceptual Splatter in Mathematics Classes* by Jack Easley

1. Try to maintain an atmosphere of freedom in the classroom, that is, an atmosphere that encourages students* to feel free to express themselves.
2. When in doubt, remain silent! Give students a chance to work through their mathematical difficulties.
3. Don't paraphrase because paraphrasing is usually a technique for pushing the students too quickly towards the teacher's point of view. Let the students' words stand by themselves. Ask students to clarify the expression of their own thoughts rather than comply with your thoughts.
4. Encourage constructive arguments. For example, ask, "Do you believe that?" "Do you agree or disagree?" "How do you know?" or say, "Tell me what you mean."
5. Play dumb, but avoid condescension. Let the students teach you as well as each other.
6. Don't focus on "right" answers. Alternative answers can create a tension that leads to lively and fruitful interaction. In addition, many good problems have more than one right answer, or at least more than one possible solution technique.
7. Let students have time to work on a problem as individuals before you ask them to share their thoughts in a small or large group, thereby encouraging each student to get involved in the problem.
8. No best way exists to form small groups. For example, you can group students at random or on the basis of ability levels or of their conflicting opinions.
9. Dialogue groups, whether small or large, can be called "meetings." Take time to model expected etiquette for the meetings.
10. Save the written work of the students to evaluate and substantiate their learning. Record the classroom dialogues on videotapes, audiotapes, and in your own journal of the activities; share these recordings with the students. And finally, bring continuity to the dialogues by basing future sessions on your evaluation of the conceptual splatter that has been expressed. (p. 36)

*Students is used here to replace "pupils," which was used in the original publication.

Arithmetic Teacher by Jack Easley. Copyright 1990 by National Council of Teachers of Mathematics. Reproduced with permission of National Council of Teachers of Mathematics in the format Textbook via Copyright Clearance Center.

For further information on developing a language-rich classroom for English Language Learners, see the Teaching the *Math Trailblazers* Student: Meeting Individual Needs section.

References

Assessment Standards for School Mathematics. National Council of Teachers of Mathematics, Reston, VA, 1995.

Burrill, G. "Changes in your Classrooms: From the Past to the Present to the Future." *Mathematics Teaching in the Middle School,* 4(3), pp. 184–190, 1998.

Chapin, S.H., C. O'Conner, and N.C. Anderson. *Classroom Discussions: Using Math Talk to Help Students Learn.* Math Solutions Publications, Sausalito, CA, 2003.

Cummins, J. "Supporting ESL Students in Learning the Language of Mathematics." *Research Says: Issues and Trends in Mathematics.* Pearson Education, New York, 2007.

Cuoco, A., E.P. Goldenberg, and J. Mark. "Habits of Mind: An Organizing Principle for Mathematics Curricula." *Journal of Mathematical Behavior,* 15, pp. 375–402, 1996.

Curriculum and Evaluation Standards for School Mathematics (1st ed.). National Council of Teachers of Mathematics, Reston, VA, 1989.

Easley, Jack. "Research into Practice. Dialogue and Conceptual Splatter in Mathematics Classes." *Arithmetic Teacher,* 37(7), pp. 34–37, 1990.

Galima, L., and T. Hirsch. "Making Mathematics Accessible to English Learners." Paper presented at the National Council of Teachers of Mathematics (NCTM) annual meeting, Atlanta, GA, March 2007.

Herbel-Eisenmann, B.A., and M.L. Breyfogle. "Questioning our Patterns of Questioning." *Mathematics Teaching in the Middle School,* 10(9), pp. 484–489, 2005.

Hiebert, J., et al. *Making Sense: Teaching and Learning Mathematics with Understanding.* Heinemann, Portsmouth, NH, 1997.

Kenney, J.M., E. Hancewicz, L. Heuer, D. Metsisto, and C.L. Tuttle. *Literacy Strategies for Improving Mathematics Instruction.* Association for Supervision and Curriculum Development, Alexandria, VA, 2005.

McIntosh, M.E. "500 Writing Formats." *Mathematics Teaching in the Middle School,* 2(5), pp. 354–358, 1997.

Polya, G. *How to Solve It: A New Aspect of Mathematical Method.* Princeton University Press, Princeton, NJ, 1973.

Principles and Standards for School Mathematics. National Council of Teachers of Mathematics, Reston, VA, 2000.

Professional Standards for Teaching Mathematics. National Council of Teachers of Mathematics, Reston, VA, 1991.

Pugalee, D.K. *Writing for Mathematical Understanding.* Christopher Gordon Publishers Norwood, MA, 2005.

Sowder, L. "Children's Solutions of Story Problems." *Journal of Mathematical Behavior* 7, pp. 227–238, 1988.

Van de Walle, J.A. *Elementary and Middle School Mathematics: Teaching Developmentally.* Pearson Education, New York, 2007.

Whitin, D.J., and P. Whitin. "Exploring Mathematics Through Talking and Writing." M.J. Burke, and F.R. Curcio, eds. *Learning Mathematics for a New Century: 2000 Yearbook,* pp. 213–222. NCTM, Reston, VA, 2000.

Wood, T. "Alternative Patterns of Communication in Mathematics Classes: Funneling or Focusing?" H. Steinbring, M.B. Bussi, and A. Sierpinska, eds. *Language and Communication in the Mathematics Classroom,* pp. 167–178. NCTM, Reston, VA, 1998.

Working with *Math Trailblazers* Parents and Families

The Parents and *Math Trailblazers* section provides suggestions and tips to help parents participate in their child's understanding of *Math Trailblazers* and to enhance its benefits for their children.

A teacher, student, and parent work together to solve a problem.

Working with *Math Trailblazers* Parents and Families

 PART I | ## *Math Trailblazers* Features

Parents' understanding and support of your mathematics curriculum plays an important role in its successful implementation and can be a key factor in children's success with mathematics. This section provides suggestions and tips to help parents understand the *Math Trailblazers* curriculum. It is arranged in three parts. The first part describes several built-in features to help you communicate with parents. The second part gives advice on preparing two types of special programs: math nights for families and parent presentations at school or district meetings. The third part provides blackline masters to copy and distribute to parents.

Parents want assurances that the content and approaches of the school's mathematics program will not only educate and interest their children now, but also benefit them later when test scores and school admissions become serious realities. Most adults experienced a mathematics curriculum that focused almost exclusively on teaching facts and standard procedures for computing. In contrast, *Math Trailblazers* maintains a careful balance between developing skills, underlying mathematical concepts, and problem solving. Parents need to understand this balance. Moreover, parents must understand the importance of teaching the other mathematics strands (algebra, geometry, measurement, and data analysis and probability). As you work with parents throughout the year, communicate the following:

> *Parents need to understand the careful balance that* Math Trailblazers *maintains between developing skills, underlying mathematical concepts, and problem solving.*

- Varied contexts for solving problems in *Math Trailblazers* help children learn to use mathematics in meaningful ways;

- The activities in *Math Trailblazers* are designed to provide children with the skills they will need in the workplace of the 21st century.

- Current research supports the approaches used in *Math Trailblazers* for teaching mathematics. In regard to computation and facts, the approaches in *Math Trailblazers* allow students to gain fluency with less drill and memorization than former methods and with better retention;

- Practice with skills and procedures is distributed between homework, Daily Practice and Problems, and within most problem-solving activities in the program;

- *Math Trailblazers* encourages students to develop varied ways to solve problems—not just the solutions that adults might select; and

- Mathematical ideas are represented with manipulatives, pictures, tables, graphs, and numbers—and how these representations allow children to access the mathematics in varied ways.

Communicating with Parents

Gaining parent support early will save effort in the long term. Anticipate potential parental concerns about a new math program and address them proactively through an ongoing parent education effort.

Math Trailblazers includes a parent brochure, letters home, homework notes, and parent information blackline masters to help you communicate about the curriculum.

Parent Brochure

The parent brochure provides an introduction to the curriculum. Blackline masters of this brochure (in English and Spanish) are at the end of this section. They are designed for you to send home at the beginning of the year or use as a handout at a fall parent meeting.

Letters Home

Parent letters are included at the beginning of each unit to give specific information about what children will study. These letters describe the concepts presented in each unit and how parents or family members can provide follow-up and encouragement at home. A sample Letter Home is shown in Figure 1.

Figure 1: *Sample letter home from Grade 1*

Homework Notes

Many homework assignments, especially in grades K–3, include a separate explanation for family members, outlining the activity's purpose and providing hints for assisting with the assignment. An example of such a note is shown in Figure 2. These explanations are to help parents feel comfortable with the curriculum's content and goals. We encourage you to supplement the parent instructions with your own notes and to provide a way for parents to get their homework questions answered (e.g., via emails, phone, or after school).

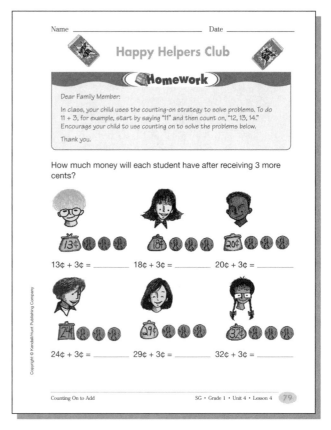

Figure 2: *Sample Grade 1 homework note for parents*

Parent Information Blackline Masters

Additional information on selected topics is available to be copied for parents at the end of this section. Topics include:

• Math Facts Philosophy

• Multiplication Methods in *Math Trailblazers*

• Long Division in *Math Trailblazers*

• Internet Resources for Families of *Math Trailblazers* Students

Roles for Parent Volunteers

Parent volunteers can support the implementation of *Math Trailblazers* in a variety of capacities.

Parent volunteers can be an important support to the implementation of Math Trailblazers in a variety of capacities.

Math Trailblazers incorporates many hands-on activities. In addition to the commercially purchased manipulatives such as base-ten pieces, many activities call for materials such as jars, container lids, paper towel cores, and so on. Parent volunteers can ease the job of gathering and managing these materials.

Parent volunteers also can assist with classroom activities. They can work on special projects or lesson extensions with small groups. Some teachers periodically invite several parents to assist with station activities, where student groups rotate from station to station. Often it is helpful to have an extra set of hands and eyes in the classroom to assist as needed.

Parents can assist students during a lesson. Assign parents to work with particular groups of students or with individual students who need extra assistance. With guidance on appropriate ways to support student thinking, this can be a great support for students, as well as educate parents in the instructional approaches used in *Math Trailblazers*.

You can obviously tailor the roles parents play in providing support to your needs and the interests and capabilities of individual parents. There is little doubt, however, that parent volunteers are a valuable asset as you work with *Math Trailblazers*.

Special Programs for Families and Parents

PART II

One way to help parents understand and support the goals and philosophy of *Math Trailblazers* is to organize special math-related programs for parents and families. One type of program is a math night, during which parents participate in math activities with their children. Another is a more formal presentation given by a teacher or other curriculum leader at a school parent night or special informational meeting. Many schools combine both types of programs by giving a short presentation as part of a math night. The following are suggestions to help you plan parent and family programs for your school.

Family Math Nights

A typical math night involves families coming to school to participate together in math activities. A variety of successful math night formats include:

- **Math Night Carnival**
  Families move from one math activity to another at their own pace. This format is typically held in a large space such as a gymnasium or lunchroom.

- **Teacher-Led Math Night**
  Families visit their child's math classroom and work together through grade-level specific activities and games.

- **Math Night Classroom Rotation**
  Families rotate through a series of classrooms. Each classroom presents a specific math activity or game. Families may encounter activities from a variety of grade levels.

> *One way to help parents understand and support the goals and philosophy of* Math Trailblazers *is to organize special math-related programs for parents and families.*

The best format of any math night differs from school to school and even from year to year within the same school. The following is what happened at one school.

The school invited parents and students to a math night designed as a carnival, held in the gym. Students and parents played a game at each booth and got a prize when they finished. As the evening progressed though, parents congregated in the middle of the gym while their children played the games alone. This event did not meet the goal of getting parents involved with and learning about Math Trailblazers.

The next year, the staff decided to reorganize the math night to keep parents involved in Math Trailblazers *activities with their children. In preparation for the math night, teachers chose primary and intermediate activities and planned them to be held in classrooms. They made a display about the activity that included information on how the activity aligned with the state and NCTM Standards. Teachers also hung estimation activities in the hallways to keep families busy as they moved through the school. As families worked their way from the primary to the middle grades, they saw how the mathematics develops across the grades. Parental involvement on this math night was a big improvement over previous years.*

Suggested Activities
When planning a math night, choose activities that illustrate key ideas from the *Math Trailblazers* curriculum and engage parents. For example, choose activities that focus on problem solving, address a range of mathematical content, or have connections to science.

Doing parts of one of the labs is an effective way for parents to experience how mathematics in the curriculum is embedded in meaningful contexts. Consider using labs you have already done in class. That way, students can lead their parents. Students won't mind repeating the lab, since in many cases, the data will be new to them.

Following is a list of activities that worked well in math night programs. We chose these activities because the concepts underlying them are easily understood, and require minimum preparation. They also show the impact of *Math Trailblazers* work with the scientific method and ways for children to practice computation in a context.

Kindergarten:
- sorting apples from *Data Collection* in the *Ongoing Content* section
- *A Garden's Area,* Month 7 Lesson 4

Grade 1:
- *Pockets* activities in Unit 3 (selected pieces)
- *More or Less Than 100,* Unit 9 Lesson 2

Grade 2:
- *High, Wide, and Handsome,* Unit 4 Lesson 1 (selected pieces)
- *Tile Designs,* Unit 2 Lesson 1
- *Marshmallows and Containers,* Unit 6, Lesson 5 (selected pieces)

Grade 3:
- *First Names,* Unit 1 Lesson 10
- *The Better "Picker Upper,"* Unit 5 Lesson 3
- *Floor Tiler,* Unit 11 Lesson 5

Grade 4:
- *Arm Span vs. Height,* Unit 1 Lesson 5 (selected pieces)
- *Investigating Area and Perimeter,* Unit 2 Lesson 1

Grade 5:
- *Three in a Row,* Unit 8 Lesson 2
- *Factor 40,* Unit 11 Lesson 1
- *Fraction Cover All,* Unit 5 Lesson 3

Tips for Math Nights
The following list of recommendations reflects the experiences of teachers in many different settings. The list is intended to help you make decisions for your own Math Night, but not all may be appropriate in your setting.

- Hold more than one math night, with different grade levels (e.g., K, 1–2, 3–5) grouped together. If you target multiple grades, families with children in different grades can participate together. On the other hand, if you offer grade-level classes, parents can learn more about their child's particular grade.

- Require that students come with an adult. Explain that this is not just a program for children, but a chance for families to enjoy mathematics together.

- If using the teacher-led classroom format, make sure there is enough room for everyone. Some schools divide participants into groups of eight to ten families, so there are about 25 people per class.

- Consider offering babysitting for younger siblings, so parents can devote their attention to their school-age children.

- Ask families to register in advance so you will know how many people to plan for. This also lets you know whether you need further recruitment efforts. However, some schools believe that asking families to register discourages some from attending.

- Involve as many people as you can. Include groups such as the parent-teacher organization. Ask high school students to help as volunteers—some schools offer credit for volunteer service.

- Involve parent volunteers in planning the event and leading the activities. This gives parents a first-hand look at the curriculum and makes the planning more manageable. Parents who are not comfortable leading activities can help with registration, shop for supplies, arrange for food, and babysit.

- Advertise. Send home fliers, have students make invitations for their parents, feature articles in school newsletters, put up posters.

- Offer rewards for coming, such as packages of manipulatives or math games that can be played at home. Offer a reward to the class that has the highest attendance.

- Provide food. Find local sponsors or ask the parent organization for donations of food or beverages.

- Have a raffle. Items can be donated by local businesses. Include information about the raffle in the flyer. Math trade books and gift certificates make great prizes.

- Be sure to try the activities yourself before leading them.

- Use manipulatives in the activities so parents can see how their children use them for meaningful math activities.

- Use one or more of the math facts games to illustrate one way to engage students in practicing math facts.

- Send home a packet of games so families can continue to play at home.

- Hand out an evaluation form to help plan for future programs.

- Have a math day, instead of math night. Parents can visit their children's math classes and stay for lunch. Or set up math stations around the school and have students as tour guides.

Content Note

Getting the most from your work with parents

Just as teachers ask students to reflect on their learning, be sure to ask parents what they learned from any *Math Trailblazers*-related parent activities. Invite parents to think about a question as the final activity. This can help provide insights into what parents have learned, but also provide feedback for the next parent session.

Here are some additional tips for programs that use a carnival or classroom rotation format:

- Hand out "passports." Ask families to get "stamped" at each station and enter their completed passports in a prize drawing.

- If you want participants to spend equal amounts of time at each station, then plan a second activity or open-ended task at short stations.

- Include stations that feature brief sessions on various aspects of *Math Trailblazers,* for example, how to use strategies to learn math facts, the TIMS Laboratory Method, and so on.

Other Resources for Planning Math Nights

- *Family Math* is an excellent resource for planning a math program for families. It describes stimulating math games and activities for a series of classes in which parents and children participate together. Included are an early childhood book and a K–8 book, and translations into Spanish. The goals of *Family Math* complement the goals of *Math Trailblazers* and as a result, parents who participate in *Family Math* are likely to have a good understanding of the approach used in *Math Trailblazers.* Whether you plan a one-night event to introduce *Math Trailblazers* or a longer series of classes, *Family Math* gives practical advice to help you plan. It also has useful handouts on topics such as math and careers that are interesting to families. For more information about the program, including training for Family Math workshop leaders, or to order a book, contact:

  Family Math
  Lawrence Hall of Science
  University of California at Berkeley
  Berkeley, CA 94720-5200
  www.lhs.berkeley.edu/equals

- As part of their continued professional development and support for *Math Trailblazers* users, Kendall/Hunt Publishing Company offers assistance in planning math nights tailored to the needs of your school. You may contact them at 1-800-542-6657.

Presentations to Parents

Since the *Math Trailblazers* program is different from what is familiar to most parents and grandparents, curriculum presentations and the reasons your school selected it can help build support. These range from formal presentations at district-wide or school-wide meetings to less formal discussions at classroom parent nights. Some schools hold monthly meetings that focus on different grade levels or different topics. Others schedule one district-wide or school-wide presentation that gives an overview of the program. Suggestions of topics to include in a presentation are discussed below. Additional resources for preparing your presentation are at the end of this section.

> **Suggested Topics for a Parent Presentation**
> - Description of *Math Trailblazers*
> - Your District's Implementation
> - A Closer Look
> - Computation and Math Facts in *Math Trailblazers*

Description of *Math Trailblazers*

The following are ways to describe *Math Trailblazers*. For further elaboration, see the Foundations section.

- *Math Trailblazers* is a *Standards*-based curriculum. It follows the recommendations of the *Principles and Standards for School Mathematics,* developed by the National Council of Teachers of Mathematics (NCTM, 2000) to improve the teaching and learning of mathematics. These recommendations outline a vision for school mathematics that includes:
  - a mathematically challenging curriculum that covers a broad range of mathematical content;
  - a strong focus on engaging students in mathematical problem solving;
  - instruction that is conceptually oriented and stresses thinking, reasoning, and the application of appropriate uses of calculators and computers; and
  - a strong commitment to promoting success in mathematics among all students—not only those who traditionally do well.

- *Math Trailblazers* is a research-based curriculum. The first edition was the result of more than six years of work by the Teaching Integrated Math and Science Project (TIMS) at the University of Illinois at Chicago, including extensive pilot- and field-testing of the materials. In developing *Math Trailblazers,* the authors drew upon research findings from a wide variety of sources, as well as from the broad experiences of the authoring group, which included mathematicians, scientists, and former teachers. The National Science Foundation funded development of *Math Trailblazers* and has continued to support research on the impact of *Math Trailblazers* on student achievement and research-based development of revised editions.

- *Math Trailblazers* is a problem-solving curriculum. A fundamental principle is that mathematics is best learned through active involvement in solving real problems. Problem solving in *Math Trailblazers* is not a distinct topic, but one that permeates the entire program, providing a context for students to apply the mathematics they know and learn new

> *Since the* Math Trailblazers *program is different from what parents and grandparents are familiar with, presentations about the curriculum and the reasons your school selected it can help build support.*

mathematics. For example, in a third grade laboratory experiment, *The Better "Picker Upper,"* students investigate which paper towel is more absorbent. They explore the absorbency of various brands of paper towels by dropping water onto each and comparing the areas of the resulting spots. In the process, they learn about area, fractions, averaging, and computation. As students work on problems such as these, they develop skills, procedures, and concepts.

- *Math Trailblazers* is a full mathematics curriculum, with a focus on science and language arts. It uses science as a context for much of the problem solving built into the program. In Kindergarten students collect and analyze data at least once every week, and in each of grades 1–5, students engage in eight to ten laboratory investigations that serve as a rich source of real-world mathematics problems. In these investigations, students identify variables, draw pictures, take measurements, organize data in tables, graph data, and look for and use patterns—all important mathematics skills that are used by scientists. *Math Trailblazers* also focuses on language arts, with lessons that emphasize reading, writing, and oral communication. Collections of original math-related stories are found in the *Math Trailblazers Adventure Book*. Math trade books are recommended to accompany many lessons.

Your District's Implementation of *Math Trailblazers*

Include some of the following as you discuss your district's implementation:

- **Selection process.** Assure parents that a careful and thoughtful process was used to select the curriculum. Consider inviting a representative from the selection committee to describe the process.

- **Reasons for choosing *Math Trailblazers* over other curricula.** Describe the features of the program that appeal to the selection committee. How does *Math Trailblazers* help meet the goals of your school? If your district pilot-tested the curriculum before adoption, discuss feedback from teachers who have piloted the program. Invite one or more of those teachers to share their experiences.

- **Professional development.** Explain the program your district has in place to assure that teachers are trained to use the curriculum effectively. Describe the professional development opportunities teachers have had or will have to support their implementation.

- **Evidence of success.** If your district has used the program for a few years, describe teacher and student experiences with it. If you are new to the program, report on some of the experiences of other districts. Information on the success of *Math Trailblazers* around the country is available on the Kendall/Hunt web site, http://www.kendallhunt.com/mtb3.

- **Examples of what students are doing.** A good way to communicate to families that their children are learning more than just computational skills is to show examples of student work. Pick samples that illustrate how students solve complex multistep problems.

A Closer Look at *Math Trailblazers*

To help parents understand some of the strengths of *Math Trailblazers,* show them examples of specific lessons. If possible, ask them to solve a problem or play a game so they can experience firsthand the problem-solving approach to *Math Trailblazers.* Debrief from the activity in the way that you would with students. Ask parents to reflect on the lesson's content, how it compares to their experience, and what this means in terms of opportunities for students to learn. Consider using student work to show the kinds of problems *Math Trailblazers* students solve. Use work collected from your own students or samples available in the *Math Trailblazers* support material.

One source of student work examples is a component of *Math Trailblazers* called the Teacher Enhancement Resource Modules (TERMs). The TERMs were designed to help staff developers assemble workshops for teachers, but portions can also be presented to parents. They contain a guide for presenters with blackline masters, explanatory text, and discussion questions and answers. A set of TERMs is usually available in each district. Check with your principal or district office or call Kendall/Hunt at 1-800-KH-Books.

Most TERMs also include videos showing *Math Trailblazers* teachers and students engaged in activities from the curriculum. These streaming videos are available through the Kendall/Hunt website, mymathtrailblazers.com. Check with your principal or district office for information on how to access these resources.

Another source of appropriate sample student work, video, and explanatory text are from a grade 2 activity, *Measuring Volume.* This source contains a selection of relevant text, blackline masters, and the video you can use to develop a presentation for parents. These materials are available on the web, www.mymathtrailblazers.com.

The following are modules that can be adapted for use with parents (found in TERMS Set #1):

- **Why Reform?**
  This TERM presents information to introduce *Standards*-based mathematics. It includes a video *How Many in the Bag?* that shows students talking with their partners about their solutions to subtraction problems that arise from pulling handfuls of cubes from a bag. The interaction of the students talking about the problems shows how communication helps students clarify their thinking, correct mistakes, and hear different strategies from fellow students.

  A selection of text, blackline masters, and the video of one TERM, *Why Reform?* is available for download at www.mymathtrailblazers.com

- **Operations: Meaning, Invention, Efficiency, Power**
  Use this TERM to help guide the discussion of how the concept of division develops across grades K–5 and to describe the *Math Trailblazers* philosophy of computation. This TERM also shows how this philosophy applies to the development of other operations and to teaching the math facts.

- **Area: A Look Across the Grades**

  Use the *Area* TERM to help parents see how science is a rich context for applying and learning mathematics. This TERM includes representative area activities from each grade to show growth in mathematics and development of the concept of area through the grades.

- **Computation and Math Facts in *Math Trailblazers***

  Many parents think of computation when they think of mathematics, so it is natural for them to be curious about the way *Math Trailblazers* teaches computation. Explain that a balanced approach fosters the development of both mathematical concepts and skills. The following points might be useful in talking with parents about computation and basic math facts.

  1. Computation. In today's world, students compute using paper-and-pencil algorithms, calculators, and mental arithmetic. They need to get exact answers to problems as well as make and recognize reasonable estimates. *Math Trailblazers* helps students develop efficient and accurate methods for computation with the four basic operations. The treatment of each operation proceeds in the following stages:

     - Developing meaning for the operation

     - Inventing procedures for solving problems

     - Becoming more efficient at carrying out procedures

     - Developing mathematical power

  2. "Mathematical power" means that students understand when to apply the operation and how to use varied computational methods to solve problems. Students practice using the operations in activities, games, and laboratory investigations. More practice is provided in the Daily Practice and Problems in Grades 1–5 and in the Home Practice in Grades 3–5. Flexible thinking and mathematical power are our goals. The above computation stages are discussed more thoroughly in the Math Facts and Whole-Number Operations section.

  3. The paper-and-pencil algorithms for multiplication and long division taught in *Math Trailblazers* are probably somewhat different from those that parents learned in school. We introduce the "all-partials method" for multiplication first since many children find it easier to learn. Then we introduce the more efficient "compact method," the algorithm traditionally taught. (See Figure 3.)

All-Partials Method	Compact Method
15	15
× 22	× 22
10 (2 × 5)	30 (2 × 15)
20 (2 × 10)	+ 300 (20 × 15)
100 (20 × 5)	330
+ 200 (20 × 10)	
330	

Figure 3: *Paper and pencil algorithms for multiplication*

For division, we teach the "forgiving method" because many students find it easier to learn than the traditional method. While this method involves making estimates about the quotient, as does the traditional method, the forgiving method encourages the use of "easy" numbers, such as division by 10 or 100 in the estimates. The forgiving method also allows underestimates so it doesn't involve as much erasing and re-calculating as done by some children when using the traditional method. In the case where the highest possible estimate is made, the two methods are essentially the same. (See Figure 4.) Parent information sheets that describe the multiplication and division algorithms used in *Math Trailblazers* are at the end of this section.

Forgiving Method		**Traditional Method**

335		335
5)‾1675‾	300 (estimate quotient 1675 ÷ 5)	5)‾1675‾
− 1500		− 15
175	30 (estimate quotient 175 ÷ 5)	17
− 150		− 15
25	5 (25 ÷ 5)	25
− 25	‾‾‾‾	− 25
0	335	0

Figure 4: *Paper and pencil algorithms for division*

4. Math Facts. The goal of the *Math Trailblazers* math facts program is for students to learn the basic facts efficiently, gain fluency with their use, and retain that fluency over time. A large body of research supports an approach that is built on a foundation of work with strategies and concepts. This leads not only to more effective learning and better retention, but also to the development of mental math skills.

The *Math Trailblazers* math facts program is characterized by the elements below. These are summarized in the *Math Facts Philosophy* Blackline master at the end of this section.
- Early emphasis on problem solving
- Use of strategies to find facts and the de-emphasis of rote work
- Gradual and systematic introduction of the facts
- Ongoing practice
- Appropriate assessment
- Facts are not gatekeepers
- Multiyear approach

As you discuss the math facts program, give parents a few examples of math fact strategies such as the subtraction strategies of "counting up" and "using a ten." Other strategies are discussed in the *Math Facts* Tutor. This tutor is available to parents on the Kendall/Hunt website, as are several other TIMS Tutors.

Other Resources for Planning Your Presentation

The *Family* section of the Kendall/Hunt Website http://www.mymath trailblazers.com has several links to documents that can help you plan your presentation. Here are a few:

- *An Introduction for Families* includes answers to the following questions:
    What is in the *Math Trailblazers* curriculum?
    What is a *Math Trailblazers* classroom like?
    What connections does *Math Trailblazers* make with other school subjects?
    Why is my child using calculators with *Math Trailblazers?*
    How can parents talk with their children about math?

- *Frequently Asked Questions* includes answers to the following questions:
    How is *Math Trailblazers* different from other mathematics curricula?
    What is the opinion of the scientific community regarding the standards set by the National Council of Teachers of Mathematics?
    What science does *Math Trailblazers* include?
    How does *Math Trailblazers* integrate mathematics with other content areas?
    What kind of assessment does *Math Trailblazers* use?
    Does *Math Trailblazers* make use of collaborative learning?
    Can *Math Trailblazers* facilitate teaching children with learning styles and ability levels in a heterogeneous classroom?

Additional resources for working with parents include:

Stenmark, Jean Kerr, Virginia Thompson, and Ruth Cossey. *Family Math.* University of California, Lawrence Hall of Science, Berkeley, CA, 1986.

Funkhouser, J.E., and M.R. Gonzales. *Family Involvement in Children's Education: Successful Local Approaches: An Idea Book.* U.S. Department of Education, Washington, DC, 1997. http://www.ed.gov/pubs/FamInvolve/

Shartrand, A.M., H.B. Weiss, H.M. Kreider, and M. Lopez, *New Skills for New Schools: Preparing Teachers in Family Involvement.* Harvard Graduate School of Education, Harvard Family Research Project, Cambridge, 1997. (Available from the U. S. Department of Education http://www.ed.gov/pubs/NewSkills/index.html.)

Mira, A. *A Family's Guide: Fostering your Child's Success in School Mathematics.* National Council of Teachers of Mathematics, Reston, VA, 2005.

National Council of Teachers of Mathematics Families Web page, http://nctm.org/resources/families.aspx

 PART III

Parent Information Blackline Masters

- Parent Brochure (English and Spanish versions)
- Math Facts Philosophy
- Multiplication Methods in *Math Trailblazers*
- Long Division in *Math Trailblazers*
- Internet Resources for Families of *Math Trailblazers* Students

Math Trailblazers™

A Mathematical Journey Using Science and Language Arts

An Introduction for Families

A TIMS® Curriculum from the University of Illinois at Chicago

Published by Kendall/Hunt Publishing Company

How can parents talk with their children about math?

Your child will have a lot to share with you about mathematics. Here are some conversation starters to help your child communicate what he or she is doing in mathematics:

☞ What problems did you solve in math today? How did you solve the problems? Are there other ways to solve that same problem?

☞ Did you use any special materials in math today? What were they? How did you use them?

☞ Did you measure anything in school today? What did you measure?

☞ Did you collect data in math today? How did you record the data?

☞ Did you hear a math story today? Please tell me the story.

> "One of the things I've noticed … is that when he [my child] brings home an activity and he brings a measuring tape or something kind of special, he's excited about doing it. The fact that we're involved in the games—he loves that—and he's proud of what he's doing."
>
> **Parent**

You can contact the developers of *Math Trailblazers* at the following address:

 UIC The University of Illinois at Chicago

TIMS Project
Institute for Mathematics and Science Education (M/C 250)
950 South Halsted Street, Room 2075 SEL
Chicago, IL 60607-7019
www.math.uic.edu/IMSE

 KENDALL/HUNT PUBLISHING COMPANY
4050 Westmark Drive   Dubuque, Iowa   52002
www.mathtrailblazers.com

Development of *Math Trailblazers* was supported in part by the National Science Foundation.

What connections does *Math Trailblazers* make with other school subjects?

> "It seems a lot of this carries over to different subject areas. It's not just isolated to math."
>
> **Teacher**

In *Math Trailblazers*, children learn mathematics, in part, by applying it in many different contexts. This makes mathematics meaningful for students and models the way mathematics is used outside of school.

Science investigations are used often in *Math Trailblazers* to provide a context for learning and applying mathematics. Children design experiments; collect, organize, and graph data; and analyze experimental results in much the same way scientists do. Measurement of length, area, volume, mass, and time is done repeatedly within the context of scientific experiments. This strong connection with science engages students in rich problem-solving activities and introduces students to the tools and methods scientists use.

Math Trailblazers also has many connections with language arts—communication of math ideas in writing and orally is an integral part of every lesson. Children write journal entries, record data, and share ideas. They also read children's books and *Math Trailblazers* Adventure Books that connect with many class lessons. As children communicate their methods for solving problems and justify their answers, they better understand important math concepts. Their writing and other communication skills also improve.

Why is my child using calculators with *Math Trailblazers*?

The calculator is a tool used in appropriate situations to help your child explore number ideas and relationships, solve more complex problems, and explore mathematics on his or her own. The use of calculators is supported by the National Council of Teachers of Mathematics.

A curriculum for your children

The mathematics curriculum being taught in many schools today is very similar to the curriculum that was taught when the parents, grandparents, and even great-grandparents of today's school children attended school. Many of the math skills in that curriculum remain important today. But the world has changed considerably since the time of our grandparents. Advances in technology have created many other essential math skills that your children will need when they complete their formal schooling and enter tomorrow's work force. The National Council of Teachers of Mathematics recognized these needs when, in 1989 and 2000, it made a series of recommendations for updating math instruction in U.S. schools. *Math Trailblazers* was developed to reflect these national recommendations.

Math Trailblazers will prepare students to:

★ know and apply basic math skills;

★ solve problems using many different strategies;

★ be independent thinkers;

★ reason skillfully in diverse situations;

★ effectively communicate solutions to problems and methods for solving them;

★ work alone and in groups to solve problems.

Math Trailblazers was developed and tested over a seven-year period by a team from the Teaching Integrated Mathematics and Science (TIMS) Project at the University of Illinois at Chicago. Using the results of educational research and over 15 years of previous experience in curriculum development, the TIMS Project has written an innovative program that will prepare your children with math skills needed for the 21st century.

What is in the *Math Trailblazers* curriculum?

Math Trailblazers is a comprehensive curriculum that maintains a balance between the development of math concepts and basic skills. Students apply basic math skills while working on meaningful and challenging tasks. The math content of the traditional math curriculum is studied; but other topics—estimation, geometry, measurement, patterns and relationships, algebra concepts, and statistics and probability—are investigated at an appropriate level in each grade.

The curriculum includes different types of lessons:

Activities—explorations of math concepts and skills that use a variety of tools and methods.

Labs—extended investigations that use a simplified version of the method scientists use.

Daily Practice and Problems—items that provide practice in math skills and concepts.

Games—math games that build familiarity with math skills and concepts.

Adventure Books—illustrated stories that deal with math and science ideas.

Assessments—activities that allow the teacher and student to assess progress.

> "When my older daughter started out, she didn't feel confident with math. And now that she's had *Math Trailblazers*, she says that she's good at math. I feel good about that."
> **Parent**

What is a *Math Trailblazers* classroom like?

When you walk into your child's *Math Trailblazers* class, you will probably notice that it does not look like the mathematics classroom you experienced when you were your child's age. Children might be working in groups, rolling cars down ramps, dropping water onto paper towels, or pulling jellybean samples from bags. As they work, children discuss different ways to solve problems. The room is filled with a feeling of excitement and discovery.

In a *Math Trailblazers* classroom, children are:

☆ learning mathematics by using it to solve many different kinds of problems;

☆ drawing on their own experiences and working with real-world problems;

☆ using concrete objects to understand abstract mathematical concepts;

☆ communicating mathematical ideas to their peers and teacher;

☆ gaining confidence in mathematics and developing an "I can do it" feeling.

> "I just love walking into a classroom when you see kids all over the room doing their data gathering. Some of them are on the floor measuring this or working with that or asking questions. It is so exciting to see children engaged in this kind of math discovery."
> **Elementary School Principal**

Math Trailblazers™*

Una Aventura en Matemáticas usando Ciencias y el Arte de Lenguaje

Una Introducción para Familias

Desarrollando por el Proyecto de TIMS—Teaching Integrated Mathematics and Science— (Integrando la Enseñanza de las Matemáticas y de las Ciencias) de la Universidad de Illinois en Chicago

Publicado por Kendall/Hunt Publishing Company

* Abriendo un camino de matemáticas

¿Qué es lo que los padres de familia pueden hacer?

Su hijo/a tendrá mucho que compartir con usted acerca de matemáticas. Aquí hay algunos temas para iniciar conversaciones que ayudarán a su hijo/a a que él o ella comunique lo que usted esté haciendo en matemáticas.

☞ ¿Qué problema resolviste el día de hoy en tu clase de matemáticas? ¿Cómo lo resolviste? ¿Hay alguna otra forma de resolver ese mismo problema?

☞ ¿Utilizaste algunos materiales especiales en tu clase de matemáticas? ¿Qué eran? ¿Cómo los usaste?

☞ ¿Mediste hoy algo en la escuela? ¿Qué fue lo que mediste?

☞ ¿Acumulaste algunos datos en matemáticas? ¿Cómo registraste esos datos?

☞ ¿Escuchaste alguna historia en matemáticas? Por favor cuéntame la historia.

> "Una de las cosas que he notado... es que cuando él [mi hijo] trae una actividad a la casa y trae una cinta métrica o algo especial, está emocionado para hacerlo. El hecho que nosotros estamos enredados en los juegos—le encanta—y está orgulloso de lo que está haciendo."
>
> **Un padre de familia**

Se puede comunicar con los diseñadores de *Math Trailblazers* a la siguiente dirección:

UIC The University of Illinois at Chicago

TIMS Project
Institute for Mathematics and Science Education (M/C 250)
950 South Halsted Street, Room 2075 SEL
Chicago, IL 60607-7019
www.math.uic.edu/IMSE

 KENDALL/HUNT PUBLISHING COMPANY
4050 Westmark Drive Dubuque, Iowa 52002
www.mathtrailblazers.com

 El desarrollo de *Math Trailblazers* fue ayudado en parte por la National Science Foundation.

¿Qué conexiones hace Math Trailblazers con otras materias escolares?

En *Math Trailblazers*, los estudiantes aprenden matemáticas, en parte, aplicándolo a diversas situaciones. De esta manera las matemáticas se hacen interesantes y adquieren sentido.

Investigaciones científicas en *Math Trailblazers* proveen la oportunidad frecuente de la aplicación de las matemáticas. Los estudiantes diseñan experimentos; acumulan y organizan datos; hacen gráficas de datos; y analizan los resultados de los experimentos en una manera semejante a lo que hacen los científicos. Se hacen mediciones de longitud, área, volumen, masa, y tiempo como parte de experimentos científicos. Esta fuerte conexión con la ciencia hace que los estudiantes resuelvan problemas como "científicos," usando métodos y herramientas de las ciencias.

Math Trailblazers también tiene muchas conexiones con el arte de lenguaje. La comunicación de ideas en matemáticas—a través de escribir, hablar, y dibujar—es una parte integral de cada lección. Los estudiantes escriben en sus diarios, registran datos, y comparten ideas. Ellos también leen libros infantiles y "libros de aventuras" que se conectan con muchas lecciones. Los estudiantes mejoran en su entendimiento de conceptos matemáticos al comunicar sus métodos de resolver problemas y explicar sus respuestas. Sus habilidades en escribir y comunicar también mejoran.

¿Por qué mi hijo/a está usando calculadoras en Math Trailblazers?

Las calculadoras son instrumentos usados para ayudar a su hijo/a a investigar ideas con números y sus relaciones, resolver problemas complejos, y explorar la matemática. El uso de estas herramientas es recomendado por el Concejo Nacional de Maestros de Matemáticas.

Un programa para sus hijos

Los programas de matemáticas que se encuentran hoy día en muchas escuelas son muy semejantes a las clases que tenían los padres, abuelos, y aún bisabuelos de los estudiantes de hoy. Mucha del material de esos programas todavía se necesita hoy. Pero el mundo ha cambiado desde el tiempo de nuestros abuelos. Avances en tecnología han creado la necesidad de desarrollar otras técnicas especiales que sus hijos necesitarán en el mundo de trabajo del futuro. El Concejo Nacional de Maestros de Matemáticas reconoció estas necesidades cuando hizo una serie de recomendaciones para mejorar la enseñanza de matemáticas en las escuelas de los Estados Unidos. Hemos desarrollado el programa *Math Trailblazers* para incorporar esas recomendaciones nacionales.

Math Trailblazers preparará estudiantes para:

★ aprender y usar técnicas básicas en matemáticas;

★ resolver problemas usando varias estrategias diferentes;

★ pensar independientemente;

★ razonar con habilidad en diversas situaciones;

★ comunicar efectivamente tanto las soluciones como los métodos;

★ resolver problemas trabajando solos y en grupos.

El programa *Math Trailblazers* fue desarrollado y ensayado por un equipo del Proyecto de TIMS—Teaching Integrated Mathematics and Science—(Integrando la Enseñanza de las Matemáticas y de las Ciencias) de la Universidad de Illinois en Chicago. Han creado un programa innovativo que proveerá a sus hijos con los bases matemáticos necesarios para poder competir en el campo del trabajo en el Siglo XXI.

¿Qué hay en el programa *Math Trailblazers*?

El programa *Math Trailblazers* es un programa integral que mantiene un balance entre el desarrollo de los conceptos y las técnicas básicas de matemáticas. Los estudiantes usan las técnicas básicas mientras están trabajando con problemas interesantes y estimulantes. Se estudian los tópicos matemáticos de un programa tradicional; pero también se investigan otras materias—estimación, geometría, medición, patrones y relaciones, conceptos de álgebra, estadística y probabilidad—en un nivel apropiado para los niños.

El programa contiene varios tipos de lecciones:

Actividades—exploraciones de conceptos matemáticos y técnicas usando diferentes herramientas y métodos.

Laboratorios—investigaciones que usan una versión simplificada del método que los científicos usan.

Prácticas y Problemas Diarios—problemas breves que proveen práctica con técnicas y conceptos matemáticos.

Juegos—juegos matemáticos que estimulan familiaridad con técnicas y conceptos matemáticos.

Libros de Aventuras—historietas ilustradas que tratan con conceptos de las ciencias y matemáticas.

Evaluaciones—actividades que permiten al maestro y a los estudiantes evaluar el progreso.

¿Cómo es una clase de *Math Trailblazers*?

Si usted entra a un salón de clases *Math Trailblazers*, probablemente notará que no se parece al que usted asistía cuando tenía esa edad. En ese salón, los niños pueden estar trabajando en grupos, poniendo gotas de agua a toallas de papel, o analizando muestras de confites. Mientras los estudiantes trabajan, ellos discuten diferentes formas para resolver los problemas matemáticos. Se percieve en clases *Math Trailblazers* los sentimientos y la emoción de descubrimiento matemático.

En un salón de estas clases los alumnos están:

☆ aprendiendo matemáticas en la resolución de problemas;

☆ usando experiencias propias y trabajando con problemas verdaderas;

☆ usando objetos concretos para entender conceptos matemáticos abstractos;

☆ comunicando sus ideas de matemáticas a sus compañeros y maestros;

☆ adquiriendo confianza en las matemáticas y desarrollando un sentimiento de, "Yo sí lo puedo hacer."

Math Facts Philosophy

The goal of the math facts strand in *Math Trailblazers* is for students to learn basic facts efficiently, gain fluency with their use, and retain that fluency over time. A large body of research supports an approach in which students develop strategies for figuring out the facts rather than relying solely on rote memorization. This not only leads to more effective learning and better retention, but also to the development of mental math skills. Therefore, the teaching of the basic facts in *Math Trailblazers* is characterized by the following elements:

Use of Strategies. Students first approach the basic facts as problems to solve rather than as facts to memorize. We encourage the use of strategies to find facts, so students become confident that they can find answers to fact problems they do not immediately recall. In this way, students learn that math is more than memorizing facts and rules that "you either get or you don't." (For information on common math fact strategies, see the *Math Facts* Tutor on the *Just for Math Trailblazers Families* page of the Kendall Hunt website http://kendallhunt.com. Click on "K–12," then "Just For Families," then "Math Trailblazers Families." Then scroll down to the list of TIMS Tutors.)

Distributed Facts Practice. Students study small groups of facts they found using similar strategies. They review the facts as they use them to solve problems in labs, activities, and games. In Grades 2–5, students are given flash cards to study each group of facts at home.

Appropriate Assessment. Teachers assess students' knowledge of the facts through observations as they work on activities, labs, and games as well as through the appropriate use of written tests and quizzes. Quizzes follow the study of small groups of facts organized around specific strategies. In Grades 2–5, students take inventory tests of facts at the end of each semester. In grades 3–5, each student records his or her progress on *Facts I Know* charts and determines which facts he or she needs to study.

A Multiyear Approach. In Grades 1 and 2, the curriculum emphasizes strategies that enable students to develop fluency with the addition and subtraction facts. In Grade 3, students gain fluency with the multiplication facts while reviewing the addition and subtraction facts. In Grade 4, the addition and subtraction facts are checked, the multiplication facts are reviewed, and students develop fluency with the division facts. In Grade 5, the multiplication and division facts are systematically reviewed and assessed.

Facts Will Not Act as Gatekeepers. Use of strategies and calculators allows students to continue to work on interesting problems and experiments while learning the facts. Thus students are not prevented from learning more complex mathematics because they do not have quick recall of the facts.

Multiplication Methods in *Math Trailblazers*

As your child learns paper-and-pencil multiplication in *Math Trailblazers,* he or she is introduced to more than one method. The **all-partials method** is introduced first since many children find it easier to learn. Then the more efficient **compact method**—the method traditionally taught in schools in the United States—is introduced. After children work with both methods, they choose which is most comfortable for them. We present both methods below so you will be familiar with them.

Both methods are based on the same idea, but the recording is different. In the all-partials method, every step is written down. In the compact method, some steps are not recorded.

Example 1. Compute 6×73.

In both methods, we break 73 into two parts: $73 = 3 + 70$. Then we multiply each part by 6 and add:

$$6 \times 73 = 6 \times 3 + 6 \times 70.$$

All-Partials Method	**Compact Method**
In this method, every step is written down on separate lines.	In this method, some steps are combined and the answer is recorded on one line.
$$\begin{array}{r} 73 \\ \times\,6 \\ \hline 18 \\ 420 \\ \hline 438 \end{array}$$ (This is 6×3) (This is 6×70)	$$\begin{array}{r} {}^{1} \\ 73 \\ \times\,6 \\ \hline 438 \end{array}$$ (This is $6 \times 3 + 6 \times 70$)
The partial products are recorded in the lines under the multiplication sign, then the lines are added.	The partial products are added as they are recorded: First compute $6 \times 3 = 18$; then write the 8 in the ones' column and carry the 1 into the tens' column (some people write down the carry, others just remember it). Next, compute 6×7 tens $= 42$ tens. Add the 1 that was carried to get 43 tens. Write the 3 in the tens' column and the 4 in the hundreds' column.

Multiplication Methods in *Math Trailblazers (continued)*

Example 2: Compute 73×46.

Again, both methods involve breaking the numbers into two parts and multiplying. Since $46 = 6 + 40$, the product is

$$73 \times 46 = 73 \times (6 + 40)$$
$$= 73 \times 6 + 73 \times 40$$
$$= (6 \times 3 + 6 \times 70) + (40 \times 3 + 40 \times 70)$$

All-Partials Method	Compact Method
In this method, every step is written down on separate lines.	In this method, some steps are combined and recorded on one line.

All-Partials Method

In this method, every step is written down on separate lines.

```
      73
    × 46
      18   (6 × 3)
     420   (6 × 70)
     120   (40 × 3)
    2800   (40 × 70)
    3358
```

The partial products are recorded in the rows under the multiplication sign, then the rows are added.

Compact Method

In this method, some steps are combined and recorded on one line.

```
       73
     × 46
      438   (This is 6 × 73)
     2920   (This is 40 × 73 or 4 tens × 73)
     3358
```

For the first line, compute $6 \times 73 = 438$ as in Example 1.

For the second line, compute $40 \times 73 = 2920$. (Some people omit the 0 in the ones' column because 2920 is 292 tens and no ones. In this case, be sure nothing is written in the ones' column.)

Here are the details for the second line:

$40 \times 73 = 40 \times 3 + 40 \times 70$. First compute $40 \times 3 = 120$; record the 20 tens by writing 2 in the tens' column and 0 in the ones' column, then carry the 1 into the hundreds' column (you can write the carry or just remember it). Next, compute $40 \times 70 = 2800$. That is 28 hundreds. Add the one 1 hundred that was carried to get 29 hundreds. Write the 9 in the hundreds' column and the 2 in the thousands' column.

Finally, add both lines.

Long Division in *Math Trailblazers*

In *Math Trailblazers,* your child will learn a long division method that may be different from the method you learned. We teach the **forgiving method** because many students find it easier to learn than the traditional method. Both methods make estimates about the quotient (the answer to the division problem), but the forgiving method allows underestimates, so it doesn't involve as much erasing and recalculating as the traditional method sometimes does.

As an example, let's divide 95 by 3. Think of dividing 95 objects such as marbles into groups of 3. How many groups will there be? (Or, think of putting the objects into 3 groups. How many will be in each group?)

First, estimate the answer. A good estimate would be 30, but lower numbers would work too. Suppose we choose 20. Then, since $3 \times 20 = 60$, we have taken care of 60 marbles. Subtract 60 from 95 and record the estimate to the right of the problem.

```
  3)95
  - 60  |  20
  -----
    35
```

Now divide the remaining 35 marbles by 3. Let's estimate that $35 \div 3$ is about 10. Since $3 \times 10 = 30$, write

```
  3)95
  - 60  |  20
  -----
    35
  - 30  |  10
  -----
     5
```

Since 3 "goes into" 5 one time, write

```
  3)95
  - 60  |  20
  -----
    35
  - 30  |  10
  -----
     5
   - 3  |   1
  -----
     2
```

Since 3 does not divide 2, there are 2 marbles left over. This is the remainder. Add up the number of 3s we took away: $20 + 10 + 1 = 31$. Thus, 95 divided by 3 is 31 with remainder 2. We write this on top of the problem, as in the traditional division method.

```
    31 R2
  3)95
  - 60  |  20
  -----
    35
  - 30  |  10
  -----
     5
   - 3  |   1
  -----
     2  |  31
```

As students become familiar with the forgiving method, they make better estimates to keep the number of steps at a minimum. Below is another way to do this problem using the forgiving method. Note that this time, making the highest possible estimates (without overestimating) results in the same number of steps as the traditional method. If the highest estimate is made each time, the two methods are essentially the same.

```
    31 R2
  3)95
  - 90  |  30
  -----
     5
   - 3  |   1
  -----
     2  |  31
```

The forgiving method allows students to underestimate as they develop their estimation skills. But, although this method forgives underestimates, overestimates are not forgiven. When students overestimate, they have to erase, just as with the traditional method.

This method can be extended to solve problems with multidigit divisors. However, *Math Traiblazers* students usually use calculators for such problems.

Internet Resources for Families of *Math Trailblazers* Students

Here are several websites that can help families support their children's learning of Mathematics:

Mymathtrailblazers.com Family section

The publisher of *Math Trailblazers,* Kendall/Hunt, maintains a website at http://www.mymathtrailblazers.com to help the families of children using *Math Trailblazers* understand the curriculum. It contains an introduction to the program and a discussion of its research basis, answers to frequently asked questions, glossaries, TIMS Tutors (which provide an in-depth exploration of the mathematical concepts and ideas behind *Math Trailblazers*), homework help, and recommended software and literature lists. Contact Kendall/Hunt regarding granting families access to this site.

NCTM Families Web page

http://nctm.org/resources/families.aspx

The National Council of Teachers of Mathematics (NCTM) Families Web page includes lessons and activities, resources, links to other family sites, as well as brochures that answer questions such as

Why does my child's math look different from the math I remember?

What can I do to make sure my child succeeds in math?

Math homework is due tomorrow—how can I help?

NCTM Illuminations

http://illuminations.nctm.org

This site contains a library of online math activities and interactive tools for students to use to explore, learn, and apply mathematics in the classroom and at home. It also has links to hundreds of online resources that an editorial panel has reviewed and rated as exemplary.

The Math Forum

http://mathforum.org

The Math Forum is a very broad-based website maintained by Drexel University. It has such features as Ask Dr. Math, where students can ask mathematical questions, and an extensive mathematics resource library for students in elementary school through graduate school. Other features include discussion groups, a collection of good problems, teacher resources, and information on issues in mathematics education.

National Library of Virtual Manipulatives for Interactive Mathematics

http://nlvm.usu.edu

Utah State University developed and maintains this web site. It includes an extensive collection of virtual manipulatives and accompanying activities. Students can work interactively with geoboards, pattern blocks, tangrams, base-ten pieces, balance scales, and other materials. This provides the opportunity to work with materials that are perhaps not otherwise available.

Helping Your Child Learn Mathematics http://www.ed.gov/parents/academic/help/math/index.html

This is a downloadable booklet available at the website of the Department of Education that contains "fun activities that parents can use with their children from preschool age through grade 5 to strengthen their math skills and build strong positive attitudes toward math."

Figure This!

http://www.figurethis.org

The Family Corner of the Figure This! website provides math challenges for families. It has downloadable brochures on topics such as Families and School, Families and Math, Families and Homework, and Math and Literature, as well as recommended books. The focus is on families of middle-school students, but much of the advice is appropriate for families of elementary-school students as well.

Manipulatives List

The Manipulatives List outlines all manufactured manipulatives and other materials needed to implement *Math Trailblazers* successfully.

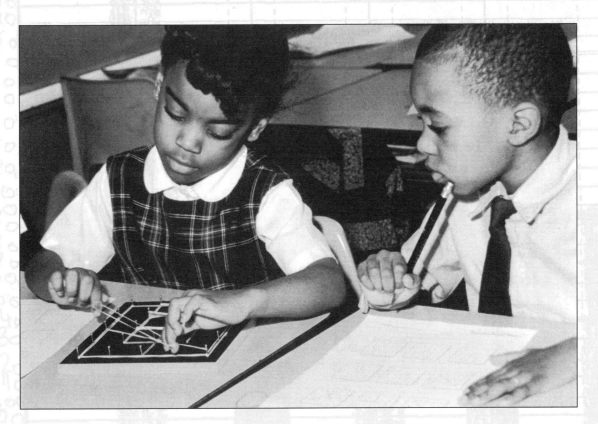

Students explore shapes using geoboards.

Manipulatives List

Following are the manipulatives for fifth grade. There are several categories of manipulatives listed here:

Manufactured Manipulatives: a list of each of the manipulatives needed to implement fully the *Math Trailblazers* curriculum. Many of these manipulatives may be available already in your classroom or school.

Manufactured manipulatives can be purchased:

- in grade-level complete kits from Kendall/Hunt Publishing Company;
- as a customized kit from Kendall/Hunt;
- or individually for your specific needs.

Please contact Kendall/Hunt directly for additional information.

Other materials are needed for the successful implementation of the *Math Trailblazers* curriculum for the entire year. These materials are listed in three categories to aid in planning for the year:

- **Consumables** (one-use items such as beans, paper towels, etc.)
- **Collectibles** (throwaway items such as magazines, egg cartons, jars, etc.)
- **School Supplies** (items usually available in classrooms such as tape, glue, markers, etc.)

Manipulatives for *Math Trailblazers* Grade 5

Manufactured Manipulative, Classroom	Number per Group	TOTAL per Classroom of 30 Students
base-ten pieces, set consists of: 2 packs (10 cm × 10 cm × 10 cm), 14 flats (10 cm × 10 cm × 1 cm), 30 skinnies (10 cm × 1 cm × 1 cm), 50 bits (1 cm × 1 cm × 1 cm)	1 set per student pair	15 sets
bubble solution	1 per student group of 3	10
bubble wands	1 per student group of 3	10
calculator	1 per student	30
compasses	1 per student	30
connecting cubes	40 per student	1200
eyedroppers	1 per student group of 3	10–15
geoboards with geobands	1 per student pair	15
graduated cylinder, 250 cc	1 per student group of 3	10–15
gram masses	1 set per student group of 3	10 sets
10 5-gram masses		
5 10-gram masses		
2 20-gram masses		
10 1-gram masses		
metersticks	1–2 per student group of 3	10–15

Manufactured Manipulative, Classroom	Number per Group	TOTAL per Classroom of 30 Students
Mr. Origin	1 per classroom	1
overhead base-ten pieces		1 set
overhead geoboard	1 per classroom	1
overhead pattern blocks		1 set
overhead ruler		1
pattern blocks, fraction (1 cm or $\frac{1}{2}$ cm to match size of standard pattern blocks used)	6 brown trapezoids, 12 purple triangles per student pair	90 brown trapezoids 180 purple triangles
pattern blocks, standard	10 green triangles, 10 blue rhombuses, 2–3 yellow hexagons, and 6 red trapezoids per student pair	150 green triangles 150 blue rhombuses 30–45 yellow hexagons 90 red trapezoids
protractors	1 per student	30
ruler, cm/inch, transparent	1 per student	30
spheres, small steel ($\frac{1}{2}$-inch diameter)	5 per student group of 3	50
spheres, medium steel (1-inch diameter)	1 per student group of 3	10–15
spheres, large steel ($1\frac{1}{4}$-inch diameter)	1 per student group of 3	10–15
spinners, clear plastic	1 per student pair	15
square-inch tiles, colored	25 per student	750
standard masses (See gram masses.)		
stopwatches	1 per student group of 3	10
two-pan balances	1 per student group of 3	10–15
*wall chart, laminated: data tables & graph	1 set per classroom	1 set

*The wall chart is available through Kendall/Hunt Publishing Company 1-800-228-0810.

Additional Materials or Equipment Needed
for *Math Trailblazers* Grade 5

Collectible Materials	Number Required
bags, paper lunch	1 per group of 3
bags, plastic self-closing	1 per group of 3
beans, baby lima	1 lb bag per group of 3–4
cardboard, 14 cm by 24 cm	1 per student
cans and lids of various sizes	2–3 per student pair

one of the following:
   piece of sod,
   nylon netting,
   window screen, or
   large beach towel
	1 per classroom

clay	1 handful per group of 3
cups/pans for holding/pouring water	1 per group of 3

small objects to measure mass/volume
   cork
   wood
   paraffin block
	1–2 per group of 3

string	1 ball (at least 200 ft)
pennies	20 per group of 3
nickels	1 per group of 3
playing cards	1 deck per group of 3
pony beads or ditali noodles	77 per student

scoops, three sizes
   small, 2 tablespoons
   medium, 4 tablespoons
   large, 6 tablespoons
	1 of each per group of 3–4

Consumable Materials	Number Required
chenille sticks	4 per group of 3
straws	10 per group of 3

Additional Materials or Equipment Needed
for *Math Trailblazers* Grade 5 (*Continued*)

School Supplies	Number Required
easel paper	50 sheets
letter-size envelopes	1 per group of 3
manila folders	2 per student
file rack	1 per classroom
paper towels	3 brands, 1 roll each
rubber bands	2 boxes per classroom
3- by 5-inch index cards	2 packages

The following supplies are used throughout the year:

masking tape

scissors

scotch tape

chalk

crayons or markers

overhead markers

glue

Literature List

The Literature List provides suggested titles and recommended reading of commercially available trade books which are used in many *Math Trailblazers* lessons.

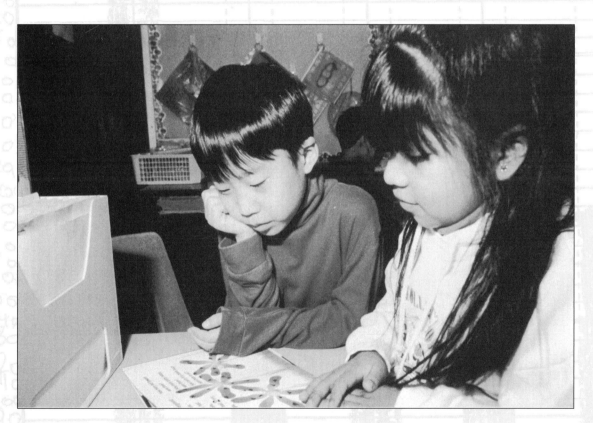

Students connect math and literature by reading a trade book.

Literature List

Many lesson guides in *Math Trailblazers* suggest the use of commercially available trade books. A listing of these trade books is provided here. These books can be used to extend or enhance a particular lesson.

Unit 1—Populations and Samples
- Bash, Barbara. *Ancient Ones.* Sierra Club, San Francisco, 1994. (Lesson 4)
- George, Jean Craighead. *One Day in the Tropical Rain Forest.* HarperCollins, New York, 1990. (Lesson 4)
- Kipling, Rudyard. *The Jungle Books.* Bantam Books, New York, 2000. (Lesson 4)
- Yolen, Jane. *Welcome to the Green House.* Scholastic, New York, 1994. (Lesson 4)

Unit 2—Big Numbers
- Cole, Joanna. *The Magic School Bus: Lost in the Solar System.* Scholastic Inc., New York, 1990. (Lesson 9)
- Jenkins, Steve. *Hottest, Coldest, Highest, Deepest.* Houghton Mifflin Company, Boston, 1998.
- Sandburg, Carl. *Complete Poems.* Harcourt, Brace, Jovanovich, New York, 1970. (Lesson 10)
- Schwartz, David M. *How Much Is a Million?* Scholastic Inc., New York, 1985. (Lesson 8)
- Schwartz, David M. *If You Made a Million.* Scholastic Inc., New York, 1989. (Lesson 9)
- Schwartz, David M. *On Beyond a Million.* Dragonfly Books, Cambridgeshire, UK, 2001.
- Simon, Seymour. *Our Solar System.* Morrow Junior Books, New York, 1992.
- *The World Almanac and Book of Facts 2000.* St. Martin's Press, New York, 1999.

Unit 3—Fractions and Ratios
- Coffland, Jack. *Football Math: Touchdown Activities and Projects for Grades 4–8.* Good Year Books, Tucson, AZ, 1995.
- Jennison, Christopher. *Baseball Math: Grandslam Activities and Projects.* Good Year Books, Parsipanny, NJ, 2001.
- Schwartz, David M. *If You Hopped Like a Frog.* Scholastic Press, New York, 1999.
- Xiong, Blip. *Nine in One, Grr! Grr!* Children's Book Press, San Francisco, CA, 1989. (Lesson 5)

Unit 4—Division and Data
- Adair, Gene. *George Washington Carver: Botanist.* Chelsea House Publishers, New York, 1989. (Lesson 7)
- Carter, Andy, and Carol Saller. *George Washington Carver.* Carolrhoda Books, Inc., Minneapolis, MN, 2001. (Lesson 7)
- Dodds, Dayle Ann. *The Great Divide: A Mathematical Marathon.* Candlewick Press, Cambridge, MA. 1999.

- Mitchel, Barbara. *A Pocketful of Goobers.* Carolrhoda Books, Inc., Minneapolis, MN, 1989. (Lesson 7)
- Moore, Eva. *The Story of George Washington Carver.* Scholastic, New York, 1995. (Lesson 7)

Unit 5—Investigating Fractions
None

Unit 6—Geometry
- Ellis, Julie. *What's Your Angle, Pythagorus? A Math Adventure.* Charlesbridge Publishing. Watertown, MA, 2004.
- Hopkinson, Deborah. *Sweet Clara and the Freedom Quilt.* Paintings by James Ransome. Alfred A. Knopf, New York, 1993. (Lesson 5)
- Kinsey-Warnock, Natalie. *The Canada Geese Quilt.* Illustrated by Leslie W. Bowman. Cobblehill Books/Dutton, New York, 1989. (Lesson 5)
- Paul, Ann Whitford. *Eight Hands Round A Patchwork Alphabet.* Illustrated by Jeanette Winter. HarperCollins, New York, 1991. (Lesson 5)
- ———. *The Seasons Sewn: A Year in Patchwork.* Harcourt Brace & Co., New York, 1996. (Lesson 5)
- Ross, Catherine Sheldrick. *Squares: Shapes in Math, Science and Nature.* Kids Can Press, Ltd., Tonawanda, NY, 1996.

Unit 7—Decimals and Probability
- Coffland, Jack and David. *Basketball Math.* Good Year Books, Tucson, AZ, 2002.
- Lowry, Lois. *Number the Stars.* Houghton Mifflin Co., Boston, MA, 1989. (Lesson 10)
- Smith, David J. *If the World Were a Village: A Book about the World's People.* Kids Can Press, Ltd., Tonawanda, NY, 2002.

Unit 8—Applications: An Assessment Unit
- Appelhoff, Mary, Mary Frances Fenton, and Barbara Loss Harris. *Worms Eat Our Garbage.* Flower Press, Kalamazoo, MI, 1993.
- Cole, Joanna. *The Magic School Bus: Lost in Space.* Scholastic, New York, 1990.
- Littlefield, Cindy A. *Real-World Math for Hands-On-Fun!* Williamson Publishing, Charlotte, VT, 2001.
- Schwartz, David M. *If You Made a Million.* Scholastic, New York, 1989.
- The EarthWorks Group. *50 Simple Things Kids Can Do to Save the Earth.* Andrews and McMeel, Kansas City, MO, 1999.
- Wilder, Laura Ingalls. *Little House in the Big Woods.* HarperCollins, New York, 2001.

Unit 9—Connections to Division
- Wilder, Laura Ingalls. *Little House in the Big Woods.* HarperCollins, New York, 2001. (Lesson 1)

Unit 10—Maps and Coordinates

- Knowlton, Jack. *Maps and Globes.* HarperCollins Publishers, New York, 1985.
- Olesky, Walter. *Mapping the World.* Scholastic Press, Inc., New York, 2002.

Unit 11—Number Patterns, Primes, and Fractions

- Dahl, Roald. *Esio Trot.* Puffin Books, New York, 1999.
- Hulme, Joy N. *Sea Squares.* Hyperion Books for Children, New York, 1993. (Lesson 3)
- Sachar, Louis. *Sideways Arithmetic from Wayside School.* Scholastic Press, New York, 1989.

Unit 12—Using Fractions

- Adair, Gene. *George Washington Carver: Botanist.* Chelsea House Publishers, New York, 1989. (Lesson 6)
- Carter, Andy, and Carol Saller. *George Washington Carver.* Carolrhoda Books, Inc., Minneapolis, MN, 2001. (Lesson 6)
- Mitchell, Barbara. *A Pocketful of Goobers.* Carolrhoda Books, Inc., Minneapolis, MN, 1989. (Lesson 6)
- Moore, Eva. The Story of George Washington Carver. Scholastic Press, New York, 1995. (Lesson 6)

Unit 13—Ratio and Proportion

- Carter, Andy, and Carol Saller. *George Washington Carver.* Carolrhoda Books, Inc., Minneapolis, MN, 2001. (Lesson 1)

Unit 14—Using Circles

- Lasky, Kathryn. *The Librarian Who Measured the Earth.* Little, Brown, and Company, New York, 1994. (Lesson 2)
- Levy, Judith (ed.). *The World Almanac for Kids, 1998.* Funk and Wagnalls, Mahwah, NJ, 1997. (Lesson 5)
- Neuschwander, Cindy. *Sir Cumference and the Dragon of Pi: A Math Adventure.* Charlesbridge Publishing, Watertown, MA, 1999.
- Neuschwander, Cindy. *Sir Cumference and the Round Table: A Math Adventure.* Charlesbridge Publishing, Watertown, MA, 1997.

Unit 15—Developing Formulas with Geometry

- VanCleave, Janice. *Geometry for Every Kid.* John Wiley & Sons, Inc., New York, 1994.

Unit 16—Bringing It All Together: An Assessment Unit

- Barbour and Davis. *Bats of America.* Books on Demand, Ann Arbor, MI, 1994.
- Cannon, Janell. *Stellaluna.* Harcourt Brace & Company, Orlando, FL, 1993. (Lesson 4)
- Lovett, Sara. *Extremely Weird Bats.* Avalon Travel Publishing, Emeryville, CA, 2002.

Games List

The Games List includes descriptions of games used in *Math Trailblazers*.

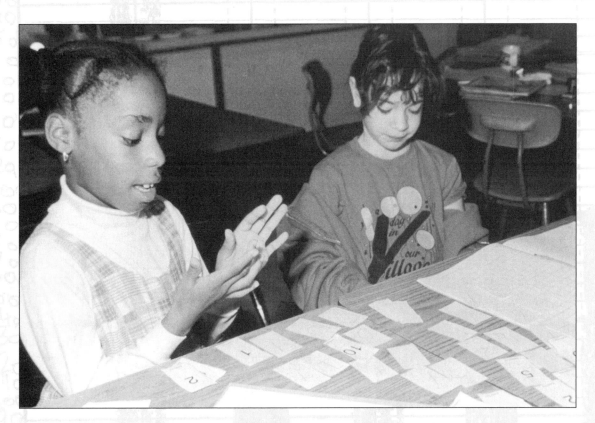

A student uses counting strategies while playing a math game.

Games List

Games are often used in *Math Trailblazers* to engage students in practicing basic arithmetic and other math concepts. A complete listing of the games for your grade and a description of the games are provided below.

Once introduced, these games can be used throughout the year for ongoing practice. We suggest that after the games have been introduced and played in class, they be added to a Games Menu, with necessary materials placed in a math center somewhere in the classroom so that students can replay the games during indoor recess, when they have completed other assignments, and at other times during the day.

Unit 1—Populations and Samples

Digits Game in *Unit Resource Guide* Unit 1 Page 25 DPP item N

To begin the game, students draw the set of boxes on their paper as shown.

The teacher chooses a digit at random from a set of *Digit Cards (0–9)*. Students place the digit in a box in such a way as to get the largest sum. Once a digit is placed, it cannot be moved. Then, the teacher chooses a second digit without replacing the first to the deck. Play continues until the teacher has read enough digits to fill the boxes. The player with the largest sum wins.

Digits Game in *Unit Resource Guide* Unit 1 Page 26 DPP item P

To begin the game, students draw the set of boxes on their paper as shown.

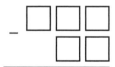

The teacher chooses a digit at random from a set of *Digit Cards (0–9)*. Students place the digit in a box in such a way as to get the largest difference. Once a digit is placed, it cannot be moved. Then, the teacher chooses a second digit without replacing the first to the deck. Play continues until the teacher has read enough digits to fill the boxes. The player with the largest difference wins.

Unit 2—Big Numbers

Spin and Read Number Game in *Unit Resource Guide* Unit 2 Lesson 1 Pages 32–48, *Student Guide* Pages 32–33, and *Discovery Assignment Book* Pages 17 and 19

A player spins a spinner and draws that number of cards from a deck. The player then lines up the cards and says the number aloud. If he or she says the number correctly, then it is recorded on a place value chart. Play continues for four rounds. At the end of the fourth round, players find the sum of the numbers on their place value chart. The highest sum wins.

Unit 3—Fractions and Ratios
None

Unit 4—Division and Data
None

Unit 5—Investigating Fractions
Fraction Cover-All in *Unit Resource Guide* Unit 5 Lesson 3 Pages 56–66 and *Student Guide* Page 157

Students draw a 3 by 4 centimeter rectangle on dot paper. One player draws a card from the game deck and reads the fraction on the card aloud. Players represent the fraction called on their rectangles. Play continues as students represent fractions from cards drawn on their rectangles. When one player fills his or her rectangle completely, the game ends. Players then write number sentences for the fractions represented on their rectangles. The winner is the player with the largest number of acceptable number sentences.

Unit 6—Geometry
None

Unit 7—Decimals and Probability
Digits Game in *Unit Resource Guide* Unit 7 Page 19 DPP item F

To begin the game, students draw the set of boxes on their paper as shown:

The teacher chooses a digit at random from a set of *Digit Cards (0–9)*. Students place the digit in a box in such a way as to try to get the largest number. Once a digit is placed, it cannot be moved. Then, the teacher chooses a second digit without replacing the first to the deck. Play continues until the teacher has read enough digits to fill the boxes. The player with the largest number wins. Play again. However, this time students try to make the smallest number.

Score One in *Unit Resource Guide* Unit 7 Lesson 2 Pages 59–77 and *Discovery Assignment Book* Page 103

This game is played in pairs. Each player makes a list of 20 decimals between 0–1 that have values in the hundredths. Each player then selects a number from his or her list and challenges his or her opponent to find it on the number line. The opponent estimates the position of the number on the number line with a toothpick and uses the decimal scale to verify the position of the number. If the number is within one-tenth of its actual location on the number line, that player earns 0.10 point. The first player to get 1 point in all, wins.

How Many Heads? in *Unit Resource Guide* Unit 7 Lesson 8 Pages 135–153 and *Student Guide* Page 258

This is a game for 3 students. Students flip two pennies. If 0 heads show, then the 0-Heads player gets a point. If 1 head shows, then the 1-Head player gets a point. If 2 heads show, then the 2-Heads Player gets a point. The first player to score 10 points wins. As students play the game several times, they record data in a table in order to determine if the game is mathematically fair.

Matching 2 Pennies in *Unit Resource Guide* Unit 7 Lesson 8 Pages 135–153 and *Student Guide* Page 264

Students flip two pennies. If the two pennies match (HH or TT), then Player 1 gets a point. If the two pennies don't match (HT or TH), then Player 2 gets a point. The first player to score 10 points is the winner. As students play the game several times, they record data in a table in order to determine if the game is mathematically fair.

Unit 8—Applications: An Assessment Unit

Three in a Row in *Unit Resource Guide* Unit 8 Lesson 2 Pages 37–41 and *Discovery Assignment Book* Pages 137–139

A player chooses two factors from the factor frame and finds the product using a calculator. He or she then places a game marker on the product on the game board that is closest to his or her product. The first player to cover three squares in a row horizontally, vertically, or diagonally is the winner.

Unit 9—Connections to Division

Digits Game: Addition with Decimals in *Unit Resource Guide* Unit 9 Page 20 DPP item L

To begin the game, students draw the set of boxes on their papers as shown:

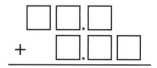

The teacher chooses a digit at random from a set of *Digit Cards (0–9)*. Students place the digit in a box in such a way as to try to get the largest sum. Once a digit is placed, it cannot be moved. Then, the teacher chooses a second digit without replacing the first to the deck. Play continues until the teacher has read enough digits to fill the boxes. The player with the largest sum wins. Play again. However, this time students try to make the smallest sum.

Digits Game: Subtraction with Decimals in *Unit Resource Guide* Unit 9 Page 22 DPP item P

To begin the game, students draw the set of boxes on their papers as shown:

The teacher chooses a digit at random from a set of *Digit Cards (0–9)*. Students place the digit in a box in such a way as to try to get the largest (or smallest) difference. Once a digit is placed, it cannot be moved. Then, the teacher chooses a second digit without replacing the first to the deck. Play continues until the teacher has read enough digits to fill the boxes. The player with the largest (or smallest) difference wins. Different configurations of boxes can also be used for addition, subtraction, multiplication, and division.

Unit 10—Maps and Coordinates

The Barrier Reef Game in *Unit Resource Guide* Unit 10 Lesson 2
Pages 36–51 and *Student Guide* Pages 323–324

On graph paper, each player hides a pod of whales (5 coordinate points), a
shipwreck (4 coordinate points), migrating turtles (3 coordinate points), and a
flock of birds (2 coordinate points). Players make a table to record their
guesses and sightings. Player 1 names an ordered pair and records it in the
table. Player 2 says "sighting" or "miss." If Player 1 gets a sighting, his or her
turn continues. If not, it becomes Player 2's turn. The first player to identify
correctly all the coordinates of all of the opponent's objects wins the game.

Unit 11—Number Patterns, Primes, and Fractions

Factor 40 in *Unit Resource Guide* Unit 11 Lesson 1 Pages 23–35, *Discovery
Assignment Book* Page 181, and *Student Guide* Pages 348–352

Player A chooses a number on the *Factor 40 Game Board* and marks the
square containing that number with his or her symbol (X or O). Player A
records this number as his or her score for this turn. Player B finds and marks
all of the remaining factors of Player A's number. Then, Player B selects
another number as his or her turn. Player B adds up all of the numbers he or
she has marked and records a score. (Note: Each player gets points two ways:
points for the factors of the other player's number and points for the number
he or she chooses.) A number can be used only once. If a player chooses a
number that has no available factors, this is considered an illegal move. He or
she earns no points. The game resumes with the opponent choosing a
number. Play continues until there are no more legal moves. Players add up
their points. The player with the most points wins the game.

Unit 12—Using Fractions

Hexagon Duets in *Unit Resource Guide* Unit 12 Lesson 1 Pages 20–29,
Student Guide Pages 376–377, and *Discovery Assignment Book* Page 193

This is a game for a group of 4 players, 2 on each team. One yellow hexagon
is one whole. Each player spins the spinner twice. Each time they spin, they
place the pattern blocks on the outline of the two hexagons and add the two
fractions together. Players may need to trade the pattern blocks for other
pattern blocks to find the sum. They write a number sentence for the sum of
the two fractions. Then, each player adds his or her sum to his or her partner's
sum to find a grand total. The team with the largest total wins the round and
earns $\frac{1}{3}$ of a point. Continue to play more rounds. The first team to earn one
whole point is the winner.

Unit 13—Ratio and Proportion

None

Unit 14—Using Circles

Fractions Digits Game in *Unit Resource Guide* Unit 14 Page 15
DPP item D

To begin the game, students draw the set of boxes on their papers as shown:

The teacher makes a set of 6 digit cards using the numbers 1, 2, 3, 4, 6, and 8. The teacher chooses one digit at random from the set of cards. Students place the digit in a box in such a way as to try to get a sum of two fractions that is closest to, but less than, 1. Once a digit is placed, it cannot be moved. The teacher chooses a second digit without replacing the first in the deck. Play continues until the teacher has read enough digits to fill the boxes. Students can use calculators to compare their sums. By comparing the decimal answers, the students can see who is the winner.

Unit 15—Developing Formulas with Geometry
None

Unit 16— Bringing It All Together: An Assessment Unit
None

Software List

The Software List outlines recommended computer software used to enhance *Math Trailblazers* lessons.

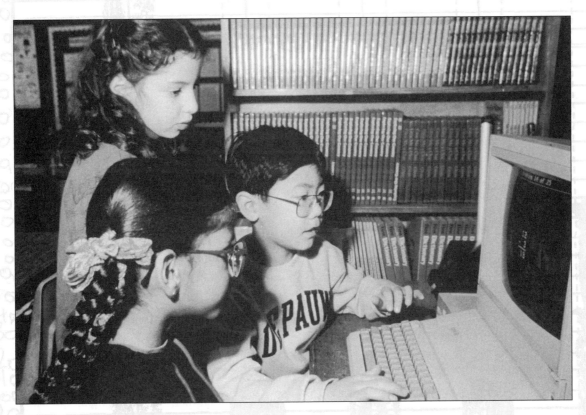

Students use software to practice math facts and solve problems.

Software List

Software Titles by Topic

Applying Mathematics to Other Disciplines
A Field Trip to the Rainforest Deluxe

Data Collection/Reading and Interpreting Graphs
A Field Trip to the Rainforest Deluxe
Graph Master
Hot Dog Stand: The Works
Ice Cream Truck
TinkerPlots

Fractions/Decimals/Percents
Fraction Attraction
Math Arena
Math Munchers Deluxe
Math Mysteries: Advanced Fractions
Math Mysteries: Fractions
Mighty Math Number Heroes
Tenth Planet: Fraction Operations

Geometry
Building Perspective Deluxe
The Factory Deluxe
The Geometer's Sketchpad
Make A Map 3D
Math Arena
Math Munchers Deluxe
MicroWorlds Ex
Mighty Math Calculating Crew
Mighty Math Number Heroes
Shape Up!
Tessellation Exploration

Integers
Mighty Math Calculating Crew

Probability
Mighty Math Number Heroes

Programs for Illustrating
Kid Pix

Logical Thinking/Problem Solving
Building Perspective Deluxe
The Factory Deluxe
Hot Dog Stand: The Works
Ice Cream Truck
Math Mysteries: Advanced Fractions
Math Mysteries: Advanced Whole Numbers
Math Mysteries: Fractions
Math Mysteries: Measurement
Math Mysteries: Whole Numbers
Number Sense and Problem Solving: Puzzle Tanks
Ten Tricky Tiles
Zoombinis Logical Journey

Number Theory (Factors and Primes)
Math Munchers Deluxe

Practice with Basic Operations
Math Arena
Math Munchers Deluxe
Number Facts Fire Zapper
Number Sense and Problem Solving: How the West
    Was One + Three × Four
Ten Tricky Tiles

Understanding of Basic Operations
Fraction Attraction
Mighty Math Calculating Crew
Number Sense and Problem Solving: How the West
    Was One + Three × Four
Ten Tricky Tiles
Tenth Planet: Fraction Operations

Websites
Bandelier National Monument: www.nps.gov/band/
Bat Conservation International: www.batcon.org
The Math Forum: www.mathforum.org
National Geographic: www.nationalgeographic.com
National Library of Virtual Manipulatives for
    Interactive Mathematics: www.matti.usu.edu
One resource for additional mathematics links and
    sites: http://illuminations.nctm.org/swr/index.asp

Recommended Software for Fifth-Grade Units

Unit 1—Populations and Samples

A Field Trip to the Rainforest Deluxe integrates mathematics with science.

Graph Master allows students to collect data and create their own graphs.

Math Mysteries: Advanced Whole Numbers is a series of structured multi-step word problems dealing with whole numbers.

Math Mysteries: Whole Numbers is a series of structured word problems dealing with whole numbers.

Number Facts Fire Zapper provides practice in number facts in an arcade-like game.

Number Sense and Problem Solving: Puzzle Tanks develops logical thinking while practicing math facts.

Ten Tricky Tiles provides practice with number facts through engaging puzzles.

TinkerPlots allows students to record, compare, and analyze data in tables and graphs.

Unit 2—Big Numbers

Ice Cream Truck develops problem solving, money skills, and arithmetic operations.

Math Arena is a collection of math activities that reinforces many math concepts.

Math Munchers Deluxe provides practice in basic facts in an arcade-like game.

Math Mysteries: Advanced Whole Numbers is a series of structured multi-step word problems dealing with whole numbers.

Math Mysteries: Whole Numbers is a series of structured word problems dealing with whole numbers.

Mighty Math Calculating Crew poses short answer questions about number operations.

Mighty Math Number Heroes poses short answer questions about fractions and number operations.

National Library of Virtual Manipulatives website (http://matti.usu.edu) allows students to work with manipulatives including geoboards, base-ten pieces, the abacus, and many others.

Number Facts Fire Zapper provides practice in number facts in an arcade-like game.

Number Sense and Problem Solving: Puzzle Tanks develops logical thinking while practicing math facts.

Ten Tricky Tiles provides practice with number facts through engaging puzzles.

Unit 3—Fractions and Ratios

Fraction Attraction develops understanding of fractions using fraction bars, pie charts, hundreds blocks, and other materials.

Graph Master allows students to collect data and create their own graphs.

Math Arena is a collection of math activities that reinforces many math concepts.

Math Munchers Deluxe provides practice in basic facts and finding equivalent fractions, decimals, percents, ratios, angles and identifying geometric shapes, factors, and multiples in an arcade-like game.

Mighty Math Number Heroes poses short answer questions about fractions, number operations, polygons, and probability.

National Library of Virtual Manipulatives website (http://matti.usu.edu) allows students to work with manipulatives including geoboards, base-ten pieces, the abacus, and many others.

TinkerPlots allows students to record, compare, and analyze data in tables and graphs.

Unit 4—Division and Data

The Factory Deluxe promotes spatial reasoning and practices finding area.

Graph Master allows students to collect data and create their own graphs.

Ice Cream Truck develops problem solving, money skills, and arithmetic operations.

Math Mysteries: Advanced Whole Numbers is a series of structured multistep word problems dealing with whole numbers.

Mighty Math Calculating Crew poses short answer questions about number operations.

Mighty Math Number Heroes poses short answer questions about number operations.

National Library of Virtual Manipulatives website (http://matti.usu.edu) allows students to work with manipulatives including geoboards, base-ten pieces, the abacus, and many others.

Number Sense and Problem Solving: How the West Was One + Three × Four provides practice in the order of operations.

TinkerPlots allows students to record, compare, and analyze data in tables and graphs.

Unit 5—Investigating Fractions

Fraction Attraction develops understanding of fractions using fraction bars, pie charts, hundreds blocks, and other materials.

Math Arena is a collection of math activities that reinforces many math concepts.

Math Munchers Deluxe provides practice in basic facts and finding equivalent fractions, decimals, percents, ratios, angles and identifying geometric shapes, factors, and multiples in an arcade-like game.

Math Mysteries: Fractions develops problem solving with fractions.

Mighty Math Number Heroes poses short answer questions about fractions, number operations, polygons, and probability.

National Library of Virtual Manipulatives website (http://matti.usu.edu) allows students to work with manipulatives including geoboards, base-ten pieces, the abacus, and many others.

Tenth Planet: Fraction Operations develops conceptual understanding of fraction operations, including finding common denominators.

Unit 6—Geometry

Building Perspective Deluxe develops spatial reasoning and visual thinking in three dimensions.

The Factory Deluxe promotes spatial reasoning and practices finding area.

The Geometer's Sketchpad allows students to construct 2-dimensional figures and explore their attributes.

Math Arena is a collection of math activities that reinforces many math concepts.

Math Munchers Deluxe provides practice in basic facts and finding equivalent fractions, decimals, percents, ratios, angles and identifying geometric shapes, factors, and multiples in an arcade-like game.

Mighty Math Number Heroes poses short answer questions about fractions, number operations, polygons, and probability.

National Library of Virtual Manipulatives website (http://matti.usu.edu) allows students to work with manipulatives including geoboards, base-ten pieces, the abacus, and many others.

Shape Up! provides activities with five different sets of shapes.

Tessellation Exploration provides opportunities to explore geometric concepts (flips, turns, slides) and to investigate tessellations.

Zoombinis Logical Journey develops thinking skills as students find patterns to solve puzzles.

Unit 7—Decimals and Probability

Graph Master allows students to collect data and create their own graphs.

Math Arena is a collection of math activities that reinforces many math concepts.

Math Munchers Deluxe provides practice in basic facts and finding equivalent fractions, decimals, percents, ratios, angles and identifying geometric shapes, factors, and multiples in an arcade-like game.

Mighty Math Calculating Crew poses short answer questions about number operations, three-dimensional shapes, and money skills.

Mighty Math Number Heroes poses short answer questions about fractions, number operations, polygons, and probability.

National Library of Virtual Manipulatives website (http://matti.usu.edu) allows students to work with manipulatives including geoboards, base-ten pieces, the abacus, and many others.

TinkerPlots allows students to record, compare, and analyze data in tables and graphs.

Unit 8—Applications: An Assessment Unit

Fraction Attraction develops understanding of fractions using fraction bars, pie charts, hundreds blocks, and other materials.

Graph Master allows students to collect data and create their own graphs.

Math Arena is a collection of math activities that reinforces many math concepts.

Math Munchers Deluxe provides practice in basic facts and finding equivalent fractions, decimals, percents, ratios, angles and identifying geometric shapes, factors, and multiples in an arcade-like game.

Mighty Math Calculating Crew poses short answer questions about number operations, three-dimensional shapes, and money skills.

Mighty Math Number Heroes poses short answer questions about fractions, number operations, polygons, and probability.

TinkerPlots allows students to record, compare, and analyze data in tables and graphs.

Unit 9—Connections to Division

Fraction Attraction develops understanding of fractions using fraction bars, pie charts, hundreds blocks, and other materials.

Math Munchers Deluxe provides practice in basic facts and finding equivalent fractions, decimals, percents, ratios, angles and identifying geometric shapes, factors, and multiples in an arcade-like game.

Mighty Math Calculating Crew poses short answer questions about number operations, three-dimensional shapes, and money skills.

Mighty Math Number Heroes poses short answer questions about fractions, number operations, polygons, and probability.

Number Sense and Problem Solving: How the West Was One + Three × Four provides practice with the order of operations.

Tenth Planet: Fraction Operations develops conceptual understanding of fraction operations, including finding common denominators.

Unit 10—Maps and Coordinates

Building Perspective Deluxe develops spatial reasoning and visual thinking in three dimensions.

Make A Map 3D introduces reading and interpreting maps, direction, distance, and scale on maps.

Math Arena is a collection of math activities that reinforces many math concepts.

MicroWorlds Ex is a drawing program that helps students develop spatial reasoning and an understanding of coordinates while making shapes.

Mighty Math Number Heroes poses short answer questions about fractions, number operations, polygons, and probability.

National Geographic has many maps and related activities for students on its website.

Tessellation Exploration develops understanding of the geometry of tessellations and allows students to create their own.

Unit 11—Number Patterns, Primes, and Fractions

Fraction Attraction develops understanding of fractions using fraction bars, pie charts, hundreds blocks, and other materials.

Graph Master allows students to collect data and create their own graphs.

Math Munchers Deluxe provides practice in basic facts and finding equivalent fractions, decimals, percents, ratios, angles and identifying geometric shapes, factors, and multiples in an arcade-like game.

Math Mysteries: Advanced Fractions develops multistep problem solving with fractions.

Mighty Math Number Heroes poses short answer questions about fractions, number operations, polygons, and probability.

Tenth Planet: Fraction Operations develops conceptual understanding of fraction operations, including finding common denominators.

Unit 12—Using Fractions

Fraction Attraction develops understanding of fractions using fraction bars, pie charts, hundreds blocks, and other materials.

Math Arena is a collection of math activities that reinforces many math concepts.

Math Munchers Deluxe provides practice with basic facts and finding equivalent fractions, decimals, percents, ratios, angles and identifying geometric shapes, factors, and multiples in an arcade-like game.

Math Mysteries: Advanced Fractions develops multistep problem solving with fractions.

Mighty Math Number Heroes poses short answer questions about different math topics including fractions.

National Library of Virtual Manipulatives website (http://matti.usu.edu) allows students to work with manipulatives including pattern blocks.

Tenth Planet: Fraction Operations develops conceptual understanding of fraction operations, including finding common denominators.

Unit 13—Ratio and Proportion

Graph Master allows students to collect data and create their own graphs.

Math Munchers Deluxe provides practice in basic facts and finding equivalent fractions, decimals, percents, ratios, angles and identifying geometric shapes, factors, and multiples in an arcade-like game.

Math Mysteries: Measurement develops multistep problem solving with distance, weight, and capacity.

TinkerPlots allows students to record, compare, and analyze data in tables and graphs.

Unit 14—Using Circles

Fraction Attraction develops understanding of fractions using pie charts and other materials.

The Geometer's Sketchpad gives students the opportunity to create their own geometric drawings.

Graph Master allows students to enter data and make graphs. (Lessons 2 and 5)

MicroWorlds Ex helps students develop spatial reasoning and an understanding of geometry.

TinkerPlots allows students to record, compare, and analyze data in tables and graphs.

Unit 15—Developing Formulas with Geometry

The Factory Deluxe promotes spatial reasoning and practices finding area.

The Geometer's Sketchpad allows students to construct two-dimensional figures and explore their attributes.

MicroWorlds Ex is a drawing program that helps students develop spatial reasoning and an understanding of coordinates while making shapes.

Mighty Math Number Heroes poses short answer questions about fractions, number operations, polygons, and probability.

National Library of Virtual Manipulatives website (http://matti.usu.edu) allows students to work with manipulatives including geoboards, base-ten pieces, the abacus, and many others.

Number Sense and Problem Solving: How the West Was One + Three × Four provides practice with the order of operations.

Shape Up! provides activities with five different sets of shapes.

Unit 16—Bringing It All Together: An Assessment Unit

Bandelier National Monument *World Wide Web site*
(http:// www.nps.gov/band/). Provides information for visitors to Bandelier
National Monument including location, hours, and fees. There is also
some specific information about climate, activities, and accessibility.

Bat Conservation International World Wide Web site
(http://www.batcon.org/). Comprehensive web site dedicated to the
conservation of bats. It includes bat activities, facts, and trivia as well
as links to other bat sites and information about bat workshops and
museum exhibits.

Graph Master allows students to collect data and create their own graphs.

TinkerPlots allows students to record, compare, and analyze data in tables and
graphs.

Recommended Software List–
Brief Descriptions of the Programs

Bandelier National Monument
website (http://www.nps.gov/band/)
This web site provides information for visitors to Bandelier National
Monument, including location, hours, and fees. There is also information
about climate, activities, and accessibility.

Bat Conservation International
website (http://www.batcon.org/)
This comprehensive web site is dedicated to the conservation of bats.
It includes bat activities and facts as well as links to other bat sites.
There is information about bat workshops and museum exhibits.

Building Perspective Deluxe by Sunburst
This program develops students' problem-solving skills, spatial perception, and
visual thinking skills. Students are presented with ground-level views of an
array of buildings. The task is to predict how the buildings will look when
viewed from above. This program is recommended for grades 4–adult.

The Factory Deluxe by Sunburst
Students are asked to produce or duplicate products in a simulated assembly
line. Students direct the machines to punch, rotate, and stripe a variety of
geometric shapes. Students explore sequences, patterns, and spatial
relationships. There are also two games in the program. *Ship It!* is a game
that develops logical thinking. Several shapes with a variety of attributes are
presented. The student must place the shapes in the best containers. The
containers are labeled with some sort of attribute. At the advanced levels, it is
possible that more than one shape fits an attribute, i.e., goes into a container.
In the second game, *Deliver It!*, students control trucks that compete on a
racecourse. The trucks move as correct answers to area problems are given.
This game develops estimating area using a grid as well as measuring and
using formulas. The program is recommended for grades 4 to 8.

A Field Trip to the Rainforest Deluxe by Sunburst
This program integrates mathematics with science. Children explore plants
and animals indigenous to a rain forest. In the activities, children use data

tables to gather information and explore various aspects of the rain forest. The program allows children to create their own tables. It is recommended for grades 2 and up.

Fraction Attraction by Sunburst
Fraction Attraction provides conceptual development of fractions in four games. Students develop understanding of equivalent fractions by turning a Ferris wheel. Other games address ordering fractions and positioning fractions on the number line. The concept of fraction as a distance is included also. In every game students can get an explanation of the mathematics in the diagnostic help section, not just correct answers. The explanations use fraction bars, pie charts, and hundreds blocks to show alternative representations. There are different levels of difficulty and students can choose to work with decimal and percent equivalents as well. The teacher's guide offers other off-computer activities and teaching suggestions to build understanding. The program is recommended for grades 3 to 8.

The Geometer's Sketchpad by Key Curriculum Press
The Geometer's Sketchpad is an interactive program that allows students to construct geometric shapes and then transform them. Shapes can be colored, labeled, and measured. The program also allows the user to record the steps of the construction. The program is recommended for upper elementary and above, but can be successfully used with younger children.

Graph Master by Tom Snyder Productions
Graph Master allows students to collect data into the program or import data from outside. There are nine different types of graphs available, depending on the type of data: bar graph, pictograph, circle graph, line graph, scatterplot, frequency chart, histogram, line plot, and box plots. The user decides on graph type, scale, variables, and labels. The program allows two graphs to be open side by side so that students can compare the same data in different formats or different data. Students can also sort and tally data, get statistics (mean, median, mode, and range), and filter data. The program provides help in interpreting the types of graphs and there are ten sample data sets available. The program is recommended for grades 4 to 8.

Hot Dog Stand: The Works by Sunburst
Hot Dog Stand: The Works combines logical thinking and planning with mathematics. Students operate a hot dog stand in an arena. They are given a certain amount of money to spend on supplies. They decide how much of each product to purchase depending on anticipated crowds, weather, and other variables. Students then must set prices. The program generates the sales at the event and shows the profits. Nonperishable leftover items can be saved from one event to the next, but perishable items like hot dogs are a loss. Students use estimation and basic arithmetic operations to make decisions. They must decide on what information is necessary and the calculations needed to get the data. The program is recommended for grades 5 and up.

Ice Cream Truck by Sunburst
Ice Cream Truck simulates a real-life business. Students own an ice cream truck and their goal is to make as big a profit as possible. Students buy ice cream from a warehouse. They decide how much to buy, what to charge, and where to sell. The program provides information about the temperature

outside and the time of day they will be selling. The program then simulates the customers and determines how much ice cream was sold that day. Students must make informed decisions. They have a spreadsheet available and must keep track of their profits and expenses, including gas. This program promotes multistep problem solving and decision making. The program is recommended for grades 3 to 6.

Kid Pix by Riverdeep—The Learning Company
This program allows students to create their own illustrations for many different applications throughout the curriculum. In mathematics, students can use this program to illustrate problems they have been given to solve or they can create and illustrate their own patterns and problems. The program is recommended for grades K–4.

Make A Map 3D by Sunburst
This program develops map-reading skills. An animated character explains many parts of a map and how to use maps. Students can then practice using directions, map symbols, keys. Students work on navigating grids, distance, and scale. Students can also investigate maps of the United States and landmarks. The program is recommended for grades 2–5.

Math Arena by Sunburst
Math Arena is a collection of 20 well thought-out problem-solving and skill-reinforcing games. Each activity begins with a short tutorial, which can be skipped. The games include practice in estimating angles, using symmetry to finish a quilt, finding a person lost in a coordinate grid, using transformations to form triangular designs, and forming arrays consisting of a given number of squares. Students practice making change and estimating if the total bill at a store is over an allotted amount of money and finding the sale price of an item, given the discount percent. Other games practice arithmetic skills. Students must recognize equivalent amounts and catch arithmetic errors. In other activities students must find equivalent fractions and find the next number in a pattern. In another game students practice forming Venn diagrams. The level of play can be changed and there are teacher options. The manual comes with worksheets to complement the computer work. This program is recommended for grades 4–7.

The Math Forum (www.mathforum.org)
The Math Forum is a very broad-based website maintained by Drexel University. The site has such features as Ask Dr. Math, where students can ask mathematical questions. There is an extensive mathematics resource library for students in elementary school through graduate school. Other features include discussion groups, an extensive collection of good problems, teacher resources, and issues in mathematics education.

Math Munchers Deluxe by Riverdeep—The Learning Company
Math Munchers Deluxe allows students to practice operations and identify primes, multiples, and factors. The student moves a Muncher around the screen as it devours expressions that fit a given criteria. For example, one task is to devour all expressions that are equivalent to .5. The Muncher tries to avoid being eaten by Troggles, but this feature can be turned off, allowing the student to focus on the mathematics. The program allows the user to choose a grade level, and choose among whole numbers, fractions,

decimals, and geometry. Within the topics students choose evaluating expressions, finding equivalent expressions, and comparing expressions. The program is recommended for students in grades 3–6.

Math Mysteries: Advanced Fractions by Tom Snyder Productions
Math Mysteries: Advanced Fractions has the same type of problems as *Math Mysteries: Fractions*. They differ in the amount of extraneous information, the number of steps, and how the questions are embedded in the stories. The program is recommended for students in grades 4–7.

Math Mysteries: Advanced Whole Numbers by Tom Snyder Productions
Math Mysteries: Advanced Whole Numbers has the same type of problems as *Math Mysteries: Whole Numbers*. They differ in the amount of extraneous information, the number of steps, and how the questions are embedded in the stories. The program is recommended for students in grades 4–7.

Math Mysteries: Fractions by Tom Snyder Productions
Math Mysteries: Fractions focuses on problem solving using fraction problems. The program is designed for group work. Students watch a short cartoon where they gather data and understand the problem. They solve the problem and check their work using provided guides. The problems involve creating fractions, adding, subtracting, multiplying, and dividing fractions. There are a total of 24 problems with reproducible pages to help structure problem solving and answers for the teacher. The program is recommended for students in grades 4–7.

Math Mysteries: Measurement by Tom Snyder Productions
Math Mysteries: Measurement focuses on problem solving using measurement problems. The program is designed for group work. Students watch a short cartoon where they gather data and understand the problem. They solve the problem and check their work using provided guides. The problems involve metric and customary length, weight, volume, and rates. There are a total of 24 problems with reproducible pages to help structure problem solving and answers for the teacher. The program is recommended for students in grades 4–7.

Math Mysteries: Whole Numbers by Tom Snyder Productions
Math Mysteries: Whole Numbers focuses on problem solving using whole numbers and time problems. The program is designed for group work. Students watch a short cartoon where they gather data and understand the problem. They solve the problem and check their work using provided guides. The problems involve adding, subtracting, multiplying, and dividing with whole numbers, working with time, working with rates, and interpreting remainders. There are a total of 24 problems with reproducible pages to help structure problem solving and answers for the teacher. The program is recommended for students in grades 4–7.

MicroWorlds Ex by LCSI
MicroWorlds is an interactive program that allows users to create geometric shapes by issuing commands. As students construct figures, they learn about the geometric properties of shapes. There are several commercially available programs. Recent versions include MicroWorlds JR and MicroWorlds Ex by LCSI. In these versions, students can add text, animation, and sound and they include web-integration. This program is recommended for grades 2 to adult.

Mighty Math Calculating Crew by Riverdeep—The Learning Company
This very versatile skills program has four sections with about 20 specific goals in each section. The Nautical Number Line presents lost treasures under a number line. Students must move a ship to the correct number to acquire a treasure. The skills here focus on locating numbers on the line, rounding, adding and subtracting whole numbers, fractions, and decimals, and working with negative numbers. The Superhero Superstore focuses on money skills and operations involving numbers with ending zeros. Dr. Gee's 3D Lab acquaints students with nets of solids. Students must match nets with solids and identify attributes of the nets and solids. Nick Knack, Supertrader develops conceptual understanding of multiplication as repeated addition and division as partitioning equally. There are long-division practice problems too. The program is recommended for 3rd to 6th grade.

Mighty Math Number Heroes by Riverdeep—The Learning Company
This very versatile skills program has four sections with about 20 specific goals in each section. Fraction Fireworks asks students questions about fractions and decimals. The questions range from identifying fractions to comparing, adding, and subtracting fractions with like and unlike denominators. It also includes multiplying fractions and questions about decimals. The GeoComputer section uses the geoboard to practice identifying different types of angles and polygons. Students answer questions about symmetry, different transformations, perimeter, area, and tessellations. In the Quizzo section students compete in a game show in various categories. Questions include multiplication and division facts, adding and subtracting 2-digit and 3-digit numbers, identifying patterns, and operations with decimals. In the probability section students answer questions with spinners, coins, and graphs. The questions range from exploring possible/impossible events to finding probabilities, comparing probabilities, and identifying independent events. The program is recommended for grades 3 to 6.

National Geographic
(www.nationalgeographic.com)
This web site provides a link to scientific and educational information and resources. The site contains a wealth of information about the world. Students can learn about geography, animals, travel, and history. There are many maps and educational games as well.

National Library of Virtual Manipulatives for Interactive Mathematics
(www.matti.usu.edu)
This web site was developed and maintained at Utah State University. It includes an extensive collection of virtual manipulatives and accompanying activities. Students can work with geoboards, pattern blocks, tangrams, base-ten pieces, balance scales, and other materials interactively. This provides the opportunity to work with materials that are perhaps otherwise not available. For students who have access to the concrete materials, using the interactive manipulatives provides opportunity to move from concrete to pictorial representations.

Number Facts Fire Zapper by Gamco
Number Facts Fire Zapper's goal is to develop proficiency and speed at basic math facts in a fun arcade-type game. Students must move firefighters around a screen and spray math facts with the correct answer in order to extinguish the flames. Students choose what operation they want to practice. The length of the game and the speed at which the number facts appear can be changed. The

program allows the teacher to keep track of individual student progress. The teacher can also see an analysis of how a student did on particular fact groups. For example, the program shows the percent correct of all problems involving the multiples of seven. The program is recommended for grades 1 to 8.

Number Sense and Problem Solving by Sunburst
  How the West Was One + Three × Four
  Students learn about order of operations as they race their stagecoach or locomotive along the number line trail. The computer generates three numbers. The players make combinations of these numbers using the four basic operations and parentheses to be the first to reach Red Gulch. Teachers can customize the program. The program is recommended for grades 4 to 8.

  Puzzle Tanks
  This program develops logical thinking. Students must fill a truck with exactly a given amount of liquid. Two tanks are used to fill the truck. The tanks hold a certain amount of liquid, which changes with each game. The tanks can be refilled indefinitely, but the entire tank is emptied at once. Students must use the basic operations to get the right amount into the tank. Besides basic operations, number sense, the concept of equality, and algebra skills are reinforced. The program is recommended for grades 4 to 8.

Shape Up! by Sunburst
Shape Up! is a versatile geometry program consisting of five sets of shapes. The user can choose to work with pattern blocks or tangrams designed to correspond to the manipulatives. Another set of shapes involves regular triangles, pentagons, hexagons, octagons, squares, and circles. These shapes can be dissected and put back together in any desired fashion. In addition, the user can choose from two sets of three-dimensional shapes. One set is the platonic solids and the other a variety of shapes. Students can explore area, symmetry, tessellations, similarity, and congruence. It allows users to view inside three-dimensional shapes using the Transparent function. Any of the shapes can be moved and rotated. The teacher's guide includes an extensive implementation guide to use the program to its fullest capacity and an in-depth reference section. This program develops student van Hiele levels with opportunities to explore shapes more easily than working with concrete materials. The program is recommended for grades K–8.

Ten Tricky Tiles by Sunburst
Ten Tricky Tiles develops understanding of number relations, addition and subtraction fact practice, and logical thinking. Students must fit number tiles 0–9 into the correct places to make number sentences true. The number tiles must be arranged so that all the sentences are correct in order to get points. The program also reinforces the concept of equality with operations on both sides of the equals sign. There are three activities to choose from. The most challenging activity is a number crossword puzzle where the number sentences are all interrelated. The ten number tiles must be placed so horizontal and vertical number sentences are true. There are accompanying worksheets and suggestions for helping students develop efficient strategies. The program is recommended for grades 2 to 6.

Tenth Planet: Fraction Operations by Sunburst
Tenth Planet: Fraction Operations develops conceptual understanding of fraction operations. The program has short video clips of fraction operations in real life and multistep fraction problem situations. The program has interactive fraction bars to help students understand common denominators. Students keep dividing a bar until they can make the given bars (fractions) with the same size parts. Several different activities practice adding and subtracting fractions. Multiplication of fractions is presented in the context of area. Division of fractions is explored as finding how many of a unit are in a given amount. The teacher's guide provides supporting blackline masters. The program is recommended for grades 4 to 7.

Tessellation Exploration by Tom Snyder Productions
Tessellation Exploration allows students to create, animate, and print their own tessellations. The program reinforces the mathematics of slide, rotation, and reflection transformations as students explore and draw connections between art and mathematics. After creating a shape, students can add artwork. Students explore the rules that govern tessellations. There are suggested class activities and worksheets in the teacher's guide. A tessellation tutorial and many examples of tessellations are included. The program is recommended for grades 4 and above.

TinkerPlots by Key Curriculum Press
This program allows students to record, explore, compare, and analyze data in tables and graphs they design themselves. The data can be entered or imported into the program. Students can edit data in tables, then display the data in a bar graph, point graph, or circle graph. Tables and graphs can be compared side-by-side to examine relationships in data. This program is recommended for grades 4–8.

Zoombinis Logical Journey by Riverdeep—The Learning Company
This program builds thinking skill. The student must guide the Zoombinis to a new land by solving logic puzzles. The zoombinis are little creatures that have different attributes (feet, hair, noses, etc.). In many of the challenges, students must discover how the attributes are grouped in order to proceed. Patterning, collecting evidence, graphing, sorting, and hypothesis testing are developed as the game progresses. There are twelve different puzzles with four levels of difficulty that change each time the program is played. The program is recommended for grades 3 to 8.

Software Companies Addresses and Telephone Numbers

Gamco
The Siboney Learning Group
325 N. Kirkwood Road, Suite 200
Saint Louis, MO 63122
1-888-726-8100
www.gamco.com
www.siboneylearninggroup.com

Key Curriculum Press
1150 65th Street
Emeryville, CA 94608
1-888-881-8885
www.keypress.com

LCSI
P.O. Box 162
Highgate Springs, VT 05460
1-800-321-5646
www.microworlds.com

Riverdeep—The Learning Company
100 Pine Street, Suite 1900
San Francisco, CA 94111
1-888-242-6747
www.riverdeep.net

Sunburst Technology
1550 Executive Drive
Elgin, IL 60123
1-888-492-8817
www.sunburst.com

Tom Snyder Productions
80 Coolidge Hill Road
Watertown, MA 02472
1-800-342-0236
www.tomsnyder.com

Glossary

This glossary provides definitions of key vocabulary terms in the Grade 5 lessons. Locations of key vocabulary terms in the curriculum are included with each definition. Components Key: URG = *Unit Resource Guide,* SG = *Student Guide,* DAB = *Discovery Assignment Book,* and TIG = *Teacher Implementation Guide.*

A

Acute Angle (URG Unit 6 p. 31; SG p. 185)
An angle that measures less than 90°.

Acute Triangle (URG Unit 6 p. 104 & Unit 15 p. 64; SG pp. 188, 468)
A triangle that has only acute angles.

All-Partials Multiplication Method (URG Unit 2 pp. 11, 139)
A paper-and-pencil method for solving multiplication problems. Each partial product is recorded on a separate line. (*See also* partial product.)

$$\begin{array}{r} 186 \\ \times\ 3 \\ \hline 18 \\ 240 \\ 300 \\ \hline 558 \end{array}$$

Altitude of a Triangle (URG Unit 15 p. 65; SG p. 470)
A line segment from a vertex of a triangle perpendicular to the opposite side or to the line extending the opposite side; also, the length of this line. The altitude is also called the height of the triangle.

Angle (URG Unit 6 p. 30; SG p. 184)
The amount of turning or the amount of opening between two rays that have the same endpoint.

Area (URG Unit 4 pp. 10, 140 & Unit 15 p. 24; SG pp. 102, 454)
A measurement of size. The area of a shape is the amount of space it covers, measured in square units.

Arc (URG Unit 14 p. 75; SG p. 441)
Part of a circle between two points. (*See also* circle.)

Average (URG Unit 1 pp. 10, 56, 66, 81 & Unit 4 p. 100; SG pp. 12, 123)
A number that can be used to represent a typical value in a set of data. (*See also* mean, median, and mode.)

Axes (URG Unit 10 p. 39; SG p. 319)
Reference lines on a graph. In the Cartesian coordinate system, the axes are two perpendicular lines that meet at the origin. The singular of axes is axis.

B

Base of an Exponent (URG Unit 2 p. 175; SG p. 60)
When exponents are used, the number being multiplied. In $3^4 = 3 \times 3 \times 3 \times 3 = 81$, the 3 is the base and the 4 is the exponent. The 3 is multiplied by itself 4 times.

Base of a Triangle (URG Unit 15 p. 65; SG p. 470)
One of the sides of a triangle; also, the length of the side. A perpendicular line drawn from the vertex opposite the base is called the height or altitude of the triangle.

Base-Ten Pieces (URG Unit 2 pp. 10, 11; SG p. 48)
A set of manipulatives used to model our number system as shown in the figure below. Note that a skinny is made of 10 bits, a flat is made of 100 bits, and a pack is made of 1000 bits.

Base-Ten Shorthand (URG Unit 2 p. 72)
A graphical representation of the base-ten pieces as shown below.

Nickname	Picture	Shorthand
bit		·
skinny		/
flat		
pack		

Benchmarks (SG p. 238)
Numbers convenient for comparing and ordering numbers, e.g., $0, \frac{1}{2}, 1$ are convenient benchmarks for comparing and ordering fractions.

Best-Fit Line (URG Unit 3 p. 115; SG p. 97)
The line that comes closest to the points on a point graph.

Binning Data (URG Unit 8 p. 73; SG p. 274)
Placing data from a data set with a large number of values or large range into intervals in order to more easily see patterns in the data.

Bit (URG Unit 2 pp. 10, 11, 70, 79; SG p. 48)
A cube that measures 1 cm on each edge.
It is the smallest of the base-ten pieces and
is often used to represent 1. (*See also* base-ten pieces.)

C

Cartesian Coordinate System (URG Unit 10 pp. 9, 40; SG p. 319)
A method of locating points on a flat surface by means of an ordered pair of numbers. This method is named after its originator, René Descartes. (*See also* coordinates.)

Categorical Variable (URG Unit 1 p. 33; SG p. 4)
Variables with values that are not numbers. (*See also* variable and value.)

Center of a Circle (URG Unit 14 pp. 29, 60; SG pp. 426, 435)
The point such that every point on a circle is the same distance from it. (*See also* circle.)

Centiwheel (URG Unit 7 p. 33; SG p. 222)
A circle divided into 100 equal sections used in exploring fractions, decimals, and percents.

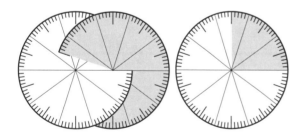

Central Angle (URG Unit 14 p. 62; SG p. 435)
An angle whose vertex is at the center of a circle.

Certain Event (URG Unit 7 p. 130; SG p. 256)
An event that has a probability of 1 (100%).

Chord (URG Unit 14 p. 61; SG p. 435)
A line segment that connects two points on a circle. (*See also* circle.)

Circle (URG Unit 14 pp. 9, 29; SG p. 426)
A curve that is made up of all the points that are the same distance from one point, the center.

Circumference (URG Unit 14 pp. 29, 62; SG pp. 427, 435)
The distance around a circle.

Common Denominator (URG Unit 5 p. 71 & Unit 11 p. 71; SG pp. 161, 364)
A denominator that is shared by two or more fractions. A common denominator is a common multiple of the denominators of the fractions. 15 is a common denominator of $\frac{2}{3}$ ($= \frac{10}{15}$) and $\frac{4}{5}$ ($= \frac{12}{15}$) since 15 is divisible by both 3 and 5.

Common Fraction (URG Unit 7 pp. 9, 35; SG p. 223)
Any fraction that is written with a numerator and denominator that are whole numbers. For example, $\frac{3}{4}$ and $\frac{9}{4}$ are both common fractions. (*See also* decimal fraction.)

Commutative Property of Addition (URG Unit 2 p. 140)
The order of the addends in an addition problem does not matter, e.g., $7 + 3 = 3 + 7$.

Commutative Property of Multiplication (URG Unit 2 p. 140)
The order of the factors in a multiplication problem does not matter, e.g., $7 \times 3 = 3 \times 7$. (*See also* turn-around facts.)

Compact Method (URG Unit 2 pp. 11, 139)
Another name for what is considered the traditional multiplication algorithm.

$$\begin{array}{r} {\scriptstyle 2\,1} \\ 186 \\ \times\ 3 \\ \hline 558 \end{array}$$

Composite Number (URG Unit 11 p. 26; SG p. 351)
A number that has more than two distinct factors. For example, 9 has three factors (1, 3, 9) so it is a composite number.

Concentric Circles (URG Unit 14 p. 64; SG p. 436)
Circles that have the same center.

Congruent (URG Unit 6 p. 74 & Unit 10 p. 90; SG p. 201)
Figures that are the same shape and size. Polygons are congruent when corresponding sides have the same length and corresponding angles have the same measure.

Conjecture (URG Unit 11 p. 38; SG p. 354)
A statement that has not been proved to be true, nor shown to be false.

Convenient Number (URG Unit 2 p. 160; SG p. 57)
A number used in computation that is close enough to give a good estimate, but is also easy to compute with mentally, e.g., 25 and 30 are convenient numbers for 27.

Convex (URG Unit 6 pp. 102, 105)
A shape is convex if for any two points in the shape, the line segment between the points is also inside the shape.

Coordinates (URG Unit 10 p. 10; SG p. 321)
An ordered pair of numbers that locates points on a flat surface relative to a pair of coordinate axes. For example, in the ordered pair (4, 5), the first number (coordinate) is the distance from the point to the vertical axis and the second coordinate is the distance from the point to the horizontal axis. (*See also* axes.)

Corresponding Parts (URG Unit 10 p. 88; SG p. 333)
Matching parts in two or more figures. In the figure below, Sides AB and A′B′ are corresponding parts.

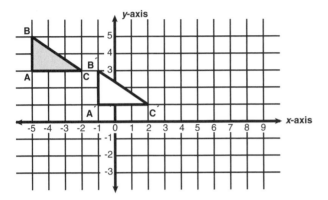

Cryptography (SG p. 354) The study of secret codes.

Cubic Centimeter (URG Unit 13 p. 66)
The volume of a cube that is one centimeter long on each edge.

D

Data (SG p. 5)
Information collected in an experiment or survey.

Decagon (URG Unit 6 p. 63; SG p. 198)
A ten-sided, ten-angled polygon.

Decimal (URG Unit 7 pp. 9, 35; SG p. 223)
1. A number written using the base-ten place value system.
2. A number containing a decimal point.

Decimal Fraction (URG Unit 7 pp. 9, 35; SG p. 223)
A fraction written as a decimal. For example, 0.75 and 0.4 are decimal fractions and $\frac{75}{100}$ and $\frac{4}{10}$ are the equivalent common fractions.

Degree (URG Unit 6 p. 30; SG p. 185)
A degree (°) is a unit of measure for angles. There are 360 degrees in a circle.

Denominator (URG Unit 3 p. 36; SG p. 68)
The number below the line in a fraction. The denominator indicates the number of equal parts in which the unit whole is divided. For example, the 5 is the denominator in the fraction $\frac{2}{5}$. In this case the unit whole is divided into five equal parts. (*See also* numerator.)

Density (URG Unit 13 pp. 59, 77; SG p. 413)
The ratio of an object's mass to its volume.

Diagonal (URG Unit 6 p. 61)
A line segment that connects nonadjacent corners of a polygon.

Diameter (URG Unit 14 pp. 29, 62; SG pp. 427, 435)
1. A line segment that connects two points on a circle and passes through the center.
2. The length of this line segment.

Digit (SG pp. 28, 29)
Any one of the ten symbols 0, 1, 2, 3, 4, 5, 6, 7, 8, 9. The number 37 is made up of the digits 3 and 7.

Dividend (URG Unit 4 p. 55 & Unit 9 pp. 50, 51; SG pp. 106, 296)
The number that is divided in a division problem, e.g., 12 is the dividend in 12 ÷ 3 = 4.

Divisor (URG Unit 2 p. 56, Unit 4 p. 55, & Unit 9 pp. 50, 51; SG pp. 37, 106, 296)
In a division problem, the number by which another number is divided. In the problem 12 ÷ 4 = 3, the 4 is the divisor, the 12 is the dividend, and the 3 is the quotient.

Dodecagon (URG Unit 6 p. 63; SG p. 198)
A twelve-sided, twelve-angled polygon.

E

Endpoint (URG Unit 6 p. 30; SG p. 184)
The point at either end of a line segment or the point at the end of a ray.

Equally Likely (URG Unit 7 p. 130; SG p. 257)
When events have the same probability, they are called equally likely.

Equidistant (URG Unit 14 p. 60)
At the same distance.

Equilateral Triangle (URG Unit 6 p. 101, Unit 14 p. 79, & Unit 15 p. 64)
A triangle that has all three sides equal in length. An equilateral triangle also has three equal angles.

Equivalent Fractions (URG Unit 3 p. 67; SG p. 77)
Fractions that have the same value, e.g., $\frac{2}{4} = \frac{1}{2}$.

Estimate (URG Unit 2 p. 160; SG p. 57)
1. To find *about* how many (as a verb).
2. A number that is *close to* the desired number (as a noun).

Expanded Form (SG p. 28)
A way to write numbers that shows the place value of each digit, e.g., 4357 = 4000 + 300 + 50 + 7.

Exponent (URG Unit 2 p. 175; SG pp. 60, 361)
The number of times the base is multiplied by itself. In $3^4 = 3 \times 3 \times 3 \times 3 = 81$, the 3 is the base and the 4 is the exponent. The 3 is multiplied by itself 4 times.

Extrapolation (URG Unit 13 p. 29; SG p. 399)
Using patterns in data to make predictions or to estimate values that lie beyond the range of values in the set of data.

F

Fact Families (URG Unit 2 p. 55; SG p. 36)
Related math facts, e.g., $3 \times 4 = 12$, $4 \times 3 = 12$, $12 \div 3 = 4$, $12 \div 4 = 3$.

Factors (URG Unit 2 p. 53 & Unit 11 p. 26; SG pp. 35, 348)
1. In a multiplication problem, the numbers that are multiplied together. In the problem $3 \times 4 = 12$, 3 and 4 are the factors.
2. Numbers that divide a number evenly, e.g., 1, 2, 3, 4, 6, and 12 are all the factors of 12.

Factor Tree (URG Unit 11 p. 60; SG p. 361)
A diagram that shows the prime factorization of a number.

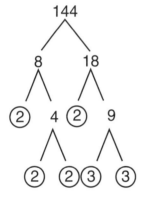

Fair Game (URG Unit 7 pp. 138, 163; SG p. 259)
A game in which it is equally likely that any player will win.

Fewest Pieces Rule (URG Unit 2 pp. 71, 80)
Using the least number of base-ten pieces to represent a number. (*See also* base-ten pieces.)

Fixed Variables (URG Unit 4 p. 117; SG pp. 96, 133)
Variables in an experiment that are held constant or not changed, in order to find the relationship between the manipulated and responding variables. These variables are often called controlled variables. (*See also* manipulated variable and responding variable.)

Flat (URG Unit 2 pp. 10, 11, 71, 79; SG p. 49)
A block that measures 1 cm $\times$ 10 cm $\times$ 10 cm.
It is one of the base-ten pieces and is often used to represent 100. (*See also* base-ten pieces.)

Flip (URG Unit 10 p. 102; SG p. 337)
A motion of the plane in which the plane is reflected over a line so that any point and its image are the same distance from the line.

Forgiving Division Method
(URG Unit 4 pp. 9, 10, 71; SG p. 113)
A paper-and-pencil method for division in which successive partial quotients are chosen and subtracted from the dividend, until the remainder is less than the divisor. The sum of the partial quotients is the quotient. For example, $644 \div 7$ can be solved as shown at the right.

```
        92
  7 ) 644
      140  | 20
      504
      350  | 50
      154
      140  | 20
       14
       14  |  2
        0  | 92
```

Formula (SG pp. 357, 431)
A number sentence that gives a general rule. A formula for finding the area of a rectangle is Area = length $\times$ width, or $A = l \times w$.

Fraction (URG Unit 7 p. 35; SG p. 223)
A number that can be written as $\frac{a}{b}$ where a and b are whole numbers and b is not zero.

G

Googol (URG Unit 2 p. 169)
A number that is written as a 1 with 100 zeroes after it (10^{100}).

Googolplex (URG Unit 2 p. 169)
A number that is written as a 1 with a googol of zeroes after it.

H

Height of a Triangle (URG Unit 15 p. 65; SG p. 470)
A line segment from a vertex of a triangle perpendicular to the opposite side or to the line extending the opposite side; also, the length of this line. The height is also called the altitude.

Hexagon (URG Unit 6 p. 63; SG p. 198)
A six-sided polygon.

Hypotenuse (URG Unit 15 p. 47; SG p. 462)
The longest side of a right triangle.

I

Image (URG Unit 10 pp. 88, 102; SG p. 333)
The result of a transformation, in particular a slide (translation) or a flip (reflection), in a coordinate plane. The new figure after the slide or flip is the image of the old figure.

Impossible Event (URG Unit 7 p. 130; SG p. 256)
An event that has a probability of 0 or 0%.

Improper Fraction (URG Unit 3 p. 56; SG p. 74)
A fraction in which the numerator is greater than or equal to the denominator. An improper fraction is greater than or equal to one.

Infinite (URG Unit 2 p. 171)
Never ending, immeasurably great, unlimited.

Interpolation (URG Unit 13 p. 29; SG p. 399)
Making predictions or estimating values that lie between data points in a set of data.

Intersect (URG Unit 14 p. 61)
To meet or cross.

Isosceles Triangle (URG Unit 6 p. 104 & Unit 15 p. 64)
A triangle that has at least two sides of equal length.

J

K

L

Lattice Multiplication
(URG Unit 9 p. 67; SG p. 300)
A method for multiplying that uses a lattice to arrange the partial products so the digits are correctly placed in the correct place value columns. A lattice for
$43 \times 96 = 4128$ is shown at the right.

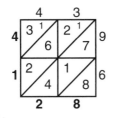

Legs of a Right Triangle (URG Unit 15 p. 47; SG p. 462)
The two sides of a right triangle that form the right angle.

Length of a Rectangle (URG Unit 4 p. 36 & Unit 15 p. 24; SG pp. 103, 455)
The distance along one side of a rectangle.

Line
A set of points that form a straight path extending infinitely in two directions.

Line of Reflection (URG Unit 10 p. 102)
A line that acts as a mirror so that after a shape is flipped over the line, corresponding points are at the same distance (equidistant) from the line.

Line Segment (URG Unit 14 p. 62)
A part of a line between and including two points, called the endpoints.

Liter (URG Unit 13 p. 66)
Metric unit used to measure volume. A liter is a little more than a quart.

Lowest Terms (SG p. 369)
A fraction is in lowest terms if the numerator and denominator have no common factor greater than 1.

M

Manipulated Variable (URG Unit 4 p. 114; SG p. 133)
In an experiment, the variable with values known at the

beginning of the experiment. The experimenter often chooses these values before data is collected. The manipulated variable is often called the independent variable.

Mass (URG Unit 13 p. 64)
The amount of matter in an object.

Mean (URG Unit 1 p. 81 & Unit 4 p. 100; SG pp. 14, 125)
An average of a set of numbers that is found by adding the values of the data and dividing by the number of values.

Measurement Division (URG Unit 4 p. 9)
Division as equal grouping. The total number of objects and the number of objects in each group are known. The number of groups is the unknown. For example, tulip bulbs come in packages of 8. If 216 bulbs are sold, how many packages are sold?

Median (URG Unit 1 pp. 57, 67, 81; SG p. 13)
For a set with an odd number of data arranged in order, it is the middle number. For an even number of data arranged in order, it is the mean of the two middle numbers.

Meniscus (URG Unit 13 p. 68)
The curved surface formed when a liquid creeps up the side of a container (for example, a graduated cylinder).

Milliliter (ml) (URG Unit 13 p. 66)
A measure of capacity in the metric system that is the volume of a cube that is one centimeter long on each side.

Mixed Number (URG Unit 3 p. 56; SG p. 74)
A number that is written as a whole number followed by a fraction. It is equal to the sum of the whole number and the fraction.

Mode (URG Unit 1 pp. 36, 81; SG pp. 6, 12)
The most common value in a data set.

Mr. Origin (URG Unit 10 pp. 9, 64; SG p. 327)
A plastic figure used to represent the origin of a coordinate system and to indicate the directions of the x- and y- axes. (and possibly the z-axis).

N

Negative Number (URG Unit 10 p. 26; SG p. 316)
A number less than zero; a number to the left of zero on a horizontal number line.

N-gon (URG Unit 6 p. 63; SG p. 199)
A polygon with N sides.

Nonagon (URG Unit 6 p. 63; SG p. 198)
A nine-sided polygon.

Numerator (URG Unit 3 p. 36; SG p. 68)
The number written above the line in a fraction. For example, the 2 is the numerator in the fraction $\frac{2}{5}$. In this case, we are interested in two of the five parts. (*See also* denominator.)

Numerical Expression (URG Unit 4 p. 103; SG p. 128)
A combination of numbers and operations, e.g., $5 + 8 ÷ 4$.

Numerical Variable (URG Unit 1 pp. 33, 53; SG p. 4)
Variables with values that are numbers. (*See also* variable and value.)

O

Obtuse Angle (URG Unit 6 p. 31; SG p. 186)
An angle that measures more than 90°.

Obtuse Triangle (URG Unit 6 p. 104 & Unit 15 p. 67; SG pp. 188, 472)
A triangle that has an obtuse angle.

Octagon (URG Unit 6 p. 63; SG p. 198)
An eight-sided polygon.

Ordered Pair (URG Unit 10 p. 39; SG p. 321)
A pair of numbers that gives the coordinates of a point on a grid in relation to the origin. The horizontal coordinate is given first; the vertical coordinate is given second. For example, the ordered pair (5, 3) gives the coordinates of the point that is 5 units to the right of the origin and 3 units up.

Origin (URG Unit 10 pp. 10, 39; SG pp. 319, 321, 327)
The point at which the *x*- and *y*-axes intersect on a coordinate plane. The origin is described by the ordered pair (0, 0) and serves as a reference point so that all the points on the plane can be located by ordered pairs.

P

Pack (URG Unit 2 pp. 10, 11, 71, 79; SG p. 49)
A cube that measures 10 cm on each edge. It is one of the base-ten pieces and is often used to represent 1000. (*See also* base-ten pieces.)

Parallel Lines
(URG Unit 6 p. 46 & Unit 10 p. 91)
Lines that are in the same direction. In the plane, parallel lines are lines that do not intersect.

Parallelogram (URG Unit 6 pp. 104–105)
A quadrilateral with two pairs of parallel sides.

Partial Product (URG Unit 2 p. 139)
One portion of the multiplication process in the all-partials multiplication method, e.g., in the problem $3 × 186$ there are three partial products: $3 × 6 = \underline{18}$, $3 × 80 = \underline{240}$, and $3 × 100 = \underline{300}$. (*See also* all-partials multiplication method.)

Partitive Division (URG Unit 4 p. 9)
Division as equal sharing. The total number of objects and

the number of groups are known. The number of objects in each group is the unknown. For example, Frank has 144 marbles that he divides equally into 6 groups. How many marbles are in each group?

Pentagon (URG Unit 6 p. 63; SG p. 198)
A five-sided polygon.

Percent (URG Unit 7 p. 35; SG p. 223)
Per hundred or out of 100. A special ratio that compares a number to 100. For example, 20% (twenty percent) of the jelly beans are yellow means that out of every 100 jelly beans, 20 are yellow.

Perimeter (URG Unit 15 p. 84; SG p. 480)
The distance around a two-dimensional shape.

Period (SG p. 29)
A group of three places in a large number, starting on the right, often separated by commas as shown at the right.

53,426,879
millions period
thousands period
ones period

Perpendicular Lines (URG Unit 14 p. 65 & Unit 15 p. 65; SG p. 437)
Lines that meet at right angles.

Pi (π) (URG Unit 14 p. 9; SG p. 431)
The ratio of the circumference to diameter of a circle. $π = 3.14159265358979....$ It is a nonterminating, nonrepeating decimal.

Place (SG pp. 28, 29)
The position of a digit in a number.

Place Value (URG Unit 2 p. 72; SG p. 28)
The value of a digit in a number. For example, the 5 is in the hundreds place in 4573, so it stands for 500.

Polygon (URG Unit 6 p. 45; SG p. 192)
A two-dimensional connected figure made of line segments in which each endpoint of every side meets with an endpoint of exactly one other side.

Population (URG Unit 1 p. 10)
A collection of persons or things whose properties will be analyzed in a survey or experiment.

Portfolio (URG Unit 2 p. 202; SG p. 64)
A collection of student work that show how a student's skills, attitudes, and knowledge change over time.

Positive Number (URG Unit 10 p. 27; SG p. 316)
A number greater than zero; a number to the right of zero on a horizontal number line.

Power (URG Unit 2 p. 175; SG p. 60)
An exponent. Read 10^4 as, "ten to the fourth power" or "ten to the fourth." We say 10,000 or 10^4 is the fourth power of ten.

Prime Factorization (URG Unit 11 p. 61; SG p. 361)
Writing a number as a product of primes. The prime
factorization of 100 is $2 \times 2 \times 5 \times 5$.

Prime Number (URG Unit 11 p. 26; SG p. 351)
A number that has exactly two factors: itself and 1.
For example, 7 has exactly two distinct factors, 1 and 7.

Probability (URG Unit 7 pp. 11, 130, 143;
SG pp. 21, 256, 261)
A number from 0 to 1 (0% to 100%) that describes how
likely an event is to happen. The closer that the probability
of an event is to one, the more likely the event will happen.

Product (URG Unit 2 p. 53; SG p. 35)
The answer to a multiplication problem. In the problem
$3 \times 4 = 12$, 12 is the product.

Proper Fraction (URG Unit 3 p. 56; SG p. 74)
A fraction in which the numerator is less than the denominator. Proper fractions are less than one.

Proportion (URG Unit 3 p. 91 & Unit 13 pp. 8, 28;
SG p. 397)
A statement that two ratios are equal.

Protractor (URG Unit 6 p. 33; SG p. 188)
A tool for measuring angles.

Q

Quadrants (URG Unit 10 p. 40; SG p. 319)
The four sections of a coordinate grid that are separated by
the axes.

Quadrilateral (URG Unit 6 pp. 45, 63; SG p. 192)
A polygon with four sides. (*See also* polygon.)

Quotient (URG Unit 4 p. 55 & Unit 9 pp. 50, 51;
SG pp. 37, 108, 296)
The answer to a division problem. In the problem
$12 \div 3 = 4$, the 4 is the quotient.

R

Radius (URG Unit 14 pp. 61, 62; SG p. 435)
1. A line segment connecting the center of a circle to any
   point on the circle.
2. The length of this line segment.

Ratio (URG Unit 3 p. 90 & Unit 12 p. 76; SG pp. 89, 396)
A way to compare two numbers or quantities using
division. It is often written as a fraction.

Ray (URG Unit 6 p. 30; SG p. 184)
A part of a line with one endpoint that extends indefinitely
in one direction.

Rectangle (URG Unit 6 pp. 101, 104; SG p. 211)
A quadrilateral with four right angles.

Reflection (URG Unit 10 p. 102)
(*See* flip.)

Regular Polygon (URG Unit 6 pp. 10, 47, 63; SG p. 199;
DAB p. 90)
A polygon with all sides of equal length and all angles equal.

Remainder (URG Unit 4 p. 57 & Unit 9 pp. 51, 53;
SG pp. 110, 296)
Something that remains or is left after a division problem.
The portion of the dividend that is not evenly divisible by
the divisor, e.g., $16 \div 5 = 3$ with 1 as a remainder.

Repeating Decimals (SG p. 290)
A decimal fraction with one or more digits repeating without end.

Responding Variable (URG Unit 4 p. 114; SG p. 133)
The variable whose values result from the experiment.
Experimenters find the values of the responding variable
by doing the experiment. The responding variable is often
called the dependent variable.

Rhombus (URG Unit 6 pp. 101, 104; SG p. 211)
A quadrilateral with four equal sides.

Right Angle (URG Unit 6 pp. 10, 31; SG p. 185)
An angle that measures 90°.

Right Triangle (URG Unit 6 p. 104 & Unit 15 p. 47;
SG pp. 188, 462)
A triangle that contains a right angle.

Rubric (URG Unit 1 p. 103)
A scoring guide that can be used to guide or assess
student work.

S

Sample (URG Unit 1 p. 10)
A part or subset of a population.

Scalene Triangle (URG Unit 15 p. 64)
A triangle that has no sides that are equal in length.

Scientific Notation (URG Unit 2 p. 176; SG p. 61)
A way of writing numbers, particularly very large or very
small numbers. A number in scientific notation has two
factors. The first factor is a number greater than or equal
to one and less than ten. The second factor is a power of 10
written with an exponent. For example, 93,000,000 written
in scientific notation is 9.3×10^7.

Septagon (URG Unit 6 p. 63; SG p. 198)
A seven-sided polygon.

Side-Angle-Side (URG Unit 6 p. 75 & Unit 14 p. 78)
A geometric property stating that two triangles having
two corresponding sides with the included angle equal
are congruent.

Side-Side-Side (URG Unit 6 p. 74)
A geometric property stating that two triangles having corresponding sides equal are congruent.

Sides of an Angle (URG Unit 6 p. 30; SG p. 184)
The sides of an angle are two rays with the same endpoint. (*See also* endpoint and ray.)

Sieve of Eratosthenes (SG p. 354)
A method for separating prime numbers from nonprime numbers developed by Eratosthenes, an Egyptian librarian, in about 240 BCE.

Similar (URG Unit 6 p. 75; SG p. 201)
Similar shapes have the same shape but not necessarily the same size.

Skinny (URG Unit 2 pp. 10, 11, 70, 79; SG p. 48)
A block that measures 1 cm × 1 cm × 10 cm. It is one of the base-ten pieces and is often used to represent 10. (*See also* base-ten pieces.)

Slide (URG Unit 10 p. 88; SG p. 333)
Moving a geometric figure in the plane by moving every point of the figure the same distance in the same direction. Also called translation.

Speed (URG Unit 3 p. 116 & Unit 5 p. 80; SG pp. 94, 165)
The ratio of distance moved to time taken, e.g., 3 miles/1 hour or 3 mph is a speed.

Square (URG Unit 6 p. 104 & Unit 14 p. 65; SG p. 211)
A quadrilateral with four equal sides and four right angles.

Square Centimeter (URG Unit 4 p. 10; SG p. 102)
The area of a square that is 1 cm long on each side.

Square Number (URG Unit 11 p. 48)
A number that is the product of a whole number multiplied by itself. For example, 25 is a square number since $5 \times 5 = 25$. A square number can be represented by a square array with the same number of rows as columns. A square array for 25 has 5 rows of 5 objects in each row or 25 total objects.

Standard Form (SG pp. 29, 61)
The traditional way to write a number, e.g., standard form for three hundred fifty-seven is 357. (*See also* expanded form and word form.)

Standard Units (URG Unit 4 p. 139)
Internationally or nationally agreed-upon units used in measuring variables, e.g., centimeters and inches are standard units used to measure length and square centimeters and square inches are used to measure area.

Straight Angle (URG Unit 6 p. 31; SG pp. 186, 194)
An angle that measures 180°.

T

Ten Percent (URG Unit 4 p. 86; SG p. 120)
10 out of every hundred or $\frac{1}{10}$.

Tessellation (URG Unit 6 p. 86 & Unit 10 p. 129; SG p. 206)
A pattern made up of one or more repeated shapes that completely covers a surface without any gaps or overlaps.

Translation
(*See* slide.)

Trapezoid (URG Unit 6 pp. 46, 104)
A quadrilateral with exactly one pair of parallel sides.

Triangle (URG Unit 6 p. 63; SG p. 198)
A polygon with three sides.

Triangulating (URG Unit 6 p. 61; SG p. 197)
Partitioning a polygon into two or more nonoverlapping triangles by drawing diagonals that do not intersect.

Turn-Around Facts (URG Unit 2 p. 53)
Multiplication facts that have the same factors but in a different order, e.g., $3 \times 4 = 12$ and $4 \times 3 = 12$. (*See also* commutative property of multiplication.)

Twin Primes (URG Unit 11 p. 41; SG p. 355)
A pair of prime numbers whose difference is 2. For example, 3 and 5 are twin primes.

U

Unit Ratio (URG Unit 13 p. 30; SG p. 399)
A ratio with a denominator of one.

V

Value (URG Unit 1 pp. 32, 53; SG p. 3)
The possible outcomes of a variable. For example, red, green, and blue are possible values for the variable *color*. Two meters and 1.65 meters are possible values for the variable *length*.

Variable (URG Unit 1 pp. 10, 32, 53; SG p. 3)
1. An attribute or quantity that changes or varies. (*See also* categorical variable and numerical variable.)
2. A symbol that can stand for a variable.

Variables in Proportion (URG Unit 13 pp. 9, 41; SG p. 402)
When the ratio of two variables in an experiment is always the same, the variables are in proportion.

Velocity (URG Unit 5 p. 80; SG p. 165)
Speed in a given direction. Speed is the ratio of the distance traveled to time taken.

Vertex (URG Unit 6 p. 30; SG pp. 184, 207)
A common point of two rays or line segments that form an angle.

Volume (URG Unit 13 p. 66)
The measure of the amount of space occupied by an object.

W

Whole Number
Any of the numbers 0, 1, 2, 3, 4, 5, 6 and so on.

Width of a Rectangle (URG Unit 4 p. 36 & Unit 15 p. 24; SG pp. 103, 455)
The distance along one side of a rectangle is the length and the distance along an adjacent side is the width.

Word Form (SG p. 29)
A number expressed in words, e.g., the word form for 123 is "one hundred twenty-three." (*See also* expanded form and standard form.)

Glossary

Grade 5 Index

This index provides the unit number in parentheses followed by the page number for the multivolume URG (*Unit Resource Guide*). It provides page references for the SG (*Student Guide*), the DAB (*Discovery Assignment Book*), the AB (*Adventure Book*), and the TIG (*Teacher Implementation Guide*). Definitions or explanations of key terms can be found on the pages listed in bold type.

Index

Bats, AB 93–106, URG (16) 33–49

Benchmarks, SG 171, **238,** URG (2) 38, URG (3) 78, URG (7) 82, URG (11) 71–72

fractions as, URG (5) 101

percents as, URG (4) 12

ten percent as, URG (4) 86

Best-Fit lines, SG **97,** 136, 167, 416, 430, 495, TIG 326–327, URG (3) 88–89, 115, 126–132, URG (4) 120–122, URG (11) 48, URG (13) 78–79, URG (14) 43, URG (16) 33, 46, 54, 57

Binning data, SG **274,** URG (8) **73,** 76, 88, 91–92

Biodiversity, URG (1) 94

Birds, URG (14) 94–95

Bits (place value), SG **49,** URG (2) **10–11, 70, 79,** URG (7) 33. *See also* Base-Ten pieces

Boll weevils, URG (4) 135

Brazilian rain forests, AB 1–12, URG (1) 94–96

C

Calculators, DAB 11–12, TIG 228, 290, URG (3) 112, URG (4) 55, **57–58, 101,** 102, 121–122, URG (8) 39, URG (9) 18, 33–35, URG (16) 81

decimals on, URG (11) 71–72

division on, SG 310–313, URG (9) 88–94

exponent key on, URG (2) 174–178, URG (11) 61

Home Practice Guide and, TIG 180

order of operations on, URG (4) **103,** URG (15) 84

pi (π) key on, URG (14) 44

square key (x^2) on, URG 34, 37, 39–40

square root key on, URG (15) 39–40

Canceling, TIG 261–262

Capacity, URG (16) 60

Capture-Recapture technique, URG (16) 54

Carpenter, Thomas, TIG 230, 306

"Carrying" in multiplication, URG (9) 68

Cartesian coordinates, SG 319–344, URG (10) **9, 40**

Great Barrier Reef example of, URG (10) 36, **39**–42

Cartesian product, TIG 309

Carver, George Washington, AB 21–34, 77–92, DAB 67, URG (4) 134–142, URG (12) 71–79

Carver Foundation, URG (12) 71–73

Categorical variables, DAB 1–6, SG **4,** 18, 22, TIG **315,** URG (1) **33**

Census figures, TIG 258

Center of circles, SG **426, 435,** URG (14) **29,** 41, **60**

Centers, in classrooms, TIG 410

Centimeters, square, TIG 336–339, URG (4) **10**

Centiwheels, DAB 219, SG 222–227, 448, URG (7) 23, **33**–38, 48–49, URG (9) 33–34

Central angles, SG **435,** URG (14) **62,** 65

Central tendency, TIG 251. *See also* Average, Mean, Median, Mode

Cents (¢), URG (3) 88, URG (7) **35**

Certain events, SG **256,** URG (7) **130**

Chicago, map of, URG (10) 118–124

Child labor, AB 47–60, URG (8) 42–50

Chords, SG **435,** URG (14) **61**

Christensen, Eric, AB 40–46, URG (7) 159, 162

Circle graphs, DAB 217–219, SG 225–227, 280, 445–449, URG (14) 91–100, **96**–97, URG (15) 19, URG (16) 13, 86–87

Circles, DAB 210, 213–215, SG **426**–451, URG (6) 30, URG (14) **9–10, 29,** 49, URG (15) 18, URG (16) 84. *See also* Circumference, Diameter

arcs of, SG **441,** URG (6) 117, URG (14) **75**

center of, SG **426, 435,** URG (14) **29,** 41,60

central angles of, SG **435,** URG (14) **62,** 65

chords of, SG **435,** URG (14) **61**

circumference of, SG **426**–**435, 427,** 445–449, URG (14) **29, 62,** URG (15) 18, URG (16) 84

concentric, SG **436,** URG (14) **64**

constructing, URG (14) 57–68, 84–86

diameter of, DAB 210, 213, SG 51, 426–**435, 427,** URG (14) 9, 16–17, 19, 26–33, 37–51, URG (16) 26–27

properties of, SG **427–451**

radius, SG 426, **435**

Circumference, SG 426–**435, 427,** URG (14) **29, 62,** URG (15) 18, URG (16) 84

diameter and, URG (14) 9–10, 16–17, 19, 26–33

diameter *versus,* DAB 210, 213, URG (14) 36–51, URG (16) 26–27

formula for, SG 432, URG (14) 44

Circumference *vs.* Diameter Lab, SG 428–434, URG (14) 36–51

Classification, URG (1) 10, URG (6) 97–107

definition of, URG (6) 100

Flatville zoo activity in, URG (6) 103–104

in geometry, URG (6) 101

Professor Peabody's zoo activity in, URG (6) 102

Classroom,

culture, TIG 131–132, 364–369

discourse, TIG 424–426

establishing norms, TIG 365–366

language, TIG 415–418

standards-based, TIG 369, 407

Classroom environment, TIG 132

Closeness, URG (4) 11–12, 80–87

in areas of irregular shapes, URG (4) 83–87

in estimates, URG (4) 88–89

relative, TIG **264**

Cloze exercises, TIG 384

Clusters, TIG 251, URG (16) 58

Cognitive competencies, TIG 389

Coin flipping

See Flipping coins

Index

extensions, URG (1) 8, URG (2) 9, URG (3) 8, URG (4) 8, URG (5) 8, URG (6) 8, URG (8) 8, URG (9) 7, URG (10) 8, URG (11) 8, URG (12) 8, URG (13) 7, URG (14) 8, URG (15) 7, URG (16) 7

games, URG (1) 7, URG (2) 9, URG (5) 7, URG (7) 8, URG (8) 8, URG (9) 7, URG (10) 8, URG (11) 8, URG (12) 8, URG (14) 8

journal prompts, URG (1) 7, URG (2) 9, URG (3) 8, URG (4) 8, URG (5) 8, URG (6) 8, URG (7) 8, URG (8) 8, URG (9) 7, URG (10) 8, URG (11) 8, URG (12) 8, URG (14) 8, URG (16) 7

laboratory experiments, URG (1) 7, URG (3) 8, URG (4) 8, URG (5) 7, URG (7) 8, URG (8) 8, URG (13) 7, URG (14) 8, URG (16) 7

Digits, SG **27–29**

decimal, TIG 268

leading, TIG 268

Digits Game, TIG 464–466, URG (1) 25–26, URG (7) 19, URG (9) 20, 22

fractions, URG (14) 15

Discourse, TIG 132, 364, 424–426. *See also* Communication

Discovery Assignment Book (DAB), TIG 48, 54

Displacement, TIG 350–351

Distance, SG 94–98, 165, 167, 182, 402–404, URG (16) 85

to define perimeter, URG (15) 83–85

predictions of, URG (10) 65

to time ratio, URG (13) 8–9, 41–42

Distance *vs.* Time Lab, URG (3) 110–132, URG (8) 30–31, 34, URG (16) 26

Distribution in populations, URG (1) 98–111

District implementation of *Math Trailblazers,* TIG 438–439

Diversity in problem types, TIG 308

Dividends, SG **106, 296,** URG (4) 55–57, URG (9) 50–51, 53–54

Divisibility rules, URG (11) 60

Division, DAB 44, 147–148, 151–155, 161, 177, 189, 201, 209, 223, 231, SG **106**–117, 294–298, 296, 304–313, URG (3) 29, URG (5) 17, 22, URG (9) 14–15, 19, URG (10) 15, 20, URG (11) 14–21, URG (12) 18, URG (14) 14, 20–21, URG (15) 16. *See also* Dividends, Divisors

of big numbers, URG (2) 12

calculator strategies for, SG 310–313, URG (9) 88–94

denominators and, SG **68,** 146–147, URG (5) 31

estimation and, TIG 260–262

fact inventory test, URG (8) 25

"Facts I Know," URG (2) 56, 62

Flash Cards, SG 37–38

forgiving method of, SG **113**–117, 296–298, URG (4) **9–10, 71,** URG (9) 47–58

fractions and, URG (9) 27–39

Math Facts on, SG 36–38, TIG 173, 288, URG (3) 16, 18, 21, 24, URG (4) 23–24, URG (5) 17, 20–21, 23, URG (6) 16, 19, URG (7) 17, 20, 22, 24, 26–27, URG (8) 16–17, 19–21, 23, URG (9) 17, 19, 23, URG (10) 16, URG (12) 14, 16–19, URG (13) 15, 17, 19, 21–22, URG (14) 16, 18, 24, URG (15) 17, 19, URG (16) 14–16, 19

measurement and, URG (4) **9**

modeling, SG 106–112, URG (4) 52–63

by multiples of ten, SG 109, 111, URG (4) 27, URG (9) 20, 22, URG (10) 17–18

numerators and, SG **68,** 147–148, URG (3) 36

partitive, TIG 309, URG (4) **9**

pencil-and-paper, SG 113–117, 294–298, URG (4) 68–76

problem solving with, TIG 308–309, URG (9) 18

quotient, SG **37, 108, 296,** URG (4) 10, 55–58, URG (9) **50–51,** 52

in recipes, AB 84

remainders in, DAB 149, SG 109–116, **110,** 296, 304–313, URG (4) 57–58, 73, 102, URG (9) 23–24, **51,** 74–82, URG (13) 17

subtraction method of, URG (4) 10

with zeros, URG (6) 24

Divisors, SG **37, 106,** 296, URG (2) **56,** URG (4) 55–57, URG (9) **50–51**

Dodecagons, DAB 91, SG 198, URG (6) **63**

Dollars and cents, URG (7) **35**

Doubling, DAB 232, TIG 284–286, URG (3) 89, URG (16) 12, 21

Drawing shapes, URG (10) 127–132. *See also* Shapes

E

Echolocation, AB 102, URG (16) 39

Ecosystems, URG (1) 94

Education Development Center (EDC), TIG 389, 394–399

Einstein, Albert, TIG 355

11-gons, DAB 91, URG (6) 63

Endangered species, URG (14) 94–95

Endpoints, SG **184,** URG (6) **30**

English language learners, TIG 3, 375–387

improving skills of, TIG 417

introduction to, TIG 375–376

language-rich approach to, TIG 378–379

lesson plan examples for, TIG 382–383

nonverbal communication and, TIG 386

outcomes, TIG 382

strategies for, TIG 385–386

support, TIG 377

teachers issues with, TIG 381

theories and, TIG 376–377

tools supporting, TIG 377

Enlargements, URG (10) 106

Environment, classroom, TIG 132

Equal arm balance, TIG 356–358, URG (13) 64

Equally likely events, SG **257,** URG (7) 130

Equal ratios, URG (3) 119

Equal sharing, URG (4) 9

Equidistant points, URG (14) **60**

Equilateral triangles, URG (6) 87, 101, URG (14) **79,**
    URG (15) **64**

Equity Principle, TIG 9, 374

Equivalent fractions, AB 105, DAB 77–78, 201, SG
    77–81, 222–223, 260, 363–368, 378, URG (3)
    63–71, **67,** 89, URG (4) 19, URG (5) 60–61,
    URG (7) 34–35, URG (8) 17, URG (9) 34–35,
    URG (11) 80, URG (13) 80, URG (16) 40

    Fractohoppers and, URG (3) 66–68

    number lines and, URG (3) 68–69

    pattern blocks and, URG (3) 66

Equivalent ratios, URG (16) 47

Equivalent sets, TIG 308–309

Eratosthenes, SG 353–355, **354,** URG (11) 17, 36, 38,
    89, 98

Erosion, AB 4

Error, URG (4) 85, 88

    experimental, TIG 276, URG (4) 117, URG (5) 82, 84

    measurement, TIG 262, URG (13) 80, URG (16) 27

    TIMS tutor on, TIG 262–267

Escher, M.C., SG 345, URG (6) 10, 87, URG (10) 10,
    127–132

Estimation, AB 13–20, DAB 153–155, SG 27, 32, 45, **57,**
    112, 118–122, 251, 253–254, 485, TIG **255,**
    URG (1) 11, 122, URG (2) **160,** URG (4) 26,
    URG (5) 24, URG (9) 16, URG (16) 12, 19.
    See also Accuracy, Approximation, Ten percent
    standard

    of angles, URG (6) 17

    of area, DAB 65, SG 131–138

    of areas of irregular shapes, URG (4) 83–87, 91–92

    of averages, URG (8) 76

    in base-ten system, URG (2) 74

    benchmarks for, SG 171, **238**

    of circumference, URG (14) 31

    closeness and, URG (4) 11–12, 88–90

    convenient numbers for, SG **57**

    decimals and, SG 249–254, URG (7) 24, 109–111

    of differences, URG (2) 77

    in division, TIG 260–261, URG (4) 55, 73

    forgiving division method and, URG (4) 10

    of fraction sums, SG **171**–181, URG (5) 101

    in Grass Act activity, URG (9) 113

    Home Practice Guide and, TIG 180

    of large numbers, SG 312, URG (2) 11, URG (3) 120

    magnitude of a measurement, TIG 266–268

of money, URG (8) 22

of populations, AB 6, 105–106

in problem solving, TIG 305, URG (6) 20

of products, SG 56, 59, 303, 388–391, URG (2)
    157–164, URG (9) 21

using proportions, URG (16) 58–59

of quotients, SG 113–117, 294–298, URG (9) 51, 54

from samples, URG (16) 47

in Score One Game, DAB 103

sums, SG 171–181, 244–246

ten percent, DAB 65, SG 120–122, 136, TIG 266,
    URG (4) 12, **86**–87

in Three in a Row Game, URG (8) 39

TIMS tutor on, TIG 255–262, 266–270

Euros currency, URG (8) 24

Events, probability of, URG (7) **130**

Expanded form, DAB 13, SG **28**–32, 34, URG (2) 32–44

Expectations, TIG 17, 365

Experimental error, TIG **262**–267, 276, URG (5) 82, 84

Experiments

    review of, DAB 135–136, 235–237, SG 270, 282, 488,
        URG (8) 26–29, URG (16) 22–30

    variables in, TIG 314–317

Exponents, DAB 178, SG 358, 361, 459, URG (2)
    172–179, **175,** URG (11) 21, **61,** URG (15) 37

    base of, SG **60,** URG (2) 175

    calculator key for, SG 362, 459, URG (2) 175–178,
        URG (11) 61

Expository writing, TIG 380

Extensions of lessons, URG (1) 8, URG (2) 9, URG (3) 8,
    URG (4) 8, URG (5) 8, URG (6) 8, URG (8) 8,
    URG (9) 7, URG (10) 8, URG (11) 8, URG (12)
    8, URG (13) 7, URG (14) 8, URG (15) 7,
    URG (16) 7

Extrapolation, SG **399,** TIG 324, **327,** URG (3) 115,
    URG (8) 31, URG (13) **29,** URG (14) 43,
    URG (16) 27

Eyelets Lab, SG 2–9, URG (1) 32–37, URG (8) 30,
    URG (16) 26–27

F

Fact families, SG **36**–37, URG (2) 54–**55.** *See also* Math
    Facts

Factor 40 Game, DAB 181, SG 348–352, TIG 467,
    URG (11) 23–32

Factors, DAB 137–139, 185, SG **35,** 348, 360–362, 373,
    URG (7) 111, 120, URG (8) 39, URG (11) 18, **26,**
    84, URG (16) 13

    to fractions, URG (11) 101–103

    multiplication, URG (2) **53**

    of numbers, SG **348**–352, 373

    prime, URG (11) 57–63, URG (14) 20

    scale, TIG 309

Factor trees, SG **361,** URG (11) 57, 60–67

Factory laws, AB 57

Facts. *See* Math Facts

Facts I Know, TIG 171, URG (2) 25–28, URG (3) 16

Fahrenheit temperature scale, URG (10) 27, 32

"Fair" coin, AB 44, URG (7) 159, **163**

"Fair" game, SG **259,** URG (7) **138**

Family math, TIG 433–437

Family math nights, TIG 433–437

Family size, URG (7) 154–157

Feedback, from field testing, TIG 18

Ferris wheel quilt pattern, URG (6) 85, 92

Fewest pieces rule, URG (2) 71, 80

Field testing of *Math Trailblazers,* TIG 18

FigureThis.org, TIG 452

Fish, URG (14) **94**–95

Fixed variables, DAB 135–136, 235–237, SG **96, 133,**
    TIG **316**–317, URG (3) 116, URG (4) 117,
    URG (8) 30–31, 87, URG (16) 26–27, 56.
    See also Manipulated variables, Responding
    variable, Variables

Flash Cards. *See* Triangle Flash Cards

Flat (place value), SG **49**–50, URG (2) **10–11, 71, 79,**
    URG (7) 33. *See also* Base-Ten pieces

Flatville zoo activity, URG (6) 103, 104

Flipping, in geometry, SG 337
    pattern blocks, URG (3) 36
    shapes, DAB 173–174, URG (10) 100–110, **102**

Flipping coins. *See also* Probability
    one coin, AB 35–46, DAB 119–123, URG (7) 126–132
    two coins, URG (7) 135–147, URG (8) 30, URG (16) 26

Flipping Two Coins Lab, SG 259–262, URG (7) 135–147,
    URG (8) 30

Floating objects, TIG 352

Florence Kelley, AB 47–60, SG 271–272, URG (8) 42–67

Fluency, in language, TIG 376

Forgiving method of division, SG **113**–117, 294–298,
    URG (4) **9–10,** 68–76, **71**

Forms of numbers, DAB 13, SG **28**–32, 34, URG (2) 32–44

Formulas, SG **357,** 431–432, TIG 273–274
    for area, TIG 337
    area of rectangle, SG 455, URG (15) 25
    area of right triangles, SG 465, URG (15) 49–50
    area of triangles, SG 473, URG (15) 61–71
    circumference and diameter, SG 432, URG (14) 44
    geometry, URG (15) 8–9
    perimeter of rectangle, SG 480

Foundations, *Math Trailblazers,* TIG 8–22
    assessment, TIG 13
    balanced approach, TIG 14–15
    collaborative work, TIG 12–13
    equity, TIG 9
    problem solving, TIG 10
    reform recommendations, TIG 8–9
    research, TIG 15–22

    school support, TIG 14
    science and language arts, TIG 10–12
    time requirements, TIG 13–14

Fraction Cover-All Game, SG 157–158, TIG 465,
    URG (5) 59–60

Fractions Digits Game, TIG 468, URG (14) 15

Fractions, DAB 28, 30, 73–74, 83, 98, 105, 107, 109, 128,
    147, 178, 190, 224, 231, SG 21–22, 99, 144–182,
    223, 260–264, 274, 280–281, 363–373, 376–393,
    447, TIG 237–241, URG (1) 99, 105, URG (4) 24,
    URG (6) 20, URG (8) 18, 22, URG (11) 9, 18, 20,
    URG (12) 9, 18, URG (13) 14, 16, 20, URG (16) 17.
    See also Denominator, Mixed numbers, Numerator
  addition and subtraction of, SG 157–159, 171–176,
    177–181, **369**–371, 376–382, URG (5) 97–105,
    110–118, URG (7) 28, URG (8) 21, URG (10) 19
  common, SG **223,** URG (7) **9**
  common denominators of, SG 160–163, 167, 171–181,
    364–367, 380–382, URG (3) 79, URG (5) 60–61,
    67–73, **71,** 103, 114, URG (11) **71,** URG (12) 23
  comparing, SG 82–84, 160–163, 169–170, 224,
    363–367, URG (3) 25, 75–81, URG (5) 25,
    URG (11) 60–74
  decimal, SG **223,** URG (7) 9, 35, 42
  from decimals, URG (9) **90,** URG (11) 16
  to decimals and percents, SG 222–231, **223,** 260–264,
    274, 286–293, URG (7) **35**–38, URG (9) 18, URG
    (14) 96–97
  denominators of, AB 84, SG **68,** 74, 83, 144, 146–147,
    URG (3) **36,** 56, URG (5) 31, URG (9) 78
  division and, SG 286–293, URG (9) 27–39
  dot paper and, URG (5) 22
  equivalent, AB 105, DAB 77–78, 201, SG **77**–81,
    222–223, 260, 363–368, 378, URG (3) 63–71,
    URG (4) 19, URG (5) 60–61, URG (7) 34–35,
    URG (8) 17, URG (13) 80, URG (16) 40
  fractohoppers and, DAB 39, SG 78–84, URG (3) 66–68,
    URG (5) 101
  geoboards and, SG 144–151, URG (5) 26–36
  greater than one, URG (3) 55–56, URG (5) 33
  of groups, SG 383–386, URG (12) 38–44
  improper, SG **74**–75, 377, URG (3) 20, 51, 55–**56,**
    URG (5) 33
  lowest terms of, SG **369**–370, URG (11) 80, 84,
    URG (12) 23–24, URG (16) 39
  in mixed numbers, SG **74**–76, 150, 376–382, URG (14) 22
  modeling, URG (5) 9–10
  multiplication of, SG 383–392, URG (12) 49–57,
    URG (14) 20–21
  numerators of, SG **68,** 74, 84, 144, 147, URG (5) 31–33
  ordering, URG (3) 22
  paper folding to multiply, URG (12) 61–68
  pattern blocks for, SG 69–72, 152–153, 376–382, 387–389,
    URG (3) 31–42
  in prices, URG (3) 30

probability and, SG **21, 261**

proper, SG **74,** URG (3) 51, **56**

in recipes, AB 84

reducing, AB 85, SG 368–373, **369,** 378–382,
URG (11) 78–84, URG (12) 23–24, URG (13)
29–30, URG (16) 39

sentences with, URG (3) 51–58

skip counting, URG (3) 21, 80

tenths and hundredths, URG (7) 33, 42–46

whole numbers multiplied by, URG (12) 49, 52–53

wholes and parts, modeling of, SG 68–72, 152–156,
URG (3) 31–41, URG (5) 44–50

from 0 to 1, URG (4) 21

Fractohoppers, DAB 39, SG 78–84, URG (3) 66–68,
URG (5) 101

Frequency, URG (8) 91

Frijoles Canyon, AB 93–106, URG (16) 36

Function machines, DAB 210, URG (14) 18–19,
URG (16) 19

Functions, TIG 275–276. *See also* Linear patterns,
Variables

TIMS tutor on, TIG 271–276

Fundamental variables, URG (5) 10

Fungi, AB 23

G

Galileo, TIG 355–356

Gallons, SG 92, 156

Games, TIG 4, 290, 463–468

Barrier Reef, The, SG 323–324, TIG 467, URG (10)
41–45

Digits, TIG 464–466, URG (1) 25–26, URG (7) 19,
URG (9) 20, 22

Factor 40, DAB 181, SG 348–352, TIG 467, URG (11)
23–32

"fair" and "unfair," URG (7) **138**

Fraction Cover-All, SG 157–158, TIG 465, URG (5)
59–60

Fractions Digits, TIG 468, URG (14) 15

Hexagon Duets, DAB 193, SG 376–377, TIG 467,
URG (12) 20–27

How Many Heads?, SG 258–259, TIG 465, URG (7)
135–147

Matching 2 Pennies, SG 264, URG (7) 144–145

Score One, DAB 103, TIG 465, URG (7) 66

Spin and Read Number, DAB 17, SG 32–33, TIG 464,
URG (2) 39

Three in a Row, DAB 137–139, TIG 466, URG (8)
37–40

Gas bubbles, URG (13) 88

General Theory of Relativity (Einstein), TIG 355

Genetics, AB 23

Genus, URG (6) 100

Geoboard fractions, URG (5) 26–36

Geoboards, SG 144–151, 462–464, 468–478,
URG (15) 44–54

Geometry, DAB 128, 232, URG (15) 19, URG (16) 20. *See
also* Angles, Constructions, Coordinates, Flipping,
Formulas, Shapes, Slides

classification in, URG (6) 101

coordinate, URG (14) 23

developmental levels of, URG (6) 9–10

formulas and, URG (15) 8–9

in unit scope and sequence, TIG 136, 138, 140, 142,
144, 146, 148, 150, 152, 154, 156, 158, 160, 162,
164, 166

George Washington Carver: Man of Measure,
AB 21–34, DAB 67, URG (4) 134–142

Gifted or talented students, TIG 374, 402–404

identifying, TIG 402–404

introduction to, TIG 402

lesson planning for, TIG 408–413

resources on, TIG 413

supporting learning of, TIG 406–408

teaching, TIG 405–407

Glossary, TIG 4, 379–387

Goldbach's Conjecture, URG (11) 38

Goldberg, H., TIG 13

Googol, AB 19–20, SG **141,** URG (2) **169,** 171

Googolplex, AB 19–20, SG **141,** URG (2) **169,** 171

Graduated cylinders, AB 33, TIG 347–349, URG (4) 140,
URG (13) 67–68

Grams (g), TIG **331,** URG (13) 65

Graphic organizers, TIG 377, 423

Graphs, DAB 129, SG 7, 167, 169, 182, 270, 406–410,
TIG 272–273, 320–327, 328, URG (3) 95.
See also Best-Fit lines, Labs

in analyzing data, URG (1) 76, URG (3) 110–132, URG
(13) 79–85

of areas, URG (4) 28

bar, AB 44–45, DAB 5, SG 6, 8–19, 23, 134, 261,
274–279, TIG 324–325, URG (1) 21, 61–63

bar *versus* point, TIG 320–322

best-fit lines, TIG 264, 321

circle, DAB 217–219, SG 225–227, 280, 445–449,
URG (14) 91–100, **96**–97, URG (15) 19, URG
(16) 13, 86–87

circumference *versus* diameter, URG (14) 42–43

of costs, URG (7) 18

data, URG (1) 53–54

of densities, URG (13) 78–79, 82–84

in Distances *vs.* Time Lab, URG (3) 117–119, 124–132

in experiments, DAB 135–136, 235–237, URG (8) 30–31,
34, URG (16) 26–27

in Flipping Two Coins Lab, URG (7) 141–142

labeling axes of, TIG 323–324

of life spans, URG (8) 74–80, 89

point, SG 86–93, 97–98, 134, 356, 416, 430, 491, 495, 497, TIG 326–327, URG (4) 116, 120, URG (7) 138, 141, URG (8) 26, 31, 57, URG (16) 22, 27, 46, 57

problem solving and, DAB 45, URG (5) 124–127

ratio and proportion from, URG (3) 88–90, 97–101, URG (13) 29–31

of samples, URG (16) 46, 57

in Searching the Forest Lab, URG (1) 104

shapes of, URG (1) 37, URG (8) 86

of speeds, URG (5) 10, 85

in Spreading Out Lab, URG (4) 116, 120, 127

from survey data, URG (8) 56–57

of variables in proportion, URG (13) 46–48

Grass Act activity, URG (9) 98–113

planning, URG (9) 102–103

solving problems in, URG (9) 104–111

Gravity, TIG 355

Great Barrier Reef, Australia, URG (10) 36, **39**–40. *See also* Barrier Reef, The, Game

Greater than **(>),** DAB 107–108, URG (4) 23, URG (7) 19, URG (10) 15

Grids, DAB 113–118

area of, URG (4) 32–44

coordinate, URG (3) 119

decimal, URG (7) 62–64, 70, 82, 97–99

Grouping data, URG (8) 69–80

Groups, estimation of, TIG 268–269

Groups, fractions of, URG (12) 38–44

Groups, student. *See* Teamwork

Height of triangles, SG **470**–472, URG (15) **65,** 67, URG (16) 86

Helping Your Child Learn Mathematics **(ed.gov/parents/academic/help/math/index/html),** TIG 452

Hendecagons, URG (6) 63

Heptagons, URG (6) 63

Heterogeneous grouping of students, TIG 366

Hexagon Duets Game, DAB 193, SG 376–377, TIG 467, URG (12) 20–27

Hexagons, DAB 89–91, SG 69, 198, URG (3) 38, 94, URG (6) 47, 62–**63**

quilt pattern of, URG (6) 85–86, 91

regular, URG (6) 93

Hierarchical classification, URG (6) **102**

Hoagies Gifted Education Page, TIG 413

Home Practice, TIG 48, 54

guide, TIG 170–180

scope and sequence for, TIG 135–167

Homogeneous grouping of students, TIG 405–406

Horizontal axis. *See* X-axis

How Many Bats in a Cave? Lab, SG 492–497, URG (16) 51–63

How Many Heads? Game, SG 258–259, TIG 465, URG (7) 135–147

How to Lie with Statistics (Huff), TIG 247, 251

How to Solve It (Polya), TIG 305

Huff, Darrell, TIG 247

Hull House, Chicago, AB 50–60, URG (8) 42

Hundreds, numbers in, DAB 10

Hundred-thousandths, URG (7) 64–65

Hundredths, URG (7) 33, 45–47, 64–65, 140, URG (9) 17

Hypotenuse, SG **462,** URG (15) **47**

I

Illinois Bureau of Labor Statistics, AB 54

Image, SG **333,** URG (10) 88, 102

Immigrants, URG (8) 42

Impossible events, SG **256,** URG (7) 130

Improper fractions, SG **74**–75, 377, URG (3) 20, 51, 55–**56,** 95, URG (5) 33

Inches, AB 31–32

Indicators, assessment. *See* Assessment indicators

Individual student needs, TIG 373–414, URG (1) 7, URG (2) 9, URG (3) 8, URG (4) 8, URG (5) 7, URG (6) 8, URG (7) 8, URG (8) 8, URG (9) 7, URG (10) 8, URG (11) 8, URG (12) 8, URG (13) 7, URG (14) 8, URG (15) 7, URG (16) 7

English language learners, TIG 375–387

introduction to, TIG 375–376

language-rich approach to, TIG 378–379

lesson plan examples for, TIG 382–385

nonverbal communication and, TIG 386

strategies for, TIG 374–387

teacher issues with, TIG 381

theory on, TIG 376–377

tools supporting, TIG 377

gifted or talented students, TIG 402–413

identifying, TIG 402–404

introduction to, TIG 402

lesson planning for, TIG 408–413

resources on, TIG 413

supporting learning of, TIG 406–408

teaching, TIG 405–407

overview of, TIG 374–375

special education students, TIG 388–401

introduction to, TIG 388–389
lesson planning for, TIG 393–399
research on, TIG 389–393
Individualized education, TIG 389. *See also* Special education students
Individuals with Disabilities Education Act of 2004, TIG 388
Infinite, AB 17, URG (2) **171**
Informal deduction, URG (6) 9
Information for parents
English, URG (2) 13
Spanish, URG (2) 14
Integer division, URG (4) 58, 102, URG (9) **90**
Integers, SG 316–318, 322–342
Interest centers, in classrooms, TIG 410
Interior angles, URG (6) **35**
International Bureau of Weights and Measures, TIG 359
Internet resources for parents, TIG 451–452
Interpolation, SG **399,** TIG **327,** URG (8) 31, URG (13) **29,** URG (14) 43, URG (16) 27
Intersection, URG (14) **61**
Intervals, data, URG (8) 16, 88, 91
Intuitive understanding, of gifted or talented children, TIG 404
Investigations, TIG 11, 317–318
IQ scores, TIG 403
Irrational numbers, URG (14) 9
Isosceles triangles, URG (6) **104,** URG (15) **64**

J

Jacob's ladder quilt, URG (6) 84, 89–90
Join situations, TIG 306
Journaling, TIG 188, 194, 201, 208
TIMS tutor on, TIG 277–280

K

Karplus, Robert, TIG 15, URG (10) 9
Kasner, Edward, AB 19
Kelley, Florence, AB 47–60, SG 271–272, URG (8) 42–67
Kerrich, John, AB 38–46, URG (7) 159, 162
Kilograms (kg), URG (13) 65
Key words, reading and, TIG 421–422
Knowing **rubric,** SG 501, TIG 195, 205, URG (1) 11, 103, URG (3) 121, URG (4) 123, URG (8) 56–63, 66, URG (9) 103–111, URG (10) 119–120

L

Labeling axes, TIG 323–324
Labor, child, AB 47–60
Laboratory equipment, AB 27–34
Labs. *See also* Experiments
assessment of, TIG 189, 208
Circumference *vs.* Diameter, SG 428–434, URG (14) 36–51
Comparing Lives of Animals and Soap Bubbles, SG 276–279, URG (8) 83–93
Day at the Races, A, SG 164–170, URG (5) 76–92, URG (8) 30–31
Distance *vs.* Time, SG 94–98, URG (3) 110–132, URG (4) 29–30, URG (8) 34
evaluation of, TIG 202
Eyelets, SG 2–9, URG (1) 32–37, URG (8) 30–31
Flipping Two Coins, SG 259–262, URG (7) 135–147, URG (8) 30
How Many Bats in a Cave?, SG 492–497, URG (16) 51–63
Mass *vs.* Volume: Proportions and Density, SG 415–422, URG (13) 74–91
review of, URG (16) 22–30
Searching the Forest, SG 17–23, URG (1) 98–113, URG (8) 30–31
Sink and Float, SG 411–414, URG (13) 54–68
Spreading Out, SG 131–138, URG (4) 110–130, URG (8) 30–31
TIMS Laboratory Method in, TIG 11, 130, URG (1) 9–10
Lambert, Johan Heinrich, URG (14) 9
Language arts connections, TIG 10, 12, 131, URG (10) 59. *See also* Communication, English language learners, Reading, Vocabulary, Writing
discourse in, TIG 424–426
incorporating, TIG 416–417
reading in, TIG 418–422
writing in, TIG 422–423
Lattice multiplication, DAB 157–158, SG **300**–302, URG (9) 8–9, **67**–68
Law of Large Numbers, URG (7) 11, 163
Lawrence Hall of Science, Berkeley, CA, URG (8) 39
Leading digits, TIG 257
Learning centers, in classrooms, TIG 405, 410
Legs of triangles, SG **462,** URG (15) **47**
Legumes, URG (12) 71, **74,** 78
Length, SG **103, 455,** URG (4) 139, URG (5) 10
addition of, URG (7) 25
in area measurement, TIG 337

M

Index

Money DAB 45, URG (5) 20–21, URG (6) 21, 24,
    URG (7) 18, 21, 35, URG (8) 22, 24, URG (9) 15,
    33, URG (10) 14, 31, URG (12) 19, URG (13) 22,
    URG (15) 20, URG (16) 17
Motivation, increasing, TIG 406
Mr. Origin, SG **327**–329, URG (10) **9, 64**–65
MTB Families, TIG 4, 429–430
    brochure for, TIG 443–444
    communication tools for, TIG 431–432
    Internet resources for, TIG 451
    Letter Home, English, URG (1–20) iii
    Letter Home, Spanish, URG (1–20) iv
    Math Facts information for, TIG 432, 447–450
    Math Facts philosophy for, TIG 432, 447
    programs for, TIG 433–437
    Spanish language materials for, TIG 445–446
Multiple representations of procedures, TIG 391
Multiple solutions, TIG 304–305
Multiplication, DAB 44, 148, 157–158, 177, 189, SG
    46–63, 299–303, URG (2) 137–143, URG (3) 29,
    URG (4) 21, URG (9) 64–70, URG (11) 14, 21,
    URG (14) 15, URG (15) 16, URG (16) 16
    all-partials method of, SG 53, URG (2) **139,** URG (9)
        66–67
    area strategies and, URG (4) 36, URG (15) 24
    of big numbers, URG (2) 12, 131–149
    commutative property of, URG (2) **140**
    compact method of, SG 53, URG (9) 66
    of decimals, SG 247–254, URG (7) 10, 27, 107–113,
        117–123
    estimation and, SG 56–59, 303, 388–391, TIG 258–260,
        URG (2) 157–164
    fact inventory test, URG (8) 25
    "Facts I Know," URG (2) 52–58, 61
    of fractions, SG 383–392, URG (12) 49–57,
        URG (14) 20–21
    lattice method of, SG 300–302, URG (9) 8–9, **67**–68
    Making Money activity for, URG (2) 147–149
    Math Facts, SG 35, TIG 173, 286–288, URG (3) 16, 18,
        21, 24, URG (4) 23–24, URG (5) 17, 20–21, 23,
        URG (6) 16, 18–19, URG (7) 17, 20, 22, 24,
        26–27, URG (8) 16–17, 19–21, 23, URG (12) 19
    by multiples of ten, SG 46–55, URG (2) 136–137,
        URG (3) 17, URG (4) 27, URG (5) 18, URG (9) 20,
        51, URG (10) 18
    paper-and-pencil method of, SG 53, 299–303,
        URG (9) 66
    problem solving with, TIG 308–309
    by two and four, URG (14) 17
    with zeros, URG (6) 24
Multiplication tables, URG (2) 146
Multi-Step logic, TIG 11
Mycology, AB 23
Mymathtrailblazers.com, TIG 451

N

NASA Ames Research Center, URG (14) 9
National Association for Gifted Children (NAGC), TIG
    403, 413
National Association of Bilingual Education, TIG 386
National Bureau of Standards, TIG 359
National Consumers League, URG (8) 44
National Council of Teachers of Mathematics (NCTM),
    TIG 2–3, 8, 15–16, 19, 21, URG (1) 12, URG (2)
    12, URG (9) 8–9, URG (12) 9
    standards, TIG 127–133
    strategies *versus* drill and, TIG 170–171
National Research Council, TIG 314
National Science Education Standards **(National**
    Research Council), TIG 314
National Science Foundation, TIG 15, 18
NCTM Families Web page, TIG 451
NCTM Illuminations Web page, TIG 451
Negative numbers, DAB 161, SG **316**–318, 322–331,
    URG (10) 9, 16, 22–33, **26,** 41
Negative sign (−), URG (10) **26**
Newton, Sir Isaac, TIG 360
N-**gons,** DAB 91, SG 199, URG (6) **63**
Nitrogen fixation, AB 80, URG (12) **74**
No Child Left Behind Act of 2001, TIG 388
Nonagons, DAB 91, SG 198, URG (6) **63**
Nonstandard units, URG (4) 10–11
Nonverbal communication, TIG 386
Norms, classroom, TIG 365–366
Number and Operations Standard **(National Council of**
    Teachers of Mathematics), URG (12) 9
Number lines, DAB 39, SG 78–84, URG (3) 68–69,
    URG (5) 101, URG (10) 26
Numbers
    on abacus, URG (2) 110–112
    big, TIG 61–66, 138–139, 209, 216
    composite, SG **351**
    convenient, TIG 260, URG (2) **160,** URG (7) 109
    forms of, DAB 13, SG **28**–32, URG (2) 32–42
    infinite, URG (2) 171
    irrational, URG (14) 9
    mixed, DAB 109, SG **74**–76, 150, 306, 376–382,
        URG (3) 20, 51, 55, URG (5) 33, URG (9) 78–79,
        URG (10) 16, URG (12) 9, 17, 24–26, 30–35,
        URG (14) 22
    negative, DAB 161, SG **316**–318, 322–331, URG (10) 9,
        22–23, **26,** 41
    positive, SG **316**–318, URG (10) **27**
    prime, TIG 103–106, 213, 219, URG (11) 17, 21, **26,**
        36–42, 89–99
    rounding, DAB 27, 105–109, 217, TIG 259, 260,
        URG (2) 38

Index

Part-Whole fractions, TIG 238
Part-Whole situations, TIG 307
Patchwork quilt pattern, URG (6) 85–91
Pattern blocks, DAB 35, 89–90, 195–197, SG 69–72,
      152–153, 206–208, 376–382, 387–389,
      URG (12) 9, 32–33, URG (16) 67–77
  for equivalent fractions, URG (3) 66
  for fraction modeling, URG (3) 31–42
  in Hexagon Duets, URG (12) 23–24
  for quilts and tessellations, URG (6) 84
  for ratios, URG (3) 94
  wholes and parts with, URG (5) 47–48
Patterns, URG (3) 119, URG (10) 10, URG (16) 20. *See
      also* Tessellations
  in density, URG (13) 60, 82–84
  in distance to time ratio, URG (13) 42
  formulas from, URG (15) 8–9
  in graphs, TIG 326–327
  in multiplication, TIG 287
  to multiply fractions, URG (12) 61–68
  number, TIG 103–106, 130–131, 187, 193, URG
    (11) 9
  in prime numbers, URG (11) 89–99
  square numbers and, URG (11) 44–54, **51**
PBS Teacherline, TIG 425
Peanut Soup (George Washington Carver), AB 77–92,
      URG (12) 71–79
Pentagons, DAB 83, 91, SG 198, URG (6) 62–**63**
Percents, DAB 98, 105–107, 190, 201, 217, 231,
      SG **223**–240, 260–267, 274–280, 286–293,
      447–449, URG (4) 11, 142, URG (7) **35**–37,
      URG (8) 22, 75, URG (13) 16, URG (15) 19,
      URG (16) 87. *See also* Ten percent estimation
  and decimals, URG (14) 96
  and fractions, SG 222–231, **223,** 260–264, 274, 286–**293,**
     URG (7) **35**–37, 107, URG (8) 18, URG (9) 18,
     URG (14) 96–97
Perimeter, DAB 224, 226, SG 479–485, **480,** URG (14)
      29, URG (15) 80–90, **84,** URG (16) 15
  of circles, URG (14) 29, 62
  quiz on, URG (15) 88–90
  of rectangles, URG (16) 20, 83
Period, SG **29**–30, URG (2) 36
Perpendicular lines, SG **437,** 469, URG (14) 65, 81–82,
      URG (15) **65,** 67
Philosophy
  assessment, TIG 181–184
  Math Facts, TIG 281–282
  TIMS, TIG 236–237
Phylum, URG (6) 100
Pi (π), SG **431**–432, URG (14) **9**–10, 17, 43–44
Piaget, Jean, TIG 343, URG (9) 8–9
Picture-Based models, TIG 392

Pictures. *See also* Labs
  in problems, TIG 302
  in TIMS Laboratory Method, TIG 317–318, 328
Pint, SG 156
Place value, SG **28, 29,** 41–44, TIG 226–228, URG (2)
      35–39
  on abacus, SG 39–45, URG (2) 116, 122
  in base-ten system, URG (2) 70–78, **72,** 79–88
  chart of, SG 235, 239
  of decimals, URG (7) 10, 64–65
  estimation and, TIG 257
  expanded, standard, and word form, DAB 13,
     SG 28–29, 34, URG (2) 32–42
  periods, SG **29,** URG (2) 36
  reading and writing numerals, SG 26–34, URG (2)
     32–42
Place value charts, DAB 19, URG (7) 69, 82, 98
Point graphs, SG 86–93, 97–98, 134, 330–331, 356, 416,
      430, 491, 495, 497, TIG 320–322, 326–327,
      URG (4) 116, 120, 127, URG (7) 141–142, URG
      (8) **31,** 34, 57, URG (16) 27
Polling, URG (1) 10
Polya, George, TIG 305
Polygons, SG 192, 197–200, URG (6) **35, 45**
  angles in, URG (6) 42–52, 58–66
  drawing, URG (6) 113–119
  regular, SG **199,** URG (6) **47,** 52, **63, 86**
Pooled data, URG (7) 135, 141
Populations, SG 17–23, 26, 31, 34, 492–497, URG (1)
      9–11, **10.** *See also* Sampling
  estimating using capture–recapture, AB 93–106,
     SG 492–497, URG (16) 51–63
Portfolios, SG **64**–65, 282–283, 498–499, TIG 191,
      194–195, 201, 209, URG (1) 107, URG (2) **202,**
      URG (16) 92–96
  in baseline assessment, URG (1) 11
  setting up, URG (2) 199–205
  review of, TIG 299, URG (8) 117–122
  TIMS tutor on, TIG 295–300
Positive numbers, SG **316**–318, URG (10) **27**
Power
  exponents, SG **60,** URG (2) **174**
Practice, TIG 289–291
Pre-algebra skills and concepts, URG (5) 10
Precision, TIG 267, URG (4) **85**
Prediction, DAB 99, URG (1) 104, URG (3) 115, URG (7)
      138, 165, URG (8) 31, 48, URG (10) 58, URG
      (16) 27
  from best-fit lines, URG (4) 121
  in coin flipping, AB 43–46
  of distance, URG (10) 65
  from point graphs, TIG 326–327

Triplets, URG (6) 62
Tripling, URG (16) 21
Turn-around facts, URG (2) 53
Turning
    angles, URG (6) 30–31
Tuskegee Institute, AB 25, URG (4) 134, 141, URG (12) 71–73, 78
Tutors. *See* TIMS tutors
Twin prime numbers, SG **355,** URG (11) **41**
200 Chart, DAB 183
Two-pan balance, TIG 356–358, URG (13) 64
Tyuonyi Pueblo, AB 934

---

u

"Unfair" coin, AB 45, URG (7) **163,** 165
"Unfair" game, URG (7) **138**
Unit planner, URG (1) 4–6, URG (2) 4–7, URG (3) 4–6, URG (4) 4–6, URG (5) 4–6, URG (6) 4–6, URG (7) 4–7, URG (8) 4–6, URG (9) 4–6, URG (10) 4–6, URG (11) 4–6, URG (12) 4–6, URG (13) 4–6, URG (14) 4–6, URG (15) 4–5, URG (16) 4–6
Unit ratio, SG 165, **399,** URG (13) **30,** 79, 81
Unit Resource Guides (URG), TIG 25–41, 54
    Adventure Book lesson guide, TIG 39
    answer key, TIG 41
    background, lesson, TIG 29
    daily practice and problems, TIG 31–32
    lesson guide, TIG 33–38
    letter home, TIG 25
    observational assessment record, TIG 30
    student pages, TIG 40
    unit outlines, TIG 26–28
Units
    of measurement, URG (3) 27, URG (5) 25, URG (8) 30
    metric, TIG 332–333, URG (13) 65–66
    nonstandard, TIG 331, URG (4) 10–11
    square, SG 146–147, URG (4) 10, 20, URG (5) 30
    standard, AB 30–34, DAB 67, URG (4) **139**
    of volume, TIG 342
Unit summary, TIG 56–125, 208–215, URG (1) 2, URG (2) 2, URG (3) 2, URG (4) 2, URG (5) 2, URG (6) 2, URG (7) 2, URG (8) 2, URG (9) 2, URG (10) 2, URG (11) 2, URG (12) 2, URG (13) 2, URG (14) 2, URG (15) 2, URG (16) 2
University of Illinois at Chicago (UIC), TIG 8, 15
Unlikely Heroes, AB 35–46, URG (7) 159–165
Using a 10 strategy, TIG 284–285

V

Values, DAB 1–6, SG **3,** 22, TIG **315**–317, URG (1) 20, 29, **32.** *See also* Place value
van Hiele, Pierre, URG (6) 9, URG (14) 9
van Hiele-Geldof, Dina, URG (6) 9, URG (14) 9
Variables, DAB 3–5, SG **3**–7, 18, 22, 48, 54, 96, 135, 164, 168, 199, 270, 357, 416, 429, 494, URG (1) **10,** 20, 29, **32**–37, URG (3) 116, URG (4) 135–142, URG (8) 87. *See also* Fixed variables, Labs, Manipulated variables, Responding variables
    in formulas, URG (15) 8–9
    fundamental, URG (4) 135, URG (5) 10
    graph types and, TIG 321–323
    measurement of, AB 28–34, DAB 67
    not in proportion, SG 406–408, URG (13) 46–47
    numerical and categorical, DAB 1–6, SG **4,** TIG 56, 315, 323, URG (1) **33,** 56
    in proportion, SG **402**–410, URG (13) **9,** 39–49, **41**
    in representing data, URG (1) 56
    in samples, URG (16) 40
    survey, URG (8) 46
Velocity, SG **165,** TIG 355, URG (5) **80**–81
Verbal representations, TIG 302
Vertebrates, URG (14) **94**–95
Vertex, SG **184,** 207, URG (6) 30–31, 35, URG (14) 65, URG (15) 67
Vertical axis. *See* Y-axis
Visualization in geometry, URG (6) 9
Vocabulary
    English language learners and, TIG 379
    special education students and, TIG 392
Volume, DAB 203, SG 405, 413–422, URG (4) 139–140, URG (5) 10, URG (13) **57, 66,** URG (16) 60, 85
    density and, URG (13) 74–91
    mass and, URG (13) 54–68, URG (16) 26–27
    standard units of, AB 32–33
    TIMS tutor on, TIG **341**–354
Volunteers, parent, TIG 432–433

W

Wagreich, Philip, TIG 15
Washington, Booker T., AB 25–26, URG (4) 134–135, URG (12) 73
Water, density of, URG (13) **60**
Watson, James, TIG 320
Weight, AB 85, TIG 360–361, URG (7) 30. *See also* Mass
Wherefore Art Thou Romeo?, AB 61–76, URG (10) 52–59

Whirligig wheel quilt pattern, URG (6) 85, 92
Whole numbers, TIG 169–173, 230–237, URG (12) 52–53
Wholes and parts, DAB 37–38, URG (3) 31–42, URG (5) 31–33, 44–51, URG (13) 16
in base-ten system, URG (7) 42–47
with pattern blocks, URG (5) 47–48
problems on, URG (3) 20, 23
with rectangles, URG (5) 48–49
Width, SG **103, 455**
in area measurement, TIG 337
of rectangles, SG **456,** URG (4) **36,** URG (15) **24,** URG (16) 20
Women's suffrage, URG (8) 44
Word form, DAB 13, SG **29**–32, 34, URG (2) 32–42
Word problems. *See* Problem solving
Words and symbols, ratios in, URG (3) 90–91
World Columbian Exposition, Chicago, 1893, URG (4) 134
Writing, TIG 189–190. *See also* Journaling
background, TIG 422
big numbers, DAB 13, URG (2) 17–23
English language learners and, TIG 377, 380

in portfolios, TIG 299
for language skills, TIG 422
strategies, TIG 423
Written assessment, TIG 185, 188–189

X-axis, SG **319**–342. *See also* Axes

Y-axis, SG **319**–342. *See also* Axes

Z

Zeros, URG (2) 76, URG (3) 78, URG (4) 56, 120, URG (6) 24, URG (7) 82, URG (10) 26

Index